Popular Influence
upon Public Policy

Contributions in Legal Studies
Series Editor: *Paul L. Murphy*

Popular Influence upon Public Policy

**PETITIONING IN
EIGHTEENTH-CENTURY VIRGINIA**

RAYMOND C. BAILEY

CONTRIBUTIONS IN LEGAL STUDIES, NUMBER 10

GP **GREENWOOD PRESS**
WESTPORT, CONNECTICUT. LONDON, ENGLAND

Library of Congress Cataloging in Publication Data

Bailey, Raymond C
  Popular influence upon public policy.

  (Contributions in legal studies ; no. 10
  ISSN 0147-1074)
  Bibliography: p.
  Includes index.
  1. Petition, Right of—Virginia—History.
2. Representative government and representation—
Virginia—History.   I. Title.   II. Series.
KFV2812.P47B34   323.4'8'09755   78-73792
ISBN 0-313-20892-1

Library of Congress Catalog Card Number: 78-73792
ISBN: 0-313-20892-1
ISSN: 0147-1074

First published in 1979
Greenwood Press, Inc.
51 Riverside Avenue, Westport, Connecticut 06880

Printed in the United States of America

10 9 8 7 6 5 4 3 2 1

TO MY WIFE JUDY

CONTENTS

FIGURES AND TABLES

FIGURES

TABLES

PREFACE

The nature of political affairs in eighteenth-century America has long
attracted considerable attention from historians, and this interest shows
no signs of diminishing. On the contrary, while recent scholarship has
significantly expanded our knowledge, much investigation remains to be
done before historians can hope to resolve the continuing debate over
the nature of eighteenth-century reality. Thus the search for additional
insights continues into such matters as the distribution of wealth, legislative voting patterns, and the degree of popular participation in the
political process. Studies on the latter topic have focused upon participation in a wide variety of forms, ranging from voting in local and provincial elections to mob activity and popular uprisings.

Despite this work, however, historians have devoted relatively little
attention to the role played by petitions sent from local citizens to their
elected representatives in the provincial legislature. This study is intended
to help fill that void, and thereby expand our awareness of the extent to
which the general public influenced public policy, by examining the role
of petitioning in eighteenth-century Virginia. My research clearly indicated
that petitioning had an extremely significant impact in the Old Dominion.
I have not attempted to prove that Virginia was either "aristocratic" or
"democratic" during the eighteenth century, for those theories involve
more than just the degree of popular participation and official responsiveness. Virginia contained theoretical and institutional elements reflecting
both concepts, and neither by itself provides an adequate description of
the Virginia experience. But examination of petitioning does demonstrate
that average citizens were neither passive nor inarticulate concerning the
legislation which affected their daily lives, and Virginia's government was
certainly not hostile or indifferent to the sentiments of the people.

In researching and writing this study I have accumulated many obligations.
I began this work under the direction of G. Melvin Herndon at the University
of Georgia, and his assistance, encouragement, and friendship have been invaluable. My professional and personal regard for this scholar and gentle-

man has continued to grow through the time it has been my privilege to
know him. Aubrey C. Land, F. Nash Boney, and William F. Holmes offered
useful suggestions and advice. I also wish to thank C. Gregg Singer for my
years under his guidance and inspiration at Catawba College. The staffs at
the various libraries were uniformly helpful, and the Georgia Chapter of
the Colonial Dames of America kindly provided a grant which helped finance
the research for this study. Finally, I am greatly indebted to my parents
and family for their unfailing encouragement and support over the years.
The book is dedicated to my wife Judy, who has been invaluable at every
stage in research and writing.

Popular Influence upon Public Policy

ABBREVIATIONS

CSPC	*Calendar of State Papers, Colonial Series*
EJC	*Executive Journals of the Council*
CO	Great Britain, Public Record Office, Colonial Office
JHB	*Journals of the House of Burgesses*
JHD	*Journals of the House of Delegates*
LJC	*Legislative Journals of the Council*
UVa	University of Virginia
VHS	Virginia Historical Society
VMHB	*Virginia Magazine of History and Biography*
VSL	Virginia State Library
WMQ	*William and Mary Quarterly*

INTRODUCTION

Government in eighteenth-century Virginia largely rested upon domestic
political institutions staffed with local people. In the years before the
Revolution, a relatively small number of wealthy and socially prominent
families held many of these leadership positions.[1] The generally benign
supervision of the English government under the Old Colonial Policy
offered few serious challenges to this planter gentry, for each new royal
governor soon discovered that the imperial authorities were quick to give
instructions and offer advice but slow to provide effective assistance.[2]

Gentry power and authority was evident everywhere. At the county
level, government depended upon the justices of the peace who made up
the county court; appointed by the governor, the "gentlemen justices"
were drawn primarily, especially in the more settled areas, from the rich
and powerful. England appointed the council which advised the governor,
served with him as the supreme court of the colony, and formed the upper
house of the legislature. Only the most influential patricians were selected.
The lower house of the assembly, the House of Burgesses, was elected,
but voting requirements generally excluded women, blacks, and the very
poor. The suffrage did extend to most white males, but Virginia voters
selected burgesses who were, as a group, nearly as aristocratic in background as the councillors.[3] The American Revolution did little to change
this pattern. England lost its supervisory authority, the upper house of
the legislature was elected, and the Assembly appointed the governor.
Moreover, voting requirements were reduced somewhat, and more middle-
class citizens were elected to office. Yet the position of Virginia's gentry
leadership was hardly shaken; they were the leaders rather than the victims of the Revolution.[4]

Virginia's economic and religious spheres further reflected the pattern
of planter domination. In the agricultural, slaveholding society they were,

of course, the large slaveholders, and frequently they also provided mercantile services upon which their smaller neighbors depended.[5] In addition,
until 1786 Virginia had an established church, the Church of England
(after independence known as the Protestant Episcopal Church). In theory
the royal governor and the commissary, who served as representative of
the bishop of London, shared supervision over church affairs, but in practice considerable control was held by the vestries which governed each
parish. Vestries, while originally elected, became self-perpetuating until
dissolved by some superior authority. As might be expected, the gentry
provided the bulk of Virginia's vestrymen.[6]

Yet examination of these institutional features alone oversimplifies
the reality of eighteenth-century life in the Old Dominion. Despite the
profits and duties extracted from the tobacco trade by English merchants
and the king, Virginia prospered in the eighteenth century. Not all shared
in this prosperity, most notably the slaves who now formed most of the
lower class, but economic opportunity and social mobility did extend
throughout much of the white population. Also, because the Virginia
economy depended heavily upon the export of staple commodities,
especially tobacco, all social classes shared many common interests. This
combination of economic opportunity, social mobility, and common
interests reduced class conflict to a minimum despite the obvious gap in
wealth and power between the common folk and their betters. The lower
ranks preferred to join, rather than to eliminate, the upper class. Virginia
in the eighteenth century saw no recurrence of the major turmoil associated with Bacon's Rebellion of the seventeenth.[7]

As for religious affairs, after 1740 Virginia held a sizable number of
dissenters, and while discrimination and even occasional persecution existed, in general dissenters were accorded enough toleration to prevent
significant conflict.[8] As chapter 7 will indicate, dissenters and Anglicans
alike frequently petitioned the assembly to express their sentiments on
important religious matters, and the legislature often responded—in the
process sometimes overturning vestry decisions or even dissolving unpopular vestries altogether. After 1786, of course, the religious establishment was completely ended.

Similarly, Virginia's political structure became increasingly responsive
to average citizens. In the late seventeeth and early eighteenth centuries
royal governors, councillors, and burgesses engaged in a significant contest
over the internal division of power. This contest reached a climax during

the stormy administration of Alexander Spotswood (1710-1722), and for the most part victory lay with the burgesses.[9] It will be recalled that the lower house of the assembly was the only branch of government elected by Virginia voters during the colonial period, a sizable majority of whom came from the middle ranks of society. While voters usually elected aristocrats to the lower house, nevertheless aristocrats unconcerned with the common good were unlikely to get elected or remain in office for long. The franchise thus served as an important defense for the many against abuse of power by the few.[10]

A growing tradition of noblesse oblige on the part of the gentry leadership further protected the common interest. Public service was the duty of the privileged, and this duty required that the leaders be responsive to the needs of average citizens.[11] The significant degree of common interests heightened this sense of responsibility and increased the trust and confidence between the people and their leaders. Moreover, the intellectual climate of eighteenth-century America was strongly affected by the Enlightenment in general and in particular by the English commonwealth ideas of Locke, Harrington, Sydney, and their followers. These republican ideals further strengthened devotion to a responsive government.[12] If the ideal of gentry responsibility was never perfectly realized by imperfect men, at least it did have a solid foundation in the social, economic, and philosophic realities of the time.

Nor did internal sectional hostility disrupt the eighteenth-century political system. Prior to the Revolution, sectional conflict was practically nonexistent. The Tidewater and Piedmont had too much in common to become enemies on many issues. Some historians, most notably Jackson Turner Main, have found relatively mild Northern Neck-Southside conflict over economic policies in the 1780s, but these differences clearly remained within tolerable limits.[13] Only the continuing westward expansion into the Valley and trans-Allegheny regions made serious sectional conflict possible, for those areas ultimately developed ethnic, religious, and economic characteristics significantly different from the East. Yet as late as 1774 one group of westerners commented that Virginia had a "government under whose protection and benign influence . . . we have enjoyed many blessings and are most desirous of continuing." East-West conflict did not begin in earnest until the second decade of the nineteenth century, when it quickly became a serious problem and ultimately, of course, resulted in the dismemberment of the state.[14]

This was the context within which petitioning occurred in eighteenth-century Virginia. As this study will indicate, the practice of citizens sending petitions to their government had roots deep in the medieval period of English history and was frequently utilized by Englishmen for centuries before the colonization of America began. The practice was transplanted to Virginia literally during the first year of settlement at Jamestown, and by 1700 petitioning had assumed an important role in the political process. Most citizens sent their petitions to their elected representatives in the House of Burgesses. The burgesses consistently encouraged citizens to present their requests and grievances with petitions by guaranteeing that all would be considered, by developing efficient procedures for investigating them, and by acting vigorously whenever necessary to protect the right of petition from potential threats. Petitioning offered a much broader means of participating in the governing process than did voting in eighteenth-century elections, for even disfranchised individuals—women, free blacks, the very poor, even an occasional slave—sent petitions to the legislature. As a result, petitioning served as the most important channel of communication between local citizens and the assembly. A typical legislative session in the 1700-1750 period received well over a hundred petitions, and the average more than doubled in the latter half of the century. Moreover, the legislature proved extremely receptive, as far more eighteenth-century laws originated directly in response to these petitions than from any other source. The aristocratic Governor Spotswood even charged that the burgesses were far *too* responsive to such "Giddy Resolves of the illiterate Vulgar."[15] In this fashion, then, Virginia citizens were able to play an active and extremely significant role in the political affairs of the Old Dominion, and the legislature's responsive attitude helped counterbalance those features of Virginia government and society which today seem so undemocratic and elitist.

Notes

1. Jack P. Greene, "Foundations of Political Power in the Virginia House of Burgesses, 1720-1776," *WMQ*, 3rd ser. 16 (October 1959): 485-506; Charles S. Sydnor, *Gentlemen Freeholders* (Chapel Hill, N.C., 1952); Louis B. Wright, *The First Gentlemen of Virginia* (San Marino, Cal., 1940).

2. Clarence Ver Steg, *The Formative Years, 1607-1763* (New York, 1964), esp. ch. 11; Jack P. Greene, *The Quest for Power* (Chapel Hill, N.C., 1963). The literature on imperial relations between England and its colonies is, of course,

extensive. A good brief summary is Carl Ubbelohde, *The American Colonies and the British Empire, 1607-1763* (New York, 1968).

3. Good descriptions of the political structure in colonial Virginia may be found in the following: Robert Beverley, *The History and Present State of Virginia,* ed. Louis B. Wright (Chapel Hill, N.C., 1947); Henry Hartwell, James Blair, and Edward Chilton, *The Present State of Virginia, and the College,* ed. Hunter D. Farish (Williamsburg, 1940); Sydnor, *Gentlemen Freeholders;* Richard L. Morton, *Colonial Virginia,* 2 vols. (Chapel Hill, N.C., 1960).

4. Thomas Jefferson, *Notes on the State of Virginia,* ed. William Peden (Chapel Hill, N.C., 1954), pp. 108-49; Robert E. Brown and B. Katherine Brown, *Virginia 1705-1786: Democracy or Aristocracy?* (East Lansing, Mich., 1964), pp. 287-95; Jackson Turner Main, "Government by the People: The American Revolution and the Democratization of the Legislature," *WMQ,* 3rd ser. 23 (July 1966): 391-407.

5. Aubrey C. Land, "Economic Behavior in a Planting Society: The Eighteenth-Century Chesapeake," *Journal of Southern History* 33 (November 1967): 469-85; Hartwell, Blair, and Chilton, *Present State of Virginia,* pp. 1x-1xii, 7-14.

6. Hartwell, Blair, and Chilton, *Present State of Virginia,* pp. 65-68; Beverley, *History and Present State,* pp. 261-64; the standard secondary account is George M. Brydon, *Virginia's Mother Church and The Political Conditions Under Which It Grew,* 2 vols. (Richmond, 1947-52); see also ch. 7 of this study.

7. Brown and Brown, *Virginia 1705-1786,* esp. chs. 1 and 2; Edmund S. Morgan, *American Slavery—American Freedom: The Ordeal of Colonial Virginia* (New York, 1975), pp. 344-80; Land, "Economic Behavior in a Planting Society," pp. 482-83; D. Alan Williams, "The Small Farmer in Eighteenth-Century Virginia Politics," *Agricultural History* 43 (January 1969): 91-101.

8. Leonard W. Labaree, ed., *Royal Instructions to British Colonial Governors, 1670-1776,* 2 vols. (New York, 1935), No. 714, 2: 494; Brown and Brown, *Virginia 1705-1786,* pp. 249-54; Rhys Isaac, "Religion and Authority: Problems of the Anglican Establishment in Virginia in the Era of the Great Awakening and the Parsons' Cause," *WMQ,* 3rd ser. 30 (January 1973): 3-36, and "Evangelical Revolt: The Nature of the Baptists' Challenge to the Traditional Order in Virginia, 1765 to 1775," *WMQ,* 3rd ser. 31 (July 1974): 345-68.

9. Morgan, *American Slavery—American Freedom,* pp. 344-69; D. Alan Williams, "Political Alignments in Colonial Virginia Politics, 1698-1750" (Ph.D. dissertation, Northwestern University, 1959); Greene, *Quest for Power,* esp. pp. 6, 22-31.

10. Lucille B. Griffith, *The Virginia House of Burgesses, 1750-1774,* rev. ed. (University, Ala., 1970); Brown and Brown, *Virginia 1705-1786,* pp. 125-242; Joyce Appleby, "The Social Origins of American Revolutionary Ideology," *Journal of American History* 64 (March 1978): 949-50.

11. Wright, *First Gentlemen of Virginia,* pp. 6, 64-69; Carl Bridenbaugh, *Myths and Realities: Societies of the Colonial South* (Baton Rouge, La., 1952), pp. 16-17.

12. Bernard Bailyn, *The Ideological Origins of the American Revolution* (Cambridge, Mass., 1967), pp. 26-54; Caroline Robbins, *The Eighteenth-Century Commonwealthman* (Cambridge, Mass., 1959); J. R. Pole, *Political Representation in England and the Origins of the American Revolution* (New York and London, 1966),

ch. 1; see James Otis, "The Rights of the British Colonies Asserted and Proved" [1764], Richard Bland, "An Inquiry into the Rights of the British Colonies" [1766], Thomas Jefferson, "A Summary View of the Rights of British America" [1774], and Thomas Paine, "Common Sense" [1776], all in *Tracts of the American Revolution, 1763-1776*, ed. Merrill Jensen (New York, 1967), pp. 19-40, 108-26, 256-76, 400-46.

13. For the absence of sectionalism before 1776, see Thomas P. Abernethy, *Western Lands and the American Revolution* (New York, 1937), pp. 160, 367; John R. Alden, *The South in the Revolution, 1763-1789* (Baton Rouge, La., 1957), pp. 143-45; Brown and Brown, *Virginia 1705-1786*, esp. pp. 234, 239. Representative of the studies on sectionalism during the 1780s are: Jackson T. Main, *Political Parties Before the Constitution* (Chapel Hill, N.C., 1973), ch. 9; Norman K. Risjord and Gorden DenBoer, "The Evolution of Political Parties in Virginia, 1782-1800," *Journal of American History* 60 (March 1974): 961-84.

14. The 1774 statement is from "Petition of Inhabitants of Augusta, Botetourt and Fincastle Counties in Virginia to Governor Earl of Dunmore," in *Documents of the American Revolution, 1770-1783 (Colonial Office Series)*, ed. K. G. Davies, 17 vols. to date (Shannon, Ireland, 1972-   ), 8: 85-86. For the growing East-West sectionalism of the nineteenth century, see Harry Ammon, "The Republican Party in Virginia, 1789-1824" (Ph.D. dissertation, University of Virginia, 1948), pp. 1-2, 21, 384-88; Fletcher M. Green, *Constitutional Development in the South Atlantic States, 1776-1860* (Chapel Hill, N.C., 1930), pp. 150-54; see also ch. 8 of this study.

15. Henry R. McIlwaine and John P. Kennedy, eds., *Journals of the House of Burgesses of Virginia*, 13 vols. (Richmond, 1904-15), 1712-1726: 167 (hereafter cited as *JHB*; the *Journals* do not carry specific volume numbers and are thus identified by the dates of the first and last sessions included in each volume).

1 ORIGIN AND EARLY DEVELOPMENT OF PETITIONING

The study of petitioning in eighteenth-century Virginia must begin with an examination of the English heritage which colonial settlers originally brought with them to the New World. The right of English subjects to petition the government for redress of grievances originated at some indeterminate point deep in the medieval past. This right was based upon the concept that the king was the source of justice and that in providing this justice he and his government must be accessible to all. Englishmen sent petitions to the highest levels of government, including the king and council, by the thirteenth century, long before Parliament assumed its ultimate organization and importance.[1]

Beginning with the reign of Edward I (1272-1307), an increasing number of these petitions was sent to Parliament, which included the king and his council plus other powerful lords and churchmen and, on occasion, elected representatives from the shires and boroughs. Parliament assumed as one of its basic functions the redressing of grievances presented by individuals from all social classes. When Edward summoned a meeting of Parliament, a proclamation was distributed throughout the kingdom advising all who wished to send petitions of the deadline for presentation. Consideration of these petitions constituted a major order of business for medieval Parliaments and occupied a great deal of their time. The number of petitions presented to a typical session by the end of the thirteenth century had grown to several hundred.[2] Parliament soon had difficulty in dealing with this quantity and decided in 1280 that action was necessary to facilitate consideration. Beginning in that year two groups of receivers and auditors were appointed to sort through the petitions and refer as many as possible to the courts and administrative departments. Nevertheless, many petitions still required action or redress by the king as he acted in Parliament, the highest authority in the land.[3]

Surviving records illustrate both the diverse character of the petitioners and the wide variety of subject matter contained in their petitions. All free subjects could petition as individuals or as groups; in the late thirteenth and early fourteenth centuries, the list of petitioners included people of all classes and occupations, from powerful nobles and bishops to poor men from all parts of the country and even a group of prisoners. Merchants, government officials, university scholars, and other petitioners fit somewhere between those two social extremes. Moreover, additional petitions came from the officials and other inhabitants of various cities and shires, petitioning as organized communities.[4] During that same period, the subjects discussed in those petitions ranged from matters of national importance to those of strictly individual concern. London asked for confirmation of the city's liberties and privileges; inhabitants of Norwich sought aid to improve local security; Hampshire offered £200 to have local lands disafforested; London inhabitants complained of injustice by local clerks and government officials; individuals asked for review of judicial proceedings or release from confinement. To quote a lawyer of that period, Parliament responded by insuring that "justice is done to every one according to his deserts."[5]

By the early fourteenth century, elected representatives from the shires and boroughs were regularly included in meetings of Parliament. Almost immediately thereafter, individuals and communities began entrusting their representatives with carrying the petitions to Parliament. Englishmen viewed their representatives almost as attorneys, charged with presenting local requests and grievances before the central authority. Although originally summoned by the crown so they could assent to tax measures, these representatives regularly presented local petitions for consideration even when taxation was not discussed. Under Edward III (1327-1377) it became the established practice at the opening of every session for the chancellor officially to declare the king's willingness to consider the petitions of the people.[6]

The House of Commons soon realized the advantages to be gained by combining all important petitions which had similar foundations. Greater pressure could then be exerted upon the king and House of Lords, who still formed the essential "core" of the medieval Parliament, to give their approval than when each petition was considered individually. The House of Commons discovered its assent to taxation to be a particularly effective bargaining weapon. The practice of consolidating important petitions into "common petitions" soon had the extremely significant consequence of securing for the knights and burgesses in the House of Commons an important role in the legislative process. The king and lords could still refuse their assent. But a majority of fourteenth- and fifteenth-century laws were enacted directly in response to the private petitions brought by the elected representatives and to the "common petitions" which the House of Commons framed from those petitions. By the mid-fourteenth century the House of Commons began drafting the "common petitions" in the form of statutes, and in this fashion it secured the power of initiating legislation. The inference to be drawn from this practice was quickly incorporated into parliamentary procedure: every action taken by Parliament, regardless of how such action originated, required the assent of the three component parts—king, lords, and commons.[7]

During the years of the Tudor dynasty (1485-1603), there occurred a constitutional development of such importance that it has aptly been described as "revolutionary." When Henry VIII initiated the English Reformation, he chose to do so by statute—through legislation enacted by the famous Reformation Parliament of 1529-1536. In the medieval Parliament, lords and commons were called together primarily to offer counsel to the king, to aid in redressing grievances, and to provide financial aid when the king required it. Now, the events of the 1530s clearly established that ultimate sovereignty within the nation rested squarely with the king-in-Parliament, or to quote King Henry, "We be informed by our judges that we at no time stand so highly in our royal estate as in the time of Parliament, wherein we as head and you as members are conjoined and knit together in one body politic."[8] In short, Parliament—which, it must be stressed, still included the king—emerged as an omnipotent legislative body. Neither Henry nor his subjects foresaw in 1529 that from this action would develop the parliamentary democracy of a later age. While acting so effectively through Parliament, Henry could hardly have realized that the omnipotence of king-in-Parliament could function only so long as the three component parts agreed on most matters and could compromise on the rest. Not until the Stuart period began in 1603 would England discover the full possibilities for conflict in such a tripartite division of authority.[9]

The enhanced authority of Parliament was obvious to all during the reigns of Henry and Elizabeth Tudor. Moreover, the House of Commons played an increasingly important role in Parliament; its members now sat

as the representatives of all the commons in the kingdom. The consideration in Parliament of the great affairs of church and state in the sixteenth
century did not, however, deter English petitioners from presenting a
multitude of requests for legislative action on matters great and small.
Considering these petitions and acting on the private bills framed from
them occupied so much time in the House of Commons that important
public business was often delayed. Englishmen also continued to petition
the king and council, and the petitions involving judicial matters were
presented to the courts.[10]

By 1571 the House of Commons often considered petitions and grievances in committee. Although procedure occasionally varied, by the beginning of the Stuart period (1603-1714) the Commons generally used a
Committee of the whole House for this purpose.[11] This procedure reflected
the conviction that consideration of petitions and redress of grievances
were primary functions of Parliament. The petitions sent to Parliament
or to the king sometimes concerned the vital questions of national policy
which were hotly debated before the English Civil War; for example,
many Puritan ministers sent the famous Millenary Petition of 1603 to
King James in order to request reformation of certain ceremonies and
abuses in the Church of England. Two thick manuscript volumes of petitions presented to the Parliaments of 1621 and 1624 have been preserved.[12]

Seventeenth-century political leaders, particularly those in the House
of Commons, placed considerable emphasis upon the importance of the
right of English citizens to petition for redress of grievances. John Pym,
a leader of the growing Parliamentary opposition to James I and Charles
I, asserted that the limitations upon royal authority and the liberties of
the people resulted from the "ancient and fundamental law." These
liberties had been confirmed in the charters assented to by kings and in
the statutes of Parliament, Pym added, both of which were founded upon
the petitions of English subjects. Pym's use of medieval history was faulty,
for he neglected to mention the vast degree of royal discretion which remained despite these limitations; the essential function of the medieval
Parliament was to assist rather than hinder or restrain the king. But Pym's
assertion does reveal the extent to which petitioning had become a fundamental part of the political system by the seventeenth century.[13] Similarly,
the Protestation of 1621, adopted by the House of Commons, insisted
that "redress of mischiefs and grievances" was one of the proper matters

for consideration in Parliament. John Pym, in a 1640 speech in the House of Commons, reiterated the constitutional necessity for frequent sessions of Parliament so that the king could make known his needs and his subjects could present their petitions.[14] Many other claims by the House of Commons in its 1603-1642 struggle with the Stuart monarchs were innovations, supported with precedents often founded upon a misreading of English history. This stress upon petitioning, however, was unquestionably justified by centuries of experience.[15]

In short, by the time England embarked upon its course of colonial expansion, the right of citizens to petition the government concerning matters of private importance and of public policy was clearly recognized. When English settlers first landed at Jamestown in 1607, their forebears had long exercised that privilege. But the revolutionary crisis of 1763-1776, plus several internal disputes in seventeenth- and eighteenth-century Virginia, later called into question the extent to which the king's subjects in America retained the rights and privileges of other Englishmen (see the discussion in chapter 2). For that reason some observations may be required to determine if petitioning was originally expected to play the significant role in the New World which it had in England itself.

The royal charters which granted official authorization for the establishing of colonies in America guaranteed that this basic political right would be transported to the New World, for those charters expressly promised that Englishmen would not forfeit their rights by migrating there. The Virginia Company charter of 1606 is typical. In it James I pledged, for himself and his successors, that all his subjects in the colony "shall have and enjoy all liberties, franchises and immunities . . . to all intents and purposes as if they had been abiding and borne within this our realme of England or anie other of our saide dominions."[16] This provision was continued in both the 1609 and 1612 Virginia charters.[17] Other colonial charters included similar terminology. The charter of the Massachusetts Bay Company guaranteed the "liberties and immunities" of the colonists;[18] the 1629 Carolina patent of Sir Robert Heath promised that settlers would enjoy all the "libertyes, franchises & priviledges" of Englishmen, and the 1663 and 1665 Carolina charters confirmed this provision;[19] the colonists of Maryland, under the 1632 charter, were to enjoy all "privileges, franchises and liberties" of the king's subjects in England.[20] Only the charter granted to William Penn failed to contain such provisions, but Penn had no intention of slighting his colonists. He wrote in 1681 that "the rights and freedoms of England (the best and largest in Europe) shall be in force there."[21]

The 1606 Virginia charter thus established the precedent that the king's subjects would carry their rights and privileges with them to America. Neither Spain nor France made the same guarantee to its colonists.[22] However, the charters did not specify exactly what constituted the rights of English citizens. A number of historians, concerned particularly with the rise of representative assemblies in the colonies, have maintained that these charter statements were understood to concern only legal, tenurial, and private rights; they were not grants of special privileges, and self-government or democracy was not promised.[23] Not only did the charters fail to enumerate the privileges involved, but the increasingly serious constitutional crisis of the early Stuart period indicated that no such clear-cut definition existed.[24] The assertion that the charter grants did not automatically guarantee the right to vote for delegates to an elected assembly is clearly correct, as the restricted franchise in England excluded many citizens from that right. Later colonial charters which did establish representative assemblies made specific mention of that authorization.[25]

However, the statement that "liberties, franchises and immunities" had limited political application should not obscure the important role played by petitioning in English political life. Since the charter grants of liberties did not contain specific enumerations, those rights which had long been recognized and which carried no restrictions of applicability must have been included.[26] In England the use of petitions was uncontested and was facilitated by, not dependent upon, the existence of an elected assembly. Thus, if the right of petition was not included in the charter provisions, then that terminology was both misleading and worthless. The colonists coming to America did not consider the guarantees of their rights to be worthless. They insisted that such provisions confirmed the inherent, inalienable nature of the rights of English citizens in the colonies as well as at home in the mother country.[27]

In light of this English tradition, it is hardly surprising that colonists quickly began to utilize the right of petition in Virginia. In fact, the first recorded instance of petitioning in the colony occurred before the original settlement was a month old. The initial group of settlers disembarked at the site which became Jamestown on May 24, 1607, where they were

governed by a president and council. A multitude of problems soon beset
the settlement. Less than a month after the landing, Gabriel Archer, recorder for the council, noted: "Satterday [6 June 1607] there being
among the Gentlemen and all the Company a murmur and grudg[e]
against certayne preposterous proceedings, and inconvenyent Courses,
[they] put up a Petytion to the Counsell for Reformatyon."[28] Although
Archer did not report what the particular grievance was, he did add that
the council considered the petition on the following Wednesday and con-
sented to it unanimously.[29] Two years later, the Virginia Company decided to obtain a revision of its charter and alter the form of government
in the colony by replacing the president and council with a single, more
powerful governor. Sir Thomas Gates was dispatched to serve as deputy
governor until Sir Thomas West, Lord De la Warr, could leave for Virginia.
The company had received petitions complaining of arbitrary conduct
by John Ratcliffe, a former president of the colonial government. Gates
was instructed to investigate the complaints and see that justice was done.[30]

For several years the colony was ruled by a series of governors who
possessed sweeping powers and utilized martial law. The company felt
that too much regard for personal rights would endanger the safety of the
colony. In 1618, however, the company instituted a more liberal policy
in an attempt to stimulate renewed migration, offer additional incentives
to those already there, and redress complaints about the arbitrary conduct
of the colonial governor. Martial law was ended, private ownership of land
was extended, greater individual freedom was allowed, and a representative
assembly was established.[31] This change in policy was emphasized in the
"Ordinance and Constitution" sent to the colony in 1621. The Company
intended the new form of government to be of "greatest benifitt and
comfort of the people and whereby all injustice, grevance and oppression
may bee prevented and kept of as much as possible from the said Colony."[32]

When the assembly met for the first time in July and August of 1619,
it became the first representative assembly to convene in the New World.
It considered the charter and instructions brought by Governor George
Yeardley in order to list any provisions not appropriate to the condition
of the colony and seek redress from the Virginia Company. Consequently,
the assembly adopted several petitions to be dispatched to London.[33]
The assembly also considered several petitions presented by citizens of
the colony. Two of these involved cases which were primarily judicial in

nature. The assembly acted upon one of them and referred the other to the governor and council for further investigation. A third petition came from the inhabitants of Argall's town, who asked to be discharged from payment of £600 in bonds which they owed to Argall for the land and another £50 in bonds to Captain Powell for clearing the land and building houses. While uncertain of its power to grant the request, the assembly promised to petition the Virginia Company in support of it.[34] From the very first session of the assembly, then, Virginians exercised their right to petition the legislature for redress of grievances or for presenting local requests.

During the years after 1619, colonists continued to petition both the governor and council and the assembly. There are no surviving records of a meeting of the assembly in 1620, but a session did convene in 1621. Although records of this meeting are fragmentary, the session received at least two petitions from citizens of the colony. In one of them, a Captain Newces proposed a new plan concerning company tenants; details of the plan are not available, but it was approved by the assembly and forwarded to the Virginia Company. A Dutchman's son also petitioned the assembly for permission to return home, and his request was granted.[35] The assembly convened only for brief periods during the 1620s, but the governor and council were always available and received numerous petitions. For example, John Pory petitioned in 1621 to request additional men and supplies for the settlement on the Eastern Shore. In response, the governor allocated additional money "for the employment and maintenance of tenants at Accowmack." The governor and council, when sitting in their judicial capacity as the General Court (which before the 1680s possessed legal jurisdiction inferior only to that of the assembly and which became the supreme colonial court after that period), also received numerous petitions which initiated legal proceedings. Land disputes, charges of slander, and suits for back wages and release from apprenticeship are but a few of the matters thus brought before the General Court.[36]

Virginians thus quickly began using petitions during the early years of settlement, and they made increasing use of that practice during the remainder of the seventeenth century to present individual and local requests to the provincial government. Following royalization of Virginia in 1624, the English government withheld official recognition of the Virginia assembly for fifteen years. During that period, however, the

governor and council continued to receive and act upon petitions seeking
executive or judicial action. The governor also convened the assembly
on several occasions prior to its formal recognition in 1639, and when
in session it received petitions from the people as usual.[37]

Although the surviving records for the 1640s are very incomplete, there
are numerous indications that the number and variety of petitions continued to increase. For example, the assembly on several occasions created
new parishes and altered parish boundaries directly in response to petitions
from local inhabitants. Other colonists petitioned the assembly in 1647
to seek an extension of the time limitation for occupying their lands; after
considering the hardships resulting from the recent Indian war and other
causes, the assembly allowed three additional years for the petitioners to
"seat" their lands. The great number of laws enacted "for the ease" of
particular groups or "upon divers informations presented to this assembly"
further suggest that Virginians during the 1640s frequently petitioned
their government in order to influence public policy. When the assembly
formally stated in 1642 that "relieving of such disorders and grievances
which are incident to all states" constituted a major reason for its very
existence, it merely provided official recognition of a centuries-old feature
of Anglo-American history. Along with the continuing flow of petitions
to the governor and council, these developments reveal that petitioning
had become firmly established in Virginia by 1650.[38]

The course of events during the 1650s further stimulated the presentation of petitions to the legislature. Virginia remained loyal to the king
during the English Civil War, but commissioners sent by the parliamentary
victors forced the colony to capitulate in 1652. From that point until the
Restoration in 1660, Virginia's House of Burgesses elected the governor
and council and exercised almost complete sovereignty within the colony.[39]
This increase in legislative authority prompted colonists to petition the
assembly concerning a host of matters. In response to these petitions the
legislature created counties and parishes and altered their boundaries,
gave permission for citizens to explore the frontier, investigated charges
of illegal election tactics, granted requests by immigrants for naturalization
as free citizens of Virginia, and in general spent much of its time absorbed
in these local and individual concerns.[40]

The pattern thus established in the first half-century of Virginia history
continued throughout the remainder of the seventeenth century. As the

number of petitions presented to the legislature continued to increase, the assembly had to develop a committee system to facilitate its investigation of these propositions and grievances (see the description in chapter 2). The assembly declared in 1664 that its primary purpose was the "making provision for the peoples safety and redresse of their Grievances."[41] While this statement constituted, at least in part, a public relations ploy of the type which politicians have always found irresistable, it nevertheless embodied a fundamental principle.

Recent investigation by a number of scholars, particularly Edmund Morgan and John Rainbolt, suggests that Virginia political life underwent a major transformation beginning in the late seventeenth century following Bacon's Rebellion. Rainbolt suggested that the political leadership of the 1660-1676 period sought to implement many major policies (especially economic ones) by "prescription." The ruling gentry formulated policies, often on its own initiative, and then expected obedience from a relatively passive or deferential public. Rainbolt then interpreted Bacon's Rebellion and the other, less dramatic, expressions of discontent in 1676-1677 largely as the response of a people dissatisfied with such a one-sided relationship between the governors and the governed. Morgan has carried this point even further, asserting that from the early years of settlement to the rebellion the leadership was too generally as interested in selfish ends as in public service. Morgan has indicated, however, that a variety of factors in the late seventeenth and early eighteenth centuries—including the increasing importance of slavery and the political struggles among the governor, council, and burgesses of the 1680-1720 period—served to produce a more responsive political leadership. Rainbolt's research supported the same conclusion. Virginia began to develop a new style of politics after 1676, he concluded, one which emphasized responsiveness to the wishes of the people. This trend was strengthened by the emergence of a native-born ruling class. By the turn of the century, there had emerged a style of politics which stressed communication and responsiveness rather than prescription.[42]

The extent of petitioning in the period from 1660 to 1676 and the creation of a committee system to aid in the consideration of petitions provide at least indirect evidence that Morgan and Rainbolt may have underestimated the degree of popular influence even before Bacon's Rebellion.[43] As this chapter demonstrates, petitioning had been an important force in legislative activity from the very beginning of settlement. But in the late seventeenth century the role of petitioning did become noticeably more significant than ever before. The house *Journals* reveal that colonists presented petitions concerning almost every conceivable subject. Among the matters presented by petition to the 1696 assembly, for example, were requests for altering the court days in Accomack County, for reducing the fees charged by clerks of courts, for preventing horse racing on the Sabbath, for amending the tobacco laws, for creating a new county, and for building bridges and improving roads. Of the fourteen laws enacted by that session, nine originated directly in response to the petitions presented by Virginia citizens.[44] The remaining chapters of this study describe the extent to which Virginia in the eighteenth century built upon this foundation to insure a significant degree of popular participation in the political process and of government responsiveness to the wishes of local citizens.

Notes

1. George O. Sayles, *The King's Parliament of England* (New York, 1974), pp. 29, 41, 49, 56-57, 64-69, 76-79; A. F. Pollard, *The Evolution of Parliament*, 2d ed., rev. (London, 1926), p. 127; William Stubbs, *The Constitutional History of England*, 3 vols., 4th ed. (New York, 1967), 2: 260-61; George L. Haskins, *The Growth of English Representative Government* (1948; reprint ed., New York, 1960), pp. 6, 8, 12.

2. Sayles, *King's Parliament*, pp. 76-81; Josef Redlich, *The Procedure of the House of Commons*, trans. A. Ernest Steinthal, 3 vols. (1908; reprint ed., New York, 1969), 1: 9, 12-13; Pollard, *Evolution of Parliament*, pp. 37, 41-42, 327; F. W. Maitland, "The Many Functions of Early Parliaments," in *Origins of the English Parliament*, ed. Peter Spufford (New York, 1967), pp. 145, 148, 149; Haskins, *English Representative Government*, pp. 8, 16-17, 43.

3. J. Franklin Jameson, "The Origin of the Standing Committee System in American Legislative Bodies," *Political Science Quarterly* 9 (June 1894): 247; Pollard, *Evolution of Parliament*, pp. 38-39; Sayles, *King's Parliament*, pp. 80-81; Stubbs, *Constitutional History*, 2: 276.

4. Pollard, *Evolution of Parliament*, pp. 42, 117; Haskins, *English Representative Government*, p. 16.

5. Quoted in Haskins, *English Representative Government*, pp. 6, 16, 21; Pollard, *Evolution of Parliament*, pp. 52-53; Redlich, *Procedure*, p. 9.

6. David H. Willson, *A History of England* (New York, 1967), pp. 174-78;

May McKisack, "The Function of Burgesses in Parliament," in *Origins of Parliament,* ed. Spufford, pp. 109-11; Stubbs, *Constitutional History,* 2: 602; Sayles, *King's Parliament,* pp. 100-08, 116-17.

7. Haskins, *English Representative Government,* pp. 85-104; Sayles, *King's Parliament,* pp. 115-25; Willson, *History of England,* pp. 177-78; Stubbs, *Constitutional History,* 2: 602-04; Pollard, *Evolution of Parliament,* pp. 117-30; Helen M. Cam, "Legislation in Early Parliaments," in *Origins of Parliament,* ed. Spufford, pp. 194-95; George B. Adams, *Constitutional History of England* (New York, 1921), p. 227; F. W. Maitland, *The Constitutional History of England* (Cambridge, 1913), p. 189.

8. Quoted in Haskins, *English Representative Government,* pp. 2, 123-26; Willson, *History of England,* ch. 12; Conyers Read, *The Tudors: Personalities and Practical Politics in Sixteenth-Century England,* Norton Library ed. (New York, 1969), pp. 65, 100; G. R. Elton, *England Under the Tudors* (London, 1955), pp. 165-75; J. J. Scarisbrick, *Henry VIII* (Berkeley and Los Angeles, 1968), chs. 10, 15; G. R. Elton, ed., *The Tudor Constitution: Documents and Commentary* (Cambridge, 1960), pp. 20-23, 228-317.

9. See the excellent discussion in Elton, *England Under the Tudors,* pp. 165-75.

10. Elton, ed., *Tudor Constitution,* pp. 101-03, 229, 245; Carl Bridenbaugh, *Vexed and Troubled Englishmen, 1590-1642* (New York, 1968), pp. 239-40, 272; Patrick Collinson, "John Field and Elizabethan Puritanism," in *Elizabethan Government and Society,* ed. S. T. Bindoff, J. Hurstfield, and C. H. Williams (London, 1961), pp. 153-54; Michael Kammen, *Deputyes and Libertyes* (New York, 1969), pp. 5-6; A. L. Rowse, *The England of Elizabeth* (New York, 1950), esp. ch. 7; for a detailed picture of parliamentary development by the end of the Tudor period, the classic accounts are the studies by John Neale—see especially Neale, *The Elizabethan House of Commons* (New Haven, Conn., 1950).

11. Jameson, "Origin of Committees," pp. 249-55; J. P. Kenyon, ed., *The Stuart Constitution: Documents and Commentary* (Cambridge, 1966), pp. 27-28, 35.

12. Kenyon, ed., *Stuart Constitution,* pp. 24-89, 132-34; Wallace Notestein, *The English People on the Eve of Colonization, 1603-1630* (New York, 1954), pp. 197-98.

13. Pym's speech of 4 June 1628, in *Stuart Constitution,* ed. Kenyon, pp. 16-18; J. W. Allen, *English Political Thought, 1603-1660,* 2 vols. (London, 1938), 1: 30-31.

14. The Protestation of 1621 and Pym's 17 April 1640 speech are found in *Stuart Constitution,* ed. Kenyon, pp. 47-48, 197-203.

15. For good discussions of the constitutional crisis of 1603-1642, see Kenyon, ed., *Stuart Constitution,* chs. 1-5; Christopher Hill, *The Century of Revolution, 1603-1714,* Norton Library ed. (New York, 1966), ch. 4; Lacey B. Smith, *This Realm of England, 1399 to 1688* (Boston, 1966), chs. 11 and 12; Sayles, *King's Parliament,* ch. 1; Haskins, *English Representative Government,* pp. 124-31.

16. Samuel M. Bemiss, ed., *The Three Charters of the Virginia Company of London, with Seven Related Documents: 1606-1621,* Jamestown 350th Anniversary Historical Booklets, ed. E. G. Swem (Williamsburg, 1957), p. 9.

17. Ibid., pp. 51, 93-94.

18. Nathaniel B. Shurtleff, ed., *Records of the Governor and Company of the Massachusetts Bay in New England,* 6 vols. (Boston, 1853-54), 1: 16.

19. William L. Saunders, ed., *The Colonial Records of North Carolina,* 10 vols. (Raleigh, 1886-90), 1: 10, 25, 107.

20. Merrill Jensen, ed., *American Colonial Documents to 1776* (New York, 1955), p. 88.

21. William Penn, "Some Account of the Province of Pennsilvania," in *Colonial Documents,* ed. Jensen, p. 126.

22. Charles M. Andrews, *The Colonial Period of American History,* 4 vols. (New Haven, Conn., 1934-38), 1: 86.

23. Ibid., 86n.; Richard L. Morton, *Colonial Virginia,* 2 vols. (Chapel Hill, N.C., 1960), 1: 5; Herbert L. Osgood, *The American Colonies in the Seventeenth Century,* 3 vols. (New York, 1904-07), 3: 11; Green, *Constitutional Development,* p. 14.

24. See the discussion in Gilman Ostrander, *The Rights of Man in America, 1606-1861* (Columbia, Mo., 1960), pp. 3-5; Allen, *English Political Thought,* 1: 3.

25. For example, the 1632 Maryland charter allowed the lord proprietor to enact legislation only "with the advice, assent, and approbation of the freemen . . . or of their delegates or deputies. . . ." Similarly, the 1665 Carolina charter contained the provision of enactment of legislation with the "advice, assent and approbation" of the freemen. Jensen, ed., *Colonial Documents,* pp. 86-87; Saunders, ed., *Colonial Records of North Carolina,* 1: 104.

26. Supreme Court Justice Joseph Story noted that England based its claim to New World territory upon the right of discovery. This claim, combined with the charter provisions and the early invitations for English subjects to settle in America, guaranteed that colonists would carry with them all applicable rights and privileges—see Story, *Commentaries on the Constitution of the United States,* 2 vols., 2d ed. (Boston, 1851), 1: 99-105.

27. Osgood, *American Colonies in Seventeenth Century,* 1: 3-11; Green, *Constitutional Development,* p. 11; Edward Channing, *A History of the United States,* 6 vols. (New York, 1905-25), 1: 161-62; Jensen, ed., *Colonial Documents,* p. 167; Thomas J. Wertenbaker, *The Government of Virginia in the Seventeenth Century,* Jamestown 350th Anniversary Historical Booklets, ed. Swem, pp. 1-2.

28. Edward Arber, ed., *The Works of Captain John Smith* (New York, 1967), p. 1iii. For standard secondary accounts of the beginnings of settlement in Virginia, see Andrews, *Colonial Period,* 1: chs. 5-10; John E. Pomfret, *Founding the American Colonies, 1583-1660* (New York, 1970), chs. 2-3; Morton, *Colonial Virginia,* 1: chs. 1-8.

29. Arber, ed., *Works of John Smith,* p. 1iv.

30. Susan M. Kingsbury, ed., *The Records of the Virginia Company of London,* 4 vols. (Washington, D.C., 1906-35), 3: 22-23.

31. Alexander Brown, ed., *The Genesis of the United States,* 2 vols. (Boston, 1897), 1: 379; Andrews, *Colonial Period,* 1: 123-24, 180-84; Darrett B. Rutman, "The Virginia Company and Its Military Regime," in *The Old Dominion: Essays*

for Thomas Perkins Abernethy, ed. Darrett B. Rutman (Charlottesville, Va., 1964), pp. 17, 20; Morton, *Colonial Virginia,* 1: 19-59.

32. Bemiss, ed., *Three Charters of Virginia,* p. 126.

33. *JHB,* 1619-1658/59: 6; Morton, *Colonial Virginia,* 1: 60; Andrews, *Colonial Period,* 1: 187; Pomfret, *Founding the American Colonies,* p. 38.

34. *JHB,* 1619-1658/59: 12, 15.

35. See the letter from the governor and council to the Virginia Company, written sometime in January 1622, in *JHB,* 1619-1658/59: 17.

36. Jennings C. Wise, *Ye Kingdome of Accawmacke, or the Eastern Shore of Virginia in the Seventeenth Century* (1911; reprint ed., Baltimore, 1967), pp. 32-33; Kingsbury, ed., *Records of Virginia Company,* 1: 169, 171; 3: 652-53, 682, 689; "Virginia in 1623-4," *VMHB* 6 (April 1899): 376; Henry R. McIlwaine, ed., *Minutes of the Council and General Court of Colonial Virginia, 1622-1632, 1670-1676* (Richmond, 1924), pp. 9, 17, 31.

37. Andrews, *Colonial Period,* 1: 192-205; Osgood, *American Colonies in Seventeenth Century,* 3: 76-77; "Decisions of Virginia General Court, 1626-1628," *VMHB* 3 (April 1896): 362-63, 367; 4 (October 1896): 160; John B. Boddie, *Seventeenth Century Isle of Wight County, Virginia* (Chicago, 1938), p. 48; William Waller Hening, ed., *The Statutes at Large: Being a Collection of All the Laws of Virginia,* 13 vols. (Richmond and Philadelphia, 1809-23), 1: 159, 161, 183-84 (hereafter cited as Hening, *Statutes*).

38. Hening, *Statutes,* 1: 245, 250, 258, 262, 277-78, 287, 335-36, 341-42, 346, 347, 349, 353, 355; *JHB,* 1619-1658/59: 69; Morton, *Colonial Virginia,* 1: 157; Clifford Lewis III, "Some Recently Discovered Extracts from the Lost Minutes of the Virginia Council and General Court, 1642-1645," *WMQ,* 2d ser. 20 (January 1940): 64.

39. Osgood, *American Colonies in Seventeenth Century,* 3: 103, 122-24, 151; Morton, *Colonial Virginia,* 1: 174-75, 187-88.

40. *JHB,* 1619-1658/59: 83, 87-88, 90-91, 95, 96, 99, 100, 101, 103, 109, 116, 117, 118.

41. Hening, *Statutes,* 1: 127.

42. Edmund S. Morgan, *American Slavery—American Freedom: The Ordeal of Colonial Virginia* (New York, 1975), chs. 4-17; John C. Rainbolt, "The Alteration in the Relationship between Leadership and Constituents in Virginia, 1660 to 1720," *WMQ,* 3rd ser. 27 (July 1970): 411-34; Rainbolt, *From Prescription to Persuasion: Manipulation of the Eighteenth [Seventeenth] Century Virginia Economy* (Port Washington, N.Y., 1974).

43. The development of a committee system is described at length in chapter 2. The sporadic quality of the house *Journals* for the 1660-1676 period makes it impossible to determine with precision the extent of petitioning in that period; nor is it possible to ascertain if the petitions which were presented retained the significant degree of influence which they enjoyed during the 1650s. It is clear, however, that the assembly did continue to receive a number of petitions in the years from the Restoration to Bacon's Rebellion.

44. See the house *Journal* for 1696 and compare the proceedings with the legislation listed in Hening's *Statutes.*

2 THE PRESENTATION AND CONSIDERATION OF PETITIONS

Virginians in the seventeenth century firmly established the practice of petitioning to influence public policy, and they made increasing use of that practice in the eighteenth century. People sent petitions to their local government and to the executive and judicial branches of the colonial or state government, but by far the most important use of petitions was to present local needs, requests, and grievances to the lower house of the legislature. A 1786 gathering of citizens in Petersburg noted that "it is the indisputable right of Freemen to assemble at any time in a peaceable and orderly manner to discuss their public grievances, and if necessity shall require, to petition or remonstrate to their Rulers thereon."[1] The procedure used in the presentation and consideration of petitions was refined and placed upon a more systematic basis in the late seventeenth century, and the stage was set for the rapidly expanding influx of eighteenth-century petitions. In colonial Virginia petitioning thus assumed an important role in the political process. Following the transformation from colony to commonwealth, the petition remained the instrument most widely used by Virginians to communicate with their government and especially with their elected representatives in the House of Delegates.

When citizens desired to express an opinion or request some action involving a matter of strictly local concern, it was a relatively simple matter to petition the county court. The county court, which possessed extensive authority in the field of local government, met at a fixed location every month. Local inhabitants seeking extension of a county road, exemption from local taxes, or a wide variety of other matters could thus present their petitions in person to the local magistrates. Similarly, urban inhabitants used petitions to present requests and grievances to their town or city government.[2] In this fashion the presentation of petitions served as a primary method of communication between citizens and their local government.

The presentation of petitions concerning executive or judicial matters to the governor and council or to the General Court was also a simple matter during the colonial period. Procedure was still relatively informal, and many requests for executive or judicial action were initiated simply by petitioning the appropriate institution. These branches of government had a fixed time and place for meeting. Petitions could be given to individual councillors before they convened or else taken directly to the capital either by the petitioner or by an agent or attorney. An executive decision or judicial proceeding followed deliberation upon the request or grievance. The council judged some of these petitions to be better suited for legislative action and referred them to the House of Burgesses. The number of such instances increased throughout the eighteenth century as the lower house expanded its share of control over the internal affairs of the colony.[3] The governor and council could also inspect petitions presented to the house, although this was rarely requested.[4] They generally preferred to consider the bills which resulted from petitions to the burgesses rather than the actual petitions.

Of the petitions sent to the governor and council, more involved requests for land or for some judicial action than any other subjects. Before 1776 the governor, acting with the advice of the council, was empowered to make land grants in accordance with conditions specified in his instructions. The most important method of securing title to public lands during the seventeenth century was through the "headright." The headright system encouraged immigration by granting fifty acres to anyone who immigrated to Virginia or who financed the transportation of an immigrant. Two other methods became more common in the eighteenth century. First, "treasury rights," each of which could be redeemed for fifty acres, could be purchased at the secretary's office; a 1705 act set the price at five shillings per right. Second, when the amount of land involved in such a transaction totaled more than four hundred acres, the purchasers were required to secure a patent by petitioning the governor and council. Large grants involving thousands or even tens of thousands of acres were sometimes made to individuals or groups by the governor and council. These speculative tracts usually were granted with extremely liberal terms.[5] Once acquired by whatever method, land had to be "seated," i.e. the legally specified improvements and planting had to be made within three years or ownership lapsed back to the king. Land escheated to the king when the owner died without leaving a will or heirs. In both cases other colonists could acquire the land by petitioning the General Court.[6]

The governor and council also sat in their judicial capacity as the General Court during the colonial period, with both original and appellate jurisdiction. In addition, the governor possessed a limited power to grant pardons or remit fines. Petitions were frequently used to seek pardon, to initiate judicial proceedings before the General Court, or to appeal county court decisions to this higher authority.[7] After 1776, of course, the judiciary receiving such petitions was an independent branch of government rather than the governor and council sitting as a court of law.

By far the greatest number of petitions sent to the governor and council belonged to these two categories and were primarily procedural in nature, but Virginians also sent them other petitions involving certain substantive issues. For example, Indian affairs and command of the militia, the location of the county courthouses, and enforcement of the Navigation Acts were matters consigned in large measure to the colonial governor. Colonists seeking protection from Indian attacks, a change in the county seat, or new stations for customs agents thus usually sent their petitions to the chief executive rather than to the legislature.[8] The number and variety of these substantive petitions steadily declined during the eighteenth century, as colonists increasingly chose to petition their elected representatives in the lower house rather than the governor and council. This trend accelerated as the House of Burgesses became increasingly powerful in domestic affairs and as it convened more frequently after 1700.

After Independence the number of petitions sent to the executive branch declined even further. The power and prerogatives of the governor and his Council of State were greatly reduced by the constitution of 1776 and by subsequent legislation, as many formerly executive functions were transferred to other agencies. The governor's power to grant pardons and remit fines was further restricted and now shared with the legislature, for example, and after 1779 sale of state land was transacted through the state's land office. Although Virginians still sent petitions to the governor and council after 1776, these petitions invariably involved procedural rather than substantive matters.[9]

The presentation of petitions to the lower house and their consideration by that body involved a more complex procedure. After 1700 far more petitions were presented to the legislature than to the other branches of government. It is hardly surprising that Virginians preferred to send their propositions and grievances to their elected representatives, a preference which grew stronger as the power of the lower house to satisfy requests or redress grievances increased rapidly in the eighteenth century.

The petitions themselves were almost as varied in appearance as the people who sent them. In form they consisted of two parts: the body of the petition, which presented the request or stated the grievance, and a list of signatures. Some of the petitions contained learned and eloquent discourses, articulately expressed with meticulous handwriting upon fine quality paper. When arguing their cases, authors of these petitions might include references to the classic works of antiquity, the colonial heritage, philosophers such as "the Great Mr. Lock," or after 1776 to the Virginia constitution. In 1816 petitioners from Wood County, seeking to prove that establishment of a public school system would be of great public benefit, even resorted to quotations of poetry in order to impress the legislature with the justice of their arguments.[10] Some petitions were published in local newspapers or by a local printer in order to insure neatness and to facilitate circulation.[11] At the opposite extreme were those petitions containing but a brief paragraph expressing the opinions of the signers. Often written upon paper of poorer quality by a hand obviously less accustomed to setting pen to paper, such petitions offer additional evidence that Virginians of all social classes felt free to communicate by petition with their elected representatives.[12] Between these extremes, however, were the bulk of Virginia petitions, consisting of a paragraph or two which stated the request or grievance, and a list of signatures which ranged in number from one to several thousand.

Since petitioners hoped to persuade the legislature to grant their requests or redress their grievances, petitions almost always were worded in a respectful and temperate manner. This was not invariably the case, however, as on occasion irate citizens expressed their anger in the most direct and forceful fashion. A 1787 Harrison County petition thus asserted that a recent tax law was "impolitic, unjust, retrospective, and unconstitutional." Obviously these petitioners were not satisfied with the legislature's response, for in 1789 another petition from Harrison County described the tax laws as "Oppressive . . . Discriminatory . . . such as Could Only be Expected to Exist in Despotick Governments. . . . This act may appear pleasing to the Contracted politician . . . , [but it is] unjust Impolitick and Dangerous in Democratick Governments."[13]

Virginians seeking the consideration and the signatures of fellow inhabitants could circulate petitions in several ways. Frequently petitions were handed about or posted at the county courthouse. Other popular locations included churches, militia musters, general stores, and other sites frequented by large numbers of people. Petitions could also be advertised in local newspapers to insure widespread circulation.[14] Petitioners often printed several duplicate copies in order to facilitate circulation and obtain the maximum number of signatures.[15] When an important topic concerned the entire colony or state rather than merely one county or local community, as in the 1776-1786 struggle for religious freedom, interested citizens often mailed copies of petitions to friends in other counties. In this manner petitions and signatures could be obtained from all across Virginia in an attempt to influence the legislature.[16] Perhaps equally numerous were those petitions which did not require widespread circulation. Those concerning strictly individual matters, such as requests for pensions or payment for services rendered to the colony or state, need not have been circulated at all. Many other topics were of sufficiently localized concern that the petition could be circulated within the community from hand to hand or carried about by a particularly zealous inhabitant.[17]

During the late seventeenth century the house developed a standard procedure for the transmitting of petitions, and in the eighteenth century the procedure was amended slightly to insure that petitioners had ready access to their elected representatives. Prior to 1660 citizens generally presented petitions in person to the assembly or gave them to the burgesses when elections were conducted. This became impractical as the colony expanded and as no new election of burgesses was held from 1662 to 1676.[18] In response, by 1664 the house inaugurated a new method. Sheriffs were ordered to post advance notice at the courthouse or at the parish churches as to when and where the county's burgesses would meet to receive petitions. The burgesses normally met for this purpose at the courthouse, though on occasion other locations were used.[19] The 1680 assembly instituted the requirement that any petition intended for presentation to the house had to be written, signed by the petitioners, and attested or certified by the clerk or chief magistrate of the county court.[20]

Eighteenth-century procedure followed these basic guidelines with only minor amendments. A 1705 election law definitely fixed the county courthouse as the site for certification and presentation of petitions, and the county court was required to hold a special session for this purpose. On election day the sheriff announced the time when this special session of the court would meet; if no election was scheduled before the legislature met, notice of the court session was posted at all churches within the county.[21] After being certified, petitions were then given to the burgesses who carried them to the assembly. However, should a petitioner fail to give his certified petition to his burgesses at the courthouse, he could still take it or mail it to them after they reached the capital.[22] Prior to 1791 the house posted notice of the deadline after which no late petitions would be accepted without special permission. Beginning with the standing order of 1791 the first fifteen days of a session (excluding Sundays) were regularly prescribed for reception of petitions. The delegates later rejected an attempt to shorten this period, and the new standing rules of 1830 eliminated the deadline altogether. Even when a deadline was in effect, however, the house frequently gave permission for late petitions to be presented if the subject was important.[23]

During the first half of the seventeenth century, the assembly investigated and considered petitions in regular meetings of the entire body. The growing number of petitions and the increasing size of the assembly made this system increasingly unwieldy. Following the emergence of a bicameral assembly in the 1650s, the burgesses developed a more efficient procedure. A Committee for Public Affairs was appointed in 1658, and a number of petitions were referred to it for preliminary investigation. The 1663 House also appointed a Committee for Public Affairs, yet some petitions were still considered in a Committee of the whole House.[24] The major development came in 1666 when the burgesses created a Committee for Propositions and Grievances to investigate petitions. The committee originally had two divisions, as propositions and grievances were evaluated separately. The house referred most petitions to this committee, which presented a report on its findings. After 1666 the two divisions were consolidated into the Committee of Propositions and Grievances, which then became a standing committee, i.e. a committee regularly appointed at the beginning of each session of the assembly. After creating this standing committee, the burgesses thereafter referred most petitions to it for investigation.[25] In the beginning a few councillors also served on the committee, but in 1682 the assembly abandoned this practice when the governor and council protested that it was contrary to English precedent.[26]

By the end of the seventeenth century, the house regularly appointed three standing committees: Public Claims, Privileges and Elections, and Propositions and Grievances. Committees of Trade and of Courts of Justice were created early in the eighteenth century, and a Committee

for Religion was added in 1769. Each standing committee generally reported on petitions specifically involving its area of concern, but the lines
dividing committee jurisdiction were not sharply drawn during the
colonial period. The great majority of petitions concerning important
topics were referred to Propositions and Grievances.[27] The Committee of
Trade was terminated in 1789 because regulation of trade had been assigned to the federal government by the new federal Constitution, and
the Committee for Religion was abolished in 1798 to reinforce the concept of separation of church and state. The remaining standing committees
remained essentially unchanged during the eighteenth century.[28] Though it
happened infrequently, on occasion petitions or other matters involving
especially controversial topics were ordered to lie on the table temporarily
for the perusal of individual members, and such petitions could then be
referred directly to a Committee of the whole House if desired. Petitions
could also be referred for investigation to select committees, i.e. special
committees consisting of a small number of delegates assigned to consider
only a single topic or petition.[29]

The manner in which petitions were received and considered further
indicates the importance attached to them by the house. When a petition
was received, it was automatically read once before the house, and there
was no "gag rule" to prevent petitions concerning even the most controversial topics from being read.[30] Ordinarily the petition was then given
to the appropriate committee for examination. The committee investigated the petition and then presented its recommendation to the house,
suggesting acceptance or rejection. Committees possessed the necessary
powers to conduct thorough investigations: they could subpoena witnesses,
papers, and records; testimony could be accepted through depositions;
witnesses were privileged from arrest while in transit and compensated
for their expenses; legal counsel could be employed by the petitioners
or by other interested parties; the house consistently promised to act
"with the utmost severity" against anyone who should "tamper with any
witness" or hinder the collection of evidence, and this promise was enforced when necessary.[31] Since committee reports usually were based
upon careful investigation, in a majority of cases the house accepted and
acted upon them. The house could reverse a committee recommendation,
however, and did so on numerous occasions, thus insuring that no individuals,
sections, or interest groups could squelch petitions which they deemed objectionable merely by dominating the committee.[32]

Burgesses often "sponsored" the petitions of their constituents, explaining the contents to committee members or to other burgesses and insuring that action on the petition would not be unduly delayed in the traditional rush of business near the end of each session. Petitioners sometimes appeared in person at the assembly to "lobby" for their request. On occasion interested parties would write to influential burgesses in an attempt to win their support for, or insure their hostility to, a controversial petition. As Thomas Jefferson discovered, however, such tactics did not guarantee success. In 1817 Jefferson wrote to Joseph C. Cabell, a delegate from Albemarle County, to seek his support for a "private matters" petition from one of Jefferson's neighbors; though Cabell then supported the petition, the house rejected it anyway.[33]

Regardless of who sponsored or opposed a petition, if it involved an important topic, then it still faced a rigorous committee investigation. Examples to illustrate the care taken in these investigations are plentiful and could be multiplied almost *ad infinitum.* In 1701 the inhabitants of St. John's Parish in King and Queen County asked to be formed into a separate county. The house, uncertain whether the number of local taxpayers in the parish was sufficient to bear the expense of a new county, appointed a committee to determine the number of freeholders and the amount of land each owned. After a lengthy investigation, the burgesses decided in favor of the petition, and King William County was created by act of assembly.[34] In a 1790 election dispute the investigating committee submitted an extremely detailed report which required four pages in the house *Journal* to quote. Many other examples of careful investigation of petitions will appear in later chapters, and others could easily be cited.[35] If the petition was accepted, a bill embodying the request or redressing the grievance was prepared, usually by the committee which made the report. The bill then had to pass three readings in the house, receive the assent of the council, and be signed by the governor before it became law. After 1776 the approval of the Senate was substituted for that of the council, and the governor no longer had veto power.

Petitions lacking the required certification or worded in an obnoxious or insulting manner were generally rejected without even being referred to a committee.[36] The house rejected other petitions following the committee report for a variety of reasons. Not all rejected petitions were refused because the house disapproved of the proposition or grievance. Some petitions failed because they were too vague for the house to act upon them. In 1752 the burgesses rejected a petition to divide Amelia

County, not because they disagreed with such a division in principle, but because the petitioners had failed to explain where they wanted the division to be made. When the petitioners responded in 1753 by clarifying their intentions, the house granted their request, and Prince Edward County was created.[37] At other times the house rejected petitions because Virginia law already contained the desired provision and made additional action unnecessary.[38]

Some petitions, though not rejected outright, were referred by the house to its next session. The assembly was on occasion called into a special session to consider some emergency; this happened several times during the French and Indian War, the American Revolution, and the War of 1812. During these special sessions the house considered only those petitions requiring immediate attention, and all others were referred to the next regular meeting of the assembly. This policy caused little inconvenience to petitioners because wartime sessions were so frequent that the delay was of brief duration.[39] Controversial petitions were sometimes referred by the house to the next session in order to allow for additional investigation of the request. In such cases the house often appointed commissioners to investigate the matter thoroughly and report to the next session, and the commissioners were instructed to accept and consider evidence and testimony from all interested parties.[40]

Petitions were frequently rejected because counterpetitions from other inhabitants revealed significant opposition to the request or proposition. Throughout the eighteenth century, for example, petitioners seeking division of a county received a full hearing before a receptive lower house. Their chances for success fell dramatically, however, if other local citizens used counterpetitions to express widespread disapproval of the proposal. In such cases the petitions served as a "polling" device, or public opinion survey, and they allowed full expression of local sentiment. When the local opposition was sizable and vocal, the house was far more likely to postpone making a decision or to reject the proposal for division.[41]

By rejecting some petitions while accepting others, the house exercised its powers of discretion. Theoretically, petitioners asked the house to consider their propositions and grievances. The house was bound to give its consideration, but it always reserved the right to reject any petition which sought, in the opinion of the house, unwise or unnecessary action. Petitions thus differed from instructions, since a petition allowed discretion and was in that sense more "deferential." Petitions sought the consideration of the entire house, while instructions gave specific commands only to one's immediate representatives. Except for two occasions, instructions were very infrequently used in Virginia. Many counties did instruct their burgesses concerning the revolutionary opposition to English policy and the issue of independence, and after 1815 western counties often instructed their delegates to seek a revision of the Virginia constitution of 1776. Because of this infrequent use, Virginians never fully debated or decided the theoretical extent to which instructions could be used with binding force, and petitions rather than instructions remained the standard practice throughout the eighteenth century.[42]

The membership of the Committee of Propositions and Grievances provides an additional indication of the importance of the right of petition. This committee always included a substantial number of the most influential burgesses and delegates. John Robinson thus started his legislative career as a member of Propositions and Grievances before beginning his long tenure as speaker of the house. Other famous and powerful committee members during the colonial period included Charles Carter, Richard Bland, Jr., Landon Carter, Archibald Cary, Richard Henry Lee, and Edmund Pendleton. The list of post-1776 members is equally distinguished, including such revolutionary leaders as Patrick Henry, Thomas Jefferson, James Madison, and George Mason, and such later powers as Edmund Randolph, Samuel Jordan Cabell, John Marshall, and Wilson Cary Nicholas.[43]

Since the house referred most petitions to Propositions and Grievances for preliminary examination, it quickly became by far the largest and most important of the eighteenth-century committees. Table 1 reveals its dramatic increase in size.[44] These figures clearly reveal that a major increase began in the 1730s and continued throughout the century. The number of members on the 1752 committee was triple that of 1730, and by 1770 Propositions and Grievances was almost six times its 1730 size. The growth after 1776 was especially rapid, until by 1790 almost every member of the house was appointed to its most important committee. Two developments in particular produced this increase in committee membership. By mid-eighteenth century the colony of Virginia, through the lower house of the legislature, had achieved substantial domestic autonomy.[45] Increased legislative control over internal policy and a growing influx of petitions on internal matters were mutually reinforcing. As the power of the legislature increased and more domestic affairs came under its control,

TABLE 1 COMMITTEE MEMBERSHIP

Year	Propositions & Grievances	Privileges & Elections	Claims	Courts of Justice	Religion	Trade	Total House Membership
1701	10	5	9				47
1705	10	4	9				50
1710	12	6	10				51
1715	11	5	11				51
1720	14	5	10				54
1726	13	7	11				58
1730	13	7	10	11			63
1736	20	12	13	17			71
1740	20	13	16	14			71
1746	28	11	19	14		12	80
1752	39	18	28	22		16	92
1755	40	17	25	16		17	104
1760	40	19	23	15		15	106
1766	49	20	30	23		16	116
1770	73	29	43	24	51	30	120
1776	66	64	41	24	55	25	126
1780	66	22	—a	21	18	27	144
1785	112	38	59	28	26	33	156
1790	141	66	103	56	39		179
1795	178b	79	155	58	31		177
1800	173	68	46	50			183

aNo Committee of Claims was appointed at this session.
bIncludes several delegates later removed following contested elections.

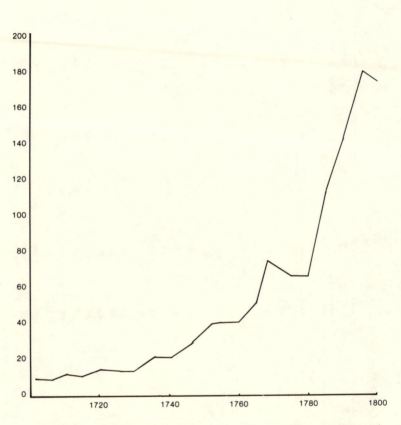

FIGURE 1 Number of Members on Committee of Propositions and Grievances, 1700-1800

Virginians responded by petitioning their representatives in the lower house concerning those matters; this popular interest and popular pressure, in turn, stimulated further legislative activity as the lower house responded to the petitions. Increased committee membership thus symbolized both the growing authority of the lower house over internal matters and the increasing importance of petitioning.

The American Revolution stimulated increased committee membership in much the same way. With British authority eliminated and the federal government deliberately denied effective internal authority, Virginia concentrated almost complete control over internal matters in the House of Delegates. In addition, the rhetoric of the Revolution emphasized such concepts as natural rights, popular government, and the ultimate sovereignty of the people. As Jackson Turner Main has illustrated, such rhetoric helped to "democratize" the system and stimulated greater popular participation in government.[46] The concentration of authority in the lower house, coupled with an increase in popular participation in government, further enhanced the importance of petitioning and thus led to a continuing dramatic increase in the size of the Committee of Propositions and Grievances.

Because Propositions and Grievances was by far the most powerful and important of the standing committees, the geographic distribution of its membership has significant implications concerning sectional relations. Had the Tidewater intended to monopolize political power and discriminate against other sections, it should have been reluctant to extend representation in the assembly to the Piedmont and West. As settlement expanded into these areas in the eighteenth century, however, the legislature proved willing—even eager—to create new counties for the convenience of these settlers.[47] Since representation in the legislature was based on the county unit, each additional Piedmont and western county meant two additional non-Tidewater members of the House. Sectional discrimination might nevertheless be present if the new Piedmont and western countries were denied equitable representation on the Committee of Propositions and Grievances. Committee members were assigned at the beginning of each session by the speaker of the house, but other members were regularly added during the session by the speaker or on motion by any other member of the house. In both cases, however, the house retained final approval over committee membership. In the eighteenth century, then, a Tidewater-dominated house could have ex-

cluded Piedmont and western members from important committee assignments.[48] As Robert Detweiler has shown, sectional discrimination was
not a significant factor in committee assignments even before 1776.[49]
Table 2 summarizes committee assignments for the sessions of 1730,
1752, 1769, and 1790.[50]

At the 1730 session the counties along the Fall Line, still "the West"
at that date, were accorded a proportionately fair share of committee
assignments. By 1752 eleven counties had been created in the Piedmont
and Valley; all eleven of them were represented on one or more of the
standing committees at that session, though there does appear to have
been some delay in placing these burgesses on Propositions and Grievances.
By 1769, however, Propositions and Grievances included burgesses from
more than three-fourths of the Piedmont and western counties, and by
1790, fifty-two of fifty-three Piedmont and western counties placed a
total of eighty-six delegates on that committee. These eighty-six delegates outnumbered their Tidewater and Fall Line counterparts on the
committee by a three-to-two margin. In short, Piedmont and western
representation on Propositions and Grievances grew rapidly during the
eighteenth century. This analysis does not necessarily indicate that there
were no sectional differences, but it does illustrate that each section had
an opportunity to be heard on the most important of all committees and
that no section dominated the house through an uncontested control of
house committees.

The attempts to facilitate the presentation and consideration of petitions served to enhance the significance of petitioning. Except on a very
few occasions, the governor, council, and House of Burgesses all agreed
that legitimate petitions concerning the requests and grievances of Virginia
citizens required official consideration and response. This belief was so
widely held by all classes that it was regarded as axiomatic. Yet challenges
occasionally arose which threatened to undermine the effectiveness of
petitioning. These challenges belonged to two general categories. On the
one hand, royal governors twice directly interfered with the presentation
of petitions; on the other, local justices of the peace occasionally attempted
to thwart the presentation of petitions which they considered objectionable. The house successfully resisted both types of challenges, however,
and its defense of the right of petition reemphasized the importance of
petitioning in the political process.

Both challenges by royal governors occurred in the seventeenth century.
The first was associated with Governor Berkeley and Bacon's Rebellion.

TABLE 2 SECTIONAL CHARACTERISTICS OF PROPOSITIONS AND GRIEVANCES

	Counties			Delegates				
	Number	Percentage on P&G	Percentage on Some Standing Committee	Number	Number on P&G	Percentage on P&G	Percentage of Total P&G Membership	Percentage of Total House Membership
1730								
Tidewater	25[a]	40.0	64.0	47	10	21.3	76.9	74.6
Fall Line	7	42.9	100.0	14	3	21.4	23.1	22.2
Piedmont	1	0.0	0.0	2	0	0.0	0.0	3.2
Valley & West	0	–	–	–	–	–	–	–
1752								
Tidewater	28[a]	64.3	100.0	52	24	46.2	61.5	56.5
Fall Line	9	77.8	100.0	18	11	61.1	28.2	19.6
Piedmont	9	33.3	100.0	18	3	16.7	7.7	19.6
Valley & West	2	50.0	100.0	4	1	25.0	2.6	4.4
1769								
Tidewater	29[a]	89.7	100.0	54	39	72.2	53.4	48.2
Fall Line	10	100.0	100.0	20	16	80.0	21.9	17.9
Piedmont	16[b]	75.0	100.0	32	15	46.9	20.6	28.6
Valley & West	3	100.0	100.0	6	3	50.0	4.1	5.4
1790								
Tidewater	29[a]	93.1	100.0	55	44	80.0	31.2	30.7
Fall Line	9	88.9	100.0	18	11	61.1	7.8	10.1
Piedmont	26	96.2	100.0	52	42	80.8	29.8	29.1
Valley & West	27	100.0	100.0	54	44	81.5	31.2	30.2

[a]Includes incorporated cities.
[b]Delegates from two additional counties did not arrive at this session.

When hostilities with the Indians erupted in 1675, many Virginians quickly lost faith in Berkeley's policy of defensive war. They sent petitions to the governor requesting that he appoint a commander to lead the armed forces in an active campaign against the Indians. Instead of granting the request, Berkeley issued a proclamation forbidding any further petitioning on that subject and threatening malcontents with heavy penalties. Berkeley's action involved only petitions to the governor, however, as he made no attempt to interfere with petitions sent to the assembly. Following the rebellion, England sent commissioners to investigate the affair and to hear the grievances of the people. Berkeley's illegal infringement of the right of petition was one of the grievances reported to the commissioners.[51]

A 1688 dispute between the burgesses and Governor Francis Howard, baron of Effingham, produced the second threat to the right of petition by a royal governor. The house received several petitions complaining of new and exorbitant fees charged by some officials, fees which were unauthorized by the assembly and had been initiated solely on the governor's authority. The burgesses vigorously protested. The controversy increased when petitioners in Northampton and Accomack counties complained that John Custis, the district customs collector, had charged the new fees and had attempted to intimidate local citizens. When a number of people presented a petition to their local burgesses complaining of his actions, Custis seized and destroyed the petition and threatened the petitioners. Upon learning of the incident, the house asked Governor Effingham to punish Custis so that citizens would not feel "hindered or molested in giveing their just grievances for redress by General Assemblies. . . ."[52]

Effingham, an autocratic and increasingly unpopular governor, refused to abolish the new fees or punish Custis. He instead demanded that all petitions and grievances received by the house be given directly to the governor and council for such redress as they deemed appropriate. The house immediately refused to comply with this demand, recognizing that such procedure would radically alter the traditional method of redress by eliminating the role of the lower house in receiving and considering petitions. While the governor and council had the right to examine petitions sent to the house, they had no authority to forbid house consideration of petitions. Effingham's conduct became so objectionable to the burgesses in this and other matters that the house sent Philip Ludwell as an agent to England in order to protest Effingham's conduct. Colonial dissatisfaction was relieved when Effingham was recalled to England;

though he was allowed to become an absentee governor, Francis Nicholson was sent to Virginia as lieutenant governor. In 1692 the council disavowed its support of Effingham and admitted that his removal had prevented a serious disturbance.[53]

The house briefly thought that it perceived a similar threat in 1753.
Shortly after his arrival as the new governor, Robert Dinwiddie initiated
a fee of one pistole for affixing his seal and signature to land patents.
When the assembly convened in 1753, it received petitions which complained of the new fee. The burgesses protested Dinwiddie's action, and
a vigorous controversy ensued until a compromise settlement was finally
achieved through the intervention of the English government. During the
debate the house suspected that Dinwiddie was questioning its right to
inquire into popular grievances. The burgesses responded:

> We do humbly, but in the strongest Terms, represent to
> your Honour, that it is the undoubted Right of the Burgesses
> to enquire into the Grievances of the People: They have con-
> stantly exercised this Right, and we presume to affirm, that
> the drawing it into Question, in any Manner, cannot but be
> of dangerous Consequences to the Liberties of his Majesty's
> faithful Subjects, and to the Constitution of this Govern-
> ment.[54]

Governor Dinwiddie did not then follow Effingham's example and frankly
question the right of the burgesses to receive petitions. He instead admitted that petitions should be heard and redressed, insisting only that
"Complaints should be well grounded, and the Grievances really felt."[55]

The other kind of challenge, where justices of the peace interfered with
petitioning, arose after passage of the 1680 law requiring that petitions
be certified by the county courts before being presented to the house.
Had local justices been allowed to reject petitions which they deemed
objectionable, the use of petitions to present grievances would have been
seriously curtailed. The 1680 requirement was enacted after the assembly
had received a massive influx of petitions following Bacon's Rebellion.
Though these petitions had expressed numerous alleged grievances, the
house considered many of them to be "false," "impertinent," "libellous,"
"scandalous," and "Rebellious."[56] The intention of the 1680 Assembly
in enacting the certification requirement, however, has remained unclear.

Philip Alexander Bruce, for example, maintained that the 1680 requirement was deliberately intended to restrict the right of petition by allowing justices to reject false or objectionable petitions. H. R. McIlwaine, on
the other hand, insisted that justices were denied discretionary power and
were required to certify all petitions presented to them; in McIlwaine's
view, the burgesses felt that merely requiring petitions to be signed and
certified would discourage frivolous petitioning.[57]

The wording of the 1680 law was so vague that the intention cannot
be clearly ascertained, as the assembly merely stated that it would accept
"all county grievances which shalbe signed by the partyes giveing the
same and attested by the clarke of the county court, or chief magistrate
soe to be. . . ."[58] By implication, at least, the clerk or chief magistrate
could refuse to attest objectionable petitions, and in 1693 the Henrico
County Court did refuse to attest a petition which it deemed "contary
to their majesties Intrest."[59] But even if the original purpose was to permit the county courts to reject petitions, the house soon abandoned that
intention. In 1705 the law was clarified. Petitions were required to be
signed and presented to the county court, "and thereupon the chief
magistrate then present, or the clerk, by the direction of the court, *shall
certify* [italics mine] the same to the General Assembly. . . ."[60]

Despite the 1705 clarification, disputes occasionally arose when justices
attempted to reject petitions, and in every instance the house condemned
such attempts and punished the justices involved. In 1715 Governor Spotswood issued a proclamation instructing the county courts to refuse certification of "Scandalous and Seditious" petitions from "ill Disposed persons." The county courts in New Kent, Richmond, and Charles City
counties did, in fact, then refuse to certify several petitions. When the
assembly convened, the uncertified petitions were presented to the house,
and the burgesses began an investigation of the affair. The house asserted
that it was the "part of the Legislature which Represents the People from
whom the Propositions and Grievances have their Rise," and it branded
the action of the justices as "Arbitrary and illegal and a Subverting of the
Rights and Libertys of the People." The offending justices were required
to appear before the house to explain their conduct. When two justices
of New Kent failed to appear, the house asked Spotswood to arrest them.
Spotswood refused to do so, since their action had been prompted by his
proclamation. The governor instructed the house that if justices were not
allowed to inspect the contents of petitions, they would be required to
certify all sorts of charges, whether true or false, lawful or seditious; this,

he added, would render certification meaningless. Neither Spotswood nor the house would concede, however, as the burgesses considered the un-certified petitions and Spotswood refused to arrest the two justices.[61]

No governor after Spotswood challenged the house interpretation, so after 1722 any justice who refused to certify a petition faced being taken into custody, reprimanded, and fined by the house. Governor Drysdale supported the house in a 1723 incident. Later, two justices from Elizabeth City County were called before the 1728 house for refusing to certify a petition which protested the conduct of the local vestry—on which the two justices sat as vestrymen. The justices defended themselves by charg-ing that the content of the petition was false, some of the signatures were not genuine, and the person who had presented the petition was not one of the signers. Even though the burgesses did not question these asser-tions, they reprimanded and fined the justices on the grounds that "it was no part of their Business to inquire into the matter of it." Similar cases in later years produced the same result. One of the guilty justices in 1746 was also a burgess, but his political power won him no privileged treatment. Like the other guilty parties, he was reprimanded for acting "illegally, arbitrarily, and contrary to the Rights of the People."[62] These and similar actions by the house confirm that certification did not become a threat to the right of petition. In effect, Governor Spotswood was correct in asserting that certification was a meaningless procedure, for if anyone felt that his petition was sufficiently important for presentation, the house guaranteed that it would be received and considered.

The significance of petitioning, both as a source of legislation and as one available means for popular participation in the political process, was considerably enhanced by its widespread use among all social classes. Had only an elite few made use of petitions, they might simply be dismissed as an additional tool for aristocratic domination. Investigation of this matter is hampered by several problems. The house *Journals* describe the subject matter of each petition but, due to limitations of space, do not list the signatures attached to the petitions. This difficulty is compounded by the unfortunate destruction in 1865 of all but a few of the petitions presented during the colonial period. Although most of the petitions presented after 1776 have survived, data on many of the signers of peti-tions is sparse and difficult to come by.

Despite these limitations, a survey of the petitions presented to the legislature both before and after Independence reveals that all classes utilized petitions to express their requests and grievances. Prominent political figures, wealthy planters and merchants, local officials, and other members of the upper class petitioned the assembly on numerous occasions. For example, Lewis Burwell in 1759 and Thomas Jefferson in 1774 both petitioned the house seeking to "dock," or terminate, the entail on certain tracts of their land. Before entails were abolished in 1776, entailing a tract of land insured that it would stay in the family, but the device more often proved to be a hindrance to sound business practices than an instrument of aristocratic privilege. Consequently, petitions by middle- and upper-class citizens to dock entails were common during the colonial period.[63] Gentlemen also sought assistance from the legislature in other matters of concern, as when Edmund Pendleton requested aid in his dispute with North Carolina over land claims, or when a group of merchants in Alexandria asked that the state establish a naval office in the town.[64]

As Charles Carter of Corotoman discovered in 1766, however, social prominence did not insure a favorable decision on the petitions of the elite. Carter petitioned the assembly in that year to seek payment for one of his slaves who had been outlawed for murder and was killed while resisting arrest. Such requests were fairly common because by law the Virginia government compensated the owners of slaves outlawed or executed by the public. Since Carter was himself a burgess in 1766, and since he was a scion of one of the wealthiest and most powerful of the "aristocratic" Virginia families, he probably anticipated little difficulty in securing payment. Carter's optimism nevertheless proved unfounded. The house soon discovered that the slave had been dead for about fourteen or fifteen years before Carter made his application. Perhaps the necessary proof had been lost in the interval, or perhaps the burgesses simply were exasperated at the delay in presenting the claim; for whatever reason, Carter's petition was rejected without even being referred to the Committee of Claims.[65]

Some petitioners apparently believed that their social rank might influence the legislature, as the signatures of prominent figures were sometimes placed in conspicuous positions on petitions. Thus when a large number of Caroline County residents decided in 1792 to petition the legislature for establishment of a tobacco warehouse in their vicinity, they approached the most influential man in the county and solicited his support. Edmund Pendleton did not write the petition himself, but his signature was first among the 170 on the petition.[66] In most cases, however, little or no consideration seems to have been given to the social rank of the signers or to the order in which they signed. In 1797, 684 Greenbrier inhabitants petitioned to protest against any attempt to divide their county, yet the very first man to sign could not write and thus "signed" with his mark. Of the eighty-six signatures on a 1783 petition from King and Queen County which protested a recent tax law, perhaps the most prominent were those of William Hill, Temple Gwathmey, John White, and Robert Hill. Each of these men belonged to the political and economic elite of King and Queen. The two Hills and White were justices of the peace. According to the 1782 tax list for King and Queen, each man possessed significant holdings in that county: William Hill was assessed for 1591 acres, valued at £556.17.0; Temple Gwathmey held 600 acres, valued at £510.0.0; John White's 957 acres were assessed at £669.18.0; and Robert Hill held 1600 acres, valued at £320.0.0. Yet these four men signed near the bottom of the petition, below the signatures of several men like James Walton (who owned eighty acres, valued at £8.0.0) and Benjamin Dean (whose tract of fifty acres was assessed at £6.5.0). Some signers owned no land; Reubin Clayton, for example, lived in the county but owned neither land nor slaves, yet he also signed before White, Gwathmey, or William Hill.[67]

The right of petition was not restricted by any requirements involving class, sex, or even race. As the assembly had proclaimed in 1705, it would accept and consider "the propositions and grievances . . . of all and every person and persons,"[68] and there were no exceptions. Petitions from poor Virginians or including the signatures of lower-class citizens were common, and many were granted. A 1696 petition from Westmoreland County complained of the high fees for probating wills and administrations for small estates. The Committee of Propositions and Grievances reported that through either "misconstruction" of the laws or an "avaritious humor," many clerks were charging excessive fees, and a bill regulating those fees was passed by the assembly and signed into law by the governor.[69] Particularly during the 1780s, when Virginia like the other fledgling states faced serious economic difficulties, a number of petitioners claimed that they were too poor to pay their taxes. Distress was so widespread at that time that the Virginia government responded with a series of measures to relieve taxpayers, such as allowing payment in commodities and tax reductions.[70] Moreover, hundreds of aged or infirm citizens, disabled veterans, widows, and other poor persons petitioned throughout the eighteenth century for public assistance or pensions, and the legislature listened sympathetically to their pleas. [71] Finally, many eighteenth-century petitions bore the "marks" of men unable to write their names along with the signatures of those who could. Although in individual cases a mark cannot be taken as conclusive evidence of lower-class status, in most cases such an inference seems to be justified. [72]

Though denied the right to vote and considered in many regards to be the "subordinate" sex, women at times also petitioned the house. Generally their petitions involved matters of strictly individual concern, as when widows of war veterans sought financial assistance from the public treasury. Occasionally, however, women would join with Virginia men in signing petitions which involved issues of public importance. This occurred most frequently in matters concerning religion, in itself perhaps a reflection of eighteenth-century notions regarding "a woman's place." One 1779 petition to the legislature, urging division of Drysdale Parish, included the signatures of a dozen ladies, and a counterpetition against division was signed by several more female church members along with their male counterparts. [73]

In eighteenth-century Virginia, blacks, whether slave or free, were denied such elementary political rights as voting and holding office, but on a few occasions even slaves used petitions to communicate with the legislature. This was especially common after 1776, when the assembly assumed the power to authorize the manumission of slaves and indicated its willingness to do so under more lenient requirements than those previously used by the colonial governor and council. Dozens of blacks thereafter petitioned to seek their freedom on the grounds of having performed some meritorious act or of carrying out the provisions regarding emancipation in the will of a deceased owner. [74]

In a few instances free blacks also petitioned regarding matters of immediate concern. A group of mulattoes and free blacks petitioned the house in 1769 to ask that their wives and daughters be exempted from paying poll taxes, a tax assessed on adult males of both races but on black females only. Both houses of the assembly and the governor agreed that the request was reasonable, and a bill ending the poll tax on black women was passed into law. [75] In 1810 and again in 1816 Harry Jackson, a free black residing in the city of Norfolk, petitioned seeking exemption from the 1802 law which forbade the employment of blacks as river and harbor pilots. Jackson's father had been a pilot and had taught the occupation to his son.

But despite a statement from forty-one other pilots, including the commissioner for the appointment of pilots, that Jackson was qualified for the occupation, his request was rejected by the house in 1810 and by the Senate in 1816. Similarly, an 1823 petition from a group of free blacks in Richmond, who desired permission to erect a church, was overwhelmingly rejected by the house.[76] It is also possible that free blacks might occasionally have signed petitions along with their white neighbors; however, it seems likely that if such cases did exist, they were the rare exception rather than the rule. It should be noted, however, that the few petitions sent by blacks were handled by the house in exactly the same fashion as the petitions of other inhabitants.

Both the elite and the underprivileged exercised the right of petition, but most petitions of general concern involved matters of interest to citizens of all social classes and were signed by everyone desiring to do so. The great majority of petitioners and signers of petitions thus came from the vast middle ranks of society, a fact emphasized most clearly in those petitions containing hundreds or even thousands of signatures. Controversies concerning division of a county or parish often led to petitions and counterpetitions signed by a sizable percentage of the local white adult male population. During the 1779 debate over division of Drysdale Parish, about 750 parishioners signed petitions to the assembly. A 1781 proposal to divide Bedford County was supported by petitions bearing the signatures of 843 county inhabitants, and the 1790 petitions and counterpetitions over division of Henry County contained 1124 signatures (which, according to the 1790 census, was 73.8 percent of the total number of free white males age sixteen and over residing in the county).[77] Though the destruction of most colonial petitions makes a precise count impossible, other evidence clearly indicates that questions of county and parish division elicited an equally widespread response from colonial petitioners. During a 1767 conflict over a proposed division of Augusta County, six petitions and counterpetitions were "very Industriously handed about" by many people, and the resulting controversy within Augusta continued amidst much confusion for more than two years before the county was finally divided.[78] Similarly, the heated debates over division of Goochland County in 1744 and Surry County in 1752 and 1753 produced a multitude of petitions and counterpetitions, and Hugh Jones reported in 1724 that similar controversy often accompanied proposals to divide parishes.[79]

Many petitions on other topics also contained extensive lists of signatures. In 1774 an Albemarle petition to establish a ferry over the Rivanna and Fluvanna rivers was signed by 190 inhabitants who were convinced that the ferry would greatly improve local transportation. Petitions and counterpetitions bearing 490 signatures precipitated a 1787 debate over the location of the county clerk's office in Accomack County, and more than 800 Amherst citizens petitioned in 1796 to support or oppose a proposal that their county needed an additional tobacco inspection warehouse.[80] Even these figures cannot rival the 1776-1786 debate over disestablishment of the Anglican Church and the attainment of religious freedom. During that debate, several sessions of the legislature were literally flooded with petitions bearing many thousands of total signatures—one famous 1776 petition alone included 125 pages of signatures.[81] In short, Virginians of all social classes were accustomed to petitioning the legislature whenever they desired to do so and concerning whatever suggestions or complaints they had. As *The Present State of Virginia, and the College,* written in 1697, noted, "to know the Pressures, Humours, Common Talk, and Designs of the People of that Country, perhaps there is no better Way than to peruse the Journals of the House of Burgesses, and of the Committee of Grievances and Propositions."[82]

Notes

1. William P. Palmer, Sherwin McRae, and Raleigh Colston, eds., *Calendar of Virginia State Papers and Other Manuscripts,* 11 vols. (1875-93; reprint ed., New York, 1968), 4: 171 (hereafter cited as *Cal. Va. State Papers*).

2. Lewis P. Summers, ed., *Annals of Southwest Virginia, 1769-1800* (1929; reprint ed., Baltimore, 1970), p. 281; Lyman Chalkley, ed., *Chronicles of the Scotch-Irish Settlement in Virginia, Extracted from the Original Court Records of Augusta County, 1745-1800,* 3 vols. (1912; reprint ed., Baltimore, 1965), 1: 16, 51, 79, 198; John F. Dorman, ed., *Westmoreland County, Virginia: Order Book, 1690-1698; Part One, 1690-1-1692* (Washington, D.C., 1962), entry for 25 March 1692; Albert O. Porter, *County Government in Virginia* (New York, 1947), pp. 47-48; May 1790 meeting of Norfolk City Common Council—see Norfolk City, Minutes of the Common Council, 1736-1798, microfilm at VSL; Warren M. Billings, ed., *The Old Dominion in the Seventeenth Century* (Chapel Hill, N.C., 1975), p. 91; George L. Chumbley, *Colonial Justice in Virginia* (Richmond, 1938), p. 60.

3. *JHB,* 1695-1702: 67; 1702/3-1712: 89, 247; 1727-1740: 354-55; 1752-1758: 39; Henry R. McIlwaine, ed., *Legislative Journals of the Council of Colonial Virginia,* 3 vols. (Richmond, 1918-19), 1: 260-61, 298, 413, 540 (hereafter cited as *LJC*). As Governor Gooch explained to the Board of Trade, petitions seeking

legislative action generally went directly to the House of Burgesses, which prepared bills from the petitions—Gooch to Board of Trade, n.d., "Virginia Under Governor Gooch," *VMHB* 3 (October 1895): 115.

   4. *LJC* 1: 40.

   5. Thomas P. Abernethy, *Three Virginia Frontiers* (1940; reprint ed., Gloucester, Mass., 1962), pp. 39-40; W. Stitt Robinson, Jr., *Mother Earth—Land Grants in Virginia, 1607-1699,* Jamestown 350th Anniversary Historical Booklets, ed. E. G. Swem (Williamsburg, 1957), pp. 30-43; Robert E. Brown and B. Katherine Brown, *Virginia 1705-1786: Democracy or Aristocracy?* (East Lansing, Mich., 1964), pp. 11-12; Aubrey C. Land, "Economic Behavior in a Planting Society: The Eighteenth-Century Chesapeake," *Journal of Southern History* 33 (November 1967): 480-85; Henry R. McIlwaine et al., eds., *Executive Journals of the Council of Colonial Virginia,* 6 vols. (Richmond, 1925-66), 3: 423, 515; 4: 2, 11, 37, 39, 83, 87, 430-31; 5: 134, 175-77, 435-36 (hereafter cited as *EJC*); *Cal. Va. State Papers,* 1: 176, 177, 198, 200, 203, 214, 216, 260, 262, 265; Edmund Pendleton to Thomas Jefferson, 3 August 1776, in *The Letters and Papers of Edmund Pendleton, 1734-1803,* ed. David J. Mays, 2 vols. (Charlottesville, Va., 1967), 1: 195-97.

   6. Henry Hartwell, James Blair, and Edward Chilton, *Present State of Virginia, and the College,* ed. Hunter D. Farish (Williamsburg, 1940), pp. 20, 29; Robert Beverley, *History and Present State of Virginia,* ed. Louis B. Wright (Chapel Hill, N.C., 1947), pp. 277-80; *Cal. Va. State Papers,* 3: 83, 149, 163, 167, 219; *EJC,* 1: 303; 5: 184; William Fitzhugh to Nicholas Spencer, 2 November 1680, in *William Fitzhugh and His Cheasapeake World, 1676-1701,* ed. Richard B. Davis (Chapel Hill, N.C., 1963), p. 77; Philip A. Bruce, *Economic History of Virginia in the Seventeenth Century,* 2 vols. (New York, 1895), 1: 564-65.

   7. Hugh F. Rankin, *Criminal Trial Proceedings in the General Court of Colonial Virginia* (Charlottesville, Va., 1965), pp. 89, 105-07; Oliver P. Chitwood, "Justice in Colonial Virginia," *Johns Hopkins Studies* 23 (1905): 442-44; Philip A. Bruce, *Institutional History of Virginia in the Seventeenth Century,* 2 vols. (New York, 1910), 1: 665, 686-87; 2: 320, 321, 360; Edmund Pendleton to John Buchanan, 18 June 1764, in *Pendleton Letters,* ed. Mays, 1: 17; William Fitzhugh to Nicholas Hayward, 3 November 1690, in *Fitzhugh Letters,* ed. Davis, p. 282; William Gooch, Answers to Queries from the Board of Trade, 1749, William Gooch Papers, 3 vols., transcripts, VHS, 3: 975; 1762 Petition of John Catlet to Gov. Fauquier, Colonial Papers, folder 46, item 4, VSL; *EJC,* 1: 27, 55, 326, 372, 522; 2: 11-12, 305, 338, 363; 3: 319, 329, 345-46; 4: 31, 64-65, 150; *Cal. Va. State Papers,* 1: 2-3, 5-6, 8-9, 19, 94, 101; Hartwell, Blair, and Chilton, *Present State of Virginia,* pp. 46-48.

   8. *EJC,* 1: 275, 284; 3: 466; 6: 203, 227; *Cal. Va. State Papers,* 1: 2, 60, 70-72, 203-04, 212-13, 221-23, 235, 252.

   9. William Waller Hening, ed., *The Statutes at Large: Being a Collection of All the Laws of Virginia,* 13 vols. (Richmond and Philadelphia, 1809-23), 10: 50-65; 11: 463; Thomas Jefferson to Samuel Huntington, 9 February 1780, in *Official Letters of the Governors of the State of Virginia,* ed. Henry R. McIlwaine, 3 vols. (Richmond, 1926-29), 2: 98; Dumas Malone, *Jefferson and His Time,* Vol. I: *Jefferson the Virginian* (Boston, 1948), pp. 257-59; Brown and Brown, *Virginia 1705-1786,* p. 284; Merrill D. Peterson, *Thomas Jefferson and the New Nation*

(New York, 1970), pp. 120-22; Edmund Pendleton to Theodorick Bland, Jr., 19 July 1782, in *The Bland Papers*, ed. Charles Campbell, 2 vols. (Petersburg, Va., 1840-43), 2: 86; Samuel Shepherd, ed., *The Statutes at Large of Virginia . . . Being a Continuation of Hening*, 3 vols. (Richmond, 1835-36), 1: 292 (hereafter cited as Shepherd, *Virginia Statutes*); Virginia, *Journals of the House of Delegates, 1776-1831* (Williamsburg and Richmond, 1776-1831), 1803: 38, 45, 101 (hereafter cited as *JHD*); *Cal. Va. State Papers*, 3: 256; 4: 77-78, 311, 504, 548; 10: 448-49.

10. Henry County Petition, 23 November 1782; Augusta Petition, 16 November 1790; Pittsylvania Petition, 10 November 1796 (oversize); Wood County Petition, 22 November 1816; Amherst, Campbell, Bedford, and Lynchburg Petition, 21 December 1826; Petition of the United Clergy of the Presbyterian Church in Virginia, 26 May 1784 (religious petitions); Petition of the Clergy of the Protestant Episcopal Church, 4 June 1784 (religious petitions); Rockingham Petition, 18 November 1784 (religious petitions); Albemarle Petition, 28 October 1785 (religious petitions). Unless otherwise noted, all petitions and religious petitions are located at VSL.

11. Loudoun, Prince William, Fairfax, and Fauquier Petition, 8 December 1797 (12 copies printed); Greenbrier Petition, 13 December 1815; Wood, Harrison, and Lewis Petition, 14 December 1818; Frederick Petition, 3 January 1832; Winchester *Virginian*, 28 December 1831.

12. Essex Petition, 2 November 1785 (religious petitions); King and Queen Petition, 5 November 1785 (religious petitions); Petition of Harry Jackson, 20 November 1816 (a free black in Norfolk City); Washington County Petition, 16 November 1822; Monongalia Petition, 4 December 1822; W. Edwin Hemphill, "Petitions of West Virginians to their General Assembly in Richmond," *West Virginia History* 18 (January 1957): 110.

13. *JHD*, 1787 (1828 reprint): 12; Harrison County Petition, 26 October 1789 — apparently such wording seemed excessive to most citizens since the petition contained only twelve signatures.

14. *JHD*, May 1784: 27, 32-33; Berkeley Petition, 25 October 1776 (religious petitions); Petition of the Baptist Association, assembled at Dover Meeting House, 11 November 1784 (religious petitions); Bedford Petition, 10 November 1785 (religious petitions); Botetourt Petition, 7 December 1830; Thomas Jefferson to James Madison, 3 August 1797, in *The Works of Thomas Jefferson*, ed. Paul L. Ford, 12 vols., Federal Edition (New York, 1904-15), 8: 334; see examples of advertising in newspapers cited below.

15. Pittsylvania Petition, 10 November 1796 (oversize); Monongalia Petitions, 4 and 5 December 1822; Montgomery Petition, 14 December 1804; Greenbrier Petition, 18 December 1798; Loudoun, Prince William, Fairfax, and Fauquier Petition, 8 December 1797.

16. James Madison to George Mason, 14 July 1826, James Madison Papers, VHS; George Mason to George Washington, 2 October 1785, Washington to Mason, 3 October 1785, Mason to Robert Carter, 5 October 1785, and Carter to Mason, 15 October 1785, all in *The Papers of George Mason, 1725-1792*, ed. Robert A. Rutland, 3 vols. (Chapel Hill, N.C., 1970), 2: 830-33; see the discussion of the general assessment controversy in chapter 7.

17. William Irvin to Thomas Jefferson, [before 1 November 1776], in *The Papers of Thomas Jefferson*, ed. Julian P. Boyd, 19 vols. to date (Princeton, N.J., 1950-   ), 1: 585-89; R. Douthat to John Preston, 9 October 1802, Preston Davie Collection of Preston Family Papers, VHS; John P. Dupuy to Asa Dupuy, 8 December 1824, letter in VHS; Thomas Lewis to William Preston, 24 February 1767, Preston Papers, Draper MSS (2QQ100).

18. Bruce, *Institutional History*, 2: 480, 491; Richard L. Morton, *Colonial Virginia*, 2 vols. (Chapel Hill, N.C., 1960), 1: 220; Jack P. Greene, *The Quest for Power* (Chapel Hill, N.C., 1963), p. 201; Oliver P. Chitwood, *A History of Colonial America* (New York, 1931), p. 90.

19. Bruce, *Institutional History*, 2: 480-82; Hening, *Statutes*, 2: 211-12; Accomack County (Upper Northampton County) Orders, Wills, Etc., 1671-1673, p. 16, VSL.

20. Accomack Petition, 25 April 1697, Colonial Papers, folder 11, item 4, VSL; Henrico County Order Book, 1694-1701, p. 47, VSL; Hening, *Statutes*, 2: 482; Bruce, *Institutional History*, 2: 481; see the additional discussion of the certification requirement later in this chapter.

21. Hening, *Statutes*, 3: 245-46; 8: 316; Beverley Fleet, ed., *Virginia Colonial Abstracts*, 34 vols. (1937-49; reprint ed., Baltimore, 1961), 5: 40, 41; Jack P. Greene, ed., *The Diary of Colonel Landon Carter of Sabine Hall, 1752-1778*, 2 vols. (Charlottesville, Va., 1965), 1: 76; Chalkley, ed., *Chronicles*, 1: 68, 72, 120, 165-66; Elmer I. Miller, "The Legislature of the Province of Virginia: Its Internal Development," *Columbia University Studies* 28 (1907): 318.

22. Speech of William Fitzhugh to the House, 24 April 1682, in *Fitzhugh Letters*, ed. Davis, p. 110; William Cabell Diary, 27 November 1783 (vol. 9), VSL; Francis Smith to John Preston, 1 January 1803, Preston Davie Collection of Preston Family Papers, VHS; Walter R. Daniel to William Brent, Jr., 5 December 1824, 17 December 1824, Cabell Papers, UVa; Douglas S. Freeman, *George Washington*, 7 vols. (New York, 1948-57), 3: 213; *JHD*, 1817: 31; Richmond *Enquirer*, 3 January 1832.

23. See especially the standing rules of 1791, 1797, and 1830, in *JHD*, 1791: 59; 1797: 16-18, 33-35; 1830: 49; see also—*JHB*, 1695-1702: 62, 213; 1702/3-1712: 242, 261; 1712-1726: 5; 1742-1749: 111; 1752-1758: 253; 1770-1772: 38; *JHD*, 1776: 69; May 1779: 40; 1786 (1828 reprint): 64; 1790 (1828 reprint): 56; 1807: 47; 1814: 82, 121, 132-33, 140; 1827: 19; Joseph C. Cabell to Thomas Jefferson, 24 December 1818, Jefferson Papers, UVa.

24. *JHB*, 1619-1658/59: 106-09; 1659/60-1693: 21-24.

25. *JHB*, 1659/60-1693: 36-37, 48-51.

26. *LJC*, 1: 24-39; Bruce, *Institutional History* 2: 484.

27. The standing committees were always appointed at the beginning of each session, so one may determine the number of such committees by examining the first few pages of the house *Journal* for a given year. For example, the standing committees at the 1752 session were appointed in *JHB*, 1752-1758: 6-12. See also Richard R. Beeman, *The Old Dominion and the New Nation, 1788-1801* (Lexington, Ky., 1972), pp. 44-45.

28. Susan L. Foard, "Virginia Enters the Union, 1789-1792" (M.A. thesis, College of William and Mary, 1966), p. 7; see also the house *Journal* for 1789 and 1798.

29. For example, at the session of 1785, when the house finally rejected the general assessment and passed the "Bill for Religious Freedom," all petitions relating to those topics were referred directly to the Committee of the whole House, where the bills were being debated. *JHD*, 1785: 4-85; Stanley M. Pargellis, "The Procedure of the Virginia House of Burgesses," *WMQ*, 2d ser. 7 (April and July 1927): 145-46.

30. Beginning in 1815, in an effort to save time, some delegates supported a change in the standing rules on this matter. They asked that the delegate presenting each petition merely summarize its contents rather than read the entire petition. This proposal was debated almost every year after 1815 until it was finally accepted in 1824. See *JHD*, 1815: 20, 25, 31; 1816: 27; 1819: 29; 1820: 231; 1821: 13, 17; 1822: 17, 24; 1824: 16-17.

31. *JHB*, 1695-1702: 254, 256, 260; 1702/3-1712: 245; 1712-1726: 260, 374; 1727-1740: 395-96; 1752-1758: 13; 1766-1769: 323-25; 1770-1772: 29, 48; *JHD*, May 1777: 18, 23; May 1784: 7, 11; 1787 (1828 reprint): 40; 1788 (1828 reprint): 6, 66-67; 1792: 150; 1814: 20, 28; 1816: 4; Greene, ed., *Diary of Landon Carter*, 1: 122; Pargellis, "Procedure of Virginia House," p. 150; Freeman, *George Washington*, 3: 120-22; Miller, "Legislature of Virginia," pp. 267-71.

32. Examples can easily be found in the *Journal* of each session. For a few examples, see: Brown and Brown, *Virginia 1705-1786*, p. 156; *JHB*, 1758-1761: 106; 1770-1772: 188.

33. Thomas Jefferson to Joseph C. Cabell, 1 January 1817, and Cabell to Jefferson, 12 January 1817, 9 February 1817, Jefferson Papers, UVa; Caleb Wallace to James Madison, 8 October 1785, James Madison Papers, Library of Congress; J. Madison to William Preston, 1 March 1767, and William Caruthers to John Preston, 1 January 1816, Preston Davie Collection of Preston Family Papers, VHS; Carter Braxton to Landon Carter, 19 December 1776, Lee Family Papers, 1761-1882, VHS; Dr. Thomas Walker to William Preston, 9 July 1778, Preston Papers, Draper MSS (4QQ179); Alexander Henderson to Zachariah Johnston, 1 December 1797, Zachariah Johnston Papers, VSL; George Mason to Patrick Henry, 6 May 1783, and Mason to Zachariah Johnston, 18 November 1791, in *Mason Papers*, ed. Rutland, 2: 772; 3: 1245-46; Greene, ed., *Diary of Landon Carter*, 1: 122; Freeman, *George Washington*, 3: 58, 69, 213.

34. *JHB*, 1695-1702: 272, 274, 289, 291, 294-95; Morgan P. Robinson, "Virginia Counties," Virginia State Library *Bulletin* 9 (January, April, and July 1916): 129.

35. *JHB*, 1712-1726: 294-95; 1770-1772: 43-44, 78; *JHD*, 1790 (1828 reprint): 7, 19-22, 66-70, 91; 1808: 20-24; J. R. Pole, "Representation and Authority in Virginia from the Revolution to Reform," *Journal of Southern History* 24 (February 1958): 31-32; Gov. Hugh Drysdale to Board of Trade, 10 July 1724, CO5/1319, p. 201. See also the following chapters for additional examples. Then as today much of the real work at any session was done in these committees, with the investigation of petitions being especially important.

36. *JHB*, 1659/60-1693: 114-15, 339; 1695-1702: 125, 225, 252, 261, 262; 1702/3-1712: 244, 250, 254; 1727-1740: xxi, 66, 71, 310, 324, 413; 1742-1749: 11; 1770-1772: 219; *JHD*, 1811: 32; 1821: 24; Pargellis, "Procedure of Virginia House," p. 147. After 1824 the house refused even to admit any petition worded in an insulting or offensive manner—see *JHD*, 1824: 16-17.

37. Greene, ed., *Diary of Landon Carter*, 1: 73; *JHB*, 1752-1758: 109, 115; Hening, *Statutes*, 6: 379. Many other examples could be given, such as the 1794 request for division of Pittsylvania County, rejected because the petitioners did not provide an accurate description of how the division was to be made—*JHD*, 1794: 7, 24, 118.

38. *JHB*, 1695-1702: 69, 77; 1702/3-1712: 56; *JHD*, 1792: 67; 1828: 48.

39. *JHB*, 1758-1761: 14, 142; *JHD*, May 1780: 21; May 1813: 7.

40. *JHB*, 1712-1726: 278, 316; 1727-1740: 356; *JHD*, 1788 (1828 reprint): 5-6, 7, 9, 46-47, 56; 1789 (1828 reprint): 64, 93; 1791: 20, 74-75, 78, 82, 95, 101, 105; 1792: 121, 185; 1793: 24, 54, 84, 103, 104, 112; Shepherd, *Virginia Statutes*, 1: 257-58.

41. William Preston to Robert Breckinridge, 1 April 1767, Breckinridge Papers, Library of Congress. Numerous examples of this process are provided in chapter 4, dealing with division of counties, and chapters on other topics reveal the same process—see especially the description of the general assessment controversy of the 1784-1786 period.

42. For two excellent discussions of this theoretical distinction, see Robert L. Nicholls, "Surrogate for Democracy: Nineteenth-Century British Petitioning," *The Maryland Historian* 5 (Spring 1974): 43-52, and Gordon S. Wood, *The Creation of the American Republic, 1776-1787* (Chapel Hill, N.C., 1969), pp. 176-96. For examples of Virginia instructions, see the following: 1776 Albemarle County instructions, in *Jefferson Papers*, ed. Boyd, 6: 284-91; William J. Van Schreeven, Robert L. Scribner, and Brent Tarter, eds., *Revolutionary Virginia: The Road to Independence*, 3 vols. to date (Charlottesville, Va., 1973-   ), 1: 109-68; Peter Force, ed., *American Archives*, 9 vols. (Washington, D.C., 1837-53), 5th ser., 2: 815-17; *Virginia Gazette or the General Advertiser*, 27 December 1783; Richmond *Constitutional Whig*, 18 August 1826. See also: Greene, ed., *Diary of Landon Carter*, 1: 90, 116-17; Brown and Brown, *Virginia 1705-1786*, pp. 155, 222-23; Robert Munford, *The Candidates*, ed. Jay B. Hubbell and Douglas Adair, *WMQ*, 3rd ser. 5 (April 1948): 222-24. In Maryland the nature of instructions was hotly debated in 1787—see Melvin Yazawa, ed., *Representative Government and the Revolution* (Baltimore, 1975).

43. *JHB*, 1727-1740: 245, 322; 1742-1749: 7; 1773-1776: 82-84; *JHD*, 1776: 5; May 1777: 5; May 1778: 6; 1785: 3; 1790 (1828 reprint): 4, 69; 1796: 4; Greene, *Quest for Power*, pp. 467-74; Beeman, *Old Dominion*, pp. 45, 249-52; Jack P. Greene, "Foundations of Political Power in the Virginia House of Burgesses, 1720-1776," *WMQ*, 3rd ser. 16 (October 1959): 485-86.

44. These figures are compiled from the respective house *Journals*.

45. See, for example, Greene, *Quest for Power*, pp. 6, 26-31; William Byrd to Peter Beckford, 6 December 1735, "Letters of William Byrd, 2d, of Westover, Va.," *VMHB* 9 (January 1902): 235.

46. Main's thesis is ably presented in such works as the following: Jackson T. Main, "Government by the People: The American Revolution and the Democratization of the Legislature," *WMQ*, 3rd ser. 23 (July 1966): 391-407; Main, *Political Parties Before the Constitution* (Chapel Hill, N.C., 1973); Main, *The Sovereign States, 1775-1783* (New York, 1973).

47. See chapter 4 and the figures for table 2.

48. Pargellis, "Procedure of Virginia House," p. 86; Robert Detweiler, "Political Factionalism and Geographic Distribution of Standing Committee Assignments in the Virginia House of Burgesses, 1730-1776," *VMHB* 80 (July 1972): 268-69.

49. Detweiler, "Political Factionalism," pp. 267-85.

50. The figures are derived from the *Journals* of the respective sessions. These particular sessions were chosen because they are separated by intervals of about twenty years. In addition, Goochland County, the first county located entirely in the Piedmont, was not formed until 1728; the session of 1752 was the first to meet in the second half of the century; the session of 1769 was representative of later colonial developments; and the session of 1790 reflects developments by the end of the century.

51. See the report of the commissioners in "Narrative of Bacon's Rebellion," *VMHB* 4 (October 1896): 121; "Charles City County Grievances 1676," *VMHB* 3 (October 1895): 136-37; Morton, *Colonial Virginia,* 1: 236-37; Wesley F. Craven, *The Southern Colonies in the Seventeenth Century, 1607-1689* (Baton Rouge, La., 1949), pp. 375, 391.

52. *JHB,* 1659/60-1693: 314; Bruce, *Institutional History,* 2: 482-83.

53. *JHB,* 1659/60-1693: 314-29; *EJC,* 1: 244-45; Morton, *Colonial Virginia,* 1: 310-34; Greene, *Quest for Power,* p. 278.

54. *JHB,* 1752-1758: 121, 129, 136, 143; Robert A. Brock, ed., *The Official Records of Robert Dinwiddie,* in Virginia Historical Society *Collections,* 2 vols. (Richmond, 1883-84), 1: 44-46; Lucille B. Griffith, *The Virginia House of Burgesses, 1750-1774* (University, Ala., 1970), pp. 22-23, 28; John R. Alden, *Robert Dinwiddie* (Williamsburg, 1973), pp. 26-36.

55. *JHB,* 1752-1758: 154.

56. *JHB,* 1659/60-1693: 87-113.

57. Bruce, *Institutional History,* 2: 480-85; *JHB,* 1712-1726: xxxii (McIlwaine's introductory comments).

58. Hening, *Statutes,* 2: 482.

59. Henrico County Order Book, 1678-1693, p. 441, VSL.

60. Hening, *Statutes,* 3: 245-46.

61. *JHB,* 1712-1726: xxxii, 124-25, 129, 145, 148-50, 153, 159-60, 165-66; Spotswood's proclamation is printed in "Prince George County Records," *VMHB* 4 (January 1897): 282-84. See also D. Alan Williams, "Political Alignments in Colonial Virginia Politics, 1698-1750" (Ph.D. dissertation, Northwestern University, 1959), pp. 161-68.

62. *JHB,* 1712-1726: 372-73, 376; 1727-1740: xvi, 11, 17, 412, 414, 429-30; 1742-1749: 188, 189, 191, 197.

63. *JHB,* 1758-1761: 138; 1773-1776: 83; Hening, *Statutes,* 3: 320; 9: 226-27; Lawrence H. Gipson, *The British Empire Before the American Revolution,* vol. 2: *The British Isles and the American Colonies: The Southern Plantations, 1748-1756* (New York, 1960), pp. 38-41. See the discussion in chapter 6 of this study.

64. Mays, ed., *Pendleton Letters,* 1: 361-62; Hamilton J. Eckenrode, ed., "A Calendar of Legislative Petitions, Accomac to Bedford," *Fifth Annual Report of the Library Board of the Virginia State Library, for Year Ending October 31, 1908*

(Richmond, 1908), Alexandria Petition, 25 October 1779, p. 62; *JHD,* October 1777: 6-7; May 1780: 11; 1785: 15, 22, 33.

65. *JHB,* 1766-1769: 36-37. See also Brown and Brown, *Virginia 1705-1786,* pp. 56-57, 234-35.

66. Mays, ed., *Pendleton Letters,* 2: 589; for other examples where prominent figures signed in a conspicuous way, see 1: 363-65; 2: 466; Rutland, ed., *Mason Papers,* 3: 1013-16; Petition of William F. Ast, 15 November 1794 (filed with Richmond City petitions).

67. Greenbrier Petition, 7 December 1797; the 1783 King and Queen Petition is found in Fleet, ed., *Virginia Colonial Abstracts,* 4: 45-46, and the tax list is in Ibid., 1-34; see also the list of justices of the peace for King and Queen in Ibid., 7: 84-85; the number of slaves owned by these men confirms their economic standing—see Augusta B. Fothergill and John M. Naugle, eds., *Virginia Tax Payers, 1782-1787* (Baltimore, 1971), pp. 25, 34, 53, 60, 132, 135.

68. Hening, *Statutes,* 3: 246.

69. *JHB,* 1695-1702: 65, 73, 75-76, 83, 88, 90, 95, 101-02; Hening, *Statutes,* 3: 153.

70. Eckenrode, ed., "Cal. Legislative Petitions," Amherst and Buckingham Petition, 1779, p. 108; Amherst, Albemarle, and Buckingham Petition, 15 October 1779, p. 108; Augusta Petition, 8 June 1784, p. 141; *JHD,* October 1783: 89-90; May 1784: 41, 70; October 1784: 30: Merrill Jensen, *The New Nation* (New York, 1950), pp. 311-12.

71. Hening, *Statutes,* 1: 287; *JHB,* 1659/60-1693: 36, 60, 87; 1742-1749: 55; 1770-1772: 8, 31; 1773-1776: 182, 189, 192, 211; *JHD,* May 1778: 9, 15, 22, 28, 29, 39, 40; Eckenrode, ed., "Cal. Legislative Petitions," Petition of John Liviston, 8 October 1779, p. 107.

72. Petition of St. Stephen's Parish, 1683, Colonial Papers, folder 3, item 31 (oversize), VSL; Northampton County Petition, no date [before 1776], Godfrey Pole Papers, VHS; 1722 Isle of Wight Petition, *Cal. Va. State Papers,* 1: 203-04; King and Queen, and Caroline, Petitions, 15 October 1779; Botetourt Petition, 13 November 1783; Culpeper Petition, 2 November 1785; Cabell Petition, 14 December 1821; see also *JHD,* 1787 (1828 reprint): 20; Churchill G. Chamberlayne, ed., *The Vestry Book of Blisland (Blissland) Parish, New Kent and James City Counties, Virginia, 1721-1786* (Richmond, 1935), pp. xlii-xlvii.

73. *JHB,* 1752-1758: 47; 1773-1776: 211; Eckenrode, ed., "Cal. Legislative Petitions," Petition of Mary Ford, 10 November 1785, p. 97; King and Queen, and Caroline, Petitions, 15 and 16 October 1779 (religious petitions); Westmoreland Petition, 2 November 1785 (religious petitions); Richard R. Beeman has shown that some Baptist churches allowed women members an equal voice in matters of discipline and secular affairs—Beeman, "Social Change and Cultural Conflict in Virginia: Lunenburg County, 1746 to 1774," *WMQ,* 3rd ser. 35 (July 1978): 471.

74. *JHD,* May 1777: 77, 150; October 1783: 12; May 1784: 20; 1785: 54-55; 1786 (1828 reprint): 47; 1792: 24; 1796: 44; 1813: 86, 96, 104, 112, 119, 130, 135, 139; Hening, *Statutes,* 4: 133-34; 9: 320-21; 11: 309, 362-63; 12: 380; 13: 619; Pole, "Representation and Authority," p. 18.

75. *JHB,* 1766-1769: 198-99, 353.

76. Petition of Harry Jackson, 10 December 1810 and 20 November 1816 (filed with Norfolk City petitions); *JHD*, 1810: 16; 1816: 34, 59, 144, 152; 1823: 17, 34, 47-48; Raymond C. Bailey, "Racial Discrimination Against Free Blacks in Antebellum Virginia: The Case of Harry Jackson," *West Virginia History* 39 (January/April 1978): 181-86.

77. King and Queen, and Caroline, Petitions, 15 and 16 October 1779 (religious petitions); Caroline Petition, 22 October 1779 (religious petitions); Eckenrode, ed., "Cal. Legislative Petitions," Bedford Petitions, 21 November 1781, p. 212; Henry County Petitions, 23 October 1790; U.S., Department of Commerce, Bureau of the Census, *Heads of Families at the First Census of the United States Taken in the Year 1790 . . . Virginia* (Washington, D.C., 1908), p. 9.

78. Thomas Lewis to William Preston, 24 February 1767, Preston Papers, Draper MSS (2QQ100); John Madison to William Preston, 1 March 1767, Preston Davie Collection of Preston Family Papers, VHS; William Preston to Robert Breckinridge, 1 April 1767, Breckinridge Papers, Library of Congress; *JHB*, 1766-1769: 37, 84, 102, 106, 146, 197, 201-02, 204, 238, 240-42, 251, 252, 253, 257, 292. The controversy is described in greater depth in chapter 4.

79. *JHB*, 1742-1749: 89, 95, 103, 106, 108, 113, 135, 148; 1752-1758: 32, 39, 44, 56, 60-64, 114, 117, 120, 123, 125, 130, 140, 142, 170; Greene, ed., *Diary of Landon Carter*, 1: 84, 90; Hugh Jones, *The Present State of Virginia*, ed. Richard L. Morton (Chapel Hill, N.C., 1956), p. 125. See the detailed discussions of county and parish divisions in chapters 4 and 5.

80. Eckenrode, ed., "Cal. Legislative Petitions," Albemarle Petition, 1774, Accomack Petitions, 22 October 1787, and Amherst Petitions, 14 November 1796, pp. 8-9, 23, 114.

81. See the extended description in chapter 7. The famous "Ten-thousand name" petition of 16 October 1776 is filed with the religious petitions in VSL.

82. Hartwell, Blair, and Chilton, *Present State of Virginia*, p. 41.

3 SOURCES OF EIGHTEENTH-CENTURY LEGISLATION

The ultimate test of the importance of petitions in the political process is to be found in the legislation enacted by the General Assembly. Eighteenth-century Virginians had reason to believe that the legislature was responsive to the requests and grievances expressed in the petitions of the people. On several occasions in the seventeenth century the assembly asserted that "the principall end of convention of assemblies is the making provision for the peoples safety and redresse of their Grievances. . . ."[1] During Alexander Spotswood's sometimes stormy tenure as governor (1710-1722), he complained that the burgesses were all too responsive to the "Giddy Resolves of the illiterate Vulgar" and to "all the Ridiculous Propositions and Grievances which the Seditious or ignorant Vulgar have Set their Marks to." When angrily dissolving the 1715 session of the legislature, Spotswood charged that "all your proceedings have been calculated to Answer the Notions of the ignorant Populace; and if you can Excuse your Selves to them, you matter not how you Stand before God, your Prince, and all Judicious men. . . ."[2] William Gooch, the popular governor of Virginia from 1727 until 1749, informed the Board of Trade that legislation was frequently a response to "petitions or Representations of ye People," and on many occasions he complimented the burgesses for "your Concern in general for the Welfare of Those you Represent."[3]

More importantly, the house itself consistently affirmed its willingness to consider and respond to the wishes of the people as expressed in their petitions. It frequently spoke of "the Duty we owe our Constituents," and as late as 1823 a house committee reported that "the right of the people to petition shall be (as it always ought to be) regarded as an axiom in our political system. . . ."[4] Many historians have agreed that the legislature did prove responsive to a significant degree, though these historians sometimes differ on whether such responsiveness was typical of the colonial period or developed to fruition in the post-revolutionary period.[5]

The degree to which the legislature responded to the petitions of the people is of such critical importance, however, that these assertions must be subjected to careful scrutiny. Such an investigation must begin by examining the various sources of legislation and then must evaluate the relative importance of petitions as one of these sources. There were, in fact, five principal sources of legislation in eighteenth-century Virginia. These were: (1) the governor's message at the beginning of each session of the assembly; (2) investigation of important matters or of the general condition of the colony or commonwealth by the Committee of the whole House; (3) bills introduced on the motion of, or at the request of, individual members of the house; (4) reports and recommendations made by standing or select committees on their own initiative or at the direction of the house; and (5) recommendations made by the various committees in response to petitions from Virginia citizens. As the following investigation demonstrates, far more eighteenth-century laws originated from this last source than from any other.

During the colonial period the assembly was called into session by the royal governor. In this matter the governor retained his discretionary power, as the lower house was never able to secure a guarantee of regular sessions. Yet even without such a guarantee, the generally good relationship between the governors and the assembly, combined with the necessity of levying and collecting taxes, resulted in frequent sessions. At the beginning of each session it was customary for the governor to address a joint session of the two houses of the assembly. In his speech the governor would confirm his willingness to cooperate in needed measures, and he generally suggested certain specific measures which, in his estimation, required legislative attention.[6] In 1710 Governor Spotswood stressed several subjects, including the need to reform the slave laws and provide better security against slave insurrections. Governor Gooch, in his opening address to the 1730 session, included the establishment of a school system among the measures which he proposed, but apparently the burgesses doubted either the wisdom or the practicality of his suggestion, and the matter was abandoned. Regulation of the tobacco trade and defense against French and Indian enemies were also frequent topics in the messages of the various royal governors.[7]

Important as these messages were, they nevertheless accounted for a relatively small percentage of the laws passed by the assembly. As a rule the governor made only a few specific suggestions, though these generally

concerned important topics. A few examples will illustrate the usual
practice. In his 1710 message to the assembly, Governor Spotswood made
four specific suggestions, and three of the seventeen laws enacted by the
legislature resulted largely from these suggestions. In 1730 Governor Gooch
mentioned five matters for legislative consideration, and three of the
twenty-nine acts originated in Gooch's message. For the seven sessions of
1710, 1720, 1730, 1740, 1752, 1760-61, and 1769-70, only 7.14 percent
(18 of 252) of the laws passed by the Virginia assembly seem to have resulted largely from the governor's proposals.[8] Though the importance of
the governor's message as a source of legislation should not be minimized,
examination of the assembly records does reveal that the great majority
of colonial laws were produced by other sources.

Following the transition from colony to commonwealth, Virginia
granted increased authority to the legislature, and especially to the House
of Delegates, at the expense of the executive and judicial departments.
This shift reflected both the culmination of the lower house's "quest for
power" and the belief that the assembly was more "democratic" or responsive to the people.[9] Among the matters affected by this shift in
power were the sources of legislation, and particularly the governor's
message. After 1776 the practice of formal opening addresses by the
governor, addresses which mentioned specific topics for legislative action,

TABLE 3 THE GOVERNOR'S MESSAGE AND LEGISLATION

Session	Laws Resulting from Governor's Message	Total Number of Laws	Percentage Resulting from Governor's Message
1710	3	17	17.65
1720	1	18	5.56
1730	3	29	10.34
1740	4	15	26.67
1752	4	53	7.55
1760-1761	2	31	6.45
1769-1770	1	89	1.12
Total	18	252	7.14

was abandoned and was not resumed until 1809. The governor did not
cease communicating with the legislature during these years; on the contrary, the weakened executive branch was seen in large measure as a
servant of the assembly and was held accountable for all actions taken
to carry out the legislative will. But this communication was more like
that of a master and servant than two equal partners discussing the ex-
igencies of the moment. The governor might still suggest the need for
action in certain areas directly involving his official functions, as in mentioning defects in the militia laws. As an important source of legislation,
however, the governor almost ceased to function in the 1776-1809
period.[10]

At the beginning of the 1809 session, Governor John Tyler reintroduced the formal address to the legislature. After discussing certain areas
under executive jurisdiction, Tyler cautiously recommended adoption
of a state-supported system of public education. His suggestion was referred to a select committee for consideration, and it was at least partially
responsible for the creation of the Literary Fund (a state endowment for
the education of poor children). Tyler's caution may be judged by his
hesitant, even defensive, language, in beginning: "The subject to which
I now beg leave to draw your attention, I touch with great delicacy, not
being certain of the propriety of the measure, since it may not be thought
to fall within the pale of Executive duty."[11]

After Tyler's action in 1809, the governor's message once again assumed an important role as a source of legislation.[12] As in the colonial
period, however, the major significance of these measures involved the
importance of the topics thus introduced rather than the number of
them. The address of Wilson Cary Nicholas in 1815, for example, stressed
only three subjects—militia reform, internal improvements, and education—and most of the 158 laws enacted during that session originated
elsewhere.[13] Governor Thomas Mann Randolph summarized very suc-
cintly the role of the governor's message, as compared with other sources
of legislation, when he observed in 1820:

> I am conscious that it is proper to use sparingly the privilege
> annually allowed by custom, to the Chief Magistrate of the
> State, at this period, to make general remarks, upon the most
> important concerns of the Commonwealth, because I am fully
> convinced, that an accurate knowledge of the actual condition

of all the main general interests can only be obtained by well
digesting the great mass of local information, brought together upon this occasion, by the Representatives of the People.[14]

During the first half of the eighteenth century, a related source of legislation was the ability of the council, sitting as the upper house of the assembly, to initiate legislation. The council nevertheless exercised this capability
only infrequently even before 1750, and after that date it no longer did
so. The Virginia constitution of 1776 denied to the Senate any right to
initiate legislation. As a source of legislation, therefore, the upper house
was insignificant.[15]

Investigation into important topics by the Committee of the whole
House provided a second major source of eighteenth-century legislation.
Committee of the whole House was a popular procedural device which
facilitated debate and action because committee rules were less rigid than
those of the house in formal session. The governor's message was generally
referred to the Committee of the whole House during the 1700-1776
period. The burgesses also used it to investigate many other important
matters, such as removal of the seat of government from Williamsburg to
a more convenient location or opposition to the post-1763 innovations
in British policy.[16] After 1776 the House of Delegates continued to use
the Committee of the whole House as a convenient instrument for insuring free and complete debate on important or controversial topics.[17]
By its very nature, however, it was not suited to initiate a significant
number of laws. The free debate and loose procedure rendered it far too
inefficient for widespread use as a source of legislation, and most noncontroversial matters simply did not require this time-consuming expedient. The Committee of the whole House thus occasionally initiated a
few important laws, but its primary function was to consider proposals
which originated elsewhere.

Bills originating on the motion of individual members constituted a
third important source of legislation. Sometimes the member already had
the bill prepared and presented it directly to the house, but often a select
committee was appointed specifically to frame the proposed bill. The
member who made the original motion was included on the select committee, usually as the chairman.[18] Bills were introduced in this fashion
throughout the eighteenth century, but the practice became increasingly
common as time passed. In the early decades of the century relatively

few bills began in this fashion, and as late as 1752 the number originating on motion was only seventeen (twelve of which ultimately were enacted into law).[19] By 1790 the number of bills produced on motion had grown to 45, and the trend accelerated in the early nineteenth century, with the number rising to 95 in 1815, 143 in 1820, and 251 in 1830. Moreover, the number enacted into law rose accordingly, to a third or more of the total.[20] Table 4 summarizes the trend as revealed in the sessions of 1720, 1752, 1790, and 1820.

Bills originating in this manner covered a wide variety of topics. Many involved matters of strictly individual or local importance. In these cases the member was, in effect, conducting business directly for his constituents by sponsoring legislation which affected them immediately. These cases often involved matters which were normally brought before the legislature by petition, but the member might simply introduce the issue on motion if he knew enough about the request and if it was of a sufficiently localized and noncontroversial nature. A select committee could then frame the bill, and enactment would be expedited by avoiding the overworked Committee of Propositions and Grievances. Alterations in the details of existing legislation, aimed at making the laws work more effectively, might also be introduced by interested members. Finally, like their twentieth-century counterparts, eighteenth-century legislators exercised their right to propose laws on the most important matters of state policy (such as the tax laws and slave codes, for example).[21]

Recommendations made by standing or select committees on their own initiative or at the direction of the house constituted a fourth source of legislation. The Committee for Courts of Justice was assigned the task of examining the laws which had expired, or were about to expire, and reporting to the house which of these laws should be reenacted. Other stand-

TABLE 4   LEGISLATION FROM MOTIONS

	1720	1752	1790	1820
Number of motions for bills	3	18	45	143
Number of laws resulting	1	12	33	62
Total number of laws	18	53	99	132
Percentage of laws resulting from motions	5.56	22.64	33.33	46.97

ing committees, such as the Committee of Trade, made occasional recommendations, and select committees were appointed as needed to investigate subjects of importance, such as the need to provide better security against slave insurrections. At periodic intervals a Committee on Revising the Laws was appointed and assigned the time-consuming task of reporting unnecessary laws which could be eliminated and suggesting alterations needed in other laws. Jefferson's work with the post-revolutionary Committee of Revisors is well known, but previous committees had also made important, if less comprehensive, efforts.[22] Though the number of laws produced in this manner varied greatly from one session to another, as a general rule only petitions and the motions of individual members accounted for a greater number.

Important as these sources were, none of them equaled the petitions of Virginia citizens in producing eighteenth-century legislation. In terms of the sheer number of issues, suggestions, and grievances brought before the legislature, petitioning far surpassed all other sources. During the first half of the eighteenth century, the House of Burgesses received an average of over a hundred petitions per session, and that average more than doubled during the latter half of the century despite the increasing frequency of sessions after 1752 (see table 5).[23]

Petitions from the citizens of Virginia thus provided a steady stream of requests and grievances to the legislature and served as the raw materials from which a great many laws could be constructed. It remains to be demonstrated, however, that the legislature did in fact utilize and respond to these petitions. The remaining chapters of this study consider this matter in depth, but some general observations are appropriate at this point in order to assess the importance of petitions as the fifth major source of legislation.

The care consistently taken by the legislature to protect the right of petition from possible threats and to facilitate the presentation and consideration of petitions is in itself one indication that petitions were an important source of legislation. Equally significant is the direct testimony of numerous political leaders. Some of the most impressive evidence is found in the correspondence between the royal governors of Virginia and the British authorities back in the mother country. England retained the right to veto colonial laws which it deemed undesirable and insisted that the legislative journals be sent back to Whitehall for inspection. The governor also customarily explained why he had signed each of the new

TABLE 5 NUMBER OF PETITIONS PER SESSION

Session	Petitions		
	General Concern	Individual Concern	Total
1701	34	53	87
1710	70	53	123
1720	68	46	114
1730	38	14	52
1740	66	49	115
1748	132	68	200
Average	68.0	47.17	115.17
1752	106	111	217
1760[a]	71	184	255
1769[b]	123	95	218
1780[c]	110	135	245
1790	139	178	317
1799	125	57	182
Average	112.33	126.67	239.0
1800	118	69	187
1810	132	161	293
1820	107	136	243
1830	221	94	315
Average	144.5	115.0	259.5

[a]Includes sessions of March, May, and October.
[b]Includes sessions of May and November.
[c]Includes sessions of May and October.

laws. In thus attempting to justify his own conduct and, at the same time, to persuade England to accept the laws, the governor frequently described the origin of the laws in question. Time and again he confirmed what the house *Journals* clearly indicated—that a large number of laws originated directly from the petitions of the people. Thus in 1726 Governor Hugh Drysdale informed the Board of Trade that the act for dividing St. Paul's

Parish in Hanover County was "made upon the petition of the people, who have lately seated that Frontier, and were too remote from the parish Church, and too numerous for the care of one Minister."[24] Similarly, in explaining a 1734 law to encourage the killing of crows and squirrels in the Northern Neck and Eastern Shore, Governor William Gooch noted that the act was passed "on the Petition of the Inhabitants of these Territorys, who it seems are more Infested with those kind of Vermin than the rest of the Colony. . . ."[25] In these and numerous other instances, royal governors confirmed that colonial laws often were "prepared upon the petition of the Inhabitants."[26]

As a source of legislation petitions retained—perhaps even increased—their important role after 1776. Again, numerous examples could be cited, but the most spectacular involved the 1776-1786 controversy over religious freedom. The struggle began in earnest in 1776, when a great influx of petitions, bearing thousands of signatures, prompted the legislature to exempt dissenters from payment of taxes to support the Anglican Church. The battle for complete religious freedom was then waged for the following decade, until in 1785 the legislature specifically asked the people of Virginia to express their wishes on the subject. The flood of petitions which followed, bearing even more signatures than those of 1776, was instrumental in the adoption of Jefferson's famous "Bill for Religious Freedom." James Madison, leader of the legislative faction supporting complete religious freedom, wrote a "Remonstrance" which served as the foundation of many of these petitions. Madison was quite explicit in describing the importance of petitions in the final victory. As he accurately noted, the petitions were "so extensively signed by the people of every Religious denomination, that at the ensuing session . . . under the influence of the public sentiment thus manifested, the celebrated Bill 'Enacting Religious freedom' [was] enacted. . . ."[27]

In addition to the testimony of individuals, eighteenth-century legislation also frequently contained direct testimony on the significance of petitions as a source of legislation. Especially during the latter half of the century, many Virginia laws included an introductory clause stating that they originated directly in response to petitions from Virginia citizens. The 1752 law creating Dinwiddie County thus began: "Whereas many inconveniences attend the upper inhabitants of the county of Prince George, by reason of their great distance from the court house, and the said inhabitants have petitioned this present General Assembly that the said county may be divided. . . ."[28] Similarly, another 1752 law, this one dissolving the present vestry of Nottoway Parish in Amelia County and providing for the election of a new vestry, said: "Whereas it hath been represented to this General Assembly, that the election of vestrymen . . . was illegal, and the inhabitants of the said parish have petitioned for a dissolution of the vestry thereof. . . ."[29]

The significance of petitions as a source of legislation is perhaps best demonstrated, however, by a detailed examination of the sessions of 1696, 1710, 1730, 1752, 1769-70, and 1790. Careful study of the origin and progress of each bill at these sessions reveals that approximately one-half or more of the laws originated from the petitions received. The figures in table 6, impressive as they are, nevertheless understate the total impact of petitions since they include neither the house resolutions passed nor the large number of public claims paid as a result of petitions. Moreover, the table omits the bills passed by the house but rejected by the council or Senate or vetoed by the royal governor.[30]

The laws enacted as a result of petitions covered a wide variety of topics, from the dividing of counties or amending the tobacco inspection or tax laws to the granting of pensions or docking of entails. The following chapters will describe this process more fully and indicate that if eighteenth-century Virginia government was dominated by "aristocrats," they nevertheless kept a willing ear open to "the voice of the people" on a great many matters.

TABLE 6   THE IMPACT OF PETITIONS ON LEGISLATION

	1696	1710	1730	1752	1769-1770	1790
Number of laws originating from petitions	9	5	17	24	49	56
Total number of laws enacted	14	17	29	53	89	99
Percentage of laws originating from petitions	64.3	29.4	58.6	45.3	55.1	56.7

Notes

1. William Waller Hening, ed., *The Statutes at Large: Being a Collection of All the Laws of Virginia,* 13 vols. (Richmond and Philadelphia, 1809-23), 1: 236-37; 2: 211.

2. *JHB,* 1712-1726: 166-70; Spotswood to Secretary Stanhope, 15 July 1715, and Spotswood to Board of Trade, 24 October 1715, in *The Official Letters of Alexander Spotswood,* ed. Robert A. Brock, Virginia Historical Society *Collections,* 2 vols. (Richmond, 1882-85), 2: 124, 134-35.

3. "Virginia Under Governor Gooch," *VMHB* 3: 115; *JHB,* 1727-1740: 234, 316; Gooch to Board of Trade, 27 May 1732, and Answers to Queries from the Board of Trade, 1749, William Gooch Papers, 3 vols., transcripts, VHS, 2: 285; 3: 973.

4. For these and similar statements, see: *JHB,* 1752-1758: 5; 1766-1769: 199; 1770-1772: 155; 1773-1776: 22; *JHD,* October 1777: 74-75; 1799: 5-6; 1819: 7; 1822: 133; Edmund Pendleton to Richard Henry Lee, 14 June 1788, in *Letters and Papers of Edmund Pendleton, 1734-1803,* ed. David J. Mays, 2 vols. (Charlottesville, Va., 1967), 2: 530-35; Henry Hartwell, James Blair, and Edward Chilton, *The Present State of Virginia, and the College,* ed. Hunter D. Farish (Williamsburg, 1940), p. 41.

5. Perhaps the best statement of colonial responsiveness is found in Robert E. Brown and B. Katherine Brown, *Virginia 1705-1786: Democracy or Aristocracy?* (East Lansing, Mich., 1964); for the interpretation that the Revolution spurred responsiveness, see Jackson T. Main, *The Sovereign States, 1775-1783* (New York, 1973), and Main, "Government by the People: The American Revolution and the Democratization of the Legislature," *WMQ,* 3rd ser. 23 (July 1966): 391-407.

6. For excellent, and more detailed, descriptions, see Lucille B. Griffith, *The Virginia House of Burgesses, 1750-1774,* Rev. ed. (University, Ala., 1970); Jack P. Greene, *The Quest for Power* (Chapel Hill, N.C., 1963); Stanley M. Pargellis, "Procedure of The Virginia House of Burgesses," *WMQ,* 2d ser. 7 (April and July 1927): 77.

7. *JHB,* 1695-1702: 245-46, 269-70; 1702/3-1712: 240-41; 1712-1726: 250; 1727-1740: xix, 58, 391-92; 1752-1758: 4-5; 1758-1761: 183-85.

8. These figures cannot be taken as exact, since legislation sometimes resulted from a combination of sources, including both the assembly's determination that certain topics were important and the governor's professed willingness to sign bills on those topics. Nevertheless, these figures reflect the maximum number of laws which resulted directly from suggestions contained in the governor's opening address to the legislature. *JHB,* 1702/3-1712: 240-41, 270, 277; 1712-1726: 250; 1727-1740: xix, 58, 391-92; 1752-1758: 4-5; 1758-1761: 183-85; 1766-1769: 226-27; 1770-1772: 4-9, 107; Hening, *Statutes,* 3: 482-540; 4: 77-95, 241-308; 5: 90-120; 6: 217-324; 7: 381-461.

9. These factors have, of course, been examined by a great many historians. Among the best brief treatments are the following: Greene, *Quest for Power;*

66   POPULAR INFLUENCE UPON PUBLIC POLICY

Main, "Government by the People," pp. 391-407; Edmund S. Morgan, *The Birth of the Republic, 1763-1789* (Chicago, 1956).

10. See the first several pages of the *Journal* for each session of the assembly, 1776-1809. Harry Ammon, "The Republican Party in Virginia, 1789-1824" (Ph. D. dissertation, University of Virginia, 1948), pp. 15-16, 16n., stated that James Monroe was responsible for reintroducing the governor's message in 1799. This statement cannot be correct, however, since Monroe was not even elected governor until after the session was under way. Moreover, during his tenure as governor (12/19/1799-12/29/1802), the *Journals* do not reveal any significant difference between Monroe's messages and those of his predecessors. The dates of Monroe's term in office can be verified in J. R. V. Daniel, *A Hornbook of Virginia History* (Richmond, 1949), p. 7.

11. *JHD*, 1809: 5-9, 25; Virginia, *Acts Passed at a General Assembly of the Commonwealth of Virginia, Begun . . . in 1809* (Richmond, 1810), ch. 14, p. 15.

12. *JHD*, 1810: 6-9, 18, 96, 104; 1812: 3-9; 1815: 5-8, 47-50, 96-97; 1816: 6-8; 1817: 6-8; 1820: 6-12; 1824: 6-8; 1828: 6-14; 1830: 8-12; Littleton W. Tazewell to Wilson Cary Nicholas, 23 April 1815, Wilson Cary Nicholas Papers, UVa.

13. *JHD*, 1815: 5-8, 25, 47-50, 58, 96, 97, 205-11.

14. *JHD*, 1820: 6.

15. Gooch to Board of Trade, n.d., "Virginia Under Governor Gooch," *VMHB* 3: 115; Griffith, *Virginia House of Burgesses*, pp. 15, 172; Ammon, "Republican Party in Virginia," p. 18; James L. Anderson, "The Virginia Councillors and the American Revolution," *VMHB* 82 (January 1974): 56-74.

16. Pargellis, "Procedure of Virginia House," pp. 149-50; *JHB*, 1702/3-1712: 61; 1742-1749: 85, 283; 1761-1765: 254, 256, 257, 350; 1766-1769: 22; 1773-1776: 74.

17. Use of Committee of the whole House by the 1790 session was typical—*JHD*, 1790 (1828 reprint): 38, 44, 51, 58, 61, 63, 70, 81, 88, 102, 107, 119, 133, 135, 144-45.

18. Pargellis, "Procedure of Virginia House," pp. 145-46, 148. The procedure can be examined by using the citations for the examples in the next several paragraphs.

19. *JHB*, 1702/3-1712: 291; 1712-1726: 273, 279; 1727-1740: 97, 100, 108; 1752-1758: 13, 19, 25, 40, 41, 45-46, 51, 54, 58, 60, 66, 67, 69, 71, 72, 77, 84, 85, 90.

20. See the house *Journal* for these respective sessions.

21. *JHB*, 1712-1726: 273; 1752-1758: 40, 51, 77, 90; *JHD*, 1790 (1828 reprint): 7, 14, 84, 92, 106, 118, 120, 131, 148, 156, 161; 1815: 22, 36, 39-40, 42, 55, 63, 71, 106, 118, 124, 129, 201; 1820: 35, 46, 60, 231.

22. Pargellis, "Procedure of Virginia House," p. 146; Dumas Malone, *Jefferson and His Time*, Vol. 1: *Jefferson the Virginian* (Boston, 1948), ch. 19; *JHB*, 1742-1749: 258-59, 275-76; 1752-1758: 15, 16, 17, 21; 1766-1769: 248-49; *JHD*, 1790 (1828 reprint): 79.

23. These figures were compiled by counting all of the petitions recorded by the house *Journals* as being presented to these respective sessions. These figures represent

the minimum possible number; an exact count is impossible, since the *Journal* on occasion mentioned several similar petitions without differentiating the exact number.

24. Hugh Drysdale to Board of Trade, 10 July 1726, CO5/1320, p. 64.

25. William Gooch to Board of Trade, 20 November 1734, Gooch Papers, 2: 374, VHS.

26. For examples, see: Hugh Drysdale to Board of Trade, 10 July 1724, CO5/1319, p. 201; Drysdale to Board of Trade, 10 July 1726, CO5/1320, pp. 64-65; William Gooch to Board of Trade, n.d. [1728?], and Gooch, Answers to Queries from Board of Trade, 1749, Gooch Papers, 1: 56-57; 3: 973, VHS. According to a significant article on colonial Pennsylvania, legislation in that colony also often originated from petitions—see Sister Joan Leonard, "The Organization and Procedure of the Pennsylvania Assembly, 1682-1776," *Pennsylvania Magazine of History and Biography* 62 (October 1948): 376.

27. See the detailed account in chapter 7. The Madison letter is to George Mason [son of the Revolutionary patriot], 14 July 1826, James Madison Papers, VHS.

28. Hening, *Statutes*, 6: 254.

29. Ibid., 272.

30. See the house *Journals* for each session and consult Hening's *Statutes* for the legislation ultimately enacted. I began with a session in the late seventeenth century and investigated eighteenth-century sessions at twenty-year intervals (there was no session in 1750 or 1751, so I used 1752).

4 PETITIONS AND THE REGULATION OF LOCAL GOVERNMENT

Petitioning played an indispensable role in the establishment and regulation of local government in eighteenth-century Virginia. The assembly frequently created new counties, altered existing county boundaries, and established and regulated towns. Almost invariably this legislation originated in petitions sent to the house by local citizens. Such petitions indicated what action was needed and why, and the list of signatures provided at least a rough indication of the degree of local support for the proposal; any citizens who opposed often sent counterpetitions. By sending these petitions Virginians took an active and important part in the political process, and for its part the assembly proved extremely receptive to the wishes of local residents in such matters.

The county unit became the basic political subdivision in 1634 and remained so throughout the period under study. Each county court possessed extensive authority over local affairs. It administered justice and rendered executive decisions, and elections, militia musters, and other public meetings were held at the courthouse. In addition, the courthouse was a favorite location for holding social activities and conducting business transactions. Since travel to the courthouse was frequently necessary and the means of transportation primitive, it was important for counties to remain reasonably compact in order to avoid seriously inconveniencing local inhabitants.[1] The difficulty of travel to the courthouse was particularly frustrating to residents living on or near the frontier because western counties were usually larger than eastern ones. This difference in size resulted during the eighteenth century not from sectional discrimination but from the rapid expansion of settlement and from the frequent outbreak of hostilities with the Indians. Larger western counties increased the size of the local militia units and spread the financial burden of Indian conflicts among more county taxpayers. Even in the older regions, however, increasing population sometimes multiplied county business to the extent that action seemed necessary to unclog the machinery of local government.

The assembly used several methods of dealing with such problems. New counties were created by dividing one or more of the existing counties as they became too large. The assembly created eighty-two new counties during the eighteenth century.[2] Care was taken not to form a new county, however, until it contained enough inhabitants to defend against attack and pay sufficient taxes to provide essential local services.[3] A second alternative involved the redrawing of county boundaries to make the respective courthouses more accessible to local citizens; a section of one county might be cut from it and added to an adjacent county where the courthouse was closer or the transportation was better. The third alternative was to change the location of the courthouse, moving it closer to the center of population.

Following the inauguration of the county system in 1634 by an act of assembly, the legislature regularly divided counties and altered their boundaries.[4] Division by statute in response to petitions of local residents remained the standard practice during the eighteenth century despite two challenges which threatened to alter that procedure or prohibit it altogether.

The first challenge occurred in the late seventeenth and early eighteenth centuries, when a series of royal governors seemed determined to diminish or eliminate the role of the lower house. After the Restoration in 1660, England had initiated a program involving closer supervision of colonial affairs, and under the last two Stuart monarchs, Charles II and James II, the English government showed little regard for Virginia rights and sensibilities. In addition to the unpopular restrictions England placed upon the tobacco trade with the Navigation Acts, it further alienated Virginians by temporarily granting proprietary rights over the entire colony to Lords Arlington and Culpeper and by threatening significant reductions in the power of the Virginia assembly (see the discussion in chapter 7). Along these lines, shortly after his arrival in Virginia as governor, the authoritarian Lord Effingham asserted in 1684 that the power to determine county boundaries was reserved to him by his commission, and no new counties were formed by legislation or otherwise during his brief tenure. Soon after Effingham's departure from the colony, however, the assembly resumed division of counties by statute.[5] Francis Nicholson, governor in Virginia from 1690 to 1692 and from 1698 to 1705, attempted to persuade the house in 1701 and again in 1703 of the necessity for altering the boundaries of several counties lying between the York and James rivers. A heated dispute followed when the burgesses refused to act and asserted that "itt is not Convenient to make any alteration in the bounds of Countyes and Parishes already setled but when representation is made from Countyes or Parishes that they are aggrieved." Despite this disagreement Nicholson did assent to legislation drawn up in the house which created several new counties.[6]

The issue involved more than just another routine struggle between the legislative and executive branches. Implicit in the efforts of Effingham and Nicholson was an assumption that the governor, as a supposedly impartial observer, should dictate when to divide or alter counties. On the other hand, in response the burgesses clearly stressed that these changes should be made only when local citizens petitioned the house to request such action. In short, the contest between the two branches of government reflected a broad difference of opinion concerning a significant issue: should policy in these matters be imposed from above or conform to the sentiments of local residents as expressed in their petitions? Because Effingham left Virginia before the issue was resolved and Nicholson did not press the matter after 1703, a final determination came only after 1710 during the turbulent administration of Alexander Spotswood.

When Spotswood arrived in Virginia as the new royal governor in 1710, his strong-willed and somewhat tactless disposition, combined with his determination to uphold the royal prerogative to the fullest extent, almost insured a continuation of the controversy. Like Nicholson before him, Spotswood soon asserted the necessity of altering the counties between the York and James rivers. When the house again failed to act, Spotswood followed Effingham's example:

> . . . I perceive my Referring Such Divisions to your Consideration is not Taken for a favourable Condesention (which I am not obliged to). . . .
> . . . I expect That you forbear for the future to Begin upon the Dividing of Either Countys or parishes untill her Majesty shall be graciously pleased to yield up That Branch of her Royal Prerogative unto Your hands.[7]

In response the burgesses again stressed that division of counties or alteration of their boundaries should not be undertaken unless the local

inhabitants petitioned to request the change, as had become the practice
in the seventeenth century despite Effingham's challenge. While denying
any desire to infringe upon the royal prerogative, the house pointed out
that the power to divide counties and parishes had always been exercised
by the legislature.[8] The resulting impasse lasted for several years. Spotswood wrote to the Board of Trade in 1710 seeking clarification on this
matter, since his action had been based solely upon Effingham's example;
actually, neither Spotswood's commission nor his instructions had expressly given him rather than the assembly the power to determine county
boundaries. He stressed that only the governor could decide such questions impartially. The Board of Trade, its attention focused upon the
more immediate problems involving the War of Spanish Succession (1702-
13), never even responded to Spotswood's inquiry, however, and he was
ultimately obliged to relent. Division of parishes by the assembly resumed
in 1713, and in 1720 Spotswood invited the assembly to consider the
need for dividing some counties. The house again replied that this would
be done in response to petitions from local inhabitants, and Spotswood
agreed. The process of creating new counties by legislative statute was
then resumed, and the position of the lower house was completely vindicated.[9] The victory of the lower house represented a victory for petitioning and thus assured that local residents would play a major role in determining when new counties were required.

The second challenge to legislative authority over division of counties
came late in the colonial period and was another example of the errors
in judgment after 1763 which cost England a major part of her empire.
In 1767 the British authorities decided to prohibit the enactment of any
future colonial laws by which the composition of assemblies would be
altered or regulated, and the royal governors were told to veto any such
act as an infringement upon the royal prerogative. The instructions given
in 1771 to Virginia's new governor, John Murray, earl of Dunmore, re-
affirmed this prohibition.[10] The English officials dictating this and other
post-1763 innovations in policy were separated from Williamsburg or
Philadelphia or Boston by three thousand miles of ocean, by tremendous
difficulties in communication, and by a one-sided attitude which continued to insist that colonies existed first and foremost to benefit the
mother country. Given these circumstances, the transition from "salutary
neglect" to imperial policy was inevitably undertaken without England's
fully understanding, or even considering, the consequences.

Because after 1661 each Virginia county elected two burgesses, the prohibition against altering the composition of assemblies, if obeyed, would have had the effect of preventing creation of any new counties on the frontier. As Governor Dunmore wrote to the British authorities, such a prohibition would produce immediate hardships for Virginia citizens because of the rapid growth of settlement in the West. For this reason Dunmore in 1772 ignored the prohibition and signed legislation which created three new counties. The Board of Trade immediately censured Dunmore and informed him that it would recommend a royal veto of the laws.[11] Consequently, new counties could be formed only if the inhabitants forfeited their right to representation in the assembly. As Edmund Pendleton wrote to William Preston, the assembly would never consent to forfeiture of "so essential a right," and the stalemate was broken only by the Declaration of Independence. In 1776 the assembly once again began creating new counties, and its right to do so was never questioned thereafter.[12]

Except for the years of these two challenges, the Virginia legislature possessed and exercised the power of creating new counties for the convenience of the people. Growing sectional antagonism jeopardized the process in the nineteenth century, as the West sought increased voting strength in the legislature and the East fought to thwart it, but such hostility was not a major factor in the eighteenth century. Some historians, notably Jackson Turner Main, have argued that sectional voting blocs appeared in the legislature by the 1780s, but such divisions apparently affected only certain issues (especially economic ones) and left many delegates totally unaffected.[13] Although an aged and embittered Landon Carter wrote in 1776 of the danger posed to the East by the rapid increase in western counties, his warning was not echoed by other eastern politicians and apparently had little or no influence. Indeed, just two years before Carter's remark a large group of western citizens referred to the Virginia government as one "under whose protection and benign influence . . . we have enjoyed many blessings and are most desirous of continuing."[14] A survey of the number of new counties created does indicate that sectional discrimination had not yet become a problem.[15] Creation of new counties, most of them in the West, at a rate of better than fifteen per decade in the 1770-1799 period hardly seems compatible with a presumption of strong eastern antagonism to increased western voting strength in the legislature. During the eighteenth century, any

underrepresentation of the Piedmont and West in the assembly resulted
from the basic principle of Virginia representation, which since 1661
had accorded two burgesses for each county regardless of size or population. As early as 1776 Jefferson wanted to abandon the traditional system
in favor of representation proportional to the number of white male inhabitants, but this proposal generally received little notice or support
before the 1790s. Barring such a fundamental alteration in the constitution, the only way to increase Piedmont and western representation was
to increase the number of counties. This the assembly was willing to do
throughout the eighteenth century. Only after 1810 did sectionalism become sufficiently widespread for a Tidewater-Piedmont coalition virtually
to halt creation of new western counties (see the discussion of this nineteenth-century development in chapter 8). Before 1800, as will be demonstrated, the major obstacle to division of a county was differing opinion
among local residents rather than eastern hostility.

During the eighteenth century, creation of new counties was, almost
without exception, a direct response to petitions from local inhabitants.[16]
Petitioners explained their reasons for desiring a division of the existing
county and often included a detailed description of the boundary line

TABLE 7 CREATION OF NEW COUNTIES IN EIGHTEENTH-
CENTURY VIRGINIA

Period	Number of New Counties Created
1700-1709	2
1710-1719	0
1720-1729	6
1730-1739	5
1740-1749	8
1750-1759	8
1760-1769	6
1770-1779	17
1780-1789	20
1790-1799	10
Total	82

they desired. The petition then underwent thorough investigation, usually by the Committee of Propositions and Grievances. If the request was deemed reasonable by the house, a bill creating the new county would be prepared. Frequently the house accepted with little or no alteration the boundary recommended by the petitioners. Thus in 1720 the "upper inhabitants" of New Kent County, i.e. those living in the "upper" or western section of the county, petitioned to report that settlement had now expanded far from the courthouse. As the people were "taking up and seating new lands on the frontiers," the result was "excessive fatigue of travelling so great a distance to their monthly Courts." The petitioners asked that St. Paul's Parish be separated from New Kent and formed into a new county. Their request was deemed reasonable by both houses of the legislature and by the governor, and Hanover County was created exactly as the petitioners had asked.[17] Similarly, in 1777 a petition from 133 inhabitants of the southeastern portion of Albemarle County reported that the petitioners were greatly inconvenienced by the "Vast extent of said County." When combined with the "extremely Bad" roads, the "Craggy and Mountainous" terrain, and the "two Rivers and many Creeks that are Rapid," the result was that a journey to the courthouse required a round trip of several days. The petitioners included a detailed map indicating the boundary by which a convenient new county could be divided from Albemarle. The assembly accepted the suggestion without amendment and created Fluvanna County.[18]

Sometimes county inhabitants agreed among themselves that a division was necessary but disagreed concerning where the division should be made. In these cases the house often received several petitions, each requesting division by a different boundary. Thorough investigation was then required before the house decided which, if any, suggestion to accept. In 1752, debate concerning division of Amelia County, prompted by a petition from local residents, was postponed because the petitioners failed to specify where the division should be made. At the next session three petitions, each suggesting a slightly different dividing line, were received and carefully investigated. The Committee of Propositions and Grievances then recommended acceptance of one of the proposals, and the assembly agreed.[19] The resulting legislation, which created Prince Edward County, specifically stated the reason for division: "Whereas many inconveniences attend the inhabitants of the county of Amelia, by reason of their great distance from the court-house and the said inhabitants have petitioned ... that the said county may be divided. ..."[20]

The house sometimes decided to accept a proposal for division but to divide by a line different from that suggested by the petitioners. This was especially common in cases in which county inhabitants failed to agree on where the division should be made. In 1776, for example, citizens in Pittsylvania County sent two petitions to the house. Both claimed that the county was too large and should be divided, but they differed as to where this should be done. Following an investigation and report by the Committee of Propositions and Grievances, the house agreed to divide Pittsylvania but decided to reject both specific proposals and instead to divide by a simple straight line.[21] In other cases the house accepted petitions for division but decided that different boundaries were preferable due to considerations of size and population density. Thus when petitioners from Monongalia County asked in 1784 that the county be divided into three parts, with the settlements of Tyger's Valley, Buchanon, and West-fork each becoming a distinct county, the house decided that such action would be premature and accepted instead a committee recommendation that only one new county be formed.[22]

Not all petitioners seeking division were successful, of course, as the house retained its discretionary power to reject petitions and as bills passed by the house might still be rejected by the upper house or vetoed by the colonial governor.[23] As table 8 indicates, however, a surprisingly large percentage of such requests were successful.[24]

Although some petitions for division were rejected by the house on its own initiative because upon investigation such action seemed unwarranted or unwise, in many cases counterpetitions against division revealed the existence of significant local opposition as well. The most common local objection was that division would result in higher taxes in both the old and new counties, as the tax base would be halved while the total number of county officials (from sheriffs to members of the legislature) would be doubled. Moreover, new public buildings would have to be constructed in the new county. The dilemma, then, was whether the increased convenience of a more compact county justified the increased expense. In many cases some county inhabitants felt that it did not.[25] Other common grounds for local opposition included charges that the new county would contain too few inhabitants, that division was intended to serve the private interests and political ambitions of a few, and that agitation for changing present boundaries was merely the work of a few disaffected troublemakers.[26] A 1790 petition from Augusta County protested vigorously against any change in the existing county boundaries:

. . . your humble Petitioners hope this Honorable house will
not suffer such an inroad to be made into this County of
Augusta By a few mal-Contents who if they were humoured
at this time, it is highly Probable they would be of an opposite
Opinion at a future Day; were such small factions in Private
Corners to be Gratified at Every time they hapen [sic] to be
out of humour we Should have nothing But anarchy and Confusion.[27]

Presentation of counterpetitions indicating a significant difference
of opinion reduced the likelihood that a petition for division would be
accepted. Thus on 2 November 1793 the house received a petition signed

TABLE 8 PETITIONS SEEKING CREATION OF NEW
             COUNTIES

Session	Specific Number of New Counties Requested[a]	Bill Passed by House[b]	Enacted into Law[b]
1701	1	1	1
1710	None accepted due to controversy with Governor Spotswood		
1720	3	3	3
1730	2	1	1
1740	3	3	0
1752	6	3	2
1760-1761	2	1	1
1769	2	1	1
1780	3	2	1
1790	6	4	3
Total	28	19 (67.9%)	13 (46.4%)

[a]This involves the number of new counties requested rather than the number
of petitions. For example, two 1730 petitions from Spotsylvania County, each
seeking division but by different dividing lines, are counted as one new county requested.

[b]These figures do not include those requests postponed or deferred to a later
session and then enacted. For example, the 1752 petition from Amelia County was
deferred to the 1753 session, when it was accepted; it is not included as passed or
enacted, however, since the action was taken in 1753 rather than 1752.

by 185 residents of Mecklenburg County which asked that the county be divided. On the same day, however, a second petition, bearing 510 signatures, protested against any division. The counterpetition asserted that Mecklenburg (which had existed without significant alteration since 1764) was actually a compact county and that division would create new and unnecessary expenses, thereby requiring higher taxes. The Committee of Propositions and Grievances reported in favor of the counterpetition, the house agreed, and Mecklenburg was not divided.[28] A similar fate befell the 1770 Accomack petition for division. Accomack had existed unchanged for over a hundred years, and the counterpetition against division was successful in preventing any such action.[29]

Counterpetitions sometimes delayed division of the county even if they did not permanently prevent it. The intense controversy over division of Augusta County in 1767-1769 provided a classic illustration of opposition not from an eastern-dominated assembly but from other county inhabitants. In 1767 Augusta was an immense frontier county stretching about three-quarters of the length of the colony and extending westward to the indefinite Virginia boundary. Augusta's internal tranquility was already disturbed by factional divisions among local politicians and by a dispute between local citizens and Loyal Company land speculators, when in 1767 petitions to divide the county began circulating.[30] Local residents were unable to agree on the need for division or upon where a division should be made, however, and six different petitions—some favoring division by one boundary, some by others, and two opposing division altogether—were sent to the 1767 session of the legislature. As William Preston, one of the Augusta burgesses, afterwards explained to another county resident, "There was Such a Confusion in the Petitions for & against a Division of the County, that the Consideration of them is refferred [sic] to the next Session of Assembly, by which Time I hope we shall have all matters amicably settled amongst ourselves."[31] The controversy continued for two more years until finally, by the end of 1769, opposition in Augusta subsided to the point that a division reasonably acceptable to all factions was agreed upon. Botetourt County was then created from the southwestern portion of Augusta.[32] Similarly, petitioners in the Limestone Settlement of Bourbon County were unsuccessful in 1786 and 1787 in seeking a division, as counterpetitions revealed the existence of sizable local opposition. In 1788, however, signatures on the petition and counterpetition ran by more than a two-to-one majority in favor of division (259 to 116). Moreover, the signers of the counterpetition opposed division primarily because they feared that Bourbon County residents would be required to repay certain tax monies to the new county. The assembly then created Mason County from a portion of Bourbon, using exactly the same boundary desired by the petitioners, but the law also alleviated the fears expressed in the counterpetition by not requiring restitution of past taxes.[33]

Although the use of counterpetitions increased the odds against a petition for division, the assembly frequently decided that the requests for division were justified and created new counties anyway. On 12 November 1796 the house received a petition seeking a division of Ohio County, but four days later a counterpetition was presented. The Committee of Propositions and Grievances reported in favor of the request for division, which was signed by 798 citizens who complained that they had to travel as much as fifty miles to the courthouse. The counterpetition, which contained 340 signatures, admitted that a division was necessary but asked that it be postponed for a few years. The assembly then passed a bill for division, and Brooke County was created by the exact dividing line suggested by the local residents in their petition.[34] Similarly, two 1734 petitions to divide Prince George, then a large frontier county in southwestern Virginia, were successful despite two counterpetitions.[35] In 1744 a counterpetition failed to halt the division of Goochland, another large frontier county, and the house also rejected a petition to divide the county by an east-west line; instead, a more normal north-south division, exactly as suggested by a petition from the "upper inhabitants" of Goochland, created the new county of Albemarle.[36]

A 1752-1753 controversy over division of Surry County provided a solid indication that the house was favorably disposed to grant requests for division unless there appeared to be sound reasons for not doing so. Two 1752 petitions requested division of Surry County, though by different boundaries, and a counterpetition asked that it not be divided at all. Landon Carter attended the investigation by the Committee of Propositions and Grievances. He reported that the matter was "so Confused that I could not form any Opinion," and the debate in the full house was also filled with "uncommon Assertions and Contradictions." Moreover, both burgesses from Surry opposed division. Although none of the debate made much sense to Carter, he and a majority of his colleagues decided to vote in favor of division anyway. A bill for that purpose then passed the house only to be rejected by the council due to a dispute over the name of the new county. At the next session, in 1753, the entire process was repeated. This time a deadlock with the council was avoided, and Sussex County was created from the southwestern portion of Surry.[37] If this incident is any indication, the house listened to requests for division with an extremely sympathetic ear, and neither counterpetitions nor the opposition of local burgesses could automatically halt a division without good reason. Whether they supported or opposed division, however, the petitions of local citizens played a crucial role in creating new counties by initiating the procedure, by suggesting a desirable dividing line, and by revealing local sentiment. For its part the house displayed a responsiveness to local needs and wishes rather than sectional hostility toward increased non-Tidewater voting strength.

When the number of citizens inconvenienced by existing county boundaries was relatively small, the house and the local residents often preferred to alter the existing boundary whenever possible rather than create a new county. Frequently in these cases the county boundary could be redrawn in a manner which added the interested citizens to a neighboring county, where the courthouse was closer or the means of transportation were better. As was the case with creation of new counties, alteration of county boundaries was almost always initiated by the petitions of local residents.

Since these petitions generally sought relatively minor adjustments, those which indicated widespread local support for the change were frequently successful. Thus in 1754 citizens living in Albemarle County on the south side of Fluvanna River, above Rock Island Creek, complained that the great distance to the courthouse was a serious inconvenience. They petitioned that their section be added to Bedford County, at that time immediately southwest of Albemarle, and their request was successful.[38] Similarly, a 1785 petition from Nansemond, asking that the section of the county south of the Blackwater and Nottoway rivers be added to Southampton, was accepted and the desired alteration was made.[39]

As was the case with dividing counties, however, local inhabitants did not always agree among themselves that an alteration was necessary or desirable. Petitions seeking to change the county boundaries were sometimes successful despite counterpetitions, as was the case with a 1790 petition and counterpetition involving a proposal to add part of Augusta to Pendleton County.[40] In many cases, however, where counterpetitions revealed a significant division of opinion among local residents, the house was reluctant to alter existing arrangements. In 1789 some residents of Hanover County petitioned to ask that the part of Hanover lying below the south branch of Pamunkey River be added to Goochland County. Though the desired modification was relatively minor, counterpetitions against the proposal were received from both Goochland and Hanover, and the house then refused to alter the boundary.[41] The same fate befell 1740 and 1793 petitions from Westmoreland and Chesterfield counties respectively when counterpetitions from other local residents disputed the need for change.[42]

Another method for redressing local complaints about the difficulty of travel to the county courthouse was to alter the courthouse location. In some cases the county seat could be moved to a more convenient location, one closer to the center of population or more accessible by existing transportation routes. During the colonial period the house normally played no role in this matter. The local justices of the peace customarily selected the location upon which the courthouse would be erected. Should other county residents be dissatisfied with the decision, or should some inhabitants later decide that the expansion of settlement dictated a change from the original location, appeal could be made to the governor and council. After considering the matter, the governor and council could order either that the present site be retained or that a new location be adopted. This procedure reflected the royal prerogative in judicial matters; the governor commissioned justices of the peace and heard any appeal of their decisions, whether involving legal or administrative matters.[43]

The governor and council gave careful consideration to any petitions seeking a change in courthouse location. On 27 February 1728, for example, a number of Surry County inhabitants petitioned that the courthouse be rebuilt closer to the center of the county, and other residents opposed the request with a counterpetition. Governor Gooch and his council postponed making a decision until the county surveyor could present them with a detailed map of Surry which indicated both the present and proposed locations and the distances to the outlying settlements. When this map was presented, it convinced Gooch and the council that the grievance was legitimate, and they ordered the new courthouse

to be constructed at a specified and more central location.[44] Similarly, a
1762 dispute over the location of the courthouse for Goochland County
caused petitions and counterpetitions to be sent to Governor Fauquier
and his council. They consulted a map of the county and decided that the
courthouse should be constructed on the land of Alexander Baine, as close
as possible to the springs.[45]

After Virginia became a state, the legislature assumed the power to
settle controversies involving courthouse locations. The house consistently
upheld the principle that the new county courthouse should be located
"at or as near the centre thereof as the situation and conveniency of the
respective counties will admit of. . . ."[46] Although within that limitation
the local justices were still allowed to select the exact location,[47] any
residents dissatisfied with the existing or proposed site could petition the
house and seek redress. When investigation upheld the petitioners' claims,
the house required the local justices to erect the courthouse at a more
convenient location; the two methods used by the delegates were to
specify a certain location in the legislation itself or else to require that a
survey be made to determine the center of the county, with the courthouse to be built as close as possible to that point.[48] As was the case
with altering existing county boundaries, changing the courthouse location
usually was a response to relatively minor problems. For major problems
associated with large counties, especially those on the frontier, creation
of new counties remained the usual remedy during the eighteenth century.

In all other respects except membership and location of the courthouse,
the county courts of Virginia were regulated by the assembly even during
the colonial period.[49] The legislature specified by statute the days when
the court of each county would hold its session, and the days were often
changed when citizens petitioned the house and requested such action.
These petitions were frequently signed by the justices and the clerk of
the county court, by local attorneys, and by other interested citizens.
They frequently asserted that the days established for holding court were
too close to those of adjacent counties and thus inconvenienced all who
might have business in more than one county.[50] Governor Spotswood's
attempt to restrict the right of altering court days to the governor rather
than to the assembly was unsuccessful. He asked the Board of Trade to
support his authority in this regard, but once again England simply ignored
his request, and in 1718 the House of Burgesses rejected a bill which

would have allowed him to alter court days upon the application of the justices of the peace.[51] After the Revolution the assembly continued to alter court days in response to the petitions of local residents.[52]

Regulation of town government was also a frequent subject of petitions to the house. Both during the colonial period and after 1776, towns were established by legislative statute. The assembly sought to encourage the growth of towns, both as an aid to commerce and a convenience for travelers, and it established some towns on its own initiative.[53] In many cases, however, the acts passed which established towns were a response to petitions. Such petitions came from speculators who owned the land where the town was to be established, from other citizens interested in purchasing lots if a town was established, and from local residents who simply believed that a town would be of general public benefit. If the assembly accepted the petition, it appointed trustees to lay off lots for the town and to manage the sale of those lots, with proceeds of the sale going to the original owner of the land.[54]

A 1728 incident illustrates the willingness of the assembly to create towns for the public benefit, for in that year it established a town in Spotsylvania County despite the opposition of the owners of the land. Spotsylvania had grown rapidly in size, and by 1728 settlement had advanced above the falls of the Rappahannock River. Planters in the upper end of the county thus brought their tobacco for storage and sale to the first navigable point below the falls. A 1728 petition from local citizens complained that the present owners of the land had erected inadequate storehouses, charged exorbitant rates, and monopolized the trade by refusing to permit other merchants to settle there. Establishment of a town below the falls, claimed the petitioners, would lead to better facilities, would increase mercantile activity, and would be a convenience to travelers. The owners of the land, John Royston and Robert Buckner, stoutly opposed the petition. The house, the council, and Governor Gooch all decided that the petition was reasonable despite this opposition, and they enacted a law to carry out the petitioners' request. Trustees were appointed to direct the establishment, though Royston and Buckner were guaranteed a selling price of forty shillings per acre and were allowed to retain two lots apiece. As the law stated and as Governor Gooch reported to England, creation of the town of Fredericksburg was thus a direct response to the petitions received by the house.[55]

Throughout the eighteenth century most of Virginia's towns were hampered by inadequate local authority for dealing with municipal affairs, for in most matters the towns were controlled by the county courts and by statutes enacted by the legislature.[56] As a result, officials and inhabitants of many towns petitioned the assembly to request passage of laws to solve particular problems or to widen the general scope of municipal power. During the eighteenth century, for example, many towns suffered from sanitation problems caused by hogs roaming loose, fouling the water supply, and in general making a nuisance of themselves. As Governor Gooch reported to the Board of Trade, "the reasons for restraining those kinds of creatures are obvious," but town trustees did not possess the authority to do so. Consequently, the assembly received numerous petitions from towns seeking legislation to prevent hogs from roaming loose within town limits. Such petitions were generally successful.[57] By the second half of the century, some of Virginia's towns had grown into healthy urban communities, and particularly after 1776 these towns began requesting legislation to increase the general authority of town trustees. Citizens living in Dumfries thus successfully petitioned in 1787 that the trustees be allowed to establish a town market and regulate the assize of bread, to maintain city streets in better repair, and to provide for a night watch. In the same fashion, in 1800 the house accepted a petition from the town of Franklin which asked that the trustees be allowed to enact rules and bylaws for preventing fires, restraining hogs, prohibiting horse racing on city streets, and "preserving in all other respects, good order in the said town."[58]

For a town continuing to grow in size and population, however, such legislative action was at best only a stopgap measure. Home rule granted by a charter of incorporation was the only long-range solution for Virginia's budding urban communities. For incorporated towns local authority was exercised by a mayor, recorder, aldermen, and common council, and the extensive powers they possessed eliminated the necessity of seeking legislative authorization before acting on important municipal concerns. During the colonial period, the granting of charters of incorporation was included in the royal prerogative and was performed by the royal governor, subject to English approval. The authority granted to incorporated cities by such charters was then detailed in a statute enacted by the General Assembly. Subsequent legislation sometimes expanded this authority;

however, due to the royal prerogative, the prior approval of the governor was required.[59] In 1736 residents of Norfolk asked the governor for a charter of incorporation, which Governor Gooch then granted. When the assembly met later that year, two additional petitions to the house secured legislative confirmation of the charter provisions.[60] Before 1776 there were only three incorporated cities in the colony—Jamestown, Williamsburg, and Norfolk—but after Independence the incorporation of Virginia's larger cities proceeded at a fairly rapid pace. With the elimination of royal authority, charters of incorporation were granted exclusively by legislative statute. Acting on petitions from town inhabitants, the assembly incorporated Winchester, Alexandria, Richmond, Petersburg, and Staunton in the 1779-1801 period. The case of Staunton is particularly instructive. The trustees of that town had been given increased powers in 1789, but this measure proved inadequate and incorporation was granted in 1801.[61]

Thus, in the vitally important area of creating and regulating local government, the assembly in the eighteenth century proved responsive to the needs and requests of local citizens as expressed in their petitions. In a positive sense creation of new counties or cities almost invariably was initiated when a petition or petitions from local inhabitants indicated the need for such action and revealed substantial popular support for it. In a passive sense creation of new counties or cities was more likely to be granted when no counterpetitions disputed the advantages to be gained or indicated that a significant number of residents were hostile to the change. In such matters, then, petitioning played an important role in terms of political participation by Virginia citizens and responsiveness on the part of their colonial and state governments.

Notes

1. George Webb, *The Office and Authority of a Justice of the Peace* (Williamsburg, 1736); Governor Gooch to Board of Trade, n.d. [1728], and 20 November 1734, William Gooch Papers, 3 vols., transcripts, VHS, 1: 56; 2: 375, 377-78; Wesley F. Craven, *The Southern Colonies in the Seventeenth Century, 1607-1689* (Baton Rouge, La., 1949), pp. 172, 269-75; Warren M. Billings, "The Growth of Political Institutions in Virginia, 1634 to 1676," *WMQ*, 3rd ser. 31 (April 1974): 225-32; Isabel Ferguson, "County Court in Virginia, 1700-1830," *North Carolina Historical Review* 8 (January 1931): 14-40.

2. Morgan P. Robinson, "Virginia Counties," Virginia State Library *Bulletin* 9 (January, April, and July, 1916): 94-112. A few of these counties were later abolished (e.g., Dunmore County, created in 1772 but abolished in 1778), while numerous others are today part of Kentucky and West Virginia.

3. For this reason, a 1705 law provided that new counties on the frontier had to contain at least 800 tithables—William Waller Hening, ed., *The Statutes at Large: Being a Collection of All the Laws of Virginia*, 13 vols. (Richmond and Philadelphia, 1809-23), 3: 284.

4. Hening, *Statutes*, 1: 224, 247, 249, 250, 352, 381, 423; 2: 151, 285, 318, 406, 421; Robinson, "Virginia Counties," pp. 36-38, 90-94, 198; Herbert L. Osgood, *The American Colonies in the Seventeenth Century*, 3 vols. (New York, 1904-07), 3: 80-82; Albert O. Porter, *County Government in Virginia: A Legislative History, 1607-1904* (New York, 1947), pp. 11-12; Elmer I. Miller, "The Legislature of the Province of Virginia," *Columbia University Studies* 28 (1907): 203, 207; *JHB*, 1619-1658/59: 101; Warren M. Billings, ed., *The Old Dominion in the Seventeenth Century* (Chapel Hill, N.C., 1975), p. 82.

5. *JHB*, 1659/60-1693: 209-10; Robinson, "Virginia Counties," pp. 93-94; Edmund S. Morgan, *American Slavery—American Freedom: The Ordeal of Colonial Virginia* (New York, 1975), pp. 288-90.

6. *JHB*, 1695-1702: 269, 272, 274, 279, 289, 291, 294, 295, 321, 325, 329; 1702/3-1712: 24; Hening, *Statutes*, 3: 211, 223.

7. *JHB*, 1702/3-1712: 263, 273, 281; Petition of Charles City County, Colonial Papers, folder 22, item 6, VSL; D. Alan Williams, "Political Alignments in Colonial Virginia Politics, 1698-1750" (Ph.D. dissertation, Northwestern University, 1959), pp. 124-37.

8. *JHB*, 1702/3-1712: 285, 344.

9. *JHB*, 1712-1726: 250, 265, 272, 273, 274, 279, 281, 316; Hening, *Statutes*, 4: 95; Spotswood to Board of Trade, 15 December 1710 and 9 March 1714, in *The Official Letters of Alexander Spotswood*, ed. Robert A. Brock, Virginia Historical Society *Collections*, Vols. 1 and 2 (Richmond, 1882-85), 1: 36-39; 2: 56; Board of Trade to Spotswood, 22 November 1711 and 18 August 1715, Great Britain, Public Record Office, *Calendar of State Papers, Colonial Series, America and West Indies*, ed. W. Noel Sainsbury et al., 44 vols to date (London, 1860-   ), no. 189, 26: 162-63; no. 575, 28: 270-71 (hereafter cited as *CSPC*). The controversy involved division of parishes as well as counties—see the discussion of the parish affair in chapter 7.

10. The 1767 circular is found in *Royal Instructions to British Colonial Governors, 1670-1776*, ed. Leonard W. Labaree, 2 vols. (New York, 1935), no. 174, 1: 107; Dunmore's 1771 instructions are contained in "Aspinwall Papers," Massachusetts Historical Society *Collections*, 4th ser. 10: 635-36; see also Board of Trade to the King, 30 January 1771, CO5/1369, pp. 47-48.

11. Board of Trade to Dunmore, 2 March 1773, CO5/1369, p. 309; Dunmore to Earl of Dartmouth, 25 May 1773, CO5/1372, pp. 241-43; Earl of Dartmouth to Dunmore, 27 October 1773, CO5/1375, pp. 191-94; Hening, *Statutes*, 8: 597, 600.

12. Edmund Pendleton to William Preston, 4 June 1774, in *Letters and Papers of Edmund Pendleton*, ed. David J. Mays, 2 vols. (Charlottesville, Va., 1967), 1: 91; George Mason to Edmund Randolph, 19 October 1782, in *The Papers of George Mason, 1725-1792*, ed. Robert A. Rutland, 3 vols. (Chapel Hill, N.C., 1970), 2: 748; Robinson, "Virginia Counties," p. 102. Jefferson listed this British policy as a major grievance in both his "Summary View of the Rights of British America"

(1774) and in the Declaration of Independence—*The Papers of Thomas Jefferson,* ed. Julian P. Boyd, 19 vols. to date (Princeton, N.J., 1950-   ), 1: 130, 430.

13. Most studies agree that sectionalism was not a problem during the colonial period. See, for example: Robert E. Brown and B. Katherine Brown, *Virginia 1705-1786: Democracy or Aristocracy?* (East Lansing, Mich., 1964), pp. 234, 239; John R. Alden, *The South in the Revolution, 1763-1789* (Baton Rouge, La., 1957), pp. 143-45; Thomas P. Abernethy, *Western Lands and the American Revolution* (New York, 1937), pp. 149-61, 367-68; Richard Hofstadter, *The Idea of a Party System* (Berkeley, Cal., 1969), pp. 47-48; Jack P. Greene, *The Quest for Power* (Chapel Hill, N.C., 1963), p. 30. For descriptions of sectionalism after 1780, see Jackson T. Main, "Sections and Politics in Virginia, 1781-1787," *WMQ,* 3rd ser. 12 (January 1955): 96-112; Main, *Political Parties Before the Constitution* (Chapel Hill, N.C., 1973), ch. 9; Norman K. Risjord and Gorden DenBoer, "The Evolution of Political Parties in Virginia, 1782-1800," *Journal of American History* 40 (March 1974): 961-84; Richard R. Beeman, *The Old Dominion and the New Nation, 1788-1801* (Lexington, Ky., 1972), pp. 91-93.

14. Landon Carter to George Washington, 31 October 1776, in *American Archives,* ed. Peter Force, 9 vols. (Washington, D.C., 1837-53), 5th ser. 2: 1306; Petition of Inhabitants of Augusta, Botetourt, and Fincastle Counties in Virginia to Governor Earl of Dunmore, in *Documents of the American Revolution, 1770-1783 (Colonial Office Series),* ed. K. G. Davies, 17 vols. to date (Shannon, Ireland, 1972-   ), 8:85-86.

15. Robinson, "Virginia Counties," pp. 94-112. This interpretation is defended by Brown and Brown, *Virginia 1705-1786,* pp. 218-24, and by Freeman H. Hart, *The Valley of Virginia in the American Revolution, 1763-1789* (Chapel Hill, N.C., 1942), pp. 62-65. See also Richard R. Beeman, "Social Change and Cultural Conflict in Virginia: Lunenburg County, 1746 to 1774," *WMQ,* 3rd ser. 35 (July 1978): 462.

16. The only exceptions involved the few instances where, for defensive purposes, frontier counties were organized prior to extensive settlement. The most notable example was the creation of Spotsylvania and Brunswick counties in 1720. See Leonidas Dodson, *Alexander Spotswood* (Philadelphia, 1932), pp. 244-45; Brown and Brown, *Virginia 1705-1786,* p. 219; Walter Havighurst, *Alexander Spotswood* (New York, 1967), p. 95.

17. *JHB,* 1712-1726: 265, 274, 281, 316; Hening, *Statutes,* 4: 95; see the Governor's report in Spotswood to Board of Trade, 6 March 1721, *CSPC,* no. 396, 32: 260.

18. *JHD,* May 1777: 9, 11; Hening, *Statutes,* 9: 325-27; see the petition and commentary in *Jefferson Papers,* ed. Boyd, 2: 14-15.

19. Jack P. Greene, ed., *Diary of Landon Carter of Sabine Hall, 1752-1778,* 2 vols. (Charlottesville, Va., 1965), 1: 73; *JHB,* 1752-1758: 56, 109, 115, 122, 124, 125, 170.

20. Hening, *Statutes,* 6: 379-80.

21. *JHD,* October 1776: 6, 14-15, 18, 19, 21-22, 30; Hening, *Statutes,* 9: 241-42. Once again, the law specifically stated that it originated in the petitions sent to the legislature.

22. *JHD*, May 1784: 18-19, 28; Hening, *Statutes*, 11: 366-68.

23. See, for example: *JHB*, 1727-1740: 73; 1752-1758: 18, 45; 1758-1761: 209; *JHD*, 1786 (1828 reprint): 27, 42, 66, 67; 1798: 21, 29, 30; Greene, ed., *Diary of Landon Carter*, 1: 121.

24. These figures are derived by examining the house *Journal* for the respective sessions and by comparing this examination with the laws listed in Hening.

25. 1710 Charles City County Petition, "Miscellaneous Documents, Colonial and State," *VMHB* 18 (October 1910): 398-99; Amelia Petition, 16 November 1789; Henry Petition, 23 October 1790; Greenbrier Petition, 20 November 1790; Pittsylvania Petition, 10 November 1796 (oversize); William Preston to William Byrd, 14 May 1774, Preston Papers, Draper MSS (3QQ24); Unsigned letter "To the Several Inhabitants of the County of Richmond," October 1769, The Carter Family Papers, 1659-1797, UVa Microfilm Publication; Beeman, *Old Dominion*, pp. 43-44.

26. Montgomery Petition, 14 December 1804; Bourbon Petition, 10 November 1787, in *Petitions of the Early Inhabitants of Kentucky to the General Assembly of Virginia, 1769 to 1792*, ed. James R. Robertson, Filson Club Publication No. 27 (Louisville, Ky., 1914), pp. 110-11; Pittsylvania Petition, 10 November 1796 (oversize); 1793 Caroline and Essex Petitions against new county, in *Pendleton Letters*, ed. Mays, 2: 616-21; Greene, ed., *Diary of Landon Carter*, 1: 121; J. Madison to William Preston, 1 March 1767, Preston Davie Collection of Preston Family Papers, VHS.

27. Augusta Petition, 16 November 1790.

28. *JHD*, 1793: 37, 79; Mecklenburg Petitions for and against division, 2 November 1793.

29. *JHB*, 1770-1772, 20, 33; Robinson, "Virginia Counties," pp. 42, 73. Numerous similar cases could be cited—see, for example, Brown and Brown, *Virginia 1705-1786*, pp. 219-20.

30. Thomas Lewis to William Preston, 24 February 1767, Preston Papers, Draper MSS (2QQ100); J. Madison to William Preston, 1 March 1767, and ? to ?, 4 April 1770, Preston Davie Collection of Preston Family Papers, VHS; *JHB*, 1766-1769: 37; Abernethy, *Western Lands*, pp. 12-13, 61, 68, 83; Brown and Brown, *Virginia 1705-1786*, p. 223.

31. *JHB*, 1766-1769: 84, 102, 106; William Preston to Robert Breckinridge, 1 April 1767, Breckinridge Papers, Library of Congress.

32. *JHB*, 1766-1769: 146, 197, 201-02, 204, 238, 240-42, 251, 252, 253, 257, 292, 297, 298, 353; Hening, *Statutes*, 8: 395-96.

33. *JHD*, 1786 (1828 reprint): 7, 11, 14; 1787 (1828 reprint): 39, 46, 53, 57; 1788 (1828 reprint): 8-9, 12, 21, 25; Hening, *Statutes*, 12: 658-59; the petitions are conveniently located in *Kentucky Petitions*, ed. Robertson, pp. 89-91, 107-11, 117-19. This compilation does not include the number of signatures, however, and for that information one must consult the original petitions in VSL.

34. *JHD*, 1796: 10, 21, 31-32, 42, 50; Ohio Petitions, 12 November 1796 (oversize) and 16 November 1796 (oversize); Samuel Shepherd, ed., *The Statutes at Large of Virginia. . . Being a Continuation of Hening*, 3 vols. (Richmond, 1835-36), 2: 54.

35. *JHB,* 1727-1740: 206, 214, 216, 222, 224, 234; Hening, *Statutes,* 4: 467-68; the Governor's report describes the legislation—Gooch to Board of Trade, 20 November 1734, Gooch Papers, 2: 377-78, *VHS.*

36. *JHB,* 1742-1749: 89, 95, 103, 106, 108, 113, 135, 148; Hening, *Statutes,* 5: 266-67; Richard L. Morton, *Colonial Virginia,* 2 vols. (Chapel Hill, N.C., 1960), 2: 537-38, 553, 581.

37. *JHB,* 1752-1758: 32, 39, 44, 56, 60-64, 114, 117, 120, 123, 125, 130, 140, 142, 170; Hening, *Statutes,* 6: 384; *Diary of Landon Carter,* ed. Greene, 1: 84, 90; William G. Stanard and Mary N. Stanard, comps. *The Colonial Virginia Register* (1902; reprint ed., Baltimore, 1965), p. 127; Brown and Brown, *Virginia 1705-1786,* p, 221.

38. *JHB,* 1752-1758: 211, 213, 226; Hening, *Statutes,* 6: 441.

39. *JHD,* 1785: 28, 38, 42, 52-53; Hening, *Statutes,* 12: 69.

40. Augusta Petition and Counterpetition, 16 November 1790; *JHD,* 1790 (1828 reprint): 65, 105, 120; Hening, *Statutes,* 13: 167.

41. *JHD,* 1789 (1828 reprint): 61-62, 93.

42. *JHB,* 1727-1740: 405; *JHD,* 1793: 47, 93.

43. For example, see the 1693 action of the justices of the peace for the new county of Essex as they selected the site for a courthouse—William M. Sweeny, ed., "Gleanings from the Records of (Old) Rappahannock County and Essex County, Virginia," *WMQ,* 2d ser. 18 (July 1938): 308; for other indications, see *EJC,* 3: 527-28; 4: 22, 167-68, 332, 396; *JHB,* 1712-1726: 152; "Henry County," *VMHB* 9: (January 1902): 262. A comprehensive 1748 act on the Virginia court system also clearly indicates that the county justices of the peace were expected to select the location, erect, and maintain the courthouse—Hening, *Statutes,* 5: 507; 8: 419-20. Only in exceptional circumstances did the legislature set the location, as in 1732 when it required the location to be changed in Spotsylvania County. Since the county was about to be divided, the legislature did set the new location and require the inhabitants of the lower county to reimburse the upper inhabitants for their expenses—see Gooch to Board of Trade, 18 July 1732, *CSPC,* no. 308, 39: 176; Hening, *Statutes,* 4: 364-65. Moreover, in 1759 the assembly specifically renounced any right to alter court locations as being contrary to the royal prerogative—Hening, *Statutes,* 7: 320. The often-repeated assertion by Albert O. Porter, *County Government in Virginia, A Legislative History, 1607-1904* (New York, 1947), p. 50, and by others, that the assembly selected the courthouse location is thus clearly in error.

44. *EJC,* 4: 167, 170.

45. Ibid., 6: 227.

46. See, for example, Hening, *Statutes,* 9: 242-43, 322-23; 12: 87.

47. Ibid., 13: 453.

48. *JHD,* May 1779: 25; 1803: 22, 57, 63; Hening, *Statutes,* 9: 229; 10: 108; 11: 432; 13: 79; Shepherd, *Virginia Statutes,* 3: 45; the 1789 Fairfax petition to move the courthouse included 558 signatures—*Mason Papers,* ed. Rutland, 3: 1179-85.

49. Greene, *Quest for Power,* pp. 332-34; Porter, *County Government in*

Virginia, chs. 1 and 2; Oliver P. Chitwood, "Justice in Colonial Virginia," *Johns Hopkins Studies* 23 (1905): 478-92.

50. *JHB*, 1695-1702: 65, 73, 76, 82, 101-02; 1742-1749: 220; 1758-1761: 140, 152; Hening, *Statutes*, 3: 140-41, 506-07; 5: 371; 7: 310, 340; William Gooch to Board of Trade, 18 July 1732, *CSPC*, no. 308, 39: 175-76.

51. Alexander Spotswood to Board of Trade, 27 January 1715 and 24 June 1718, in *Spotswood Letters*, ed. Brock, 2: 98-99, 281.

52. *JHD*, October 1784: 51; 1786 (1828 reprint): 19, 31, 32, 38; Hening, *Statutes*, 9: 439-40, 580; 11: 431; 12: 407, 408, 606.

53. Hening, *Statutes*, 3: 53-69, 404-15; Brown and Brown, *Virginia 1705-1786*, pp. 129-30; John W. Reps, *Tidewater Towns: City Planning in Colonial Virginia and Maryland* (Charlottesville, Va., 1972), chs. 4 and 9.

54. *JHB*, 1752-1758: 27; *JHD*, May 1777: 47; 1785, 15; 1786 (1828 reprint): 8, 11, 14, 31, 126; Harrison Petition, 26 November 1784; Hening, *Statutes*, 6: 268-70; 9: 425-26; 12: 217, 361, 396-97; Katherine G. Greene, *Winchester, Virginia, and Its Beginnings, 1743-1814* (Strasburg, Va., 1926), pp. 20-34; Reps, *Tidewater Towns*, p. 194.

55. *JHB*, 1727-1740: 12, 52; Hening, *Statutes*, 4: 234-39; Gooch to Board of Trade, [8 June?] 1728, *CSPC*, no. 241, 36: 120-21.

56. Carl Bridenbaugh has illustrated many of the general problems which confronted colonial towns, including their need for increased powers—Bridenbaugh, *Cities in the Wilderness* (New York, 1938), pp. 7, 36, 144. See also E. Lee Shepard, "Courts in Conflict: Town-County Relations in Post-Revolutionary Virginia," *VMHB* 85 (April 1977): 184-99.

57. Douglas S. Freeman, *George Washington*, 7 vols. (New York, 1948-57), 3: 58-59; *JHB*, 1727-1740: 9-10, 52; *JHD*, 1789 (1828 reprint): 20-21, 56, 58; 1801: 41, 55; Staunton Petition, 28 October 1789; Franklin Petition (Pendleton County), 9 December 1800; Hening, *Statutes*, 4: 180, 240; 13: 89-90; Shepherd, *Virginia Statutes*, 2: 350; Gov. Hugh Drysdale to Board of Trade, 10 July 1726, CO 5/1320, p. 65; Gov. Gooch to Board of Trade, [8 June?] 1728, *CSPC*, no. 241, 36: 122.

58. *JHB*, 1752-1758: 10, 28, 31, 98; *JHD*, 1787 (1828 reprint): 55, 74-75, 81, 86; 1789 (1828 reprint): 20-21, 37-38, 56, 58; Staunton Petition, 28 October 1789; Franklin Petition (Pendleton County), 9 December 1800; Hening, *Statutes*, 6: 285-86; 12: 630-31; 13: 89-90; Shepherd, *Virginia Statutes*, 2: 258.

59. Hening, *Statutes*, 3: 427; 4: 138-39, 541-42; 5: 204-07; 7: 136-39; Gooch to Board of Trade, 5 December 1736, *CSPC*, no. 480, 42: 364-65; Brown and Brown, *Virginia 1705-1786*, pp. 127, 129.

60. *Virginia Gazette*, 26 November 1736; *JHB*, 1727-1740: 255, 316; Hening, *Statutes*, 4: 541-42; Gooch to Board of Trade, 5 December 1736, *CSPC*, no. 480, 42: 364-65; Thomas J. Wertenbaker, *Norfolk: Historic Southern Port* (Durham, N.C., 1931), pp. 7-9.

61. *JHD*, May 1779: 30, 47; May 1784: 31-32, 53; 1789 (1828 reprint): 20-21, 37-38, 56, 58; 1801: 7-8, 11, 30-31, 40; Hening, *Statutes*, 10: 172-76; 11: 45-51, 382-87; 13: 89-90; Shepherd, *Virginia Statutes*, 2: 335-37.

5 PETITIONS AND ECONOMIC LEGISLATION

During the colonial period and in the years following the Revolution, the people and government of Virginia accepted the principle of government regulation in some phases of the economy.[1] The assembly enacted a host of laws to control the agricultural, industrial, and commercial activity of the Old Dominion. The government acted to forbid the exportation or engrossing of staple foodstuffs during periods of domestic shortage. An elaborate network for the inspection and quality control of tobacco was constructed by mid-eighteenth century, and a number of other commodities intended for export were inspected before shipment on a less systematic basis. Production of several domestic manufactures, including iron, naval stores, and wine, was encouraged by bounties and other favorable policies. Much of this economic legislation was enacted and later amended on a trial-and-error basis. In several cases the assembly introduced these regulations when citizens requested them, and later amendments frequently incorporated suggestions or redressed complaints presented in the petitions of interested people.

War, drought, or other calamities occasionally forced the Virginia government to act to prevent temporary food shortages. When the colony suffered a severe shortage of corn in 1699, citizens in several counties petitioned the house for an embargo on the exportation of corn until the crisis passed. The assembly accepted the suggestion and prohibited the exportation of corn until December 25, 1700. When the crisis persisted longer than anticipated, the next session of the legislature extended the prohibition for five additional years. In 1728 the assembly enacted legislation authorizing the royal governor to issue proclamations prohibiting export of provisions during domestic shortages, and the legislation established stiff penalties for violators. When the governor took such action in 1755, the assembly added a law to fix the price of corn during the coming year so that sellers could not extort excessive prices "from the poor and necessitous." A severe 1759 shortage of corn, confined to the region around Albemarle County, led local inhabitants to petition the house seeking assistance. The legislature responded by appropriating £1000 to purchase corn or grain and transport it to the area. Trustees were appointed to sell the provisions at cost to those who could afford to pay, but the poor and indigent received the supplies free of charge. In 1778 the assembly authorized the governor to forbid export of foodstuffs during domestic shortages, just as the colonial governor had been authorized to do.[2]

Virginia also took preventive action against damage to crops and livestock by encouraging the destruction of wolves, crows, and squirrels. The assembly provided bounty payments from the public treasury for wolves' heads, and at times additional legislation authorized county courts to supplement the bounty with local tax funds. Such laws were frequently enacted or amended in response to petitions from local citizens. In 1720 the assembly granted petitions from Stafford and New Kent counties by increasing the bounty to 200 pounds of tobacco per wolf. During the 1760s residents of Hampshire, Frederick, and several other counties in the western Piedmont and Valley successfully petitioned to allow the county courts in that area to supplement the established bounty for a limited time. A similar petition from Hampshire County in 1789 was equally successful.[3] The assembly also responded to complaints that large numbers of crows and squirrels threatened the production of corn and other crops. Generally when petitioners asked for legislation to encourage the killing of such pests, the assembly passed laws which applied only to the specific counties where the problem existed. The standard remedy involved a temporary requirement that each tithable kill a certain number of crows and squirrels or be assessed a penalty by the county court. Residents who killed more than their quota often received bounties from these fines. Legislation of this description was enacted periodically throughout the eighteenth century in direct response to petitions.[4]

Much legislative attention focused upon the production of agricultural staples for export. Tobacco was the most important export staple throughout the seventeenth and eighteenth centuries. Falling prices, caused by failure to control quality and by overproduction, plagued colonial planters within a few years after John Rolfe's introduction of the tobacco culture. In response, the 1619 assembly enacted a law for inspecting tobacco and burning that of poor quality, and other legislation followed during the next few years. In 1630 production was restricted, and colonists were specifically prohibited from using bad tobacco in payment of debts, and a 1633 act required inspection of all tobacco at warehouses to be erected. These specific measures aroused considerable dissatisfaction and were soon repealed, but other laws designed to control quality and quantity soon followed. A number of statutes prohibited replanting tobacco after a certain date because any replanted then would be of poorer quality. Additional legislation forbade the tending of second-growth tobacco or the curing of suckers, since both practices produced an inferior product. A third category of restrictions limited the number of leaves that could be harvested from each plant or the number of plants that each laborer could cultivate.[5]

In part this early regulation was suggested by English officials. Of greater significance were the debates within the assembly itself concerning the requirements of the tobacco trade.[6] Unfortunately, the assembly *Journals,* the statutes, and other surviving legislative records are brief and incomplete for much of the early seventeenth century; this makes it impossible to determine precisely the extent to which early tobacco regulation included suggestions presented by colonial planters through petitions. There are some indications, however, that these petitions played an important role. The 1633 provisions for inspection of tobacco at warehouses before exportation were repealed following petitions of protest by Virginia planters.[7] During the seventeenth century, Virginia planters sent a number of petitions concerning the tobacco trade directly to the authorities in England. These petitions emphasized the absolute necessity for reducing production, and some even proposed a temporary prohibition against planting any more tobacco in Virginia and Maryland.[8] In 1663, 1666, and 1681 the assembly attempted to prohibit planting for one-year periods. In each of those years the burgesses received a large number of petitions, at least some of which concerned the tobacco regulations. Governor Berkeley reported in 1666 that "its the voice of all" that a cessation of planting would be a great advantage.[9] Despite these efforts, each attempt to halt planting failed, sometimes because Maryland refused to cooperate and on other occasions because of royal opposition on the grounds that English customs duties would decline.[10] By 1700 the tobacco laws had been explained or altered on numerous occasions to include suggestions or to redress complaints expressed by colonists in their petitions. In 1686 the assembly enacted a statute which specifically forbade packing tobacco stalks or other trash in hogsheads to be exported; the provision was intended to close a loophole in previous laws and thereby settle the uncertainty as to whether shipping tobacco stalks was actually illegal. Similarly, in 1696 some petitioners successfully requested repeal of the law forbidding the planting or replanting of tobacco after the last of June; some planters apparently wanted to try increased production again as the answer to falling prices.[11]

During the eighteenth century, colonists presented a large number of petitions concerning tobacco regulations to their burgesses. The suggestions included in these petitions often produced amendments to the tobacco laws, as Governor Gooch noted in 1734.[12] A 1704 petition from inhabitants of King and Queen County urged that the colony establish public warehouses in each county where tobacco could be stored until sold and exported. Although establishment of such warehouses by statute had been discussed, and some had been provided by a 1680 law, no systematic approach had been undertaken. The assembly rejected this 1704 petition, but in 1712 the King and Queen petitioners tried again. This time the house proved receptive, and the assembly enacted the measure into law.[13] For the remainder of the period under study, tobacco warehouses were constructed for the convenience of planters and merchants and became the foundation of the new inspection system attempted in 1713 and finally established in 1730. Other tobacco laws in the first quarter of the eighteenth century were frequently suggested to the house in petitions. These included laws for regulating the size of tobacco hogsheads and for preventing exportation of inferior grades of tobacco.[14]

The major eighteenth-century addition was the creation of a comprehensive inspection system. This system reflected a century of experimentation in quality and quantity control, and it replaced much of the older legislation which had proven largely unsuccessful and unenforceable. Governor Spotswood initiated the effort in 1713 by drawing up and sponsoring a proposal to license inspectors who would serve at the warehouses already established. The inspectors would view all tobacco intended to be exported or used within the colony as legal tender and would reject and burn the inferior grades. The plan aimed at reducing the quantity of exported tobacco and guaranteeing acceptable quality to the buyer. The notes issued to the owners of the hogsheads stored in the warehouses would pass as currency, thus benefiting both commercial transactions and payment of taxes. Spotswood used all his influence to win approval for the scheme, and the assembly did enact it. But continued internal opposition from planters concerned about the expense and inconvenience of the system, combined with English fears that the measure might reduce the tobacco trade too much, ultimately doomed this first attempt. England disallowed the law in 1717, and final creation of an inspection system was postponed for over a decade.[15]

The 1720s saw little improvement in the tobacco trade, as prices remained below what many colonists considered to be a fair and reasonable return.[16] William Gooch, who arrived in 1727 to become the new royal governor, quickly acquired a conviction that Spotswood's inspection scheme was the only solution to falling prices. Only an increase in prices, he felt, could restore the colony's economic health and prevent Virginians from turning to manufacturing (which, of course, would violate a basic principle of mercantilist theory). For their part, many colonists were reluctant to act; while recognizing that some action had to be taken, they were hesitant to try radical measures. Gooch's "interest" or influence proved decisive. He introduced the proposal for a comprehensive inspection system to the 1730 assembly. The same session received a number of petitions from planters who felt that some action was absolutely necessary. Somewhat reluctantly, the assembly agreed that decisive action was required, and the inspection system was created. The 1730 law did include several suggestions from the petitions, such as provisions for better preventing the planting of second-growth tobacco or destruction of warehouses. The essential features, however, remained similar to the 1713 plan. Tobacco was inspected and stored in public warehouses, where inferior leaves were destroyed. Planters received tobacco notes representing ownership of hogsheads which passed inspection, and these notes served as currency in public and private transactions. England accepted the 1730 law, and although minor details were frequently altered afterwards, the essential features remained constant for the remainder of the century.[17]

The periodic amendments made in the tobacco laws after 1730 were often a response to suggestions or complaints from petitioners. In 1732 the assembly enacted several minor alterations in order to clarify certain sections of the law. Confusion had arisen concerning the transportation of tobacco to warehouses and use of tobacco notes in payment of public levies. As the preamble to the new law mentioned, the amendments were enacted in response to the petitions for clarification. According to Governor Gooch, such alterations improved the inspection system and rendered it "agreable [sic] to the people and easy to the Trade."[18] Also in 1732 a number of citizens in Westmoreland County petitioned that the inspectors should be elected by local voters rather than appointed by the governor (who had thus acquired a potentially important source of patronage). The burgesses rejected this 1732 request, but the demand for local selection continued. In 1738 the assembly provided that the governor had to select the inspectors for any given county from a list of men nominated by that county court. This helped to insure that the inspectors were acceptable to the local communities.[19] The need for alterations diminished, though it never completely abated, as the inspection system was improved and as planters and merchants became more accustomed to its operation. The assembly continued to receive and consider minor suggestions and grievances throughout the eighteenth century, however, and a number of these petitions were successful. A 1752 case was typical. According to a statute enacted four years earlier, inspectors were required to be on duty at their warehouses from the tenth of November through the following August. The house in 1752 received several petitions on the tobacco laws, one of which asked that inspectors begin taking tobacco earlier. The burgesses agreed that the proposal was reasonable, and the 1752 law required inspectors to be on duty beginning on the twentieth of October.[20]

A few petitions on the tobacco laws met a less hospitable reception. In 1769, for example, a group of planters in Hanover County argued that the tobacco trade had declined and that the best remedy was to eliminate the inspection system and thus abandon the efforts at quality control. The burgesses quickly rejected the petition; while they were willing to consider minor amendments, by 1769 the burgesses, like most Virginians, were firmly committed to the basic principle of inspection. Also rejected was a 1772 petition from Mecklenburg County which asked that the importation of tobacco from North Carolina be prohibited. This suggestion had been considered several times before, as Carolinians lacked adequate port facilities and were compelled to rely heavily upon shipment through Virginia. By prohibiting importation of North Carolina tobacco, Virginia could both reduce the absolute quantity of exports and increase its share of the total market at the expense of its southern neighbor. The assembly rejected the petition, however, because an earlier law for that purpose had been vetoed in England.[21]

Perhaps the most significant alterations in the tobacco laws after 1730 involved the locations selected for official inspection warehouses. Although

the warehouses were normally privately owned, the legislature established
the locations and otherwise regulated their operation by statute. The 1730
act provided over seventy inspection sites for the convenience of planters.
As people moved west from the older regions, however, they carried the
tobacco culture with them; by mid-eighteenth century many Piedmont
farmers grew tobacco for export. Moreover, tobacco was particularly hard
on the soil and exhausted old fields within a few years. Many areas in the
Tidewater switched to other crops, especially wheat, by mid-century, and
after the Revolution tobacco was seldom grown in the Tidewater. As a
result of this changing agricultural pattern, some of the existing warehouses became unnecessary while new ones were often needed elsewhere.[22]

In most cases the assembly established new locations in response to
petitions from local planters and merchants. In 1762, for example, citizens
in the counties of Dinwiddie, Amelia, Brunswick, Lunenburg, and Halifax
petitioned for the establishment of a new inspection warehouse on the
land of Robert Bolling, between the towns of Petersburg and Blandford.
This site, the petitioners noted, "will have every possible Advantage of
a fine Situation, a good Road, and very convenient to a safe Landing."
The counties involved in this request were located along the Fall Line and
in the southwestern part of the Piedmont—at that time one of the fastest
growing tobacco centers in the colony. The Petersburg area, situated below
the falls on the Appomattox River just before it enters the James, was thus
a convenient inspection and export center, and the petitioners wanted additional facilities established to handle the increasing volume of tobacco. The
assembly agreed that the request was reasonable and established a new
inspection station on the site proposed by the petitioners.[23] Earlier, in 1744,
petitioners in King William County were equally successful with their request for creation of an inspection warehouse at Waller's Ferry on the
Mattapony River. This stream divided King William from King and Queen
County and provided convenient transportation for planters in the York
River district, an important tobacco-growing region around mid-century.
Similarly, the assembly regularly established numerous other new or
additional warehouses after 1730. For example, it authorized warehouses
in the towns of Dumfries in 1769, Manchester in 1773, and Petersburg
in 1789 directly in response to the petitions of local citizens.[24]

Legislative deliberation concerning warehouse locations was complicated at times by conflicting requests. Thus in 1762 some petitioners
from James City and Charles City counties wanted to discontinue the

warehouse at Hog Neck and establish a replacement at Barrett's Ferry, but other residents counterpetitioned against the proposal. The Hog Neck warehouse was located on the James River. Barrett's Ferry was several miles above Hog Neck, on the Chickahominy River just before it empties into the James. Committee investigation indicated that the original site was more convenient, so the house accepted the counterpetition against any change in location. On other occasions the house accepted the proposal for change. In 1785 residents of Westmoreland, Richmond, and Northumberland counties petitioned to move the inspection site from Rust's warehouse, a relatively small one, to the town of Kinsale. Businessmen and other inhabitants of Kinsale recognized the increase in activity, commercial and otherwise, which an inspection warehouse would bring to their town, and other area residents agreed that the new site would be more convenient. A counterpetition against removal failed to convince the delegates that the original site was still preferable, and the change was made.[25]

Despite expansion of the tobacco culture into the Piedmont and the apparent desire of the legislature to place inspection sites where they were needed, it appears that none were established above the Fall Line until after the Revolution. Several factors seem involved in this delay. Large-scale exportation from the Piedmont was impossible because the falls in the rivers and the shallow depth of water above the falls restricted ocean-going vessels to the Tidewater. Until the falls were cleared or canals were dug around them (projects which began only in the 1780s), it made little sense to establish export stations at places where ships could not reach them. Piedmont residents during the colonial period apparently recognized this difficulty, for their petitions almost always requested establishment of inspection sites at locations below the falls.[26] Moreover, the assembly may have been concerned that inspection warehouses spread out into the Piedmont and West would be more difficult to supervise properly than those concentrated in the Tidewater. Governor Dinwiddie informed the house in 1753 that the neglect or dishonesty of some inspectors was a major problem, and Dinwiddie proposed that warehouses be reduced in number and controlled more carefully. Although reduction in the number of sites was dismissed by the house as impractical, many burgesses apparently shared Dinwiddie's concern about the problem of supervision.[27] The need for inspection locations above the Fall Line was at least partially alleviated by a 1748 statute which allowed county courts in the Piedmont or elsewhere to establish public storehouses where commodities could be stored while awaiting sale or shipment. If the Piedmont farmer sold his tobacco from these storehouses to merchants or factors, then the merchants had to transport it to the east for inspection.[28] It is also possible that a degree of economic discrimination against the Piedmont was involved as well, since an inspection warehouse brought considerable economic benefit to the local community.[29] However, the absence of any conclusive supporting evidence and the failure of the Piedmont to protest or complain render it impossible to assess the degree, if any, to which sectional discrimination was involved; apparently the Piedmont did not feel discriminated against in this matter.

The continuing shift in tobacco production from the Tidewater to the Piedmont finally required that action be taken after the Revolution to establish inspection sites above the Fall Line. In 1783 the assembly authorized three sites in the western counties of Jefferson, Fayette, and Lincoln (subsequently a part of Kentucky).[30] Inhabitants of Bedford, Campbell, and Amherst (a major tobacco-producing area) petitioned in 1785 for establishment of an inspection warehouse at Lynch's Ferry, on the James River in Campbell County. Citizens from Botetourt County, just west of Bedford, and Hampshire County, now in West Virginia, also requested creation of inspection warehouses at certain locations in their respective counties. At the same time, David Ross, one of the wealthiest merchants in the state and the owner of vast tracts of Piedmont land, was working to secure establishment of an inspection site on his land at Point of Fork in Fluvanna County, on the Rivanna River. The assembly accepted all four proposals and established the warehouses as desired by the petitioners and by Ross.[31] After 1785, establishment of inspection warehouses in the Piedmont in response to petitions was a commonplace occurrence.[32]

The assembly also regulated and encouraged other agricultural, commercial, and industrial activities, although these regulations were not nearly so systematic or extensive as the tobacco laws. In the eighteenth century, colonial Virginia enacted inspection requirements or other quality control measures to encourage exportation of flour, naval stores (especially tar, pitch, and turpentine), hemp, and salted meats, and several additional commodities were added to the list after 1776. In some cases this regulation was combined with monetary incentives for producers in the form of bounties, as Virginia sought to diversify its economy. In the case of hemp and naval stores, Virginia's interest was further stimulated by English mercantile policies aimed at fostering production of valuable military materiel in her colonies.

As was the case with tobacco legislation, the petitions of Virginia citizens also played a significant role in the initiation or amendment of these regulations, as the assembly sought to incorporate suggestions and redress grievances. The legislature was especially interested in fostering the production and exportation of hemp, which became a staple of considerable commercial significance in the eighteenth century. From 1722 until the revolutionary period, the production of hemp was promoted by bounty payments from the colonial government and at times by additional bounties offered by the British government for hemp imported into England. Many farmers, particularly those in the backcountry and Valley, produced sizable quantities of hemp both for domestic consumption and for export, with the 1730s and the years after 1765 being "boom" periods.[33] Yet until 1784 the official inspection of hemp was much less systematic than that of tobacco or several other commodities. From 1722 until 1748 the inspecting and weighing were done by county court officials, and such inspection was required in order to receive the bounty. After 1748, however, an oath by the producer that the hemp was of acceptable quality replaced the inspection by local officials, although they still certified the weight. Hemp growers in Lunenburg and Frederick counties (located in southwestern Virginia and in the Valley respectively) petitioned in 1748 for creation of an inspection system similar to that used for tobacco. Valley producers in Augusta County petitioned to echo that request in 1769. Both requests failed to secure creation of such a system. Although after 1748 the legislature did provide for the establishment of convenient storehouses for the reception of hemp, not until 1784 did it create an inspection system modeled along the lines of the tobacco laws. Then, following requests from such Valley and Piedmont counties as Botetourt, Frederick, and Amelia, the assembly established inspection warehouses and regulations for packaging and exporting hemp.[34]

Although the Virginia economy remained predominantly agricultural throughout the eighteenth century, some manufacturing for commercial purposes developed, in addition to the traditional amount of "home industry." The assembly enacted legislation designed to foster industrial development, thus further reflecting the conviction that economic diversification was needed to reduce the overdependence upon tobacco and thereby benefit both the colony and England. During the colonial period, such

legislation could operate only within the limits defined by English mercantilism, which sought to prevent the development of any colonial industries that would compete with those of the mother country. England
did encourage its colonies to develop complementary industries, such as
naval stores and pig iron, which could provide raw materials for British
use. Thus it encouraged the colonies to export pig iron, which could be
refined into finished products in English factories, but restricted colonial
production of iron machinery or steel.[35]

The interest in promoting the manufacture of such products as linen
and woolen cloth, naval stores, and salted meats was reflected in legislation enacted during the last two decades of the seventeenth century.
For example, Virginia used bounties and tax incentives to stimulate
cloth production. A number of petitioners supported the effort and requested that additional measures be enacted. In response to several such
1693 petitions, the assembly enacted a law providing that each county
must offer annual premiums to the local citizens who made the three
best pieces of linen during the next six years. But this law, like the other
1680-1700 provisions for creating a domestic cloth industry, failed to
stimulate production in commercial proportions; production of homespun
for domestic purposes continued, but no export trade developed. Even if
the attempt had succeeded, the Woolens Act of 1699 was designed by
England to prohibit this form of competition with English industries.
Victor Clark has shown, however, that the colonial cloth trade had failed
to assume export proportions even before the Woolens Act was passed.[36]
After 1699 Virginia abandoned her effort to develop a cloth industry.

The colony's attempt to stimulate production of naval stores, salted
meats, and flour as export commodities was much more successful. By
the end of the seventeenth century, Virginia exported modest quantities
of tar, pitch, and salted pork and beef, mostly at that time to the West
Indies. In a 1696 petition citizens in Elizabeth City County (located along
the coast, between the James and York rivers) successfully requested that
the barrels used for packing these products be standardized in gauge and
the contents required to be of good quality. The 1696 statute regulated
barrel size, required inspection of meat exports by persons appointed by
the county courts, and established fines for exporting naval stores of
inferior quality. After 1722 Virginia also offered bounty payments to
stimulate production of tar, and England gave additional bounties after
1704 for tar it imported from the colonies. A 1745 amendment required
inspection of naval stores as well because, as Governor Gooch observed,

some exporters added trash into the barrels and thus threatened the reputation of all Virginia producers.[37] Several amendments to the laws were suggested by petitioners interested in the export trade. In 1755 citizens in Nansemond County complained of abuses caused by allowing inspectors of naval stores to purchase those commodities—apparently instances of discrimination by inspectors in favor of their own products led the petitioners to protest. In response, the assembly prohibited inspectors of naval stores from purchasing or trading in those products. Other persons interested in the trade petitioned in 1769 to request additional measures for insuring compliance with the inspection laws. The Committee of Trade investigated the matter and discovered that amendments were needed to state the duties of inspectors more clearly and to strengthen the penalties for violation of the laws. The house accepted the report, and the desired changes were made.[38] Aided by this encouragement and regulation, export of naval stores and salted meats reached significant proportions by the mid-eighteenth century. In 1742, for example, the value of these exports exceeded £20,000.[39]

The export of flour also became a major commercial activity during the eighteenth century. By the 1740s a significant number of Tidewater farmers grew wheat, either as an alternative or as a supplement to tobacco, and farmers in the Valley also grew considerable quantities of wheat. In 1745 the assembly responded to this development by including flour among the products to be inspected before exportation by persons appointed by the county courts.[40] By the 1780s, however, this method of quality control seemed inadequate because of the great increase in flour exports and the favorable prospects for a further increase. A growing number of farmers, particularly in the Tidewater but elsewhere as well, were discouraged by the worn-out lands and low prices which characterized the tobacco culture. The outlook for an improved European market for grain and flour thus convinced many farmers to convert to wheat. In 1781 Virginia created a comprehensive network for the inspection of flour and bread exports. The assembly then made extensive amendments in 1787 to incorporate suggestions presented in a petition from merchants and other interested citizens in Alexandria (a major export center). As a result of their suggestions, the assembly increased the number of inspection sites, elaborated the regulations concerning milling, packing, and shipping, and instituted four quality grades for export flour.[41]

A series of public and private actions in 1759 and 1760 further revealed a significant degree of interest in promoting economic diversification through the growth of manufacturing. An ambitious 1759 statute "for encouraging Arts and Manufactures" appointed a committee of nineteen prestigious gentlemen and authorized it to spend up to £1000. The committee could offer premiums to any person who provided "any useful insight or intelligence in any art or manufacture." Information obtained in this fashion was to be disseminated to the public in the *Virginia Gazette*. A number of prominent Virginians, led by Governor Fauquier, began a private subscription in 1760 to supplement the effort by offering bounties for the production of wine and silk. Unfortunately, both the public and private acts produced disappointingly meager results.[42]

Virginians engaged in "infant industries" sometimes petitioned directly to the assembly for governmental assistance, and on several occasions the legislature responded in the hope of fostering further economic diversification. Virginia did develop a growing iron industry which attained commercial significance by 1728 and continued to expand under official encouragement thereafter. The 1728 assembly received a petition from the management of the Bristol Iron-mine Company, asking that the manufacture of iron be encouraged. The legislation adopted in response by the assembly was then amended in 1730 to redress complaints by other colonists that some of the original provisions were excessive. As amended, the statute exempted all persons who owned or worked at any ironworks from militia duty (except in emergencies such as slave rebellions) and road work. Owners and workers at all ironworks subsequently established also received a seven-year exemption from public taxation. Aided by these provisions, which were continued throughout the eighteenth century, the Virginia iron industry developed by 1776 to serve domestic needs and to export a sizable quantity of pig and bar iron to England.[43]

Colonists seeking to engage in wine production were considerably less successful. In 1770 Andrew Estave, a French winemaker who had immigrated to Virginia, petitioned the assembly for a grant of one hundred acres of land, a house, and three slaves to aid his winemaking project. The assembly appointed trustees to oversee the venture and authorized the expenditure of up to £450 to meet Estave's request. If he could produce ten hogsheads of good wine within six years, he would receive title to the property and slaves. Three years later Robert Bolling petitioned for a "moderate assistance," as he was "thoroughly convinced, that the culture of Grapes may be propagated in the upper part of the Country." Bolling had already hired an experienced Swiss winemaker to assist in the project. The legislature again responded favorably, this time by granting Bolling

£50 annually for five years. Despite all efforts, however, Virginia did not develop a satisfactory wine industry. Estave, for example, failed to make the stipulated amount of wine, and in 1776 the assembly ordered the property and slaves to be sold.[44]

The colonial policies for encouraging the growth of manufacturing were supplemented during the Revolution by a more systematic attempt to stimulate the production of such war materials as iron, lead, salt, and saltpeter. The legislature regularly accepted petitions seeking assistance from individuals and companies involved in this effort. For example, John and Meade Anderson sought to establish a lead mine and petitioned in 1779 for permission to pay the property tax in lead. Because a steady supply of that material was indispensable for the war effort, the legislature accepted the request by guaranteeing a reasonable tax valuation of the property and allowing payment in lead.[45] Similarly, when John Dixon petitioned for aid in establishing a salt works, and Charles Carter and the Dumfries Saltpeter Company asked for encouragement to produce salt-peter, the legislature responded with public loans on generous terms. Bounties were added as inducement for others to produce salt. Virginia even established some public salt works for a time, but they never produced salt in adequate quantity and were discontinued even before the war ended. Private ventures into saltmaking also failed to attain commercial significance.[46]

Virginia also made a concerted effort during the war to stimualte further development of ironworks for providing cannon, shot, military utensils, and other necessities. The wartime contracts awarded by both the state and national governments served to encourage existing operations, but demand always exceeded supply, and the legislature authorized additional means for developing new and bigger foundries. When James Hunter requested assistance in 1777 to insure an adequate supply of iron ore for his new ironworks in Stafford County, the assembly authorized him to use the ore at a discontinued mine nearby. This same statute further aided all ironworks by exempting their horses, wagons, and wagoners from impressment. Hunter's operation flourished and soon filled contracts for the state and the American army.[47] Virginia also accepted an ambitious 1776 proposal by John Ballendine and John Reveley, who petitioned for a loan of £5000 to aid in constructing a large-scale iron mine and blast furnace along the James River above Richmond. Virginia then established a state-owned foundry at Westham to manufacture ordinance from the pig iron to be supplied by Ballendine and Reveley, who were to repay the loan in pig iron at a stipulated rate. By 1779, however, the state had spent almost £10,000 to support the Ballendine-Reveley venture and had increased the valuation of the iron to be accepted in payment of the loan; nevertheless, the project remained far from completion. The state-owned foundry, operated under Reveley's leadership, did ultimately produce some equipment until it was destroyed by the British army in 1781. The Ballendine-Reveley furnace never supplied much pig iron, however, and the loan was never repaid. The standard account of this affair, by Kathleen Bruce, suggests that the assembly should have given this kind of massive financial support to Hunter (who was extremely talented and patriotic) rather than to these two adventurers.[48]

After the war ended, Virginia's approach toward fostering industrial development returned for the most part to prewar channels. As already mentioned, after 1776 the state continued and even expanded the policy of inspection and quality control of numerous products intended for export. But, perhaps at least in part because of the Ballendine-Reveley fiasco, the assembly was reluctant to undertake direct financial involvement to stimulate the growth of manufacturing. The state-supported scheme for improving the navigation of the James and Potomac rivers, discussed in the next chapter, would indirectly benefit industry as well as agriculture, but the legislature refused to finance strictly industrial projects after the Revolution. Thus when Thomas Douthat petitioned in 1793 and again in 1794 for an interest-free loan of $1000 to aid him in constructing a woolen cloth factory in Staunton, the house rejected both requests.[49]

While avoiding direct financial involvement, the state did continue to encourage manufacturing in other ways. On several occasions the legislature authorized new manufacturing companies to raise capital by holding lotteries. For example, in 1776 the assembly rejected a petition from Smyth Tandy, who sought financial assistance in establishing a linen factory near Staunton. Tandy tried again in 1791, when he petitioned for permission to conduct a lottery for raising the money needed to repair and complete his business. The assembly accepted this suggestion, appointing trustees authorized to raise up to $4000 for Tandy by that method.[50]

Of much greater significance than lotteries as a means of raising capital was the granting of charters of incorporation to businesses by the legislature. Corporations possessed two significant advantages over other forms of business organization: large sums of money could be raised by selling stock to investors, and the principle of limited liability restricted a stockholder's maximum loss in case of failure to the amount originally invested in the corporate stock. Although the old joint-stock companies (such as the Virginia Company after 1609) were very similar to later corporations, the corporate form of organization made only an occasional appearance in colonial America and was not used by Virginians until after the Revolution. Colonial legislatures were reluctant to create such concentrations of economic power, and indeed incorporation was needed only in the largest industrial and commercial operations—such as banking, insurance, and transportation. Virginia had little need for such organizations until the 1780s. At that time, the Virginia legislature and its counterparts in many states began granting such charters, rather hesitantly at first, by special legislative statute. Incorporation by the legislature in response to individual petitions then remained the rule in Virginia and elsewhere until the widespread acceptance of general state incorporation laws by the 1850s provided uniform standards and procedures.[51]

In Virginia the first projects which required incorporation of businesses involved transportation improvements. Making the James and Potomac rivers navigable into the Piedmont was obviously going to require extensive capital expenditure, and in response the 1784 assembly incorporated two companies to undertake the projects. Incorporation of other transportation companies for clearing rivers and building turnpikes followed after 1785 (see the extended discussion in the next chapter).[52] The assembly then gradually took similar action in other fields as well, almost always in response to petitions from interested citizens. In 1792 a petition from business firms, individual merchants, and other residents of Alexandria asked the legislature to incorporate a bank in that city, with an authorized capital stock of $150,000. The Alexandria petitioners had previously asked the president and directors of Hamilton's new Bank of the United States to establish a branch bank in Alexandria, but the national bank refused to cooperate. The state legislature finally agreed to incorporate a bank in Alexandria, accepting the petitioners' contention that "the experience of commercial Nations for several ages has fully evinced that well regulated Banks are highly useful to Society. . . ."[53] The incorporation bill passed the house and Senate by only narrow margins, however, as some agricultural spokesmen remained convinced that banks were unrepublican and of no benefit to farmers. But other politicians felt that state banks could reduce dependence upon Hamilton's bank, and the 1792 session ultimately chartered a second state bank also, this one in Richmond. The Richmond bank never began operations because subscriptions were inadequate, but the Alexandria bank functioned effectively, though on a relatively small scale despite a subsequent increase in capital stock. Not until creation of the Bank of Virginia in 1804 did the state incorporate a bank intended to operate on a large scale.[54]

Beginning in the 1790s the legislature incorporated insurance companies. William F. Ast petitioned in 1794 to propose a scheme for creating a fire insurance company to protect homes and businesses, and his petition was signed by a number of prominent citizens. The assembly, impressed with Ast's plan, chartered an insurance corporation along the lines he proposed. Following another petition from Ast to the next session, the assembly incorporated an insurance company to protect the contents of businesses and homes, and the 1797 session incorporated a marine insurance firm in Alexandria.[55]

Adoption of the corporate form of organization by manufacturing firms proceeded more slowly in Virginia and in the other states also. Most manufacturing firms in the eighteenth and early nineteenth centuries operated on a relatively small scale and did not require an extensive amount of capital. In Virginia, directors and stockholders of a few manufacturing companies petitioned for incorporation in the early nineteenth century, and the legislature generally granted such requests. Most of these ventures were very modest in scope. For example, the assembly accepted an 1808 petition from John B. Scott and others for incorporating the "Halifax Manufacturing Society." Authorized capital stock was only $5000, however, far below that of banks, insurance firms, and transportation companies.[56]

Overall, the eighteenth-century desire to stimulate economic diversification had only limited success. Virginia did develop several additional agricultural staples, notably wheat and hemp, so that the heavy dependence upon tobacco was reduced somewhat. Tobacco accounted for a smaller share of total exports by 1781 than forty years earlier (58 percent by value as opposed to 80 percent in 1742).[57] Virginia had less success in stimulating the growth of manufacturing; while production of iron, naval stores, and flour reached significant proportions, on balance Virginia remained predominantly an importer rather than an exporter of manufactured goods. Thus in 1800, as a hundred years before, Virginia retained considerable resemblance to Jefferson's ideal—a republic of farmers.

Although Virginia citizens frequently petitioned to make suggestions or express grievances concerning other economic regulations, the tax laws aroused little attention and elicited few petitions after 1700. This lack of concern about taxation reflected the extremely modest level of public taxes in eighteenth-century Virginia. During the 1700-1776 period, the colonial government required little revenue to perform its limited functions. The moderate trade duties, supplemented by an occasional poll tax of relatively inconsequential size, proved adequate for normal expenditures.[58] Only briefly during the French and Indian War did additional taxes become necessary, but even these taxes were so limited and of such short duration that they caused almost no controversy.[59]

Only during and immediately after the Revolution, a period of economic distress and heavy taxation, did the tax laws cause any appreciable public debate and stimulate the use of petitions. Numerous historians, most notably Jackson Turner Main, have analyzed this debate in detail. Main observed that even at the height of the controversy in the mid-1780s, Virginia experienced far less disagreement than any other state, and the issue involved differences of opinion over means rather than ends.[60] When the economy improved and the new federal government assumed the state war debts, Virginia again reduced state taxes to a low level, and taxation again ceased to arouse controversy. In 1818 Governor James Preston observed that Virginia's taxes "subtract so small a portion from the labour and industry of the community, that they are scarcely felt, and are paid by the people with alacrity and satisfaction."[61] While Preston perhaps exaggerated the "satisfaction" which citizens derived from paying taxes, his observation nevertheless reveals why, except for the 1776-1790 period, taxation produced so little controversy during the eighteenth century and why people sent almost no petitions about taxation to the legislature.

In summary, through their petitions to the legislature Virginia citizens often made suggestions or raised complaints concerning economic regulations. These petitions were especially important in initiating or amending the various export and commodity inspection laws and in establishing tobacco inspection sites. Petitions were not the exclusive source of economic legislation, as suggestions from England and from royal governors, as well as deliberations within the legislature itself, also had an important impact.

But petitioning did provide an important means whereby local citizens could communicate with the legislature concerning the various economic matters of importance to them, and the assembly proved most receptive to these suggestions.

Notes

1. For good general discussions, see: Richard B. Morris, *Government and Labor in Early America* (New York, 1947), esp. pp. 18-21; William A. Williams, "The Age of Mercantilism: An Interpretation of the American Political Economy to 1828," *WMQ*, 3rd ser. 15 (October 1958): 419-37.

2. *JHB*, 1695-1702: 154, 172, 190; 1758-1761: 73, 128; William Waller Hening, ed., *The Statutes at Large: Being a Collection of All the Laws of Virginia*, 13 vols. (Richmond and Philadelphia, 1809-23), 3: 185-86, 200; 6: 553-54; 7: 312-14; 9: 530-32; William Gooch to Board of Trade, [8 June?] 1728, *CSPC*, no. 241, 36: 120; Lewis C. Gray, *History of Agriculture in the Southern United States to 1860*, 2 vols. (1933; reprint ed., Gloucester, Mass., 1958), 1: 163, 172.

3. *JHB*, 1712-1726: 264, 272, 281, 316; 1761-1765: 183, 243, 325, 363; *JHD*, 1789 (1828 reprint): 41, 51, 67, 96, 100; Hening, *Statutes*, 4: 89-91; 6: 152-54; 8: 48, 147-48; 13: 33, 561; Alexander Spotswood to Board of Trade, 27 January 1715, in *The Official Letters of Alexander Spotswood*, ed. Robert A. Brock, Virginia Historical Society *Collections*, Vols. 1 and 2 (Richmond, 1882-85), 2: 98; Hugh Jones, *The Present State of Virginia*, ed. Richard L. Morton (Chapel Hill, N.C., 1956), p. 85; Thomas Jefferson, *Notes on the State of Virginia*, ed. William Peden (Chapel Hill, N.C., 1954), p. 135.

4. *JHB*, 1727-1740: 181, 234; 1766-1769: 217, 251, 272; *JHD*, 1790 (1828 reprint): 8, 30, 90, 139; Hening, *Statutes*, 4: 446; 8: 389-90; 13: 188-89; Harrison Petition, 21 October 1790; Gooch to Board of Trade, 20 November 1734, William Gooch Papers, 3 vols., transcripts, VHS, 2: 374.

5. Hening, *Statutes*, 1: 152, 164, 190, 203-07, 209-13, 399, 478, 487, 496, 524; 2: 119; 3: 34-35, 142; G. Melvin Herndon, *Tobacco in Colonial Virginia*, Jamestown 350th Anniversary Historical Booklets, ed. E. G. Swem (Williamsburg, 1957), pp. 14, 22-23, 26-28, 42-44; Arthur P. Middleton, *Tobacco Coast* (Newport News, Va., 1953), pp. 112-13; Gray, *History of Agriculture*, 1: 224-26; Edmund S. Morgan, *American Slavery—American Freedom: The Ordeal of Colonial Virginia* (New York, 1975), pp. 134-36.

6. See, for example, Governor Francis Wyatt's 1639 instructions, in "Virginia in 1638-39," *VMHB* 11 (July 1903): 56; *JHB*, 1659/60-1693: 22-23. For the extent to which tobacco regulation was discussed in the assembly, see Jerome Hawley to Sec. Windebanke, 20 March 1638, "Virginia in 1637-38," *VMHB* 9 (April 1902): 409; Governor Wyatt to Whitehall, 25 March 1640, "Virginia in 1639-40," *VMHB* 13 (April 1906): 381.

7. Hening, *Statutes*, 1: 203-07, 210; Herndon, *Tobacco*, pp. 22-23, 27-28.

8. "Virginia in 1638," *VMHB* 10 (April 1903): 425; "Virginia in 1654-56,"

VMHB 18 (January 1910): 44-46, 50; "Virginia in 1658-62," *VMHB* 18 (July 1910): 299-300; "Virginia in 1662-65," *VMHB* 18 (October 1910): 422-23.

9. *JHB,* 1659/60-1693: 22-23, 35-36, 41, 137.

10. Middleton, *Tobacco Coast,* pp. 113-14; Herndon, *Tobacco,* pp. 43-44; "Virginia in 1662-65," 423-24; Joseph C. Robert, *The Story of Tobacco in America* (New York, 1949), pp. 11-12.

11. *JHB,* 1659/60-1693: 264-65; 1695-1702: 67, 101-02; Hening, *Statutes,* 3: 33, 142; Gray, *History of Agriculture,* 1: 224-25; Middleton, *Tobacco Coast,* p. 112.

12. See the speech of Governor Gooch at the close of the 1734 session—*JHB,* 1727-1740: 234; for a similar comment, see Robert Wormeley Carter to Landon Carter, 20 March 1770, Carter Family Papers, 1659-1797, UVa microfilm publication.

13. *JHB,* 1702/3-1712: 54-55; 1712-1726: 11, 30, 42; Hening, *Statutes,* 4: 32-36; Herndon, *Tobacco,* pp. 28-30.

14. *JHB,* 1702/3-1712: 54, 56, 70; 1712-1726: xlvi, 327, 329; Hening, *Statutes,* 3: 225; 4: 106.

15. *JHB,* 1712-1726: 47, 54-68, 73; Hening, *Statutes,* 4: 37; Spotswood to Board of Trade, 29 December 1713 and 27 January 1715, in *Spotswood Letters,* ed. Brock, 2: 48-51, 96; D. Alan Williams, "Political Alignments in Colonial Virginia Politics, 1698-1750" (Ph.D. dissertation, Northwestern University, 1959), pp. 141-77; Richard L. Morton, *Colonial Virginia,* 2 vols. (Chapel Hill, N.C., 1960), 2: 423-24, 454, 456, 471; Leonidas Dodson, *Alexander Spotswood* (Philadelphia, 1932), pp. 51-57; John C. Rainbolt, "The Case of the Poor Planters in Virginia Under the Law for Inspecting and Burning Tobacco," *VMHB* 79 (July 1971): 315.

·16. Gooch to Board of Trade, 29 June 1729, *CSPC,* no. 796, 36: 417-18; Middleton, *Tobacco Coast,* p. 121; see the price trend for the 1720s as listed in Herndon, *Tobacco,* p. 48.

17. *JHB,* 1727-1740: 57-58, 61, 63; Hening, *Statutes,* 4: 241-44, 247-73; Gooch to Board of Trade, 29 June 1729, 23 July 1730, 10 May 1731, 27 May 1732, *CSPC,* no. 796, 36: 417-18; no. 348, 37: 202-06; no. 164, 38: 101; no. 241, 39: 125-26; Gooch to the Bishop of London, 28 May 1731, "The Virginia Clergy," *VMHB* 32 (October 1924): 325; Joseph C. Robert, *The Tobacco Kingdom* (Durham, N.C., 1938), pp. 7-8, 76-77; Morton, *Colonial Virginia,* 2: 511-17; Herndon, *Tobacco,* p. 31; Middleton, *Tobacco Coast,* pp. 120-26.

18. *JHB,* 1727-1740: 122, 123; Hening, *Statutes,* 4: 331, 333; Gooch to Board of Trade, 27 May 1732 and 18 July 1732, *CSPC,* no. 241 and no. 308, 39: 125-26, 174-75. See the similar action taken in 1734—*JHB,* 1727-1740: 234; Hening, *Statutes,* 4: 380-93.

19. *JHB,* 1727-1740: 122; Hening, *Statutes,* 5: 10; Herndon, *Tobacco,* p. 34.

20. *JHB,* 1752-1758: 10-11, 29-30; Hening, *Statutes,* 6: 162, 224.

21. *JHB,* 1766-1769: 195, 206, 207; 1770-1772: 188; Gooch to Board of Trade, 26 August 1728, Board of Trade to the King, 25 August 1731, and Order in Council, 25 November 1731, *CSPC,* no. 372, 36: 187-89; no. 382 and no. 516, 38: 239-40, 356; Middleton, *Tobacco Coast,* pp. 114-15.

22. Herndon, *Tobacco,* pp. 8-10, 35-36; Robert, *Tobacco Kingdom,* pp. 6, 77-78; Thomas P. Abernethy, *The South in the New Nation, 1789-1819* (Baton Rouge,

La., 1961), pp. 23-26; Avery O. Craven, *Soil Exhaustion as a Factor in the Agricultural History of Virginia and Maryland, 1606-1860* (1926; reprint ed., Gloucester, Mass., 1965), pp. 32, 56, 76-77.

23. *JHB*, 1761-1765: 83; Hening, *Statutes*, 7: 531; Herndon, *Tobacco*, p. 9.

24. *JHB*, 1742-1749: 119; 1766-1769: 292, 306-07; 1773-1776: 14, 18, 25, 28, 35; Hening, *Statutes*, 5: 233; 8: 320, 654; 13: 41; Amelia Petition, 4 November 1789.

25. *JHB*, 1761-1765: 97; *JHD*, 1785: 5, 15, 16, 17; Hening, *Statutes*, 11: 211; 12: 64.

26. See, for example, the 1762 petition from Dinwiddie, Amelia, Brunswick, Lunenburg, and Halifax already cited, and the similar cases in 1744 and 1773— *JHB*, 1742-1749: 80, 100; 1761-1765: 83; 1773-1776: 14, 18, 35. A 1769 petition from southern Augusta and Bedford counties, asking for an inspection site above the Fall Line at New London, was rejected by the house without explanation. This rejection aroused no protest, however, and Piedmont farmers almost never requested such sites before the 1780s—*JHB*, 1766-1769: 271-72, 279-80; Freeman H. Hart, *The Valley of Virginia in the American Revolution* (Chapel Hill, N.C., 1942), pp. 11, 11n.

27. Dinwiddie's address is found in *The Official Records of Robert Dinwiddie*, ed. Robert A. Brock, in Virginia Historical Society *Collections*, 2 vols. (Richmond, 1883-84), 1: 38-39; see also Herndon, *Tobacco*, p. 37. This view is supported by the care taken by the assembly to spell out as carefully as possible the rules for shipment from Piedmont sites when they were first established in 1785—see *JHD*, 1785: 60, 64, 76, 78, 92, 97, 103, 143, 144; Hening, *Statutes*, 12: 61-63.

28. Hening, *Statutes*, 6: 60-64. Scottish traders were particularly active in the tobacco trade of the interior—Herndon, *Tobacco*, p. 39.

29. Herndon, *Tobacco*, pp. 37, 51-52.

30. Hening, *Statutes*, 11: 345.

31. *JHD*, 1785: 19, 31, 47-48, 60, 64, 76, 78, 92, 97, 103, 108, 117, 143, 144; Hening, *Statutes*, 12: 61-63, 66-67; William Tatham, "An Historical and Practical Essay on the Culture and Commerce of Tobacco," in *William Tatham and the Culture of Tobacco*, ed. G. Melvin Herndon (Coral Gables, Fla., 1969), pp. 70n., 70-71; Ross's wealth is described in Jackson T. Main, "The One Hundred," *WMQ*, 3rd ser. 11 (July 1954): 363, 381.

32. See, for example, the Piedmont and western warehouses established in the 1788-1790 period—Hening, *Statutes*, 12: 666, 717-18; 13: 41-42, 155.

33. Hening, *Statutes*, 4: 96-99; 5: 358; 6: 144; 8: 363; Gray, *History of Agriculture*, 1: 179-82; Hart, *Valley of Virginia*, p. 9; Middleton, *Tobacco Coast*, pp. 162-65; G. Melvin Herndon, "Hemp in Colonial Virginia," *Agricultural History* 37 (April 1963): 90-91; Herndon, "A War-Inspired Industry: The Manufacture of Hemp in Virginia," *VMHB* 74 (July 1966): 311.

34. Hening, *Statutes*, 4: 96-99, 301-02; 6: 60-64, 144-46; 8: 253-54, 363-64; 10: 508; 11: 412-15; 13: 167-70; *JHB*, 1742-1749: 262-63, 298-99, 380; 1766-1769: 210, 253, 264; *JHD*, October 1783: 40-41, 90; Augusta County Order Book, 20 March 1764, in *Chronicles of the Scotch-Irish Settlement in Virginia, Extracted*

from the Original Court Records of Augusta County, 1745-1800, ed. Lyman Chalkley, 3 vols. (1912; reprint ed., Baltimore, 1965), 1: 111.

35. Morton, *Colonial Virginia,* 1: 299-300, 306; Victor S. Clark, *History of Manufactures in the United States,* Vol. 1: *1607-1860* (1929; reprint ed., New York, 1949), chs. 2 and 3. John C. Rainbolt's *From Prescription to Persuasion: Manipulation of the Eighteenth [Seventeenth] Century Virginia Economy* (Port Washington, N.Y., 1974) and Morgan's *American Slavery—American Freedom* reveal both the extent of Virginia's interest during the seventeenth century in securing economic diversification and the extent to which this interest was thwarted by British opposition. See N. Blakiston to Philip Ludwell, 10 July 1711, "Some Colonial Letters," *VMHB* 4 (July 1896): 20.

36. *JHB,* 1659/60-1693: 205, 213, 227, 265, 270, 272, 346, 354, 358, 454, 456, 462, 484; Hening, *Statutes,* 2: 503-07; 3: 16, 30, 50-51, 121-22; Herndon, "Hemp in Colonial Virginia," p. 91; Clark, *History of Manufactures,* pp. 22-23.

37. *JHB,* 1695-1702: 69, 82, 101-02; Hening, *Statutes,* 3: 148-49, 254-57; 4: 96-99; 5: 164-68, 350-51; Gooch to Board of Trade, 4 July 1746, Gooch Papers, 3: 856, VHS; Gray, *History of Agriculture,* 1: 152-54; Newton B. Jones, "Weights, Measures, and Mercantilism: The Inspection of Exports in Virginia, 1742-1820," in *The Old Dominion: Essays for Thomas Perkins Abernethy,* ed. Darrett B. Rutman (Charlottesville, Va., 1964), p. 125; Morton, *Colonial Virginia,* 2: 528-29; Rainbolt, *From Prescription to Persuasion,* p. 163; Sinclair Snow, "Naval Stores in Colonial Virginia," *VMHB* 72 (January 1964): 75-93.

38. *JHB,* 1752-1758: 264, 265, 272, 293; 1766-1769: 296-97, 305, 353; Hening, *Statutes,* 6: 484; 8: 351-52.

39. See the figures given in Morton, *Colonial Virginia,* 2: 528-29; Rainbolt, *From Prescription to Persuasion,* pp. 163-64; Jefferson, *Notes on Virginia,* pp. 166-67.

40. Hening, *Statutes,* 5: 352; 6: 146-51; 7: 40, 570-75; 8: 143-45, 511-14; Gooch to Board of Trade, 4 July 1746, Gooch Papers, 3: 856-57, VHS; Augusta County Order Book, 19 November 1763, *Chronicles,* ed. Chalkley, 1: 111; Jefferson, *Notes on Virginia,* pp. 166-69; Hart, *Valley of Virginia,* p. 10; Gray, *History of Agriculture,* 1: 164-69; Arthur G. Peterson, "Flour and Grist Milling in Virginia," *VMHB* 43 (April 1935): 101.

41. Hening, *Statutes,* 10: 496-98; 12: 515-18; *JHD,* 1787 (1828 reprint): 9, 14, 45, 65; Jefferson, *Notes on Virginia,* pp. 166-69; Jackson T. Main, *The Sovereign States, 1775-1783* (New York, 1973), pp. 11-12, 38-39; Myra L. Rich, "The Experimental Years: Virginia, 1781-1789" (Ph.D. dissertation, Yale University, 1966), pp. 219-20; Peterson, "Flour and Grist Milling," p. 102. For contemporary statements about the prospects for a "wheat and flour boom" in the 1780s, see: Jefferson to C. W. F. Dumas, 20 May 1785, Jefferson to Brissot de Warville, 16 August 1786, William Short to Jefferson, 28 April 1789, Stephen Cathalan, Jr., to Jefferson, 2 August 1789, and Robert Crew to Jefferson, 31 August 1789, all in *The Papers of Thomas Jefferson,* ed. Julian P. Boyd, 19 vols. to date (Princeton, N.J., 1950-   ), 8: 158; 10: 262; 15: 77, 323, 353.

42. Hening, *Statutes,* 7: 288-90, 563-70; Clark, *History of Manufactures,* p. 38;

Douglas S. Freeman, *George Washington*, 7 vols. (New York, 1948-57), 3: 83, 83n.

43. *JHB*, 1727-1740: xxi, 19, 66, 67; Hening, *Statutes*, 4: 228-31, 296-300; 6: 137-40; Gooch to Board of Trade, [8 June?] 1728, *CSPC*, no. 241, 36: 121; Jefferson, *Notes on Virginia*, pp. 135, 167. The standard secondary account is Kathleen Bruce, *Virginia Iron Manufacture in the Slave Era* (New York, 1930), ch. 1; see also—Clark, *History of Manufactures*, pp. 24, 96-97; Hart, *Valley of Virginia*, pp. 13-14; Morton, *Colonial Virginia*, 2: 529.

44. *JHB*, 1770-1772: 17, 19, 107; 1773-1776: 16-17, 36; *JHD*, 1776: 52-53; Hening, *Statutes*, 8: 364-66.

45. *JHD*, October 1779: 37, 47-48; Hening, *Statutes*, 10: 193-94; Rich, "Experimental Years," pp. 225, 225n.

46. Virginia, *The Proceedings of the Convention of Delegates, held . . . the 1st of December, 1775* (Williamsburg, 1776), pp. 4, 5, 7, 8; *JHD*, May 1779: 75; Hening, *Statutes*, 9: 122-26, 310-12; Governor Patrick Henry to Benjamin Harrison, 21 May 1778, in *Official Letters of the Governors of the State of Virginia*, ed. Henry R. McIlwaine, 3 vols. (Richmond, 1926-29), 1: 277-78; Clark, *History of Manufactures*, pp. 222-23.

47. Hening, *Statutes*, 9: 303-06; William P. Palmer, Sherwin McRae, and Raleigh Colston, eds., *Calendar of Virginia State Papers and Other Manuscripts*, 11 vols. (1875-93; reprint ed., New York, 1968), 1: 531; Bruce, *Virginia Iron Manufacture*, pp. 19, 63-76.

48. *Proceedings of the Convention, 6 May 1776*, pp. 34-35, 50-51, 111-12, 156; *JHD*, May 1778: 24-25, 31, 33-34; May 1779: 39, 74, 75; October 1779: 77; 1787 (1828 reprint): 119, 128, 130; 1791: 37, 42; Governor Jefferson to Benjamin Harrison, 30 October 1779, plus the statute of 1779 and the editorial commentary on the entire affair, in *Jefferson Papers*, ed. Boyd, 3: 125-47; Bruce, *Virginia Iron Manufacture*, ch. 2.

49. *JHD*, 1793: 34, 40, 65; 1794: 9.

50. *JHD*, 1776: 52, 58; 1791: 28, 87; Hening, *Statutes*, 13: 316.

51. Clark, *History of Manufactures*, pp. 182-84, 265-68; George R. Taylor, *The Transportation Revolution, 1815-1860* (New York, 1951), pp. 240-41.

52. Hening, *Statutes*, 11: 450-62, 510-25; Samuel Shepherd, ed., *The Statutes of Virginia . . . Being a Continuation of Hening*, 3 vols. (Richmond, 1835-36), 1: 244-53, 378-88, 390-94; 2: 249-54.

53. "Petition of Alexandria Merchants, 1792," *WMQ*, 2d ser. 3 (July 1923): 206-08; see also the earlier petitions from Alexandria, Norfolk, and Richmond to the Bank of the U.S., seeking establishment of branch banks in Virginia—reprinted in "The Bank of the United States: Petitions of Virginia Cities and Towns for the Establishment of Branches, 1791," *VMHB* 8 (January 1901): 287-95.

54. *JHD*, 1792: 25, 94-95, 103, 129-30, 138, 145, 148, 181, 201, 209; Hening, *Statutes*, 13: 592-98, 599-607; Shepherd, *Virginia Statutes*, 1: 373-74; 2: 292; 3: 100-08; Susan L. Foard, "Virginia Enters the Union" (M.A. thesis, College of William and Mary, 1966), pp. 145-51; George T. Starnes, *Sixty Years of Branch Banking in Virginia* (New York, 1931), pp. 18-25.

55. Petition of William F. Ast and others, 15 November 1794 (filed with Rich-

mond City petitions); *JHD*, 1794: 12, 30, 97, 108, 111; 1795: 30, 44, 63, 68;
Shepherd, *Virginia Statutes*, 1: 307-10, 412-14; 2: 89-92.

56. Taylor, *Transportation Revolution*, pp. 240-43; *JHD*, 1808: 15, 40, 41, 49,
55, 75, 82; 1827: 17, 24, 98, 145; Virginia, *Acts Passed at a General Assembly of
the Commonwealth of Virginia, Begun . . . in 1808* (Richmond, 1809), ch. 46, pp.
46-49.

57. Rainbolt, *From Prescription to Persuasion*, pp. 163-64; Jefferson, *Notes on
Virginia*, p. 167.

58. Both standard accounts of government taxation and expenditure in colonial
Virginia are old but still quite useful: Percy S. Flippin, "The Financial Administration of the Colony of Virginia," *Johns Hopkins Studies*, 23 (1915), 177-272;
William Z. Ripley, "The Financial History of Virginia, 1609-1776," *Columbia University Studies*, 4 (1893), 1-170. The calculations in Morgan, *American Slavery —
American Freedom*, pp. 345-46, indicate that the public levy was minimal after
1700. Also helpful are: Henry Hartwell, James Blair, and Edward Chilton, *The
Present State of Virginia, and the College*, ed. Hunter D. Farish (Williamsburg,
1940), pp. 53-60; Robert A. Becker, "Revolution and Reform: An Interpretation
of Southern Taxation, 1763 to 1783," *WMQ*, 3rd ser. 32 (July 1975): 418-25.

59. Becker, "Southern Taxation," pp. 418-25; Flippin, "Financial Administration," p. 250; Ripley, "Financial History," pp. 38-44, 154-61; Robert E. Brown
and B. Katherine Brown, *Virginia 1705-1786: Democracy or Aristocracy?* (East
Lansing, Mich., 1964), pp. 114-19; E. James Ferguson, *The Power of the Purse*
(Chapel Hill, N.C., 1961), ch. 1.

60. Jackson T. Main, *Political Parties Before the Constitution* (Chapel Hill,
N.C., 1973), ch. 9; Merrill Jensen, *The New Nation* (New York, 1950), ch. 15;
Norman K. Risjord and Gorden DenBoer, "The Evolution of Political Parties in
Virginia, 1782-1800," *Journal of American History* 60 (March 1974): 961-84;
Forrest McDonald, *E Pluribus Unum* (Boston, 1965), pp. 70-77; James A. Henretta,
The Evolution of American Society, 1700-1815 (Lexington, Mass., 1973), pp. 158-
64.

61. *JHD*, 1816: 6.

6 PETITIONS AND OTHER LEGISLATION

One indication of the significance of petitioning involves the wide variety of subjects thus presented for legislative consideration. These subjects ranged from matters of colonial or statewide importance to minor local issues and even matters of purely individual concern. This chapter will examine how Virginians used petitions to influence legislation on such major issues as internal improvements, the slave codes, and defense policy, and such local and individual concerns as fighting outbreaks of smallpox, docking entails, and paying public claims. Whether involving matters great or small, such petitions were an important part of the political process.

The assembly played an active role in establishing and regulating the public ferries needed for crossing Virginia's rivers and streams. The legislature authorized public ferries to be maintained at key locations and regulated the rates charged by those ferries. The county courts supervised the operators of public ferries, and each court could establish such additional ferries as were needed for crossing any other creeks and streams within the county.[1]

In most cases the assembly established these public ferries directly in response to the petitions of local residents. Creation of new ferries followed the westward expansion of settlement, although in some cases additional ferries became necessary and were established in the older regions as well.[2] Petitions for new ferries generally included the signatures of the man or men who owned the land at the proposed location and would operate the ferry. In many cases numerous other citizens signed also, expressing their conviction that the proposed ferry would greatly improve local transportation. For example, over two hundred residents of Albemarle County petitioned in 1774 for a ferry to operate from the confluence of the Fluvanna and Rivanna rivers to Cumberland County.[3]

When no local citizens opposed such requests and when committee investigation substantiated the need for a new ferry, the house usually accepted the request. A 1786 case was typical of the normal process. Robert Parker and several other residents of Hampshire County petitioned for a ferry over the south branch of the Potomac River, where it intersected the road from Winchester to Pittsburgh, Pennsylvania. Parker owned the land on both sides of the river, there was no local opposition, and investigation indicated that travelers and trade would benefit from creation of a ferry at that point. The assembly then established the ferry as requested.[4] Similarly, petitioners in the counties of Isle of Wight, Nansemond, and Southampton successfully asked in 1755 that a public ferry be established from Hog Island on the south bank of the James River to Higginson's Landing in James City County. In a 1776 petition to the house, citizens of Amherst and Bedford counties stated that they often traveled between the two courthouses but were required to go far out of their way in order to cross the Fluvanna River. The petitioners asked that a ferry be established from the land of Henry Trent in Amherst to that of Nicholas Davies in Bedford. No other citizens objected, and the advantages of the proposed ferry seemed obvious to the assembly, which established the ferry as desired.[5]

Legislative decisions were more difficult to make in those occasional instances where some local residents counterpetitioned against creating a new ferry. Usually such counterpetitions came from the owner of the land across from the proposed location or from owners of adjacent lands who did not want roads built through their property. Also, operators of nearby ferries sometimes protested against establishment of rival facilities. A more detailed investigation was required in such cases, for while promoting the public good, the house tried to avoid imposing unreasonable sacrifices upon any local citizens. The assembly sometimes established the ferry despite some local opposition, but on other occasions, when impressed by the arguments in the counterpetition, it refused to do so. Fortunately, in the vast majority of cases such disputes did not arise, and the assembly's decision was a reasonably easy one.[6]

The assembly's role in other phases of the transportation network was more sporadic. While many citizens recognized the need for better transportation, the responsibility for maintaining roads and clearing navigable waterways fell largely within the jurisdiction of the county courts. The comprehensive legislation enacted in 1748 consolidated previous provisions and stated the local responsibility in detail. Each county court was to construct convenient public roads leading to Williamsburg, the county courthouse, the parish churches, and all public mills and ferries. Additional roads were provided whenever local residents petitioned the court and demonstrated the need. When roads between counties were necessary, the respective courts were required to cooperate in building them. In order to keep the roads in repair, local citizens occasionally worked in road gangs under the direction of a road surveyor appointed by the county magistrates. The county court also was responsible for keeping the navigable rivers and creeks free of debris, with the funds to be raised through the county levy. If the river or stream passed through two or more counties, the respective courts shared the expense.[7] These provisions had but mixed success. The quality of Virginia's roads varied considerably, ranging from adequate to atrocious, and obstacles to navigation remained all too common in the rivers and streams.[8]

Beginning around the middle of the eighteenth century, the colonial government assumed a more active role in building roads and clearing waterways. In most instances legislative action in this field responded to suggestions presented in the petitions of Virginia citizens. When inhabitants of King William and Hanover counties petitioned in 1728 that public funds be used for clearing the Pamunkey River, the house rejected the petition without comment.[9] By 1746, however, the official attitude towards such petitions was clearly changing. In that year citizens in Albemarle County asked for public assistance in clearing the Fluvanna River, which runs through much of what was Albemarle territory in 1746. The petitioners noted that the river was useful for transporting tobacco to the warehouses below the falls, but in a few places obstacles rendered navigation hazardous. The house accepted the petition, and the assembly appropriated £100 to certain trustees for making the improvements.[10] In 1748 the assembly accepted an Augusta petition which sought financial assistance in opening roads through the Blue Ridge at Swiftrun Gap and two additional places. The legislature again appointed trustees to supervise the expenditure. That same session rejected a petition from Prince William County that a road be constructed at public expense to connect Prince William to the Valley county of Frederick; however, the legislature did authorize the county court of Prince William to construct the road at county expense.[11]

Virginia's interest in internal improvements further increased following the French and Indian War. With the backcountry again secured and the need for heavy wartime expenditures eliminated, Virginia was free to seek new ways for improving trade and communication throughout the colony.

For example, much of the Valley trade still had to go north to Pennsylvania rather than east, over the mountains. Better east-west transportation thus offered distinct commercial advantages to the whole colony.

Augusta County residents petitioned in 1764 and 1765 that the county court be authorized to levy an additional tax to finance construction or improvement of roads over Rockfish and Swiftrun gaps. The assembly accepted both requests; after all, neither would cost the colonial government anything, and there was no opposition from the local taxpayers who would bear the expense.[12] But the assembly recognized that some projects simply could not be completed solely with local funds, and it proved receptive to proposals requiring moderate expenditures by the colonial government. In 1767 petitioners in Frederick and Hampshire counties (situated in the northwestern part of the colony) suggested that the colonial government repair Braddock's Road. The road connected the north branch of the Potomac with Fort Pitt, and if it was repaired, Virginia could increase its share of the Indian trade and sell supplies to the British garrison. The assembly, impressed with the proposal and cognizant that western citizens needed assistance in the plan, appointed trustees to supervise the project and authorized £200 in government expenditures.[13] Similarly, the legislature accepted a 1772 petition from the Piedmont and western counties of Augusta, Botetourt, Hanover, and Albemarle which sought assistance in constructing a turnpike to connect Warm Springs in Augusta with the road from the Piedmont to Jenning's Gap. At the time Warm Springs held commercial possibilities for its bath and mineral waters, and the turnpike would provide access to the rest of the colony. The assembly appointed trustees to oversee the expenditure of £300 in public tax monies. In response to another 1772 petition, the legislature appointed commissioners to investigate the feasibility of constructing a public road over South Mountain to connect Botetourt with the Piedmont county of Bedford.[14]

Proposals for improving the navigation of Virginia's rivers also seemed to offer great benefits to trade and communication, and beginning in 1764 the colony initiated steps which ultimately culminated in the famous James and Potomac River canal schemes of the 1780s. A 1764 petition from Buckingham County asked that the legislature appoint trustees to take voluntary subscriptions for clearing the falls of the James River near Richmond and removing obstructions above the falls. If the project was successful, light craft could then travel without hindrance from the Tidewater to within a few miles of the Blue Ridge. Since the James formed the northern and western boundaries of Buckingham, the petitioners obviously had a major interest in the project. The petition arrived too late in the 1764 session for action to be taken, but in 1765 the assembly enacted legislation which appointed trustees and authorized them to receive private subscriptions. Although some individuals contributed money and part of the Rivanna River was cleared of obstructions, nothing was accomplished towards clearing the falls on the James.[15] Recognizing that considerable expense could be required to complete the plan, the assembly in 1772 passed additional legislation allowing the subscribers to elect directors for supervising the project. As another incentive, when a canal around the falls was completed, the subscribers could collect tolls from users. The assembly established a similar plan for clearing the falls of the Potomac River. Considerable sums were subscribed and John Ballendine was hired to go to England and learn how to build canals. But Ballendine's character has already been described, and the confidence in his abilities proved misplaced. Though he ultimately began work on a canal above the James River falls, nothing substantial was accomplished under either of the 1772 acts.[16] A petition from sundry Tidewater residents seeking construction of a privately financed canal near Williamsburg to link the James and York rivers was also accepted in 1772, but once again little was accomplished.[17] Attention and financing were diverted from all these projects during the Revolutionary War, but the groundwork had been prepared for the renewed interest which followed the conclusion of hostilities.

In the 1780s Virginia resumed work on internal improvements on a scale which quickly surpassed the modest colonial efforts. This interest was promoted by numerous petitions from citizens interested in better transportation. Virginia used three different methods to carry out the program: the assembly sometimes appointed trustees to raise subscriptions or chartered private corporations to construct turnpikes, clear rivers, and build canals; the assembly chartered other transportation corporations which combined private investment and public support, as the state purchased a sizable minority of the corporate stock; and the assembly financed some projects entirely through the expenditure of tax revenue. This program enjoyed considerable support during the late eighteenth century from petitioners and from such powerful public figures as Washington, Madison, Jefferson, and Benjamin Harrison. Despite the optimism

of the 1780s and 1790s, however, several factors limited the overall effectiveness of the state's efforts. The legislature relied upon private financing
as much as possible, and with a couple of exceptions state expenditures
remained relatively modest. This policy is understandable, in light of the
economic distress of the 1780s and the nearly universal desire to keep
taxes as low as possible, but it limited the accomplishments which could
realistically be expected. Moreover, again with a few exceptions, the
assembly provided little central planning or overall direction for the program. In most cases the legislature merely responded to specific proposals
presented by petitions from local citizens; rarely did it initiate action,
and not until creation of the Board of Public Works in 1816 was anyone
responsible for coordinating the individual projects to achieve a unified
transportation network.

Within these limitations, however, the legislature acted to improve
Virginia's roads and rivers in the 1784-1800 period. It accepted a 1793
petition from the western county of Harrison asking that trustees be
appointed to accept subscriptions for clearing the Monongahela River,
but the work was to be financed entirely by private funds. The legislature
also accepted a 1793 petition from residents of Culpeper and Madison
(two counties in the western Piedmont) and created a private corporation
for clearing the Rappahannock River. The Rappahannock Company was
authorized to clear the river from the falls to the highest practical point
upstream, and when the improvements were finished, the company could
then collect tolls from river traffic.[18] The assembly also accepted petitions
from Piedmont and Valley counties for chartering turnpike companies to
build toll roads connecting the two sections. The efforts made after 1748
to improve the roads between the Valley and Piedmont had considerable
success, for much of the Valley trade turned east, toward Alexandria and
other Virginia cities, and away from the Pennsylvania towns which had
previously dominated this commerce.[19]

The failure of the 1765 and 1772 plans for clearing the James and
Potomac rivers clearly indicated, however, that for some projects state
assistance was indispensable. George Washington had long advocated
clearing those rivers (particularly the Potomac) and possibly even linking
them via short roads or canals to the "western waters" which flowed
into the Ohio River and thence to the Mississippi. Washington had supported the 1772 legislation, and in 1784 he resumed his efforts. After
personally viewing the terrain and then securing the approval of the

Maryland legislature for improving the Potomac, Washington presented his plan to the Virginia assembly.[20] Madison and other political leaders immediately added their support, a number of Virginia and Maryland citizens petitioned in favor of the proposal, and the legislature responded favorably. As a result, two companies were incorporated in January 1785, one for clearing the James and the other for the Potomac. Although both were private corporations with the majority of stock to be purchased by investors, the assembly provided public assistance by authorizing government purchase and control of about $20,000 of stock in each company. The legislature also purchased a similar amount of stock in each as a gift for Washington, in recognition of his public service. (Washington, very much embarrassed by the gift, then donated the stock to worthy public projects.) The immediate goal of both corporations was restricted to building a canal around the falls and extending navigation "to the highest place practicable" on the river. The companies could then charge tolls for river traffic. But the general hope was that upon this foundation Washington's broader plan would eventually be constructed. If accomplished—and in 1785 hopes were high—the waterway would cover half the continent, thereby cementing the American union of East and West and securing the western trade for Virginia.[21] The assembly granted similar assistance, though on a smaller scale, to several other companies. For example, in 1795 it incorporated the Appomattox River Company to build a canal around the falls and clear the river for navigation as far as possible above that point, and the following year the assembly subscribed for one hundred shares of stock (an investment of $10,000) in the company.[22]

Some minor projects offered too little prospect for an immediate return on investment to attract much private capital through incorporation of a turnpike or canal company. In such cases the assembly on occasion financed the project entirely with state funds. This method was often used for repairing or completing western roads through relatively rough and sparsely populated terrain. In almost all such cases, the assembly took this action directly in response to petitions from local citizens, who reported that their community would derive great benefit from the project or that it would link the western counties more closely to the rest of the state. For example, residents of Greenbrier and Kanawha counties, located in the trans-Allegheny region (now West Virginia), petitioned in 1796 to ask that the state repair the road leading from the town of Lewisburg to the Kanawha River. The Kanawha was one of the major navigable rivers in the West, and below its falls the river provided a water route to the Ohio River. The assembly recognized the importance of the connecting road to Lewisburg and appropriated $500 for making the repairs. Similarly, in response to a petition from inhabitants of Lee County, the 1794 assembly authorized the expenditure of $1,000 in state funds to complete an important road from the western counties of Lee and Washington to the state of Kentucky.[23]

In short, the effort to improve Virginia's transportation network during the eighteenth century exhibited two major characteristics. First, most of the projects originated directly from the suggestions presented to the assembly in the petitions of local citizens. Second, the assembly sought to utilize private capital as much as possible and restricted government expenditures to a minimum. In 1816 Virginia took a major step forward by establishing a permanent fund for internal improvements to be administered by a Board of Public Works. Yet that fund also proved inadequate, and Virginia was then forced to confront a serious dilemma. Many citizens, particularly in the West, desired a costly program of internal improvements. Many other citizens, particularly taxpayers in the East where rivers already provided cheap transportation, either refused to support such schemes by adequate taxation or insisted that most of the funds be spent on the James River project and other eastern measures. As the final chapter of this study will indicate, failure to resolve these conflicting opinions sparked increasing sectional hostility within the Old Dominion.[24]

As slavery became an increasingly significant institution in eighteenth-century Virginia, citizens sent a number of petitions to the house concerning the slave codes and the position of blacks in society. Importation of African slaves on a large scale was under way by the end of the seventeenth century, and the percentage of blacks in the total population rose fairly quickly to perhaps 40 percent or more. Blacks constituted a much larger share of the population in the Tidewater and Piedmont than in the Valley and West. East of the Blue Ridge a significant number of white farmers owned slaves, and in a number of counties between half and two-thirds of the population was black; west of the mountains the percentage of slaveholders in the population was much smaller, and blacks formed a small minority of the population.[25]

The assembly received several petitions in the early eighteenth century calling for more stringent regulation of slaves and free blacks—perhaps an indication that some persons were concerned over the growing influx of slaves. Petitioners in James City and New Kent counties asked in 1700 that more efficient procedures be established for capturing runaway slaves. Virginia laws of that period indicate why the petitioners were concerned; a 1691 statute noted that "many times negroes, mulattoes, and other slaves unlawfully absent themselves from their masters and mistresses service, and lie hid and lurk in obscure places killing hoggs and committing other injuries to the inhabitants of this dominion."[26] While the house rejected this petition on the grounds that existing provisions were adequate, a 1705 statute did establish more efficient guidelines for outlawing runaways.[27]

In the years from 1699 to 1704 the assembly received several petitions from citizens in the counties of Surry, Prince George, and Accomack asking for stronger measures to prevent interracial marriages. The Accomack petitioners suggested that legal sanctions be imposed on any minister performing such marriages. Existing statutes already provided that any white person who married a Negro, mulatto, or Indian would be banished forever from the colony. Nevertheless, "for a further prevention of that abominable mixture and spurious issue," the 1705 assembly added that any white person marrying a Negro or mulatto faced a fine and six-month prison sentence. Any minister performing such a marriage was to be fined 10,000 pounds of tobacco.[28] In 1720 petitioners in Surry County requested that all further importation of slaves into the colony be prohibited. The petitioners' motives, however, cannot be determined from the surviving records. Perhaps the request reflected a growing fear of slave rebellions or other ill consequences from the steady increase in slaves; in 1710 a planned slave rebellion in Surry County had been discovered just in time to prevent it. On the other hand, the petitioners may simply have owned enough slaves already and desired to increase the value of the existing supply. At any rate, the house rejected the petition.[29]

During the half-century after 1720, the assembly received very few petitions concerning the slave laws—except, of course, petitions from the owners of slaves outlawed and killed or executed by the public, for the law provided compensation to the owners in such cases. The slave codes as developed by 1720 allowed slaveholders a considerable degree of latitude in the treatment of slaves. For example, even if a slave died as a result of punishment inflicted by the owner for the "correction" of some "offense," the owner was exempted from prosecution unless some "credible" witness could prove that the death was intentional.[30] Apparently most Virginians approved of this policy, and antislavery sentiment was not strong enough to mount an effective challenge to the "peculiar institution" during the colonial period. Consequently, the 1752 requests from the counties of James City and Richmond asking that slaves be forbidden from keeping dogs stand as exceptions to the general pattern of satisfaction with the status quo.[31]

The slavery question aroused an increasing amount of attention, however, during the revolutionary period, and the topic of emancipation was widely discussed. By that time a number of Virginians, including many Quakers, Methodists, Baptists, "enlightened" statesmen, and others, agreed with Jefferson that slavery was a wicked institution, damaging to both whites and blacks. Similar debates raged, of course, in all of the other states, and those north of the Mason-Dixon line abolished slavery. But in Virginia, as in the other southern states, the antislavery sentiment was not strong enough to overcome several major obstacles. First, while Jefferson and numerous citizens attacked slavery, many others accepted it without question as a natural and beneficial institution. Second, almost all white Virginians accepted the same basic racial assumptions—blacks were inferior to whites, and freeing the slaves without somehow deporting them might well destroy the foundations of white civilization.[32] In short, the strong proslavery sentiment of some and the common conviction that blacks and whites were incapable of living together in freedom doomed the emancipation proposals of the 1780s.[33]

Distrust of free blacks had long received legal expression in the many restrictions placed upon that class of citizens and in the provisions, first adopted in 1691, limiting manumission of slaves. The 1691 statute required that anyone freeing a slave must transport him out of the colony within six months. This provision was replaced in 1723 with another: no slave could be freed "except for some meritorious services, to be adjudged and allowed by the governor and council. . . ."[34] In 1759 a group of petitioners in Northampton County, which had a sizable black population, even asked that all free blacks be immediately expelled from the colony. The petition, though rejected by the house, nevertheless reflected a widespread conviction among whites about the undesirability of black citizens.[35] During the antislavery discussion of the 1780s, however, Virginia did enact a significant law in 1782 which permitted any slaveholder to free his slaves, provided only that he furnish support for any young, elderly, or disabled slave so emancipated. Although some individual legislators supported emancipation in principle, the assembly was willing to go no further than allowing voluntary manumission. Even so, an estimated ten thousand slaves were freed during the decade following passage of the 1782 statute.[36]

A proslavery reaction soon challenged the manumission law. Petitioners in Henrico and Hanover counties asked unsuccessfully in 1784 for repeal of the law, but a much stronger effort came in 1785. Prompted by a new Methodist proposal for emancipation, the proslavery forces launched a vigorous counterattack. Almost 1250 petitioners from the counties of Mecklenburg, Amelia, Brunswick, Pittsylvania, Halifax, and Lunenburg defended slavery, asked that emancipation be rejected, and reiterated the call for repeal of the manumission law. The proslavery petitions all came from counties located in the tobacco-producing southern Piedmont region, and all of these counties contained heavy concentrations of slaves. Some petitioners based their defense of slavery upon the Bible, while others argued that the Revolution had been fought in defense of property rights and slaves were property. All agreed that blacks could never become first-class citizens. The 1785 assembly ultimately sidestepped the issue entirely; it rejected the emancipation proposal and at the same time refused to repeal the manumission law.[37] Nevertheless, the slavery issue refused to fade away. The free Negro population continued to grow rapidly in the 1790s and early 1800s, and following Gabriel's Rebellion in 1800 an increasing number of Virginians in the areas with large black populations became alarmed. In 1806 the assembly passed a law requiring all blacks subsequently manumitted to leave the state within six months or be sold back into slavery.[38] Yet some antislavery sentiment remained in Virginia, especially in the West, and the most famous legislative debate on emancipation and colonization came in the early 1830s.

Eighteenth-century Virginians petitioned much less frequently about education than internal improvements or the slave codes. Except for the College of William and Mary, established in 1691, education during the colonial period remained an individual and local responsibility. Virginians generally agreed with their New England counterparts that education was a matter of great importance, but the rural pattern of settlement prevented the creation of any effective network of public schools. Wealthy parents frequently hired private tutors or sent their children to private schools (often taught by local ministers) or to England. Education was also available to many other children, though on a sporadic and limited basis. Tutors hired by wealthy families often taught other neighborhood children as well, and the private schools were available to children whose parents could afford the tuition. Some counties were fortunate in having an endowed free school, subsidized by a gift from some wealthy patron, which provided free education to poor children. And, of course, educated parents often taught their children. Considering the difficulties of the environment and the inadequacies of this system, a surprisingly large number of children received at least a rudimentary education.[39] The difficulties confronting establishment of a comprehensive public school system seemed so great that serious discussion of the matter was minimal before 1776. Petitioners in New Kent and Princess Anne counties asked the 1720 assembly to establish public schools in every county, but both petitions were rejected with little discussion. Similarly, in 1730 Governor Gooch asked the legislature to consider creating a school system, but after only a brief investigation the burgesses indefinitely tabled the matter.[40]

Proposals for public education attracted much greater attention during and after the Revolution. Jefferson's famous "Bill for the More General Diffusion of Knowledge" proposed establishing primary schools throughout the state and guaranteeing at least three years of schooling to all children, with poor children to receive this education at public expense. The most gifted children would then advance to public secondary schools, and a select few to college, also at public expense. After considerable discussion, however, the 1786 assembly rejected Jefferson's plan because in its opinion the cost was prohibitive.[41] A 1796 statute did allow each county to establish public schools supported by local taxes, but compliance was voluntary, and few counties took any action.[42] After 1776 the assembly acted on occasion to support existing schools, particularly academies, but in doing so it relied primarily upon private rather than public funds. It often accepted petitions from the trustees of academies and other interested citizens who asked permission to raise funds by lottery or subscription. Granting permission to hold lotteries was especially popular with the delegates, as lotteries offered a convenient way to raise money for worthwhile causes without resorting to taxation.[43] In 1787 petitioners from the Kentucky region asked that part of the local surveyor's fees be granted to Transylvania Seminary. The assembly accepted this proposal even though it normally rejected petitions for giving public funds to private schools. For example, the trustees of Liberty Hall

Academy (which eventually became Washington and Lee University) unsuccessfully petitioned for financial assistance on several occasions between 1786 and 1800.[44] The state did create the Literary Fund in 1810 as an endowment to help educate poor children, but the funds were inadequate even for that limited purpose. Creation of a comprehensive public school system came only after the Civil War.[45]

Virginians also petitioned the assembly on occasion concerning military defense against Indians or foreign enemies. While the royal governor served as commander-in-chief of the colonial militia and other armed forces, any significant military venture required the additional revenue which only new taxes could provide. The assembly used its "power of the purse" to acquire an increasingly important role in determining defense policy.[46] Frontier inhabitants often petitioned the assembly to take additional measures for protecting local residents from the Indians. The house carefully considered these petitions when it drew up bills for appointing rangers to patrol the frontier or for appropriating money for colonial defense.[47] During the Revolutionary War, the executive branch kept in close communication with militia officers throughout the state, and especially on the frontier, so most proposals on specific defense measures were sent to the governor. But petitioners did sometimes ask the legislature to amend certain features of the militia or defense laws. Citizens in Greenbrier County, for example, petitioned in 1780 for an increased allowance to scouts serving on the frontier, and the assembly accepted the proposal.[48]

Virginians also used petitions to protest alleged violations of the election laws. Voters in each county selected two representatives in open elections, either by voice vote or by signing the polls of their favorite candidates. The election laws prohibited candidates or other persons from influencing voters by bribery or intimidation; however, a rather fine line separated bribery from "treating," an accepted campaign tactic whereby a candidate offered food or drink (especially the latter) to all voters on election day without regard to their choice of candidates. When everyone had voted, the sheriff counted the votes and announced the winners.[49] The results were often contested on various grounds, including charges that the sheriff miscounted the vote or influenced voters, that unqualified persons voted, and that candidates or their supporters "treated" beyond the limits permitted by law and custom. In such cases a defeated candidate or other concerned citizens could petition the house to investigate. The Committee of Privileges and Elections conducted these investigations with a scrupulous determination to uncover the facts and insure that justice was done, for the house considered corrupt or unfair electioneering intolerable. The committee had full power to send for evidence of every description. If the contested election occurred in a county close to the capital, witnesses were often summoned to testify before the committee. When longer distances were involved, local justices of the peace were allowed to take depositions from all parties involved and send them to the committee.[50]

Although the house could reject the committee report, it did so rather infrequently and then mostly when questions involving interpretation of the law were involved, because the committee conducted such thorough investigations. The house reacted quickly if anyone attempted to suppress evidence or if a member sought to block presentation of petitions contesting his election. In 1736 Richard Bland challenged the election of Robert Munford as a burgess for Prince George County. Munford interfered with the investigation and threatened Bland's witnesses. Even though Bland withdrew his petition, the house still severely reprimanded Munford for his conduct, concluding: "And you and others, will hereafter be satisfied, That no Member of this House can use his Privilege for insulting or maltreating Mankind."[51] In 1752 the house adopted a standing rule that any burgess interfering with the presentation of such petitions would be punished.[52]

When the committee discovered complaints to be groundless, it recommended that the house uphold the election. If the investigation substantiated the charges made by the petitioners, the committee made one of two recommendations. When a defeated candidate actually received more legitimate votes than a candidate declared by the sheriff to be elected, the committee suggested that the contested seat be awarded to the legitimate victor. In his 1798 petition, for example, Joshua Chaffin charged that he had received more legitimate votes than Alexander Jones in the recent Amelia County election. Investigation revealed that Jones's margin of victory was provided by sixty-one voters who were not legal freeholders. As a result, Jones was dismissed and Chaffin took his place in the house. In many cases, however, illegal or unfair tactics so disrupted the election that the committee recommended holding a new one. A number of petitioners from Pittsylvania County reported in 1797 that the recent election had been disrupted by the "riotous and disorderly proceedings" of certain individuals who attempted to permit only their friends to vote. The committee was unable to determine which candidate was responsible for the disturbance, so it recommended that the election be invalidated and a new one held.[53] In a majority of cases, the house ultimately upheld the original election, but a significant number were overturned following investigation of these petitions.[54] The election process served as an important means of insuring that the house represented the people and acted in a responsive manner, for those members who failed to do so could be rejected by the voters at the next election. The ability of citizens to contest election results by petitioning the house helped insure that the election process could not be undermined by fraud or corruption.

Citizens also petitioned the assembly concerning a host of other issues which had only local or temporary significance, but such petitions also received careful legislative attention. Two 1769 petitions were typical of this type. Both petitions complained of the dangers involved in smallpox inoculation and asked that the practice be strictly regulated or prohibited. One of the petitions had been circulated among "sundry of the Inhabitants" of the colony, while the other came from the town of Norfolk and the surrounding county. Both petitions reflected the bitter controversy then raging in certain parts of Virginia concerning inoculation for smallpox, still a dreaded and deadly disease in the eighteenth century. An epidemic broke out in parts of Virginia, especially in the Williamsburg area, in 1768 and 1769. Although apparently introduced from the West Indies, the epidemic may have been spread by careless inoculation. In 1769 the Norfolk area was still unaffected, but several prominent citizens decided to inoculate their families as a precautionary measure. Their decision produced a heated debate in the city between those favoring and those opposing the introduction of smallpox into a community still free of the disease, with majority sentiment strongly opposed. The controversy also included political overtones, for the families seeking inoculation were associated because of previous actions with pro-English sympathies in the current imperial dispute. When some of them proceeded to be inoculated despite the uproar, a mob drove the affected individuals through a storm to the local pest house. At this point the house received the two petitions. After considering the matter, the house decided that inoculation, when properly administered in an area already threatened by the disease, was of considerable value. But the burgesses agreed that "the wanton introduction of the Small-Pox into this colony by inoculation, when the same was not necessary, hath, of late years, proved a nuisance to several neighbour-hoods. . . ." The assembly then enacted legislation to permit inoculation only by qualified persons, and then only when approved by local authorities.[55]

Virginians also petitioned concerning matters of strictly individual con-cern. Among the most common sources of private bills in the eighteenth century were petitions to "dock," or terminate, the entail on property. By entailing his lands the owner decreed that the property must remain in the possession of a designated line of heirs (usually descending from father to legitimate son) and could not be sold or otherwise transferred. The device was most often used in attempts to keep large estates intact, but small as well as large estates were sometimes entailed. For many years historians exaggerated the importance of entail as an "aristocratic" tool, but studies have now revealed that most land was not entailed. Moreover, entail often became a burden to later generations, for it prevented sub-sequent owners from selling unproductive land or consolidating scattered holdings into a compact and more efficient unit. After 1727 slaves could also be entailed, thus compounding the inconvenience for later owners.[56]

Many owners of entailed property sought to dock the entail in order to sell the land or move the slaves to other locations. A 1705 statute provided that an act of assembly was required to break an entail, though a 1734 statute allowed entails on lands valued at less than £200 to be docked simply by acquiring a writ from the secretary's office.[57] The assembly received a large number of petitions for this purpose after 1705. If the petitioner informed other family members and interested parties of his intention to dock the entail, and if none of them objected, then his petition was almost certain to be accepted. Over a hundred such acts were passed in the 1711-1776 period. The fifteen petitioners success-ful from 1756 to 1763 included Lewis Burwell, Ralph Wormeley, and Archibald Cary.[58] By 1776 Virginians were accustomed to breaking en-tails on estates large and small, either by writ or by private bill founded upon petition. This explains why Jefferson's successful effort to abolish entails in 1776, rather than overthrowing a "landed aristocracy," actually met with almost no opposition at all.[59]

The presentation of petitions to the house was also instrumental in the payment of public claims. The colonial government appropriated funds in advance for certain major projects, such as military expeditions or construction of public buildings, and the permanent revenue arising from the duties on tobacco and on certain imports covered the regular, continuing expenses (such as the salary of the governor and council). Most extraordinary expenditures were handled on a deferred-payment basis. When an individual sold goods to or provided services for the colony, he had the county court certify his claim, and he sent it by petition to the next session of the assembly. The house usually received dozens of these petitions at each session, and during periods of war or other unusual circumstances the number often rose to a hundred or more. Some claims involving routine matters were immediately accepted by the house, but most of them were given to the Committee of Public Claims for investigation. If the house accepted a claim, it was listed for payment in the Book of Public Claims which was presented to the council for acceptance at the end of the session. Disputes between the two houses over specific claims were surprisingly infrequent. In most cases, a favorable report by the Committee of Public Claims insured that both houses would approve payment.[60]

Public compensation for owners of slaves outlawed and killed or executed for committing crimes constituted a special category of public claims. In such cases the county court certified the value of the slave, and the owner petitioned the assembly for compensation. If both houses accepted the petition, the claim was added to the Book of Public Claims for payment.[61] In 1792 western delegates, representing counties with relatively few slaves, attempted to end such payments but were defeated by the eastern delegates, sixty-three to fifty.[62]

With the outbreak of the Revolution and the great increase in expenditures which followed, the legislature took steps to facilitate the settling of public claims. It created a Board of Auditors in 1776 to examine claims and authorize payment. Anyone not satisfied with the auditors' decision could still petition the house and receive legislative consideration, and many claimants did so. Despite creation of the auditors, the Committee of Public Claims stayed busy investigating claims presented by petitioners.[63]

In conclusion, it should be emphasized that the discussion in this and the other chapters of various types of petitions has of necessity focused upon the most important categories. A comprehensive listing of all the subjects presented by petitioners for legislative attention would involve a prohibitive amount of space and time. A multitude of minor issues, important only to the individual or group immediately involved, were presented in such petitions. Considered individually these minor petitions may seem unimportant, but collectively they too were of major significance. For whether the issue was great or small, petitioning provided a means whereby average citizens could communicate with their government and frequently receive favorable action on matters which concerned them.

Notes

1. William Waller Hening, ed., *The Statutes at Large: Being a Collection of All the Laws of Virginia,* 13 vols. (Richmond and Philadelphia, 1809-23), 3: 469-76; 4: 93-94, 112-14; 6: 13-23; Lewis P. Summers, ed., *Annals of Southwest Virginia, 1769-1800* (1929; reprint ed., Baltimore, 1970), pp. 703-04, 733, 811, 1369; Thomas Jefferson, *Notes on the State of Virginia,* ed. William Peden (Chapel Hill, N.C., 1954), p. 152; Douglas S. Freeman, *George Washington,* 7 vols. (New York, 1948-57), 1: 151-52.

2. Hugh Drysdale to Board of Trade, 10 July 1726, CO5/1320, p. 65; see also William Gooch to Board of Trade, 20 November 1734, William Gooch Papers, 3 vols., transcripts, VHS, 2: 373.

3. Hamilton J. Eckenrode, ed., "Calendar of Legislative Petitions," *Fifth Annual Report of the Library Board of the Virginia State Library for the Year Ending October 31, 1908* (Richmond, 1908), Albemarle Petition, 1774, p. 23. The governor's dissolution of the assembly, due to the house resolves opposing British policy, prevented final action on the petition—*JHB,* 1773-1776: 99, 125, 126, 132. See also Freeman H. Hart, *The Valley of Virginia in the American Revolution* (Chapel Hill, N.C., 1942), pp. 22-23; Ohio County Petition, 29 October 1787.

4. *JHD,* 1786 (1828 reprint): 8; Hampshire Petition, 27 October 1786; Hening, *Statutes,* 12: 403.

5. *JHB,* 1752-1758: 247; *JHD,* 1776: 14, 26, 36, 38, 106, 113; Hening, *Statutes,* 6: 494; 9: 233-35. For similar instances, see: *JHB,* 1702/3-1712: 21; 1712-1726: 265, 267, 274, 281, 316; 1742-1749: 171, 220; 1766-1769: 238, 258; 1773-1776: 11, 24, 27, 36, 202, 211; *JHD,* May 1779: 9; May 1780: 6; May 1784: 8, 21; Hening, *Statutes,* 3: 219; 4: 92-94; 5: 364-65; 8: 368-71, 658-59; 10: 124-25, 365; 11: 370-71.

6. Halifax Petition, 30 November 1803; *JHB,* 1773-1776: 99; *JHD,* 1785: 81, 109; 1791: 119; Hening, *Statutes,* 12: 83; 13: 282; Hart, *Valley of Virginia,* p. 22.

7. Hening, *Statutes,* 6: 64-71; Freeman, *George Washington,* 1: 147-50; Jefferson, *Notes on Virginia,* pp. 151-52; Albert O. Porter, *County Government in Virginia: A Legislative History, 1607-1904* (New York, 1947), pp. 20-22, 57-61; Lyman Chalkley, ed., *Chronicles of the Scotch-Irish Settlement in Virginia, Extracted from the Original Court Records of Augusta County, 1745-1800,* 3 vols. (1912; reprint ed., Baltimore, 1965), 1: 123, 130, 132-33.

8. See the excellent description in Freeman, *George Washington,* 1: 147-54; George R. Taylor, *The Transportation Revolution* (New York, 1951), p. 16.

9. *JHB,* 1727-1740: 12-13; the Committee of Propositions and Grievances decided to reject the petition after very little consideration, indicating that projects

of this nature were still considered to be a local responsibility—see the committee minutes for 6 February 1728, in Godfrey Pole Papers, VHS.

10. *JHB*, 1742-1749: 184, 196, 213, 216, 217, 220; Hening, *Statutes*, 5: 377-80; Jefferson, *Notes on Virginia*, p. 6.

11. *JHB*, 1742-1749: 307, 312, 315, 316, 319, 321, 323, 324, 326, 328; Hening, *Statutes*, 6: 210, 211.

12. *JHB*, 1761-1765: 207, 275; Hening, *Statutes*, 8: 16-17, 152, 548; Hart, *Valley of Virginia*, pp. 20-22.

13. *JHB*, 1766-1769: 109, 129; Hening, *Statutes*, 8: 252-53.

14. *JHB*, 1770-1772: 167, 233, 315; Hening, *Statutes*, 8: 546, 552.

15. *JHB*, 1761-1765: 275, 326, 363; Hening, *Statutes*, 8: 148-50; Jefferson to Benjamin Harrison, 30 October 1779, in *The Papers of Thomas Jefferson*, ed. Julian P. Boyd, 19 vols. to date (Princeton, N.J., 1950-   ), 3: 128; Jefferson, *Notes on Virginia*, p. 6; Dumas Malone, *Jefferson and His Time*, Vol. 1: *Jefferson the Virginian* (Boston, 1948), pp. 115-16.

16. *JHB*, 1770-1772: xxxv, 154, 192-93, 218-19, 222, 292, 295, 303, 316; Hening, *Statutes*, 8: 564-79; Jefferson to Harrison, 30 October 1779, in *Jefferson Papers*, ed. Boyd, 3: 128-29; George Washington to Rev. Jonathan Boucher, 4 May 1772, in *The Writings of George Washington*, ed. John C. Fitzpatrick, 39 vols. (Washington, D.C., 1931-44), 3: 81; Richard Jackson to Board of Trade, 16 February 1773, in *Documents of the American Revolution, 1770-1783 (Colonial Office Series)*, ed. K. G. Davies, 17 vols. to date (Shannon, Ireland, 1972-   ), no. 973, 4: 251.

17. *JHB*, 1770-1772: 183-84, 187, 316; Hening, *Statutes*, 8: 556-63; Alexander C. Brown, "Colonial Williamsburg's Canal Scheme," *VMHB* 86 (January 1978): 26-32.

18. *JHD*, 1793: 9, 26, 93, 111, 114, 129; Samuel Shepherd, ed., *The Statutes at Large of Virginia . . . Being a Continuation of Hening*, 3 vols. (Richmond, 1835-36), 1: 242-43, 244-53.

19. *JHD*, 1795: 10, 11, 61, 127; Shepherd, *Virginia Statutes*, 1: 378-88; Hart, *Valley of Virginia*, pp. 20-22, 149-58.

20. Washington presented his observations in a letter to Governor Harrison, which he intended to be circulated among the legislators—Washington to Harrison, 10 October 1784, in *Washington Writings*, ed. Fitzpatrick, 27: 471-80. See also: Freeman, *George Washington*, 6: ch. 1; Charles H. Ambler, *Sectionalism in Virginia from 1776 to 1861* (Chicago, 1910), pp. 46-48.

21. *JHD*, October 1784: 13, 55, 58, 60, 65, 66, 73, 93, 94, 96; Hening, *Statutes*, 11: 450-62, 510-26; Washington to Jefferson, 25 February 1785, Jefferson to Washington, 4 January 1785 [1786], Jefferson to Washington, 10 May 1789, in *Jefferson Papers*, ed. Boyd, 8: 3-6; 9: 151; 15: 117; Henry Lee to Washington, 21 April 1786, Lee Family Papers, 1742-1795, UVa microfilm publication; Wayland F. Dunaway, "History of the James River and Kanawha Company," *Columbia University Studies* 104 (1922): 245-70; see the editor's note in *The Papers of James Madison*, ed. William T. Hutchinson et al., 11 vols. to date (Chicago and Charlottesville, Va., 1962-   ), 8: 191-92, 215-16.

22. Shepherd, *Virginia Statutes*, 1: 390-94; 2: 34-35; *JHD*, 1796: 23-24, 27, 34.

23. *JHD*, 1795: 21, 61-62, 118, 123, 125; 1796: 54, 86, 91, 95; see also: 1786 (1828 reprint): 87, 109, 139; 1794: 17, 33-34, 72, 95, 103; Hening, *Statutes*, 12: 295-97; Shepherd, *Virginia Statutes*, 1: 314-15, 389; 2: 63-64.

24. *JHD*, 1815: 73-78, 107, 125, 158, 184; Harry Ammon, "The Republican Party in Virginia, 1789-1824" (Ph.D. dissertation, University of Virginia, 1948), pp. 369-70, 444-69; Fletcher M. Green, *Constitutional Development in the South Atlantic States, 1776-1860* (Chapel Hill, N.C., 1930), pp. 150-54; Ambler, *Sectionalism in Virginia*, pp. 97-99, 104-07; Charles S. Sydnor, *The Development of Southern Sectionalism, 1819-1848* (Baton Rouge, La., 1948), pp. 18-19, 271, 273n. See the discussion in the final chapter of this study.

25. Robert E. Brown and B. Katherine Brown, *Virginia 1705-1786: Democracy or Aristocracy?* (East Lansing, Mich., 1964), ch. 3; Gerald W. Mullin, *Flight and Rebellion: Slave Resistance in Eighteenth-Century Virginia* (New York, 1972), pp. 6, 15-16; James C. Ballagh, *A History of Slavery in Virginia* (Baltimore, 1902), pp. 9-12, 22-25; Thomas J. Wertenbaker, *The Planters of Colonial Virginia* (Princeton, N.J., 1922), ch. 8; Kenneth M. Stampp, *The Peculiar Institution* (New York, 1956), pp. 24, 32.

26. Hening, *Statutes*, 3: 86.

27. *JHB*, 1695-1702: 224; Hening, *Statutes*, 3: 460.

28. *JHB*, 1695-1702: 148, 266; 1702/3-1712: 56; Hening, *Statutes*, 3: 453-54; 6: 361-62. For the extent to which such liaisons occurred, whether with or without the sanction of law, see: Eugene D. Genovese, *Roll, Jordan, Roll* (New York, 1974), esp. pp. 413-31; John W. Blassingame, *The Slave Community* (New York, 1972), pp. 82-85,

29. *JHB*, 1712-1726: 266; Brown and Brown, *Virginia 1705-1786*, pp. 71-72; Hening, *Statutes*, 3: 537-38.

30. Hening, *Statutes*, 3: 447-62; 4: 126-34; 6: 104-12; Stampp, *Peculiar Institution*, esp. ch. 4; Blassingame, *Slave Community*, ch. 6.

31. *JHB*, 1752-1758: 20. Both petitions were rejected.

32. For standard accounts, see: Winthrop D. Jordan, *White Over Black* (Chapel Hill, N.C., 1968); Robert McColley, *Slavery and Jeffersonian Virginia* (Urbana, Ill., 1964); Mullin, *Flight and Rebellion*, ch. 4; Fredrika T. Schmidt and Barbara R. Wilhelm, "Early Proslavery Petitions in Virginia," *WMQ*, 3rd ser. 30 (January 1973): 133-46. Jefferson, of course, is a classic example of this combination of antislavery sentiment and a desire for deportation of emancipated slaves—see his autobiography, in *The Works of Thomas Jefferson*, ed. Paul L. Ford, 12 vols., Federal ed. (New York, 1904-05), 1: 76-77; Jefferson, *Notes on Virginia*, pp. 137-43, 162-63.

33. Jefferson was hopeful in 1786 that emancipation would come "in my day," but by 1805 he had abandoned his hope for a quick and easy solution—see Jefferson's answers to queries of Demeunier, 24 January 1786, in *Jefferson Papers*, ed. Boyd, 10: 18; Jefferson to William A. Burwell, 28 January 1805, and Jefferson to Dr. Thomas Humphreys, 8 February 1817, in *Jefferson Works*, ed. Ford, 10: 126; 12: 53-54. Virginia did prohibit further importation of new slaves in 1778—Hening, *Statutes*, 9: 471-72.

34. Hening, *Statutes,* 3: 87-88; 4: 82; 6: 112.

35. *JHB,* 1758-1761: 73.

36. Hening, *Statutes,* 11: 39-40; Quaker Petitions, 29 November 1780 and 29 May 1782 (religious petitions); Brown and Brown, *Virginia 1705-1786,* pp. 284-85; Schmidt and Wilhelm, "Early Proslavery Petitions," p. 135; Mullin, *Flight and Rebellion,* ch. 4.

37. *JHD,* October 1784: 23; 1785: 25, 28, 64, 91, 107, 108, 142; Schmidt and Wilhelm, "Early Proslavery Petitions," pp. 133-46; Madison to Washington, 11 November 1785, and editor's commentary, in *Madison Papers,* ed. Hutchinson et al., 8: 403-05; Jackson T. Main, *Political Parties Before the Constitution* (Chapel Hill, N.C., 1973), pp. 258-59.

38. Shepherd, *Virginia Statutes,* 3: 251-53.

39. Louis B. Wright, *The Cultural Life of the American Colonies, 1607-1763* (New York, 1957), ch. 5; Philip A. Bruce, *Institutional History of Virginia in the Seventeenth Century,* 2 vols. (New York, 1910), 1: 293-361, 450-59; Porter, *County Government in Virginia,* pp. 97-98; Malone, *Jefferson the Virginian,* pp. 39-46, 280-85; "Virginia's Cure: or An Advisive Narrative Concerning Virginia" [1662], in *Tracts and Other Papers Relating Principally to the Origin, Settlement, and Progress of the Colonies in North America,* ed. Peter Force, 4 vols. (Washington, D.C., 1836-46), 3: 6; William Cabell Diary, 27 September 1775 and 6 April 1776 (vol. 5); Hunter D. Farish, ed., *Journal and Letters of Philip Vickers Fithian, 1773-1774* (Williamsburg, 1943). A series of reports made in 1724 by twenty-eight Virginia parishes reveals that at least half had some private schools—see the reports in George M. Brydon, *Virginia's Mother Church and The Political Conditions Under Which It Grew,* 2 vols. (Richmond, 1947-52), 1: 372-73.

40. *JHB,* 1712-1726: 264; 1727-1740, xix, 58, 63.

41. Jefferson, *Notes on Virginia,* pp. 146-49; Jefferson to Samuel Stanhope Smith, [March?] 1779, Jefferson to George Wythe, 13 August 1786, Madison to Jefferson, 15 February 1787, in *Jefferson Papers,* ed. Boyd, 2: 246-49; 10: 244-45; 11: 152; the bill itself is reprinted in Ibid., 2: 526-33; Malone, *Jefferson the Virginian,* pp. 280-85.

42. Shepherd, *Virginia Statutes,* 2: 3-5; Porter, *County Government in Virginia,* pp. 218-19.

43. *JHD,* 1786 (1828 reprint): 58-59, 88, 93; 1803: 21, 37-38, 62; Hening, *Statutes,* 12: 364-65, 406; Shepherd, *Virginia Statutes,* 3: 34-36, 47; John Ezell, "The Lottery in Colonial America," *WMQ,* 3rd ser. 5 (April 1948): 194, 199-200.

44. *JHD,* 1786 (1828 reprint): 20; 1787 (1828 reprint): 84, 95, 97; 1789 (1828 reprint): 34; 1799: 31-32; Susan L. Foard, "Virginia Enters the Union" (M.A. thesis, College of William and Mary, 1966), pp. 122-23.

45. *JHD,* 1809: 5-9, 25; Virginia, *Acts Passed at a General Assembly in 1809* (Richmond, 1810), ch. 14, p. 15; Porter, *County Government in Virginia,* pp. 219-21; Sydnor, *Development of Southern Sectionalism,* pp. 57-64. The general inadequacy of the Literary Fund is evident from the annual reports made by the 2nd auditor to the General Assembly. See especially the school commissioners' reports contained in the auditor's 1828 report, and the 1830 report which shows that less than half of

the state's eligible poor children participated in the program during 1829. The state in 1829 spent an average of only $3.33 per poor child receiving aid—the reports are contained as an appendix to the house *Journals* for those sessions. While education was vastly underfinanced and taxes were kept to a minimum, the Committee of Finance reported to the assembly in 1830 that the state could expect a massive surplus during the coming year—the committee then recommended a further tax cut: *JHD*, 1830: 288-92.

46. See Jack P. Greene, *The Quest for Power* (Chapel Hill, N.C., 1963), pp. 297-309.

47. *JHB*, 1695-1702: 11, 69, 88, 94, 101-02; 1702/3-1712: 99, 309; 1712-1726: 266-67, 278; 1752-1758: 202, 226; Hening, *Statutes*, 3: 126-28, 164; 6: 435-40.

48. *JHD*, May 1779: 53, 63, 70; October 1779: 10, 13; May 1780: 18; May 1781: 4, 7, 9, 26, 27, 35; Hening, *Statutes*, 9: 375; 10: 287; see the correspondence in *Official Letters of the Governors of the State of Virginia*, ed. Henry R. McIlwaine, 3 vols. (Richmond, 1926-29), 1: 76-77, 117-18; 2: 33-34, 250-53; 3: 293, 339-40.

49. Charles S. Sydnor, *Gentlemen Freeholders* (Chapel Hill, N.C., 1952), esp. ch. 2; Lucille B. Griffith, *The Virginia House of Burgesses, 1750-1774*, Rev. ed. (University, Ala., 1970), chs. 3-6; Brown and Brown, *Virginia 1705-1786*, ch. 8. The election laws of 1705, 1762, and 1785 are in Hening, *Statutes*, 3: 236-46; 7: 517-30; 12: 120-29.

50. *JHB*, 1712-1726: 259-60, 275, 294; 1727-1740: 9; 1742-1749: 7; 1752-1758: 344; 1766-1769: 190; 1773-1776: 10; *JHD*, 1789 (1828 reprint): 6, 7, 8, 38, 67-68; 1793: 9-10, 60-61, 66.

51. *JHB*, 1727-1740: 246, 250, 282, 298-99.

52. *JHB*, 1752-1758: 15, 18, 41, 58, 62; Jack P. Greene, ed., *Diary of Landon Carter of Sabine Hall, 1752-1778*, 2 vols. (Charlottesville, Va., 1965), 1: 73-74.

53. *JHB*, 1702/3-1712: 245, 256-57; 1712-1726: 259-60, 270, 275, 294; 1727-1740: 15-16; 1742-1749: 334; 1752-1758: 62, 160; *JHD*, 1789 (1828 reprint): 7, 20, 36, 38, 67-68; 1797: 7, 10-11, 14, 44, 51; 1798: 9, 25.

54. Examples of elections overturned as a result of petitions can easily be found in the *Journals*—for a few cases, see: *JHB*, 1702/3-1712: 245, 256-57; 1712-1726: 260, 270, 294; 1742-1749: 334-35; 1752-1758: 62, 160; *JHD*, 1793: 9-10, 60-61, 66; 1798: 9, 25.

55. *JHB*, 1766-1769: 203, 246, 269; 1770-1772: 107; Hening, *Statutes*, 8: 371-74; John Duffy, *Epidemics in Colonial America* (Baton Rouge, La., 1953), pp. 7-10, 16-17, 24-26, 35-41, 99-100. See the discussions of the Norfolk riots in: Pauline Maier, "Popular Uprisings and Civil Authority in Eighteenth-Century America," *WMQ*, 3rd ser. 27 (January 1970): 6-7; Patrick Henderson, "Smallpox and Patriotism: The Norfolk Riots, 1768-1769," *VMHB* 73 (October 1965): 413-24.

56. Brown and Brown, *Virginia 1705-1786*, pp. 83-92; C. Ray Keim, "Primogeniture and Entail in Colonial Virginia," *WMQ*, 3rd ser. 25 (October 1968): 545-86. For the old view, see Ambler, *Sectionalism in Virginia*, p. 33.

57. Hening, *Statutes*, 3: 320; 4: 400; Gooch to Board of Trade, 20 November 1734, *CSPC*, no. 389, 41: 301-02.

58. *JHB*, 1712-1726: 268, 269, 316; 1727-1740: 299; 1758-1761: 138; 1770-

1772: 9, 108; 1773-1776: 16, 36, 83; Hening, *Statutes*, 4: 95, 534-37; 7: 157, 159, 293, 343, 377, 440, 455, 458, 478, 480, 483, 488, 514, 628, 634; 8: 468-70, 665.

59. Hening, *Statutes*, 9: 226-27; Malone, *Jefferson the Virginian*, pp. 251-57; Brown and Brown, *Virginia 1705-1786*, pp. 286-87.

60. Two excellent descriptions of the procedure are: *JHB*, 1758-1761: xvii-xviii; Stanley M. Pargellis, "The Procedure of the Virginia House of Burgesses," *WMQ*, 2d ser. 7 (April and July, 1927): 144-45. For examples of the claims presented to the house by petition, see the first several pages of the *Journal* for any session.

61. *JHB*, 1712-1726: 324; 1727-1740: 425; 1752-1758: 27, 31; 1766-1769: 39, 42; 1770-1772: 158-59, 166, 168; 1773-1776: 98, 189, 192; *JHD*, October 1783: 95; Greene, ed., *Diary of Landon Carter*, 1: 119; Hening, *Statutes*, 6: 107; see the petition and supporting documents presented by Thomas Patterson in 1774, reprinted in "Miscellaneous Colonial Documents," *VMHB* 18 (July 1910): 279-81.

62. *JHD*, 1792: 179; see the similar vote in 1800—*JHD*, 1799: 84.

63. Hening, *Statutes*, 9: 245-46; *JHD*, October 1777: 12, 18; October 1780: 55; May 1784: 92, 120; 1787 (1828 reprint): 8, 18, 40; 1788 (1828 reprint): 58.

7 PETITIONS AND RELIGIOUS AFFAIRS

During the eighteenth century, as in the preceding one, religion played
a major role in the lives of many Virginians. The importance of spiritual
concerns was reflected not only in the daily lives of individuals, but also
in the laws and institutions of the day. The Church of England was the
established church during the colonial period, although after 1689 the
colony generally tolerated dissenters so long as they obeyed colonial
laws and caused no disturbances. Since Virginia contained relatively few
dissenters before 1740, the church-state relationship did not become a
heated issue until the Revolutionary period. Within this Anglican framework, a significant degree of colonial religious autonomy resulted from
a combination of the distance from England, the rural pattern of settlement, and the colonial desire for the maximum degree of local control
over religious matters. Most religious questions—ranging from the location of chapels to the degree of toleration afforded dissenters—were determined within the colony, and in these determinations the wishes of local
citizens as expressed in their petitions played a major role.[1]

As in England, the parish was the basic ecclesiastical unit of the established church. A vestry governed each parish; while originally elected,
usually from among the most prominent parishioners, vestries became
self-perpetuating until they were dissolved by the colonial government
and new elections were held. Vestries were also responsible for a number
of secular as well as religious duties, particularly in the field of poor relief.
In each parish a tract of land, known as a glebe, was provided for the
support of the minister, and the vestry levied taxes upon parish inhabitants
to finance the minister's salary, poor relief, and other expenses.[2]

Overall supervision of religious life in general, and of the Anglican
Church in particular, was theoretically shared by the royal governor and
by the bishop of London through his agent, the commissary. England
instructed royal governors to "take especial care that God Almighty Be
devoutly and duly served" by insuring that Virginia follow the rites and
rituals of the Church of England, build and maintain churches in good

repair, and provide ministers a suitable maintenance.[3] The commissary could call conventions of the clergy and was supposed to supervise the character of ministers, and as he normally was a member of the council, he could offer advice to the governor concerning religious matters. His authority extended only to the clergy as individuals, however, and institutional supervision continued in the hands of the governor.[4]

Despite the great theoretical grants of ecclesiastical power given to the governor and commissary, in actual practice the local vestries retained a considerable degree of autonomy. Moreover, the status and organization of the church had from the beginning in 1619 been defined by legislation enacted by the assembly, and in eighteenth-century Virginia general authority to regulate church affairs progressively shifted into the hands of the legislature.[5] This development was part and parcel of the broader "quest for power" by which all of the colonial assemblies won considerable control over internal policy even before the Revolution. Laws to divide parishes or alter their boundaries, to dissolve vestries and to conduct new elections, and to overturn unpopular vestry actions became increasingly common after 1700 and almost always originated from the petitions of Virginia citizens.

Colonial Virginia generally computed the size of a parish in terms of population rather than geography, for it was essential to include within each parish a sufficient number of taxpayers to bear the necessary expenses. Particularly during the seventeenth century, but in some areas even in the eighteenth, settlement was so scattered that parish boundaries incorporated extensive tracts of land. In the early years settlement had concentrated along the rivers, which furnished a convenient transportation network. The original parishes thus often extended for great distances along these rivers. As settlement spread inland thereafter, or as settlement in frontier parishes expanded westward, many parishes grew to very inconvenient sizes. Some included an entire county, while others stretched across parts of several counties. In 1724 Lawne's Creek Parish was reportedly 120 miles long and 10 miles wide; Southwalk Parish was 20 miles by 100; and several others were almost as large. This pattern of settlement presented the church, and local parishioners, with a dilemma. In a large parish several "chapels of ease" were often constructed, but there was only one resident minister. The minister traveled among his churches, performing at each in turn and allowing lay readers to lead the services at the other chapels. In this and all his other clerical functions, then, even the most dedicated man faced tremendous difficulties in ministering the needs of his flock. Yet a parish smaller in geographic size, and therefore more convenient, sometimes contained too few taxpayers to support parish services without an excessively high levy per taxpayer.[6]

The remedy for such difficulties involved dividing large parishes into smaller ones whenever the population had grown sufficiently to give each an adequate tax base. As was the case with creation of new counties, however, local taxpayers did not always agree upon the time or manner for such divisions. This continuing compromise between convenience and expense produced many heated contests among Virginia parishioners.

The General Assembly exercised the power of dividing parishes or altering parish boundaries during most of the colonial period. Most of the standard secondary accounts suggest that the colonial assembly always did so,[7] but authority to create new parishes actually passed through three distinct stages. In the first period, which lasted from the formal establishment of the first parishes in the early seventeenth century until 1674, parishes were divided, combined, or otherwise altered by the assembly. Surviving records are fragmentary, but they do indicate that such action was frequently a response to petitions from local inhabitants. In this fashion the legislature delineated the boundaries of Lynnhaven Parish in 1643, created Marston Parish from the upper part of Hampton Parish in 1654, and established Southwark and Stratton Major parishes in 1647 and 1655 respectively.[8] In several instances during this period, economy-minded inhabitants petitioned to combine two small parishes into a single, larger one. The assembly created Middletown Parish in 1658, for example, when citizens in the parishes of Harrop and Middle Plantation petitioned for consolidation, and Lancaster and Peanckatanck parishes were combined in 1666 into Christ Church Parish.[9] In a few cases the assembly delegated the responsibility for creating new parishes to the county courts. Captain Thomas Pritchard petitioned the assembly in 1656 that the inhabitants of Nuttmeg Quarters Parish desired that it be combined with Denbigh Parish. Uncertain that Pritchard's petition did in fact have widespread support, the assembly ordered the next county court to conduct an election and to perform the consolidation only if the majority of parishioners voted to do so. The 1656 assembly also authorized the courts of certain new counties to establish the local parishes. In these cases, however, the county courts clearly acted as agents for the assembly and possessed no independent power to act.[10]

In the second period, which lasted from 1674 to 1713, the authority to create new parishes vacillated between the governor and the assembly. Charles II, who in 1649 and 1669 granted to a group of cronies certain proprietary rights to the Northern Neck, further alienated Virginians in 1674 by granting such rights over the remainder of the colony to Lords Arlington and Culpeper. Among the terms in this 1674 grant was a statement that the proprietors could establish necessary towns, counties, and parishes.[11] Such authority conflicted, of course, with that exercised by the royal government then functioning in the colony. Perhaps the conflict was resolved in English eyes when Lord Culpeper was appointed governor of Virginia shortly thereafter. The commission took effect upon the death of Governor Berkeley, although Culpeper did not arrive in Virginia until 1680.[12] Culpeper had by 1683 purchased the remaining proprietary rights both to the Northern Neck and to the rest of the colony from Lord Arlington. But his chronic absence from Virginia cost him his governorship in 1683, and Culpeper then sold most of his claims back to the king, retaining only the quitrents and escheats from the Northern Neck.[13]

Although revocation of the Arlington-Culpeper grant resolved the potential conflict between royal and proprietary rights, it did not end the clash with previous colonial practice involving the establishment of parishes. In the latter part of the seventeenth century, the authorities in London began to define much more carefully the commercial and colonial policy of the empire and to implement that policy.[14] The instructions issued by the Lords of Trade in 1683 to the new royal governor of Virginia, Lord Effingham, reflected the new interest in central supervision. For the first time, a royal governor of the colony was specifically directed "to see the laws for support of the ministry enforced; to limit the parishes and eject scandalous ministers."[15] During the remainder of the colonial period, the instructions of Virginia governors included the sentence: "And you are to take care that the parishes be so limited and settled as you shall find most convenient for the accomplishing this good work."[16] Exactly how much thought went into this statement by English authorities is uncertain, and they provided no clarification as to whether the governor was now to possess *exclusive* authority to settle parish boundaries or was to continue sharing it with the assembly. If the latter was to be the case, however, there would seem to have been no need to add such a statement to the instructions. But for the governor to exercise this power alone, or even to do so with the advice of his council, would radically alter the previous practice by rendering division of parishes an executive rather than a legislative function.

That such was in fact the original intention is suggested at least by the other English innovations of the early 1680s. Three significant features of the new policy affecting Virginia were the coerced enactment of legislation to provide the royal governor with a permanent revenue independent of legislative action (the two-shilling duty on tobacco exports), the loss of the assembly's previous position as the supreme court of appeal in the colony, and Effingham's assertion of sole authority to set the boundaries of counties. Culpeper's infamous 1680 commission and instructions had even required prior English consent before the assembly could convene and had eliminated the right of the lower house to initiate legislation. Those two provisions had proven so impractical, however, that Culpeper had ignored them from the beginning, and England soon repealed them.[17] Nevertheless, if these new features of policy may be taken as an indication, after 1674 England originally intended for the governor to assume the power of creating or altering parishes.

Because the governor's instructions concerning parish boundaries were so vague, confusion apparently resulted in Virginia from the failure of English officials to clarify their intentions. As a result, for the next several years parishes were created or altered on some occasions by the assembly and on other occasions by the governor and council. On April 29, 1679, the governor and council granted a petition from Blisland Parish for a division, and they intervened ten years later to settle a boundary dispute between Blisland and St. Peter's parishes.[18] Moreover, an act passed by the assembly in 1696 specifically authorized the governor to consolidate small parishes upon the application of the respective vestries, and the governor and council exercised the authority granted in that act on at least one occasion in 1707.[19] Yet in 1680, just a year after the governor and council authorized division of Blisland Parish, the assembly used a joint resolution to grant a petition from "the Inhabitants of *Pamunkey* Neck praying that they be made a Parish," and the boundary between St. Peter's and St. John's parishes was altered by statute in 1691.[20]

With the exception of action taken under the 1696 act allowing the governor to consolidate small parishes upon their application, authority to establish or alter parishes seems to have reverted back to the assembly by the 1690s. The instructions sent from England still contained the same wording, but in practice any attempt to exclude the lower house from the process was abandoned. The reasons for this must unfortunately remain a matter of speculation, but several factors apparently were involved. England was in the 1690s involved in a major European war, with the threat of a Jacobite Restoration backed by French arms hanging over its head. Under such conditions the attention of English authorities naturally focused upon the more important questions of national and imperial security, and we might well imagine that the issue of who had the authority to establish new parishes in Virginia fell well down on the list of English priorities. For its part, the House of Burgesses had reacted strongly to Effingham's assertions of increased executive power, and in the 1690s it must have welcomed the opportunity to restore some of its former privileges and powers. Colonel Francis Nicholson, who served as royal governor from 1690 to 1692 and again from 1698 to 1705, was an ardent friend of the Anglican Church, and he earnestly sought to improve the state of religion in Virginia. For the good of the church, and perhaps also because of his reluctance to strengthen the power of the great men who sat on the council, Nicholson may well have been willing to accept the traditional method of establishing parishes by legislative act.[21]

For whatever reason, the power of the legislature to establish or alter parishes went unchallenged for twenty years after 1690. Even the 1696 act authorizing the governor to consolidate small parishes under certain conditions was in itself an assertion of the general authority of the assembly, since it obviously could not delegate authority which it did not possess. For his part, Governor Nicholson strongly believed that a number of Virginia parishes required alteration for the greater convenience of church members. Significantly, Nicholson sent a message to the house in 1701 urging the burgesses to consider the need for such alterations. Equally significant was the house response that such action should be undertaken only "when representation is made from Counties or Parishes that they are aggrieved."[22] The house did act upon those petitions which it received, as in 1704 when parishioners in St. Peter's Parish of New Kent County requested a division. The burgesses accepted the proposal as suggested by the petitioners, and a bill for carrying out their request passed the house without difficulty and was enacted into law by the assembly. But the house refused to accept a 1705 petition seeking a division from the "housekeepers and freeholders" of the upper part of St. Stephen's Parish. The Committee of Propositions and Grievances reported that the petition contained few signatures, that the upper end was still thinly populated, as two-thirds of the parishioners lived in the lower part of the parish, and that the county burgesses insisted that division was unpopular. The house then rejected the petition.[23]

So things remained until the arrival in 1710 of Alexander Spotswood as the new royal governor of Virginia. Spotswood's character and exalted view of the royal prerogative were discussed in chapter 4 in relation to his unsuccessful efforts at securing executive rather than legislative control over the creation of new counties. Since his instructions contained the provision regarding parish boundaries, Spotswood felt even more certain of his authority in this area than in regard to county boundaries. When the dispute arose in 1710 over the refusal of the burgesses to comply with his wishes on county boundaries, Spotswood announced that division of both counties and parishes was a branch of the royal prerogative and was to be abandoned by the house.[24] Even so, Spotswood felt compelled to justify his conduct to the Board of Trade and to seek its advice. He reported that controversies over proposals to divide parishes often caused "Partys and Factions" to arise during elections, and although such divisions had previously been enacted by the assembly, his instructions seemed to render this an executive matter. The governor would be the most impartial judge of such disputes, Spotswood continued, and thus the people would benefit:

> Yet because my Predecessors (tho' they had the same Instruc-
> tion) have hitherto allowed this matter to be handled and deter-
> mined by the Assembly, I humbly desire Yo'r Lord'ps' directions
> therein, for as I resolved never to suffer any encroachments
> on her maj'ties Prerogative, So on the other hand I would very
> unwillingly be engaged in a dispute with the Assembly unless it
> be thought worth the contending for.[25]

As in the case of county division, the English authorities apparently decided that the matter was not "worth the contending for," and they did not even respond to Spotswood's request for further instructions. By 1713 he felt compelled to capitulate. When the assembly met, it received a petition from the vestry of St. Mary's Parish in Essex and Richmond counties. The petition expressed the earnest desire of the parishioners for a division as the only remedy for the present inconveniences. The house ordered the burgesses of Essex and Richmond to prepare a bill

as requested by the petitioners, and the bill quickly passed its three readings in the house. Spotswood and the council accepted the bill; when
signed into law in 1713, it signified the final confirmation of the Assembly's
authority in such matters.[26] The governor explained to the Board of
Trade that "having receiv'd no answer from y'r Lo'ps [your Lordships]
to what I writt concerning the power of bounding and dividing Countys
and parishes, I could no longer resist the importunity of the People in
this Case."[27] Spotswood did succeed in getting an amendment to the bill
stating that such applications ought first to be given to the governor, but
even he must have recognized that this face-saving device would prove
meaningless. When the upper inhabitants of St. John's Parish in King
William County petitioned for division in 1718, and the lower inhabitants
counterpetitioned against any division, Spotswood merely referred their
petitions to the house without comment. The house referred the matter
to the next session in order to allow more time for investigation. At the
next session, the burgesses passed a bill to divide the parish in a manner
intended to satisfy both groups, and the governor and council accepted
the bill without question. Several other parishes were divided by statute
in 1720 as a direct response to petitions. Soon even Spotswood's clause
for having such petitions first go to the governor was abandoned.[28]

In the third period, from 1713 to the final separation of church and
state after the Revolution, authority to divide or alter parishes was again
lodged firmly in the hands of the legislature. Spotswood's successors for
the next quarter century, Hugh Drysdale (1722-1726) and William Gooch
(1727-1749), were both even-tempered and popular gentlemen who lacked
the fiery Scotsman's exalted notions of prerogative. Drysdale and Gooch
cooperated with the assembly rather than challenging it, and they had no
inclination whatever to renew a contest where even Spotswood had been
forced to surrender. The Drysdale-Gooch approach was perfectly in keeping with the contemporary English attitude of "salutary neglect" held by
the duke of Newcastle and his colleagues in London. In this circumstance
the lower house's "quest for power" gained momentum, and unchallenged
legislative control over creation of parishes was one of the fruits of victory.[29]

Division of parishes after 1713 almost invariably was a direct response
to petitions from local inhabitants. On many occasions parishioners agreed
among themselves on the need for such action, and in those cases the
house had little difficulty in granting the request. Thus in 1734 the inhabitants of Henrico Parish petitioned that the parish was too large. The

petitioners asked that the parish be divided along the James River, with
the territory on the north side to become a separate parish and that on
the south side to be joined with a portion of Bristol Parish to create
another. Investigation by the Committee of Propositions and Grievances
failed to discover any sign of local opposition, and the law enacted as a
result contained the exact boundary desired by the petitioners.[30] The
assembly divided St. Mark's Parish in 1752 exactly as desired by the uncontested petition of "the minister, vestry, and other inhabitants" of the
parish, and petitioners in St. Paul's Parish (1726) and St. James's Parish
(1744) likewise had no difficulty since there was agreement among local
parishioners.[31] Similarly, the uncontested 1773 petition of the vestry
in Dale Parish successfully led to an alteration in the parish boundaries.
Manchester Parish had recently been created from a portion of Dale, but
by that division the new parish was given too much of the territory and
too many of the tithables; Dale Parish was left too small to bear the
necessary expenses. The burgesses proved responsive when committee
investigation failed to uncover local opposition, and the law enacted by
the assembly granted exactly the new boundary desired by the petitioners.[32]

The house had greater difficulty responding to such petitions when
significant local opposition to the proposed division appeared in the form
of counterpetitions. Writing in 1724, Hugh Jones noted that, in many
cases, "works of this nature, where great numbers are concerned, are not
affected without great opposition and difficulty."[33] A 1720-1723 controversy over a proposed dissolution of Wilmington Parish in James City and
Charles City counties illustrates the difficulties sometimes encountered.
The affair began with a 1720 petition to the house which asked that the
parish be dissolved and added to adjacent parishes in order to save money.
Since the house received the petition too late in the session to act upon
the request, it referred the petition to the next session. At the next session,
in 1722, the house actually passed a bill for dissolving the parish, but the
bill died in a dispute between the house and the council over proposed
amendments.[34]

The issue heated up considerably at the 1723 session, when parishioners
supporting dissolution sent four separate petitions to the burgesses; the
petitioners living below Hooker's Mill asked to be added to James City
Parish, for example, while those living above Diascum Creek, on the north
side of "Chicohominy" River, asked to be joined to St. Peter's Parish in
New Kent County. The house then appointed a select committee to

investigate the matter thoroughly. All seven members on the committee
came from the counties and borough involved—James City, Charles City,
New Kent, and Jamestown—and the house gave them complete authority
"to send for persons papers & Records for their Information." The burgesses
soon received at least three more petitions, this time from parishioners
firmly opposed to dissolution. The emotional atmosphere apparently
clouded the judgment of one group of petitioners, for the house condemned their petition for being "drawn up in terms very rude and indecent." The burgesses then ordered the petition to be "torn and Thrown
under the Table." After what Governor Drysdale described, with considerable understatement, as "a full hearing of all parties concerned," the
select committee reported in favor of dissolving Wilmington and adding
the parts to the neighboring parishes. A bill for that purpose then passed
the house, was amended slightly by the council, and was signed into law
by the governor. Even then the affair had not ended, for by the dissolution the minister of Wilmington Parish would lose his job. The council
amendment had postponed final dissolution for two years so that the
governor could seek a new job for the minister. As late as mid-1724,
however, the minister was still threatening to seek English intervention
to nullify the law. Governor Drysdale was thus forced to send the Board
of Trade a detailed justification explaining that the act was desired by,
and would benefit, at least three-fourths of the parish residents.[35]

Sizable and vocal opposition could prove fatal to a proposal for division, as inhabitants of Drysdale Parish discovered in 1744. Drysdale
stretched across parts of King and Queen County and Caroline County,
and some parishioners felt that division was required. Many others remained unconvinced, however, and their counterpetition persuaded the
Committee of Propositions and Grievances to report against division.
The house agreed with the committee and rejected the request for division. So the matter remained for thirty-five years, until in 1779 inhabitants from the western end of the parish tried again. Though citizens
in the eastern part of the parish sent two counterpetitions, this time the
house accepted the need for division, and such a bill was enacted into
law by the assembly. The law specifically stated that it was a response
to the petition, and it accepted without alteration the boundary desired
by the petitioners. The parishioners in the eastern end of Drysdale were
not totally defeated, however, as they were allowed to keep the larger
church building without making compensation to the new parish.[36] The

TABLE 9   SUCCESSFUL PETITIONS REGARDING PARISH
BOUNDARIES

Session	Number of Boundary Alterations	Number of New Parishes Created
1720	2	2
1730	0	2
1740	0	1
1752	1	2
1761 (March)	0	5
1769 (November)	1	6
1780 (October)	1	0
1790	0	1
Total	5	19

house often sought a compromise acceptable to both parties in such cases,
as in the 1723 dispute over a proposal to divide St. Stephen's Parish in
King and Queen County. The upper inhabitants wanted a division, but
the lower inhabitants opposed or at least wanted a dividing line west
of that proposed by the upper inhabitants. The Committee of Propositions
and Grievances reported in favor of a compromise line, the house accepted
the report, and St. Stephen's was divided.[37]

The extent to which the house responded to petitions regarding creation or alteration of parishes is indicated in table 9. The table surveys the
period after 1713 to the final separation of church and state at the end
of the century, when the legislature abandoned its authority over parish
affairs.

Legislative supervision of parish affairs extended beyond determination of boundaries. Because of the considerable powers and responsibilities
exercised within each parish by the local vestry, occasional disputes inevitably arose between vestrymen and other parishioners. Vestries were
composed of members of the local elite, and most behaved responsibly.
Yet on some occasions parishioners indicted vestrymen with a host of
charges, ranging from illegal election, poor health, and senility to factionalism, bad judgment, and outright fraud. Such disputes were perhaps

less significant in the early seventeenth century than later because a new election of vestry members by parishioners was held every three years; unpopular vestrymen could then be voted out of office. After 1662, however, each vestry became a self-perpetuating body until dissolved by some superior authority and a new vestry was elected.[38] The lines of jurisdiction for exercising such supervisory authority were quite unsettled in the seventeenth and early eighteenth centuries, as the governor and council, the assembly, and even the county courts all dissolved vestries or overturned vestry actions at various times.[39]

This overlapping jurisdiction was particularly noticeable in the early eighteenth century. The 1708 election of a new vestry in Charles Parish left many parishioners so dissatisfied that they petitioned the governor and council to overturn the "undue and irregular" election. When their investigation confirmed the charges of voting irregularities, the governor and council ordered a new election to be held. The new election also sparked heated controversy, expressed in a new wave of petitions and counterpetitions, but this time the governor and council upheld the results.[40] Similarly, a 1732 petition signed by "the greater part of the Freeholders & Inhabitants" of St. John's Parish in King William County asked the governor and council to overturn a recent decision made by the vestry. Originally two churches were to be constructed in the parish, but the vestry then decided instead to authorize only one church, to be built near the center of the parish. When the governor and council examined a map of the parish, they agreed with the petitioners that two chapels were necessary because of the distance involved in traveling from the extremes to the center of the parish. The vestry was ordered to carry out the original plan and construct two churches "in the most convenient places in the sd parish for the general Ease of the Inhabitants."[41] A 1705 law provided also that all vestrymen could be prosecuted in the General Court "for the breach of any penal law, relating to their office."[42]

For its part, the house had always taken part in enacting statutes for establishing church regulations in the colony. Although the burgesses stated in 1695 that vestry elections lay outside their jurisdiction, they acted in 1699 and in 1703 to overturn arbitrary actions by the vestries in Lower Norfolk and Westmoreland counties respectively.[43] In 1720 a group of parishioners in Accomack County petitioned the house to ask that the vestry be required to build the new church near the center of the county rather than at the location selected by the vestrymen. The house then passed a bill for that purpose and the council agreed also, but

Governor Spotswood withheld his assent. Spotswood felt that other
parishioners might not have been aware of the proceedings, and he persuaded the assembly to postpone the matter to the next session in order
to insure that all parties could be heard. The next session, meeting in
1722, reconsidered the affair and again passed a bill requiring the vestry
to construct the church near the center of the county. This time Spotswood agreed, and the bill became law.[44] Similarly, in 1728 a number
of inhabitants in Elizabeth City Parish petitioned the house to complain
of the "arbitrary & illegal proceedings" of the vestry. When investigation by the Committee of Propositions and Grievances substantiated the
charges, a bill to dissolve the present vestry and elect a new one was prepared. The bill quickly passed both houses of the legislature and was
signed by Governor Gooch. In explaining the act to the Board of Trade,
Gooch observed that the complaint had been widespread among local
parishioners, that investigation confirmed the charges, and that he
deemed it advisable to yield to "popular Humours" in such cases.[45]
Yet, as mentioned above, the governor and council continued to exercise
similar authority at least into the 1730s.

By mid-century, however, control over such matters had settled firmly
into the hands of the legislature, which then regularly dissolved vestries
or overturned unpopular vestry actions. Almost invariably such action
was taken directly in response to petitions from local parishioners. Irate
inhabitants of Frederick Parish petitioned the house in 1752 to charge
the vestry with misapplication of parish funds. The vestry had collected
more than £1570 in taxes for the purpose of building and equipping new
churches. The house investigation confirmed that at least some of the
money had instead been used by the vestry for private purposes while
the half-finished chapels decayed for lack of weatherboarding. The petitioners asked that the present vestry be dissolved and forced to restore
the misappropriated money to the parish. The law enacted by the assembly
did exactly that, with a new vestry to be elected and the churchwardens
to bring suit if necessary to recover the missing funds.[46] The assembly
dissolved many other vestries following accusations by petitioners of
"irregular Election," "inconvenient and illegal actions," and "unwarrant-
able proceedings." Some vestries sent counterpetitions in defense of
their conduct, but others agreed that a new election was necessary. A
1772 petition from the vestry of St. John's Parish in King William County
admitted that the members were "divided among themselves by Party
Spirit, which prevents their meetings [and] interrupts their proceedings

in the affairs of the Parish. . . ."[47] The assembly continued to exercise its authority in such matters until final separation of church and state at the end of the century, at which time the composition and activities of Episcopal vestries became a concern of that particular denomination rather than a matter for legislative supervision.

This procedure for dividing parishes and dissolving vestries or nullifying their actions was extremely significant. It made regulation of parish affairs much more responsive to popular wishes than might be suggested merely by the institutional composition, authority, and tenure of the vestry. In form, parish government was controlled by a few members of the local elite. Yet in practice the petitions of local parishioners played a major role in creating parishes or altering parish boundaries and in reversing arbitrary or unpopular vestry conduct. As a result, despite the theoretically undemocratic features of parish government, the public interest was safeguarded and considerable popular participation was encouraged.

Finally, in the years immediately before and after the Revolution, religious issues produced perhaps the most significant and widespread use of petitions in all of Virginia history. At stake was the disestablishment of the Anglican Church and the transition from mere toleration of dissenters to complete religious freedom. In this struggle the leadership of enlightened statesmen such as James Madison and Thomas Jefferson received the absolutely indispensable support of a massive petitioning campaign waged by thousands of Virginia citizens. This struggle for religious freedom produced widespread internal controversy in the Revolutionary period, and it has been described in great detail by numerous historians.[48]

By 1750 Virginia included a large number of dissenters, especially Presbyterians and Baptists, and the numbers continued to grow at an accelerating pace. Along the frontier, in the Shenandoah Valley and beyond, dissenters far outnumbered Anglicans. Even the Valley vestries were frequently dominated by dissenters, and except in the center of Anglican strength near Winchester, there were few Anglican chapels to be found. Many western dissenters had been encouraged to migrate to the colony by Virginia's policy of offering them great toleration—regardless of their Presbyterian beliefs, hardy Scotch-Irish settlers would prove valuable in the defense of Virginia's frontiers from the French and Indians. Yet even though the dissenter strength was proportionally strongest in the West, by the 1750-1776 period dissenters had made substantial gains even in the traditional Anglican stronghold east of the Blue Ridge. Under the able and active leadership of ministers like the Presbyterians' Samuel

Davies and the Baptists' John Leland, strong dissenter communities
sought their spiritual salvation outside the established church in such
counties as Hanover, Henrico, Lancaster, Caroline, Westmoreland, Lunenburg, and many others.[49]

Following enactment of the famous Toleration Act of 1689, dissenters
in England enjoyed a regulated toleration. Since English legislation passed
after 1607 applied in the colonies only when Parliament specifically included provisions to that effect, Virginia confirmed its acceptance of
toleration by enacting a similar law in 1699. Dissenters were exempted
from required attendance at Anglican churches, and they were allowed
to maintain their own churches and ministers provided that the locations
were registered and the ministers were licensed by the government.
Originally such licenses were obtained from the county courts, but by
mid-eighteenth century the governor and council had assumed that function. Such requirements permitted dissenter congregations to exist undisturbed, but they did prohibit the activities of itinerant ministers.
Moreover, as was the case in the Anglican Church, there were not enough
dissenter ministers to serve each of the scattered churches; consequently,
ministers sought licenses to preach at several congregations. Samuel Davies
secured official permission to serve Presbyterian churches in five different counties, but the steady growth of dissenter strength alarmed some
champions of the Anglican establishment and led to a crackdown on such
practices. Other forms of legal discrimination existed as well. Dissenting
ministers were not allowed to perform marriage ceremonies, though in
practice "gentlemen's agreements" were sometimes arranged whereby
the dissenting minister conducted marriages but gave the fees to his
Anglican counterpart. In addition to these restrictions, like all other parish
inhabitants the dissenters paid the annual parish levy which was used to
provide local services and to support the Anglican Church. Since this requirement forced dissenters to provide financial support for doctrines and
practices which they rejected, and since they also had to support their
own churches, by 1776 they were determined to end the practice.[50]

The issue of the church-state relationship became increasingly critical
after 1768, when legal persecution of some itinerant New Light Baptist
ministers commenced. Between 1768 and 1774 perhaps as many as thirty
were jailed on charges of "disturbing the peace," since they refused to
obtain licenses and insisted upon their right to conduct an evangelical
ministry free from secular interference.[51] In 1774 the young James
Madison had just returned to Virginia after obtaining his college educa-

tion at Princeton under the tutelage of John Witherspoon. There he was much influenced by Witherspoon's defense of religious freedom. After observing the persecution of some local dissenters, Madison wrote to a college friend: "That diabolical, hell-conceived principle of persecution rages among some; and to their eternal infamy the clergy can furnish their quota of imps for such business. . . . So I must beg you to pity me, and pray for liberty of conscience to all."[52]

Nevertheless, the movement which would soon destroy the religious establishment was already under way. The house created a new standing committee, the Committee on Religion, in 1769 and quickly instructed it to draw up a new toleration bill. Conflict with England and internal uncertainties and disagreements concerning the degree to which toleration should be extended prevented any final action on the measure. But already by 1776 a growing number of dissenter petitions demanded increased toleration—and a few even expressed the conviction that only complete religious freedom would be an acceptable solution.[53]

A giant step in the direction of religious freedom was taken by the Virginia Convention which met in May 1776, and proceeded to adopt a state constitution and a Declaration of Rights. Any bill of rights had to include some statement concerning religion. Dissenter wishes in this regard were expressed in a 20 June 1776 petition to the convention from the Baptist church in Prince William County. In this petition the Baptists asked for full religious freedom, and they concluded the petition with an implied threat: "that, *these things granted* [italics mine], they will gladly unite with their brethren, and to the utmost of their ability promote the common cause."[54] After considerable debate between the more conservative members, such as Edmund Pendleton and Carter Braxton, and their more liberal colleagues, led particularly by Patrick Henry and George Mason, a constitution and Declaration of Rights were adopted. Mason wrote much of the declaration, but his original draft offered only "the fullest toleration in the exercise of religion." Under Madison's prodding, the final statement went much further:

That religion, or the duty which we owe to our CREATOR, and the manner of discharging it, can be directed only by reason and conviction, not by force or violence, and therefore all men are equally entitled to the free exercise of religion, accord-

ing to the dictates of conscience; and that it is the mutual duty
of all to practice Christian forebearance, love, and charity,
towards each other.[55]

The full significance of this statement remained a matter of heated controversy during the following decades, for the declaration did not specify
what alterations in the existing establishment would be required. Not until
1786, with the passage of Jefferson's celebrated "Bill for Religious Freedom," was the controversy finally resolved.

The first General Assembly which met under the new constitution, in
October of 1776, received a multitude of petitions seeking disestablishment. These included the famous "Ten-thousand Name" petition, nearly
two hundred feet long. A number of progressive leaders, most notably
Jefferson, had intended to take action anyway, but their efforts were
strengthened by the strong support of these widely circulated petitions.
Perhaps equally significant was the relative absence of protests from
Anglicans. Except for petitions from Anglican and Methodist ministers
and meetings in Charles City and Accomack counties, the established
church took surprisingly little action to prevent disestablishment.[56]

Nevertheless, the debate in the house produced what Jefferson later
described as "the severest contest in which I have ever been engaged."
The bill finally enacted into law did not go as far as Jefferson or most
dissenters wished. It did grant complete toleration to dissenters, ending
such requirements as the licensing of their ministers and repealing the
statutes which imposed penalties for not attending church. Dissenters
were also exempted from taxation to support the Anglican Church. But
compulsory taxation of Anglicans to support their church was only suspended, and it was not finally abolished until 1779. Finally, the legislature specifically deferred final judgment on the issue of voluntary religious
contributions versus a general tax assessment whereby each taxpayer would
designate the denomination to receive his support.[57] During the next few
years after 1776, dissenter petitions secured additional concessions, such
as legal recognition of marriages performed by dissenting ministers.[58]
With this legislation an important step towards complete religious freedom
was taken, but the final goal was still to be achieved.

After 1776 the religious question centered upon two alternatives.
Virginia could enact the general assessment in support of Christianity,
or the state could complete the process of disestablishment and provide

for full religious freedom. Deciding between these two alternatives required a full decade of heated debate. The general assessment scheme
had the support of the Anglican clergy, as well as the initial support of
some Presbyterian clergy, and of many political leaders, including Patrick
Henry, Richard Henry Lee, and Edmund Pendleton. These men denied
any intention of reestablishing the Protestant Episcopal Church (in 1784
the Anglican Church in Virginia was officially incorporated under this
new name) or of violating the Declaration of Rights; they were convinced,
however, that Christianity was the chief guardian of public morality and
required adequate financial assistance.[59]

The movement for complete religious freedom was led by Jefferson
and Madison, ably assisted by men like George Nicholas and George
Mason, and with the increasingly active support of petitioners seeking
the same end. Jefferson's "Bill for Religious Freedom" was written in
1777, first presented before the house in 1779, and widely distributed
throughout the state. In it Jefferson asserted, in majestic and sweeping
terms, the natural right of the human mind and spirit to remain free and
unshackled by restraints imposed by civil government.[60]

The proponents of a general assessment nearly won the struggle in 1784.
By a recorded vote of forty-seven to thirty-two, the Committee of the
whole House voted on November 11 in favor of such a measure, and the
House appointed a select committee to prepare the bill. Madison led the
opposition, but in mid-November he was writing to associates that some
form of assessment scheme seemed "probable."[61] The bill passed its
second reading by only two votes, however, and the election of Patrick
Henry as governor removed the ablest champion of an assessment from
the house. Moreover, though some petitioners had supported the concept,
others had opposed, and the house was uncertain of public sentiment
concerning the measure. By a vote of forty-five to thirty-eight the delegates finally decided to postpone consideration until the next session.
Copies of the bill, plus a tally of the vote for postponement, were distributed throughout the state. The house specifically asked the people
of Virginia to "signify their opinion respecting the adoption of such a
Bill."[62]

The decision to submit the issue directly to the people quickly produced
the most spectacular and successful example of direct popular influence
upon legislation in all of Virginia's history up to that time. Madison carefully reported the course of events to Jefferson and Monroe, both of

whom were out of the state on public business. He wrote to Monroe, in April 1785, that the "only proceeding of the late Session of Assembly which makes a noise thro' the Country is that which relates to a Genl. Assessmt." The dissenter laity were unanimously opposed, he added, while even the Episcopal laity were losing their enthusiasm for the measure. By June, Madison was reporting to Monroe: "A very warm opposition will be made to this innovation by the people of the middle and back counties, particularly the latter. They do not scruple to declare it an alarming usurpation on their fundamental rights. . . ."[63] Madison himself, at the urging of George Nicholas, wrote his famous "Remonstrance" against the assessment, and Nicholas, Mason, and several others began distributing copies of it throughout the state to secure as many signatures as possible. Other individuals and groups, particularly the dissenter denominations, took similar steps.[64]

When the assembly convened in October 1785, even the most ardent foes of the assessment were astonished at the public response. The legislature was flooded with an unprecedented number of petitions which clearly revealed public sentiment to be overwhelmingly opposed to adoption of the bill. Petitions against the bill came from fifty-one counties located in all sections of the state. Other petitions against the assessment came from Presbyterian societies and organizations, from the Baptist Association, and from groups of Quakers. Only ten counties (five in the Tidewater, five in the Piedmont) sent petitions in support of the assessment, and in nine of these ten counties other petitioners opposed the measure. Petitions opposing the assessment contained far more signatures than those favoring the bill. The house received at least thirteen copies of Madison's "Remonstrance," which included a total of over fifteen hundred signatures. Copies of another widely circulated petition, prepared by some equally zealous but anonymous opponent, contained almost five thousand signatures. All told, signatures on petitions opposed to the assessment outnumbered those on petitions in favor of it by a ten-to-one margin, approximately eleven thousand against to twelve hundred in favor.[65]

Analysis of the counties sending—and not sending—petitions is most instructive. The extensive opposition to the assessment was predictable in those areas where the dissenters were strongest. The Presbyterian Convention and the Baptist General Committee both issued strong statements against the assessment in 1785, and the Baptist General Committee specif-

○ FAYETTE   ○ MONONGALIA
○ GREENBRIER   ○ NELSON
○ HAMPSHIRE   ○ OHIO
○ HARRISON   ⊚ WASHINGTON
○ JEFFERSON   ⊚ ACCOMACK
○ LINCOLN   ○ NORTHAMPTON

⊚ Counties sending petitions against general assessment

▥ Counties sending petitions in favor of general assessment

⊜ Counties sending petitions both against and in favor of general assessment

○ Counties sending no petitions

FIGURE 2 PETITIONS CONCERNING GENERAL ASSESSMENT
BILL—OCTOBER 1785

ically asked fellow Baptists to petition against the bill. The flood of petitions from counties with sizable dissenter elements was thus to be expected. Valley counties like Augusta, Berkeley, and Rockbridge, Piedmont counties like Hanover, Orange, and Prince Edward, and Northern Neck counties like Westmoreland and Northumberland all had active dissenter congregations, and all sent extensively signed petitions against the assessment.[66] The counties where Nicholas and Mason conducted their campaign to circulate copies of Madison's "Remonstrance" (counties such as Fairfax, Prince William, Albemarle, Buckingham, and Culpeper) also responded in an impressive fashion.[67]

The failure of those western counties which later became Kentucky and West Virginia to send petitions apparently resulted from their isolation. When delegates from those counties returned home after the 1784 session, no general decision had yet been reached on precisely how the people should "signify their opinion" concerning the assessment. Not until the spring and summer of 1785 did opponents of the measure definitely decide upon a widespread petitioning campaign, and the counties in the Kentucky and West Virginia sections apparently did not receive notice of this decision. In addition, Kentucky's attention was distracted by its drive for independent statehood, and concentration upon that subject may have reduced awareness of events in the other sections of Virginia. Westerners evidently assumed that county delegates were to transmit local sentiment directly to the house. Certainly these counties vigorously opposed the assessment, as Madison and others had noted; delegates from the Kentucky and West Virginia sections, for example, voted eleven to nothing in favor of Jefferson's "Bill for Religious Freedom" at the 1785 session.[68]

Perhaps the most surprising feature of the petitioning campaign was the meager response in favor of the assessment, even from the eastern counties where Anglicanism was strongest. The Episcopal clergy and a few prominent laymen had supported the assessment plan from the beginning, but the 1785 petitions clearly revealed that the Episcopal laity did not share that enthusiasm. Only ten counties sent petitions in favor of the bill. Five of these were Southside counties, where Henry's influence was still strong, and the other five were Northern Neck and Tidewater counties. Yet in nine of these counties other petitioners protested against the bill. Moreover, even in the former Anglican strongholds of the Tidewater and Northern Neck, far more counties remained totally silent or opposed the assessment than supported it. Methodists, Baptists, and other dissenters had established congregations even in those counties, but some attempt must be made to explain the refusal of Anglicans to support the assessment scheme.

George Washington's response to Mason's inquiries revealed two reasons for this lack of support. Washington reported that he tended to support the assessment plan in principle, but the agitation which it had created was so great that he wished the issue had never been raised and would prefer to see it simply abandoned. Washington then expressed a conviction which may well have become increasingly common among former champions of the bill when he added that, given the great opposition to the measure, it could never be enforced and would only produce convulsions throughout the state.[69]

Finally, the economic problems of the 1780s undoubtedly played a major role in diminishing enthusiasm for *any* proposal which would result in higher taxes. The 1780s, with the declining tobacco prices and the heavy taxes required to fund the war debt, were unfavorable years for seeking popular support for compulsory church contributions. After 1779 both dissenters and Anglicans had been exempted from payment of levies, and the assessment plan would thus have reintroduced a tax measure. The very session of 1785 narrowly rejected a plan to postpone or reduce collection of existing taxes.[70]

In effect, then, a coalition of "enlightened" statesmen, dissenters, and overburdened taxpayers responded with a resounding "no" on the assessment issue. This overwhelming expression of public sentiment proved to be decisive, and the bill was quickly abandoned without even being brought to a vote. Madison then brought forward Jefferson's "Bill for Religious Freedom," which passed both the House (by a vote of seventy-four to twenty) and the Senate early in 1786 with only minor amendments. Another bill passed by the same session transferred the secular duties of the parish to triennially elected "overseers of the poor."[71] Minor details still remained to be settled, but with the victory in 1786 Virginia accepted the concept of complete religious freedom. As Madison always insisted, the petitions of Virginia citizens had played an indispensable role in the struggle.

Notes

1. After 1682, royal governors were instructed to permit "liberty of conscience" to all quiet and peaceable persons "Except Papists"—*Royal Instructions*

to British Colonial Governors, 1670-1776, ed. Leonard W. Labaree, 2 vols. (New York, 1935), no. 714, 2: 494; Henry Hartwell, James Blair, and Edward Chilton, *The Present State of Virginia, and the College,* ed. Hunter D. Farish (Williamsburg, 1940), p. 65; Robert Beverley, *History and Present State of Virginia,* ed. Louis B. Wright (Chapel Hill, N.C., 1947), p. 261; Hugh Jones, *The Present State of Virginia,* ed. Richard L. Morton (Chapel Hill, N.C., 1956), pp. 25, 125; Hamilton J. Eckenrode, "Separation of Church and State in Virginia," *Sixth Annual Report of the Library Board of the Virginia State Library, 1908-1909* (Richmond, 1910); George M. Brydon, *Virginia's Mother Church and the Political Conditions Under Which It Grew,* 2 vols. (Richmond, 1947-52); Rev. Sam. Davies to Dr. Doddridge, 20 October 1750, Robert Dinwiddie to the Bishop of London, 5 June 1752, [Anonymous] to the Bishop of London, 1 February 1754, The Clergy of Virginia to the Bishop of London, 25 February 1756, all in *Historical Collections Relating to the American Colonial Church,* ed. William S. Perry, Vol. 1: *Virginia* (Hartford, Conn., 1870), pp. 368-71, 395-96, 408, 445; Wesley M. Gewehr, *The Great Awakening in Virginia, 1740-1790* (Durham, N.C., 1930), pp. 34, 40-43, 52, 93-95, 101, 106; Robert E. Brown and B. Katherine Brown, *Virginia 1705-1786: Democracy or Aristocracy?* (East Lansing, Mich., 1964), ch. 11; William H. Seiler, "The Anglican Parish in Virginia," in *Seventeenth-Century America,* ed. James M. Smith (Chapel Hill, N.C., 1959), p. 141.

2. Hartwell, Blair, and Chilton, *Present State of Virginia,* pp. 65-67; Beverley, *History and Present State,* pp. 262-63; Park Rouse, Jr., *James Blair of Virginia* (Chapel Hill, N.C., 1971), p. 53; William H. Seiler, "The Anglican Parish Vestry in Colonial Virginia," *Journal of Southern History* 22 (August 1956): 314-15, 332-35; Virginia Bernhard, "Poverty and the Social Order in Seventeenth-Century Virginia," *VMHB* 85 (April 1977): 147-55.

3. Labaree, ed., *Royal Instructions,* no. 694, 2: 482-83; 1641 Instructions to Governor Berkeley, in *The Old Dominion in the Seventeenth Century,* ed. Warren M. Billings (Chapel Hill, N.C., 1975), p. 51; Hartwell, Blair, and Chilton, *Present State of Virginia,* pp. 65-66; Evarts B. Greene, *The Provincial Governor in the English Colonies of North America* (New York, 1898), pp. 128-32.

4. Jones, *Present State,* pp. 95, 96, 120, 256; Hartwell, Blair, and Chilton, *Present State of Virginia,* pp. 67-68; Brydon, *Virginia's Mother Church,* 1: 280-87; Labaree, ed., *Royal Instructions,* no. 708, 2: 489-90; Spencer Ervin, "The Establishment, Government, and Functioning of The Church in Colonial Virginia," *Historical Magazine of the Protestant Episcopal Church* 26 (March 1957): 76, 80.

5. For discussions of the actual powers of the commissary and of the governor, see the following: Brown and Brown, *Virginia 1705-1786,* ch. 11; Jones, *Present State,* pp. 95, 96, 120, 256; Brydon, *Virginia's Mother Church,* 1: chs. 19-22; Percy S. Flippin, "The Royal Government in Virginia, 1624-1775," *Columbia University Studies* 84 (1919): 172, 204; William H. Seiler, "The Church of England as the Established Church in Seventeenth-Century Virginia," *Journal of Southern History* 15 (November 1949): 478-508.

6. Hartwell, Blair, and Chilton, *Present State of Virginia,* pp. lv, lxvi, 65; Jones, *Present State,* pp. 96-97, 100, 125, 226-27; Beverley, *History and Present State,* p. 261; Thomas J. Wertenbaker, "The Attempt to Reform the Church of

Colonial Virginia," *The Sewanee Review* 25 (July 1917): 257-58; Alexander Spotswood to Board of Trade, 6 March 1721, *CSPC*, no. 396, 32: 260; see also the
parochial reports made in 1724 by Virginia ministers to the bishop of London, contained in Brydon, *Virginia's Mother Church*, 1: 370-93; Spotswood to Board of
Trade, 15 December 1710, in *The Official Letters of Alexander Spotswood*, ed.
Robert A. Brock, Virginia Historical Society *Collections*, Vols. 1 and 2 (Richmond,
1882-85), 1: 38.

    7. For examples of standard accounts, see: Richard L. Morton, *Colonial Virginia*,
2 vols. (Chapel Hill, N.C., 1960), 2: 469-70; Brydon, *Virginia's Mother Church*,
1: 81-82, 135-36, 227; Seiler, "Anglican Parish in Virginia," p. 125; Flippin,
"Royal Government in Virginia," pp. 172, 204; Philip A. Bruce, *Institutional
History of Virginia in the Seventeenth Century*, 2 vols. (New York, 1910), 1: 55-59.

    8. William Waller Hening, ed., *The Statutes at Large: Being a Collection of
All the Laws of Virginia*, 13 vols. (Richmond and Philadelphia, 1809-23), 1: 250,
347, 388, 404; Churchill G. Chamberlayne, ed., *The Vestry Book of Stratton Major
Parish, King and Queen County, Virginia, 1729-1783* (Richmond, 1931), p. viii;
Bruce, *Institutional History*, 1: 55-59.

    9. *JHB*, 1619-1658/59: 109; Hening, ed., *Statutes*, 1: 498; 2: 252; Billings,
ed., *Old Dominion in Seventeenth Century*, pp. 317-18.

    10. *JHB*, 1619-1658/59: 101; Bruce, *Institutional History*, 1: 55, 58; Churchill
G. Chamberlayne, ed., *The Vestry Book of Petsworth Parish, Gloucester County,
Virginia, 1677-1793* (Richmond, 1933), pp. x-xi.

    11. Thomas J. Wertenbaker, *Virginia Under the Stuarts* (New York, 1959), p.
124; Morton, *Colonial Virginia*, 1: 208. The 1674 charter granted to Arlington and
Culpeper is conveniently reprinted in Hening, *Statutes*, 2: 569-78.

    12. Hening, *Statutes*, 2: 565-67; Wesley Frank Craven, *The Southern Colonies
in the Seventeenth Century, 1607-1689* (Baton Rouge, La., 1949), pp. 391-92;
Wertenbaker, *Virginia Under the Stuarts*, pp. 124, 212.

    13. Morton, *Colonial Virginia*, 1: 209; Craven, *Southern Colonies in Seventeenth
Century*, pp. 397-98.

    14. Charles M. Andrews, *The Colonial Period of American History*, 4 vols. (New
Haven, Conn., 1934-38), 4: 272-74, 291; Leonard W. Labaree, *Royal Government
in America* (New Haven, Conn., 1930), p. 29; Oliver M. Dickerson, *American
Colonial Government, 1696-1765* (Cleveland, Ohio, 1912), chs. 1 and 2; George L.
Beer, *The Old Colonial System, 1660-1754*, Part One: *The Establishment of the
System, 1660-1688*, 2 vols. (1912; reprint ed., Gloucester, Mass., 1958), 1: 256-
315; James A. Henretta, *"Salutary Neglect": Colonial Administration Under the
Duke of Newcastle* (Princeton, N.J., 1972); Lawrence H. Gipson, *The British Em-
pire Before the American Revolution*, Vol. I: *The British Isles and the American
Colonies; Great Britain and Ireland, 1748-1754* (New York, 1958), ch. 1.

    15. See Lord Culpeper's Representations Concerning the Church, 27 September
1683, and the Journal of the Lords of Trade, 25 September 1683 and 2 October
1683, *CSPC*, no. 1264, no. 1272, no. 1290, 11: 503, 504-05, 511; Labaree, ed.,
Royal Instructions, no. 694, 2: 482-83.

    16. Labaree, ed., *Royal Instructions*, no. 694, 2: 482-83; the instructions given
to the earl of Orkney, absentee governor of Virginia from 1714 to 1737, contain

almost the exact wording—Instructions dated 15 April 1715, "The Randolph Manuscript," *VMHB* 21 (October 1913): 349.

17. Labaree, ed., *Royal Instructions*, no. 199, 1: 125; all pertinent paragraphs from Culpeper's commission and instructions are reprinted in full, with editorial comment, in *JHB*, 1659/60-1693: xxix-xxx; Craven, *Southern Colonies in Seventeenth Century*, pp. 396-97; Edmund S. Morgan, *American Slavery—American Freedom: The Ordeal of Colonial Virginia* (New York, 1975), pp. 288-90; Wertenbaker, *Virginia Under the Stuarts*, pp. 226-43; John C. Rainbolt, "A New Look at Stuart 'Tyranny': The Crown's Attack on the Virginia Assembly, 1676-1689," *VMHB* 75 (October 1967): 387-406. See chapter 4 for a discussion of Effingham's attempt to control regulation of county boundaries.

18. William Palmer, Sherwin MacRae, and Raleigh Colston, eds., *Calendar of Virginia State Papers and Other Manuscripts*, 11 vols. (1875-93; reprint ed., New York, 1968), 1: 11-12; Churchill G. Chamberlayne, *The Vestry Book of Blisland [Blissland] Parish, New Kent and James City Counties, Virginia, 1721-1786* (Richmond, 1935), pp. xxxiii-xxxiv.

19. Hening, *Statutes*, 3: 152-53; *EJC*, 3: 140.

20. *JHB*, 1659/60-1693: 150, 353, 354; Hening, *Statutes*, 3: 94; Chamberlayne, ed., *Vestry Book of Blisland Parish*, p. xix.

21. Seiler, "The Anglican Parish in Virginia," p. 126; Brydon, *Virginia's Mother Church*, 1: 232-34; Stephen S. Webb, "The Strange Career of Francis Nicholson," *WMQ*, 3rd ser. 23: (October 1966): 535-36; Morton, *Colonial Virginia*, 1: 310-41.

22. *EJC*, 2: 181-82; *JHB*, 1695-1702: 269, 279, 321, 325, 329.

23. *JHB*, 1702/3-1712: 55, 70, 93, 104; Hening, *Statutes*, 3: 225.

24. *JHB*, 1702/3-1712: 281. See the discussion in chapter 4.

25. Spotswood to Board of Trade, 24 October 1710 and 15 December 1710, in *Spotswood Letters*, ed. Brock, 1: 20, 38-39; Brydon, *Virginia's Mother Church*, 1: 333-34; Leonidas Dodson, *Alexander Spotswood* (Philadelphia, 1932), p. 227; Morton, *Colonial Virginia*, 2: 469-70.

26. *JHB*, 1712-1726: 49, 51, 52, 54, 63, 66, 73; Hening, *Statutes*, 4: 49; William G. Stanard and Mary N. Stanard, comps., *The Colonial Virginia Register* (1902; reprint ed., Baltimore, 1965), p. 99.

27. Spotswood to Board of Trade, 9 March 1714, in *Spotswood Letters*, ed. Brock, 2: 56.

28. Ibid.; *JHB*, 1712-1726: 224, 225, 226, 253, 256-57, 274, 276, 278, 283, 286, 287, 289, 291, 296, 316; Hening, *Statutes*, 4: 94.

29. Herbert L. Osgood, *The American Colonies in the Eighteenth Century*, 4 vols. (New York, 1924), 4: 83; Henretta, "Salutary Neglect," esp. p. 162n.; Jack P. Greene, *The Quest for Power* (Chapel Hill, N.C., 1963), p. 6.

30. *JHB*, 1727-1740: 184, 234; Hening, *Statutes*, 4: 443; William Gooch to Board of Trade, 20 November 1734, William Gooch Papers, 3 vols., transcripts, VHS, 2: 374.

31. *JHB*, 1712-1726: 280, 411, 412, 415, 417, 425; 1742-1749: 89, 95, 103, 106, 108, 113, 135, 148; 1752-1758: 10, 84, 98; Hening, *Statutes*, 4: 180; 5: 267; 6: 256-57; Hugh Drysdale to Board of Trade, 10 July 1726, CO 5/1320, p. 64.

32. *JHB*, 1773-1776: 22, 25, 30, 31, 35; Hening, *Statutes*, 8: 655.

33. Jones, *Present State*, p. 125.

34. *JHB*, 1712-1726: 311, 336, 339, 343, 347, 350.

35. *JHB*, 1712-1726: 376, 377, 382, 387, 390, 391, 393, 394, 395; Hening, *Statutes*, 4: 141; Hugh Drysdale to Board of Trade, 10 July 1724, CO5/1319, p. 201; Stanard and Stanard, *Colonial Virginia Register*, pp. 104-05.

36. *JHB*, 1742-1749: 92; *JHD*, October 1779: 11, 14, 24, 42; Hening, *Statutes*, 10: 209-10, 213-14; King and Queen, and Caroline, Petitions, 15, 16, and 22 October 1779 (religious petitions).

37. *JHB*, 1712-1726, 367, 368, 371, 384, 389, 391, 395; Hening, *Statutes*, 4: 141.

38. Hartwell, Blair, and Chilton, *Present State of Virginia*, p. 66; Jones, *Present State*, p. 96; Emory G. Evans, "The Rise and Decline of the Virginia Aristocracy in the Eighteenth Century: The Nelsons," in *The Old Dominion*, ed. Darrett B. Rutman (Charlottesville, Va., 1964), p. 67; Seiler, "Anglican Parish Vestry," pp. 314-15.

39. A bewildering variety of descriptions can thus be obtained from the standard secondary sources. Spencer Ervin merely asserted that the governor and council exercised the authority to hear and determine complaints against vestries, while William Seiler, Albert Porter, and Robert and Katherine Brown noted that the legislature possessed such authority. George Brydon stated that an appeal could go to either the General Court or to the assembly, while Percy S. Flippin maintained that appeals normally went to the executive in the seventeenth century, but the legislature usurped that authority in the eighteenth century. Finally, Philip A. Bruce cited examples where the county court, the governor and council, and the assembly all acted at various times to supervise vestry conduct. See the following: Ervin, "Establishment of The Church," pp. 86-87; Seiler, "Church of England as Established Church," p. 507; Seiler, "Anglican Parish Vestry," p. 317; Brown and Brown, *Virginia 1705-1786*, p. 216; Albert O. Porter, *County Government in Virginia: A Legislative History, 1607-1904* (New York, 1947), pp. 89-91; Brydon, *Virginia's Mother Church*, 1: 98; Flippin, "Royal Government," pp. 89, 172, 204; Bruce, *Institutional History*, 1: 65-77.

40. *EJC*, 3: 197-98, 207-08.

41. *EJC*, 4: 272-73, 344, 359.

42. Hening, *Statutes*, 3: 289.

43. *JHB*, 1695-1702: 10; 1702/3-1712: 34; Bruce, *Institutional History*, 1: 76-77; Hening, *Statutes*, 1: 240, 290; 2: 25, 44, 356; Ervin, "Establishment of The Church," pp. 87-91, 100-02.

44. *JHB*, 1712-1726: 278, 289-90, 291, 293, 304, 315-16, 334, 337, 344, 353; Hening, *Statutes*, 4: 116; Spotswood to Board of Trade, 6 March 1721, *CSPC*, no. 396, 32: 262.

45. *JHB*, 1727-1740: 11, 18, 23, 25, 26, 27, 29, 47, 52; Hening, *Statutes*, 4: 240; Gooch to Board of Trade, n.d. [8 June? 1728], Gooch Papers, 1: 57, VHS.

46. *JHB*, 1752-1758: 25, 71, 75, 82, 98; Hening, *Statutes*, 6: 258-60.

47. *JHB*, 1770-1772: 10, 52, 82, 94, 169, 199; *JHD*, October 1777: 49; Hening, *Statutes*, 7: 416; 8: 432, 607; 9: 439, 525; Seiler, "Anglican Parish Vestry," pp.

317-19; Brown and Brown, *Virginia 1705-1786*, pp. 243-44.

48. Eckenrode's "Separation of Church and State in Virginia" is marred by a too-strong Progressive interpretation which places far too much emphasis upon social and sectional conflict. It has been largely superseded by Thomas E. Buckley, *Church and State in Revolutionary Virginia, 1776-1787* (Charlottesville, Va., 1977). See also: Brown and Brown, *Virginia 1705-1786*, chs. 11 and 13; Brydon, *Virginia's Mother Church*, 2: chs. 17 and 18; an excellent brief treatment is Freeman H. Hart, *The Valley of Virginia in the American Revolution* (Chapel Hill, N.C., 1942), chs. 2 and 8.

49. Richard R. Beeman, "Social Change and Cultural Conflict in Virginia: Lunenburg County, 1746 to 1774," *WMQ*, 3d ser. 35 (July 1978): 455-76; Rhys Isaac, "Evangelical Revolt: The Nature of the Baptists' Challenge to the Traditional Order in Virginia, 1765-1775," *WMQ*, 3d ser. 31 (July 1974): 345-68; and "Religion and Authority: Problems of the Anglican Establishment in Virginia in the Era of the Great Awakening and the Parsons' Cause," *WMQ*, 3d ser. 30 (January 1973): 3-36; Hart, *Valley of Virginia*, ch. 2; Brown and Brown, *Virginia 1705-1786*, ch. 11; Gewehr, *Great Awakening in Virginia*, pp. 34, 40-43, 52, 93-95, 100-01, 106, 155-56; Harold W. Gardner, "The Dissenting Sects on the Southern Colonial Frontier, 1720-1770" (Ph.D. dissertation, University of Kansas, 1969), pp. 169-71, 251-55; Richard B. Davis, *Intellectual Life in Jefferson's Virginia* (Chapel Hill, N.C., 1964), pp. 131-40; Brydon, *Virginia's Mother Church*, 2: chs. 4-8.

50. Labaree, ed., *Royal Instructions*, no. 714, 2: 494; Buckley, *Church and State*, ch. 1; Seiler, "Church of England as Established Church," p. 497; Eckenrode, "Separation of Church and State in Virginia," pp. 32-40; Hening, *Statutes*, 3: 170-71; Brydon, *Virginia's Mother Church*, 2: 370-73; George W. Pilcher, "Samuel Davies and Religious Toleration in Virginia," *The Historian* 27 (November 1965): 48-71.

51. Buckley, *Church and State*, pp. 13-14; Eckenrode, "Separation of Church and State in Virginia," pp. 37-40.

52. Madison to William Bradford, Jr., 24 January 1774 and 1 April 1774, in *The Papers of James Madison*, ed. William T. Hutchinson et al., 11 vols. to date (Chicago and Charlottesville, Va., 1962-   ), 1: 104-06, 111-13.

53. *JHB*, 1770-1772: 160-61, 182-83, 185-86, 188, 189; 1773-1776: 92, 189; Brown and Brown, *Virginia 1705-1786*, pp. 260-65; see the commentary in *The Papers of Thomas Jefferson*, ed. Julian P. Boyd, 19 vols. to date (Princeton, N.J., 1950-   ), 1: 525-30.

54. Virginia, *The Proceedings of the Convention of Delegates, held . . . the 6th of May, 1776* (Williamsburg, 1776), pp. 142-43; Prince William Petition, 20 June 1776 (religious petitions).

55. Hening, *Statutes*, 9: 111-12; Irving Brant, *James Madison*, 6 vols. (Indianapolis, 1941-61), 1: 234-50; see the text of the various drafts, and the editor's commentary, in *The Papers of George Mason, 1725-1792*, ed. Robert A. Rutland, 3 vols. (Chapel Hill, N.C., 1970), 1: 274-91.

56. *JHD*, 1776: 9, 20, 28, 32-33, 35, 40, 46-47, 63-65; Peter Force, ed., *American Archives*, 9 vols., 5th ser. (Washington, D.C., 1837-53), 2: 815-17; the petitions

are found in the collection of religious petitions, VSL—some have been printed in "Virginia Legislative Papers," *VMHB* 18 (January 1910): 38-44; Brydon, *Virginia's Mother Church*, 2: 396-401.

57. *JHD*, 1776: 85, 102-03; Hening, *Statutes*, 9: 164-67, 312, 387-88, 469, 578-79; 10: 197-98; Dumas Malone, *Jefferson and His Time*, Vol. 1: *Jefferson the Virginian* (Boston, 1948), pp. 274-77; see Boyd's commentary in *Jefferson Papers*, 1: 525-29.

58. *JHD*, October 1779: 28; May 1780: 8, 35; October 1783: 15; May 1784: 27, 48-49; Hening, *Statutes*, 10: 362-63; 11: 503-05.

59. Edmund Pendleton to Richard Henry Lee, 28 February 1785, in *The Letters and Papers of Edmund Pendleton, 1734-1803*, ed. David J. Mays, 2 vols. (Charlottesville, Va., 1967), 2: 474-75; Richard Henry Lee to James Madison, 26 November 1784, in *The Letters of Richard Henry Lee*, ed. James C. Ballagh, 2 vols. (New York, 1911-14), 2: 304-07; George Mason to Patrick Henry, 6 May 1783, in *Mason Papers*, ed. Rutland, 2: 770; James Madison to Richard Henry Lee, 14 November 1784, Lee Family Papers, 1638-1867, VHS; Madison to James Monroe, 14 November 1784, in *Madison Papers*, ed. Hutchinson et al., 8: 136-37; John Page to Thomas Jefferson, 23 August 1785, in *Jefferson Papers*, ed. Boyd, 8: 428; Buckley, *Church and State*, pp. 5-6, 38-143; Brown and Brown, *Virginia 1705-1786*, pp. 297-98; Lunenberg Petition, 3 November 1779 (religious petitions).

60. Boyd's text of the bill, and his commentary upon it, are definitive—Boyd, ed., *Jefferson Papers*, 2: 545-53; see also: George Nicholas to James Madison, 22 April 1785, in *Madison Papers*, ed. Hutchinson et al., 8: 264-65; George Mason to George Washington, 2 October 1785, in *Mason Papers*, ed. Rutland, 2: 830-31; Augusta Petitions, 20 and 27 October 1779 (religious petitions); Amherst Petitions, 1 November 1779 (religious petitions).

61. *JHD*, October 1784: 17; Madison to Richard Henry Lee, 14 November 1784, Lee Family Papers, 1638-1867, VHS; Madison to James Monroe, 14 November 1784, in *Madison Papers*, ed. Hutchinson et al., 8: 136-37.

62. *JHD*, October 1784: 9, 13, 26, 29, 46, 51, 78-79; Madison to Monroe, 4 December 1784 and 24 December 1784, and Madison's Notes on the debate, in *Madison Papers*, ed. Hutchinson et al., 8: 175, 197-200; Buckley, *Church and State*, pp. 102-12.

63. Madison to Monroe, 12 April 1785, Madison to Jefferson, 27 April 1785, Madison to Monroe, 29 May 1785 and 21 June 1785, in *Madison Papers*, ed. Hutchinson et al., 8: 261, 268, 286, 306; others agreed that the issue had produced "considerable clamours"—see, for example, Edmund Pendleton to Richard Henry Lee, 18 April 1785, in *Pendleton Papers*, ed. Mays, 2: 478.

64. George Nicholas to Madison, 22 April 1785 and 7 July 1785, Madison to Edmund Randolph, 26 July 1785, Madison to Jefferson, 20 August 1785, in *Madison Papers*, ed. Hutchinson et al., 8: 264-65, 316, 327-28, 345; Mason to Washington, 2 October 1785, Washington to Mason, 3 October 1785, Mason to Robert Carter, 5 October 1785, Carter to Mason, 15 October 1785, in *Mason Papers*, ed. Rutland, 2: 830-33; Madison to George Mason [son of the Revolutionary patriot], 14 July 1826, Madison Papers, VHS; Madison's "Remonstrance" is printed,

with excellent editorial commentary, in *Madison Papers,* ed. Hutchinson et al., 8: 295-306; for dissenter action, see Charles F. James, ed., *Documentary History of the Struggle for Religious Liberty in Virginia* (1900; reprint ed., New York, 1971), pp. 136-38.

65. The petitions both for and against the assessment are contained in the file of religious petitions, VSL; see also Hutchinson et al., eds., *Madison Papers,* 8: 295-306. Buckley, *Church and State,* pp. 113-56, is excellent.

66. Buckley, *Church and State,* pp. 113-56; James, ed., *Documentary History,* pp. 136-38; Hart, *Valley of Virginia,* pp. 35-38; Brown and Brown, *Virginia 1705-1786,* pp. 251-54; Gewehr, *Great Awakening in Virginia,* pp. 93-95, 101, 106.

67. Nicholas to Madison, 22 April 1785 and 7 July 1785, in *Madison Papers,* ed. Hutchinson et al., 8: 264-65, 316; Mason to Washington, 2 October 1785, and Mason to Carter, 5 October 1785, in *Mason Papers,* ed. Rutland, 2: 830-33.

68. *JHD,* 1785: 7-8, 94.

69. Washington to Mason, 3 October 1785, in *The Writings of George Washington,* ed. John C. Fitzpatrick, 39 vols. (Washington, D.C., 1931-44), 28: 285; George Nicholas went even further in asserting that any attempt to enforce the bill would produce a "revolution," and the angry wording of some petitions indicates that this concern was justified—Nicholas to Madison, 22 April 1785, in *Madison Papers,* ed. Hutchinson et al., 8: 264-65.

70. Eckenrode, "Separation of Church and State in Virginia," p. 113; Jackson T. Main, *Political Parties Before the Constitution* (Chapel Hill, N.C., 1973), pp. 250-53; Merrill Jensen, *The New Nation* (New York, 1950), esp. ch. 15.

71. *JHD,* 1785: 93, 94, 115, 137, 141, 142; Hening, *Statutes,* 12: 27-30, 84-86; Madison to Mason, 14 July 1826, Madison Papers, VHS; Madison to Monroe, 17 December 1785 and 24 December 1785, Madison to James Monroe, Sr., 24 December 1785, Madison to Jefferson, 22 January 1786, *Madison Papers,* ed. Hutchinson et al., 8: 445-46, 454-56, 473-74.

CONCLUSION

This study has described the origin and development of the right of petition, the procedure used in the presentation and consideration of petitions, and the impact of petitions upon the political process. Investigation revealed that by 1607 the right of petition had long been recognized as a fundamental right of free Englishmen, and Virginians quickly initiated its use in the colony. During the eighteenth century, citizens of all classes and sections used petitions to communicate their requests and grievances to the lower house of the assembly. Petitioning thus played an extremely important role in the government of eighteenth-century Virginia. Average citizens did not merely elect their representatives and then passively "defer" to the leadership of the elite, taking little part or interest in politics between elections.[1] On the contrary, the process of petitioning for favorable legislation and redress of grievances provided an open and frequently utilized channel of communication between the people and the provincial government, especially the lower house of the assembly. By this method many citizens took an active participatory interest in the political process.

Even though petitioning served as an important means of participation and communication, it would have had little significance had eighteenth-century legislators assumed a posture of aristocratic indifference towards the sentiments of local citizens. As this study has demonstrated, however, such was clearly not the case. A significant amount of legislation, concerning a wide variety of topics both great and small, originated directly in response to these petitions—far more laws than from any other single source, and roughly as many as from all other sources combined.

The legislature's responsive attitude towards these petitions helped counterbalance those institutional features in the government of eighteenth-century Virginia which today seem so undemocratic and elitist. The suffrage eliminated blacks, women, and the very poor; the governor, whether appointed by the king (before 1776) or the legislature (after 1776), was not directly responsible to the people; many local officials, including the

powerful justices of the peace who made up the county court, were
appointed rather than elected. Despite these features, however, numerous
historians have asserted that colonial and state government in eighteenth-
century Virginia was relatively responsive to the wishes of average citizens.
In particular there existed what Richard L. Morton described as a "close
association" between the lower house and the people, or in different
words what John Rainbolt called "a political style . . . of familiarity with
all orders and frequent subservience to the sentiments of the common
planters."[2] This study confirms that provincial government was even
more responsive in practice than historians have generally realized, and
to a major degree this responsiveness operated through the action taken
by the legislature upon the petitions presented to it for consideration.
As previously noted, for example, the creation of new counties was a
matter of primary importance to Virginians, but in theory the people
played no part in the procedure. In practice, however, citizens played
an extremely important role. In a positive sense creation of a new county
almost invariably originated in petitions from local residents, indicating
the need for division of the existing county, revealing substantial popular
support for such action, and suggesting suitable new boundaries. In a
passive sense the assembly was more likely to act when the absence of
counterpetitions indicated no significant local opposition. To reiterate
another example, parish government during the colonial period in theory
provided little opportunity for popular participation and few safeguards
for the public interest. Yet in practive unpopular vestry actions were frequently overturned by the legislature in response to petitions from parish
inhabitants; when a vestry persisted in unwise or unpopular conduct, local
parishioners often petitioned successfully to dissolve it and elect a new one.

After describing how petitioning played such a major role in eighteenth-
century political affairs, it remains to offer some suggestions at least as
to why it worked so well. The answer involves certain commonly accepted
ideas concerning the nature of eighteenth-century society and politics.
Four factors in particular seem responsible for creating a climate of
opinion within which the petitions of the people might play a major role.

First, eighteenth-century Virginia society remained fundamentally
stable and remarkably free of class conflict. Even if the degree of economic,
social, and geographic mobility was less extensive than some have asserted,
it was nevertheless sufficiently broad to prevent major social strains from
developing within the society. Moreover, Virginia remained essentially an

agrarian, slaveholding society in which planters of all social classes had much in common. For example, the desire to create a workable and convenient tobacco inspection system and thereby raise tobacco prices was a matter of common concern.[3] Similarly, sectionalism had not yet destroyed this stability in the eighteenth century. Sectional hostility was practically nonexistent prior to the Revolution, for despite the old myths of bitter Tidewater-Piedmont antagonism, those two sections had too much in common to become enemies on many issues. Potentially dangerous sectional conflict began to develop only after significant westward expansion into the Valley and trans-Allegheny regions (which developed different ethnic, religious, and economic characteristics from the East) and after economic issues (such as taxation and the British debts question) temporarily assumed disproportionate significance during the Confederation period. Even then, sectionalism clearly remained within tolerable limits in the 1780-1800 period.[4]

Second, by and large the gentry leaders recognized that obligations and responsibilities went with their privileged position in society. The eighteenth-century ideal insisted that the upper class must govern in the public interest, and this standard was strengthened by the Enlightenment philosophy of the day. On the whole, most historians have agreed that this leadership functioned rather well.[5]

Third, as Gordon Wood has demonstrated, eighteenth-century political thought in the colonies contained elements of two separate concepts regarding the role of elected representatives. On the one hand, American thought and practice increasingly stressed the concept of "actual representation." The representative brought the petitions of his constituents to the legislature and informed the assembly of his constituents' opinions on major issues. If they so desired, the people could issue binding instructions to their representative, requiring him to vote or act as they directed on certain issues. This concept had much in common with the practice in medieval England, where representatives served almost as local attorneys.[6] Yet a second concept, similar in many ways to the English idea of "virtual representation," remained strong in eighteenth-century America. This concept stressed that legislators should act to promote the general welfare rather than to win special concessions for their districts at the expense of the whole community. It could survive, however, only so long as the different groups and localities within the community had interests not too dissimilar, for "virtual representation" stressed that in promoting the good of the whole all the parts would ultimately benefit. Indeed, as Wood has cogently demonstrated, the fundamental American disagreement with England's "virtual representation" defense of her post-1763 colonial policy was "the disparity of interests between mother country and colonies that was inherent in their emerging conception of empire. . . ." Petitioning fit perfectly into this second concept, for it required representatives from all sections to consider each petition impartially. Petitioning could no longer function effectively if each representative was determined to accept only those measures of immediate interest to his constituents.[7]

Fourth, eighteenth-century government was much simpler in organization and more limited in its goals and programs than government in the twentieth century. Government in 1750 did less because people demanded less of it—indeed, in that relatively homogeneous agrarian society, there was less that government needed to do. Here again, Enlightenment philosophy, with its stress upon limited government, meshed neatly with eighteenth-century reality in the Old Dominion. The opportunities for corruption or for special-interest legislation favoring the few at the expense of the many or one section at the expense of another were thus considerably reduced in comparison with the nineteenth and twentieth centuries.[8] Conversely, the opportunity for direct popular influence upon legislation was enhanced. Many problems were relatively simple to understand and localized in significance, such as the need to divide an excessively large county or prevent hogs from roaming loose in town. For local citizens to identify those problems and suggest possible solutions by petitioning the legislature was thus a logical response to existing conditions.

For these reasons, provincial government in eighteenth-century Virginia worked rather well—or, as Richard Hofstadter put it, "One may argue whether the government of colonial Virginia was brilliant, but it was certainly competent as governments went then and as most of them go now. . . ."[9] And within this context petitioning worked very well. Again, the key words in analyzing the significant role of petitioning are "participation" and "responsiveness."

In succeeding years, however, petitioning did not retain its eighteenth-century significance. During the years from 1800 to 1831, it declined significantly in importance as Virginia society and politics underwent some fundamental changes. In particular, sectionalism became increasingly pronounced as the Valley and trans-Allegheny counties grew more rapidly in population than their eastern counterparts and as the East and West developed divergent views on a growing number of major issues. For example, Virginians living west of the Blue Ridge strongly supported increased expenditures for a program of internal improvements. Westerners quickly decided that the Fund for Internal Improvements (a trust fund established in 1816 to support internal improvement projects) was inadequate for the program they desired. But many easterners opposed spending large sums of money, most of it raised by taxing eastern land and slaves,[10] for opening access to the fresher lands of western farmers. Eastern farmers faced economic problems of their own in the early nineteenth century, such as low prices for farm products and worn-out lands; the increasing interest in better agricultural techniques and the emigration of many easterners to the new lands of the southwest territories and states provide indications of the problems. For these reasons, some easterners (particularly residents of the Piedmont) were willing to support internal improvements provided that much of the money was spent in their section, but many refused to support major appropriations for the West.[11]

The increasingly heated issue of legislative reapportionment also reflected the growth of sectionalism. The old system of county-unit representation no longer worked very well after 1800 because easterners became reluctant to create new western counties and thereby increase western voting strength in the legislature. In the 1770-1799 period, Virginia added forty-seven new counties; in the 1800-1830 period, only fourteen were created.[12] Westerners responded by demanding constitutional revision to institute proportional representation based upon white population— thereby not counting the eastern slaves. The drive for proportional representation actually originated even before 1800 (Jefferson, for example, advocated the principle in 1776), but the western campaign did not begin in earnest until 1806. Most easterners feared that if the West gained control of the assembly, it would quickly adopt an expensive program of internal improvements and other measures to benefit the West at the expense of the East. Consequently, most eastern delegates opposed calling a state constitutional convention to establish proportional representation.[13]

Other issues also served to divide the sections. The West wanted the capital moved from Richmond to a site beyond the Blue Ridge, and as might be expected the East was almost unanimous in its opposition.[14] The West also wanted more banks and more currency. The eastern-

TABLE 10 SECTIONAL VOTING PATTERNS IN THE ASSEMBLY,
1815-1832

Issue	East				West			
	Tidewater		Piedmont		Valley		Trans-Allegheny	
	Aye	Nay	Aye	Nay	Aye	Nay	Aye	Nay
1	6	34	21	21	21	0	34	2
2	14	34	19	31	19	5	28	8
3	9	45	20	21	15	2	35	5
4	0	70	1	52	18	8	34	13
5	14	35	14	31	20	6	26	16
6	0	56	4	53	19	7	33	12
7	26	35	28	19	22	3	27	13
8	3	32	6	35	17	6	32	0
Total	72	341	113	263	151	37	249	69

Code of Issues:
  1, 15 January 1816 vote to create a new county in the Trans-Allegheny section
      (passed house 82-57; rejected by Senate)
  2. 6 January 1817 vote to charter two banks, one in the Valley and one in the
      Trans-Allegheny section (passed house 80-78; accepted by Senate)
  3. 1 February 1817 vote to poll the electorate about holding a constitutional
      convention (passed house 79-73; rejected by Senate)
  4. 22 January 1822 vote on moving the capital from Richmond to the West
      (rejected by the house 143-53)
  5. 3 January 1823 vote on state financial aid for building a turnpike from the
      Valley to the James River in the Piedmont (rejected by house 88-74)
  6. 12 December 1823 vote on creating a new county in the Trans-Allegheny
      section (rejected by house 128-56)
  7. 21 February 1824 vote to borrow money for additional internal improve-
      ments (passed house 103-70; accepted by Senate)
  8. 25 January 1832 vote on adopting measures to abolish slavery (rejected by
      house 73-58)

dominated assembly did charter a few relatively small banks beyond the
Blue Ridge, but never enough to satisfy the western demand. Virginia's
two large banks, the Bank of Virginia and the Farmer's Bank of Virginia,
were both controlled by Easterners and both operated largely in the East.[15]
Moreover, the slavery question also poisoned Virginia's sectional relations.
The West contained relatively few slaves, and antislavery sentiment re-

mained strong there. While some easterners still supported the emancipation and colonization of blacks, for the most part eastern Virginia closed
ranks in defense of the "peculiar institution" after the Revolutionary
period. Easterners feared that a western-dominated assembly might destroy
the institution either by heavy taxation or by abolition. When the 1831
assembly debated the slavery question following Nat Turner's Revolt,
a motion to adopt measures for abolishing slavery was defeated by a vote
of seventy-three to fifty-eight. The voting was largely sectional in nature.[16]

The effect of sectionalism upon voting patterns in the legislature is
strikingly revealed in table 10, which examines a few representative votes
for the 1815-1832 period.[17]

The growth of sectionalism after 1800 quickly damaged the effectiveness of petitioning. For petitioning to work properly, the legislature had
to give careful and relatively unbiased consideration to petitions on all
major issues and from all sections. The comparatively homogeneous nature
of eighteenth-century society had promoted just this sort of atmosphere.
Because of the increasing sectionalism, however, nineteenth-century
delegates quickly judged petitions on many issues according to precon-
ceived biases. Contemporary observers frequently commented on the
damaging effects of sectionalism, but easterners blamed the West and
vice versa. Thus Joseph C. Cabell (an eastern delegate) wrote to Jefferson
in 1818: "All that I have ever told you about these people is true. But
few of them legislate for the state: they legislate for the back country."[18]
Many westerners responded in kind. A meeting of concerned citizens in
Ohio County (now part of West Virginia) resolved in 1827: "Virginia is
under the dominion of an oligarchy, whose misrule, if it has not actually
impoverished and depopulated the territory, has certainly retarded its
growth in wealth and population to an alarming degree."[19] In this kind
of atmosphere, petitioning simply could not retain its previous significance.[20]

Although the growth of sectionalism was the most important factor
responsible for the declining importance of petitioning, several others
were also involved. Gordon Wood indicated that the trend away from
"virtual representation," stressing the responsibility of the legislator to
serve the overall public interest, was already under way by the late
eighteenth century. That trend accelerated after 1800, as representation
became increasingly a matter of legislators fighting for the particular
interests of their constituents. The trend toward "actual representation"
was more in keeping with the pluralistic society of competing interest

groups which the growing sectionalism reflected.[21] Again, petitioning did not work as well under these new conditions.

"Actual representation" might also be interpreted as a more "democratic" political style which was thus in keeping with the temper of the times. Early nineteenth-century Virginia politics became more democratic, and certainly more sophisticated, than eighteenth-century practice in several ways. Though the legislature continued to receive large numbers of petitions, Virginians began using instructions with increasing frequency as well; in particular, western citizens often instructed their delegates after 1800 to introduce or support measures for constitutional revision. Gordon Wood maintained that the growing use of instructions symbolized the shift towards "actual representation," and instructing one's delegates also reflected the concept of ultimate popular sovereignty more obviously than did petitioning to *ask* for the consideration of the entire legislature.[22] Moreover, the number of bills introduced directly upon the motions of individual members increased dramatically after 1800, from 45 in 1790 to 258 in 1831.[23] In part this technique developed from a desire to avoid the overworked standing committees, especially Propositions and Grievances. But in most cases, when a delegate introduced a bill on motion, it involved some issue of immediate concern to his constituents. The delegate was, in effect, acting directly to carry out the wishes of his constituents, and this procedure was perhaps more "democratic" than having local citizens petition to ask the assembly for consideration. Also significant were the methods used by the legislature to discover the sentiments of the people concerning important issues. In 1784, when the assembly asked for public reaction to the general assessment scheme, it expected the people to send petitions;[24] in the nineteenth century, whenever the legislature considered polling Virginians about holding a constitutional convention, it always proposed to do so by holding a referendum. Legislative procedure thus mirrored developments in society by becoming more complex, more sophisticated, and more in keeping with the spirit of democracy after 1800. The legislature continued to receive substantial numbers of petitions, but they no longer played the prominent role of the previous century. In short, petitioning was a casualty of the growing sectionalism and the continuing process of political evolution.

Nevertheless, during the eighteenth century petitioning provided a significant method of political participation for local citizens and was used even by individuals who were disfranchised by the voting requirements. Petitioning provided by far the most important channel of communication between the people of Virginia and their elected representatives in the assembly. The house guaranteed consideration of all petitions, and far more eighteenth-century legislation originated directly in response to these petitions than from any other source. It was primarily by responding to their petitions that the assembly maintained its close association with Virginia citizens.

Similarly, there was a direct relationship between petitioning and the successful eighteenth-century "quest for power" of the lower house. The increasing authority of the lower house prompted Virginia citizens to send even more petitions to the burgesses; at the same time, this growing influx of petitions presenting requests and grievances further stimulated the increase in legislative activity and gave added significance to the "quest for power." The process of petitioning and response allowed the house to maintain, and justifiably so, that it was the "part of the Legislature which Represents the People from whom the Propositions and Grievances have their Rise." As the 1710-1720 controversy between Governor Spotswood and the lower house over creation of counties and parishes vividly demonstrated, the victory of the burgesses represented more than just a transfer of power from one branch of government to another. Because of petitioning, the burgesses' success reinforced the ability of average citizens to play an important role in the decision-making process. The burgesses themselves clearly recognized this relationship between their growing authority and their responsibility to act on the petitions of the people. As they explained in 1753 to Governor Dinwiddie:

> We do humbly, but in the strongest Terms, represent to
> your Honour, that it is the undoubted Right of the Burgesses
> to enquire into the Grievances of the People: They have constantly exercised this Right, and we presume to affirm, that the
> drawing it into Question, in any Manner, cannot but be of
> dangerous Consequences to the Liberties of his Majesty's faithful Subjects, and to the Constitution of this Government.[25]

Notes

1. Those historians who have placed great emphasis upon the concept that the colonies were "deferential" societies often used Virginia as an example, but they failed to recognize the significance of petitioning. For examples of the argument in support of "deference," see: Roy N. Lokken, "The Concept of Democracy in

Colonial Political Thought," *WMQ,* 3rd ser. 16 (October 1959): 568-80; J. R. Pole, "Historians and the Problem of Early American Democracy," *American Historical Review* 67 (April 1962): 626-46; James A. Henretta, *The Evolution of American Society, 1700-1815* (Lexington, Mass., 1973), pp. 92-94, 112-14, 169; Jackson T. Main, *The Sovereign States, 1775-1783* (New York: 1973), pp. 103-04.

2. Richard L. Morton, *Colonial Virginia,* 2 vols. (Chapel Hill, N.C., 1960), 2: 503; John C. Rainbolt, "The Alteration in the Relationship between Leadership and Constituents in Virginia, 1660-1720," *WMQ,* 3d ser. 27 (July 1970): 412; Thomas J. Wertenbaker, *The Planters of Colonial Virginia* (Princeton, N.J., 1922), p. 109; Charles S. Sydnor, *Gentlemen Freeholders* (Chapel Hill, N.C., 1952), esp. chs. 4 and 9; Robert E. Brown and B. Katherine Brown, *Virginia 1705-1786: Democracy or Aristocracy?* (East Lansing, Mich., 1964), esp. ch. 10; Dumas Malone, "The Great Generation," *Virginia Quarterly Review 23* (Winter 1947): 108-22.

3. In his study of the economic structure of Chesapeake society, Aubrey C. Land observed: "Probably never since in American history has top wealth enjoyed a more harmonious relationship with the rest of society." Land, "Economic Behavior in a Planting Society: The Eighteenth-Century Chesapeake," *Journal of Southern History* 33 (November 1967): 482-83; Jack P. Greene, *The Quest for Power* (Chapel Hill, N.C., 1963), pp. 29-31; Brown and Brown, *Virginia 1705-1786,* pp. 7-57; Arthur M. Schlesinger, "The Aristocracy in Colonial America," *Proceedings of the Massachusetts Historical Society* 74 (1962): 14-15, 19-21; Carl Bridenbaugh, *Myths and Realities* (Baton Rouge, La., 1952), pp. 5-8, 18, 51; D. Alan Williams, "The Small Farmer in Eighteenth-Century Virginia Politics," *Agricultural History* 43 (January 1969): 91-92; Emory G. Evans, *Thomas Nelson of Yorktown* (Charlottesville, Va., 1975), pp. 3-4. Even those historians who believe that Virginia did experience some class or sectional conflict after 1776 generally admit that the degree of conflict was small in comparison to other states. For example, Jackson T. Main observed: "Stability, continuity, consensus: these terms more nearly apply to Virginia than to any other state during the Confederation." Main, *Political Parties Before the Constitution* (Chapel Hill, N.C., 1973), p. 244.

4. For statements concerning the absence of serious sectional divisions in Virginia before 1776, see: John R. Alden, *The South in the Revolution, 1763-1789* (Baton Rouge, La., 1957), pp. 143-45; Brown and Brown, *Virginia 1705-1786,* pp. 234, 239; Sydnor, *Gentlemen Freeholders,* pp. 90-97; Greene, *Quest for Power,* p. 30; Thomas P. Abernethy, *Western Lands and the American Revolution* (New York, 1937), pp. 160, 367. The best recent studies of sectional blocs in the legislature after 1780 are: Main, *Political Parties Before the Constitution,* ch. 9; Norman K. Risjord and Gorden DenBoer, "The Evolution of Political Parties in Virginia, 1782-1800," *Journal of American History* 60 (March 1974): 961-84.

5. Sydnor, *Gentlemen Freeholders,* esp. ch. 9; Malone, "Great Generation," pp. 108-22; Louis B. Wright, *The First Gentlemen of Virginia* (San Marino, Cal., 1940), p. 6; Bridenbaugh, *Myths and Realities,* pp. 16-17; Schlesinger, "Aristocracy in Colonial America," pp. 19-21.

6. Gordon S. Wood, *The Creation of the American Republic, 1776-1787* (Chapel Hill, N.C., 1969), esp. pp. 183-84, 189; Bernard Bailyn, *The Origins of American Politics* (New York, 1968), pp. 84-85.

7. Wood, *Creation of American Republic,* pp. 176-80, 189, 195-96. See also the discussion in Main, *The Sovereign States,* pp. 104-14.

8. See, for example, the observations in Sydnor, *Gentlemen Freeholders,* p. 108; Main, *The Sovereign States,* pp. 42-43.

9. Richard Hofstadter, *The Idea of a Party System* (Berkeley, Cal., 1969), p. 47; for similar comments, see Bridenbaugh, *Myths and Realities,* pp. 16-17; Sydnor, *Gentlemen Freeholders,* ch. 9.

10. The Tidewater and Piedmont paid far more taxes than did the Valley and West. For example, in 1810 Virginians living east of the Blue Ridge paid 82.81 percent of total state taxes; in 1830 the figure was still 75.47 percent. See the figures conveniently collected in Virginia, *Documents, Containing Statistics of Virginia, Ordered to be Printed by the State Convention Sitting in the City of Richmond, 1850-51* (Richmond, 1851).

11. Harry Ammon, "The Republican Party in Virginia, 1789-1824" (Ph.D. dissertation, University of Virginia, 1948), pp. 1-2, 21, 384-88; Fletcher M. Green, *Constitutional Development in the South Atlantic States, 1776-1860* (Chapel Hill, N.C., 1930), pp. 150-54; Charles H. Ambler, *Sectionalism in Virginia from 1776 to 1861* (Chicago, 1910), pp. 98, 105; Norman K. Risjord, *The Old Republicans* (New York, 1965), pp. 177-78; for accounts of the agricultural difficulties of the East, see such standard accounts as Clement Eaton, *The Growth of Southern Civilization, 1790-1860* (New York, 1961), esp. pp. 4-5, 177-80; Avery O. Craven, *Soil Exhaustion as a Factor in the Agricultural History of Virginia and Maryland, 1606-1860* (1926; reprint ed., Gloucester, Mass., 1965), esp. chs. 3 and 4.

12. Morgan P. Robinson, "Virginia Counties," Virginia State Library *Bulletin* 9 (January, April, and July 1916): 94-116.

13. Green, *Constitutional Development,* pp. 162, 168-74, 203-10; Charles S. Sydnor, *The Development of Southern Sectionalism, 1819-1848* (Baton Rouge, La., 1948), esp. ch. 12; Dumas Malone, *Jefferson and His Time,* Vol. 1: *Jefferson the Virginian* (Boston, 1948), pp. 238-39; *Niles' Register,* 20 August 1842, p. 25.

14. The legislature regularly received western petitions on this subject—see, for example, *JHD,* 1821: 70, 137-38.

15. Ammon, "Republican Party in Virginia," pp. 372-77; Ambler, *Sectionalism in Virginia,* p. 104; *JHD,* 1816: 22, 24, 30, 36, 133, 174, 195-97.

16. Richard B. Davis, *Intellectual Life of Jefferson's Virginia, 1790-1830* (Chapel Hill, N.C., 1964), pp. 415-17; James C. Ballagh, *A History of Slavery in Virginia* (Baltimore, 1902), pp. 94-95; Ambler, *Sectionalism in Virginia,* pp. 189-201; *JHD,* 1831: 15, 16, 19, 21, 26, 29, 32, 34, 37, 41, 45, 51, 56, 65, 69, 75, 81, 90, 93, 95, 98, 100, 101, 102, 106, 107, 109-10, 114.

17. *JHD,* 1815: 118-19, 149; 1816: 133, 184, 195-97, 203; 1821: 137-38; 1822: 99; 1823: 45, 181, 217; 1831: 109.

18. Joseph C. Cabell to Jefferson, 6 February 1818, Jefferson Papers, UVa.

19. *Richmond Constitutional Whig,* 27 April 1827.

20. For other observations by contemporaries which reveal the extent of sectionalism in the nineteenth century, see: *JHD,* 1816: 87; Isaac A. Coles to Joseph C. Cabell, 8 February 1802, Cabell Papers, UVa.; Linn Banks to Henry Edmundson, 20 April 1829, Edmundson Family Papers, VHS; Francis Preston to John Preston,

20 April 1817, Preston Davie Collection of Preston Family Papers, VHS. See the excellent article by Robert P. Sutton, "Sectionalism and Social Structure: A Case Study of Jeffersonian Democracy," *VMHB* 80 (January 1972): 70-84.

21. Wood, *Creation of the American Republic*, pp. 176-96. See the especially cogent remarks on Virginia politics in *Niles' Register*, 12 March 1831, p. 40.

22. Wood, *Creation of the American Republic*, pp. 176-96.

23. See chapter 3. In 1752 only 18 bills were introduced directly on motion by individual members, and in 1790 the number had risen only to 45. By 1815, however, 95 bills originated in that fashion. The number grew to 144 by 1820, and at the 1831 session 258 bills were introduced on motion.

24. The assessment controversy has already been discussed. For nineteenth-century proposals to hold referendums on the issue of constitutional revision, see: *JHD*, 1815: 60, 167-68; 1816: 86-88, 184; 1822: 143-44; 1824: 67, 148-50; 1825: 103; 1827: 16, 33-34, 131.

25. *JHB*, 1752-1758: 143.

BIBLIOGRAPHY

A Note on Sources and Methodology

Investigating the impact of popular petitions on the legislative process
requires detailed examination of the lower house journals, since it was
the branch of the assembly which normally received and first acted upon
them. Fortunately these journals for the eighteenth-century sessions are
complete and readily available. For the pre-revolutionary years historians
have long relied on *Journals of the House of Burgesses of Virginia*, edited
by Henry R. McIlwaine and John P. Kennedy. The post-1776 journals are
available in a variety of forms, perhaps most conveniently through *Records
of the States of the United States. A Microfilm Compilation Prepared by
the Library of Congress in Association with the University of North
Carolina*, edited by William S. Jenkins. The record of each petition introduced into the lower house, including committee reports and the outcome
of any bills resulting, can thus be followed. This record can then be compared with the legislation ultimately enacted, available in William W.
Hening, ed., *The Statutes at Large: Being a Collection of All the Laws of
Virginia . . .* , in Waverly K. Winfree, ed., *The Laws of Virginia: Being a
Supplement to Hening's The Statutes at Large,* and in Samuel Shepherd,
ed., *The Statutes at Large of Virginia . . . Being a Continuation of Hening.*

Since eighteenth-century sessions usually received a hundred or more
petitions, the legislative journals of necessity included only a summary
of each petition's contents and did not include the list of signatures. To
examine these individual petitions requires use of the manuscript collections of petitions preserved and available for scholarly use at the Virginia
State Library in Richmond. The 1865 Richmond fire destroyed all but
a few of the colonial petitions. Those that survived are included in the
collection of Colonial Papers, and most have been published in the first

volume of *Calendar of Virginia State Papers and Other Manuscripts,* edited by William Palmer, Sherwin McRae, and Raleigh Colston. However, the collection of post-1776 legislative petitions is remarkably complete, numbering an estimated twenty thousand or more. Part are separated into a special collection of Religious Petitions, 1774-1802, which can even be purchased inexpensively on microfilm. The legislative petitions are arranged by county of origin in chronological order. A convenient guide is Hamilton J. Eckenrode, ed., "A Calendar of Legislative Petitions, Accomac to Bedford," in *Fifth Annual Report of the Library Board of the Virginia State Library, for the Year Ending October 31, 1908.* Scholars seeking to follow the advice of Jesse Lemisch and others, that we increase our understanding of American history "from the bottom up," will find this collection of petitions to be invaluable. It provides a significant way to uncover the ideas and aspirations of those average people who usually did not leave manuscript collections of letters and other documents for the convenience of later historians.

Now for some observations on methodology. In my research I did not use statistical techniques to produce a "scientific" sample for study, nor have I attempted to relate my findings to any hypothetical or quantitative model. Instead I reviewed the records of every legislative session from 1619 to 1831, including every page of every lower house journal. Then I have relied upon my professional judgment in selecting which portions of this data to include in the book. In that sense, of course, every historian selects a sample—hopefully an accurate and meaningful one—of the material at his disposal for presentation. When the occasion called for it I have stressed the more significant events, as in describing procedural developments and important instances where petitioning played a dramatic role in shaping public policy (such as the 1776-1786 struggle for religious freedom). However, because petitioning was used to express public sentiment on almost all matters rather than on just a few significant ones, I have also frequently been required to summarize or describe vast quantities of data. In doing so my objective has been to present the most complete description possible within the necessary limitations of research time and book space, and I have used a variety of methods in doing so. My work is, then, more of the "traditional" than the "quantitative" or "cliometric" variety, but I did not hesitate to "quantify" data when it seemed appropriate to do so.

Primary Sources

MANUSCRIPTS

Great Britain, Public Record Office
    Colonial Office Papers (microfilm)
Library of Congress, Washington, D.C.
    Breckinridge Papers
    James Madison Papers (microfilm)
    James Monroe Papers (microfilm)
    George Washington Papers (microfilm)
Virginia Historical Society, Richmond, Virginia
    John P. Dupuy Letter
    Edmundson Family Papers
    William Gooch Papers (3 vols., transcripts)
    Lee Family Papers, 1638-1867
    Lee Family Papers, 1761-1882
    James Madison Papers
    Godfrey Pole Papers
    Preston Davie Collection of Preston Family Papers
Virginia State Library, Richmond, Virginia
    Accomack County (Upper Northampton County) Orders, Wills, Etc., 1671-1673
    William Allason Letter Book, 1770-1789
    William Cabell Diaries, 1751-1825
    Colonial Papers
    Henrico County Order Books, 1678-1693, 1694-1701
    Zachariah Johnston Papers
    Legislative Petitions
    Norfolk City, Minutes of the Common Council, 1736-1798 (microfilm)·
    Religious Petitions, 1774-1802 (microfilm)
University of Virginia, Charlottesville, Virginia
    Cabell Papers
    Carter Family Papers, 1659-1797 (microfilm)
    Thomas Jefferson Papers
    Lee Family Papers, 1742-1795 (microfilm)
    Wilson Cary Nicholas Papers
Wisconsin Historical Society, Madison, Wisconsin
    Preston Papers, Draper MSS (microfilm)

PRINTED SOURCES

Arber, Edward, ed. *The Works of Captain John Smith.* New York, 1967.
"Aspinwall Papers." Massachusetts Historical Society, *Collections,* 4th ser., Vols. 9
    and 10, 1871.

Ballagh, James Curtis, ed. *The Letters of Richard Henry Lee.* 2 vols. New York, 1911-14.

"The Bank of the United States: Petitions of Virginia Cities and Towns for the Establishment of Branches, 1791." *VMHB* 8 (January 1901): 287-95.

Bemiss, Samuel M., ed. *The Three Charters of the Virginia Company of London, with Seven Related Documents: 1606-1621.* Jamestown 350th Anniversary Historical Booklets, edited by E. G. Swem. Williamsburg, 1957.

Beverley, Robert. *The History and Present State of Virginia.* Edited by Louis B. Wright. Chapel Hill, N.C., 1947.

Billings, Warren M., ed. *The Old Dominion in the Seventeenth Century: A Documentary History of Virginia, 1606-1689.* Chapel Hill, N.C., 1975.

Boyd, Julian Parks, ed. *The Papers of Thomas Jefferson.* 19 vols. to date. Princeton, N.J., 1950- .

Brock, Robert A., ed. *The Official Letters of Alexander Spotswood.* Virginia Historical Society *Collections,* Vols. 1 and 2. Richmond, 1882-85.

_____. *The Official Letters of Robert Dinwiddie.* Virginia Historical Society *Collections,* Vols. 3 and 4. Richmond, 1883-84.

Brown, Alexander, ed. *The Genesis of the United States.* 2 vols. Boston, 1897.

Campbell, Charles, ed. *The Bland Papers: Being a Selection from the Manuscripts of Colonel Theodorick Bland, Jr.* 2 vols. Petersburg, Va., 1840-43.

Chalkley, Lyman, ed. *Chronicles of the Scotch-Irish Settlement in Virginia, Extracted from the Original Court Records of Augusta County, 1745-1800.* 3 vols. 1912. Reprint. Baltimore, 1965.

Chamberlayne, Churchill G., ed. *The Vestry Book of Blisland (Blissland) Parish, New Kent and James City Counties, Virginia, 1721-1786.* Richmond, 1935.

_____. *The Vestry Book of Petsworth Parish, Gloucester County, Virginia, 1677-1793.* Richmond, 1933.

_____. *The Vestry Book of Stratton Major Parish, King and Queen County, Virginia, 1729-1783.* Richmond, 1931.

"Charles City County Grievances, 1676." *VMHB* 3 (October 1895): 132-47.

Davies, K. G., ed. *Documents of the American Revolution, 1770-1783 (Colonial Office Series).* 17 vols. to date. Shannon, Ireland, 1972- .

Davis, Richard Beale, ed. *William Fitzhugh and His Chesapeake World, 1676-1701: The Fitzhugh Letters and Other Documents.* Chapel Hill, N.C., 1963.

"Decisions of Virginia General Court, 1626-1628." *VMHB* 3 (April 1896): 359-67; 4 (October 1896): 154-60.

Dorman, John F., ed. *Westmoreland County, Virginia: Order Book, 1690-1698; Part One, 1690-1692.* Washington, D.C., 1962.

Eckenrode, Hamilton J., ed. "A Calendar of Legislative Petitions, Accomac to Bedford." *Fifth Annual Report of the Library Board of the Virginia State Library, for Year Ending October 31, 1908.* Richmond, 1908.

Elton, G. R., ed. *The Tudor Constitution: Documents and Commentary.* Cambridge, 1960.

Farish, Hunter Dickinson, ed. *Journal and Letters of Philip Vickers Fithian, 1773-1774: A Plantation Tutor of the Old Dominion.* Williamsburg, 1943.

Fitzpatrick, John C., ed. *The Writings of George Washington.* 39 vols. Washington, D.C., 1931-44.

Fleet, Beverley, ed. *Virginia Colonial Abstracts.* 34 vols. 1937-49. Reprint. Baltimore, 1961.

Force, Peter, ed. *American Archives.* 9 vols. Washington, D.C., 1837-53.

_____. *Tracts and Other Papers Relating Principally to the Origin, Settlement, and Progress of the Colonies in North America.* 4 vols. Washington, D.C., 1836-46.

Ford, Paul L., ed. *The Works of Thomas Jefferson.* 12 vols. Federal Edition. New York, 1904-05.

Fothergill, Augusta B., and Naugle, John M., eds. *Virginia Tax Payers, 1782-1787.* Baltimore, 1971.

Great Britain. Public Record Office. *Calendar of State Papers, Colonial Series, America and West Indies.* Edited by W. Noel Sainsbury et al. 44 vols. to date. London, 1860-   .

Greene, Jack P., ed. *The Diary of Colonel Landon Carter of Sabine Hall, 1752-1778.* 2 vols. Charlottesville, Va., 1965.

Hartwell, Henry; Blair, James; and Chilton, Edward. *The Present State of Virginia, and the College.* Edited by Hunter Dickinson Farish. Williamsburg, 1940.

Hening, William Waller, ed. *The Statutes at Large: Being a Collection of All the Laws of Virginia.* 13 vols. Richmond and Philadelphia, 1809-23.

"Henry County." *VMHB* 9 (January 1902): 262-66.

Hunt, Gaillard, ed. *The Writings of James Madison.* 9 vols. New York, 1900-10.

Hutchinson, William T. et al., eds. *The Papers of James Madison.* 11 vols. to date. Chicago and Charlottesville, Va., 1962-   .

James, Charles F., ed. *Documentary History of the Struggle for Religious Liberty in Virginia.* 1900. Reprint. New York, 1971.

Jefferson, Thomas. *Notes on the State of Virginia.* Edited by William Peden. Chapel Hill, N.C., 1954.

Jensen, Merrill, ed. *American Colonial Documents to 1776.* New York, 1955.

_____. *Tracts of the American Revolution, 1763-1776.* New York, 1967.

Jones, Hugh. *The Present State of Virginia.* Edited by Richard L. Morton. Chapel Hill, N.C., 1956.

Kenyon, J. P., ed. *The Stuart Constitution: Documents and Commentary.* Cambridge, 1966.

Kingsbury, Susan M., ed. *The Records of the Virginia Company of London.* 4 vols. Washington, D.C., 1906-35.

Labaree, Leonard Woods, ed. *Royal Instructions to British Colonial Governors, 1670-1776.* 2 vols. New York, 1935.

"Letters of William Byrd, 2d, of Westover, Va." *VMHB* 9 (January 1902): 225-51.

Lewis, Clifford, III, ed. "Some Recently Discovered Extracts from the Lost Minutes of the Virginia Council and General Court, 1642-1645." *WMQ,* 2d ser. 20 (January 1940): 62-78.

McIlwaine, Henry R., ed. *Legislative Journals of the Council of Colonial Virginia.* 3 vols. Richmond, 1918-19.

_____. *Minutes of the Council and General Court of Colonial Virginia, 1622-*

1632, 1670-1676. Richmond, 1924.

_____. *Official Letters of the Governors of the State of Virginia.* 3 vols. Richmond, 1926-29.

McIlwaine, Henry R. et al., eds. *Executive Journals of the Council of Colonial Virginia.* 6 vols. Richmond, 1925-66.

McIlwaine, Henry R., and Kennedy, John P., eds. *Journals of the House of Burgesses of Virginia.* 13 vols. Richmond, 1904-15.

Mays, David John, ed. *The Letters and Papers of Edmund Pendleton, 1734-1803.* 2 vols. Charlottesville, Va., 1967.

"Miscellaneous Colonial Documents." *VMHB* 18 (July 1910): 272-89.

"Miscellaneous Documents, Colonial and State." *VMHB* 18 (October 1910): 394-407.

Munford, Robert. *The Candidates.* Edited by Jay B. Hubbell and Douglass Adair. *WMQ,* 3rd ser. 5 (April 1948): 217-57.

"Narrative of Bacon's Rebellion." *VMHB* 4 (October 1896): 117-54.

Palmer, William P.; McRae, Sherwin; and Colston, Raleigh, eds. *Calendar of Virginia State Papers and Other Manuscripts.* 11 vols. 1875-93. Reprint. New York, 1968.

Perry, William S., ed. *Historical Collections Relating to the American Colonial Church.* Vol. I: *Virginia.* Hartford, Conn., 1870.

"Petition of Alexandria Merchants, 1792." *WMQ,* 2d ser. 3 (July 1923): 206-08.

"Prince George County Records." *VMHB* 4 (January 1897): 272-92.

"The Randolph Manuscript." *VMHB* 21 (October 1913): 347-58.

Robertson, James R., ed. *Petitions of the Early Inhabitants of Kentucky to the General Assembly of Virginia, 1769 to 1792.* Filson Club Publication No. 27. Louisville, Ky., 1914.

Rutland, Robert A., ed. *The Papers of George Mason, 1725-1792.* 3 vols. Chapel Hill, N.C., 1970.

Saunders, William L., ed. *The Colonial Records of North Carolina.* 10 vols. Raleigh, 1886-90.

Shepherd, Samuel, ed. *The Statutes at Large of Virginia . . . Being a Continuation of Hening.* 3 vols. Richmond, 1835-36.

Shurtleff, Nathaniel B., ed. *Records of the Governor and Company of the Massachusetts Bay in New England.* 6 vols. Boston, 1853-54.

"Some Colonial Letters," *VMHB* 4 (July 1896): 15-23.

Summers, Lewis P., ed. *Annals of Southwest Virginia, 1769-1800.* 1929. Reprint. Baltimore, 1970.

Sweeny, William M., ed. "Gleanings from the Records of (Old) Rappahannock and Essex County, Virginia." *WMQ,* 2d ser. 18 (July 1938): 297-313.

U.S. Department of Commerce. Bureau of the Census. *Heads of Families at the First Census of the United States Taken in the Year 1790 . . . Virginia.* Washington, D.C., 1908.

Van Schreeven, William J.; Scribner, Robert L.; and Tarter, Brent, eds. *Revolutionary Virginia: The Road to Independence.* 3 vols. to date. Charlottesville, Va., 1973-

Virginia. *Acts Passed at a General Assembly of the Commonwealth of Virginia, Begun . . . in 1808.* Richmond, 1809.

Virginia. *Acts Passed at a General Assembly of the Commonwealth of Virginia, Begun . . . in 1809.* Richmond, 1810.

Virginia. *Documents, Containing Statistics of Virginia, Ordered to be Printed by the State Convention Sitting in the City of Richmond, 1850-51.* Richmond, 1851.

Virginia. *Journals of the House of Delegates, 1776-1831.* Williamsburg and Richmond, 1776-1831. These are available in various forms, the most convenient being *Records of the States of the United States. A Microfilm Compilation Prepared by the Library of Congress in Association with the University of North Carolina.* Collected and edited under William Sumner Jenkins. Library of Congress, 1949.

Virginia. *The Proceedings of the Convention of Delegates, held . . . the 1st of December, 1775.* Williamsburg, 1776.

Virginia. *The Proceedings of the Convention of Delegates, held . . . the 6th of May, 1776.* Williamsburg, 1776.

"The Virginia Clergy." *VMHB* 32 (October 1924): 321-37.

"Virginia in 1632-4." *VMHB* 6 (April 1899): 373-78.

"Virginia in 1637-38." *VMHB* 9 (April 1902): 407-10.

"Virginia in 1638." *VMHB* 10 (April 1903): 423-28.

"Virginia in 1638-39." *VMHB* 11 (July 1903): 46-57.

"Virginia in 1639-40." *VMHB* 13 (April 1906): 375-88.

"Virginia in 1654-56." *VMHB* 18 (January 1910): 44-57.

"Virginia in 1658-62." *VMHB* 18 (July 1910): 290-303.

"Virginia in 1662-65." *VMHB* 18 (October 1910): 408-27.

"Virginia Legislative Papers." *VMHB* 18 (January 1910): 24-44.

"Virginia Under Governor Gooch." *VMHB* 3 (October 1895): 113-23.

Webb, George. *The Office and Authority of a Justice of the Peace.* Williamsburg, 1736.

Winfree, Waverly K., ed. *The Laws of Virginia: Being a Supplement to Hening's The Statutes at Large.* Richmond, 1971.

Yazawa, Melvin, ed. *Representative Government and the Revolution: The Maryland Constitutional Crisis of 1787.* Baltimore, 1975.

NEWSPAPERS

Niles' Register, 12 March 1831; 20 August 1842.

Richmond Constitutional Whig, 18 August 1826; 27 April 1827.

Richmond Enquirer, 1815-1832.

Virginia Gazette, 1736-1774.

Virginia Gazette or the American Advertiser, 27 December 1783.

Virginia Gazette and General Advertiser, November-December, 1799.

Winchester Virginian, 28 December 1831.

Secondary Sources

BOOKS

Abernethy, Thomas P. *The South in the New Nation, 1789-1819*. Baton Rouge, La., 1961.
_____. *Three Virginia Frontiers*. 1940. Reprint. Gloucester, Mass., 1962.
_____. *Western Lands and the American Revolution*. New York, 1937.
Adams, George Burton. *Constitutional History of England*. New York, 1921.
Ahlstrom, Sidney E. *A Religious History of the American People*. New Haven, Conn., 1972.
Alden, John R. *Robert Dinwiddie: Servant of the Crown*. Williamsburg, 1973.
_____. *The South in the Revolution, 1763-1789*. Baton Rouge, La., 1957.
Allen, J. W. *English Political Thought, 1603-1660*. 2 vols. London, 1938.
Ambler, Charles Henry. *Sectionalism in Virginia from 1776 to 1861*. Chicago, 1910.
Ames, Susie M. *Studies of The Virginia Eastern Shore in the Seventeenth Century*. Richmond, 1940.
Andrews, Charles M. *The Colonial Period of American History*. 4 vols. New Haven, Conn., 1934-38.
Bailyn, Bernard. *The Ideological Origins of the American Revolution*. Cambridge, Mass., 1967.
_____. *The Origins of American Politics*. New York, 1968.
Ballagh, James Curtis. *A History of Slavery in Virginia*. Baltimore, 1902.
Beeman, Richard R. *The Old Dominion and the New Nation, 1788-1801*. Lexington, Ky., 1972.
Beer, George Louis. *The Old Colonial System, 1660-1754*. Part One: *The Establishment of the System, 1660-1688*. 2 vols. 1912. Reprint. Gloucester, Mass., 1958.
Blassingame, John W. *The Slave Community: Plantation Life in the Antebellum South*. New York, 1972.
Boddie, John Bennett. *Seventeenth Century Isle of Wight County, Virginia*. Chicago, 1938.
Brant, Irving. *James Madison*. 6 vols. Indianapolis, 1941-61.
Bridenbaugh, Carl. *Cities in the Wilderness*. New York, 1938.
_____. *Myths and Realities: Societies of the Colonial South*. Baton Rouge, La., 1952.
_____. *Vexed and Troubled Englishmen, 1590-1642*. New York, 1968.
Brown, Robert E., and Brown, B. Katherine. *Virginia 1705-1786: Democracy or Aristocracy?* East Lansing, Mich., 1964.
Bruce, Kathleen. *Virginia Iron Manufacture in the Slave Era*. New York, 1930.
Bruce, Philip Alexander. *Economic History of Virginia in the Seventeenth Century*. 2 vols. New York, 1895.
_____. *Institutional History of Virginia in the Seventeenth Century*. 2 vols. New York, 1910.
Brydon, George Maclaren. *Virginia's Mother Church and the Political Conditions Under Which It Grew*. 2 vols. Richmond, 1947-52.

Buckley, Thomas E. *Church and State in Revolutionary Virginia, 1776-1787.* Charlottesville, Va., 1977.

Channing, Edward. *A History of the United States.* 6 vols. New York, 1905-25.

Chitwood, Oliver P. *A History of Colonial America.* New York, 1931.

Chumbley, George Lewis. *Colonial Justice in Virginia.* Richmond, 1938.

Clark, Victor S. *History of Manufactures in the United States.* Vol. I: *History of Manufactures in the United States, 1607-1860.* 1929 ed. Reprint. New York, 1949.

Craven, Avery O. *Soil Exhaustion as a Factor in the Agricultural History of Virginia and Maryland, 1606-1860.* 1926. Reprint. Gloucester, Mass., 1965.

Craven, Wesley Frank. *The Southern Colonies in the Seventeenth Century, 1607-1689.* Baton Rouge, La., 1949.

Daniel, J. R. V. *A Hornbook of Virginia History.* Richmond, 1949.

Davis, Richard Beale. *Intellectual Life of Jefferson's Virginia, 1790-1830.* Chapel Hill, N.C., 1964.

Dickerson, Oliver M. *American Colonial Government, 1696-1765.* Cleveland, 1912.

Dodson, Leonidas. *Alexander Spotswood: Governor of Colonial Virginia, 1710-1722.* Philadelphia, 1932.

Duffy, John. *Epidemics in Colonial America.* Baton Rouge, La., 1953.

Eaton, Clement. *The Growth of Southern Civilization, 1790-1860.* New York, 1961.

Elton, G. R. *England Under the Tudors.* London, 1955.

Evans, Emory G. *Thomas Nelson of Yorktown: Revolutionary Virginian.* Charlottesville, Va., 1975.

Ferguson, E. James. *The Power of the Purse: A History of American Public Finance, 1776-1790.* Chapel Hill, N.C., 1961.

Freeman, Douglas Southall. *George Washington.* 7 vols. New York, 1948-57.

Gaustad, Edwin S. *A Religious History of America.* New York, 1966.

Genovese, Eugene D. *Roll, Jordan, Roll: The World the Slaves Made.* New York, 1974.

Gewehr, Wesley M. *The Great Awakening in Virginia, 1740-1790.* Durham, N.C., 1930.

Gipson, Lawrence Henry. *The British Empire Before the American Revolution.* Vol. I: *The British Isles and the American Colonies; Great Britain and Ireland, 1748-1754.* New York, 1958.

———. *The British Empire Before the American Revolution.* Vol. II: *The British Isles and the American Colonies; The Southern Plantations, 1748-1756.* New York, 1960.

Gray, Lewis Cecil. *History of Agriculture in the Southern United States to 1860.* 2 vols. 1933. Reprint. Gloucester, Mass., 1958.

Green, Fletcher M. *Constitutional Development in the South Atlantic States, 1776-1860.* Chapel Hill, N.C., 1930.

Greene, Evarts Boutell. *The Provincial Governor in the English Colonies of North America.* New York, 1898.

Greene, Jack P. *The Quest for Power: The Lower Houses of Assembly in the Southern Royal Colonies, 1689-1776.* Chapel Hill, N.C., 1963.

188   BIBLIOGRAPHY

Greene, Katherine G. *Winchester, Virginia, and Its Beginnings, 1743-1814.* Strasburg, Va., 1926.

Griffith, Lucille Blanche. *The Virginia House of Burgesses, 1750-1774.* Rev. ed. University, Ala., 1970.

Hart, Freeman H. *The Valley of Virginia in the American Revolution, 1763-1789.* Chapel Hill, N.C., 1942.

Haskins, George L. *The Growth of English Representative Government.* 1948. Reprint. New York, 1960.

Havighurst, Walter. *Alexander Spotswood: Portrait of a Governor.* New York, 1967.

Henretta, James A. *The Evolution of American Society, 1700-1815: An Interdisciplinary Analysis.* Lexington, Mass., 1973.

_____. *"Salutary Neglect": Colonial Administration Under the Duke of Newcastle.* Princeton, N.J., 1972.

Herndon, G. Melvin. *Tobacco in Colonial Virginia: "The Sovereign Remedy."* Jamestown 350th Anniversary Historical Booklets, edited by E. G. Swem. Williamsburg, 1957.

_____. *William Tatham and the Culture of Tobacco.* Coral Gables, Fla., 1969.

Hiden, Martha W. *How Justice Grew: Virginia Counties.* Jamestown 350th Anniversary Historical Booklets, edited by E. G. Swem. Williamsburg, 1957.

Hill, Christopher. *The Century of Revolution, 1603-1714.* Norton Library ed. New York, 1966.

Hofstadter, Richard. *America at 1750.* New York, 1971.

_____. *The Idea of a Party System: The Rise of Legitimate Opposition in the United States, 1780-1840.* Berkeley, Cal., 1969.

Jensen, Merrill. *The New Nation.* New York, 1950.

Jordan, Winthrop D. *White Over Black: American Attitudes Toward the Negro, 1550-1812.* Chapel Hill, N.C., 1968.

Kammen, Michael. *Deputyes and Libertyes: The Origins of Representative Government in Colonial America.* New York, 1969.

Labaree, Leonard Woods. *Royal Government in America.* New Haven, Conn., 1930.

McColley, Robert. *Slavery and Jeffersonian Virginia.* Urbana, Ill., 1964.

McDonald, Forrest. *E Pluribus Unum: The Formation of the American Republic, 1776-1790.* Boston, 1965.

Main, Jackson Turner. *Political Parties Before the Constitution.* Chapel Hill, N.C., 1973.

_____. *The Sovereign States, 1775-1783.* New York, 1973.

Maitland, F. W. *The Constitutional History of England.* Cambridge, 1913.

Malone, Dumas. *Jefferson and His Time.* Vol. I: *Jefferson the Virginian.* Boston, 1948.

Middleton, Arthur Pierce. *Tobacco Coast: A Maritime History of Chesapeake Bay in the Colonial Era.* Newport News, Va., 1953.

Morgan, Edmund Sears. *American Slavery—American Freedom: The Ordeal of Colonial Virginia.* New York, 1975.

_____. *The Birth of the Republic, 1763-1789.* Chicago, 1956.

Morris, Richard B. *Government and Labor in Early America.* New York, 1947.

Morton, Richard L. *Colonial Virginia.* 2 vols. Chapel Hill, N.C., 1960.

Mullin, Gerald W. *Flight and Rebellion: Slave Resistance in Eighteenth-Century Virginia.* New York, 1972.

Neale, John Earnest. *The Elizabethan House of Commons.* New Haven, Conn., 1950.

Notestein, Wallace. *The English People on the Eve of Colonization, 1603-1630.* New York, 1954.

Osgood, Herbert L. *The American Colonies in the Seventeenth Century.* 3 vols. New York, 1904-07.

———. *The American Colonies in the Eighteenth Century.* 4 vols. New York, 1924.

Ostrander, Gilman. *The Rights of Man in America, 1606-1861.* Columbia, Mo., 1960.

Peterson, Merrill D. *Thomas Jefferson and the New Nation.* New York, 1970.

Pole, J. R. *Political Representation in England and the Origins of the American Revolution.* New York and London, 1966.

Pollard, A. F. *The Evolution of Parliament.* 2d ed., rev. London, 1926.

Pomfret, John E. *Founding the American Colonies, 1583-1660.* New York, 1970.

Porter, Albert O. *County Government in Virginia: A Legislative History, 1607-1904.* New York, 1947.

Rainbolt, John C. *From Prescription to Persuasion: Manipulation of the Eighteenth [Seventeenth] Century Virginia Economy.* Port Washington, N.Y., 1974.

Rankin, Hugh F. *Criminal Trial Proceedings in the General Court of Colonial Virginia.* Charlottesville, Va., 1965.

Read, Conyers. *The Tudors: Personalities and Practical Politics in Sixteenth Century England.* Norton Library ed. New York, 1969.

Redlich, Josef. *The Procedure of the House of Commons.* 3 vols. 1908. Reprint. New York, 1969.

Reps, John W. *Tidewater Towns: City Planning in Colonial Virginia and Maryland.* Charlottesville, Va., 1972.

Risjord, Norman K. *The Old Republicans: Southern Conservatism in the Age of Jefferson.* New York, 1965.

Robbins, Carolyn. *The Eighteenth-Century Commonwealthman.* Cambridge, Mass., 1959.

Robert, Joseph C. *The Story of Tobacco in America.* New York, 1949.

———. *The Tobacco Kingdom: Plantation, Market, and Factory in Virginia and North Carolina, 1800-1860.* Durham, N.C., 1938.

Robinson, W. Stitt, Jr. *Mother Earth—Land Grants in Virginia, 1607-1699.* Jamestown 350th Anniversary Historical Booklets, edited by E. G. Swem. Williamsburg, 1957.

Rouse, Park, Jr. *James Blair of Virginia.* Chapel Hill, N.C., 1971.

Rowse, A. L. *The England of Elizabeth.* New York, 1950.

Sayles, George Osborne. *The King's Parliament of England.* New York, 1974.

Scarisbrick, J. J. *Henry VIII.* Berkeley, Cal., 1968.

Smith, Lacey Baldwin. *This Realm of England, 1399 to 1688.* Boston, 1966.

Stampp, Kenneth M. *The Peculiar Institution: Slavery in the Ante-Bellum South.* New York, 1956.

Stanard, William G., and Stanard, Mary N., comps. *The Colonial Virginia Register.* 1902. Reprint. Baltimore, 1965.

Starnes, George T. *Sixty Years of Branch Banking in Virginia.* New York, 1931.

Story, Joseph. *Commentaries on the Constitution of the United States.* 2 vols. 2d ed. Boston, 1851.

Stubbs, William. *The Constitutional History of England.* 3 vols. 4th ed. New York, 1967.

Sweet, William W. *Religion in Colonial America.* 1942. Reprint. New York, 1965.

_____. *Religion in the Development of American Culture, 1765-1840.* New York, 1952.

Sydnor, Charles S. *The Development of Southern Sectionalism, 1819-1848.* Baton Rouge, La., 1948.

_____. *Gentlemen Freeholders.* Chapel Hill, N.C., 1952.

Taylor, George Rogers. *The Transportation Revolution, 1815-1860.* New York, 1951.

Ubbelohde, Carl. *The American Colonies and the British Empire, 1607-1763.* New York, 1968.

Ver Steeg, Clarence L. *The Formative Years, 1607-1763.* New York, 1964.

Wertenbaker, Thomas Jefferson. *The Government of Virginia in the Seventeenth Century.* Jamestown 350th Anniversary Historical Booklets, edited by E. G. Swem. Williamsburg, 1957.

_____. *Norfolk: Historic Southern Port.* Durham, N.C., 1931.

_____. *The Planters of Colonial Virginia.* Princeton, N.J., 1922.

_____. *Virginia Under the Stuarts.* New York, 1959.

Willson, David Harris. *A History of England.* New York, 1967.

Wise, Jennings Cropper. *Ye Kingdome of Accawmacke, or the Eastern Shore of Virginia in the Seventeenth Century.* 1911. Reprint. Baltimore, 1967.

Wood, Gordon S. *The Creation of the American Republic, 1776-1787.* Chapel Hill, N.C., 1969.

Wright, Louis B. *The Cultural Life of the American Colonies, 1607-1763.* New York, 1957.

_____. *The First Gentlemen of Virginia: Intellectual Qualities of the Early Colonial Ruling Class.* San Marino, Cal., 1940.

ARTICLES

Anderson, James L. "The Virginia Councillors and the American Revolution." *VMHB* 82 (January 1974): 56-74.

Appleby, Joyce. "The Social Origins of American Revolutionary Ideology." *Journal of American History* 64 (March 1978): 935-58.

Bailey, Raymond C. "Racial Discrimination Against Free Blacks in Antebellum Virginia: The Case of Harry Jackson." *West Virginia History* 39 (January/April, 1978): 181-86.

Becker, Robert A. "Revolution and Reform: An Interpretation of Southern Taxation, 1763 to 1783." *WMQ*, 3rd ser. 32 (July 1975): 417-42.

Beeman, Richard R. "Social Change and Cultural Conflict in Virginia: Lunenburg
    County, 1746 to 1774." *WMQ*, 3rd ser. 35 (July 1978): 455-76.
Billings, Warren M. "The Growth of Political Institutions in Virginia, 1634 to 1676."
    WMQ, 3rd ser. 31 (April 1974): 225-42.
Blatcher, Marjorie. "Touching The Writ of Latitat: An Act 'Of No Great Moment.' "
    In *Elizabethan Government and Society: Essays Presented to Sir John Neale,*
    edited by S. T. Bindoff, J. Hurstfield, and C. H. Williams. London, 1961.
Brown, Alexander C. "Colonial Williamsburg's Canal Scheme." *VMHB* 86 (January
    1978): 26-32.
Cam, Helen M. "Legislation in Early Parliaments." In *Origins of the English Parlia-
    ment,* edited by Peter Spufford. New York, 1967.
Chitwood, Oliver P. "Justice in Colonial Virginia." *Johns Hopkins University
    Studies in Historical and Political Science* 23 (1905): 399-522.
Collinson, Patrick. "John Field and Elizabethan Puritanism." In *Elizabethan Govern-
    ment and Society: Essays Presented to Sir John Neale,* edited by S. T. Bindoff,
    J. Hurstfield, and C. H. Williams. London, 1961.
Detweiler, Robert. "Political Factionalism and Geographic Distribution of Standing
    Committee Assignments in the Virginia House of Burgesses, 1730-1776."
    VMHB 80 (July 1972): 267-85.
Dunaway, Wayland Fuller. "History of the James River and Kanawha Company."
    Columbia University Studies in History, Economics and Public Law 104 (1922):
    241-491.
Eckenrode, Hamilton J. "Separation of Church and State in Virginia." *Sixth Annual
    Report of the Library Board of the Virginia State Library, 1908-1909.* Rich-
    mond, 1910.
Ervin, Spencer. "The Establishment, Government, and Functioning of The Church
    in Colonial Virginia." *Historical Magazine of the Protestant Episcopal Church*
    26 (March 1957): 65-110.
Evans, Emory G. "The Rise and Decline of the Virginia Aristocracy in the Eighteenth
    Century: The Nelsons." In *The Old Dominion: Essays for Thomas Perkins
    Abernethy,* edited by Darrett B. Rutman. Charlottesville, Va., 1964.
Ezell, John. "The Lottery in Colonial America." *WMQ*, 3rd ser. 5 (April 1948):
    185-200.
Ferguson, Isabel. "County Court in Virginia, 1700-1830." *North Carolina Historical
    Review* 8 (January 1931): 14-40.
Flippin, Percy Scott. "The Financial Administration of the Colony of Virginia."
    Johns Hopkins University Studies in Historical and Political Science 23 (1915):
    177-272.
_____. "The Royal Government in Virginia, 1624-1775." *Columbia University
    Studies in History, Economics and Public Law* 84 (1919): 7-393.
Greene, Jack P. "Foundations of Political Power in the Virginia House of Burgesses,
    1720-1776." *WMQ*, 3rd ser. 16 (October 1959): 485-506.
_____. " '*Virtus et Libertas*': Political Culture, Social Change, and the Origins of
    the American Revolution in Virginia, 1763-1766." In *The Southern Experience
    in the American Revolution,* edited by Jeffrey J. Crow and Larry E. Tise.
    Chapel Hill, N.C., 1978.

Hemphill, W. Edwin. "Petitions of West Virginians to their General Assembly in Richmond." *West Virginia History* 18 (January 1957): 105-15.

Henderson, Patrick. "Smallpox and Patriotism: The Norfolk Riots, 1768-1769." *VMHB* 73 (October 1965): 413-24.

Herndon, G. Melvin. "Hemp in Colonial Virginia." *Agricultural History* 37 (April 1963): 86-93.

———. "A War-Inspired Industry: The Manufacture of Hemp in Virginia." *VMHB* 74 (July 1966): 301-11.

Isaac, Rhys. "Evangelical Revolt: The Nature of the Baptists' Challenge to the Traditional Order in Virginia, 1765 to 1775." *WMQ*, 3rd ser. 31 (July 1974): 345-68.

———. "Religion and Authority: Problems of the Anglican Establishment in Virginia in the Era of the Great Awakening and the Parsons' Cause." *WMQ*, 3rd ser. 30 (January 1973): 3-36.

Jameson, J. Franklin. "The Origin of the Standing Committee System in American Legislative Bodies." *Political Science Quarterly* 9 (June 1894): 246-67.

Jones, Newton B. "Weights, Measures, and Mercantilism: The Inspection of Exports in Virginia, 1742-1820." In *The Old Dominion: Essays for Thomas Perkins Abernethy*, edited by Darrett B. Rutman. Charlottesville, Va., 1964.

Keim, C. Ray. "Primogeniture and Entail in Colonial Virginia." *WMQ*, 3rd ser. 25 (October 1968): 545-86.

Land, Aubrey C. "Economic Behavior in a Planting Society: The Eighteenth-Century Chesapeake." *Journal of Southern History* 33 (November 1967): 469-85.

Leonard, Sister Joan de Lourdes. "The Organization and Procedure of the Pennsylvania Assembly, 1682-1776." *Pennsylvania Magazine of History and Biography* 62 (October 1948): 376-412.

Lokken, Roy N. "The Concept of Democracy in Colonial Political Thought." *WMQ*, 3rd ser. 16 (October 1959): 568-80.

McIlwaine, Henry R. "The Struggle of Protestant Dissenters for Religious Toleration in Virginia." *Johns Hopkins University Studies in Historical and Political Science* 12 (1894): 172-235.

McKisack, May. "The Function of Burgesses in Parliament." In *Origins of the English Parliament*, edited by Peter Spufford. New York, 1967.

Maier, Pauline. "Popular Uprisings and Civil Authority in Eighteenth-Century America." *WMQ*, 3rd ser. 27 (January 1970): 3-35.

Main, Jackson Turner. "The Distribution of Property in Post-Revolutionary Virginia." *Mississippi Valley Historical Review* 41 (September 1954): 241-58.

———. "Government by the People: The American Revolution and the Democratization of the Legislature." *WMQ*, 3rd ser. 23 (July 1966): 391-407.

———. "The One Hundred." *WMQ*, 3rd ser. 11 (July 1954): 354-84.

———. "Sections and Politics in Virginia, 1781-1787." *WMQ*, 3rd ser. 12 (January 1955): 96-112.

Maitland, F. W. "The Many Functions of Early Parliaments." In *Origins of the English Parliament*, edited by Peter Spufford. New York, 1967.

Malone, Dumas. "The Great Generation." *Virginia Quarterly Review* 23 (Winter 1947): 108-22.

Miller, Elmer I. "The Legislature of the Province of Virginia: Its Internal Development." *Columbia University Studies in History, Economics and Public Law* 28 (1907): 163-344.

Nicholls, Robert L. "Surrogate for Democracy: Nineteenth Century British Petitioning." *The Maryland Historian* 5 (Spring 1974): 43-52.

Pargellis, Stanley M. "The Procedure of the Virginia House of Burgesses." *WMQ*, 2d ser. 7 (April and July 1927): 73-86, 143-57.

Peterson, Arthur G. "Flour and Grist Milling in Virginia." *VMHB* 43 (April 1935): 97-108.

Pilcher, George William. "Samuel Davies and Religious Toleration in Virginia." *The Historian* 28 (November 1965): 48-71.

Pole, J. R. "Historians and the Problem of Early American Democracy." *American Historical Review* 67 (April 1962): 626-46.

――――. "Representation and Authority in Virginia from the Revolution to Reform." *Journal of Southern History* 24 (February 1958): 16-50.

Rainbolt, John C. "The Alteration in the Relationship between Leadership and Constituents in Virginia, 1660-1720." *WMQ*, 3rd ser. 27 (July 1970): 411-34.

――――. "The Case of the Poor Planters in Virginia Under the Law for Inspecting and Burning Tobacco." *VMHB* 79 (July 1971): 314-21.

――――. "A New Look at Stuart 'Tyranny': The Crown's Attack on the Virginia Assembly, 1676-1689." *VMHB* 75 (October 1967): 387-406.

Ripley, William Zebina. "The Financial History of Virginia, 1609-1776." *Columbia University Studies in History, Economics and Public Law* 4 (1893): 1-170.

Risjord, Norman K., and DenBoer, Gorden. "The Evolution of Political Parties in Virginia, 1782-1800." *Journal of American History* 60 (March 1974): 961-84.

Robinson, Morgan P. "Virginia Counties: Those Resulting from Virginia Legislation." Virginia State Library *Bulletin* 9 (January, April, and July 1916): 1-283.

Rutman, Darrett B. "The Virginia Company and Its Military Regime." In *The Old Dominion: Essays for Thomas Perkins Abernethy*, edited by Darrett B. Rutman. Charlottesville, Va., 1964.

Schlesinger, Arthur M. "The Aristocracy in Colonial America." *Proceedings of the Massachusetts Historical Society* 74 (1962): 3-21.

Schmidt, Fredrika Teute, and Wilhelm, Barbara Ripel. "Early Proslavery Petitions in Virginia." *WMQ*, 3rd ser. 30 (January 1973): 133-46.

Seiler, William H. "The Anglican Parish in Virginia." In *Seventeenth-Century America: Essays in Colonial History*, edited by James M. Smith. Chapel Hill, N.C., 1959.

――――. "The Anglican Parish Vestry in Colonial Virginia." *Journal of Southern History* 22 (August 1956): 310-37.

――――. "The Church of England as the Established Church in Seventeenth-Century Virginia." *Journal of Southern History* 15 (November 1949): 478-508.

Shepard, E. Lee. "Courts in Conflict: Town-County Relations in Post-Revolutionary Virginia." *VMHB* 85 (April 1977): 184-99.

Snow, Sinclair. "Naval Stores in Colonial Virginia." *VMHB* 72 (January 1964): 75-93.
Sutton, Robert P. "Sectionalism and Social Structure: A Case Study of Jeffersonian
   Democracy." *VMHB* 80 (January 1972): 70-84.
Webb, Stephen Saunders. "The Strange Career of Francis Nicholson." *WMQ*, 3rd ser.
   23 (October 1966): 513-48.
Wertenbaker, Thomas Jefferson. "The Attempt to Reform the Church of Colonial
   Virginia." *The Sewanee Review* 25 (July 1917): 257-82.
Williams, D. Alan. "The Small Farmer in Eighteenth-Century Virginia Politics."
   Agricultural History 43 (January 1969): 91-101.
Williams, William Appleman. "The Age of Mercantilism: An Interpretation of the
   American Political Economy to 1828." *WMQ*, 3rd ser. 15 (October 1958): 419-37.

UNPUBLISHED MATERIAL

Ammon, Harry. "The Republican Party in Virginia, 1789-1824." Ph.D. dissertation,
   University of Virginia, 1948.
Foard, Susan Lee. "Virginia Enters the Union: A Legislative Study of the Common-
   wealth, 1789-1792." M.A. thesis, College of William and Mary, 1966.
Gardner, Harold Warren. "The Dissenting Sects on the Southern Colonial Frontier,
   1720-1770." Ph.D. dissertation, University of Kansas, 1969.
Rich, Myra Lakoff. "The Experimental Years: Virginia, 1781-1789." Ph.D. disserta-
   tion, Yale University, 1966.
Williams, D. Alan. "Political Alignments in Colonial Virginia Politics, 1698-1750."
   Ph.D. dissertation, Northwestern University, 1959.

INDEX

71, 81, 143-44. *See also*
England; Old Colonial Policy
Bolling, Robert, 96, 102-3
Botetourt County, 98, 117; cre-
ated, 77; and establishment of
hemp inspection system, 99
Bourbon County, divided, 77-78
Bristol Iron-mine Company, 102
Brooke County, created, 78
Bruce, Kathleen, 104
Bruce, Philip Alexander, 40
Brunswick County, 96; pro-
slavery sentiment in, 124
Buckingham County, and internal
improvements, 117-18
Burwell, Lewis, 42, 129

Cabell, Joseph C., 30; and sec-
tionalism, 172
Cabell, Samuel Jordan, 32
Campbell County, 98
Caroline County, 42
Carter, Charles, of Cleve, 32
Carter, Charles, of Corotoman,
42, 103
Carter, Landon, 32; and sec-
tionalism, 72
Cary, Archibald, 32, 129
Certification of petitions, 27-28,
30, 39-41
Charles City County, 40, 96-97
Charles Parish, 148
Charter, of colonial Virginia,
13-14
Chesterfield County, 80
Christ Church Parish, created,
139
Church of England, role of in
eighteenth-century Virginia,
4, 137-58. *See also* Religious
freedom

Cities: local governments of
receive petitions, 23; establishment, regulation, and incorporation of, 68, 82-84
Clark, Victor, 100
Classes: degree of conflict among,
4, 5, 167-68; petitions presented by all, 26, 41-46, 166,
173-74
Clayton, Reubin, 43
Cloth industry, 100
College of William and Mary,
124
Commissary, powers of, 4, 137-
38
Committee of Propositions and
Grievances, membership and
duties of, 28-29, 32-36, 60
Committee of the whole House,
as source of legislation, 56, 59
Committees, legislative: origin of
in England, 9-14; origin of in
Virginia, 18, 28-29; standing,
28-29, 56, 60-61, 127-28,
130, 152; select, 29, 56, 59-
61
Constitution of 1776, 26, 152; revision of sought by westerners,
32, 170-71
Convention of 1776, 152-53
Council: executive duties of, 3,
148-49, 151; judicial duties of,
3, 16, 25, 80-81; legislative
duties of, 3, 30, 59, 64; presentation of petitions to, 24;
powers of reduced after independence, 25
Counterpetitions, use of, 31, 68,
75-79, 145-47
Counties: alteration or division of,
17, 19, 31, 63, 68-80; legislative

Representation: in Virginia legisla-
ture, 72-73; theories of "actual"
and "virtual," 168-69, 172-
73; and sectional conflict, 170-
71
Republican government, ideal of, 5
Reveley, John, 103-4
Richmond, city of, 45, 106
Richmond County, 97, 123; and
certification controversy, 40
Rivers, clearing obstructions to
navigation of, 115-21
Roads, construction and mainte-
nance of, 19, 23, 115-21
Robinson, John, 32
Ross, David, 98

St. James's Parish, divided, 145
St. John's Parish, 30, 141, 148,
149; divided, 144
St. Mark's Parish, divided, 145
St. Mary's Parish, divided, 143-44
St. Paul's Parish: divided, 62-63,
145; mentioned, 74
St. Peter's Parish, 141; divided,
142
St. Stephen's Parish, 142-43;
divided, 147
Salt, production of, 103
Salted meat, production and ex-
portation of, 98, 100-1
Scott, John B., 106
Sectionalism: lack of before 1800,
5, 35-36, 72-73, 168; growth of
after 1800, 5, 72-73, 121, 169-72
Senate, 30, 59
Slavery, 3-4, 44, 56, 61, 121;
and compensation to owners
of slaves executed by government, 42, 122, 130; petitions
about, 121-24; and section-

alism, 171-72; and debate over
emancipation, 172
Smallpox, 128-29
Southampton County, 79, 115
Southside, 5
Southwalk Parish, 138
Spotswood, Alexander, Governor,
56, 148-49; and domestic political conflict, 5, 55, 70-71,
81-82, 174; and certification
controversy, 40; and dispute
over creation of counties and
parishes, 70-71, 143-44, 174;
and creation of tobacco inspection system, 93-94
Squirrels, killing of encouraged,
91
Stafford County, 91, 103
Staunton, city of, incorporated,
84
Storehouses for commodities,
built by county courts, 97-98
Stratton Major Parish, created,
139
Suffrage, 3, 5
Surry County: divided, 45, 78-79;
dispute over courthouse location of, 80-81; seeks to halt interracial marriages, 122; seeks to
halt further importation of
slaves, 122
Sussex County, created, 79

Tandy, Smyth, 104
Taxes, 23, 26, 43, 107
Tidewater, common interests
with Piedmont, 5, 168
Tobacco, production of, 4, 96,
106; laws regulating, 19, 42,
46, 56, 90-98; and English
commercial policy, 92-94

Trans-Allegheny, and sectional
conflict, 5, 168-73
Transylvania Seminary, 125
Tyler, John: supports creation of
public school system, 58; and
governor's message to legislature, 58

Upper house of the legislature.
See Council; Senate

Valley, and sectional conflict,
5, 168-73
Vestries: membership and duties
of, 4, 137-38, 147-50, 158;
supervision of by colonial and
state government, 64, 137,
147-50
Virginia, general political structure of, 3-6
Virginia Company of London, 13,
15-16

Walton, James, 43
Washington, George: and internal
improvements, 118-20; and
religious freedom, 158

West, Thomas, Lord De la Warr,
Governor, 15
Western counties, and sectionalism,
32, 35-36, 72-73, 121, 169-
72
Westmoreland County, 43, 80,
97
Wheat, production of, 101
White, John, 43
Williamsburg Canal, plan for con-
struction of, 118
Wilmington Parish, dispute over
dissolution of, 145-46
Wine, attempts to encourage
production of, 102-3
Witherspoon, John, and religious
freedom, 152
Wolves, killing of encouraged,
91
Women: denied suffrage, 3, 166;
use petitions, 44
Wood, Gordon, 168, 172-73
Wood County, supports creation
of public school system, 26
Wormeley, Ralph, 129

Yeardley, George, Governor, 15

About the Author

Raymond C. Bailey is Assistant Professor of History at Northern Virginia Community College. He has published articles and reviews in a number of historical journals, including *West Virginia History* and *The Historical Magazine of the Protestant Episcopal Church.*

BAREND VAN NIEKERK

THE
CLOISTERED VIRTUE

THE
CLOISTERED VIRTUE

Freedom of Speech and the
Administration of Justice
in the Western World

BAREND VAN NIEKERK

I cannot praise a fugitive and cloistered virtue, unexercised and
unbreathed, that never sallies out and sees her adversary, but
slinks out of the race, where the immortal garland is to be run
for, not without dust and heat.

John Milton, *Areopagitica*

PRAEGER

New York
Westport, Connecticut
London

Financial support toward publication of this volume was
granted by the Alexander von Humboldt-Stiftung.

Library of Congress Cataloging-in-Publication Data

Van Niekerk, Barend.
  The cloistered virtue.

  Bibliography: p.
  Includes index.
  1. Freedom of speech. 2. Justice, Administration of.
I. Title.
K3254.V36   1986   342'.0853   86-25570
ISBN 0-275-92082-8 (alk. paper) 342.2853

Library of Congress Catalog Card Number: 86-25570
ISBN: 0-275-92082-8

First published in 1987

Praeger Publishers, 521 Fifth Avenue, New York, NY 10175
A division of Greenwood Press, Inc.

Printed in the United States of America

∞

The paper used in this book complies with the
Permanent Paper Standard issued by the National
Information Standards Organization (Z39.48-1984).

10 9 8 7 6 5 4 3 2 1

To the children of Africa,
Kristine Naëtt and Marijke Annette

CONTENTS

FOREWORD

In 1981, shortly after completing the manuscript of *The Cloistered Virtue*, Barend van Niekerk died at the age of 42. He left a wife, Traute, and two small daughters, Kristine and Marijke. An inveterate traveler, he died of a heart attack on a visit to Lake Titicaca in Bolivia, some 12,500 feet above sea level, where he had gone despite medical warnings that his high blood pressure would not permit travel to high altitudes. Thus South Africa lost its most active and controversial civil rights campaigner, whose interventions had raised the temperature of debate in almost every civil rights issue for over a decade. In a country in which human rights violations are many and activists are few, Barend van Niekerk succeeded in stimulating public debate on so wide a range of subjects as the country's archaic Sunday observance laws, capital punishment, race discrimination in law enforcement, police torture, censorship, press freedom, and the role of the judge, lawyer, and academic in an unjust society. He wrote prolifically and spoke courageously in a manner that was often considered neither politic nor polite by his own staid profession. Many disagreed strongly with his writings, his speeches, and his actions. But no one could ignore him. He was a vital, vibrant force who demanded a response. On occasion the South African government responded in a heavy-handed manner, but all its attempts to silence him failed. The present study bears eloquent testimony to this failure.

Barend van Niekerk was born into the White Tribe of Africa – the Afrikaners, whose political mouthpiece, the National Party, has governed South Africa since 1948, with its policy of apartheid or separate development, as it is now euphemistically called. He attended an Afrikaans school and university and devoted himself energetically to the cause of Afrikaner nationalism throughout his high school and undergraduate days. Indeed, when I first met Barend as a fellow student at the University of Stellenbosch in the 1950s, his zealous support for the National Party exceeded that of his peers. For not only was he active in the work of the National Party youth movement, but he proudly advertised this allegiance by flying a party flag on his motor scooter. Characteristically, political change came to him not through reflection but through action. Incensed by student rudeness at a meeting addressed by the liberal Anglican archbishop of Cape Town, the Right Reverend Joost de Blank, he publicly disavowed the National Party demonstrators and apologized for their insulting behavior. That night he made his choice. He was not to conform again.

After graduating from the University of Stellenbosch, Barend van Niekerk studied abroad in Germany, France, and Italy. His studies were not limited to law, but spread into the fields of politics, philosophy, history, language, and literature. He traveled widely in Europe and Africa and became proficient in German, French, Spanish, and Italian. In 1965, a doctorate in history was conferred on him by the University of Strasbourg for a dissertation on

Pan-Africanism, with special reference to the roles of W. E. B. du Bois and Kwame Nkrumah. He developed an interest in the poetry of Léopold Senghor, the president of Senegal, and in 1970 he published *The African Image (Negritude) in the Work of Léopold Sedar Senghor*. Later, he became a good friend of President Senghor and visited him in Senegal on many occasions.

The effect of foreign travel on Afrikaner attitudes is an oft-debated topic in South Africa. Certainly it had a radical impact on Barend van Niekerk. The young man who returned to South Africa in 1966 was no longer the committed, narrow Afrikaner of his student days. In January of 1968, in an article in *New Nation,* he described himself as a "detribalized Afrikaner," who had rejected the hallmarks of nationalist Afrikanerdom, particularly as reflected in its racist policies, but who nevertheless remained bound to Afrikanerdom in a community of destiny and by ties of sentiment and history.

On his return to South Africa, Van Niekerk applied for a post in the law faculty of the University of Fort Hare, a university for blacks rigidly controlled by the Nationalist government, but, despite his impressive academic qualifications, he was not successful. In the interview that preceded this decision he was questioned about his religious affiliations and church attendance and his response that he had applied for a post in law and not theology was not lightly dismissed by the selection committee. He was more successful in his application to the University of Zululand, another government-controlled university for blacks, but after a year's sojourn there he was appointed to a senior lectureship in law in mid-1967 at the University of the Witwatersrand.

The University of the Witwatersrand, the largest English-language university in South Africa, prides itself on its commitment to the liberal and humanist academic tradition. Situated in the city of Johannesburg, it gives the academic easy access to the media and to the main platforms of legal and political debate. It was the ideal environment for the detribalized Van Niekerk.

During his early years at the University of the Witwatersrand, Van Niekerk pursued the life of an ambitious young academic: he lectured in a wide range of subjects and started to write prolifically. His writings provided abundant evidence of his knowledge and understanding of foreign legal systems, but they ruffled few feathers. Even his first foray into legal controversy, an article ridiculing South Africa's primitive Sunday observance laws (which are deeply rooted in the Calvinist theology that provides the spiritual force for Afrikaner nationalism) was soon forgotten. His espousal of the cause of abolition, which was to bring him into national prominence, was not to be so easily forgotten.

Despite the fact that the death penalty still figures prominently as a punishment in South Africa, there is little support for the abolitionist cause. Van Niekerk set out to remedy this situation almost single-handed in the late 1960s as the execution rate mounted to exceed the hundred mark each year. He formed the Society of the Abolition of Capital Punishment and began to campaign passionately. In 1970, he was prosecuted for contempt of court for an article on the death penalty. This prosecution, so central to an understanding of

Van Niekerk's crusade for freedom of expression in the administration of justice, is, however, one that can be understood only in the context of that time.

The South African Supreme Court, comprising several provincial divisions and an Appellate Division, is modeled on English lines. The judges pride themselves on their independence, and in the early 1950s this independence was amply demonstrated when the Appellate Division refused to approve a legislative scheme aimed at disenfranchising colored voters and insisted on strict compliance with the separate but equal doctrine in the field of public amenities at a time when the government had set about implementing a policy of "separate but unequal." In response, the government set about reconstituting the Supreme Court, and more particularly the Appellate Division. The nature of this division was radically transformed by its enlargement from five to eleven judges and important changes were also made in the membership of the provincial divisions. These changes did not go unnoticed in legal quarters, but little public attention was given to them. Consequently, it did not surprise the public to find the new Supreme Court basking in the reputation established by its predecessor. Nor did it appear incongruous that the same government that had vigorously assailed the Appellate Division in the 1950s should now join in singing the praises of the independent judiciary. In 1968, the same government that had openly criticized the Appellate Division and enlarged its membership in the 1950s declared in a publication for foreign consumption that "South Africa is proud of its judges" who "exercise their functions independently of the Executive" [*South Africa and the Rule of Law* (Department of Foreign Affairs, Pretoria) 20].

By the mid-1960s, when the Supreme Court was called upon to hear a number of cases arising out of the political subversion of that period, it had grown accustomed to its reputation for independence. Its performance in the 1950s had won the hearts of liberals and its new composition, coupled with its policy of restraint in matters affecting the state, had won favor with the government. Therefore, it was totally unprepared for criticism directed at its interpretation of the security laws; and it was particularly offended to find itself – a court with a reputation for independent action hitherto criticized mainly by the government – now being questioned by liberal critics on the grounds of "executive-mindedness."

In 1964 and 1965, the Appellate Division delivered a number of pro-government decisions that gave the court's blessing to the system of detention without trial introduced in 1963 to deal with persons suspected of political offenses. These decisions were vigorously condemned by Professors Tony Mathews and Ronald Albino of the University of Natal. In an article published in the leading South African legal periodical, the *South African Law Journal*, they declared:

We have to face the fact that some South Africans may have lost faith in the courts. The line of cases discussed in this article does not present a picture of judges fired by ideas of individual liberty or personal sanctity. There is no assertion that the judges are partial or that they lack integrity. What does seem to have been lacking in the cases analysed above is an imaginative grasp of the implications of solitary confinement and of Western ideals of individual freedom. [(1966)83 *South African Law Journal* 16 at 37]

This criticism was not allowed to go unanswered. In April 1967, Chief Justice Steyn expressed regret at the "intemperate, derogatory language" of the court's critics, who had by implication accused the court of "something in the nature of a dereliction of duty, due to an inadequate concern for basic rights and liberties." He then pleaded for a neutral approach to the judicial function and added that "it would be an evil day for the administration of justice if our courts should deviate from the well recognized tradition of giving politics as wide a berth as their work permits."

Both the government and the judges were concerned about this criticism of the courts, and there were signs that a prosecution of Professor Mathews on a charge of contempt of court was seriously contemplated. The judges and the government were now clearly on the lookout for academic lawyers who went too far in their questioning of the judicial role in an apartheid society.

In 1969, Barend van Niekerk published an article in the *South African Law Journal* under the title ". . . Hanged by the Neck until You Are Dead" [(1969)86 *SALJ* 457, (1970)87 *SALJ* 60], advocating the abolition of the death penalty. In it he discussed a questionnaire he had circulated among the judiciary and advocates soliciting their views on capital punishment. One of the questions posed in the questionnaire was, "Do you consider, for whatever reason, that a Non-European tried on a capital charge stands a better chance of being sentenced to death than a European?" This was followed by the question, "If your answer (to the previous question) is 'yes' or 'only for certain crimes', do you think that the differentiation shown to the different races as regards the death penalty is conscious and deliberate?" In his article, Van Niekerk reproduced these questions and the replies of advocates, and commented, "Whatever conclusion one may draw from the results of these two questions, the fact which emerges undeniably is that a considerable number of replying advocates, almost 50 per cent in fact, believe that justice as regards capital punishment is meted out on a differential basis to the different races, and that 41 per cent who so believe are also of the opinion that such differentiation is 'conscious and deliberate'."

For these comments Van Niekerk was charged, apparently on the complaint of the judge president of the Transvaal, Mr. Justice P. M. Cillié, with contempt of court, on the ground that his statement was calculated to bring the judiciary into contempt, to violate their dignity and respect, and to cast suspicion on the administration of justice. He was acquitted by Judge Claassen as he was found not to have had the necessary intention to commit the crime, but the judge took the opportunity to rebuke Van Niekerk. More disturbing still, he found that the statements published could, standing on their own, be viewed as being contempt of court, as

> a reasonable person reading the article in question would understand that advocates are persons who have an intimate knowledge of the way justice is meted out and their opinions are entitled to great respect and if the reader accepted the views set out he could possibly hold the judges and the administration of justice in low esteem.... If the interpretation suggested be correct then the judges could no longer be treated with due respect for they could no longer be universally thought of as being impartial. [*S* v. *Van Niekerk* 1970(3) SA 655(T)]

The prosecution failed to silence Van Niekerk. On the contrary, he became more outspoken on matters affecting the administration of justice in general, and the abolitionist cause in particular. He was now a national figure whose pronouncements on issues of justice were featured regularly in the popular press. He was also much in demand as a public speaker as his oratory, a blend of compassion, hyperbole, and sardonic humor, could be entertaining and yet moving.

In 1970, Van Niekerk was appointed to the chair of public law in the University of Natal, Durban, a position he was to hold until his death, June 21, 1981. Controversy surrounded his appointment, and, indeed, his tenure of the post as a result of his prosecution and his high profile in public debate. Moreover, he was soon to become embroiled in another prosecution that was further to alienate him from the legal establishment.

In November 1971, at the height of a public outcry following the death of Ahmed Timol while a detainee under Section 6 of the Terrorism Act, a protest meeting was held in the Durban City Hall attended by several thousand people. At this meeting Professor van Niekerk delivered a scathing attack on Section 6 of the Terrorism Act, which authorized the police to detain a person suspected of participation in terrorist activities indefinitely, in solitary confinement, for the purpose of interrogation. Inter alia, he declared:

> [The] very purpose of the detention clause of the Terrorism Act is to procure evidence by way of torture. It is an accepted fact in any civilized land but ours that solitary confinement over a long period, even if unaccompanied by any of its possible frills, is torture *per se*. In one of the landmark decisions in American law (that of *Miranda* v *Arizona*) incommunicado interrogation was itself regarded as third degree.

He then went on to criticize lawyers and judges for their failure to condemn this statute.

> The Terrorism Act ... is a negation of what any true lawyer would call justice. And yet our lawyers, the guardians of our nation's legal

heritage, have done so very little to mitigate its crudities. What then, you ask, can our lawyers do? In the very first place our lawyers, all our lawyers from judges downward, can make their voices *heard* about an institution which they must surely know to be an abdication of decency and justice. No doubt, they will tell you, it is not their function to criticize the law, but to apply it. This is the very understandable retort of our judges to the demand sometimes made upon them to have their influential voices heard when the rule of law is trampled into the dust. But we must surely ask these lawyers, when will a point *ever* be reached when their protests would become justified? Will they still make this facile excuse for abject inactivity if it is decreed that public flogging be introduced for traffic offences, . . . burning at the stake for immorality and decapitation for the use of abusive language? Surely we have reached the stage that we are no longer merely dealing with a nicety of jurisprudence but with the essential quality and survival of justice itself! Surely also lawyers should realize that by remaining silent at the helm of their clinking cash registers they are not only perpetuating these palpable injustices but they are indeed also lending them the aura of respectability. Above all, they should realize that by remaining silent in the face of what they know to be inherently unjust, cruel and primitive, they are indeed sullying themselves and the reputation of their profession.

Finally, Van Niekerk turned his attention to the judiciary and asked:

In the face of the grotesqueness of the situation as regards the application of the Terrorism Act, has not the time come for them to stand up more dynamically in the defence of the hallowed principles of the rule of law in the Western sense? . . . Cannot our judiciary . . . in effect kill one aspect of the usefulness of the Terrorism Act for our authorities? They can do so by denying, on account of the built-in intimidatory effect of unsupervised solitary confinement, practically all creditworthiness to evidence procured under those detention provisions. It is a grave solution I am asking them to take, but the situation is also a very grave one.

For some time prior to the protest meeting in the Durban City Hall, a criminal prosecution (*S* v. *Hassim and Others*) under the Terrorism Act had been in progress in Pietermaritzburg. The accused and most state witnesses in this case had previously been held for lengthy periods under the Terrorism Act, and it was alleged by defense counsel that several state witnesses had been physically ill treated by the police while in detention. Considerable publicity had been given to these proceedings and to the allegations of police brutality, and Van

Niekerk was clearly aware of the proceedings although he did not mention them in his speech.

In December 1971, Professor van Niekerk was indicted before Judge Fannin in the Durban and Coast Local Division on charges of contempt of court and attempting to defeat or obstruct the course of justice as a result of his speech. On the first count the state alleged that Van Niekerk had committed contempt of court, first, by insulting or scandalizing the court, and second, by making comments "with intent . . . to prejudice and influence the judgment in the case of *S* v. *Hassim and Others.* " (The comments referred to here were those calling upon the judiciary to "kill" the usefulness of the Terrorism Act by denying "practically" all evidence procured under its detention provision.) On the second count the prosecution averred that he had attempted to defeat or obstruct the course of justice

> by calling upon the Judges of the Supreme Court of the Republic of South Africa and other judicial officers not to admit or attach any credence to evidence given or statements made by persons detained in accordance with the provisions of the Terrorism Act, during judicial proceedings before them, thus seeking improperly to influence the said judges and judicial officers in their judgements and the administration of justice by them in accordance with the law and customs of the Republic of South Africa.

Judge Fannin acquitted Van Niekerk of the charge of scandalizing the court on the first count, but found him guilty of publishing comments that had a tendency to prejudice or interfere with the proceedings in the *Hassim* case, despite the fact that he nowhere referred to this case in his address. The judge acquitted him on the second count on the ground that the state had failed to prove that he had the necessary intention to interfere with or obstruct the course of justice in any judicial proceedings which might then or in the future be pending. Professor van Niekerk was sentenced to a fine of 100 rands, with an alternative of one month's imprisonment, in respect of his conviction on the first count. The trial court gave leave to appeal against this conviction and, on the application of the attorney-general for Natal, reserved a question of law on whether the speech "[did] not in law, constitute the crime of attempting to defeat or obstruct the course of justice."

The Appellate Division, like Judge Fannin, held that Van Niekerk's speech did not constitute the species of contempt known as "scandalizing the court," but found that it did have a tendency to interfere with the proceedings in the *Hassim* case and therefore dismissed his appeal. Furthermore, it found in favor of the state on the point of law reserved and convicted Van Niekerk of attempting to defeat or obstruct the course of justice [see *S* v. *Van Niekerk* 1972(3) SA 711(A)].

The judgment of the Appellate Division had a traumatic effect on Van Niekerk. The court's decision, which reflected a clear determination to be rid of the turbulent Van Niekerk, imposed severe restraints on the right to criticize the administration of justice, and Van Niekerk rightly believed that the press and the legal fraternity did not treat it with sufficient concern. He saw it as his task to alert the media and the legal profession to the curb that had been placed on free speech by the Appellate Division and from this time he devoted much of his energy to speaking and writing on this subject. The cause of abolition was not forgotten, but relegated to second place.

The third of Van Niekerk's trials, like the first, arose out of his concern over the racial factor in the system of capital punishment. This time, however, it took the form of a civil action for defamation (libel). The case arose out of a comment by Van Niekerk, in which he condemned the decision of the Executive Council (cabinet) to reprieve a white killer but not his black colleague, who had been convicted of the same crime. According to Van Niekerk, in an interview published in the Johannesburg *Sunday Times,* the execution of the black man in this case

> must fill all South Africans with shame. Two persons of different races commit the same crime and are sentenced to the same punishment by a court of law: yet they are treated differently by the Executive on the plea of mercy. One would have expected the Government to save the life of Makinitha [the black man], to avoid the obvious inference of discrimination; that they did not do so speaks volumes for their lack of concern for justice and the reputation of our law.

These remarks resulted in defamation proceedings being instituted against Van Niekerk and the *Sunday Times* by the minister of justice, Mr. P. C. Pelser, acting in a personal capacity. On behalf of the two defendants, it was argued that this article was not defamatory as it would be understood by the reasonable reader as a legitimate exercise of the subject's right to criticize the executive and its policies. The Appellate Division, however, in an appeal on a preliminary question of law, rejected this contention and held that the words were defamatory as they imputed racial discrimination and a lack of concern for justice in the exercise of the discretion to reprieve persons sentenced to death. Moreover, although the Executive Council itself could not sue, it was open to the minister of justice, as the minister in charge of the administration of justice, to sue in his personal capacity.

This decision, like the earlier Van Niekerk cases, had serious implications for freedom of expression in South Africa, as in effect it meant that critics of the government might now be exposed to defamation proceedings at the instance of ministers acting in their personal capacities. Unfortunately the Appellate Division chose not to see it in this light and failed to refer to the leading American decision on this subject, *New York Times* v. *Sullivan* 376 U.S.

254(1964), despite the fact that this authority featured prominently in the argument of counsel for the defendants [see *South African Associated Newspapers Ltd and Van Niekerk* v. *Estate Pelser* 1975(4) SA 797(A)].

Van Niekerk was deeply troubled by this action as he feared that he might be ruined by a large award against him and by the costs of the proceedings. Before the conclusion of the proceedings, however, Mr. Pelser died with the result that no award was made, and the *Sunday Times* agreed to bear the full burden of the costs of the proceedings.

The three Van Niekerk cases were undoubtedly the inspiration for the present comparative study. Van Niekerk was outraged that he, a member of the Afrikaner elite and a professor of law, should be persecuted by the government and ostracized by the legal establishment. Moreover, he was distressed that many of his colleagues in the law failed to support him publicly or to appreciate the enormity of the restrictions on freedom of speech expounded in the Van Niekerk cases. On the other hand, his direct pronouncements on social justice, so unlike the polite murmurs of the liberal establishment, won him new friends and admirers in the black community, who saw in Van Niekerk a campaigner prepared to "tell it as it is" and to face the consequences.

Gradually, Van Niekerk's anger gave way to reflection on the forces in Western societies that wittingly or unwittingly conspire to protect the judiciary from robust criticism. He came to realize that law, convention, legal mythology, taboos, and professional codes of conduct together ensured that the administration of justice remained a "cloistered virtue," even in societies that enjoy a greater measure of free speech than South Africa. This new understanding obsessed him and the last years of his life were devoted mainly to the study of the subject. Although he became more understanding of the nature of the judicial function, Van Niekerk did not let up in his campaigning of the cause of justice. He continued to publish regularly in legal periodicals, to make pronouncements in the popular press, and to address meetings. And, running like a golden thread through all these writings, speeches, and utterances on the subject of the injustices in South African society, was the clear message that freedom of speech is a democratic value that should not be allowed to fall into disuse – even, or particularly, where the courts and judges are concerned.

Van Niekerk clearly believed that his crusade for freedom of speech in matters affecting the administration of justice had met with little success in his native land. Indeed, readers of the present work will have little difficulty in identifying this mood of despondency. But here Van Niekerk was too pessimistic, for there is no doubt that he did succeed in expanding the bounds of free speech. The judiciary gained nothing from the contempt of court prosecutions. On the contrary, they lost much public support as they were seen to be petty minded in their readiness to invoke the criminal sanction to protect their own reputation. Furthermore the prosecutions failed to curb academic criticism of judicial decisions in the areas of race and security as writers, including Van Niekerk, simply became more artful in the formulation of their criticism. Some judges came to appreciate that robust and frank comments on their decisions from academic quarters were perhaps justified and constructively intended. Indeed, Van Niekerk came to be respected by a number of judges and could proudly boast that "some of my best friends are judges." There is no question that today there are more lawyers in South Africa prepared to speak out against injustice in the courts; and subjects that were taboo ten years ago – such as race and sentencing, the torture of detainees, and the appointment of judges – are debated more openly.

The new freedom to discuss the administration of justice in South Africa stands as a lasting monument to Barend van Niekerk. But there are other memorials. His advocacy of the abolitionist cause constitutes a lasting reminder of the barbarous nature of this punishment. And his passionate, at times sardonic, appeals to practicing and academic lawyers to concern themselves more with the broader issues affecting justice have left their mark.

Barend van Niekerk could not be typecast. Politically he espoused the values of liberalism, but no political movement in South Africa was free from the strictures of his tongue or pen. He was interested in issues and causes, not political parties or ideologies. The right of the lawyer to criticize the administration of justice in an open and robust manner became his main cause and this he pursued with energy and fervor.

In this brief biographical introduction, I have sought to give a picture of Barend van Niekerk within the setting of *The Cloistered Virtue*. In the process of concentrating on Van Niekerk the public figure I have, inevitably, neglected Barend the private man, the friend. Unlike most South Africans, whose friendships are forged by ethnic loyalties or political affiliations, Barend had friends from all racial groups and political factions. He prized these friendships dearly and he was a loyal and concerned friend to many. Surrounded by his family – his wife Traute and his daugthers Kristine and Marijke – he loved to play the role of the host, the warm Afrikaner family man, whose main task was to feed and entertain his friends. For those who knew this side of him, his early death was a double blow.

The Cloistered Virtue has its roots in the soil of an apartheid society. Its inspiration is to be found in the tribulations of the author. But in its completed form it is the work of a citizen of the world, of a scholar who discarded the boundaries of state and language in his mission to advance the free exercise of speech in the cause of justice.

John Dugard
Director
Center for Applied Legal Studies
University of the Witwatersrand
Johannesburg, South Africa

EULOGY FOR
PROFESSOR BAREND VAN NIEKERK

This eulogy was delivered by Dr. Alan Paton at the funeral service held for Professor van Niekerk in Durban on July 6, 1981.

It is an honor that has been given to me today, by Traute van Niekerk, to deliver the eulogy on the occasion of the funeral of her husband Barend, our gifted, tempestuous, brave, reckless, friend and brother.

It is a cliché often used on occasions such as these to say that we shall never see his like again. But it is not a cliché today, for we shall never see his like again. Traute, like you I have a belief in a Creator, and that we are His creatures, and a part of his creation. And Barend was one of the most extraordinary creatures that this creation has ever seen. His enemies could see only his faults, but those of us who loved and honored him saw rather his virtues, and they were as extraordinary as Barend himself.

He was born, like myself, in Pietermaritzburg, the lovely city, although some 36 years later. His father was a government servant at Cedara, just outside the city. When Barend was a small boy the family moved to Cintsa, a small village near East London, and he went to the Grens school in that city. After he had matriculated he went to the intellectual Mecca of Afrikanerdom, the nursery school of prime ministers and rugby champions, the University of Stellenbosch, where he graduated in law. His academic career could not be described as anything but brilliant, but this intellectual eminence was hidden from many by his downright earthiness, and by the downright earthiness of his language. It is a striking characteristic of Afrikaners that when they pray, they pray in Afrikaans, but when they swear, they swear in English.

Barend was brought up therefore in an Afrikaner world, but by this time he was equally a master of English, I mean intellectual English, as well as the other. I do not need to tell a congregation like this that if you deify your race and your language and your culture and your history, you suffer a great mental and spiritual impoverishment. And even if you do not deify them, but if you exalt them excessively, you suffer the same impoverishment. But Barend broke out of it all, finally, decisively, irrevocably. It would never occur to me to think of him as an Afrikaner. There were no doubt foolish and bigoted people who thought that he had become English. One cannot think of a greater absurdity. It will no doubt come as a surprise to many to learn that his home language, I mean the language of his home with Traute and their two daughters, was German.

After Stellenbosch he went to Heidelberg to study international law and comparative law, and then to Bonn. He became the master of German in the same way that he was already the master of Afrikaans and English. He went to Strasbourg where he became a doctor in political science and a fluent speaker of

French. He learned to speak Spanish and campaigned for the teaching of Spanish at the University of Natal. That was in the 'seventies and it is interesting to note that Roy Campbell, who had much of Barend's tempestuousness but not so much of Barend's deep love of justice, claimed that he had learned Spanish at the Natal University College fifty years before. As I recount this story of Barend's academic career, I marvel again to think how this intellectual eminence was hidden by his earthiness. Not only his earthiness, but an absence of all cant and pretension.

Barend returned to be admitted as an advocate although he never practiced. He went in 1968 to the University of Zululand as senior lecturer in law, and in 1969 to the University of the Witwatersrand in the same capacity. On the thirty-first day of May, 1970, he married Traute von Oehsen, whom he had met long before in Germany. As you all know, the thirty-first day of May is an historic day in the history of South Africa, but Traute and Barend did not marry on that day because of that, but because it was Traute's birthday. It was soon after that the state proceeded against Advocate van Niekerk for contempt of court. No advocate likes to be proceeded against for contempt of court and Barend was no exception. He didn't like it, but it was characteristic of the whole restless tempestuous irrepressible personality that he was brought before the court on three more occasions. One is reminded of the famous story of F. E. Smith, who when asked by an angry judge if he was trying to show contempt of court, replied "No, my lord, I am trying my best to conceal it."

Barend now entered the second phase of his adult life, that of the crusader. The death penalty, the statistical fact that if you were black you were more likely to incur the death penalty than if you were white, the whole question of imprisonment and especially the treatment in prison, freedom of speech and communication, the functions and duties and derelictions of judges, all these provided him with his causes. They didn't make him universally popular. In fact they made him enemies. They rebuked him for his bluntness, his invective, his slaughter of the sacred cows, and many of them failed completely to recognize him as a crusader. Of them Barend said, "If you don't make enemies, you don't make anything." He spoke about them in good, powerful, earthy language. What indeed could be more scathing than this? "Another factor which moves me to sadness and incomprehension is that with many people in high places in Durban – high especially in municipal and commercial places – one finds a delight in their own cultural ignorance and vandalism befitting some cabal in a Central American Republic."

One should not close this catalogue without mentioning his crusade in defense of the old buildings and historic places of his adopted city. He was tireless in their defense, and thought it quite fitting that he, graduate of Stellenbosch and Heidelberg and Bonn and Strasbourg, should climb up a ladder in Soldiers' Way in order to put a coat of paint on the peeling roof of the Old Station that he was trying to save.

It is time for me to come to an end, but I want to make a point that to me is very important. This country is ruled by an authoritarian government. It does not really care for freedom of speech or communication, it believes that literature, especially the novel, should be controlled. It is highly suspicious of the press. It treats harshly those who are militant in opposition to the policies of racial separation, even while – and this is a great paradox – it itself is telling the world that it is moving away from discrimination. It administers security laws that are not to be found elsewhere in the Western world, to which world it desperately wants to belong. It has the power to frighten people, to make them keep silent, to make them say "I don't discuss politics," to make a white man afraid to show a black woman a courtesy, to make us afraid to protest against any injustice, to make us afraid to go into a police station to make some perfectly legitimate enquiry about some detained person, to make us shadows of ourselves. Yet it is this same country that throws up a Barend van Niekerk, who refused to go down on his belly before the state, who espoused something far greater than the cause of law, namely the cause of justice. And I could mention many others but I shall not do so. When people call this the greatest tyranny in the world, they are talking nonsense. Barend van Niekerk would have soon been dead under Hitler or Stalin or Amin or the Ayatollah Khomeini. There are many injustices in this country, but we can thank God that we have so many people who condemn them, and who use their lives to try to remove them from the life of our society. That is why we are here today to give thanks for the life of Barend van Niekerk.

Barend,

Aan God se reddende genade
En aan Sy beskerming
Dra ons jou op.
Die Here sal jou seën
En jou behoed
Die Here sal Sy aangesig
Oor jou laat skyn
En jou genadig wees
Die Here sal Sy aangesig
Oor jou verhef
En jou vrede gee
Nou en vir altyd.*

---

*To God's saving mercy/And to His protection/We deliver you./The Lord will bless you/And preserve you/The Lord will let His countenance/Shine upon you/And be merciful to you/The Lord will let His countenance/Rise over you/And give you peace/Now and forever.

I have one last word to say about this blessing. It asks God to give Barend peace, now and for ever. Well I am not sure that Barend would want peace for ever. Rather let us ask that he should rest for a week or two before he starts campaigning for improvements in heaven.

Traute, many people bring their love to you, and your daughters on this day. And not only love, but a salute.

PREFACE

I place on record my abiding gratitude for the generous assistance of the Alexander von Humboldt-Stiftung in Bonn, which made the research for this work possible, and for the research facilities of the Max-Planck Institüt für ausländisches und internationales Strafrecht in Freiburg, where I spent one of the most rewarding periods of my life. I also record here with warmth and deep respect and gratitude the succor of the band of lawyers who stood by me when the principles and beliefs upon which this work are based were rudely and crudely tested in the cases where the seeds for this work were sown. As to the research and writing of this work, devouring as it did a major slice of my time and energies and patience, I remember here those nearest to me both at home and at work who generously bore so much of my cross. Literally scores of people in at least a score of countries were consulted and gave me of their time in my quixotic endeavor to portray a slice of the law and practice of free speech in the West. Some names are recorded in the work, many more are not. I remember them here whether or not they will ever know it.

All the translations in English, apart from a handful relating to Greek, Polish, and Hungarian, are my own. For reasons of space and largely also of common sense, I inserted only the translations and not the original text. My apologies in advance to students of the languages concerned.

Very generous use – perhaps too generous use – was made of cross-references in footnotes with a cross-reference referring to an *approximate* location of the footnote concerned and not to a page. Some may like this innovation, others may not. I believe it assists meaningfully with the integration of the overall text and with its usefulness for reference purposes.

Because the research for this work was done in various countries at various times, the time frame as regards either the legal or the de facto situation concerning free speech in the legal domain varies from country to country. The bulk of my research ought to reflect at least the situation up to the end of 1977. As regards South Africa, the United States, and Britain the situation depicted would reflect that obtaining at the end of 1980.

INTRODUCTION

Justice is not a cloistered virtue: she must be allowed to suffer the scrutiny and respectful, even though outspoken, comments of ordinary men.

Lord Atkin, *The* Ambard *case*[1]

This is a work about one of humanity's most cherished freedoms – freedom of expression. However, only one particular aspect, or bundle of aspects, concerned with that freedom will be discussed here: the freedom of expression in relation to the administration of justice. Moreover, we shall be concerned mainly with the most common form of humanity's mode of expression: speech. An attempt will be made to provide a comparative bird's-eye view of how freedom of speech concerning the administration of justice – *legal free speech* for short – has fared or is presently faring in the world, and particularly in the so-called Western world. The world – or for that matter, just the Western world – has become, as far as the use of the comparative legal method is concerned, very complex indeed. Therefore, in the nature of things, nothing more than a limited view of the major legal systems will be given. This limitation is dictated by the availability of sources and by my personal inclinations, not to speak of limitations dictated by the need to keep the work within reasonable and readable bounds.

·This work is concerned with one of humanity's great liberties and it is written by a fervent believer in that particular liberty. This is as much an admission as it is the framework within which the entire content of this work must be seen. To this writer, at least, it is one of the minor marvels of jurisprudence to see how in many instances and in many legal systems – by no means limited to the most repressive countries – this important part of this important right has been suppressed, circumvented, or simply left unused. As I hope to show, no perceptible social advantages seem to have come from this situation.

In yet another way have I become deeply committed to this particular aspect of freedom of speech, a commitment that will not fail to become abundantly apparent to the reader. In no fewer than three cases in under four years, two of which were followed by appeals to the highest court in the land, I had to face trial in my country, South Africa, for pronouncements on matters purely related to the administration of justice. It is quite possible that my critics, particularly those in South Africa who have become so psychologically inured to their own lack of freedom, may see in these personal curial experiences a built-in absence of objectivity and detachment. Inasmuch as we are all the product of our experiences, I cannot of course hope to escape such a charge. The experience of standing trial on those three occasions, under the particular circumstances of each case, obviously could not fail to imprint on my mind more than any abstract argument the pivotal importance of that crucial part of freedom of speech, an importance which, I think, will speak for itself when those cases – milestones in their own right – are detailed. The origins of this work, more than is generally the case with works on legal subjects, are therefore undoubtedly also deeply personal in nature. I offer no apologies.

This work must not be seen as a legal textbook, although the greater part of it is concerned with law and legal values. Instead, I intend to focus attention on the social and political dynamics of freedom of speech in the administration of justice in a complex modern democratic society. Important as that freedom may be to lawyers, it is even more important to the citizenry in general. In fact, it would seem that, as a profession, lawyers have done more than any other group to limit, to circumscribe, or simply to ignore – and hence to smother – that freedom, much to the detriment of the public weal. It is one of the recurring themes of court judgments, both those which contribute to the edification and those which bespeak the erosion of that freedom, that the public at large is vitally concerned with freedom of speech in legal matters. Yet, it is also true that innumerable judgments touching on that freedom and many practices of impeccable legal standing and respectability cannot stand an objective and incisive scrutiny against the yardstick of the public weal. It is hoped, therefore, that the essential message of this work will appeal not only to lawyers interested in civil rights but even more to concerned members of the public at large and especially those manning the journalistic ramparts of our liberties.

The possible appeal of the thoughts contained herein to nonlawyers merits illumination from yet another angle. The civil liberties of the citizens in the West are too often left in the hands of the legal profession, including those of the judiciary, to develop and protect. No doubt, *legal* thinking in matters concerned with civil rights in general and with freedom of speech in particular has contributed very profoundly to the expansive evolution of those rights; but it is my firm conviction that much more is needed for those rights to take firm root than merely the focus of the legal or judicial mind upon them. Professor Thomas Emerson states in his seminal work from which much inspiration was drawn for the first part of this work, "The theory of freedom of expression is a sophisticated and even complex one. It does not come naturally to the ordinary citizen, but needs to be learned. It must be restated and reiterated not only for each generation but for each new situation. It leans heavily upon understanding and education, both for the individual and the community as a whole."[2]

A corollary of this view is certainly that, despite the importance of legal contributions to the development of legal free speech, the initiative to utilize that freedom and to turn it into an effective check on the exercise of power rests ultimately with the informed citizen and especially the media, who must ensure that that freedom becomes part of the common store of beliefs and expectations in society. Until recently, judges and justice were essentially nontopics even in a deeply democratic country like Britain, and the social climate thus created certainly contributed to a further narrowing of the basic right of freedom of speech by the courts. Only when public opinion, especially through the medium of the press, started to take an interest in the subject – to the point of even deliberately flouting the law and generally accepted journalistic customs – the scene was set for changes brought about mostly judicially but also legislatively.[3] In South Africa, by contrast, the three Supreme Court decisions and the two Appellate Division decisions on legal free speech against this writer could really only be effectively grafted onto a society in which the public and its media were characterized by a deep ignorance of the implications involved and by a casual and even cavalier unconcern for the rights of a critic. Even in a modern and dynamic constitutional setup, such as that in Germany,[4] a judge could very recently find himself in considerable difficulty for the expression of mildly critical ideas about the judiciary: ideas that have been commonplace in the United States at least since the birth of the realist tradition. In a book on the English judiciary that appeared in 1976 the editor – himself a coauthor of a leading textbook on a related subject – has to state almost apologetically (but probably quite realistically) that "[no] public institution should be beyond study and examination."[5] In the Netherlands, a country often praised for its liberal values, a journalist lamented not long ago the extent to which certain aspects of that country's legal system had become veritable sacred cows.[6] The fact is simply that the viability of freedom of speech in legal matters depends even more on a vigilant public than may be the case with many other civil rights.[7] It is my fervent hope that this contribution may be of avail somewhere in contributing something toward whetting the intellectual appetite of nonlawyers, and particularly of journalists, to slaughter some of the sacred cows in the administration of justice, which in so many climes have resisted that fate successfully for so long.

This work is ultimately directed at lawyers, who for better or for worse – and so often for the worse! – remain the primary expounders of the ideas and ideals of justice. Despite the fact that in most Western societies lawyers unmistakably belong to the status quo-oriented governing elite, the individual lawyer who, either alone or in the company of peers, is prepared to stick out his or her neck can sometimes produce changes and amelioration out of all proportion to the loneliness of the effort. During the long constitutional night of the regime of the Greek colonels, the voices of a few lawyers on specific legal issues were almost the only audible voices of dissent in the country, and the occasional commendable civil courage of Spanish lawyers during the Franco regime undoubtedly had a democratizing effect in much wider circles in the country at large.[8] One of the most inspiring recent examples of lawyers' dissent came from Africa, when the lawyers in Ghana, by way of an unprecedented strike, set the example for other professional groups to exact a promise from the military rulers there to return the country to civil rule.[9] Because the processes of law are often well-nigh impenetrable to the layperson – a question not entirely unrelated to the theme of this work – it is still to the lawyer that society will look for guidance in many legal matters. The phenomenon of the iconoclastic lawyer who will be prepared to question the myths and the taboos of the profession – a figure well established on the legal front in the United States since the early 1920s when the modern realist school made its appearance – is still relatively rare in most societies, including highly developed Western European societies.[10] It is especially to these actual and potential verbal iconoclasts of the legal profession that I wish to direct this work as a minor tool in their struggle to open the eyes – and the mouths! – of society.

Ultimately, the gravamen of the message of this work is to be found in my belief and basic thesis that, although the administration of justice is one of the most crucial areas on which the actinic qualities of free speech can be used for the benefit of society, this area in actual fact is the one most seldom exposed to those qualities. Through a peculiar mixture of restrictions and taboos of both a legal and a societal nature, this area often constitutes a veritable vacuum of semiuncontrolled power with abiding and profound negative consequences for the quality of justice.

The relatively frequent use of South African examples of restrictions and reactions to such restrictions throughout this work is dictated not only by its South African origins but also, I submit, by the comparative relevance there of such restrictions and reactions. The peculiar mix of the South African society and the South African legal system offers the prospective inquirer in the field of legal free speech especially good examples both of liberty and suppression. Endowed with a legal system that has roots deep in Western libertarian thought but exposed to several generations of gradual but inexorable decline of Western standards, South Africa presents almost the full gamut, on the one hand of imaginable examples of controls and dilutions of free speech, and on the other hand of examples of challenges to the abdication of critical standards. It is also a country whose press still clings – sometimes valiantly but sometimes less than honestly – to the mirage of liberty in the field of our inquiry. Especially in the field of the growth and influence of subtle and imperceptible informal restrictions and taboos in the legal field, the South African situation offers a number of model specimens that have excellent heuristic qualities for the world at large, offering documentable instances that testify with great clarity to the potency of the effects and consequences of a phenomenon which, for the West, has very curiously remained unexplored for a very long time. Negative as its story may be, South Africa has a story of some originality to tell on the matter. In essence, however, this work is concerned with the West as a whole or at least with those parts of the West whose legal systems and literature were accessible to me, either directly or (in a number of cases) indirectly through the assistance of colleagues and journalist contacts. As regards legal free speech, no two situations in the West are alike but – and this is the crucial benefit of using the comparative method on this topic – almost every situation has to a greater or lesser extent its comparable counterpart somewhere else and hence its relevance to other systems of law. It is with the modest hope that this work will stimulate further inquiry into specific areas of the law and society in countries of the West on this quintessential but oft-ignored liberty of Western humanity that I present here the results of my odysseys through various legal systems.

THE
CLOISTERED VIRTUE

1

The Concept of Freedom of Speech in the Legal Domain and Its Premises

The choice is ours whether, if we hear the pipes of Pan, we shall stampede like a frightened flock, forgetting all those professions on which we have claimed to rest our polity. God knows, there is risk in refusing to act till the facts are all in; but is there not greater risk in abandoning the conditions of all rational enquiry? ... The mutual confidence on which all else depends can be maintained only by an open mind and a brave reliance upon free discussion.... [W]e must not yield a foot upon demanding a fair field and an honest race to all ideas.

Judge Learned Hand[1]

INTRODUCTION

Formal and Informal Approach

It is not easy to research the biography of a Swiss traitor and it is even more difficult to get it published in Switzerland.[2]

Through the centuries, there has been a very marked reluctance in most parts of the world to give meaningful recognition to the right of the citizen to speak his or her mind freely on the administration of justice. Strengthening this official reluctance and acting at times as a corollary to it there has also been an ingrained reluctance on the part of society generally to concern itself very much with the administration of justice. One is really confronted here with a vicious circle: official animosity (expressed at times by sanctions) toward legal free speech leads to a popular reluctance as far as the critical broaching of legal matters is concerned, and this popular reluctance (partly based on fear but partly also on unconcern) again strengthens the hand of authority in the maintenance of its repressive stance. Bolstering this repression is the fact that the law and its administration do not inherently command the interest of most members of the public and hence of their media even in sophisticated societies, despite superficial impressions to the contrary as symbolized by the crowds at public executions in repressive regimes or by saturation publicity in the yellow press. A climate of unconcern by its nature is a notoriously fertile soil for the growth of suppression of liberties.

The underlying idea of free speech in legal matters, that is, the free imparting of information about the processes of the law, is often subjected to profuse lip service – even on the part of those very judges involved in its actual suppression – but there is a profound lack of communication between citizens and their administration of justice. With rare exceptions that prove the rule, justice administrations have not been forthcoming in promoting knowledge about themselves and even those who could give a lead to foster more knowledge about the machinery of justice, such as academics, have often failed to respond to the challenge. The situation in Germany has been pointedly described as follows by a group of reformist judges:

> But it is not only the politicians who wish to have nothing to do with the administration of justice; the administration of justice also wishes to know nothing about itself. The law professors look down upon the judges, the judges as people of practice look down upon the university theoreticians and the law students are told that they would later on their own steam comprehend that which they cannot be told about today and they hastily retreat into the commentaries and textbooks and are simply content with having passed one of the lesser or more important examinations. The editors of legal periodicals fill the columns of their publications with complicated trivia of a technical nature which they call "practical problems"; these editors, however, are hopelessly overcommitted when a somewhat starry-eyed legal scatterbrain wishes to ruminate in their journals about the deeper meaning of his own activities or wishes meekly to pose the question as to when the twentieth century will dawn in the German administration of justice.[3]

The situation in Germany has most recently undergone certain changes in the field of legal free speech, with the appearance of voices of fundamental and critical dissent from within the legal ranks regarding the administration of justice. However, there has also appeared a vast new web of restrictions particularly applicable to the legal profession that has generated a heavy pall of uncritical silence in the one profession that should have an institutional and professional interest to have much to say, and to say it loudly, about the law and the legal processes. In Britain, where the flow of judicial rhetoric in support of free speech is probably only surpassed by the United States, outspoken and robust comment about the administration of justice, and especially the judiciary, was until recently conspicuous only by its absence or by the infrequency of its use. Abel-Smith and Robert Stevens, who contributed much to the demystification of the justice machinery, comment about the way in which the judiciary attempted to put themselves above criticism:

> Once the power [of punishing outspoken critics of the judges with contempt of court proceedings] had been re-enacted the judges seemed to

take pleasure in using it. Within a decade the criticism of judicial behaviour which had been so outspoken was replaced in the press by almost syncophantic praise for the judges.

And later, writing of the post-World War Two period, the same authors state:

As the judges removed themselves from sensitive areas where their discretion or law-making activities had previously been obvious, criticism of the judiciary, which earlier in the century had been open, began to disappear. The absence of criticism was partly the result of the development of what may felt to be an excessive power to commit for contempt of court those who criticized judges. It was also to some extent due to the improving standards of the judiciary. But the general absence of criticism ensured that even bad judges were protected from any sort of criticism. The fact that the judges gradually came to be regarded as above any type of criticism may well have led them to believe in their own infallibility.[4]

Whatever changes may have come about in the interim in Britain, the fact remains that the laborious human rights machinery of the Council of Europe had until recently been seized for some seven years of an appeal from the London *Sunday Times* under the sub judice contempt rule for its publication of the plight (while a civil action was pending) of the thalidomide children, many years after tragedy first struck. Even in conservative continental or U.S. legal circles, which decry so-called trial by newspaper, this case does not fail to produce shrieks of incredulity.[5] It is also not so long ago that the *Times*, one of the most persistent public watchdogs over legal matters in the West, printed a bitter lament on restrictions of access to prisons.[6]

As an abstract concept, freedom of speech in general receives generous recognition in the constitutions of the world, whether in the East or West, and also in several international instruments like the Universal Declaration of Human Rights, the European Convention on Human Rights, and (indirectly) in the Rome treaty creating the European Economic Community. As a viable doctrine of meaningful control of state power, it exists in varying degrees of efficacy only in a small number of Western states. However, as far as freedom of speech specifically relates to scrutiny of the administration of justice, it does not even apply fully and effectively in that small minority of countries. Apart from scattered references in judgments and books on either wider or more specialized topics, the *concept* of this freedom has nowhere really commended itself at all to serious study. It can hardly even be said that a separately identifiable concept of freedom of speech concerning the administration of justice has evolved in legal literature.[7] Even in Britain, with its alert press concerning legal matters, it is a saddening experience for a civil libertarian to see that erudite text-books on a subject such as contempt completely ignore the underlying jurisprudential principles on which that restrictive instrumentality is intrinsically based.[8]

In literature dealing with specific restrictions on legal free speech, there is also very scant recognition of the sociopolitical consequences of having a wide measure of freedom of speech in legal matters or of the consequences of making use (or of failing to make use) of that liberty as provided by law. Visitors to South Africa, for instance, are usually very surprised by the robustness of critical comment on political matters and although allowance is made for certain oppressive legal restrictions in the country's freedom of the press, the picture that emerges of free speech in that country is often quite flattering. Yet one will search in vain for comment and analysis in South Africa of the crucial, controversial, and sensitive areas of the law such as class justice, white justice, the appointment and promotion of judges, and the subtle (and not so subtle) executive control of judicial officers. It is significant to note that a recent critical study of the South African press,[9] although published abroad, did not refer to the very strong tradition of the South African press to refrain from incisive reporting on controversial legal matters, despite the veritable sea of injustice that is thus allowed to go uncharted by the press. However, this experience is not unique to South Africa. For the last few years, there has been wave upon wave of speech repression of certain groups of lawyers in Germany concerning their views on the administration of justice. Although this repression, especially in the form of disciplinary proceedings, has produced a spirit of inhibition of free speech in the legal domain, it has as yet received practically no attention in the country's numerous law reviews, which very frequently deal with the constitutionally protected right of free speech.

The situation in South Africa and Germany may perhaps appear entirely explicable on the basis of the former country's repressive internal spirit as far as dissent to the established order is concerned and by the latter's security problems concerning a new brand of urban terrorism that has unnerved the legal system in recent years and under whose shadow lawyers have been speaking out about certain controversial issues in German justice. However, in several other countries with very respectable democratic credentials, there is a similar lack of concern in the public media and legal textbooks for certain basic questions relating to the administration of justice. The freedom that is theoretically available in the constitution or in the general laws as far as free speech is concerned is simply left untapped and unused. Despite the reputation of Switzerland, for instance, as a haven for democratic values, my scrutiny of three of that republic's major newspapers over a period of three months did not produce one single critical and discordant note worth recording on the administration of justice. One would also vainly search the country's legal periodicals for articles outspokenly critical of the country's legal order. Unless one adheres to the logically untenable view that the situation in Switzerland, and in other democratic countries similarly unruffled by probing comments on the administration of justice, is devoid of *any* problems calling for outspoken critique, one must conclude that freedom of speech in the legal domain, despite its formal existence in the constitutions concerned, is practically and creatively inoperative.

The difference between such a situation of *unused freedom* and a situation of *suppressed* or *limited freedom* largely loses its sting and importance. For instance, the inability to find a reputable publisher for a critical work – as was the case with the work by Meienberg from which the opening quotation was taken – produces a situation that in substance and effect is not much different to outright censorship.[10] The fact that Swiss or German judges are sacrosanct either due to the fear or effect of informal taboos, or due to the fear of indirect sanctions, or due simply to inertia or to ignorance, ultimately matters very little *as far as the public is concerned*, whose interests are being flouted or ignored.[11] Against this background the sanctions of the contempt institution in Britain and elsewhere – sanctions that at times "may seem quiescent . . . [but are nevertheless] there in the background available to be used when occasion demands"[12] – lose much of their uniqueness as far as their actual *effect* is concerned and from the point of view of the reduced public interest. Under all these sets of circumstances we have the situation where the public are, in the words of Jerome Frank, treated as children:

I am unable to conceive . . . that in a democracy, it can ever be unwise to acquaint the public with the truth about the workings of any branch of government. It is wholly undemocratic to treat the public as children, who are unable to accept the inescapable shortcomings of man-made institutions. The public, I think, can "take it."[13]

From the above it should be clear that I will endeavor to take an approach that is inspired as much by technical legal restrictions as it is by informal restrictions of freedom of speech in the legal domain. It will be an underlying premise of this work that from the point of view of the intrinsic social importance of that right it is the *effect* and not the *nature* of the restrictions that really matters. Although formal legal restrictions may at times constitute more difficult obstacles to overcome than informal sanctions, partly because such formal restrictions may at times be selectively applied against unpopular critics and so escape general condemnation, the dilution of encrusted customs in venerable institutions such as the press and the legal profession may often prove to be more difficult and time-consuming than the removal or bypassing of legal restrictions. At times the dilution of these customs may require the use of a kind of shock therapy in which the verbal sting may have an important role to play.

The Concept of Legal Free Speech Defined

I recognize contempt when I hear it.

Courtroom wisdom

The concept of freedom of speech concerning the administration of justice, when viewed in a strictly legal context, presents no undue definitional difficulties. In that particular context it is simply part of the right of free speech, recognized and limited by law, and focused on the administration of justice in its entirety. For practical purposes, we limit our attention to *speech* although it is easy to conceive of other modes of communication of ideas concerning the legal domain, in which case one would rather speak of freedom of *expression*. A study of the concept of legal free speech will thus primarily involve a study of the legal limitations on the use of that freedom. A comparative study of such limitations in a number of legal systems and the effects of these limitations where they are identifiable will thus be one of the major objects of this work. However, because of the ubiquitous presence of nonlegal or semilegal checks and inhibitions it is necessary also to view the concept in a societal or sociological context, in which case it assumes a more variegated complexion which is replete with many subtleties. Like the concept of freedom of speech generally, it is largely dependent for its vitality, efficacy, and creativity on relatively *free access to important or meaningful information* about the administration of justice, a reality that will likewise receive attention.

Against the backdrop of this wide connotation of legal free speech, it can thus be tentatively redefined as that part of freedom of expression that is concerned with the expression of views by way of speech and speech-related means about all aspects of the administration of justice and with the restrictions on such expression, whether they be of a legal, semilegal, or societal nature, as well as with restrictions on the access to information about the administration of justice upon which the meaningful exercise of the right to free speech is based. The term administration of justice is understood here in its widest connotation, including not only the judicial but also the executive aspects of the administration, and such institutions as prison and mental facilities.

THE PREMISES OF A SYSTEM OF FREE SPEECH IN THE LEGAL DOMAIN

> *Free discussion of the problems of society is a cardinal principle of Americanism – a principle which all are zealous to preserve.*
> From the contempt judgment of *Pennekamp* v. *Florida*[14]

An analysis of freedom of speech in the legal domain only on the basis of its legal and societal limitations – a kind of "thou shalt not" approach – will do but scant justice to the concept as an inherent and dynamic ingredient of a democratic society. It is also necessary to look at the concept within the ambit of certain premises on which it is predicated. A submission that will very perceptibly thread its way through this entire work is that these premises have an inherent and basic validity that puts a high value on the interests of the individual, on the protection of his or her basic rights and human expectations, as well as on the edification of the personality of the individual. Although it is possible to argue the validity of these premises on generally acceptable rational principles, it is also well worthwhile to remember that they are largely based on articles of faith of a believer in that freedom and can therefore ultimately find their basis more in belief than in proof. Thomas Emerson speaks of four premises on which "the system of freedom of expression in a democratic society rests": as "a means of assuring individual self-fulfillment"; as "an essential process for advancing knowledge and discovering truth"; as an essential means "to provide for participation in decision making by all members of society" and, finally, as "a method of achieving a more adaptable and hence more stable community." He continues:

> The validity of the foregoing premises has never been proved or disproved, and probably could not be. Nevertheless our society is based upon the faith that they hold true and, in maintaining a system of freedom of expression, we act upon that faith.[15]

All four premises of free speech outlined by Professor Emerson generally would apply with undiminished force also as far as the legal domain is concerned. However, in our particular field of enquiry it is not difficult to postulate yet two further interlocking premises, both of which seem to allow a tolerably accurate and objective enquiry. First, there is what may be regarded as the major premise on which a vital system of legal free speech is based: that without a vigorous degree of free speech for the legal domain the entire apparatus of the administration of justice, on the basis of the documentable or observable experi-ence of many nations over long periods, is ultimately unable to function in a way that will respond to the need for justice of the individual. Moreover, in the vast majority of instances where free speech has been suppressed or rendered more onerous, the *public interest* has also manifestly suffered or, at the very least, has not been meaningfully advanced when seen in relation to the social price paid for the effort.

Second, and not unconnected with this major premise on which a system of legal free speech is based, there is the important but often ignored concomitant premise: that most, if not all, serious attempts to suppress free speech in the legal domain remain futile gestures which are often counterproductive to the very interests that are theoretically protected. If such a futile attempt to curb legal free speech would simply remain a *brutum fulmen* devoid of further serious consequences for society, the effort of the attempt may perhaps not be entirely wasted, since law, and especially criminal law, is replete with dramatic gestures that are essentially futile. However, the cost to society (not even considering for the moment the cost to the individuals) of such gestures will often be considerable.

The notions on which these premises are based are not easily marketable commodities in the marketplace of emotionally charged ideas, and because they are not always readily recognizable by a public that is badly informed on legal matters it would be foolish to pretend that we are dealing here with a kind of wisdom that invariably commends itself to human reason. Indeed, when confronted by the full gamut of restrictions on freedom of speech in the legal domain even in countries with impeccable democratic traditions, the opposite may even seem to be true. Emerson neatly summarizes the difficulty of selling these premises in the market halls of society:

> [I]t is clear that the problem of maintaining a system of freedom of expression in a society is one of the most complex any society has to face. Self-restraint, self-discipline, and maturity are required. The theory is essentially a highly sophisticated one. The members of the society must be willing to sacrifice individual and short-term advantage for social and long-range goals.[16]

He could well have added vague, illusive, and ill-defined goals.

As far as the application of these premises is concerned in relation to the legal domain, the problem of complexity and of social marketability may be more pronounced than is the case with freedom of speech in general. The law, its processes, and the scrutiny of its officers have traditionally been off limits to the public at large, partly as a consequence of the alleged complexity of these topics and partly as a consequence of the blaze of glory and mystique with which the law has traditionally been surrounded. An "insult" to the "dignity" of a judge, or an infringement of the "respect" in which the administration of justice "ought" to be held, or a concern for information about the happenings in the jury chamber, in mental asylums, or in the dank cells of prisons, or an understanding of the need for lawyers to indulge in fearless and robust speech when pitted in a tussle against the power of the state (and often of the judiciary), or an appreciation for the vital role that newspapers and the other media should play in keeping the vast justice apparatus of a modern society under check are all matters in which the proverbial man on the street has little interest. If it is partly true (quoting Justice William Douglas again) that in the face of burning issues "most [American] lawyers have remained silent,"[17] how much less inclination will there not be on the part of the so-called public at large in many other societies to indulge in discussions concerning abstruse or contentious legal issues?

The premises on which a system of free speech in the legal domain are based in a democratic society merit detailed analysis. This is so not only because such analysis will by itself afford a valuable overview of the dynamics of a system of free speech but also because it can provide a useful framework for the making of value judgments concerning the use made of legal free speech, the formulation of possible restrictions, and the importance that a society generally and the legal profession in particular should accord to such freedom. This is so because these premises are not only inherently reflective of democratic values and expectations but also because they constitute tolerably useful yardsticks and intellectual tools with which to assess the use to which legal free speech should be put.

The need for such yardsticks and intellectual tools for the making of value judgments concerning the use or limitation of free speech in the legal domain is apparent on every level of decision making in all legal systems. The truth of the matter is simply that if an *Ehrengericht* in Germany, which exercises control over the ethical code of lawyers, wishes to tighten the reins over offensive lawyers,[18] or if a court in Argentina or Spain wishes to apply the *desacato* provisions in their criminal codes,[19] or if an Italian court has to interpret the *oltraggio* provisions in articles 342 and 343 in the penal code,[20] or if a French court wishes to give meat to the vague and controversial articles 226 and 227 of the penal code on *outrage à la justice*,[21] or if some farflung and erstwhile island colony in Her Majesty's crown wishes to silence the critics of the judiciary,[22] or if the courts in South Africa wish to allow themselves to be used by the authorities to get even with one of their critics, or if a German court uses the ordinary criminal defamation article to give a somewhat irreverent critic a knock,[23] and even if Her Majesty's judges, in a forlorn question for the good old days when inquisitive journalists knew their "proper" place, wish to recreate the distilled atmosphere that reigned around the operations of the courts[24] – if under any of these or other circumstances a decision is called for, a conscious value judgment has to be made in relation to free speech that involves a selection between various options. The same kind of value judgment is also made by the potential critic or commentator of the legal scene who elects to comment (or perhaps *not* to comment) on a particular question concerned with the administration of justice or, having decided to comment, has to select appropriate weapons from his or her verbal arsenal. It is submitted that conscious reference to these premises, to which we now turn our attention, can assist meaningfully in the making of selections that would enhance the substance of democracy, the public interest, and individual justice.

THE FIRST PREMISE: THE ACHIEVEMENT OF INDIVIDUAL SELF-FULFILLMENT

I endure not an instructor that comes to me under the wardship of an overseeing fist.

John Milton, *Areopagitica*

It is a distressing phenomenon to observe how many liberal people and institutions in the West have been willing to silence themselves on legal matters "under the wardship of an overseeing fist." This premise of Emerson's may at first blush seem to relate more to artistic expressions of free speech but a careful analysis of the actual use made of legal free speech would reveal the application of this premise also in this field. Many of the documented instances of the use of the limitation of legal free speech flow from facts where the operation of this premise can be detected.

In an average Western society, there would be two groups especially that would consciously, at least, seek part of their self-fulfillment in speaking out about the administration of justice: lawyers and journalists. This does not detract from either the right or the ability of other groups to scrutinize legal issues; it means only that in the normal run of affairs in a Western democracy these two groups would have the most obvious professional and emotional need to express themselves fearlessly and robustly on the administration of justice, a reality or a need reflected in a considerable part of the case law on the limitation of legal free speech.

The Self-Fulfillment of the Lawyer

Ultimately the task and duty and responsibility for legal knowledge and legal conscience of the nation . . . belong to the legal profession and particularly to the law faculties of our universities.

Gustav Radbruch[25]

Lawyers – and this would include lawyers from all branches of the profession – who conceive of their role in society as something more than that of blind or narrow interpreters of the extent and ramifications of state power, but as that of creative architects of justice with positive duties toward the protection of that concept in its widest and fullest Western connotation, will need and regard fearless free speech on all matters as an important – indeed the most important – tool. It is not suggested that this model is necessarily the only one for a lawyer in the West but it undoubtedly constitutes a vital aspect of the ideal of many, perhaps even most, Western lawyers in their better moments; an ideal moreover in terms of which these lawyers, despite many blemishes, profess to act. The suggestion here is that a lawyer who predicates his or her role and professional raison d'être on the defense and edification of individual liberty, will demand, as a necessary corollary of this role (in the pregnant phrase of the German *Grundgesetz*)[26] an undiminished *"Recht auf die freie Entfaltung seiner Persönlichkeit"* – a right to an unfettered development of one's personality *as a lawyer*. A substantial part of this claim will revolve around one's rights to free speech as regards every and any aspect of the entire administration of justice apparatus.

Some aspects of this demand concerning the self-fulfillment of the lawyer relate simply to the normal (or what ought to be normal) exercise of professional duties toward one's client as accepted in theory by lawyers in every clime. Other aspects clearly relate to a more elevated and idealistic interpretation of the lawyer's duties, both toward the client and society. The question of the true role of the democratic lawyer in the West is one that must be divorced from the pious and after-dinner-speech cant so often indulged in by judges of the British tradition. The truth is that lawyers in the West have preponderantly been attached to the status quo in their respective societies. This has almost invariably had an inhibitive effect on their willingness to speak out on controversial or sensitive legal issues, a situation that in the nature of things could not fail to insinuate its corrosive influence into the legal fabric by way of institutionalized speech restrictions. These restrictions do not necessarily find their entry into the legal fabric through the front door of substantive law but also through devious side alleys of the law, such as professional ethics, or through simple intolerance toward iconoclastic ideas within the profession as manifested, for instance, in de facto censorship in academic law journals and in career disadvantages. These indirect restrictions and inhibitions will often constitute more potential forces of persuasion and dissuasion of lawyers to express themselves freely than the known legal pitfalls. They constitute not so much an abdication to "an instructor ... under the wardship of an overseeing fist" but to an inherent psychological impulse and weakness of people to buy peace at the cost of principle and duty.

The weak and exposed position of an accused person in certain criminal trials, especially with political overtones, calls for a particular kind of commitment and role for defense attorneys, particularly in relation to speech. This commitment and role are often misunderstood, and the situation in Germany today affords the best heuristic example of this failing. At the time of writing, literally a score or more lawyers in Germany have faced either criminal or disciplinary actions for statements or activities related to their defense methods, mostly in trials concerned with the spate of politically motivated violent incidents that have strained the social fabric in that country in recent years. Although one may not wish to defend all the activities or utterances of some of these lawyers – the use of deliberate insult, delaying tactics, harassment of court and police officials, and the like – there is a substantial number of instances of purely verbal excess that are clearly commendable examples of lawyers living up to the finest traditions of their profession. Some of these cases will be discussed in the next chapter, but an instance worth documenting at this stage and that is exemplary for the patent lack of understanding of certain German authorities for the crucial role of the lawyer in the Western tradition and for the enlightened lawyer's view of his or her own role is one that has been documented in a recent publication, *Die Verteidigung auf der Anklagebank*[27]: the case of attorney Elfferding of Berlin.

In March 1976, the state prosecutor of West Berlin initiated disciplinary proceedings before the local *Ehrengericht* or disciplinary court against attorney Elfferding on the basis of the fact that together with a number of prominent citizens of Berlin he had published a statement in a newspaper announcing the fact that a client of his had on that day been awaiting trial for five years, mostly in isolation. The statement itself was couched in almost excessively courteous language in relation to the almost grotesque nature of the injustice this lawyer was assailing, an injustice that in my submission would have justified almost any nonscatological language fit to print.[28] The state prosecutor submitted inter alia to the disciplinary tribunal that the attorney had failed to refer to certain facts concerning the detainee and he also stated that the respondent attorney had infringed his professional duty by falsely describing the solitary confinement of the detainee as "torture," which mode of detention, in any event, was not "unique" in Germany as far as its length was concerned:

> Through his public appeal, based on false allegations and interpretations, attorney Elfferding finally attempted by the use of improper means and public obloquy to affect judicial decisions contrary to the ethical rules of the legal profession.[29]

The *Elfferding* case illustrates a number of points within the context of our present enquiry. There is, first, the example of the use of slightly unorthodox but wholly reasonable means to defend a client's vital interests. Second, irrespective of the outcome of the disciplinary proceedings, the perilously inhibitive effect of this kind of case on an average member of the legal profession cannot be overestimated. If this kind of mild indulgence in free speech can lead to such difficulty, one can easily visualize the intimidating effect on lawyers generally. Third, whatever mild penalty may perhaps have ensued, the spirit from which the proceedings emanated would be a strong deterrent against lawyers pursuing their calling fearlessly and, at times, robustly.

It would often be the *academic lawyer* in the West – and indeed also in certain East European and third world countries – who would be in the best position to say what has to be said and to say so clearly as regards vital or controversial aspects of the administration of justice. Protected, as often is the case, against the strong pressures toward conformism within the practicing profession and, it is hoped, equipped with the means of arriving at valid comparisons with situations in other legal systems, the legal academic has a uniquely important role to play in the administration of justice as a fearless and outspoken scrutineer of aspects of the justice machinery. This role is one that the legal academic in the West has not always shouldered too voluntarily and the "responsibility . . . for legal conscience," (in the words of Radbruch) is one that is often shirked.

This role of the legal academic flows not only from a sense of duty but also constitutes an exciting challenge and a source of emotional enrichment, affording at times the satisfaction of knowing that *his or her* voice will often be the only one of fundamental dissent, speaking the unspeakable and mentioning the unmentionable. To the academic lawyer who conceives of a role within the context of the Radbruchian ideal, robust free speech is the lifeblood of his or her credo and the major tool toward achieving innermost self-fulfillment as lawyer.

For a second heuristic example of what this right to free speech may mean to a lawyer who seeks self-fulfillment in the quest for justice, the scene now switches to South Africa and to this writer's second case for contempt of court before the Supreme Court of South Africa, a case that raises important questions on the subject of lawyers' quest for professional self-fulfillment.

As essential background to this case and its implications, one must consider the almost total taboo around the judiciary of the Supreme Court who are all white and who, with only minor gradations, belong to the upper social class. Until most recently, the number of lawyers who were willing to subject the judiciary and controversial aspects of the administration of justice and the quality of law to fundamental criticism could literally be counted on the fingers of one hand. The allegiance of the judiciary to the status quo as conceived by the class makes them live in a world of genteel make-believe, allowing them to believe in their own impeccable impartiality on the cases presented to them and inducing them to ignore and remain silent to the fact that in practically all crucial issues of political justice the executive has almost totally usurped the functions normally entrusted to a judiciary in a democratic society; for example, a person may legally be "banned" (that is, subjected to almost any conceivable restriction, including the restriction to be quoted or to meet with more than one person at a time) or detained in solitary confinement without any identifiable reason and without any restriction of time by simple fiat of the government, which is unquestionable in a court of law. And during such detention, in terms of a law aptly called the Terrorism Act,[30] there is no *effective* guarantee whatever against abuse, torture, and even killing and some fifty persons have in less than a decade died under mysterious circumstances while in detention. All this happens outside the official ken of the judge and without his or her having any effective control whatever in curbing abuse of power. Against this background it may come as no startling surprise to find a lawyer calling injustice by its name.

The immediate origin of the contempt case against me was yet another mysterious death of a Terrorism Act detainee that gave rise to a protest meeting of some 5,000 people in the city of Durban.[31] The circumstances, I seriously believed then as I believe now, called for the clearest possible expression both of legitimate ire and of commitment to the fundamental principles of the legal profession and my criticism was strident and harsh. I excoriated with particular virulence lawyers who had become slack in their opposition to injustice and in their commitment to the higher ideals of their profession:

> The Terrorism Act . . . is a negation of what any true lawyer would ever call justice. And yet our lawyers, the guardians of our nation's legal heritage, have done so very little to mitigate its crudities . . . [for instance to] make their voices heard about an institution which they must surely know to be an abdication of decency and justice.[32]

In concluding my address, I directed my attention to the judiciary and also implored them in effect to face up to the dictates of justice and of their profession and to deny all credence to evidence procured under solitary confinement and so to "kill" the usefulness to the authorities of the Terrorism Act.

This would not be the place for a plea to history to understand my ire in that address. At most I wish to submit that there should be more than just a theoretical scope for ire in the Western lawyer's armory and that a viable system of legal free speech that is premised in part on the self-fulfillment of the legal profession must be able to accommodate and under extreme circumstances even promote such ire. The presiding judge in the ensuing prosecution for contempt of court seriously disagreed. In a judgment unique in the annals of contempt in the English-speaking world, he acquitted me for reasons related to free speech on the charge for contempt for "scandalizing the courts" and proceeded to convict me *on the very same words* for contempt under the sub judice rule.[33] A court case then proceeding in a neighboring city to which I nowhere referred provided the basis for this conviction because of the theoretical possibility of "unconsciously" influencing the presiding judge in that case.

The relevance of this case for the law of sub judice contempt will be considered in a later chapter. What is relevant here is merely the decrying by the presiding judge of my assessment of the roles of judge and lawyer in a Western society. These views, as expressed in my address, he found to be

> illogical, perverse or just plain silly . . . [and] express a point of view
> with which I, as a judge . . . profoundly disagree and which, in my
> humble opinion, exhibit a misunderstanding of the functions of a judge
> in a society such as ours which, especially in the case of a man in the
> accused's position, is both surprising and, indeed, disturbing.

It is very instructive from the point of view of understanding the dynamics of a viable system of free speech in the legal domain to examine the phenomenon, very visibly at work here, of decrying the piercing of a taboo as "disturbing," "surprising," "illogical," etc. In an atmosphere where the unmentionable about the law is hardly ever mentioned and where blatant discrepancies exist between theory and practice concerning free speech and where, especially, the judiciary would psychologically have very little *rapport* with and understanding for such "disturbing" views, there would be a natural tendency when generating judicial standards to elevate the social taboo into a legal prohibition. Because of the reality that in many legal systems there is a tendency or tradition of aloofness toward certain controversial aspects of the judiciary, the phenomenon so clearly observed here will be operative also in other more libertarian legal systems, where unmentioned opinions become filtered through the judicial process and so become legally unmentionable.

My appeal to the Appellate Division, the highest court in the land, not only confirmed the contempt conviction but added another conviction for "obstructing the course of justice" because of my appeal to the judiciary. These technical niceties have no bearing on our present enquiry, but the judgment of South Africa's chief justice (C.J.) added new and important insights into the way the courts viewed the self-fulfillment urge of the academic lawyer. In his judgment to which two fellow judges concurred without any dissent, Ogilvie Thompson, C.J., animadverted on the accused's conception of a lawyer's social duties.

> For some years past an increasing tendency has manifested itself on the part of certain academic lawyers to criticise the judiciary from time to time for failing to comment adversely upon certain statutory provisions. That question was, *inter alia*, with special mention of interrogation under solitary confinement, pointedly referred to by Chief Justice Steyn in 1967 ... and again ... by myself in 1971.... It suffices to say that, while I disagree with the appellant's concept of the duty of a judge as reflected in ... his speech ..., and although I regard some of the phraseology employed by him (e.g. "This facile excuse for abject inactivity") as bordering upon the deliberately offensive, I do not consider that counsel for the state's above mentioned submission [that the judges were scandalised] should be upheld.[34]

In his judgment, the chief justice avowed his belief that the true basis for the existence of contempt is the public interest but refrained from analyzing the application of that interest as far as the sub judice rule is concerned to the circumstances of the case in hand. As in so many other instances of suppression of legal free speech that are documented in this work, he paid his respects to the concept of free speech but failed to analyze the content of that concept to the circumstances that had called forth the offending statement. Nor is there any indication that he even vaguely visualized the debilitating and intimidating effect of this kind of action on freedom of speech as regards the administration of justice. In reading somewhat between the lines and relying also on hints that came my way, it seems as if the real sting to the authorities and the two courts lay less in the substance of the remarks than in the outright and embarrassing form in which they were presented and the awkward publicity they generated. Given the difficulties at times of breaking through a particularly strong taboo, a system of legal free speech must include also the right to be robustly forthright and embarrassingly effective.[35]

The question of being able to be *effective* – in the sense particularly of attracting public attention and sympathy – in the use of speech can be particularly relevant for a defense lawyer in a political or politicized case and the temptation on the part of authorities to thwart his or her freedom of expression will be considerable. It is therefore not surprising to find that a large proportion of attempts documented in this work of reducing the scope of the free speech of lawyers have their basis in political trials. In a mature society (or in courts manned by persons with a mature outlook on freedom of speech), it will be readily appreciated that in cases where a person stands trial for his or her ideas – often in a hostile social atmosphere and in terms of statutory provisions framed with such latitude as really to incorporate or anticipate a conviction – in a realistic (albeit not in the legal) sense a defense lawyer who, in the client's hour of greatest need and solitude, indulges in a certain amount of verbal saber rattling will in fact be making use of practically the only defense mechanism available. This lawyer will be acting in the highest professional tradition by portraying to the court, but in reality to the world and to the verdict of history, the bases of his or her client's criminal action.[36] Difficult as it may well be for a court to recognize that it has, perhaps inevitably so, become a mere rubber stamp of the prosecution, it can at least reinforce the appearance of its independence and integrity by allowing counsel the fullest possible use of verbal aggressiveness that is compatible with order in court and by being conscious that history is replete with examples of the wheel of destiny turning in a manner that changes the criminals of yesterday into the heroes of today.[37]

A celebrated case of the self-fulfillment of the lawyer on behalf of a politically unpopular and exposed client is that of *Dennis*[38] in the United States, where a summary conviction for contempt of court of the lawyers at the end of a hotly contested political trial was upheld by the Federal Court of Appeals for the Second Circuit.[39] In *Dennis*, members of the American Communist Party were charged under the Smith Act of 1940 with conspiring in effect to organize a party teaching the overthrow of the government. The case itself is a milestone in the evolution of free speech – or, rather, the suppression of it[40] – but our concern here is with the conduct of the personalities in the trial, which "was accompanied by considerable publicity, much of which was devoted to a running controversy between Judge Medina and attorneys for the defendants."[41] A dispassionate study of the preamble and the forty specifications of contempt[42] will reveal a phenomenon also present in the spate of disciplinary cases of German lawyers and the disciplinary cases involving French lawyers for their trial tactics in the Algerian cases during the late fifties and early sixties in the security cases following on the decolonization of Algeria[43]: a commitment of the lawyers to present their clients within the framework of the latter's political ideas and, especially, a commitment to exhaust every possible legal remedy and stratagem to make the inevitable victory of the prosecution a costlier affair – a commitment entirely in line with Western legal ideals.

It would be the so-called civil rights lawyer who would imperatively need and demand the protection and advantages of a vital system of legal free speech for the fulfillment of the role he or she conceives. Although one would often hear sanguine thoughts to the contrary, this model is certainly not one to which the average lawyer adheres. The average lawyer in most Western countries is not conspicuous for challenging the existing order or for supporting those who do. The average lawyer would for average purposes very seldom need more than just a modicum of speech freedom to satisfy the demands of his or her métier and his or her normal duties would seldom require throwing down the verbal gauntlet to the powers within the administration of justice. The ideas and ideals, however, of government under the rule of law and of free speech itself are predicated substantially on the need for the protection of the rights or expectations of those who challenge the existing order or who say the things most people hate. To give just a semblance of reality to these ideas and ideals, however imperfectly, there will be a need for lawyers who will be prepared on behalf of their clients to avail themselves, especially as regards speech, of every conscionable measure and means to promote the interests of these clients.

Readily as all this may be accepted in theory by most Western lawyers, in reality these civil rights lawyers will often expose themselves to the opprobrium of their peers and even to the sanctions of the law when they pursue the interests of their clients too robustly with the speech they use. Nowhere has this opprobrium been more pronounced than in Germany, where as we will later see in some detail there has been a spate of proceedings especially before professional tribunals or *Ehrengerichte* as well as before criminal courts relating to the kind of speech of which certain lawyers availed themselves on behalf of their clients. In many instances the phraseology used against these lawyers could have been borrowed from an English textbook on contempt and in some instances professional sanctions were invoked where merely a judicial frown would have been forthcoming in Britain.[44] And very seldom were the free speech implications raised, let alone applied in these cases. The same, on a greatly reduced scale however, holds true for disciplinary proceedings in Holland in instances where lawyers displayed robust outspokenness in their speech.[45] In short, the use of free speech as a means whereby the lawyer can seek self-fulfillment as a lawyer has only inchoately and haltingly been identified as a legitimate premise or basis for a system of free speech in the legal domain. It seems that only in Italy, where the right of defense has been given preferred status as "an inviolable right at all stages and levels of legal proceedings,"[46] has there been an overt recognition that this may also involve profound free speech implications of a constitutional nature.

The Self-Fulfillment of Other Groups, Particularly Journalists

Nor ever be ashamed
So we be names
Pressmen; Slaves of the Lamp; Servants of Light.
        Sir Edwin Arnold [47] (1832-1904), scholar, poet, and pressman

It is possible that the majority of lawyers never consciously consider a need for untrameled legal free speech based inter alia on their need or desire for self-fulfillment as lawyers. For the average activities of practicing lawyers, merely an adequate modicum of free speech is required and what was said about the self-fulfillment of lawyers really only applies to relatively exceptional situations. This is not the case, however, with at least three other categories of persons whose right of free speech in legal matters may have a vital bearing on their personal and professional self-fulfillment: first, those individuals of whatever profession who make justice their business and who refuse to take injustice good-naturedly – a group who would rarely, if ever, be considered as having any particular claim to free speech concerning the legal domain; second, the legal academics whose role has tangentially been alluded to[48]; and finally, the journalists who in the true spirit of their calling illuminate injustice and scrutinize the fiat of all authority.

The role of the press as a critical scrutinizer of the justice administration is really the only aspect of legal free speech that has received meaningful attention in the West. The awe-inspiring rallying cry "freedom of the press" together with the acute sensitivity of many journalists about their duty to nose around festering social ills of the community they serve have contributed toward a measure of judicial recognition of the basic importance of the press as a necessary control over the administration of justice. In Germany as we will see, for instance, there is a crass distinction between the levels of speech tolerance allowed the press on the one hand and the legal profession on the other, flowing partly from the more immediate identification of the press with free speech.

Perhaps the most inspiring recent recognition of the importance for the press of free speech in the legal domain is that of Lord Denning, Master of the Rolls, in the famous thalidomide case on contempt of court over the deliberate infringement of the sub judice rule by the *Sunday Times* of London.[49] This case, which has recently only reached the end of its time-consuming trek through the labyrinthine procedures of the European Convention on Human Rights – some twenty years after, (to quote Lord Denning) "overwhelming tragedy befell hundreds of families"[50] in Britain – will as far as its more technical aspects are concerned receive attention at a later stage.[51] Of concern here is the unequivocal recognition Lord Denning gave to the professional duties of a conscientious journalist.

The full impact of Lord Denning's judgment can only be appreciated when projected against the oppressive backdrop of the precedent on the sub judice principle in English law and when seen thus the judgment in *AG* v. *The Times* may yet be regarded as one of the most impressive defenses of the freedom of the press concerning the administration of justice. Lord Denning actually expresses regret that the *Sunday Times* ever submitted the offending article to the Attorney General who, as might have been expected, then cranked the ancient contempt law into motion.[52] Although the Master of the Rolls expressed his desire that "the law . . . [as it had developed in England] should be maintained in its full integrity" by not allowing "trial by any medium other than the courts of law,"[53] he proceeded to knock a massive aperture into the law as it had previously been understood. Apart from considering such practical considerations as the fact that the litigation was "dormant" or that Parliament had debated the problem in fully reported sessions or the long delay that had lapsed since tragedy struck or that similar cases had been disposed of that could then legitimately be commented on, Lord Denning clearly considered the *public interest* as being of paramount importance:

And when considering the question [of "a real and substantial danger of prejudice" to a pending trial], it must always be remembered that besides the interest of the parties ... there is another important interest to be considered. It is the interest of the public in matters of national concern, and the freedom of the press to make fair comment on such matters. The one interest must be balanced against the other.

Take this present case. Here we have a matter of the greatest public interest. The thalidomide children are living reminders of a national tragedy. There has been no public inquiry as to how it came about.... On such a matter the law can and does authorise the newspapers to make fair comment. So long as they get their facts right, and keep their comments fair, they are without reproach.... If the pending action is one which, as a matter of public interest, ought to have been brought to trial long ago, or ought to have been settled long ago, the newspapers can fairly comment on the failure to bring it to trial or to reach a settlement. No person can stop comment, by serving a writ and letting it lie idle.[54]

Concluding his judgment Lord Denning makes the unanswerable case for a journalist's right to a forceful scrutiny of the administration of justice:

No doubt the article was intended to bring pressure to bear on Distillers [the marketing company] to increase their offer – but that pressure was legitimate in the light of all that had happened. *It would be open to Distillers to reply to it.* If they had submitted their reply to "The Sunday Times" *I should expect it to have received equal publicity.* But, all in all, it was a matter which warranted debate, not only in Parliament, but also in the press. I would not restrict it.[55]

Although more forceful language in defense of free speech may well have been called for in the almost bizarre circumstances of the *Times* case, the judgment is clearly heavily premised on a recognition of the essential role of the press in a democratic society as an agency of control of the justice machinery. Its historic significance becomes even more apparent when the judgment is seen against the deliberate flouting both of the letter and the spirit of the English law of contempt on the part of the *Sunday Times*, and by giving overt support to this act of defiance Lord Denning in effect struck a devastating blow against encrusted old customs and taboos inhibiting free speech in the legal domain. Although subsequently overruled again on appeal by the House of Lords, Lord Denning's approach ultimately commended itself – not unexpectedly – to the Court of Human Rights in Strasbourg.[56]

As previously stated there is substantial recognition of the right of the press to indulge in a degree of free speech toward the administration of justice and the most cited authority in the contempt jurisdictions in the English-speaking world is that of the Privy Council in the *Ambard* case.[57] In his oft-quoted judgment, Lord Atkin expresses strong support for the actinic role of the press toward the seat of justice and for the journalist who uses verbal skills in communicating and reporting about the justice machinery:

> But whether the authority and position of an individual judge, or the due administration of justice, is concerned, no wrong is committed by any member of the public who exercises the ordinary right of criticising, in good faith, in private or public, the public act done in the seat of justice. The path of criticism is a public way: the wrong headed are permitted to err therein: provided that members of the public abstain from imputing improper motives to those taking part in the administration of justice, and are genuinely exercising a right of criticism, and not acting in malice or attempting to impair the administration of justice, they are immune. Justice is not a cloistered virtue: she must be allowed to suffer the scrutiny and respectful, even though outspoken, comments of ordinary men.[58]

And then later, referring to the press, Lord Atkin adds:

> Their Lordships have discussed this case at some length because, in one aspect, it concerns the liberty of the Press, which is no more than the liberty of any member of the public, to criticise temperately and fairly, but freely, any episode in the administration of justice.[59]

There is, however, another side to the *Ambard* case: the fact that much of the praise it has been wont to receive for so long has partly been ill-conceived. Far from being a clarion charter of legal free speech, *Ambard* is often invoked where that freedom is contracted. Seen against the tenor of a mild and reasoned article on the perennial topic of discriminatory sentences, the judgment with its array of qualifications hardly bespeaks a penetrating understanding of the role of the press as practically the only effective agency of control and public accountability. The array of qualifications in the passages quoted above – "ordinary" right of criticism, "good faith," the abstention from imputing "improper motives" to the judiciary, "genuinely" exercising a right of criticism, "not acting in malice," not acting with the intention "to impair the administration of justice," "respectful" comments, to criticize "temperately and fairly" – have mostly been glossed over under the impact of their poetic qualities. In a viable system of legal free speech, the "wrong headed" must, concerning acts done officially "in the seat of justice," be given more than just a right "to err." To serve journalism *effectively* and to give substance to the freedom of the press in matters that really matter, nothing but the highest possible degree of unfettered freedom of speech will suffice. At the very least the journalist must be legally permitted and should feel socially free to comment as freely and with as little good taste and with as much vehemence on matters done "in the seat of justice" as he or she would be able to do on matters done in the seat of political power.

The freedom of the journalist to watch over the administration of justice is customarily projected against inhibitions based on the criminal law. However, contrary perhaps to popular belief, journalistic freedom in that area may at times be even more seriously curtailed by inhibitions based in civil law. This point – which will be developed later – was crisply put by Justice Brennan in the celebrated *New York Times* v. *Sullivan* case where an attempt was made to sidestep the constitutional protection of free speech by instituting civil proceedings to curb critical comment of official action:

> What a state may not constitutionally bring about by means of a criminal statute is likewise beyond the reach of its civil law of libel. The fear of damage awards . . . may be markedly more inhibiting than the fear of prosecution under a criminal statute.[60]

Freedom of speech in the legal domain like free speech generally can obviously not be limitless if regard is given to other valid social claims in a vital democracy, and vital as the institution of a free press may be it must respect – and if need be forced to do so – those other values, as will be argued elsewhere in this work.[61] One pivotal value a press dedicated to individual liberty must respect is that of the privacy of the individual. This aspect is seldom brought to play on the question of legal free speech but is one that is of special significance in the context of modern media of communications such as television. In an important judgment of the German *Bundesverfassungsgericht* – the Federal Constitutional Court – this potential clash of values of the media's free speech in legal matters on the one hand and of the privacy of the individual on the other received incisive attention.

The facts of the *Lebach* case[62] can be briefly stated. The applicant had indirectly participated in the murder of four soldiers in 1969 and was sentenced to a period of six years' imprisonment. The crime and the subsequent case generated considerable publicity in the media. At a time when the applicant had served two-thirds of his sentence and was about to be released on parole it became known that the "Second Program" of the German Television Service was preparing a 160-minute documentary of a reconstruction of the murders and the police investigations. Shots of the applicant and the main perpetrators were to be shown at the outset, but the dramatization was to be undertaken by professional actors. A book on the events had been published even before the termination of the original case. The applicant applied unsuccessfully first to the *Landgericht* and then to the *Oberlandesgericht*[63] for an injunction to prevent the screening of the documentary, and in view of the constitutionally protected rights involved an appeal was allowed to the *Bundesverfassungsgericht*, which upheld the appeal and banned the broadcast of the documentary.

The judgments of both the *Oberlandesgericht* and of the *Bundes-verfassungsgericht* are lengthy and involved essays on the reach and the limitations of the fundamental rights enshrined in the German constitution in which the conflicting interests of privacy of the applicant – an unlawful infringement of his right to an unimpaired personality and an infringement of his right to the exclusiveness of his name and image[64] – were weighed against society's need for information and the constitutionally protected freedom of speech.

The basic argument presented on behalf of the applicant was that after putting him in a modern version of the pillory by his exposure to millions of viewers his reintegration into society would be rendered virtually impossible. Such an exposure would also conflict with the constitutional protection of the individual's personality. In any event, he contended, the legitimate interest of the public to information ceases "at the time of judgment or at a time closely connected with the judgemt."[65] The respondent television chain on the other hand relied on the full thrust of the constitutional provision of free speech and on the duty of the media to satisfy the need for information, including information about the chances of detection of serious crime that would satisfy the aim of general deterrence.[66]

In its closely reasoned judgment the *Bundesverfassungsgericht* delicately balanced the conflicting social values and arrives at the conclusion that despite

> the weighty considerations militating in favour of the fullest information on the part of the public, including information about past crimes which encompasses also the personality of the perpetrator, and the possible roots of such crimes ... [and despite the fact that] generally speaking the contemporaneous reporting of crimes and the [public's] right to information would outweigh the inevitable intrusion into the private sphere of the perpetrator[67]

this right to information was a qualified one and the problem had to be solved with recourse to the principle of *Verhältnismässigkeit* or proportionality. Because of the substantial perils that would beset the social reintegration of the applicant if the documentary was screened, the television service was enjoined from doing so.

The *Lebach* judgment,[68] unlike most other judgments relating to legal free speech, is heavily premised on liberal principles of individual liberty, albeit of a person who had only himself to blame for his predicament. As such, the judgment has libertarian merits that speak for themselves. However, on balance, I submit that a more subtle use of the proportionality yardstick would have produced the opposite result. The question of the openness of the justice machinery is far too peripherally dealt with in relation to the modern medium of television.[69] The judgment seems also to be too optimistically premised on an individual's potential for betterment and too pessimistically premised on the role that a single documentary may play in its prevention. The Constitutional Court also too easily rejected the contention that the injunction would seriously affect the constitutionally protected freedom of the arts in relation to the creative use of television in that sphere.[70] There was further an overly unrealistic comparison between the massive penetration of television and the more limited but potentially more durable impression that the written word would have made in the relatively small circle where it really mattered.[71] There is also an unrealistic air about the unexpressed but latently present assumption that but for the documentary the applicant could slip back inconspicuously into his little community of yore.[72] Paradoxically, the bringing of the action itself would, as would very often be the case, effectively have ended the applicant's subsequent anonymity, affording him thus merely with the meaningless shell of theoretical protection.[73] Against these considerations one must finally weigh the undoubted consequence that the ban unduly, and without sufficient compensatory advantage, restricted creative journalism in the legal sphere in the most important journalistic medium of our time.[74]

In conclusion, it must be stressed that there is much more to a journalist's self-fulfillment as far as legal reporting is concerned than merely living with the array of formal legal free speech restrictions. Of much greater importance than legal impediments to legal free speech is the journalist's positive commitment to it. As will be seen in the last part of this work, the failure of many newspapers and other media in the West to give the administration of justice the attention it inherently deserves is due less to legal restrictions than to the potent pull either of societal pressures on journalists to treat the administration of justice with more deference than other concentrations of power or to simple indifference. In many countries, there are only minimal effective legal restrictions on reporting in the legal domain and the explanation for the substantial silence of the press on sensitive legal issues must be sought in such extra-legal considerations. In the context of extra-legal considerations inhibiting the flowering of a vital doctrine of legal free speech, the work of the *individual journalist* who makes the legal domain his or her business or of the *individual newspaper* that concentrates on quality and incisive analyses of the workings of the legal machinery become profoundly relevant. At various parts of the work attention will be given to individual examples such as Bernard Levin of the *Times* of London, Gerhard Mauz of *Der Spiegel*, Jac van Veen in the Dutch paper *Het Parool*, and the quality reporting generally of *Le Monde* in France and of *Der Spiegel* in Germany.

THE SECOND PREMISE: FREEDOM OF SPEECH AS AN ESSENTIAL INSTRUMENT FOR THE ADVANCEMENT OF KNOWLEDGE AND TRUTH IN THE ADMINISTRATION OF JUSTICE

> *Silence is not an option when things are ill done.*
> Lord Denning in the *Quintin Hogg* case[75]

It is a trite proposition that the administration of justice is better served by knowledge than by ignorance and it must also follow that freedom of speech in the legal domain would be a prerequisite for the acquisition of such knowledge.[76] There has been a remarkable tendency in many legal systems at various times to devalue this truth as a consequence both of formal restrictions on speech freedom and of the pull of informal taboos as well as indifference or ignorance on the part of those in society who are in the best position to keep the administration of justice under control and observation. Jerome Frank, who did so much to foster a tradition of openness about the workings of courts, partly justified his legal iconoclasm in the search for truth on this premise. In his *Courts on Trial* he lamented the inactivity of the media concerning the imparting of truthful information about the workings of the law with the result that "what may be called 'court-house government' still is mysterious to most of the laity."[77]

The American realist tradition in which Jerome Frank played such an important role was largely predicated on the premises of legal free speech under discussion here and particularly that of the search for truth, which was an ever-present undercurrent of the tradition. But it was not only truth for its own sake – a kind of *l'art pour l'art* approach – that moved Frank and his fellow iconoclasts but also the belief inherent in their democratic faith that the search for truth would also facilitate the search for the *graal* of justice: "I am – I make no secret of it – a reformer. . . . I see grave defects in some of the ways courts operate . . . but [defects] that will never be intelligently dealt with unless they are publicised."[78]

The realist approach concerning the search for truth in the law and the willingness to publish it regardless of provoked susceptibilities has, more than is the case in any other country, become part and parcel of American scholastic and journalistic methodology, although pockets or aspects of self-censorship or repression of legal free speech persist.[79] In Britain the situation as regards the conscious use of free speech in the legal domain is more equivocal, as is evident from an authoritative joint report of lawyers and journalists where the conclusion is reached that the lack of incisive reporting on contentious legal matters must not entirely be laid at the door of the contempt law and that something akin to a deviation of duty is at work in the British press[80]:

> We are . . . of the opinion that the law of contempt is not nearly as threatening as some editors and journalists imagine it to be, and need

not be as inhibiting.... [W]e believe that it would be of great advantage to ... [the Press] and to public interest if newspapers could devote more continual and serious attention to matters concerning the administration of justice and employ more experienced reporters and editorial staff for this purpose.[81]

Instances in the form of judgments or other occurrences (or nonoccurrences) in which we can detect either an attempt to suppress the truth or a failure to serve the truth in legal matters are plentiful and a few illustrative instances can be documented here.

In at least three recent scholarly publications in Britain the imputation of bias to a judge is considered a *proper* occasion for the invocation of contempt proceedings.[82] In the report by Justice on *Contempt of Court,* a curious concession is made to freedom of speech inasmuch as it concedes that such an imputation is one that ought to be made with impunity although the forum for such an allegation should not be the press.[83]

Against the background especially of the *New Statesman* case, which is still regarded as the leading case on the point, the question is indeed a proper one as to why the press is not the ideal vehicle in a democratic society for airing an imputation of partiality as it would be for other incumbents of state authority. True to his name, the editor of the *New Statesman,* Mr. Sharp, excoriated a particularly ill-conceived judgment and suggested that in the particular matter a fair judgment was not to be expected from Justice Avory.[84] Looking as objectively as one can at the facts of the case, one would think that either Mr. Sharp's deduction was an obvious one or at least one that ought to be made with impunity in a democratic society. In making the inevitable bow in deference to the dictates of free speech, the lord chief justice proceeded to hand down a judgment that still to this day maintains its truth-undermining thrall in Britain and elsewhere.[85] Compared to the catastrophic influence of this precedent the mild sentence imposed fades into obscurity. [86] Even more surprising perhaps is the continued academic deference to this precedent.[87]

What has been described in an English textbook as "one of the most interesting [cases] to emerge in this area [of contempt] for many years,"[88] that of this writer in 1970 in South Africa, illustrates as few reported instances do both the elaborate attempts made at times to suppress the truth concerning the administration of justice and the consequences of such attempts. Moreover, it also illustrates with a rare degree of clarity how even an acquittal on a criminal charge relating to legal free speech can produce inhibitions not materially different to those that would flow from a conviction. An article on capital punishment in the *South African Law Journal* "expressed in sober and responsible language"[89] included the results of a questionnaire directed at advocates,[90] including those of two questions relating to the possible obtrusion of the racial element in the imposition of death sentences.[91] The asking of these two questions was made the object of a contempt prosecution before the

Transvaal Supreme Court, the attorney-general appearing in person, because of their alleged tendency of "bringing the South African judiciary into contempt and/or of violating the dignity of the judges."[92] The backdrop to these questions of and the contempt charge have been fully developed elsewhere,[93] but suffice it to say that by drawing attention to the racial factor I had breached two very important taboos: first, that the senior judiciary, being the ordinary mortals they are, inevitably reflect the racial prejudices of the white society to which without exception they all belong; second, that race is an obvious and, in many respects, particularly in cross-racial crimes, the one factor that determines who would take the last fateful leap from the scaffold in Pretoria where at the time almost half of the world's official executions were taking place.[94] Over and above these facts hovered the fact, or rather the incontrovertible truth, that race is a stronger factor or reality in South African society than in any other in the world, despite the oft-proclaimed theory that it did not prejudicially enter the judicial lawmaking process.[95]

Although the prosecution ended in an acquittal (but only because of the absence on the part of the accused of mens rea in the form of intention), the judgment of Justice Claassen held not only that the prosecution was justified but in effect also that, objectively, contempt had been committed.[96] The justification of truth so prominently raised by the defense with the help of masses of statistics and so clearly relevant in view of undeniable realities[97] was not only laconically brushed aside but has in fact since become hazardous to pursue as a consequence of the prosecution and the judgment. Indeed, it would seem as if the truth, if anything, acted as a kind of aggravating factor that increased the potency of the sting.[98]

It is particularly in the identifiable consequences of the first *Van Niekerk* contempt case as regards the search for the truth that we may detect this case's most important contribution in the annals of legal free speech. It drew attention as nothing before had to the racial realities of the death penalty in South Africa, and despite a rising curve of capital crime the infliction of capital punishment fell by some 50 percent in two years.[99] On the negative side, however, it effectively stopped any further inquiry into sensitive areas both by journalists and academics by its legal reinforcement of what had hitherto largely been a social taboo. The result is that, for all the freedom of speech that still exists in the political arena in South Africa, all the sensitive areas of the administration of justice have become almost total no-go areas, often to an extent that goes far beyond the reasonably foreseeable reach of even the imagination of the prosecuting authorities, as we will again see below.[100]

The undermining of the search for the truth will occur not only when penal sanctions are invoked, but also when for whatever other reason a person with a story to tell in the legal field feels muzzled or inhibited. One obvious source of muzzling or inhibition is simply the commentator's peers and their peculiar philosophical makeup; this could apply to journalists and lawyers alike, but it is in the mores and peculiarities of the legal profession especially where these inhibitions are strongest and at times most visible. And nowhere would the inclination to refrain from speaking out be stronger than with the judicial profession in most Western countries.[101] Silence, discretion, and equivocation as regards controversial issues have largely become the rule with most judiciaries in the West, and they are enforced by an array of subtle sanctions. An instance – a very rare one – where such sanctions assumed a less subtle and a readily documentable form concerned a senior German judge, Dr. Theo Rasehorn, which, strangely enough, has never been adequately documented and analyzed in Germany on the basis of its constitutional implications.[102] This case is but one manifestation of a much more involved phenomenon, but for our purposes it has interesting heuristic implications, especially as an indication of the brittle substance of free speech in legal matters vis-à-vis social and political pressures in a particular society – quite apart from legal restrictions – in the perennial quest for the truth.

The possible promotion of Dr. Rasehorn to the chairmanship of the *Oberlandesgericht* in Frankfurt unleashed a furor in certain public and judicial circles. The reason for the furor was simply that Dr. Rasehorn had become known – and, it should be added, also respected in many quarters – for his role, a very rare one in Germany at the time, as judicial critic of the administration of justice. Apart from a number of critical press reports that appeared at the time, the *Richterverband* or professional organization of judges in the province of Hesse wrote to the minister of justice of the province taking a strong stand against the possibility of Dr. Rasehorn's promotion. The content of the letter was communicated to the press. Dr. Rasehorn applied unsuccessfully for an injunction against the *Richterverband*, compelling it to desist from further publication of its criticism, and in an appeal to the *Oberlandesgericht* in Frankfurt Dr. Rasehorn was once again unsuccessful. The judgment of the court need not detain us here; based as it was on the constitutional right of free speech of the *Richterverband* and on the fact that the latter body had expressed itself in a factual and not in an excessively hurtful manner that may have exceeded that right, one can have no qualms with the judgment on policy grounds.[103] The interesting aspect of this case resides in the fact that it documents and reflects the crucial importance of extra-legal inhibitions on free speech and the crippling effect such inhibitions must inevitably have on the already difficult search for truth in the labyrinthine recesses of the machinery of justice.[104]

In its reply to the application of Dr. Rasehorn, the *Richterverband* provided certain examples of the writings of the applicant that in their view documented "the controversial reputation of Dr. Rasehorn to the effect that he has indefatigably propagated both in writings and in speeches extremist views which question the existing legal order and the fundamental constitutional principles."[105]

It is quite obvious that Dr. Rasehorn's views, coming as they did from within the most conservative part of the German legal profession, may have appeared extremist at the time, but even in comparison with the views of a comparable judicial maverick of our time, Jerome Frank, they pale into conservative respectability.[106] Not only has time been kind to Dr. Rasehorn's views on the importance of opening up the judicial apparatus to critical inquiry, but amid the din of a much more vociferous and fundamentalist questioning along neo-Marxist lines of the premises of German justice, these views have an almost conservative ring today, less than a decade later. Dr. Rasehorn, incidentally, did receive the promotion![107]

The crucial point of the Rasehorn episode in the present context is that it underlines tellingly the brittle substance of free speech in legal matters vis-à-vis social and political pressures in a particular society, quite apart from any legal restrictions on free speech. One needs no great gifts of imagination to understand how, even in a functioning democracy (which Germany surely is), the potential well-meaning and nonrevolutionary judicial critic of the law will be deterred from seeking the truth in the administration of justice by pressures such as those that were brought to bear on Dr. Rasehorn. Fortunately, not only for Dr. Rasehorn but also for our inquiry, the most blatant of these pressures – the attempt to block his professional advancement – was exercised relatively openly. In that respect it must be conceded, much as I disagree with its analysis of material that I have also had at my disposal, that the *Richterverband*'s initiative was well-covered by the minimum requirements of free speech – a view reflected in the judgment of the court – and that Dr. Rasehorn's attempt to have it stopped, understandable and subjectively justifiable as it might have been, was misplaced and unfortunate. Undoubtedly, in the majority of instances of a similar nature the pressures will be less direct, less open, and more subtle.

The use of legal free speech as an instrumentality in the search for truth in the final analysis depends not only on the degree of speech freedom permitted by the law – including the indirect operation of the law as evidenced by the Rasehorn episode – but by the atmosphere surrounding the law, which in turn is created by the willingness or otherwise of the commentators (mostly journalists and lawyers) to avail themselves of the fullest possible measure of freedom permitted by the law. The reality of deeply ingrained social taboos and simple indifference that inhibit and circumscribe free speech forms the topic of a major part of this work, but suffice it to say at this juncture that in most societies the operation of these taboos and indifference probably constitutes a greater impediment to the search and proclamation of the truth than legal sanctions. An important side effect of these taboos and indifference is that channels of access to information may become blocked, whereby important institutions such as prisons, mental institutions, and judiciaries become so isolated from the kind of scrutiny normally expended on important institutions that the question of the legality of speech as regards them will not arise in the first place. This is part of the wider question of access to information on which free speech ideally depends to which we will also turn our attention.

THE THIRD PREMISE: FREEDOM OF SPEECH AS A DEVICE OF DEMOCRATIC PARTICIPATION IN THE ADMINISTRATION OF JUSTICE

It is the inalienable right of everyone to comment fairly upon any manner of public importance. This right is one of the pillars of individual liberty – freedom of speech, which our courts have always unfailingly upheld.

Lord Justice Salmon in the *Quintin Hogg* case[108]

There is little, if any, recognition anywhere of the fact that freedom of speech on all matters concerned with the operation of the machinery of justice is the only real form of participation that the public has, either directly or indirectly through the media, with the judiciary. Undoubtedly, the jury system provides a slight corrective in certain societies, but there is little doubt that even in those societies, and a fortiori in the others, much more is needed if the most important premise of a democratic society – the active participation of the people in decisions affecting themselves – is to be translated into some semblance of reality. Like democracy as such, this premise can claim for itself no inherent justification beyond the belief of those who profess faith in that form of government.[109]

There is, however, considerable recognition, in theory at least, for considering the so-called *public interest* when invoking or interpreting speech controls over legal free speech. The so-called public interest is really on closer analysis nothing other than the democratic expectation of society that the justice administration would be as adequately scrutinized as other concentrations of power. Paradoxically, the public interest has almost invariably been invoked in cases where there has been a blatant suppression of free speech. This was the case when, in the famous case of *New York Times* v. *Sullivan*, the Alabama Supreme Court initially awarded $500,000 damages to the plaintiff for certain criticisms of the police – a decision subsequently overruled in one of the great legal free speech decisions in the West.[110] In Britain, it was so also in the final judgment in the famous *Sunday Times* thalidomide case, when the sub judice rule was invoked under bizarre circumstances.[111] It was so in both *Van Niekerk* contempt cases, where for all practical purposes an almost total ban was put on scrutiny of the judicial apparatus in South Africa.[112] It was inevitably so also in the Liberian case of *Cassell*, which clamped down on mild criticism of the bench with possibly the most strident judicial invective in the long and rich history of the Anglo-Saxon contempt instrumentality.[113] It is submitted that, in these and most other cases where the public interest was invoked within the ambit of legal free speech, a more socially alert scrutiny would have revealed that the democratic ethos imperatively demanded the protection and not the contraction of free speech. Indeed, in these instances free speech constituted the only real, albeit minimal, check on the exercise of power in the administration of justice.

That the exercise of this right of democratic participation and of control of decision making within the administration of justice will for practical purposes mostly be exercised on behalf of the citizenry by the press and by the legal profession detracts not a whit from the validity of the premise in those societies claiming allegiance to the democratic faith. That those within the administration of justice who traditionally have been insulated from criticism may find such "democratic" control or scrutiny neither helpful nor pleasant must be expected, but the resentment will seldom be as openly expressed as it was in the official letter of the *Deutscher Richterbund* to the German ministers of justice after the publication of an article in *Stern* on German judges[114] in which it requested protection against such criticism: "Even private persons no longer hesitate of late to turn to the public with pamphlets and to describe judges as 'bums and criminals who ought to be in jail'." The article itself consisted of a critical exposé of a kind regularly found – and lauded – on other concentrations of power in the state.

In the light of the role of the press and the legal profession (including the judiciary) of being really the only instruments of control, critique, and scrutiny over the administration of justice, the informal restrictions and limitations on these professions assume added importance. If, for some reason or another, legal or societal, formal or informal, the voices of these persons or institutions were silenced or muffled on legal matters, there would be no meaningful scrutiny of the administration of justice.[115] Decision making, and especially judicial decision making, would take place in a kind of intellectual vacuum, which would inevitably entail an absence of effective control over such decision making as well as a blunting of the critical faculties of the decision makers.[116] Moreover, this intellectual vacuum constitutes the ideal breeding ground for the stuff of which myths and an inflated sense of self-importance of those decision makers – the judiciary particularly – are made.

It is not difficult to find many instances of suppression of legal free speech where the need for democratic control of judicial decision making was either ignored or heeded. It can in fact be argued that all instances of speech restrictions over the legal domain involve an application of this principle in one form or another. In the leading contempt case of *Ambard*,[117] in perhaps the most quoted passage in contempt law, Lord Atkin echoes John Milton's view[118] on free speech in relation of the legal domain – a passage obviously derived from the democratic ethos:

But whether the authority and position of an individual judge, or the due administration of justice, is concerned, no wrong is committed by any member of the public who exercises the ordinary right of criticizing, in good faith, in private or public, the public act done in the seat of justice. The path of criticism is a public way. . . . Justice is not a cloistered virtue: she must be allowed to suffer the scrutiny and respectful, even though outspoken, comments of ordinary men.[119]

It is really as a device for the control of authority – judicial authority in the present instance – that a viable system of free speech in the legal domain performs its most important democratic function. It can undoubtedly be argued that judicial power even in a fully functioning democratic state, for all the safeguards and appeal possibilities, remains the most uncontrolled of the three organs of government.[120] The very notion of a fully independent judiciary testifies to this fact, and it will most often be only the existence of an informed and critical public opinion that will keep the judicial power under some form of control, conscious as well as unconscious.[121] It is in this light, I submit, that much more is needed than a doctrine that guarantees only the "ordinary" right of criticism, or is "temperately and fairly" conceived, or refrains from imputing "improper motives," to mention just a few of Lord Atkin's qualifications in the *Ambard* case.[122] The universal phenomenon that uncontrolled power is of an encroaching nature[123] is one that exists also in the field of what may be termed psychological control of institutions in the form of subtle and less subtle kinds of feedback from the critical forces in society. On the basis of this somewhat evasive verity, I submit that, in cases where it is confronted even by intemperate criticism that is manifestly ill-conceived, it would be better for a court to react with a shrug instead of a shriek.

One of many instances where such a shrug was in fact forthcoming – albeit a qualified one – is found in French Polynesia, where the *Cour de Cassation* of Papeete was called on to apply Articles 226 and 227 of the French Criminal Code[124] to a newspaper editor who had published an article, very respectful in tone, on the unequal justice meted out in the courts of the island, with special reference to a particular case in which a high official had been charged with a driving offense.[125] The court held that the general way in which the relevant provisions are framed – Article 226 speaks of bringing discredit on a judicial (*"juridictionnelle"*) act or decision in circumstances of a kind that assails the authority or the independence of the administration of justice (*"la justice"*) – did not, despite the "rather indecent nature of the article" render the latter criminal.[126]

The article of the editor in Papeete was *"peu décent,"* with the judicial shrug merely a qualified one; the same cannot be said of the judgment of the Irish High Court in O'Ryan and Boyd's case.[127] The offending attack was sulphuric indeed, but instead of a shrug the court followed with its own bag of vitriolic epithets – "monstrous ebullition"; "afflicted with a frenzied indignation"; ". . . had not recovered his sanity"; etc. Following a brawl in "an agrarian dispute," a number of persons were charged and found guilty of "riot." The letter of a clergyman pleading for leniency induced the presiding judge to wonder aloud whether the former "expected that [he] . . . should get no punishment." This remark prompted a follower of the man of the cloth to compose a letter to the judge – which letter was also read at a county council meeting – in which Irish wrath and Irish historical memory combined to produce one of the minor masterpieces of invective in the rich annals of the contempt institution in the English-speaking world.[128] However, it is submitted that in the very acrimony of its tone and in the choice of its words, the letter carried its own neutralizing antidote and that a dignified statement by a senior judge would have redounded more to the status of the impugned judge than the inevitable apology, the light sentence, and the scathing judgment, as well as the inevitable certificate of good conduct issued by the judge's brethren in their judgment.

It may seem incongruous and farfetched to relate democratic values to an attack of this kind, but I submit that it is equally farfetched to believe that penal sanctions could ever contribute to a strengthening of the reputation of either the impugned judge or of his office. It may well be argued that even an extravaganza of the kind documented here can serve purposes of a democratic nature: to give the aggrieved citizen the psychological satisfaction of blowing off steam about a grievance; to illuminate even more clearly the excellence and qualities of the impugned judge and his office; to provide food for thought on the basis of the belief that even an unreasonable attack may contain germs of wisdom. And then of course there is ultimately no real distinction between extravagance of words and extravagance of errors as far as criticism of the administration of justice is concerned; the dictum of Lord Denning as regards the latter kind of extravagance in the *Quintin Hogg* case must in a mature society also apply to the former: "We [the judges] must rely on our conduct itself to be its own vindication."

By their very nature, the existence and the invocation of legal instrumentalities, such as contempt, with which respect for the judiciary is enforced seem to indicate that the judiciary concerned cannot be trusted to be its own vindication. Nowhere does this assumption come clearer to light than in the *Cassell* contempt case of Liberia, where mild, respectful, indirect, and academic criticism of the senior judiciary by a former attorney-general was met by a barrage of abuse rarely seen in the cold print of the judgments of senior courts.[129] The stark contrast between the mild critique and the thirty-six page rambling vituperation of the court, in which the public interest and democratic control also figure prominently, tellingly underlines the need for some form of democratic control over judicial power.[130] A court capable of such strident overreaction is visibly in need of some form of control in the wider public interest as conceived in democratic terms.

THE FOURTH PREMISE: FREEDOM OF SPEECH AS A METHOD OF MINIMIZING CONFLICT AND MAXIMIZING STABILITY IN THE ADMINISTRATION OF JUSTICE

Finally, freedom of expression is a method of achieving a more adaptable and hence a more stable community, of maintaining the precarious balance between healthy cleavage and necessary consensus. This follows because suppression of discussion makes a rational judgment impossible, substituting force for reason; because suppression promotes inflexibility and stultification, preventing society from adjusting to changing circumstances or developing new ideas; and because suppression conceals the real problems confronting a society, diverting public attention from the critical issues. At the same time the process of open discussion promotes greater cohesion in a society because people are more ready to accept decisions that go against them if they have a part in the decision-making process. Moreover, the state at all times retains adequate powers to promote unity and to suppress resort to force. Freedom of expression thus provides a framework in which the conflict necessary to the progress of a society can take place without destroying the society. It is an essential mechanism for maintaining the balance between stability and change.

Thomas Emerson[131]

Not only is this last of Emerson's democratic premises of free speech probably the most elusive of all to pin down analytically, it constitutes in effect a summary of the one principle that underlies all premises of a system of free speech: that free speech is good, indeed essential, for democratic government in the widest sense of the word. Naturally this premise is based on or inspired by an even wider premise or principle – that the democratic form of government is indeed the preferred form for a particular society.

It can hardly be denied that we are dealing here, as was also the case with the preceding premises, with an inherently sanguine hypothesis that, at least in the long run, truth (including the unpleasant truth) serves the forces of justice and stability better than the suppression of it and the maintenance of myths and lies. It is an assumption of free speech in a democracy as much as it is a tacit goal for and article of faith of democrats. John Milton's celebrated aphorism sums up this goal and this faith:

For who knows not that Truth is strong, next to the Almighty? She needs no policies, nor stratagems, not licensings to make her victorious: those are the shifts and the defences that error uses against her power. Give her but room, and do not bind her when she sleeps, for then she speaks not true.[132]

Transposed to the narrow domain of the administration of justice, it cannot be said that this premise is readily recognized in practice for the truth it is so facilely assumed to be in theory. Secrecy, discretion, and stultifying moderation are very much the stuff of which many attitudes and commentaries are made in this field, as it sometimes still is in the wider field of government and politics. One can effectively argue that any restriction of free speech – direct and indirect, formal and informal – that applies to the administration of justice is ultimately based on or inspired by a belief either that truth will not prevail or that truth ought not to prevail in the first place and that social stability may in effect be undermined by knowledge and truth.[133]

It is not difficult to document how this fundamental premise is traduced or attenuated in practice in most countries of the world. A comment by Judge Archie Simmonds of Madison, Wisconsin, – that a rape victim may have contributed to the assault – led to the women's lobby initiating recall procedures (allowed in a small number of American states), which ultimately led to his electoral defeat.[134] His reasoned and unemotional statement under the circumstances may have been inopportune or misplaced (as it certainly was in the opinion of the lobby that immediately drew itself into battle formation) or wrong (in which event the appeal court might have said something) or simply insensitive (as the truth often is), but it certainly incorporated a viewpoint that is not intrinsically outrageous, evil, or erroneous and that society can do better to ponder (together with other opposing ones) than to suppress. And so, albeit in a small way, the truth – or rather the quest for truth – on the particular question was smothered, and, what is more grievous, it will also be smothered as far as other judges and other sensitive and contentious policies are concerned in an area much wider than Madison, Wisconsin.[135]

To return to the Rasehorn episode[136]: it is also clear against the backdrop of the premise presently under discussion that Dr. Rasehorn's writings, which for present purposes we may summarize as being largely in the vein of the American realist tradition, ultimately substantially cleared the German academic and judicial air as regards the ability of the German judiciary to cope with the problem of renewal of attitudes from the time of the Third Reich and with the problem of being more critical – and more modest – about its ability and its efforts to cope with the changing needs of German society. Proof of this can be found in the simple fact that Rasehorn's views have not only largely entered the mainstream, but they are even regarded as conservative in many quarters. From a situation where, as it has been recorded,[137] the official journal of the judicial profession refused to publish his articles, Dr. Rasehorn has progressed – or, rather, perhaps German society has progressed – to a point where only a lustrum later his views were regularly reported and published in the same journal.[138] It is widely recognized today that attempts by Rasehorn and a few others to discuss and criticize the working of the judiciary openly have led to a general improvement in judicial standards and judicial accountability.[139]

Without writing a comprehensive historical gloss on the iconoclastic achievements of the American jurisprudential school of realism of Jerome Frank and others – a school or approach whose force is not yet spent – it is not difficult to see how the approach of being both willing and legally able to say practically anything about the law has gone into the mainstream of American judicial methodology, leading in turn to something akin to a spirit of adventurous boldness where the unshakeable wisdom of yesterday is questioned today to be overturned tomorrow.[140] Despite Frank's lament as late as 1950 that American "court-house government" was still wrapped in myths,[141] there is no doubt that the extensive degree of legal free speech claimed and actually used in America – coupled to improve access to information about the periphery of the justice administration, such as prisons, mental institutions, and juries – constitutes a most important element in the continuous reform-oriented questioning of these institutions.[142]

Two instances of the unorthodox use of legal free speech documented in this work that illustrate the potentially reformationist and ameliorative operation of this premise are the *Sunday Times* thalidomide case in Britain[143] and the first *Van Niekerk* contempt case in South Africa.[144] In the first instance, the dedicated, costly, and time-consuming application of the *Sunday Times* to free speech in the legal domain ultimately led to probably the most important blow ever struck against the suppression of that freedom in Britain by the contempt institution. This happened in 1979 when the European Court of Human Rights[145] ruled for the *Sunday Times* on the basis of free speech in its open flouting of the sub judice restrictions in the law by its publication of the full horror of the plight of the thalidomide children at the hands of a party to the litigation for damages. However, the first operation of the premise presently under discussion came about when under the pressure of the *Sunday Times* some correction of the injustice took place, an achievement conceded in the official Phillimore Report on contempt.[146]

The majority judgment of the European Court of Human Rights in Strasbourg drew attention to the fact that a strict sub judice rule cannot stand the test of logic, justice, or the democratic value system.[147] Indeed, it was specifically on its understanding of the demands of the democratic ethos that the majority on the court[148] decided that the legitimate interest of "maintaining the authority and impartiality of the judiciary" did not outweigh the "public interest in freedom of expression within the meaning of the Convention":

> The Court therefore finds the reasons for the restraint imposed on the applicants not to be sufficient under Article 10(2) [of the Convention]. The restraint proves not to be proportionate to the legitimate aim pursued; it was not necessary in a democratic society for the authority of the judiciary.[149]

In substance, what the courageous and vigorous exercise of free speech rights by the *Sunday Times* brought about was not only the righting of a grievous wrong but also the most serious challenge and indeed frontal attack on the contempt institution that had been hallowed by time and uncritically passed over by generations of jurists.[150]

The first *Van Niekerk* contempt case in South Africa, although highly suppressive of a vital system of free speech,[151] drew attention to the racial realities of the application of capital punishment and the considerable drop in the rates of executions before and after the case can really not be explained with reference to any other factor, least of all to the steadily climbing rate of capital crimes.[152] It is one of the ironies of the ameliorative operation of legal free speech that is suppression – including successful suppression – could often lead to an achievement of the substantive aim sought, whether it be the reduction of capital punishment in South Africa, the achievement of justice to the thalidomide children in Britain, or the wider dissemination of the kind of ideas propagated by Dr. Theo Rasehorn. Although by breaking through the conspiracy of silence around some of the taboo subjects of the death penalty – especially the racial factor – the offending article probably made its own contribution to the dramatic change in the statistical pattern of executions in South Africa, it was especially the court case and the aggressive defense methods used there that gave an extra sharp edge to the original – and rather conservative – indulgence in legal free speech and brought about the dramatic amelioration (albeit temporary) in the statistical pattern of the death penalty in South Africa.

THE FIFTH PREMISE: FREE SPEECH IN THE LEGAL DOMAIN AS A PREREQUISITE FOR JUSTICE TO AND THE LIBERTY OF THE INDIVIDUAL

If there is any principle of the Constitution that more imperatively calls for attachment than any other, it is the principle of free thought – not free thought for those who agree with us, but freedom for the thought we hate.

Justice Holmes in the *Schwimmer* case[153]

Professor Emerson's four premises that have been discussed above, taken together, mean nothing more than that free speech is a necessary prerequisite for the achievement of justice and individual liberty in the Western democratic sense. It is submitted, however, that when free speech is specifically linked to the administration of justice it assumes a relevance more precise and more specific as a prerequisite for justice to the individual and for the liberty of the individual in the much narrower sense of those terms.

Trite though it be, once more it must be pointed out that law and its processes are fraught with importance to the well-being and liberty of the individual. What happens in both civil and criminal courts of first instance, or in the lofty chambers of courts of final appeal, what is decided in obscure crannies of departments of justice or what goes on behind the high and often impenetrable walls of police stations, prisons, or mental asylums will in almost every instance touch on the liberty or well-being of a particular individual. It is simply a fact of life that, without a system of meaningfully free speech in the legal domain, the administration of justice, particularly so far as the individual is concerned, can easily become enveloped in semisecrecy. It is too late to have to argue the demerits of secret justice, which is almost universally regarded as a contradiction in terms, and even the most authoritarian regimes seem to accept that there should be physical openness of and access to court proceedings to bolster the pretence of justice and fairness. However, as is also evident from a number of contemporary examples, mere open, visible, or accessible procedures often are not effective countervailing force against injustice, whereas the possibility to direct open, free, and general comment on and criticism of such procedures would be a useful counterweight under such circumstances. Open or accessible as court and legal procedures may be in many countries in the purely physical sense, the absence of the legal and the social ability or the willingness of the persons concerned, or of interested persons on behalf of others, to express themselves vigorously and critically on those procedures renders mere physical accessibility to be of relatively little importance as an effective, as opposed to a theoretical, guarantee against injustice. In the world in which we live justice will be done not only, in the words of the old maxim, when it is seen to be done, but also when one can be sure that informed and concerned persons will both be able and willing to speak out when (according to their views) justice is *not* done. It is when these points are carefully pondered that the irreplaceable role of a vigilant, informed, and outspoken press becomes obvious – a press, moreover, that is unrestricted not only by inhibitive legal restrictions but also by debilitating social taboos. Here it is also necessary to note that, in most instances where issues relating to legal free speech arise, they do so not in relation to the interests of the speaker (or writer) but in relation to his or her championing of someone else's cause and the premise now under discussion will relate more often to justice vis-à-vis others than to the speaker.

Due to a variety of reasons, some relating to education (with few people having the necessary expertise to speak on legal matters), others to psychology (with law having certain inherently unpleasant associations), and others again to practical problems (especially in the face of drawn-out or complicated proceedings or concerning the sense of powerlessness felt by an individual who is dealing with matters of justice), the legal processes do not inherently commend themselves to the interest of the average citizen.[154] One consequence of this situation is that without the ability and willingness of the media and interested individuals to express vigorous dissent, substantial secrecy descends on the justice administration that will make the purely physical openness of court proceedings substantially meaningless. This raises involved questions in a modern society, such as the access of the courts to the medium of television,[155] but it especially raises the issue of interested parties – lawyers and journalists particularly – turning the concept of an open court into something more dynamic. It is not just an issue that justice must be *seen to be done* but that the possibility must actually exist that the public would be able to *hear* when justice has *not been done*.

One aspect of free speech as a prerequisite of justice for an individual that never receives attention is that of providing the individual with a kind of psychological method of attenuating or blunting his or her wrath or frustration in the often luckless world of litigation. It is a fact of life in the process of litigation that there is on every level of decision making a rich array of possibilities for error or false judgments that may never be discovered or provable to the satisfaction of a court. Allowing an individual – or his or her supporters – a measure of robust comment in and out of court will, far from undermining the administration of justice, actually redound to its advantage by constituting a kind of crude but psychologically highly effective appeal procedure – an appeal, in other words, to the public at large or even to history.[156] Numerous cases of contempt in facie curiae[157] or of criminal insult in Continental systems[158] may well merit consideration from this point of view, as well as some scandalization cases.[159] The leading commentary on the ethical code of German lawyers makes a mild gesture in this direction by suggesting a tolerant attitude toward a lawyer who uses insulting language under certain circumstances.[160] In pleading for a tolerant attitude toward some verbal excess, it is necessary to emphasize the obvious fact that such protection is claimed for speech and speech alone, and that when words turn into action – riot or disturbance – completely different considerations should prevail.[161] In that hypothetical mature society of which we have already spoken, it would be intuitively felt and accepted that, in the words of Lord Denning, the reputation of courts "must rest on surer foundations"[162] than suppressive procedures against critical, even excessively critical, speech. Excessive speech would in such a society be regarded as incorporating its own condemnation and rejection, with which the reputation of the judicial dramatis personae or the administration of justice itself should be able to live. In any event, there is almost invariably a pious avowal that the particular judicial officer impugned by the offending remarks does not really need protection in the first place![163]

The premise that free speech in the legal domain constitutes a prerequisite for the achievement of justice in the Western sense is in reality a corollary of one of the basic touchstones of the democratic faith: that free speech is a sine qua non for the control of *all* authority and power. If it is accepted that important powers are vested in the administration of justice and that the control of power is intrinsically linked to the achievement of individual liberty, it follows axiomatically that the role of a system of free speech as a necessary means of controlling power within the justice machinery is of much more than passing interest to the liberty of the individual. Important as the powers of appeal courts or of legislatures may be, the individual will in reality often have very little besides his or her own voice and that of public opinion generally to countervail the powers vested in the administration of justice. In essence we are dealing here with an extension and a refinement of the premise of democratic participation discussed above.[164]

The need in terms of the democratic ethos to control the power of the judicial arm of government is graphically illustrated by a number of contempt cases from Britain's erstwhile colonies. These cases, based as they so clearly are on facts that manifest the clear need for the control of judicial power, also possess heuristic value for those working in situations where criticism of judiciaries is muted or inhibited. It is interesting, however, to see that in the leading case of *McLeod*[165] in 1899, the Privy Council justified the use of contempt powers specifically in colonial countries as opposed to the mother country under circumstances where the democratic ethos today may demand a greater degree of understanding toward robust criticism of a semisacrosanct colonial judiciary.[166] This overt elitism – including its undisguised racial element – tellingly underlines the need to control the judicial arm of government through the use of free speech. No other agency of government is in a position to exercise such control.[167]

A more recent case in Fiji[168] involved a political speech in which, in the broadest terms, it was hinted that the judiciary under the chief justice had to be "cleaned up once and for all," a statement that would in most climes be perfectly innocent if addressed to other incumbents of power.[169] In sentencing the politician to six months' imprisonment, the chief justice – the very object of the attack! – adduced no arguments when he found the accused guilty of contempt for having in effect intimated "that the court is subservient to the government of the day and that under that government the court denies the citizens of Fiji their fundamental human rights."

At least three important cases – from Germany, Britain, and the Bahamas – illustrate a dimension of the legal free speech problem that hardly ever receives attention: the use of pointed wit and satire to control and limit judicial power. Two of these cases display an even rarer quality – the use of satire *by lawyers* in their watchdog capacity over the administration of justice. Although the use of the political joke as a legitimate form of social comment is a well-known phenomenon, it would seem that no such liberties are generally taken with holders of judicial office, a situation that undoubtedly enhances the general spirit of untouchability around certain crucial areas of the administration of justice. The dearth of contempt cases involving genuine satire – especially by lawyers – underlines the uniqueness of these three cases.

In the Bahama case,[170] the Privy Council made short shrift of the conviction of a newspaper editor for publishing a scathing letter on the colony's chief justice and for refusing to reveal the identity of the correspondent.[171] The originality of this case must be seen in the plucky courage of a newspaper editor in a small colonial outpost to print what is really perhaps the gem of satire in · the dreary history of contempt, rather than in the unsubstantiated judgment of the Privy Council.[172]

The more recent *Quintin Hogg* case in England, which has done much to strengthen the right of the critic to let fly at the judiciary with the kind of verbal punches normally reserved for politicians and other repositories of state power, constitutes one of the rare examples where a prominent lawyer in the West availed himself of the medium of a satirical journal, *Punch*, to deliver himself of a stinging attack on a particular group of judges. Writing about the Court of Appeal, Mr. Hogg – later to become lord chancellor as Lord Hailsham of St. Marylebone – spoke of the "blindness which sometimes descends on the best of judges."[173] Unfortunately his attack, which has become a veritable classic in the contempt literature, was directed at the wrong court. Nonetheless, the Court of Appeal went out of its way to stress the high premium it put on the right to comment on courts and judges. Said Lord Denning in a momentous phrase:

> We do not fear criticism, nor do we resent it. For there is something far more important at stake: It is no less than freedom of speech itself. It is the right of every man ... to make fair comment, even outspoken comment, on matters of public interest. Those who comment can deal faithfully with all that is done in a court of justice.[174]

If the example of a prominent British lawyer descending into pointed criticism of the judiciary in a satirical journal is rare, the same phenomenon in Germany, where the legal processes are even more humorless, is even rarer. Therefore, the example of attorney Heinrich Hannover of Bremen[175] writing in the leading satirical magazine *Pardon*[176] is unique. Using heavy satire, he berated the conduct of a particular judge in a way that, if justified, would undoubtedly, have been more effective as a device for the check of judicial power than any appeal or learned article. Ironically, the article concerned the "punishability of mirth" in a courtroom![177] Charged by the state prosecutor with unprofessional conduct before a disciplinary tribunal, he was fined DM 1,500 because of his failure to be "factual and dignified" in his public activities and the article's "tendency to destroy the respect of the readers for the administration of justice, a respect which is necessary for an orderly society."[178] Mr. Hannover described the juvenile judge in the case he discussed as *lebensfremd* (literally "foreign to the ways of life"); *lebensfremd* was also the justice he got. The judgment ends with a reference to the article in the German *Grundgesetz* guaranteeing freedom of expression and with an affirmation that the offending article is not covered by the *Grundgesetz*. Too bad that the *Ehrengericht* had not apparently heard of Quintin Hogg![179]

Finally, concerning the power controlling role of legal free speech, especially in relation to individual lawyers, it is necessary to note that, in several of the instances of the suppression of legal free speech documented thus far, the fact that the speaker or writer was a lawyer acted as a kind of aggravating factor.[180] This attitude is clearly based on a philosophy that does not tally with that on which a viable system of legal free speech is based, especially in view of the leadership qualities that often only the lawyer can give to intricate or controversial matters within the justice administration. Restrictive as each of these precedents may be in its own right, its effect on the legal profession generally, which is known in most climes for its conservative rather than liberal attitudes, should be obvious. Once again we are touching on the amorphous area where formal and informal sanctions and taboos coincide and reinforce each other.[181]

THE SIXTH PREMISE: THE INEFFICACY AND FREQUENT COUNTERPRODUCTIVITY OF FREE SPEECH RESTRICTIONS CONCERNING THE ADMINISTRATION OF JUSTICE

Most attacks of this kind [against judges] are best ignored. . . . To take proceedings in respect of them would merely give them greater publicity, and a platform from which the person concerned could air his views further.

Phillimore Report on Contempt of Court[182]

It will be the thesis of this discussion that, as a matter of simple observation and common sense, formal restrictions on free speech will very often be illusory as far as their effectiveness is concerned and in most instances even counterproductive to the interests whose protection are being sought. However, the social price of such restrictions will in most cases be considerable and, in a social sense, be magnified by the resultant inefficacy or counterproductivity. This latter proposition, which once again is to be sustained by reference to democratic values rather than to empirical evidence,[183] can be stated also as follows: the social price a society pays in lost debate, lost stimulation, lack of reform, maintenance of myths, and the like is rendered even greater by the inefficacy of both the restrictions and the sanctions to protect the values to which they are ostensibly geared. The existence of the majority or perhaps all of the formal sanctions – whether they are of the direct kind, as with contempt of court (or the approximate equivalents in other legal systems), or of the indirect kind (as with professional sanctions over lawyers) – is generally justified on the social grounds that these sanctions protect the reputation of the administration of justice generally (or of its individual members) or its independence, as in the case of trial publicity restrictions. When, however, these objectives are impartially and critically considered, especially within the methodological framework of the American realist approach, it is impossible to conclude that in most documented cases of restrictions or sanctions being invoked the actual objectives were achieved or were even achievable. If one considers the ways in which the contempt power in English-speaking countries and the disciplinary powers over lawyers in Germany have been invoked and interpreted, particularly also considering the selectivity of the recipients of the sanctions,[184] it is clear that the actual objective must often have been only to induce potential critics and commentators to stay clear of sensitive issues in the administration of justice altogether, or at least to treat the legal decision-making processes with a greater sense of detachment than, say, similar processes in the political or social field.

Can it be said, for instance, that the restraints on comments about pending or current litigation – inherent in the sub judice restrictions of the contempt law and in the self-imposed restraints of the press in Scandinavian countries[185] and

Holland[186] – succeed in the ordinary run of affairs to achieve an inherently purer and more just form of judicial decision making than when information of a more subtle but legally irreproachable kind is covertly and insidiously insinuated into judicial decisions? In the revealing case of *Tonks*[187] – revealing particularly for its sheer unrelatedness to the realities of life – the New Zealand Supreme Court deemed it necessary, among other things, to consider the possible *unconscious* stimulus of a newspaper editorial on a judge in order to prevent the pollution of the pure stream of justice.[188] Much as we know today about judicial decision making as a consequence of the work of the realists, we are still substantially in the dark about the relative persuasive force or strength of various social and other influences on the judicial mind. Despite this possibly insoluble uncertainty, many societies have been willing either to retain or adopt,[189] to experiment with,[190] or at least to envy the existence in other societies[191] of a number of restrictions on some of the West's most hallowed civil rights – freedom of the press, freedom of speech, control of power, etc.

By the same token, it is also untenable to suggest that most of the speech restrictions on comment or critique of the administration of justice or of the judiciary – whether the particular restriction was related to general comments,[192] or was attuned to a specific case,[193] or was ill conceived,[194] or constituted an expression of personal ire,[195] or of heavy satire[196] – actually brought one iota of additional respect or protection to those values whose protection was ostensibly sought. If silence based on fear or exaggerated praise or tongue-in-cheek avowals of respect can be regarded as worthy of these persons and institutions, then truly it can be said that those sanctions and restrictions have fully justified their existence. If, however, we look at the real results and effect of those sanctions and restrictions and at the price society pays for their existence, it is difficult not to agree with Krishna Iyer J. in the leading Indian Supreme Court decision of *Mishra*, when he stated:

> Vicious criticism of personal and administrative acts of Judges may indirectly mar their image and weaken the confidence of the public in the judiciary but the countervailing good, not merely of free speech but also of greater faith generated by exposure to the actinic light of bona fide, even if marginally over-zealous, criticism cannot be overlooked.[197]

Three further examples, already documented, can be referred to here that demonstrate even more blatantly the inefficacy of formal speech restrictions in achieving their avowed or theoretical purpose. First, did the ban on the publication of the full horror of the thalidomide tragedy achieve the kind of pristine purity for the legal stream to which it was geared?[198] Second, only a sanguine soul would think – and be able to show – that the elaborate attempt to suppress a discussion of the racial factor in the imposition of capital punishment in South Africa – inherent in the first *Van Niekerk* contempt case – added as much as a whit of additional respect among blacks for the procedures that produced the statistical pattern in that country.[199] And third, recent history has certainly proved that the elaborate attempt to silence and blackball Dr. Rasehorn in Germany[200] was not only a total failure but in fact contributed to the introduction of his ideas into the mainstream of juridical thought there. It is also ironic that any overt suppression of criticism of the administration of justice invariably emphasizes, publicizes, and, more often than not, ridicules the very value whose protection is sought. In a community like South Africa, which is known for its reticence concerning legal matters and court decisions, no fewer than fourteen critical editorials appeared after my first contempt case, all of them critical and most of them calling for an inquiry into the death penalty, the very raison d'être of the offending article! It is also difficult to conceive of anything more amusing and more calculated to draw attention to the original criticism than hauling a prominent German lawyer before a disciplinary tribunal and going through all the motions of a court procedure to stamp out a bit of pointed satire in a periodical read only by a small percentage of the intelligentsia in the country. And if anything was calculated to undermine respect for the law it was the attempt to silence the *Sunday Times* from performing its basic journalistic duty regarding the thalidomide scandal.

It does not follow – and this point merits emphasis – from what has been said hitherto that *anything* said about the legal administration inherently deserves protection, a qualification that will be elucidated in a later chapter.[201] However, I submit that the values whose edification are mostly sought will seldom be achieved or even be achievable by formal sanctions. Speech being just that and not action will often – in the word of the Phillimore Report quoted above – "be best ignored . . . [since taking] proceedings in respect of [it] would merely give [it] greater publicity." It is undoubtedly possible that even an unredeemed lie in relation to the justice administration would be best left alone instead of prosecuted. A heuristic judgment in this context is that of the prosecution in Germany for the so-called *üble Nachrede* for a falsehood (assuming it to be such) of a political nature in relation to the Federal Constitutional Court. Only an allegation of unconscionable consultations between the government and the president of the court was at issue.[202] One truly wonders whether affording this kind of protection to such an institution equates it with the meanest traffic court in a banana republic in Central America. It is obvious that this kind of allegation would in a democratic state best be left to the judgment of public opinion.[203]

Finally, and perhaps most important, the inefficacy of achieving the theoretical or philosophical aims on which formal speech restrictions are based must not lead one to believe that sanctions are not effective – grievously so at times – in stamping out or inhibiting legal free speech. The spate of German disciplinary cases on legal free speech has resulted in a general unwillingness on the part of mainstream lawyers to concern themselves critically and outspokenly with controversial legal issues.[204] The same is true of German judges as a result of the problems Dr. Rasehorn encountered. Although not one iota of respect would in reality have been added to the renown of the South African courts by the first *Van Niekerk* contempt case, it has inaugurated an almost unbroken tradition of silence and circumspection about the controversial aspects of justice administration among academics and journalists – despite the acquittal of the accused![205] So also has the interpretation by a court of the plausible-sounding provision in South African law to punish the dissemination of *untrue* statements about prisons and prisoners effectively sealed off prison institutions, where society accommodates its most vulnerable citizens from practically *all* meaningful scrutiny on the part of the press.[206] It remains one of the strange ironies of the West that, despite its theoretical commitment to liberty, it has raised so many sanctions against free speech concerning the administration of justice – for advantages that are mostly so illusory, and a gain that is often so trifling and at a social cost that can be so crippling.

2

The Formal Restrictions on Legal Free Speech: The Protection of the Prestige and Standing of Legal Officers and of the Administration of Justice

If men, including judges and journalists, were angels, there would be no problems of contempt of court. Angelic judges would be undisturbed by extraneous influences and angelic journalists would not seek to influence them.

Justice Felix Frankfurter in the *Pennekamp* case[1]

INTRODUCTION

Because people are not angels, there have always been attempts in most legal systems to control the relationship between the administration of justice and its potential critics and commentators by some form of formal restrictions on free speech. This chapter will take a broad and critical look at representative examples of formal speech restrictions in the legal domain pertaining to the protection of officials within the administration of justice and evaluate these restrictions on the basis of the premises discussed in the first chapter. The same approach will be followed in the third chapter as regards various formal restrictions on comments and reports on trials that are imminent or proceeding. The object will not be to furnish all the technical details of these restrictions on free speech, but only to provide their essential outline, particularly the identifiable consequences of their enforcement on the values inherent in a system of government claiming allegiance to Western democratic traditions.

One important point is that the existence and/or mode of application of formal restrictions have a fallout effect far outside the primary point of impact. The contempt law of England, for instance, has created an atmosphere of self-censorship far beyond the scope of the probable intention of the prosecuting authorities.[2] In addition, the excessively restrictive jurisprudence of the German *Ehrengerichte* in matters pertaining to comments about the courts has very considerably inhibited the willingness of lawyers in Germany to speak out forthrightly on controversial matters within the administration of justice. In certain countries, the legal advisers to newspapers are often the invisible but highly influential éminences grises who determine the reach, and often the excessive reach, of formal restrictions by their decisions to print or not to print. Inquiries into the South African prison conditions have to all intents and purposes completely stopped[3] – and inhibition has been rendered even more total by the strict interpretation of newspaper legal advisers.[4] Here once again is an example of the curious interreaction of formal and informal speech restrictions, with the latter reinforcing and extending the reach of the former.

Given the inherent vagueness and elasticity of almost all formal speech restrictions – and especially speech restrictions in the legal domain – there would, as far as criminal sanctions are concerned, be an obvious temptation to use the sanctions against unpopular people and causes with the result that often the crucial determining factor for the invocation of sanctions would not be *what* was said but by *whom* it was said. In many of the documented instances in this work where restrictions on legal free speech were invoked, there are clear indications that speech sanctions are differentially applied. This has certainly been the case in South Africa, and there is little doubt that in Germany many of the disciplinary proceedings before lawyers' professional tribunals were dictated by considerations of bringing the particular lawyers into disrepute over their defense methods in the Baader-Meinhoff urban terrorism cases. In the Australian *Fairfax* decision,[5] the High Court of Australia drew attention to the ulterior motives for which restrictions concerning legal free speech could be used:

There may be occasions where it will be material to remember that there may be attempts to abuse the [contempt] jurisdiction. There have been occasions where summary proceedings for contempt have been commenced, or threatened, not with the real object of ensuring the impartial administration of justice, but solely for the purpose of stopping public comment on, or even public enquiry into, a matter of public importance.

The temptation on the part of prosecuting or other decision-making authorities to invoke restrictions on legal free speech in a discriminatory or an intimidating fashion against uncomfortable critics of the legal order will not often be as openly assailed as in the *Fairfax* case, but if one looks at the case law referred to in this work as a whole, there is little doubt that such discriminatory use of speech restrictions constitutes perhaps one of the most important, albeit invisible, realities in the majority of cases relating to legal free speech. The obvious use of double standards in the invocation of the contempt law in South Africa has been documented.[6] Even in the *Sunday Times* thalidomide case, there was ample evidence of double standards and this accusation actually constituted one of the original complaints in the appeal to the European Court of Human Rights.[7] And in Argentina, the history of the recent use of the *desacato* provisions of the criminal code, which covers much of the same social terrain as the contempt law on the scandalization of courts, has been described by one commentator as constituting "one of the most instructive chapters of the dictatorship."[8] However, one can witness in Germany the most consistent use in recent times of speech restrictions relating to the administration of justice –

albeit of the indirect kind relating to professional ethics – against critics of the legal mainstream.[9]

Late in 1980, in an almost unbelievable attempt to get even with one of his most consistent critics as regards his dubious diamond transactions with an African dictator, President d'Estaing of France ordered (so it is widely accepted by friends and critics alike) the prosecution of one of the world's most prestigious newspapers, *Le Monde*, under France's almost forgotten contempt law. The touching of that untouchable and august newspaper by prosecuting the editor, Mr. Jacques Fauvet, and the legal correspondent, Mr. Philippe Boucher, is in itself an event of incredible boldness. But more important in the present context is the fact that even supporters of the president accept that "the deeper motives of Giscard and [justice minister] Peyrefitte appear to . . . [flow from] the resentment of Giscard against a paper which has become his most dangerous critic, and of Mr. Peyrefitte for Mr. Boucher, a writer who has been very rude, indeed, about the minister for a long time.[10]

CONTEMPT OF COURT

The friendly relations between you and the judges are governed by the law of contempt of court.
Justice Brian McKenna of the English High Court[11]

The issuing of attachments by the Supreme Court of Justice in Westminster Hall, for contempts out of court stands upon the same immemorial usage as supports the whole fabric of the common law; it is as much the "lex terrae", and within the exception of Magna Charta, as the issuing of any other legal process whatsoever.
Wilmot J. in the *Almon* case (1765)[12]

In the Anglo-Saxon countries, it is the institution of contempt of court – the origins of which are lost in the mists of early English history – that has always been the most important means of protecting the prestige of the administration of justice and the dignity of the personalities involved therein. The protection afforded individual officers, especially judges, is invariably based and justified on the protection of the *institutions* of the administration of justice. There is little doubt that this is but a camouflage behind which sensitive judicial officers would often ensconce themselves from criticism.

The origins of the contempt power are avowedly elitist. Although one may not wish to go so far as Goldfarb does in linking it with the same kind of protection flowing from the "sanctity of the medicine man,"[13] there is much truth even today in his statement that "the law of contempt is not the law of men, it is the law of kings."[14] Indeed, until very recently (and even to this day), this royal link of the institution is stressed. Says Oswald in the *locus classicus* of contempt law: "In its origin all legal contempt will be found to consist in an offence more or less direct against the Sovereign as the fountain-head of law and justice."[15]

As can be expected, this elitist and even royal antecedent of the contempt institution has been downplayed and overshadowed in recent times by arguments that are socially and democratically more acceptable in an age that pays allegiance to the dictates of reason and individual liberty. Therefore, the emphasis shifted from the fortuitous protection of the individual judge to the protection of the standing and independence of the administration of justice, although as so many cases in all contempt jurisdictions reveal, this shift in emphasis was often based on a transparent fiction: the possibility or indeed the need to protect the administration of justice with the contempt sanctions. Stripped of some of their rhetoric and camouflaging semantics, these cases seem to indicate that, as was the case at the time of *Almon* in the eighteenth century, the major consideration remains (in the famous words of that famous judgment that was actually never delivered)[16] "to keep a blaze of glory around . . . [the judges], and to deter people from attempting to render them contemptible in the eyes of the public."

The part of the protean contempt institution we are concerned with here is that part of so-called criminal contempt that relates to the protection of the dignity and reputation (and associated attributes) of individuals within the administration of justice, particularly of judicial officers, and also of the institutions on which they serve. Excluded here, therefore, is that part of criminal contempt relating to comments on trials that are sub judice – a topic that will be explored in the next chapter – as well as so-called civil contempt, which is untouched by free speech considerations.[17] A broad sociologically oriented description of the contempt institution follows, with special emphasis on free speech considerations flowing from the democratic premises of free speech described above and without much concern for the technical rules characterizing the institution where it operates.[18]

After looking at the leading contempt cases in the leading contempt jurisdictions of the world, one cannot but be struck by the continuing echo of the elitist origins of the institution, with the heavy stress put on the protection of legal institutions and with a corresponding underselling of the interests of the civil libertarian rights of the public and individuals. In fact, whenever the institution still operates relatively intact, it has the inevitable consequence of isolating the machinery of justice from the kind of scrutiny reserved for other concentrations of power in the state. The only major exception in the English-speaking world is the United States, where the part of the institution that will be discussed here – the so-called scandalization of judges whether in or out of court – has largely been expunged by constitutional developments in the realm of free speech. Of all the countries in the English-speaking world, the United States stands alone in its almost unswerving emphasis – at least since the watershed *Pennekamp*[19] case – of "the self-righting process, recommended by the writings of men like Locke and Milton, as the more democratic way to resolve individual-governmental conflict" in the legal domain.[20]

Contempt *in the face of the court*,[21] which is directed at the judiciary or other personnel and constitutes *behavior* other than speech, or speech that has crossed over into overt acts would mostly fall outside the reach of any ordinary doctrine of free speech, irrespective of any other protection to which it may be entitled. This point merits emphasis because the distinction that must be drawn between contempt involving and not involving free speech considerations is often blurred. To recognize and evaluate the problems inherent in a system of legal free speech, a strict and almost hermetic distinction must be maintained between speech (whether conveyed by mouth, in writing, or by technological means) and overt action. From the dawn of recorded contempt history down to our day, a considerable part of the contempt law has been concerned with overt acts that fall outside the scope of legal free speech as conceived within or defensible on the premises discussed above.[22]

As would be clear from the way in which the well-known American *Dennis* case was discussed in the first chapter,[23] the situation may well arise whereby so-called contempt in the face of the court by counsel should be covered by cogent and socially defensible free speech considerations. This would be particularly true as regards the use of aggressive but *nondisruptive* defense tactics in political trials, where the accused stands charged under widely framed laws or circumstances where guilt is widely presumed or made oppressively evident.

It should also be clear to any well-balanced, responsible, and confident judicial officer that the use of an oversensitive approach toward speech in the course of the proceedings, and especially in defense argument, will hardly contribute to reinforce the respect in which the officer will be held, regardless of any action taken or not taken to curb what may appear to be too robust speech, including comments that are critical of judicial rulings. In most instances, a dignified reply will probably do more to reinforce the inherent dignity of the judicial officer and the administration of justice in general than any reaction in the form of penal sanctions. Indeed, a citation for contempt will often and quite properly be regarded as an act of desperation by a person unable to handle a difficult situation. In most cases, an apology should be sufficient balm for the seared feelings of the judicial officer in the event of unjustified verbal excess. As for the impairment of public respect for the legal institutions in general, one would assume that their reputation is not so brittle stuff that they would be damaged by a degree of verbal violatility. This should be particularly so in view of the fact that judicial officers almost invariably deny or understate their own protection or concern in the matter, an attitude that is often embellished with the somewhat unctious dictum from the old English case of *Davies*[24]:

> The object of the discipline enforced by the court in the case of contempt of court ... is not to vindicate the dignity of the court or the person of the judge, but to prevent undue interference with the administration of justice.

If the inherent implications of the principle in *Davies*, which is so often made the object of lip service in contempt cases, are carefully pondered there will be very few instances in ordered civilized societies – rare cases of an extremely obnoxious nature obviously excepted – where it would be necessary to invoke criminal sanctions to vindicate the reputation of the court *system*. This would apply to scandalization contempt both in and out of court. Indeed, it is probably more correct to say that the reputation of the administration of justice can *never* be vindicated by an enforcement of certain behavioral standards on pain of punishment, except in the purely negative sense of encompassing the justice machinery in an atmosphere of fear and untouchability in which the spirit of criticism will be markedly absent. It is only when speech becomes disruptive and when the disruption becomes a serious and a real danger to the functioning of the courts that it should invite the sanction of the law, not to protect the unprotectable – the reputation of the courts – but to protect the public's right to a viable and smoothly functioning public institution against a debilitating public nuisance.

It is illuminating to compare contempt *in facie curiae* in English-speaking countries with the situation in Germany, where the judicial officer does not have recourse to such an immediate sanction as a contempt citation and where, in the case of a simple personal insult, the officer must stand in line with ordinary citizens and proceed with a claim of criminal insult.[25] Information obtained from judges and prosecutors makes it clear that the dearth of German defamation cases involving judges is partly due (as in most countries of the world) to the natural respect and/or awe that people have toward judges who are seen to be doing their duty and partly to the robust and rather philosophical way judges react to taunts or insults from emotionally worked-up counsel or litigants. However, as far as the Germany situation is concerned, it is also necessary to consider that an important potential source of outspoken comment, the legal profession, is subjected to an extremely strict regime of professional sanctions as far as speech is concerned. Apart from the excessive sensitivity that is evident in some of the German cases involving professional misconduct on the part of lawyers, it would seem that verbal excess on the part of counsel is best reported to and dealt with by professional bodies where the possible justification of such speech can be assessed with reference to considerations applicable to the legal profession in particular. Paradoxically, as we will later see, Polish lawyers, when dealt with by their peers in circumstances such as these, have been shown a degree of tolerance not evident in many German cases of professional misconduct.[26] All in all, there is much to be said for a degree of maturity and a philosophical attitude on the part of judges toward the occasional outburst in court by litigants or lawyers.[27]

Judges need to understand that, for a criminal defendant or counsel acting on his or her behalf, speech remains substantially the *only* weapon at their disposal to counter the infinitely greater resources of the state. Where the defendant acts as his or her own counsel, one would assume – as apparently the Privy Council ultimately did in the illuminating *Parashuram* case from India – that the forensic forum is not the place for an "undue degree of sensitiveness" and that often it would be "more consonant with the dignity" of the court to ignore the odd foolish or excessive remark.[28] In any event, in every other forum such remarks would belong to the normal verbal give-and-take of life and there is no justification why this should not also be so in the forensic forum, where speech plays such an important role.

Ultimately, despite the need for a more robust attitude toward speech in those jurisdictions where such robustness would normally invite contempt citations, there remains a value that brooks little compromise in an ordered society: the smooth and efficient functioning of court proceedings. It is also on this score that the *Dennis* case is deficient, since the penal sanctions were invoked not at the time of the alleged transgressions but at the end of the trial when the damage – if there was any – had already been done and where the sanctions were not geared to the maintenance of order in court.[29] What is at stake here is not the dignity of the judges or the reputation of the administration of justice, but simply the functioning of an essential part of the state. Noisy, boisterous and disruptive behavior, including verbal behavior, falls clearly in this category, but the cutting remark or the aggressive use of legal procedures does not. That certain remarks on the part of lawyers may be regarded as unbecoming to the profession may well be a matter that legitimately justifies the invocation of professional sanctions – with due cognizance taken always of the realities of life, such as frayed tempers and the need at times for lawyers to act more robustly than Sunday school teachers – but then not to protect the dignity of or the aura of mystique around the judges and courts but solely to achieve efficiently functioning institutions, including the institution of the bar.

When it comes to scandalizing a judge or a court *out of court*, the considerations militating for a degree of robustness of speech would apply a fortiori.[30] Indeed, as will be clear in what follows, there are cogent reasons why in this sphere the sanctions of contempt of court on a balance of social considerations have overstayed their welcome in legal systems predicated on the democratic ethos.

The institution of contempt has, as far as criticism and scrutiny the administration of justice and of individual judges are concerned, undoubtedly caused a certain isolation and mystification of judges and their office. This will become clear from certain landmark decisions that are noted below, but it is clear also from the virtual absence in most English-speaking countries, barring the United States, of widespread public criticism of judges and their qualities to hold office. Although it is true (as is also commonly said) that a verbal attack on a judge purely in his or her private capacity ought not to lead to any criminal or civil action that would not ensue if the object were anyone else, there is a considerable social reluctance in English-speaking countries to accept the full implications of this rule. We are in effect witnessing here a manifestation of the fringe of awe that is at least partially the result of the contempt institution to insulate the judicial office from the kind of criticism reserved for other incumbents of high office. This informal taboo may well, as will be shown in a later chapter, have its origins in a number of social factors other than the contempt power, but at least part of the mystique flows inevitably from a kind of spillover effect of the contempt institution, especially in view of the amorphous nature of its limitations. At times there has been a willingness by judges to pull their rank on issues where their office was not remotely involved. The *Bahama* case discussed above is clearly such an instance where the vitriolic attack in the Nassau *Guardian* was directed at the judge in his nonjudicial capacity.[31] A rather amusing and recent incident documented by the inimitable Bernard Levin[32] in the *Times* of London of a judge hauling a man from the street over the coals for making a mildly nasty finger sign in the judge's direction would seem to flow from the kind of pristine isolation in which the awe of the contempt power has put judicial incumbents in many parts of the English-speaking world.

If, as is theoretically the case, criticism of judges in their private capacity is not contempt, there seems in effect less social necessity for considering it as such when the attack is directed at the judge's execution of official functions. One would assume, arguing purely on the basis of the democratic ethos that puts such a high theoretical premium on the need to control the encroaching tendencies of power, that there would even be less pressing social reasons to limit critical and offensive speech directed at the official seat of judicial power than at the incumbent privately. This would hypothetically seem to follow for at least two reasons. First, by being ensconced by an office that can act as a kind of verbal lightning conductor, the judicial officer should be able to face criticisms and attacks with greater equanimity than if the attacks were personal. Second, verbal criticism or an attack on an office of a part of the public administration should never entail penal or civil consequences in a functioning democratic setup on the basis of the simple democratic premise that such criticism or attack is the citizen's democratic birthright. In reality, however, with the sole exception of the United States, the judicial arm of government is not equated for purposes of critique and attack with other repositories of state power in a single country in the English-speaking world. This situation results from the presence of the contempt power – and mostly through its mere presence and not its invocation.

As a point of departure for a sociologically oriented discussion of the operation of the contempt institution *ex facie curiae*, it is useful to scrutinize the assumption, sanguinely repeated in almost every case, that (to quote the formulation of the old case of *Davies* again) the "object of the discipline enforced by the court in the case of contempt of court . . . is not to vindicate the dignity of the court or the person of the judge, but to prevent undue interference with the administration of justice."[33] It is interesting to note that in the English judgment of *McLeod* in 1899, which we have encountered above in the ambit of the discussion of free speech as a prerequisite for the achievement of individual justice, the social justification for contempt of court was very narrowly defined:

"It [the contempt power] is not to be used for the vindication of a judge as a person. He must resort to an action for libel or criminal information."[34] Indeed, the *McLeod* case almost sounded the death knell for scandalization contempt by stating that, except for colonies with their different "racial" setup,[35] contempt had "become obsolete" in Britain since the "Courts are satisfied to leave to public opinion attacks or comments derogating or scandalous to them."[36]

However, in looking at the case law of England and of the English-speaking world in this century, it becomes clear that the emphasis in practice shifted heavily toward a protection of judges and the judicial office per se, although lip service has invariably been paid to the public interest on which such protection was predicated. In the *Gray* case,[37] which involved what seems like a thoroughly deserved newspaper attack on Justice Darling – "the impudent little man in horse-hair, a microcosm of conceit and empty-headedness" – the very defective authority in the *Almon* case in 1765 was chosen as inspiration for the judgment, with *McLeod* being totally ignored, despite the fact that it had been handed down only a year before:

> It is not too much to say that it is an article of scurrilous abuse of the judge in his character of judge; scurrilous abuse in reference to his conduct when acting under the Queen's Commission, and scurrilous abuse published in the town in which he was sitting in discharge of the Queen's Commission.[38]

The authority of the *Gray* case is still substantially intact in Britain, if reference is made to the leading commentaries and also to an extracurial statement of Lord Denning. This case underlines clearly how untenable the oft-proclaimed social justification for contempt really is, that is, the protection of the institution as opposed to the incumbent of judicial office. It was Justice Darling and nobody else who was lambasted under circumstances where a politician or a bureaucrat in any functioning democracy would have been subjectable to the same kind of critique. Leaving sophistries aside, the object of the prosecution could only have been to vindicate Justice Darling in his personal capacity, since it is difficult to imagine that the attack constituted any serious "interference with the administration of justice" (in the words of *Davies*) that necessitated the intervention of criminal law. What applies to the *Gray* case applies also to the *New Statesman* case concerning, as we have already seen,[39] an indirect accusation of bias on the part of Justice Avory in a particular kind of case. It is indeed more than just arguable that it is in the public interest for any serious accusation of bias against a judge to be made in public rather than in private so that it can be countered if thought necessary, and it could only really have been Justice Avory's reputation that could be vindicated by a prosecution, if it could be vindicated at all.

Somewhat paradoxically, if regard is given to the underlying philosophy of his own judgment in the *Quintin Hogg* case,[40] Lord Denning issues, essentially on the basis of the *Gray* and *New Statesman* cases, a rather warm justification for the existence of scandalization contempt:

> The judges must of course be impartial: but it is equally important that they should be known by all people to be impartial. If they should be libelled by traducers, so that the people lost faith in them, the whole administration of justice would suffer.[41]

It is difficult to see why the administration of justice would suffer if "libelled by traducers" unless, to paraphrase Lord Denning himself in the *Quintin Hogg* case, their conduct was such that it could not be its own vindication. Legal free speech can ultimately only be meaningful as an instrument of social improvement if it covers not only stupid or erroneous remarks, as in the *Hogg* case, but also pointedly accurate remarks of the most pernicious kind, including the allegations of prejudice. This, however, is a view favored neither in mainstream academic scholarship in Britain nor in the recommendations of an authoritative British commission, largely because of the still loud echo of the *Gray* and *New Statesman* cases, as well as that of the two relatively underreported cases of the *Daily Worker* in 1930[42] and the *Truth* in 1931.[43]

There is a sometimes openly expressed assumption that judges, especially judges in the English mold, cannot easily, if indeed at all, reply to their detractors.[44] This is a proposition more easily stated than proved. Judges and courts start out with a number of potent advantages as compared to their critics: they are mostly highly respected, they have a ready platform for their own views – a platform not necessarily limited to the courts – and they are ensconced in possibly the most secure job available in any state. Criticism that is therefore outrageous or factually off the mark should not unduly perturb them, since such criticism would almost invariably carry within itself its own condemnation or refutation. This is at least one of the assumptions on which the democratic ethos is made – that the people can, or must, be trusted as far as their ability and willingness to distinguish between truth and untruth is concerned. It is simply part of the hazards of free speech in a viable democracy that exaggeration and falsehood will tend to circulate more freely than in authoritarian societies. However, the antidote is not suppression but indeed more argument or better argument that, as the history of contempt illustrates, also tends to be inhibited when any attempt is made to suppress what may appear to some as exaggeration or falsehood.

The fact that a democratically inspired and intelligent court ought to stress the effect of falsehood or exaggeration concerning judges on intelligent rather than on gullible people finds strong support in the interesting and also revealing Canadian case of *Hébert*. In this case, which concerned the prosecution of a writer over a book on an alleged miscarriage of justice in the imposition of capital punishment and which is also illustrative of the potential overreach of the contempt sanction into the legitimate literary search for truth, Trembly J. makes the following point:

I feel that the average resident of Quebec is more highly developed intellectually today than he was 50 years ago. His ability to criticize intelligently has been refined, and he does not "swallow" everything which is written, nor everything which is said to him.[45]

There is a natural tendency not restricted to the English-speaking world to react with shock when strident language or far-reaching implications are involved in criticism directed at judicial officers, and such language or implications have a tendency to trigger off a kind of intellectual short circuit, whereby important civil libertarian issues are overlooked under the impact of the shock in opting for a prosecution. *Hébert*'s judgment makes a telling point that is often ignored in such cases of emotional reaction to strident criticism:

> [His emotional] style carries within itself its own antidote, for the reader immediately grasps the meaning of the terms and places them on a less elevated and more reasonable level. . . . [W]e cannot analyse accurately French justice in the last century, by examining Daumier's caricatures.[46]

It is particularly the allegation of bias, however gently put, that has often triggered the above mentioned short-circuit reaction.[47] Perhaps this reaction is surprising in view of the universal expectation from judges of the impossible in this regard, but it is seldom, if ever, considered that one of the most effective antidotes to bias is the free discussion of its possible presence. Where it is evidently present, the mention or discussion of it can clearly do no further harm but may possibly countervail it; where the allegation is clearly false or exaggerated, the absence of bias on the part of the judicial officer concerned must be its own vindication. Then the truth must also be considered that it is a simple fact of life, and also thus of the law, that human beings are consciously and subconsciously subject to prejudices, including prejudices that may be regarded by many as positive – for example, a prejudice against certain types of immorality or certain types of criminals.[48] In any mature society, it is inconceivable that this basic truth will be denied, and yet it is common in legal systems that have adopted the contempt institution to deny in practice the right of expression of this truth about people who exercise a wide measure of discretionary power over the liberty and welfare of the citizen. Only through the use of open discussion and argument and counterargument can judicial officers in fact start approaching the ideal of being as free of prejudice as is humanly possible or even desirable.[49]

Although the Phillimore Report on contempt sensibly recommended that certain attacks on judges "are best ignored [since] . . . to take proceedings in respect of them would merely give them greater publicity,"[50] and although it actually recommended the scrapping of the scandalization contempt law in favor of a new statutory crime in Britain, it nevertheless recommended that publication of bias or corruption was best dealt with not by publication (as would be the case with other incumbents of power), but by reporting it to the "proper authority," that is, the Lord Chancellor in England and the Secretary of State for Scotland. The truth of such allegations would not itself be a defense (as is also presently the case) unless accompanied by proven public benefit in making such allegations. It seems obvious that this approach fundamentally contradicts some basic civil rights and the larger interests of the administration of justice in a system where the premises of legal free speech are allowed free play. It is almost inconceivable that any similar hushing up or cozy in camera procedure would be seriously advocated concerning any other public official. This kind of attitude can only be explained by an adherence to the belief that judicial officers are somehow more worthy of being spared embarrassment than other members of the community.[51]

The only country in the English-speaking world where the use of contempt in cases of scandalization has entirely lost its sting is the United States. This development has largely taken place under the banner of the First Amendment to the U.S. Constitution, which enshrines free speech. This same right is theoretically also enshrined in the common law of Britain and other English-speaking countries and in the constitutions of all Western countries, but it has seldom been extended meaningfully to cover the legal domain. The result, which has been achieved without overly much travail and is accepted largely without question today, is that the concept of scandalizing the courts (or judges) has no place in a legal system that puts a high premium on free speech and that the use of such an intimidatory device is in any event largely unproductive and often counterproductive. In 1946, the U.S. Supreme Court handed down a decision that really sounded the death knell for this ancient form of enforced conformism as far as the administration of justice is concerned. It is interesting that, in the *Pennekamp v. Florida*[52] decision, the two major forms of contempt – scandalizing the courts and interference with a current or pending trial – were subjected to the same practical and fact-oriented test and criterion to establish whether the facts of the case were such that they could overcome the formidable constitutional barricades that the First Amendment had built up around freedom of speech. The result has been the adoption of the "clear and present danger" test, an intellectual tool with which to assess the potential damage of an offending statement to the administration of justice and thus also the permissibility of that statement. Whereas this test has not been unquestioned in other areas of the law, it remains the valid yardstick for contempt in the United States and as such is an almost insuperable hurdle for prosecutors to overcome.

Relying on the older authority of *Bridges* v. *California* involving sub judice contempt,[53] the Supreme Court unanimously found in favor of striking down the contempt citation that had been upheld by the Florida Supreme Court because of the absence of any clear and present danger to the administration of justice. In words that ring in their simplicity, the Court held: "Freedom of discussion should be given the widest range compatible with the essential requirement of the fair and orderly administration of justice."[54]

The underlying philosophy of *Pennekamp* is essentially simple, based as it almost entirely is, not on empirical evidence, but on the article of faith inherent in the democratic ethos: "Free discussion of the problems of society is a cardinal principle of Americanism – a principle which all are zealous to preserve."[55]

Partly flowing from this "cardinal principle" and partly elaborating it further, and constituting the essence of the "clear and present danger" method of analysis, there is the further assumption to which the Supreme Court gave eloquent expression: courts and judges simply do not need this kind of protection. This belief is but a refinement of Lord Denning's famous dictum as expressed in the *Quintin Hogg* case and on which that watershed judgment is philosophically predicated[56]: "We [judges] must rely on our conduct itself to be its own vindication." In rejecting what it termed "too many fine-drawn assumptions against the independence of judicial action," the Court in effect pleaded for a greater trust in the judiciary and less reliance on the efficacy of sanctions to achieve overt compliance with speech laws.[57]

The readily observable results of this freer approach to critical speech as it is directed at the administration of justice in the United States is that there is no overt or covert fear of legal repercussions in the criticism and scrutiny of the performance of judges and courts. Whereas sensitive souls may at times be offended by the viciousness of criticism directed toward individual judges, especially in publications emanating from the periphery of mainstream America, the overall beneficial effect of this robust approach is that courts and judges are by and large equated with other institutions and repositories of power. Therefore, what may be regarded as wrong with the status of American free speech in the legal domain flows simply from what is wrong with the status of free speech generally in America. In the wake of this greater availability of legal free speech, scholars and journalists have become more willing to question and analyze the judicial process on a scale unknown anywhere else in the world.

One must seek the basis for the major objections against the contempt power in relation to scandalization in both the observable and the less-observable social and legal consequences of the contempt instrumentality (and its approximate equivalents outside the English-speaking realm). In a word, and at the lowest, whenever this instrumentality has been invoked or invocable, it has resulted in a situation where the judiciaries concerned are substantially off limits to incisive and critical scrutiny. Although it is undoubtedly true that there has recently been a much greater willingness – for instance, in Britain – to subject the judiciary to more robust criticism,[58] credit for this change of attitude is due more to the willingness of individual journalists, who have been prepared to write more robustly about judges than had been the case before, than to the prosecuting authorities for their more mature attitude. Naturally, the spirited proclamation of the Quintin Hogg principle, whereby judges must look to their own conduct and not to penal sanctions for a vindication of their reputations, has considerably raised the judicial toleration level of criticism.

Nonetheless, the Phillimore Report's finding that because of the rarity of proceedings for contempt the press was not "unduly inhibited by this aspect of the law"[59] is naive, overly broad, and open to dispute. Indeed, from the continued academic and judicial deference paid to the major scandalization authorities,[60] it would seem that the rarity of the invocation of the contempt sanctions must be attributed rather to the *efficacy* of such sanctions than to their reputedly inoffensive nature. Admittedly, the whole array of informal sanctions and taboos inhibiting robust comment in the legal domain would also constitute a factor of considerable importance in this regard, which would explain the relative dearth of recent cases.[61] The Phillimore Committee's recommendation to enact a new scandalization law also seems to contradict its sanguine belief in the nontoxic nature of the instrumentality of contempt within the ambit of Britain's civil liberties. The pointed comment of Brian Abel-Smith and Robert Stevens that the contempt institution had much to do with the general absence of criticism of the judges in Britain seems to be a more realistic assessment.[62] In his work dealing with an earlier period, Professor Arthur Goodhart notes the intimidating effect of judges acting in their own interest in limiting criticism.[63]

In Canada, the Law Reform Commission has also recently commented that "contempt for scandalising the court is rarely invoked in England" whereas it is still "quite frequently used" in Canada, possibly as a consequence of "greater feelings of insecurity in the face of criticism."[64] One merely has to consider the mountain made out of the molehill by the New Brunswick Supreme Court when it came down heavily on a student newspaper over an accusation of class justice[65] to understand both the efficacy and the deleterious social consequences of the contempt sanction in Canada. One needs but a modicum of imagination to deduce from this successful prosecution the very narrow scope of meaningfully robust critique allowed by the judicial order in Canada. The commission's advocacy of retaining the substance of the offense adds to this doleful assessment.[66] Without developing the point, the commission nevertheless hints at the high social price the Canadian public pays for entertaining the contempt instrumentality within the law's fabric when the commission sardonically concedes that it "conflicts with certain very important principles of Canadian society, notably the right freely to criticize the system of justice and judicial institutions."[67] A reading of the quality Canadian press will indicate the more than ample ground for supposing that the contempt institution acts as a potent inhibiting factor on the scrutiny of the administration of justice, particularly in comparison with the press south of its border.

Against the background of the ultimate acquittal in the Canadian case of *Hébert* over the publication of a book over an alleged miscarriage of justice,[68] a crucial but perhaps less obvious point worth considering is that an acquittal in contempt cases does not per se constitute a blow for free speech. Because of the inherently amorphous nature of the boundaries of indictable contempt, it will often be the *fact of prosecution* more than the *outcome* of the case that will determine the prevailing atmosphere around the administration of justice and that will in turn determine the degree of free speech permissible.[69] An acquittal that is too strictly predicated on the facts of the case, and not on the values being protected, would do little toward liberalizing the atmosphere. Journalists and academics are not by nature given to experimenting with the degree of latitude that they may be able to expect from the courts, and unless an acquittal constitutes something in the form of a ringing declaration of principle – the *Quintin Hogg* and *Pennekamp* judgments spring readily to mind – a narrow acquittal on the facts would not invariably be conducive to strengthening free speech in the legal domain. As will presently become clear, nothing has done more to insulate the South African judiciary from criticism than the acquittal in the first *Van Niekerk* contempt case.

The high price a society pays in democratic terms for the presence of a readily invocable contempt law, irrespective of the relative rarity of such invocation, is nowhere more observable than in South Africa, especially in view of the two contempt cases in which I was involved.[70] This book is not the proper place to examine all the social consequences of these two cases, which have for all practical purposes totally ensconced the South African judicial scene from any meaningful scrutiny despite the meticulous pretense that the press remains a relatively free institution.[71] There is, however, little doubt in the minds of most knowledgeable observers that for the time being at least freedom of speech in the legal domain will be a lost cause for yet a long time to come.

The two *Van Niekerk* contempt cases did not happen in a vacuum but came after a long tradition where for all practical purposes the press, the legal academics, and the legal profession had consistently abdicated their critical faculties relating to the judiciary in favor of an almost unbroken record of sycophancy of the same kind that characterized the situation in Britain for the greater part of this century.[72] Undoubtedly, this sycophancy indirectly influenced the ultimate shape of the law as laid down by the courts. Barring the fortuitous intervention of an individual judicial maverick who writes legal free speech demonstratively on his banner and had the opportunity to apply it in court – an event that did not take place – it should really have been a foregone conclusion that this intellectual vacuum surrounding the judiciary would influence the kind of attitude one could expect from the judiciary when it is called on to determine the location of the fluid boundaries of the mercurial contempt institution.[73] This happened in almost textbook fashion in South Africa and put a damper on any of the rare manifestations of free legal speech that a few individual commentators had previously indulged in from public platforms and, less frequently, in print.

After the first *Van Niekerk* case, which resulted from an academic study of capital punishment, the Council of the University Teachers of Law prophetically predicted that there was "every prospect that in future no one will be prepared to discuss even tangentially or indirectly, and without personal agreement, the possibility that the actions of the judiciary might imply bias, albeit unconsciously, against certain races, classes or groups, for fear of a prosecution for contempt of court."[74] The prophecy was totally fulfilled not only in relation to allegations of bias – the same kind of allegation that English commentators still regard as being potentially worthy of the intervention of criminal law – but indeed in relation to almost any controversial question concerning the judiciary and even the administration of justice in its widest context. Although the second *Van Niekerk* contempt case concerned the sub judice rule,[75] the conviction there massively strengthened what a commentator called the "warning against academic enquiry into the judicial process in sensitive areas."[76]

The legal reinforcement of the already strong social taboo on critical comments on the judiciary has led to the situation where at present one would look in vain for any incisive analysis of almost any sensitive issue relating to the administration of justice. This comment applies equally to academic journals and newspapers and a fortiori to any contribution, in speech or writing, by practicing lawyers. At the same time, however, one finds a steady stream of panegyrical outpourings on the excellence of the country's judiciary. Even the mildest criticism of the legal system is de rigueur prefaced by a degree of sycophantic praise singing of the judiciary. The overall effect is that the judiciary has for all practical purposes become totally exempt from being subjected to the kind of scrutiny reserved for ordinary incumbents of state power. The symptoms of this aloofness are sometimes momentarily visible in the illusions of grandeur to which some judges fall prey.[77] Without entering into detail, it should be clear to any dispassionate outside observer that the almost insane pronouncements made within the all-pervasive system of apartheid laws remain essentially unchallenged even in the so-called liberal media because of the fear flowing from the brooding presence of the contempt law. The result is that huge gaps are created in academic scholarship, journalism, and public affairs about such crucial matters as the influence of race, class bias, incompetence, and institutionalized injustice in the administration of justice, especially about the quality of judicial appointments.[78] It cannot be argued that the wider public interest and the cause of democracy are not served under these circumstances.

It is not impossible to visualize circumstances where the invocation of the contempt law is plausible. The American case of *Pennekamp*, it will be recalled, relied on the intellectual tool of the "clear and present danger" test, which means that circumstances are theoretically conceivable where such a danger may justify the intervention of criminal sanctions.[79] The drawing of such limits would naturally be an invidious task, despite the available guidelines that are inherent in the premise of a democratic system of free speech. But what should at least be clear is that the kind of critical, abrasive, or embarrassing speech we have encountered in *all* the contempt cases hitherto alluded to in this work could not, with reference to the philosophy inherent in the premises of a democratic system of legal free speech, conceivably be construed as constituting a real and pressing danger to the orderly running of the administration of justice. It is, of course, not impossible that in certain societies the circumstances may be such that there may still be the need to ensconce the judiciary behind the barricade of the contempt law, as was conceded in the *McLeod* case, which prematurely sounded the death knell of scandalization contempt in Britain.[80] In those societies there would thus be no question of leaving "to public opinion attacks of comments derogatory or scandalous to [judges],"[81] in the democratic expectation that such public opinion would be able either to digest the occasional scandalous remark or, on a more sanguine level, be able to realize that grossly exaggerated or untruthful remarks carry their own antidote.[82] What would really be involved in those circumstances is, first, an abandonment of a core area of the democratic ethos, and second, an admission that, in the words of Jerome Frank, the situation is such that it is necessary "to treat the public as children who are unable to accept the inescapable shortcomings of man-made institutions."[83]

It follows from the pivotal distinction between speech and *action* alluded to at the outset[84] that speech which crosses over the subtle and amorphous borderline into action and thereby constitutes a real danger to the functioning of the administration of justice may be a legitimate ground for redress, especially where such speech may have an intimidatory effect on witnesses or the judiciary. But here one is already moving into the realm of the sub judice rule. Speech that grossly offends morals or reaches into the private sphere of the judge may also perhaps be a proper cause for redress, but then on grounds other than those that theoretically form the basis for the contempt power. By the same reasoning, invasions of the privacy or the honor of the judge in a form that is irrelevant to the performance of his or her duties need not be tolerated any more than what they would be as far as any other official is concerned, either in criminal law (where, in the European systems of law, the major protection is afforded to such officials)[85] or civil law. Whatever redress may under such circumstances be regarded as justifiable, no distinction can be made in principle between judges and other incumbents of power, especially politicians. Where such distinctions – whether subtle or overt – are made on principle, one invariably witnesses the beginnings of a process of mystification of the processes of the law.

Ultimately, whether or not the circumstances are such that on a balance of social considerations there may be a justification for the invocation of the contempt power – albeit only, as the Canadian Penal Reform Commission seemed to indicate, to allow judges to overcome their "feelings of insecurity"[86] – it is still true that wounding and vicious criticism may in fact produce a strengthening of the judicial system by directing on it, in the words of Iyer J in the Indian case of *Mishra*, "the actinic light of . . . criticism."[87] But once more we have here an article of democratic faith rather than a piece of empirical experience.

SANCTIONS COMPARABLE TO CONTEMPT OF COURT

Justice constitutes a need of all at all moments; but in the same way as it demands respect it must inspire confidence.

Compte de Mirabeau (1749-1791)

It is generally, but erroneously, believed that the kind of suppression of freedom of speech concerning the administration of justice associated with contempt of court is unique to countries that inherited their legal systems from England.[88] Although it is true that the comparable legal institutions in countries not heir to the British legal influence lack the overall character of the English contempt institution, which encompasses almost all aspects of "unwanted" commentary on the administration of justice, many of the salient features of the various aspects of the contempt institution are nevertheless substantially present in one form or another in all of these other systems. Because these systems lack an all-encompassing instrumentality of speech control over the legal domain, there has probably been less of a tendency to differentiate judicial processes from other operations of the state as subject matters for speech restrictions, although in many respects the net difference *in effect* between certain speech controls in these countries and the equivalent aspects of contempt do not seem very substantial. At times, these speech controls may even be more inhibiting than the equivalent aspects of contempt in countries such as Britain, Canada, Australia, New Zealand, and Israel, not to mention India, South Africa, and other African contempt jurisdictions where the erosion of free speech generally had a disastrous fallout effect on the legal domain.

In the following sections I will attempt to describe the broad outline and effect of a number of devices used to achieve speech control in the legal domain in countries outside the Anglo-American legal family. Most attention will be devoted to two countries, West Germany and the Netherlands, in which detailed free speech guarantees are constitutionally entrenched and about whose democratic standing there is general agreement. In these two case studies an attempt will also be made to look sociologically at the actual operation of the law as is evidenced in the press and elsewhere. They will be followed by more or less formal descriptions of the legal situation in a number of other countries, the choice of which was dictated largely by language accessibility and availability of sources.

GERMANY: A CASE STUDY OF CRIMINAL AND PROFESSIONAL SANCTIONS RELATING TO THE SCANDALIZATION OF JUDGES AND COURTS

The German has no talent for defence in criminal cases.

Gerhard Mauz[89]

Introduction

The situation in German law offers the researcher the widest scope for interesting comparisons with the scandalization form of contempt. Formally, the situation in that country differs *toto caelo* from the situation in any common law country as far as the restriction of comment, criticism, or scandalization of the administration of justice and its officers is concerned. In substance, there are certain similarities that are nevertheless striking, especially in relation to their social effect.

It is interesting that there has for a considerable time been almost a fascination with the institution of contempt of court in certain circles in Germany. A scholar mentions four serious discussions or attempts to create a crime along the English model of contempt, particularly as far as scandalization and sub judice restrictions are concerned.[90] It remains to this day a favorite topic for comparative theses and research. This fascination and interest is not surprising in view, first, of the undoubted respectability that the notion of the protection of the dignity of judges retains in certain judicial[91] and academic circles,[92] and second, in view of the de facto acceptance in German practice of many of the consequences inherent in the Anglo-Saxon institution of contempt of court.

Scandalization of Judges in Court

"The Court" is no magical bearer of dignity; the court is no more than the judge, who fortuitously happens to be presiding.

Judge Sarstedt[93]

Concerning the scandalization type of activities *on the part of the criminal accused* committed *in facie curiae,* it is necessary to note that certain courts in Germany have recently displayed a willingness to tolerate behavior that would not have been tolerated in any of the contempt countries mentioned above, including the United States. In the trials of the main leaders of the Baader-Meinhof urban terrorist group, there were many scenes reminiscent of the Chicago contempt trial and some of the language directed at the judges, quite apart from other harassing behavior, was downright scatological with "old sow" and "arse hole" being among the more polite epithets directed at the court.[94] No action was taken in the vast majority of instances where these verbal delicacies were hurled at the court and its officers, no doubt as a consequence of the palpable inefficacy of any permissible form of punishment for people facing several life sentences and rejecting every fiber of the raison d'être of the court sitting in judgment on them.

It is a matter of common sense that court proceedings must be allowed to proceed without undue disturbance. Speech used in a way that causes harassment or disturbance will probably never be able to lay claim to protection in terms of the basic premises of legal free speech.[95] In the absence of a legal bludgeon of the all-embracing nature of the contempt law, there are detailed provisions in German law with which to regulate unruly behavior by the accused with due reference to the legal values involved.[96] The chairman of the court decides all questions relating to the maintenance of order as far as persons not involved in the proceedings are concerned; in matters concerning the behavior of accused, witnesses, experts, and others (the list is exhaustive), the court as a whole decides the issue. Refusal on the part of persons not involved in the proceedings to obey the chairman's orders constitutes the ordinary crime of *Hausfriedensbruch* (disturbance of domestic peace or trespassing) in terms of articles 123 or 124 of the penal code. Mainly spectators would be involved in such violations. In terms of article 177, outsiders refusing to obey the orders of the chairman can be removed from the court or detained in *Ordnungshaft* (detention for the maintenance of order) for a period not exceeding 24 hours.

In the case of persons involved in the proceedings disturbing the order, the decision is taken by the court as a whole in view of the more serious consequences. The ultimate sanction involving the accused in a criminal trial is exclusion from the trial.[97]

Apart from removal and temporary detention, article 178 of the G.V.G. authorizes the chairman or the court (according to the same criteria mentioned above) to impose a summary penalty (*Ordnungsgeld*) of DM 2,000 or detention of one week on persons "guilty of an impropriety [*Ungebühr*] during proceedings."

The interpretation of the concept of *Ungebühr* will, as can be expected, depend on the mores and spirit of the time, but a number of reported examples[98] eerily resemble the jurisprudence one finds in contempt jurisdictions where overt stress is placed on the "dignity of the court." In one case where there was no question of a disturbance of proceedings, the concept of impropriety was defined thus: "An *Ungebühr* is a culpable act on the part of a participant in court proceedings which is irreconcilable with the dignity of the court or with the order of the proceedings."[99] In a case not concerned with speech, the highest court in Germany, the Federal Constitutional Court, went far toward creating a general contempt provision for court behavior from the *Ungebühr* concept when it stated: "Every person is obliged to show the necessary respect to the judges who, according to the Constitution, exercise their judicial functions in the name of the people."[100]

In the event that the impropriety constitutes a punishable offense – for instance criminal defamation of the judge – the law will take its normal course, with the court recording the facts and referring the matter to the appropriate authorities.[101]

The interpretation in Germany of the *Ungebühr* concept concerning statements and other contemptuous acts *in facie curiae* has in effect brought about the situation whereby speech and acts not jeopardizing the orderly proceedings, but showing contempt for the courts or judges, have been brought within the reach of the provision. In many cases, the courts have manifested a profound sensitivity, which accords poorly with the robustness that citizens may expect from court institutions in a democratic society.[102] Although contemptuous or critical remarks *in facie curiae* would generally not involve considerations of great importance for a viable system of legal free speech,[103] the development of the *Ungebühr* concept to cover essentially the same field as contempt *in facie curiae* is not without heuristic value.[104] It formalizes a tendency we will encounter again, where the difference in substance and social effect between the situation in Germany as regards legal free speech and that in the contempt jurisdictions has been considerably narrowed. The strong dissent of Judge Werner Sarstedt, in terms reminiscent of Lord Denning in the *Quintin Hogg* case that "the dignity of the court lies not in the hand of any boorish individual who behaves improperly before the court,"[105] seems for the time being to express a lost cause.

Speech Restrictions on Counsel in and out of Court

Subject to the limitation only that counsel's trial methods must not be immoral or geared to achieving immoral ends, the freedom of defence must be radical *and if the need arises include the right to give a hearing to the unheard of.*

Adolf Arndt[106]

Unlike the situation in contempt jurisdictions where the ordinary law of contempt also applies to statements of counsel,[107] the situation in Germany is substantially different despite superficial similarities in the formal situation. Whereas the general contempt law is, in practice, the only effective instrumentality inhibiting scandalization of the courts by counsel in Anglo-Saxon countries, it is in the realm of professional sanctions that one must seek the major source of speech inhibitions affecting German lawyers. Although professional sanctions would also marginally operate as inhibiting forces in common law jurisdictions, there is simply no comparison between those countries and Germany as far as their inhibiting effect on the free speech of practicing lawyers is concerned. What will emerge here is that as far as counsel in criminal cases is concerned – for obvious reasons the problem is practically nonexistent in civil cases – there is ultimately no substantial difference between the *efficacy* of the contempt law on the one hand[108] and the German professional sanctions on the other.

Lawyers committing an *Ungebühr* in court are not dealt with under the provisions outlined above. Where counsel behaves in a way that precludes further proceedings, the court can only adjourn the case and complain to the disciplinary authorities.[109] The case would then proceed as outlined below with the application of the standards adumbrated there as well as some minimal allowance being made for the frailty of human temper.[110]

As a background to a description of the situation regarding the ethical control of the free speech of German lawyers, it is necessary to point out that the ethical code of German attorneys has traditionally been enforced very strictly, especially when compared to speech and activities that are common in America. The discipline is exercised by an *Ehrengericht*, a disciplinary court of peers, and is subject to a further appeal to an *Ehrengerichtshof* and ultimately to a special chamber of the federal court. The details of the court structure do not concern us here. It is important to note, however, that the structure and operations of these courts and tribunals is regulated by statute and ties in with the ordinary court structure.

The jurisprudence of the speech control over a practicing lawyer is based on two laconic provisions in the Federal Statute for Attorneys, which enjoin the lawyer, first, to act in a manner "worthy of respect" and, in dealings outside the scope of duties, in a manner that would not prejudice the reputation of his or her profession.[111] This jurisprudence, massively augmented in recent times as a consequence of a spate of politicized urban terrorist cases, hails in fact from the relatively distant past, when a strong line was taken on critical comments by lawyers concerning the administration of justice. If one makes allowance for the different idiom of the age, it is evident that some of the authorities from the twenties and thirties do not seem entirely out of line with the attitudes of the disciplinary tribunals today regarding critical comments on the administration of justice.[112] Even the humorless attitude in the *Hannover* case detailed above,[113] where an attorney wrote an article in a satirical journal, had its counterpart in 1936.[114] And whereas in the latter case there was undoubtedly an element of craven but understandable self-defense involved concerning official policy in view of the fact that the defendant was Jewish, one has to wonder what philosophy of heartless conformism went into the recent charge against attorney Elfferding when he respectfully drew public attention to the ongoing miscarriage of justice against his defenseless client.[115]

A social reality alluded to above in relation to contempt sanctions merits restatement here, namely, the relative unimportance of the actual *outcome* of criminal or disciplinary proceedings involving speech restrictions, particularly in relation to lawyers.[116] Lawyers generally are not usually militant challengers of the existing order and very few from the mainstream would be willing to court problems over utterances that they wish to make. In view specifically of the narrow confines of legitimate comment on the legal domain in Germany as they emerge from the case law that will be discussed here, and in view also of the fact that the constitutional free speech guarantees have largely remained ignored or ineffective in the area of professional speech control, the mere fact that a lawyer can land in difficulties over speech concerning the justice machinery is by itself an effective deterrent, regardless of the outcome of an eventual disciplinary case. The temptation to maintain silence, whether it be unconscious or conscious, is considerable. When this reality is considered in conjunction with the additional reality that, apart from journalists, lawyers effectively constitute the only group in society with an ongoing brief to speak about the law,[117] the serious civil libertarian consequences flowing from these ethical restrictions become self-evident.

Many of the disciplinary cases that have recently diluted the substance of legal free speech in Germany considerably – largely unseen and hence unconsidered by the public and the media and in scholarly publications – have flowed from the activities and defense methods of a group of lawyers defending a group of highly organized urban terrorists loosely referred to as the Baader-Meinhof group. The deep social revulsion against this criminal group and the willingness of these lawyers – often but not always accurately referred to as leftist or radical lawyers – to exhaust all the normal legal remedies and also to explore new avenues of defense of persons whose guilt was universally accepted combined to create an atmosphere of hysteria against these lawyers. This atmosphere also spread into the ruling echelons of the legal fraternity, leading to a further heightening of tension that often manifested itself in a viciousness of language previously unknown in the halls of judicial power in Germany. In their concern to come to grips with what may have been temporary exaggerations and aberrations, the prosecuting authorities overreacted in a way that effectively silenced – or attempted to do so – the legal profession as a critical source of outspoken verbal dissent toward the administration of justice.[118]

Four representative cases from the multitude of disciplinary action involving the free speech of lawyers out of court follow. One such case – or rather series of cases, including criminal cases – concerned one of the Baader-Meinhof lawyers, Mr. Kurt Groenewold of Hamburg, who more than any other lawyer has been singled out for official attention and who has had some case or another pending against him for about eight years. One disciplinary case that led to his disbarment – subsequently revoked – related to his "unbridled criticism" of the administration of justice by calling solitary confinement "torture" and by his rhetorical use of the word "murder" in the case of the death of a detainee.[119] Many of Groenewold's activities that gave rise to the plethora of disciplinary proceedings against him were subsequently reduced to a criminal charge against him that was entirely based on the allegation that his defense methods aided and abetted a criminal association of persons then all in jail.[120]

Special disciplinary cases resulted in the disbarment of lawyers for belonging to far-left organizations that manifested a disloyalty to the constitutional order. The *Gildemeir* case, as did most others of this genre, also involved speech "offenses," for instance allegations of "class justice," "fascist hate and state terror" and the like.[121]

The various disciplinary cases against Dr. Klaus Croissant, one of the main defenders of the Baader-Meinhof gang, also involved a number of critical extracurial statements about the legal order, such as equating judges and prosecutors with "murderers"[122] and declaring that prison controls are "real fascism."[123]

In a disciplinary case against three Munich attorneys,[124] the charge emanated from two long statements made in open court in which they drew attention to a number of problems inherent in the defense of persons regarding themselves as political prisoners within the framework of the German state. In essence, the statements amount to little more than a reasoned (albeit misplaced, according to reigning ideas) political declaration that, unusual as it may be, should be easily digestible by a court, a profession, and a society sure of their own values. In any event, the expression of such ideas in a responsible fashion so that, if need be, they can be openly countered in or out of court would seem to *promote* rather than destroy fair judicial procedures and should be countered, if at all, by something more discerning than the statement in the charge sheet that the attorneys "had made an unqualified attack on the court in question and on the administration of justice in general," a statement not unreminiscent of certain contempt indictments.

The cases mentioned above had heavy political overtones and the language used was often strident. The *Elfferding* case points to intolerance of a more general nature not connected with the emotionally loaded Baader-Meinhof scene. So also does the disciplinary case of attorney Moller over his phraseology in an official letter to a court in which the strongest phrase was the proverbial exclamation "You must be joking!" but where the retort of the disciplinary court manifested a kind of elitism not readily associated with noncontempt jurisdictions.[125] Add the *Hannover* case, which has been detailed above,[126] and a host of others that are readily available and the picture that emerges bespeaks a considerable intolerance toward the free speech of attorneys on the part of the prosecuting authorities and a deference to judicial authority that is as pronounced as one would find in any contempt jurisdiction. Because these disciplinary cases are decided outside the ambit of the general law, there is widespread ignorance about their very existence, let alone an understanding of their intimidating importance. Constitutional free speech considerations are practically never considered. The peculiar problems pertaining to the defense in political or politicized matters in a hostile atmosphere where guilt is widely presumed are likewise never credited with any attention.[127]

If one compares the overall effect of the jurisprudence of the German disciplinary proceedings on the state of legal free speech with the contempt law, one finds more than superficial similarities. To a significant extent we simply find a shift of the speech sanctions from the official level, where they apply generally (but in actual fact chiefly to the groups mainly interested in the administration of justice, the press, and the legal profession), to the level of the internal (but highly effective) machinery of ethical control of the group most interested in the administration of justice – the lawyers. It is even possible that for several reasons the latter method may act as an even more potent inhibiting force than possible criminal action before the ordinary courts, for instance, because of the greater ease with which a conviction can be obtained, because of the pronounced absence of a constitutional approach to matters on that level, and perhaps because of the added humiliation of being arraigned before and censured by one's peers and to be found wanting in one's professional qualities.

As far as practicing lawyers are concerned, the end result of both systems is eerily similar, with the German system in effect having a more intimidating effect than contempt jurisdictions. The temptation to invoke the contempt provisions in Germany against a selective group of lawyers championing unpopular causes is also uncannily similar to the situation in certain contempt jurisdictions.[128]

Criminal Defamation of Judges and Other Officers of the Law

It is monstrous that the incumbent of the judicial office who . . . can scarcely be called to account for the discharge of his judicial duties . . . must counter the most subjective press attacks like an ordinary private citizen, perhaps even on the thorny path of a private prosecution.

Eberhardt Schmidt[129]

There is widespread unease in certain academic and judicial circles in Germany about the "monstrous" nature of strident criticism of judicial officers and about the need to afford them with a kind of protection modeled on English contempt law, which would obviate the need for them to stand in line like "an ordinary private citizen" for protection under the criminal defamation laws.

Apart from the inhibitions flowing from the ethical control of the free speech of lawyers, the major source of speech restrictions in Germany that would tend to inhibit fearless and open scrutiny of the judicial arm is to be found in the various criminal defamation laws. Of course, these laws also apply to lawyers, and they have been generously invoked in recent years within the ambit of the psychological war waged against the Baader-Meinhof lawyers.[130]

A relevant peculiarity of German law in contrast to the Anglo-American legal systems is the effective nonavailability of civil sanctions for nonpatrimonial damage for the kind of scandalization to which officers of the law may at times be subjected.[131] The invocation of civil sanctions for defamation as practiced in the English and related legal systems is unknown in Germany. The exceptions to this rule, marginal as they are in any event, have no relevance here.

Unlike the situation in the contempt jurisdictions, the situation that obtains in Germany as regards *Richterkritik* – the criticism of judges – is theoretically based on the premise of an equality of the victims of defamation, whether they be judges or ordinary private citizens.[132] On the basis of the democratic ethos that stresses the principles of equality and deprecates the kind of elitism of which the contempt law is a manifestation, this identity between the common man and judicial officer may be welcomed. Whether this equality promotes or destroys individual liberty in the widest sense will, however, depend on the way in which these defamation laws are interpreted and especially on the way in which the overwhelming public interest in the free flow of information about the legal domain is affected.

The ambit within which one must make an assessment of the importance or otherwise of the defamation instrumentality for the concept of legal free speech is predicated by the premises of legal free speech outlined in the first chapter. Flowing from these premises, one must draw the ineluctable conclusion that criticism and excoriation of judges for the duties they perform cannot conceivably be equated with similar criticism directed at the proverbial man in the street without prejudicing a core area of the democratic control of state power. Put differently, if the application of the defamation laws produces a result that entails a muffling of criticism or a hushing up of inadequacies or simply a mystification of judicial power, the quality of democracy and the application of the criminal defamation laws in Germany to the protection of judicial officers has at least partly contributed toward achieving the above result as well as the narrowing of differences between the substance of the English contempt law and the effective legal situation in Germany concerning scandalization of the courts.

From the relatively small number of recently reported cases, the situation in Germany as regards *Richterkritik* may superficially not seem as serious as the above assessment indicates.[133] It is, however, necessary to consider that the sociological phenomenon alluded to as regards both the law of contempt[134] and professional sanctions[135] indicates that the dearth of reported cases or convictions is more than likely a result of the *effectiveness* rather than of the ineffectiveness of the sanctions concerned. Despite the fact that many German judges prefer not to invoke the defamation laws – a position that would be shared by enlightened judges in contempt jurisdictions – one finds a sensitivity in some of the reported cases to a degree unknown in England at least since the *Quintin Hogg* decision. Parenthetic reference was made above to two German cases where relatively mild criticism of judges emanating from dissatisfied litigants was made the object of prosecutions under circumstances that a prosecutor would probably have ignored in Britain.[136] We also saw the paradoxical attempt of the foremost judicial critic of the day, Dr. Theo Rasehorn, proceeding – albeit unsuccessfully – with an interdict based on defamation against his critics under circumstances that blatantly show the hypersensitivity of German judicial offices.[137]

From within the penumbra of the Baader-Meinhof cases come a number of prosecutions and/or convictions of lawyers for defamation of judges and court officials that would be unthinkable in the United States and very unlikely in Britain under the contempt law. The following are statements that have actually led to convictions: calling detention "torture" and "torment,"[138] referring to compulsory anesthesia for purposes of fingerprinting as "Gestapo methods,"[139] accusing the prosecutor of having "prepared and coached witnesses,"[140] referring to the prosecutor's ignorance about the law,[141] and comparing the arguments of the prosecutor with those of Roland Freisler, a notorious Nazi judge.[142]

Two cases involving contempt of the Federal Constitutional Court can also be dealt with here in view of the obviously intimidating effect these provisions may have on judicial criticism. The one case involving a conviction for qualified defamation for alleging consultations between a Constitutional Court judge and the government was noted above.[143] The other resulted in a conviction for "contempt of the state" for alleging that the Federal Constitutional Court "glorified torture" by deciding to authorize certain forms of detention.[144]

Looking at the overall picture presented by these and a host of similar cases, it seems clear that the picture presented is not one that bespeaks a high tolerance of free speech and vigorous verbal dissent in the domain of the administration of justice, or an understanding of the importance of paying some price in frayed nerves and hurt feelings to avoid impairing one of the highest goods in free society: an open and a fearlessly critical and fiercely criticized administration of justice. A number of the verbal incidents that took place in the shadow of this complex of political or politicized cases may well have caused a lifting of eyebrows in countries like Italy, Britain, or the United States, but it is highly unlikely that these incidents would in those countries have been visited by criminal sanctions. It is also clear that the substance of the law of defamation and related crimes in so far as it relates to judicial criticism and indeed to other officers of the administration of justice[145] reaches as far into the core area of free speech – and often further – as the law of contempt in Britain and the Commonwealth.

Criminal Defamation of Judicial Officers and the German Press

> *In the same way as is the case with the press, radio and television constitute indispensable means of mass communication which are therefore entitled to play a dominant role in the control of those institutions and in the integration of the community in all spheres of life. They provide the citizen with the necessary detailed information on contemporary events and on developments in the political and social spheres.*
>
> From the *Lebach* judgment of the Federal Constitutional Court[146]

The barrier of sensitivity and at times of virtual untouchability thrown up around the German courts regarding critical comments, especially by lawyers, about judges and their performance is not matched by comparable restraints concerning the press. In fact, the situation as regards the scrutiny by the press (or rather sections of the press) of the judicial administration in Germany is highly satisfactory with reference to the best the Western world has to offer in this respect.

There is a strong and obvious reluctance on the part of state authorities to proceed criminally against the press for attacks on the judiciary or the administration of justice, even under circumstances where the criticism directed at identified members of the judiciary or the judicial order make some of the offending statements of the lawyers we have noted above fade into respectability. The importance of press freedom, strongly anchored in the jurisprudence of the German Constitutional Court and the sensitivity (including a sensitivity about international opinion) toward anything smacking of censorship restrictions undoubtedly constitute the main reasons for the hands-off attitude of the prosecuting authorities toward the press when it comes to a consideration of criminal proceedings for contemptuous attacks on the administration of justice and its officers. The prosecution of a small publication of the far left, noted above for its allegation of consultations between a Federal Constitutional judge and the government, must be seen as a temporary aberration.[147] It is in this context that one must see the refusal of the authorities to prosecute a newspaper for statements concerning the leniency displayed by a judge in a trial of a doctor who had participated in the Nazi euthanasia program. The offending statement intimated that such leniency and "crafty sophistry" may promote "the return of the rule of injustice and of criminals."[148] The maligned judge proceeded with a private prosecution for simple defamation on the basis that he had been made out to lack intelligence, to be impervious to new ideas in political questions, and to be inspired by malice to minimize the facts of the case. From the laconic report, it seems that the *Landgericht* of Frankfurt based the major part of its argument on the need for a free press and a free flow of information to the public. These, the court held, constituted "justified interests" that one is entitled to defend, despite the inevitable consequence that such defense must necessarily lead to the plaintiff being insulted. In light of the higher public interest involved, the court held that the plaintiff had to suffer the affront to his dignity.

In a note accompanying this judgment, which could hardly have been decided in a different way in a country where free speech and a free press are effectively enshrined constitutionally, a senior judge lamented the failure of the judgment to take cognizance of yet another public interest, namely "the necessary general respect for judicial office." What is particularly revealing here is the writer's equation of the German criminal defamation law in cases such as this and the law of contempt.[149]

It is significant that so-called "alternative" or "underground" student newspapers, relatively vulnerable targets for suppressive measures in most countries, have not been harassed with prosecutions for criticism of courts that, given the right provocation, literally knows no limits. In Canada, by contrast, it will be recalled that a mild accusation of "class justice" invited a contempt prosecution in New Brunswick.[150] It is quite possible, however, that in contrast to the willingness to prosecute unpopular lawyers, there is a reluctance to add fuel to the smoldering social fires at German universities with prosecutions that, if the lawyers' cases are any guide, should easily succeed in the lower courts.[151]

That the freedom to scandalize judges in Germany is, in effect, as wide as the press itself may wish it to be is clear if one scrutinizes the incisive legal reporting of two major institutions on the German journalistic scene: *Der Stern*[152] and *Der Spiegel*.[153]

Der Stern regularly concerns itself with legal matters, especially with controversial aspects of the administration of justice and at times with a heavy bias toward investigative reporting.[154] It seems to have no hesitation to come forward regularly with mordantly critical views on individual judges or the judiciary in general. For instance, an article that appeared in 1972[155] affords an interesting, revealing, and somewhat curious insight into German thinking about criticism of the judiciary. The article constituted a frontal attack on the judiciary as it was organized at the time and on the prevailing attitudes in it. It was accused inter alia of being wedded more to the maintenance of order than to justice, of oozing with a Nazi spirit, of practicing class justice, of being unqualified for its task, and of being influenced by outdated norms in the field of morality. The overall picture that emerges was that of a class-conscious elite applying and interpreting law in an antisocial and antiquated way and in a manner often contrary to the obvious interests of society. The article unleashed a torrent of recriminations in the official journal of the judiciary, the *Deutsche Richterzeitung*, and an official request by the chairman of the German Organization of Judges to the federal and provincial ministers of justice for "protection of the reputation" of the judiciary was a clear hint at prosecution.[156] No prosecution followed. An editorial in the *Richterzeitung*[157] likewise hinted at the possible illegality of such criticism, and compared with some of the formulations of the dissident lawyers noted above that actually culminated in convictions, there was clearly substance in the point.[158]

In 1974, under the evocative title "The Ugly German," *Der Stern* took on the highest court in the land, the Federal Constitutional Court,[159] indicating inter alia that the court was deliberately flouting the Constitution to dilute the constitutional protections of the citizens. Given the German crime of *Rechtsbeugung*,[160] it is difficult to imagine, short of alleging the taking of a bribe, a more serious charge against a court that is specifically entrusted with the protection of the Constitution and of the basic rights of the citizen.

Ad hominem criticism of individual judicial officers occurs frequently, especially in relation to actual trials – to the point of even alleging bias[161] – and also at times against the whole weight of popular prejudice.[162] This kind of criticism, published as it is in a popular family magazine and in a popular style, must naturally have a potentially far greater and wider effect than anything said or written by the dissident German lawyers who have so obviously been singled out as targets for a psychological war.[163] However, such an approach in this kind of magazine (so one must assume if one shares the democratic hope in the cleansing and liberating effect of knowledge and variety of ideas) must result in a more informed citizenry that looks more critically on the judicial arm of government and therefore contributes to the making of a more responsive democracy.

As far as the critical incisive and regular scrutiny of the administration of justice is concerned, *Der Spiegel* does not have a peer in the West and, therefore, the world. Examples of biting and indeed highly injurious personal criticism of judges are massively available. Its reporting and commentaries on matters within the legal domain is both general – in other words, related to trends and national events – and very specific and very often ad hominem. Its legal correspondent, Mr. Gerhard Mauz, has obtained a national reputation as watchdog over judicial excesses and abuse of legal procedures and his biting style is as much feared as it is respected. As a previous German government discovered to its chagrin and embarrassment when it arrested and prosecuted its editor for divulging defense secrets, *Der Spiegel* is a formidable foe to have and it is more than unlikely that even a fraction of the energy spent on the array of lawyer cases will ever be spent on silencing this wide-awake, outspoken critic of the administration of justice. From a reference in the letter of the *Richterverband* to the ministries of justice about the *Der Stern* article it is clear that this style is highly resented in certain judicial quarters.[164]

The unique role of *Der Spiegel* as critical watchdog over the administration of justice will be analyzed in another context,[165] but in the present context it is relevant to stress that in its reporting and interviews it spares no personalities and protects no sacred cows. At times it seems also to be the lone voice of rational thinking – or of any thinking at all that finds its way into print – in highly emotional cases. It made no bones about the fact, for instance, that it believed that the presiding judge in the sensational Baader-Meinhof trial was prejudiced – a bold allegation concerning the protection of the country's most universally hated criminals.[166]

About the trial of a particularly gruesome murderer who had kidnapped and then murdered his six-year-old victim after claiming the ransom, Mauz directs a shaft of biting and bitter irony and accusation at the defense, the judge, the prosecutor, the expert witness, the press, and the administration of justice generally, and ends as follows: "In the hall [outside the court] there is a sign ... 'No dogs allowed.' Against the dogs at least the dignity of the court is protected in Augsburg."[167]

From these and literally dozens of other available examples of *Der Spiegel's* legal reporting, some of which will be analyzed later, it is possible to say that on the basis of any comparable journalistic yardstick in the West, there is no topic, taboo, and personality within the administration of justice to which it will not devote its most incisive attention in the most outspoken terms if it so chooses. Within this context one can say that legal free speech is indeed a vital article of faith of this institution equaled by no other journalistic medium in the world. If extreme legal free speech is a danger to the administration of justice, there can be no better social laboratory to study this danger than Germany, where literally almost every social leader reads *Der Spiegel*.[168] There is no available evidence to suggest that anything but social advantages have hitherto flowed from *Der Spiegel*'s concern with the law and its method of reporting and analysis. It would indeed be impossible to find anywhere in the world a social leadership better informed about the administration of justice than that in Germany, largely as a consequence of the reportorial method of one single periodical.

The freedom of speech claimed and actually used by *Der Spiegel* and *Der Stern* – and to a lesser but still significant extent by *Die Zeit*[169] – regarding the personalities involved in the administration of justice is in stark contrast with the lack of such freedom for members of the legal profession in terms of their professional ethics and also for members of the public in terms of the general defamation laws. In this sphere of legal free speech, we thus find in Germany a unique combination of suppression and of liberty. As far as the legal profession and the public at large is concerned, one finds a lack of legal free speech that in some respects at least, is even more restrictive than in Poland[170]; as far as the press is concerned, the freedom is as extensive as that in any country of the West. No immediate explanation commends itself beyond that of the greater social prestige attaching to the freedom of the press in comparison with freedom of speech generally.

THE NETHERLANDS: A CASE STUDY OF CRIMINAL AND PROFESSIONAL SANCTIONS RELATING TO THE SCANDALIZATION OF JUDGES AND COURTS

It is necessary to be careful when dealing with judges and with the administration of justice.
                    Editorial in the official journal for Dutch advocates[171]

An inquiry into the situation in Holland concerning the legal restraints on the vigorous scrutiny of judicial officers and the administration of justice is problematical for two reasons. First there is a deep-seated popular belief that in a viable democracy such as Holland "anything on the courts can be printed." Second, to a considerable extent the problem of robust criticism of judges is taken care of *informally*; because of certain taboos, scandalizing criticism tends not to arise at all. Added to these realities is the presence of professional speech restraints on lawyers inhibiting legal free speech.

As point of departure for the scandalization of judges, it is appropriate to consider the provision in the penal code that increases by a third the potential penalties for the defamation of "an official during or in relation to the exercise of his duties."[172] Judges are regarded as "officials,"[173] but they are not singled out for special protection concerning defamatory speech,[174] and there seems to have been only one reported instance in recent times where this provision was invoked under circumstances relevant to legal free speech. Surprisingly enough, the article was invoked against a newspaper – a situation relatively unthinkable in Germany – for a critical article over a judge's "childish, insulting and annoying conduct . . . [and] open provocation to the people of Frisia. . . . for displaying repeatedly his personal inferiority complexes against free Dutch citizens" by insisting in the use of the Frisian language in court.[175]

The language and tone bear some resemblance to the *New Statesman* case in Britain,[176] including the hint at general bias. The judgment deals purely with the facts and totally ignores the constitutional relevance of the case in terms of freedom of speech and the press, a situation not totally unexpected in view of the rarity of this kind of strident criticism in the Dutch press – even more so at the time of its occurrence – and the tendency that such criticism has to become the social, and ultimately the legal, norm.[177] Strident as the criticism in the *Schurer* case may well have been, it nevertheless constituted an entirely cogent and *potentially* meritorious point of view that would undoubtedly have been legally acceptable if it had been made vis-à-vis a politician. One would expect that a viable democracy could live with such criticism.

Unique as the *Schurer* case may be in the context of legal free speech, its underlying philosophy is not entirely unrepresented in the Dutch penal code itself, in the light of a vague provision geared to the "protection" of the reputation of all public institutions. This provision has occasionally been used to penalize criticism of the administration of justice.[178] Although the repeal of this "contempt" provision has been mooted and although its invocation is so rare, the very presence of such a protean speech crime on the statute book must undoubtedly inhibit criticism, especially of judges and courts, whose operations are enwrapped in social restraints and seldom questioned.

The locus classicus under this provision could well have emanated from a contempt jurisdiction in the Caribbean and, as in so many contempt cases, it concerned a charge of the application of class justice in a particular court. The judgment is jurisprudentially meaningless and even laughable, but the precedent could not have been without some effect.[179]

Of more recent vintage, and also more illustrative, is the 1958 case against a national newspaper, *De Telegraaf*, where the freedom of the press was prominently argued – and rejected.[180] The case has heuristic value outside the narrow confines of article 137(a), since it illustrates vividly the kind of rigorous and robust, but nevertheless responsible and potentially beneficial criticism, that one should be able to level at a court and a particular judge in a viable democratic setup. The offending article lambasted the procedures used against an accused in a military tribunal. The strongest expressions (certainly in the Dutch context) were the accusation that the war ministry had used "Gestapo and MVD methods" and that the court helped to make "a dash for the goal" in order to put the troublesome major behind bars."[181] As is wont in contempt jurisdictions, the court made the customary bow in the direction of press freedom and in no way disputed the facts. Still, the court found that as a "precondition" for being entitled to free speech, the injurious criticism "must not be cast in a disparaging form."[182] Translated into plain language, this statement means that freedom of speech for criticism of authorities – particularly of courts – can only be claimed if the speech is correct and polite. What this means is that truth about the law will only be allowed to emerge if it emerges gently and politely and is expressed in the language of the court room. In the absence of a kind of Richter scale to measure the intensity of the contempt, this criterion – especially as it was applied in the *Telegraaf* case, where the language used should have been easily digestible in a democratic society – would make legal free speech both unworkable and unsafe as an instrument of creative dissent and change.

From the 1958 *Telegraaf* case and from an almost identical case in 1960,[183] as well as from the *Schurer* case on aggravated contempt of officials, it is very clear that the formal situation concerning scandalization of courts and judges is uncannily similar to the comparable aspect of the contempt power. The sanguine assumption generally made by Dutch lawyers that one can say anything one likes about Dutch judges is simply not correct. The strong reluctance there would obviously be in the present climate to prosecute persons and, especially, newspapers for scandalizing courts is the equivalent of a similar reluctance in Britain, particularly after the *Quintin Hogg* case. The possibility, however, is still real.

In personal communications, several Dutch lawyers supported their contention about the virtual immunity of all criticism of judges by citing a well-publicized incident in 1977, in which a prominent trade union leader publicly and very directly cast aspersions on the fairness and impartiality of a judge involved in the adjudication of a labor dispute. Apart from being subjected to strong criticism in the press, no action was taken against him.[184]

However, the immunity granted this trade union leader is in all probability more predicated on the virtual political impossibility on the part of *any* authority in Western Europe to take a prominent trade union leader to court for a speech offense relating to union activities than on free speech considerations. In any event, the very strong reactions against his statement indicated that this kind of comment is still regarded as highly improper. A similar inference can be drawn from the reactions to an allegation of class justice made in a technical journal.[185] Robust and incisive criticism of judges and the courts in newspapers and legal periodicals occurs too rarely to allow one to conclude that legal free speech has come of age in Holland or that the legal restrictions have become obsolete. In any event, such criticism as exists is only of relatively recent vintage in the opinion of a veteran court reporter, Jac van Veen, whose critical reports have done much to open up the legal processes to the public.[186]

An analysis of an absent element – in this instance, incisive and regular criticism of judges and courts – is inherently problematical, but it would be wrong to attribute the full blame for this absence to the deterrent value of the criminal code. A substantial part of the explanation must certainly be sought in extralegal or social inhibitions, especially as far as the press and the legal profession are concerned, but the narrow limits of legal free speech allowed in or promoted by the law undoubtedly strengthens the atmosphere of discretion around the judicial process. Van Veen mentions a series of problems that ought to receive regular media attention but seldom if ever do: class consciousness of lawyers, inability to comprehend social changes, lack of realism on the part of judges, incomprehensible rituals. Van Veen contends that one reason for this absence of meaningful analysis of these problems lies in the exaggerated deference of lawyers to judicial power, which robs society of the benefit of the influence of the group best equipped to give leadership in legal matters[187]; another reason for that abdication lies in what Van Veen in a different context calls the lawyers' beholdenness to the typical Dutch bourgeois morality or *burgermansfatsoen.*[188]

The most direct way in which the Dutch lawyer's attachment to the *burgermansfatsoen* would have a relatively direct bearing on the shape of the system of legal free speech would be through the interpretation of the legal profession's ethical code and the kind of leadership input made into society by lawyers in their extracurial activities. Concerning the latter, one can use the official professional journal as yardstick, on the assumption that this journal, the *Advocatenblad,* would broadly reflect some of the attitudes of the profession vis-à-vis problems in relation to the judiciary. A scrutiny of the journal between 1958 and 1977 is quite revealing.

There is, first, the unquestionable reserve toward all criticism of judges that is obvious in all references – and they are rare – to the judicial office. In an editorial under the title "Careful," this reserve is unequivocally stated: "It is necessary to be careful when dealing with judges and with the administration of judges."[189]

In the two decades under review, only two articles appeared that referred to – without indulging in – criticism of the judiciary and it can be said that they displayed the vaguest element of controversiality. The one contribution on "The Bar and the Judicial Power" constitutes a criticism on the "one-sidedness of the relationship between advocates and judges as far as mutual treatment is concerned."[190] The article very pertinently draws attention to the fact that judges are hardly ever criticized and that the "elevated nature of their office stands in the way of . . . a discussion" between lawyers and judges concerning the latter's frequent criticism of the former. The article makes no attempt to correct the imbalance and contains no judicial criticism whatever.

An article by Professor Verpaalen, "Respect for the Judicial Office," records the need for judges to be criticized occasionally "since . . . no human institution is perfect," provided only there is no criticism of the "integrity or the impartiality" of a judge.[191] Although the article underlines the need for judicial criticism, it is unhelpful in indicating the circumstances when such criticism may be required.[192] Although making the case for more criticism of judges, neither this article nor any other sets an example or even tangentially indicates how the situation can be alleviated.

The major reason – or is it but a symptom of the *burgermansfatsoen*? – for the lack of judicial criticism is indirectly alluded to in a third article, where the writer addresses himself to new advocates and parenthetically touches on the "strange and generally accepted fact of the veneration for the judiciary" among advocates.[193] And in a mild call to arms, we obtain just a whiff of understanding of what legal free speech is about:

> [T]he judgment of a judge is after all a simple human judgment, something which young advocates would do well to remind themselves of. . . . [This is especially so since] we as young advocates probably have the tendency to have too much veneration for a judicial judgment and for the judicial power. This is so at least in the sense that we are not [sufficiently] conscious of our function. This function, in my modest opinion, is to influence the judgment of the judge in the interest of our client.[194]

Mild and anemic as this statement is, it nevertheless provoked a contributor in a subsequent issue to exclaim: "The contribution of colleague Ribbink . . . , particularly in so far as it relates to the relationship advocate-judge, filled me with a very profound sense of shock."[195]

During the same period under review, a number of heated controversies raged in the *Advocatenblad* – but all on foreign issues, notably the German emergency laws, the Vietnam War, and the situation in Greece after the military coup. The use of foreign controversies to keep critical faculties alive in the legal sphere is a phenomenon that has been recorded elsewhere in the world[196] and is probably not devoid of some psychological significance in Holland, where such outspokenness is totally uncommon concerning Dutch legal institutions.

The influence of the Dutch *burgermansfatsoen* on the interpretation of the lawyers' ethical restrictions regarding speech is evident from the disciplinary cases reported regularly in the *Advocatenblad*. Very few of these cases, however, concern the area of our discussion, which is indicative of the rareness of any criticism of the judicial order. In light of the exceedingly low toleration level of criticism evidenced in the *Meester X* case, to be discussed below, this is no cause for surprise. The extent of the discretion of the profession toward legal free speech generally is also evident in the regular complaints about publicizing these ethical cases![197] The case of *Mr. X* is greatly indicative of the depth of the restrictive spirit of discretion prevailing in the legal profession around the judicial office.[198] This case resulted from critical statements he had made under oath about the Dutch judiciary as an expert witness abroad[199] and seem in any event to have been manifestly true, quite apart from their laughably trivial nature. The only sting in the words of Mr. X was his contention that judicial officers in Holland constitute a "close-knit group . . . [in which] not all the aspects of Dutch life are represented."[200] The tribunal waived the imposition of a penalty due to certain mitigating factors such as inexperience and the use of a foreign language, but its finding that the language used under the particular circumstances constituted a breach of ethics cannot fail to radiate an ominous and chilling influence in determining how far a lawyer can go in responding to Mr. Roessel's invitation – noted above – to young lawyers to manifest a critical spirit toward the bench.[201] The one consideration that did not enter into the discussion was free speech.

The dreary catalogue of disciplinary cases that make their lugubrious way month after month through the *Advocatenblad*, often regarding small verbal indiscretions in court, need not detain us beyond enunciating the finding that they manifest a strange hypersensitivity to free speech in one of Europe's most renowned democracies. As previously stated, these cases rarely concern criticism of the judicial order. The situation in Holland assumes ironic and even disturbing dimensions when it is compared to that in Poland, where one expects so much less and finds so much more.[202]

The spirit of discretion concerning the administration of justice generally in Holland is also evidenced by the fact that, although there is no sub judice rule as regards trial publicity, there is for all practical purposes a totally self-imposed ban in the Dutch press on any comment concerning pending or proceeding trials. It is submitted that this voluntary withdrawal syndrome, which will be discussed below, is at least partly a consequence of the pervasive spirit of the Dutch *burgermansfatsoen* toward the judicial arm of government.

It must be recorded that the conscious or subconscious effort on the part of the ruling elite within the legal administration to keep controversial aspects of the judiciary under wraps is not altogether successful in maintaining confidence in the judiciary and that there is a growing awareness that the absence of criticism is not predicated on an absence of problems and disquiet about such problems.[203] However, if *Ars Aequi*, a national law journal for Dutch students, is any yardstick[204] of a growing awareness among the younger generation of lawyers to question the hitherto unquestionable, there is still a long road to go before reaching a viable and vital system of legal free speech.

SCANDALIZATION OF COURTS IN FRANCE

> *To be above criticism means for the judiciary to be at the zenith of its mission – a terrible mission which induced Lamennais to emit this cry of anguish: "When I think that there are people who dare judge other people, I am outraged and a big shiver goes down my spine. . . ." Voltaire, Rousseau and Dante succeeded in unrobing the world; they could not unrobe the judge; the judge still has on his shoulders the mantle of the gods! Such a garment obliges; it requires hearts which are*

more than human; it is either an apotheosis or it is a carnival! Let it be
an apotheosis; the judiciary represents our supreme hope. May it
tremble and shudder with us!

Emile de Sante-Auban, French advocate[205]

There was indeed some trembling and shuddering in many quarters when it became known in the late fifties that two criminal provisions, eerily resembling and indeed inspired by the English law of contempt, were to be incorporated into the French penal code. Of all the formal restrictions in Western Europe limiting free speech in the legal domain, the French restrictions are indeed the nearest equivalent to the law of contempt both in scope and potential effect. However, whereas the English law of scandalization contempt has lost some of its sting in the postwar period, and whereas the Italian *oltraggio* and *vilipendio* provisions have largely remained a dead letter regarding the personalities and the institutions of the administration of justice, and whereas the absence also of any direct restrictions on the contempt model has been maintained for Germany (despite occasional calls for their introduction and the presence of a number of legal instrumentalities that have been used for similar purposes), France offers the rare example of a legal system moving in the opposite direction through the creation of new formal legal restrictions on legal free speech by putting the administration of justice on a different footing to other concentrations of power.

In 1958, two new crimes were inserted into the French penal code, generally now referred to as *atteintes à l'autorité de la justice* (or as *outrages à la justice*) – translatable as infringements of the authority of the administration of justice – which, on the one hand, criminalized public acts that discredit the administration of justice and, on the other hand, introduced a kind of rudimentary sub judice rule.[206] Not surprisingly, the French press saw in these innovations a serious challenge to their freedom of legal free speech.[207] Predictably, the proponents also spoke of the need to protect free speech against abuse.[208]

Taken at face value, article 226 of the French penal code is potentially almost as wide, amorphous, and inhibitive as scandalization contempt in English law, with its penalization of any act that "impairs the authority or the independence of the administration of justice."[209] Although inspired by the same underlying philosophy as contempt of court, article 226 contains a number of novel dimensions. Linked as it is only to the "authority" of the administration of justice, it is different from the normal continental or Hispanic approach – where the point of departure is the protection of *all* state authority – but is similar to the contempt institution with its built-in emphasis of the elitism of the judicial office. The requirement that the offending act must be *public* contains a restrictive safeguard of limited importance against the criminalization of all acts injurious to judicial authority. In practice, however, a viable system of legal free speech is overwhelmingly concerned with *public* criticism and scrutiny, with the result that this minimal concession to criticism is really meaningless in the context of such a system. It must be recalled that the general object of Articles 226 and 227 was to control critical *press* reports, which would of course always be public.

One element of the French contempt article that constitutes a real limitation of its scope as compared to scandalization contempt is the requirement that the contempt must relate to "an act or decision of the courts." This requirement would exclude from the ambit of this article disparaging comments of a general nature about the state of the courts or the quality of their personnel and decisions. The object of limiting certain kinds of reporting in newspapers on *specific* cases shines through this requirement.[210]

The inherent bias of the French *atteinte* provisions against the press is evident from yet another limitation that would seem to be quite original in the annals of the formal limitation of legal free speech: the exclusion from the article's ambit of "purely technical commentaries." Looked at positively, the limitation can be regarded as recognition for the potentially important ameliorative role that academic criticism can have within the legal processes of a country – a topic discussed in some detail above.[211] More negatively, however, this provision may well be predicated on the realization that academic criticism would seldom have the same potent effect on the general public than would incisive newspaper criticism. When this proviso is viewed in the context of formal and professional speech control that has been documented so far, it is clear that few of the situations cited would have qualified for protection.[212] To exist at all, meaningful free speech in the legal domain must exist for nontechnical criticism and for the benefit of the press.[213]

The interpretation of discredit or contempt in practice would inevitably determine the extent of the intimidating effect of article 226. From the reported cases and my own inquiries, it is clear that the general reluctance in Europe to proceed against the press[214] acts as a strong deterrent on the prosecuting authorities in France against invoking articles 226 and 227 too readily, as does the possibility that the press now has of appealing to the legal machinery of the Council of Europe as a last resort. Nonetheless, from the relatively small number of reported cases, it is clear that the kind of situations that have been prosecuted are reminiscent of some of the contempt cases. Not surprisingly, the *Procurateur de la République* referred to the analogy in one of the first prosecutions, that of *Schroedt*,[215] in justifying the prosecution.

The contribution, as we saw, of Britain's erstwhile island dependencies in the realm of contempt is considerable; perhaps not surprisingly therefore we find that one of the first *atteinte* cases originated from Papeete, in French Oceania. These Pacific origins moved one commentator to exclaim that "as far as the facts are concerned the judgment emitted the typically Polynesian fragrance."[216] Almost predictably, the case also concerned – in the words of Lord Atkin concerning the most famous contempt case from the islands – "the perennial topic of the inequality of sentences."[217] A newspaper article couched in mild and humorous language under the title "Two Justices" drew attention to the very lenient attitude of the prosecutor toward a drunken driving charge against a person in an "eminent position," taking that eminence as a mitigating factor.[218] In acquitting the writer – one Gervais – the *Tribunal d'Appel* of Papeete held that to enter the ambit of the provision the article also had "to strike at the authority or the independence of the administration of justice viewed as a basic institution of the state," which, the court held, the article did not do; hence, the acquittal.[219] For once the breeze from the islands also had the fragrance of liberty!

The *Schroedt* judgment[220] clearly illustrates the potentially far-reaching and socially pernicious nature of the *atteinte* provisions, with its clear hint of being used for ulterior purposes.[221] Under the title "Class Justice," the writer of a mimeographed publication was convicted over his accusation vis-à-vis a labor tribunal of committing a "parody of justice . . . [and] a mockery of the working class."[222] The "unequivocal wish of Schroedt to discredit the judgment in the eyes of the workers" and so to attack the "authority and independence of the justice administration" constituted the basis for the conviction.[223] No considerations of free speech or the beneficial effect of allowing disgruntled litigants the possibility of a kind of rudimentary appeal and the opportunity to blow off steam entered the discussion,[224] something that would be of special relevance in this kind of case, where the application and the accusation of class justice in some form or another is almost inevitable. The mountain made out of this proverbial molehill indicated how premature the sanguine assessment was that the French *atteinte* provisions "are not as dangerous as they may look."[225]

A tendency to look at the purely semantic *form* and not at the *substance* of criticism of judges and courts is subliminally evident in many contempt cases and in the Dutch *Telegraaf* case, as we saw, this tendency was spelled out categorically.[226] What it means in effect is that criticism will often cross the borderline of criminal contempt, if it is pungent and outspoken instead of mild and polite. In the *Coulouma* case, the court pointed at the two *atteinte* provisions and specifically stressed the form of the criticism as being one of the major criteria for invoking these provisions. The criticism appeared in a mainstream newspaper, *La Defence du Midi*, and but for the emotive language, the basic suggestion was that a judgment was wrongly decided with no indication of prejudice or class bias.[227] Rejecting the "technical commentary" defense (undoubtedly on account of the evocative language), the court on appeal upheld the decision and doubled the fine, holding that the "outrageous, abusive and excessive . . . form and . . . terms . . . bring evident discredit upon the law and . . . the authority of the administration of justice."[228] There is little doubt that it was a taboo of language more than anything else that the accused had breached and the candid recognition thereof in the judgment has illustrative value for legal free speech in the West. Excepting obvious instances of obscenity and vulgarity – where other considerations may apply – there seems to be no logical reason why relevant and necessary criticism must be rendered impermissible for reasons only of form and language, irrespective of substance.

There is no indication that articles 226 and 227 (which, despite their differing ambit, are invariably invoked in tandem) presently constitute much of a threat to the major newspapers in France. As will be seen later from a case study of the legal reporting of *Le Monde* in relation to informal taboos, there is no hesitation on the part of that newspaper to become vicious at times as regards legal personalities and institutions, with the use of strong and sarcastic but unemotive language.[229] Although official harassment of the press has not been unknown in France, to the point even of bugging editorial offices in recent times, it would seem that the roots of the *atteinte* provisions are still shallow, and several journalists were surprised to hear of their existence. The very existence of these provisions on the statute book may, however, act as sufficient deterrent, at least on the part of the legal advisers of the media, against certain kinds of criticism, which would partly explain the dearth of reported cases. The focus of the provisions on comments concerning specific court cases has the tendency to leave the overall administration of justice unaffected. In any event, apart from *Le Monde*, which is regarded by many as one of the three or four best and most influential newspapers in the world and would for that reason alone be almost untouchable, the general level of concern for legal matters in France is low, a situation that would in itself tend to obviate recourse to these provisions.

A number of provisions in the penal code under the generic title of outrage may be peripherally relevant in the present context, but related as they are to all "officials ('magistrates')" of the administrative or judicial order, they are of secondary importance to legal free speech, an area in which they have not been conspicuously applied.[230]

The importance of these formal devices of speech control over the administration of justice cannot be established exactly, but that they have tended, by way of singling out the judicial administration, to underline the aloofness of the French judiciary seems obvious. In a series of outspoken articles on the state of the French administration of justice, even the French justice minister spoke of the fact that the "judiciary seems to be cut off from the world around them . . . and insufficiently open to contemporary society."[231] Given the natural inhibitions and enforced deference toward the administration of justice, it is reasonably predictable that the mere presence of the French *atteinte* articles would reinforce the mutual aloofness between the public and the third estate.

A Postscript: Touching the Untouchable

As already indicated above,[232] late in 1980 the impossible happened and not only were the French *atteinte* provisions taken out of mothballs but they were applied against none other than *Le Monde*'s editor and legal correspondent, whose legal columns had in recent times acquired more and more of the kind of pungent acerbity associated with the legal reporting of *Der Spiegel* in Germany. The crux of the charge is that *Le Monde* had brought discredit on the French courts by its reporting on a specific case, but friend and foe of *Le Monde* alike accept that the prosecution was in fact intended as punishment for the newspaper's critical stand toward the French president.

Whatever the outcome of the case, there will be little doubt that it will boomerang both against the government and the continued existence of the contempt provision in French law, not unlike the *Sunday Times* thalidomide case in relation to the English contempt law. The use of suppressive devices against the truth – or a reasonable version of the truth – can simply not be defended in respectable democratic company, least of all when a prestigious institution such as *Le Monde* is involved, which on that basis can lose any battle and always win the war. This overreach on the part of the government may ironically turn out to be of very considerable benefit to the cause of legal free speech in Europe.

SCANDALIZATION OF COURTS IN ITALY

> *Here in Italy people will now say the most outrageous things about judges but you will not easily find someone to print them.*
>
> An Italian judge to the writer

A study both of mainstream Italian newspapers[233] and the official organ of the Italian Communist Party[234] reveals neither a robust attitude nor a significant concern on the part of the press toward the administration of justice. On the other hand, certain groups of lawyers can be heard and seen indulging in strident criticism unheard of in, say, Holland or Germany, and in most recent times certain judges also – loosely referred to as leftist – have likewise distinguished themselves in their acrimoniously critical utterances toward the administration of justice.[235] Also, Italian lawyers in court avail themselves with impunity of formulations that in Germany at least would entail the imposition of ethical sanctions and would be unthinkable in Holland.[236]

In the field of formal penal sanctions it is the crimes of *oltraggio*[237] and, but to a lesser extent, *vilipendio*[238] that can in theory be invoked in relation to certain kinds of criticism of the administration of justice. However, from the dearth of reported cases on the one hand and from the ready availability of viciously critical statements about the courts on the other, especially on the part of neo-Marxist student extremists, it is clear that these provisions have little influence in practice on legal free speech. The extent that the existence of these crimes affect the subdued tone of legal reporting in mainstream newspapers is a matter for speculation.

Oltraggio alla publica amministrazione[239] protects the "honour or reputation" of certain public officials, including judges.[240] In a 1939 case, which apparently still enjoys some value as precedent, an *oltraggio* conviction was upheld for a critical letter to a judge about the latter's seemingly unreasonable behavior.[241] More important than the sketchy details of this case is the spirited academic attack in an accompanying note on this judgment, delivered as it was at the height of the fascist regime.[242] The equivalent of contempt in the face of the court constitutes an aggravated form of *oltraggio*.[243] That *oltraggio* would at times be invoked simply to assuage the hurt feelings of sensitive souls on the bench is clear from a case in 1953, where an *oltraggio* conviction was upheld when a person, on being asked to remove his hands from his pockets, replied: "It seems to me that just about everybody here has his hands in his pockets."[244]

The constitutional challenge leveled at the *oltraggio* institution on the basis that it creates a constitutionally unconscionable inequality in society is of some heuristic significance in a wider context.[245] Although the challenge has been made on several occasions, the courts have hitherto refused to respond positively.[246] Paradoxically, the constitutional right of free speech seldom figures seriously in the challenge.[247] The constitutional challenge in Italy of *oltraggio* on grounds other than free speech underlines the possibility of also challenging institutions such as contempt on a variety of grounds. Although the challenge in Italy has hitherto been unsuccessful, it may well serve as a basis for viewing these institutions of speech control in other Western countries on a much wider constitutional canvas than that of free speech.

The crime of *vilipendio* of certain institutions, including the Constitutional Court and the "judicial order," is another major potential restriction on legal free speech,[248] although the crime seems to have had little importance in practice in that realm. In one of the rare reported cases relating to the administration of justice, the Bologna Court went far toward recognizing a social interest in the responsible criticism of courts.[249] For the crime of vilification there has to be some "grossly offensive" act "which manifests . . . a total denigration of the public function of the . . . person or institution."[250]

Considering both the extremely rotten state of the Italian administration of justice on the one hand and the absence of a regular scrutinizing function of the ordinary press regarding the justice administration on the other, the mere presence of these broadly framed provisions in the penal code may well constitute a deterrent effect of some importance on certain potential critics other than the press. As is the case in Germany, the mainstream press finds itself in a virtually untouchable situation. As regards the legal profession, these provisions are practically devoid of any importance, especially vis-à-vis their statements in court.[251] It is finally of some interest to note that the Italian jurisprudence relating to *oltraggio* and *vilipendio* institutions have exerted some influence in the Hispanic world.[252]

AN OVERVIEW OF RESTRICTIONS OF LEGAL FREE SPEECH IN HISPANIC COUNTRIES

The history of desacato *is one of the most instructive chapters of the dictatorship [in the Argentine].*

From an Argentine textbook on criminal law[253]

In Spain as well as in the Hispanic countries in the Americas, the most important penal institution of control of free speech in the legal domain is *desacato* – literally disrespect or contempt. The concept of *desacato* in the legal sense is only used in relation to state officials, although a valiant but unsuccessful attempt is made in academic and judicial pronouncements to stress that the legal value that is protected is the social order.[254] Inasmuch as the *desacato* provisions apply to judicial officers, it is clear from decided cases that the protection is afforded to the individuals manning the judicial ramparts and not, or only to a lesser extent, to the institutional ramparts themselves. By affording state officials, including judges, extra protection to that received by other citizens, *desacato* is inherently based on the principle of the inequality of officials and citizens, a situation that has led to several constitutional challenges of the Italian equivalents.

The Spanish *desacato* provision for its part makes it clear that it is not the office of an official that is protected against verbal criticism and threats, but the official himself. The essentially elitist nature of the provision is underlined by the increased penalty imposed when one official insults another.[255]

Both from the ambit of the *desacato* provision and from the justification thereof by Professor Rodriguez referred to above, it is clear that the essential object is to protect the authority or prestige of officials by a degree of enforced silence or respect not required for ordinary citizens. From the dire and dreary list of insults – many of which display all the inventiveness at verbal skills of a warm-blooded society with its roots in a recent agricultural past – that generated the massive Spanish case law under this article, it becomes clear that in the vast majority of instances the office or the efficacy of public administration were not remotely involved.[256]

One positive aspect of the Spanish provision in the context of legal free speech is that no special protection is given judicial officers above that given to other state officials and, as is the case in Italy, the protection is so generously distributed to so many individuals down to the rank of municipal guards and postmen that (so this writer was informed) it may in fact be considered to be *infra dignitatem* for a self-respecting judicial officer to seek protection for *desacato*.[257]

In analyzing those reported instances of *desacato* that relate to judicial officers, one finds almost no instance relating to a democratic system of free speech. The free speech suppressed here was mostly in the nature of invective, abuse, and obscenities, and although one may be surprised at the sensitivity displayed by judges, it is a sensitivity they share with a host of other officials. In the final analysis, we have here simply an instrument of glorification of state power and it is particularly in this sense that the role of *desacato* instrumentality, together with other glorification devices, must be seen during the Franco regime. In an authoritarian regime, all official power tends to be left uncriticized; hence, the absence of reported instances where legal free speech was meaningfully involved. A general spirit of deference to authority will axiomatically strengthen the taboos surrounding the administration of justice, leading to a situation where the actual invocation of the *desacato* sanctions will hardly be necessary. With a new critical spirit now sweeping the Iberian peninsula changes may, however, be imminent.[258]

Looking at the *desacato* provision in Argentina, one is again struck by the wide ranks of officialdom accorded this protection in relation to acts against their dignity or decorum, including speech not directed at them in the course of their duties, as is required in Spain. However, a qualified contempt exists for the protection of a small number of high officials, including all judges.[259] Even indirect *desacato*, where there is no link whatever between the actor and the victim or class of victims, is possible, not unlike the possibility in contempt jurisdictions of scandalizing the entire administration of justice. It is not astonishing to find the *desacato* provision being used in recent times by repressive regimes to prohibit or inhibit the operation of a free press.[260] The facile equation of *all* judges with the highest state officials introduces an elitist element unknown in the contempt law of Spain and Italy. Criticism or even meaningful scrutiny of the administration of justice by the Argentinian press is therefore virtually unknown, and even mild criticism of the confiscation on judicial orders of Ingmar Bergman's film, *The Silence*, was penalized,[261] properly adorned with the customary bow to free speech and – the height of irony – even with a comparative reference to the free speech jurisprudence of the American Supreme Court.[262]

In Chile, a requirement in the *desacato* provision in the penal code limits the operation of the instrumentality to *grave* insults of certain high officials, including the superior courts of law.[263] Until the advent of political extremism both from the left and the right, Chile constituted one of the most democratic societies in the Americas, with a legal system that tolerated and protected a significant measure of dissent. More for social than for legal reasons, a spirit of dissent never seemed to have flowered regarding the administration of justice, and it is not clear whether the *desacato* provision was the cause, especially since indirect *desacato* is likewise possible.[264] An attempt was made to extend the protection afforded to the institution (and indirectly to the incumbents) of the Supreme Court to lower echelon courts. Conflicting decisions seem to hold the scales in balance on this point.[265]

In Peru, the *desacato* provision is a verbatim copy of its counterpart in Argentina.[266] It is not surprising, in view of the source of its inspiration, that the relevant Peruvian article has often been applied to critical comments in newspapers on the administration of justice.[267] Perez documents a rather unique contribution of Peruvian law in the form of a circular of the Supreme Court judges to lower echelon judges stressing the "need, if insulted and disparaged in periodicals, to lay the required criminal charges in order to sanction the actor with the full rigor of the law"[268] – a veritable exercise of generating judicial sensitivity!

In Ecuador, the *desacato* provision strikes an original note by its emphasis not of the nature of the disparaging words or act but of the failure to show the necessary respect to the protected authorities, a formulation that is potentially more far-reaching.[269] This formulation seems to bring out an idea subliminally present in many speech restrictions in the legal domain: the idea that irrespective of their own behavior certain authorities, especially members of the judiciary, are per se deserving of respect.[270]

Continuing our South American *tour d' horizon* of *desacato* provisions, the penal codes of Bolivia,[271] Venezuela,[272] and Uruguay[273] provide nothing new or original regarding the provisions. In Venezuela, the protection, as far as the administration of justice is concerned, is limited to judges of the highest courts with a hierarchical "fixed rate of exchange" prescribed for penalties, depending on the rank of the offended judge. Public contempt or vilification of the institution of the Supreme Court as such is separately punished.[274] In Uruguay and Bolivia, all public officials are protected, with the concept of official statutorily defined in Uruguay in the broadest terms,[275] a situation that constitutes a populist element in a basically elitist institution.

Finally, reference can be made to the interesting *desacato* provisions in Colombia, where it would seem the only genuine attempt in Latin America is made to protect certain legal values that merit protection in any state: the undisturbed and peaceful functioning of "legislative, judicial or administrative bodies."[276] Another provision, unlike any we have noted so far, concerns a person who commits *any* crime against an official's functions; such an offender is subjected to an increased penalty.[277]

What is interesting here – and striking a very different note – is, first, the fact that *desacato* is equated with violence against officials and, second, the justification of the increased sentences on the basis of the entirely acceptable jurisprudential ground of positive obstruction to the functions of the officials. It is clear from Arenas that the major importance of this provision is in the field of the crimes of calumny and injury.[278]

From the reported court decisions, it would not seem as if any use has been made of these provisions concerning criticism of the administration of justice.[279] In taking these provisions at face value, it is difficult to conceive of a prosecution being brought for situations comparable to those dealing with legal free speech that have been alluded to in this work. The protected legal value here is simply the peaceful and uncorrupted conduct of public affairs and the independence of decision-making officials.[280]

SWITZERLAND AND AUSTRIA

Here in Switzerland we do not have any real problem as regards strong criticism of judges since people here don't criticize the judiciary.

A Swiss judge to the writer

The federal criminal system of Switzerland has no provision with any direct or meaningful application to our inquiry, which is somewhat paradoxical when one considers the situation in the neighboring countries. The restrictions in Switzerland – and they are far from being unimportant – are entirely informal, which make them more difficult to establish and almost impossible to analyze.

In terms of free speech in the legal matters, it is necessary to keep in mind the considerable amount of federal decentralization in legal matters, which affects the extent of free speech in that domain. In particular, the legal profession, which, as argued earlier in this work, constitutes one of the two most important bulwarks in defense of legal free speech, is split along and organized according to cantonal lines. As a result of this strong decentralization, there is a close interaction between local communities (which, for the most part, are extremely conservative according to West European standards) and the legal profession, a situation that results in a much greater degree of cozy conformism and lack of critical scrutiny of the administration of justice.

This cozy conformism is equally characteristic of the mainstream press, and nothing even approximating robust criticism of the judicial order ever sees the light of day there.[281] It is not surprising, therefore, to find that there is practically no case law pertaining to contempt of court. That this placid atmosphere of uncritical conformism, which almost inevitably meets the eye of even a casual observer of the Swiss scene, does not necessarily indicate an absence of problems within the administration of justice becomes clear from a study of a mimeographed publication (recently discontinued), *Schwarzpeter*, that concentrated on prison conditions and reform.[282] Even if a generous allowance is made for a certain amount of polemical exaggeration that is typical of alternative publications, enough purely factual material emerges indicating that ample opportunity exists for a more vigorous expression of criticism in the legal domain than exists in the conventional Swiss press.

The basic point of departure in Swiss law is that the individual member of the Swiss judiciary (or any other authority) who seeks to protect his reputation or standing (and indirectly that of his office) must take his place in the queue of ordinary litigants and avail himself of the remedies available to the ordinary citizen.[283] Not even the limited institutional protection vested in the highest judicial authority such as the *Bundesverfassungsgericht* in Germany – referred to above[284] – is available. There seems to be no problem if one considers the small number of defamation cases relating to a contempt situation. In one of the rare contempt cases under the criminal defamation law, the following was stated: "Criticism of the manner in which a magistrate exercises his office does not constitute an assault on his honour if such criticism does not impinge on the honourableness of the magistrate as a private individual."[285] There is no doubt that the existence of defamation procedures to protect judicial officers against overly robust criticism is no secret, but because of the strong social taboos against such criticism and its publication, the problem of adjudication seldom arises.[286]

The situation regarding legal free speech in Austria seems to follow the Swiss rather than the German model, with potent social and journalistic inhibitions rather than penal and professional sanctions ensuring a considerable degree of conformism. Judicial personalities must seek their protection as any ordinary citizen would in terms of the defamation laws. A vague form of contempt of authorities similar to *desacato* seems in practice to be of little relevance to legal free speech, although its presence may not be lost on potential critics.[287] Even before and during the *Anschluss* period, there seems to have been no reported recourse to this provision.[288]

A NORDIC OVERVIEW

To suggest that there are other nations engaged in similar, meaningful debate over the boundaries of a relatively unfettered press freedom detracts perhaps from the grandeur that the American sees in his own debate. In fact, the debate thrives throughout Scandinavia, and nowhere more prominently than in Sweden, whose constitutional guarantee of free press predates the first amendment.

Dennis Campbell[289]

Limited access to Scandinavian materials and the existence of language barriers obliged me to survey the Scandinavian scene more formalistically than other areas hitherto discussed in relation to scandalization of courts.[290] It would, however, seem that the free speech-free press debate referred to by Professor Campbell has not in any meaningful sense been extended to the vigorous scrutiny by the press of the administration of justice. Except for sensational trials that would receive wide coverage in any country, there is no major newspaper in Sweden that regards itself as having a special brief for the scrutiny of the administration of justice.[291] Although criticism will from time to time be directed at court judgments – more or less a common practice in all countries with a modicum of institutionalized democracy – the criticism will almost invariably be muted and gentle. The great degree of freedom of speech theoretically existing in Sweden does not readily show up in the columns of newspapers concerning the administration of justice.

The most important Swedish provision that could cover the scandalization contempt situation relates to insults to *any* public servant, as was the case with *desacato*.[292] Likewise, courts are not singled out for the protection of all public authorities against the spread of false rumors that undermine respect for such authorities.[293] In view of the latitudinous nature of this provision and especially of the difficult nature of establishing the truth, it is not surprising to find that the repeal of this "despair and despondency" type of contempt has been mooted.[294] The striking discrepancy in sentences for personal contempt on the one hand and the institutional contempt of this provision on the other is perhaps not without significance.

In the Danish penal provision relating to the protection of public officials, judicial officers are specifically mentioned but do not receive any qualified protection in addition to that afforded other officials against "contempt, abusive language or other insulting behaviour."[295]

In Norway, there is no article in the penal code that deals with abusive language regarding officialdom as such, let alone the administration of justice. Article 130, in a similar concern for truth about public authorities manifested in the Swedish code, penalizes a person attributing intentional or grossly negligent falsehoods to authority "against his own better conscience."[296]

In Finland, the protection afforded in the general contempt clause is potentially very wide and includes not only public officials, but also the government, the popular representation, and the social and public order. It does not specifically refer to the administration of justice or to courts. Following what seems a Scandinavian penchant for truth in comments about officialdom, it also penalizes the spreading of false information regarding the protected persons, authorities, and institutions.[297]

AN EAST EUROPEAN GLOSS

There is no problem concerning what you can say about our judges since you can only praise them.

An East German legal academic[298]

Freedom of speech, including freedom of speech in the legal domain, does not exist anywhere in Eastern Europe in any meaningful form. And yet it would seem that over the last decade a subtle change has come about to indicate that the West's inherent critical spirit is slowly asserting itself again in Eastern Europe. A few aspects, mostly formal, on legal free speech in some Eastern European countries will be illuminated here to show that the monolithic nature of legal free speech there has not been impervious to change.

Limited access of material and language barriers proved less important impediments to research than the deep chasm between theory and reality in civil rights matters in Eastern Europe. Nevertheless, outside of the Soviet Union there seems to have been a gradual narrowing down of this discrepancy and in certain circles, notably academic, loyal criticism has become relatively free and outspoken.

Of the four countries to which reference will be made here, the German Democratic Republic (East Germany) presents by far the most depressing scene. The free availability of and accessibility to East German materials together with incisive discussions with East German legal scholars in Berlin and relatively extensive coverage of East German events in the West German press convinced me that legal free speech is for all practical purposes nonexistent in East Germany, either in the press or in academic and journalistic circles. The situation today – unlike perhaps a decade and more ago – flows as much from the radiation of legal restrictions as it does from the omnipresent and pervasive peril that a potential critic may face in terms of career and social advancement. With a press whose critical faculties are only marginally different from a telephone directory,[299] and with a general taboo operating in *all* media as regards *all* state institutions, and with law faculties and the legal profession totally geared to the active defense of the sociopolitical status quo, legal free speech in East Germany is still a distant dream.

The major legal instrumentality that enforces silence on all aspects of the state administration is the celestially latitudinous penal provision on *Staatsverleumdung*, which for good measure equates such "state defamation" with "fascist or militaristic statements."[300] Given the inherently fragile nature of legal free speech under the best of circumstances, it is not surprising to find no criticism in print of any aspect of the justice administration.

On the other extreme, we have the situation in Poland. The provisions relating to insults of officials and state organs are framed in terms not in excess of that found in certain Western countries[301] and have apparently not been invoked for well over a decade. Although the absence of reported decisions is not necessarily tantamount to a manifestation of legal free speech, it does assume some significance in view of the considerable latitude allowed under the professional code of lawyers.

It is in the field of the ethical restrictions on lawyers that the de facto situation in Poland assumes an interesting dimension, even when compared to the situation in countries like Holland and Germany. In looking at all the reported ethical cases over a decade involving speech indiscretions, one is struck both by the way in which a dissenting and critical spirit seems to have survived among Polish lawyers and by the mature attitude displayed toward legal free speech. During the same period, there was no reported instance of an overly sensitive attitude toward outspoken lawyers.

In a 1967 case, for instance, a lawyer who accused a judge of exceeding his legal powers by his reprimands of the lawyer's use of language was completely exonerated by a disciplinary tribunal. On appeal, the acquittal was reversed and referred back to the original disciplinary tribunal for judgment.[302] In an academic journal, this *noli me tangere* attitude toward criticism of the appeal court came under strident attack for its reversal of the acquittal and its admonition that the "reputation and the honour" of the court had to be respected regardless of whether such courts deserve such respect.[303]

In a 1969 case,[304] the statement by a lawyer to a judge in chambers that another judge "cannot be trusted" with a certain case resulted in the lightest possible professional penalty: the lawyer was reprimanded. In an appeal by the public prosecutor to the ordinary court of appeal, the matter was referred back to the disciplinary tribunal for a stiffer punishment. Precisely the same thing happened when a lawyer wrote in a written argument for appeal that a judge had conducted the trial "provocatively" and had demonstrated his "incompetence." The court of appeal, in referring the case back to the disciplinary tribunal, described the said formulation as unnecessarily "vindictive" toward the person of the judge of the trial court.[305] The same mild treatment – a reprimand, which was not altered on appeal – befell the sharp-tongued attorney in 1974, when in his written argument for appeal he expressed himself in lurid terms about the incompetence of a trial judge.[306]

Whatever significance one may attach to these and similar cases and to the general absence of an overly sensitive attitude concerning lawyers using robust language toward the administration of justice, these facts do afford an insight into the way in which the Polish legal profession seems to have carved out for itself under exceptionally onerous conditions a small but palpable refuge for free speech.[307]

In an internationally reported case, the authorities of Yugoslavia displayed an infinitely harsher and more uncompromising attitude toward speech, admittedly of a political nature, used by counsel in his argument. The case, which was fully documented by the International Commission of Jurists,[308] not only demonstrates the obviously fragile nature of legal free speech in that country, but also the patent need for a lawyer to enjoy the widest possible scope of free speech in his or her commitment to the interests of the client and to the lawyer's ethos of at times mentioning the unmentionable.[309] In defending his client against the charge of making "hostile propaganda" against the state in relation to economic conditions in Yugoslavia, Attorney Srdja Popovic attempted to prove the truth of the propaganda.[310] Eighteen months after his client was convicted, the attorney was charged with the same crime and convicted, but the prosecutor's request for disbarment was refused. Apart from the fact that, in the words of the International Commission of Jurists, it "seems incredible and . . . profoundly disturbing that a defence speech . . . should form the basis of a charge of spreading false information," the case demonstrates with uncommon clarity a widespread, albeit unexpressed, feeling ingrained in many legal systems that lawyers are first and foremost technicians whose primary duty is to oil the cogs of the legal machinery without becoming involved too creatively and, especially, too *outspokenly* in the defense of higher social values that would disturb the traditionally placid atmosphere around the exercise of judicial functions. This unusual invocation of indirect speech restrictions in the legal domain makes the laconic contempt provision in the Yugoslav penal code seem innocuous.[311]

In Hungary, which after Poland has the greatest toleration of gentle dissent toward the political status quo, the justice administration still remains off limits to any penetrating and critical gaze, not so much because of the fear of legal repercussions but simply on account of the impossibility of finding a platform from which to proclaim critical views. There also seems to be only one reported instance over the last two decades where the relevant contempt article of that country's penal code has been used to protect the dignity of personalities involved in the administration of justice, and then under circumstances of no great heuristic value other than to show the familiar sensitivity of judges to scathing criticism from the ranks of ordinary folk.[312] From an abusive postcard to a judge criticizing his attitude in a case, the court drew the farfetched conclusion that it not only constituted an attack on the dignity of the judge but also undermined the functions of the state.[313]

In drawing a tentative conclusion from these scattered examples of indulgence in and suppression of legal free speech in Eastern Europe and from the general atmosphere surrounding those legal systems, one is struck by the now-familiar problem of defining the shifting limits of legal free speech because the situation is regulated by informal sanctions. If one considers the lack of an independent press and academic institutions in those countries, this similarity with the situation in many Western countries is more an unflattering commentary on the state of legal free speech in the West than on that in the East.

CONCLUSION: SO WHAT?

To wind up, the key word [for invoking sanctions for criticism of a judge or of the administration of justice] is "justice", not "judge"; the keynote thought is unobstructed public justice, not the self-defence of a judge.

Justice Krishna Iyer in the *Mishra* case[314]

After looking at the picture of all the speech restrictions relating to scandalization of courts that have been documented in this chapter, one must be an incorrigible believer in legal fairy tales to believe that one iota of respect for the legal processes was purchased in the vast majority of instances. It will also be difficult when looking at the various invocations of speech restrictions and at the legal provisions on which they are based to assume that any meaningful societal interests befitting the democratic ethos were promoted by the enforcement of these provisions or are being promoted by their presence. Only in the narrow category of cases or penal provisions where speech verges on or passes into action that disrupts the administration of justice would there be justification for protective measures, and even in those instances there is overwhelming merit in being conscious of the therapeutic social effect of allowing more rather than less critical speech and critical activities in relation to the least-controlled and least-scrutinized part of the trichotomy of government. It is also useful to be conscious of the fact that all speech restrictions, and perhaps even more particularly speech restrictions in the legal domain, have an inherent tendency to feed on themselves and to bolster informal restrictions and taboos, and that a slight and perhaps even considerable inconvenience and annoyance with robust language vis-à-vis the justice administration would generally be a fair price to pay for the undoubted advantages that free speech would bring to the justice administration in a free society.

An unmistakable undercurrent in many of the recorded instances of punishing the robust use of free speech in relation to judicial authorities is an intolerance not toward criticism per se but toward what is regarded as excessively blunt language of an embarrassing nature. The notion that for legal free speech to be a viable instrumentality of control it must indeed be *free* and at the very least be as free as would be permissible in relation to political institutions and personalities is one that does not seem to commend itself easily to both prosecuting and judicial authorities in the West. Specifically, statements that tend to lay bare the raw nerves of the political commitments or shortcomings of judges tend to invoke sanctions. Several such cases have been documented in this work, but one that is probably more striking than any of them was brought in Greece for insult to officials by a newspaper editor in his blunt but reasoned excoriation of the judges of the Greek Supreme Court for their accommodating attitude toward the "traitors" who had seized power and for having themselves been the minions of the dictatorship.[315]

The offending article itself is a classic of robust criticism of a particular court, accusing it among other things of being "doormats . . . for the barbarian boots of the tyrants."[316] The reported judgment did little more than to record that the words used were excessive and that the respect of the citizen is a prerequisite for the effective functioning of a court. However, the facts of the case raise the ever-recurring question as to whether criminal sanctions can *ever* be an effective and a democratically acceptable foundation for achieving respect and honor and whether, all things considered, it is not politically, socially, and psychologically better for all concerned, including the protected judges, to have more rather than fewer outspokenly critical and honest views expressed about judges. What the accused verbalized in his editorial was nothing more than an idea intrinsic to all dispassionate thinking about a judiciary that sits in judgment on people for their political crimes. By allowing such speech, wounding as it may well be, a court will not only contribute to those ideals inherent in the premises of a system of legal free speech but also to the demystification, dedeification, and humanization of those judges who in so many senses of the word hold sway over the fortunes of their people. This particular case does more than any other available instance of scandalizing the courts to exemplify the need for what may be called a psychological appeal procedure that could allow someone who feels aggrieved by the often luckless pursuit of justice to make a public appeal to the verdict of history. Few societies, however, seem to have the maturity to see that what may appear to be insulting language constitutes a palliative and even a strengthening device of the administration of justice. The Areopagus lost a rare opportunity to strike a blow for this elusive wisdom as well as for the notion, inherent in the words of Thucydides's funeral oration by Pericles, that in a society that "is called democracy . . . the public estimation in which each man is held in any field . . . [depends] on his true worth."[317] Inasmuch as the West may have progressed toward recognizing this seemingly elusive truth in other areas, the legal domain is far from a haven for outspoken dissent and toleration.[318]

3

Trial Publicity Restrictions

There has long been and there still is in this country a strong and generally held feeling that trial by newspaper is wrong and should be prevented. . . . What I think is regarded as most objectionable is that a newspaper or television programme should seek to persuade the public, by discussing the issues and evidence in a case before the court, whether civil or criminal, that one side is right and the other wrong.

Lord Reid in the *Sunday Times* thalidomide case[1]

INTRODUCTION

The formal and informal limitation of various forms of publicity relating to court trials that are either pending or in progress – referred to henceforth simply as *trial publicity* – relates to the other major cluster of restrictions, prohibitions, or inhibitions operative in the West relating to the administration of justice. Whereas the principle of free speech in relation to the protection of the honor or reputation of the personalities of the administration of justice – or of the administration itself – has largely been accepted either as well-nigh total in the United States, and at least as desirable in principle elsewhere, free speech in relation to trial publicity remains a disputed topic even in the United States and most European countries and an almost impregnable no-go zone in the balance of the English-speaking world. Unlike the situation regarding free speech in relation to the scandalization of the courts, there has been no dearth of fundamental debate on the topic of trial publicity. However, not even a theoretical consensus has been achieved. Whereas the potential theoretical benefits of free speech in relation to the personalities and institutions of the justice machinery are almost universally accepted in democratic societies, there is considerable academic or theoretical support for an absolute or quasiabsolute legal prohibition on trial publicity. In a number of countries, the legal problems are simply ignored and left to the media to regulate on an informal basis, if at all.

Although the problem of the legal regulation of trial publicity historically had little to do with the role of the media – especially the press – it has in this century become very closely interlinked with the influence and the role of the modern mass media in democratic societies.[2] Especially in recent times, the role of the most pervasive forms of the media – television and the mass circulation press (and especially those sections specializing in sensationalism) – has become exceptionally important within the ambit of what has become known as the free speech-fair trial debate. Indeed the problem of trial publicity has become almost totally enmeshed with the influence and the social perils of the modern mass media.

The problem of limiting or controlling trial publicity involves a number of deeply significant psychological aspects of which very little is known. This is true especially regarding the possible effect such publicity may have on the minds of those officers of the law involved in judicial decision making. It is indeed ironic that much of the discussion on trial publicity in the English-speaking world – takes place without recourse to psychology.[3] Nevertheless, it is on psychological dangers, albeit largely unproven ones, that trial publicity prohibitions are largely predicated or advocated.

Another aspect of pivotal importance in the so-called free speech-fair trial debate that is seldom considered is the question of public interest in the access to information in the public domain. The same is true of the need, in the interest of defensible democratic values, to restrict public access to certain kinds of information in relation to trials, especially in matters involving the core area of an individual's privacy. This problem is seldom considered both in a situation such as occurs in the United States, where restrictions are practically nonexistent, or in relation to those countries that are particularly strict, whether as a consequence of legal sanctions or as a result of informal taboos or rules of journalistic ethics.

It is of course particularly the so-called sub judice rule in English-speaking countries outside the United States that the problem of trial publicity has presented itself on the legal level, especially that of criminal law. However, the problem has still not resolved itself even in the United States, with a number of new restrictions having been created recently now that so-called gagging writs had fallen on evil days. Even in some European countries where there is a bemused incomprehension in legal circles about sub judice restrictions, there are informal restrictions. Most of the discussion here will be devoted to the situation in the English-speaking world, where the problem has been most incisively disputed, and Germany, where trial publicity is not regulated by formal restrictions but has been subjected to some critical consideration.

The best and perhaps only circumstance in which an intelligent discussion of the free speech-fair trial conflict situation can take place is based on a conscious attempt at *Güterabwägung*, or social balancing.[4] It will become clear that in many instances of free speech repression such a social balancing has not taken place at all or not with a cogent understanding of the basic values involved. Moreover, in some instances there was a bland assumption of the presence of a public interest when it was manifestly absent. Indeed, in most cases there seems to be very little public interest involved at all, and even less interest of the state, in restricting most kinds of trial publicity that would normally be forthcoming in responsible media of most Western countries. Where social balancing between conflicting ideals in this debate is called for, it will mostly involve not a straight balancing of social advantage against social evil but a balancing between various evils (or assumed evils) that will demand an intelligent social quantification of such evils.

Naturally, such quantification and balancing of conflicting evils will take place against the general backdrop of the reigning philosophy as regards legal free speech in a particular country. Where the legal domain is regarded as a legitimate area of social concern, the balancing between conflicting social evils will be deeply affected by the general assumption of the cleansing properties of free speech and free debate, whereas in other systems, albeit respectable democratic ones, those propensities may well be obscured or denied with a corresponding underplaying of the need for free speech in relation to trial publicity. Inherent in the arguments that follow here is the belief that free speech also has a role to play as regards trials and that restrictions imposed thereon must be such that they will be defensible in terms of democratic values and the major premises of a system of legal free speech.

THE FUNDAMENTAL CONFLICT IN TRIAL PUBLICITY

A responsible press has always been regarded as the handmaiden of effective judicial administration, especially in the criminal field. Its function in this regard is documented by an impressive record of service over several centuries. The press does not simply publish information about trials but guards against the miscarriage of justice by subjecting the police, the prosecutors, and judicial processes to extensive public scrutiny and criticism.

Justice Clark in *Sheppard* v. *Maxwell*[5]

Responsible "mass media" will do their best to be fair, but there will also be ill-informed slapdash or prejudiced attempts to influence the public.

Lord Reid in the *Sunday Times* thalidomide case[6]

The popular albeit not overly enlightening term "trial by newspaper" expresses the fear that under the glare of certain kinds of publicity independent and effective court procedures may be prejudiced. Inherent in this fear are a number of tacit but largely unproven assumptions that have in certain countries – and specifically in the English-speaking worked – given rise to certain restrictions. Inter alia, these assumptions include: that media (and of late, especially, television) publicity possesses a tendency to warp the independence of persons, including judicial officers; that media publicity is necessarily more destructive to fair procedures than other less-visible and less-controllable forms of "mind pollution" on judicial officers; that the possible advantages of publicity are outweighed by the disadvantages; and that, despite its deep psychological implications, the problem is indeed amenable to rational analysis. All of these assumptions can, however, be challenged both on cogent logical ground and, especially, on grounds relating to the democratic ethos.

There can be no question that in a democratic society the citizen who ventures as a litigant into a court has the well-nigh inviolable right to a trial as fair as frail human nature and formal procedural guarantees can make it. It is, therefore, not surprising that there is in wide and respectable democratic circles an almost automatic sympathy for trial publicity restrictions inspired by this concern. It is not surprising to find that even in those instances where restrictions on trial publicity were taken to excessive and illogical lengths, there is a pious allegiance to this ideal. This was so in the leading New Zealand case of *Tonks*,[7] the second *Van Niekerk* contempt case in South Africa, [8] and also in the *Sunday Times* thalidomide case. In the remarkable *Tonks* judgment, Chief Justice Meyers made a statement that is exemplary for many trial publicity restrictions:

> The publication of the matter complained of is a contempt of court only if it was calculated to prejudice, obstruct, or interfere with the due administration of justice. . . . The court must not only *be* free – but must also *appear* to be free – from any extraneous influence. The appearance of freedom from any such influence is just as important as the reality. Public confidence must necessarily be shaken if there is the least ground for any suspicion of outside interference in the administration of justice.[9]

When seen against the facts of the case – a mild newspaper appeal after judgment but before sentence that an accused should "meet with the utmost rigour of the law" when he comes up for sentence – this undoubtedly laudable concern for correct appearances becomes more problematic. Correct procedures and correct appearances may in fact be worthless, unless there is correct action – as well as general public confidence therein – on the part of the court concerned. The remarkable aspect of the *Tonks* judgment is, however, that it takes this concern for correct appearances to its full and logical but, therefore, slightly ridiculous conclusion by extending the reach of the contempt restrictions into the sphere of subconscious stimuli that may affect the judicial mind, even where there is not the least likely possibility of such mind being influenced.[10]

This candid defense of the extended reach of the sub judice rule into the sphere of subconscious stimuli in the *Tonks* case[11] is valuable and heuristically useful. It indicates on the one hand of what is both popularly and also at times judicially regarded as the true and acceptable basis of trial publicity restrictions – that is, the protection of the proverbial clean stream of justice – and on the other hand it indicates the essential futility of the exercise in most instances because of the inability to reach and control (despite the reasoning of the *Tonks* case) the subconscious stimuli on the judicial mind. The largely unspoken assumption on which this approach of speech control is predicated is that courts must – or can –

operate in a kind of diluted atmosphere free of extraneous, nonlegal influences that may corrupt or influence – or be *seen* to be doing so – the judicial process. The statement in *Tonks* is further useful because it stresses, albeit unwittingly, the possible influence on the judicial process of unconscious stimuli that is basically uncontrollable. And, as will be shown later, it is this emphasis on controllable visible or audible stimuli over the substantially uncontrollable invisible (or inaudible) stimuli that results in the fact that protection of the judicial order by trial publicity restrictions is for the most part inconsequential from the point of view of protecting the substance of fair court procedures.

Nowhere in recent times did the legitimate concern for fair trial procedures on the one hand and the absurdity and social unacceptability of an overly strict approach on the other hand come more clearly into focus than in the *Sunday Times* thalidomide contempt case in Britain to which detailed reference has already been made.[12] The publication of the details by the *Sunday Times* in Britain of the foot-dragging by the drug company in paying out reasonable compensation to the victims of the thalidomide tragedy undoubtedly brought public pressure to bear on a litigant in a pending civil trial and the further publication of material, which was enjoined, would undoubtedly have involved various public prejudgments. It was the danger of this kind of trial by newspaper that moved the House of Lords[13] to overrule the finely balanced judgment of the Court of Appeal,[14] which would have lifted the injunction and allowed the publication, probably with little effect on the substance of the English sub judice rule. In their judgment, the House of Lords followed the customary line of disallowing comments from the street or the media that can potentially affect the course of pending litigation.[15] But one aspect of Lord Reid's judgment breaks new ground with a new justification for the banning of trial publicity: "If people are led to think that it is easy to find the truth, disrespect for the processes of the law could follow, and, if mass media are allowed to judge, unpopular people and unpopular causes will fare very badly."[16]

What the first part of this latter statement seems to mean, if anything, is that the elusive search for the grail of the truth is for the courts alone to undertake. The second part is an admission that courts will succumb to overt pressure to treat unpopular causes unfairly. The House of Lords then continues to make a statement that gets to the crux of its misunderstanding of the issues involved: "I do not think that the freedom of the press would suffer, and I think that the law would be clearer and easier to apply in practice if it is made a general rule that it is not permissible to prejudge issues in pending cases."[17]

That a total ban on all trial publicity would be "clearer and easier to apply" than a differentiated ban that tries to balance conflicting values is obvious, but the bland contention that it would not affect freedom of the press must be attributed to a grievously restrictive view of the role of the press (and of free speech generally) in the legal domain. No better example can in fact be found for the defective understanding of the role of free speech as regards the legal domain than the very *Sunday Times* thalidomide case, where an almost grotesquely unjust situation became rectified only through the activist role of the press.[18]

It is especially the public's right to access of information within the legal domain and its right to legal free speech that are encumbered and often rendered totally ineffective by trial publicity restrictions, and when viewed superficially, it is the right of free speech that appears to vie with the right to a fair trial. It is, of course, a matter of debate as to whether on the one hand the public indeed has an interest in a trial beyond that of being factually informed of the details – especially in matters of a salacious and personal nature published only for purposes of sensationalism – and on the other whether there could be a vital public interest involved that is strikingly evident from the facts of, for example, *Sunday Times* case. The same observation would be true even of the facts of the *Tonks* case, where a newspaper propounded a certain line to be followed in sentencing a convicted person. That excessive trial publicity restrictions can in fact blanket out whole areas of public interest is particularly clear from the example of the second *Van Niekerk* contempt case in South Africa, which potentially shuts out from discussion any issue – even a legal issue – that is the subject of a trial somewhere and may, albeit unconsciously, influence any judicial officer.[19] The selective invocation of such sub judice restrictions regarding judicial commissions of enquiry in South Africa has likewise excised from public discussion vast areas of the public domain,[20] a situation that is also theoretically possible under British law.[21]

Naturally, it is usual to view trial publicity restrictions against the backdrop of the persuasiveness of modern communications,[22] but it is sobering to recall that in their origins the sub judice restrictions of the English-speaking world predate by centuries the advent of the modern media, a fact that tends to underline the truth that in their essence these restrictions flow from the same tendency (in the words of the nondelivered but seminal decision in the *Almon* case[23]) "to keep a blaze of glory" around the courts that is similar to scandalization restrictions. It is not surprising that in the same breath Oswald deals with the origins of the two major glory-blazing manifestations of the "legal thumbscrew" of contempt of court.[24]

The attempts by American courts to come to grips with certain forms of trial publicity highlight the importance of freedom of speech – particularly of the press – in relation to trial publicity and also the imaginativeness of the attempts to control or limit that freedom. It is, of course, under the protective penumbra of the right of free speech of the First Amendment of the U.S. Constitution that the battle for the dilution and ultimately the effective elimination of sub judice restrictions has been waged in recent years. Although echoes of that battle are still heard, it has become a hard row for a prosecutor to hoe to overcome the bulwarks thrown up around the First Amendment regarding trial publicity. To a significant extent, the focus of this battle recently has shifted to other issues such as the right of access of television media and speech restrictions on the dramatis personae in the litigation, chiefly prosecutors and lawyers – problems with which almost all other legal systems have not yet started to deal. Contrary perhaps to superficial reactions, the American experience in this field is of abiding relevance elsewhere in the world, since it flows from the only genuine attempt by a nation's courts to balance the real conflicting interests and to look hard at some of the underlying issues involved.

In the 1976 *Nebraska Press Association* case,[25] the U.S. Supreme Court squarely faced up to the problem of trial publicity restrictions. The unanimity of the Court regarding the result (although not the reasoning) bode ill for future restrictions, and the decision itself probably constitutes the most impressive landmark on the legal landscape of the world as a whole concerning free speech regarding the administration of justice.[26] It struck down a gagging writ of a Nebraska court and refused to see trial publicity as an inherent and axiomatic danger to a fair trial under the Sixth Amendment.

> It is unnecessary, after nearly two centuries, to establish a priority [between competing First and Sixth Amendment rights] applicable in all circumstances. Yet it is nonetheless clear that the barriers to prior restraint remain high unless we are to abandon what the Court has said for nearly a quarter of our national existence and implied throughout all of it.[27]

The various opinions in the *Nebraska Press Association* case concur on the basic philosophy of allowing free speech the greatest possible scope within the legal domain despite the obvious presence of those "problems . . . [which] are almost as old as the Republic"[28] but that have been heightened by the pervasiveness of modern communication techniques. The opinions all manifest an alertness to the basic issues involved, such as the watchdog role of the press within the administration of justice, the inefficacy of restraints, the possibility of using less-restrictive measures than gagging orders, the unlikelihood of not finding a fair and unbiased jury, etc. Although the barrier erected by this case around press freedom in the legal domain is a high one, the majority consciously elected not to follow the minority view of three judges, who believed such freedom had to be absolute and total.[29] Therefore, the possibility persists that under certain extreme but unspecified circumstances a future Supreme Court majority may hold that certain kinds or forms of trial publicity may constitute an unacceptable prejudice to the inherent fairness of a trial. What the majority probably had in mind was the kind of carnival atmosphere at the trial in the older *Sheppard* v. *Maxwell* decision.[30] However, as will presently be pointed out, this raises other implications that have little to do with a viable system of legal free speech. Another important aspect of the *Nebraska* decision is the constitutional abhorrence to prior restraints as opposed to subsequent punishment for contravening speech restrictions.[31] What is unexpressed but patently present in the philosophy of the various opinions is an awareness that the mere counterposing of First Amendment free speech rights and Sixth Amendment fair trial rights is too simplistic and too unsubtle a way of solving a problem as multidimensional and elusive as that of the balancing of the demands of free speech and fair trial under circumstances where intelligent precautions could not ensure a fair trial, even under circumstances of pervasive publicity. There is no underplaying of the "gravity of the evil [which] pretrial publicity can work," but merely an overriding emphasis that countervailing steps of a more discerning nature than a blanket ban are called for. And as far as the lessons for other legal systems are concerned, it must be remembered that the kind of facts of the *Nebraska* case – including the geographical realities of impaneling an unbiased jury in that area – would not occur too frequently. Also underlying the judgment is the problem flowing from the use of juries.[32]

That publicity and especially some of the side effects of publicity may at times cause problems for a fair trial is obvious and by leaving the authority of the *Sheppard* case substantially intact, the Supreme Court underscored this truth. But the "carnival atmosphere in court" was pervasive in the *Sheppard* case, a situation that, it is submitted, must be divorced from the free press, in which fair-trial debate can be controlled without undue contraction of the core area of legal free speech if careful consideration is given to the real alternatives and real issues involved in trial-publicity problems, namely, free speech and independent judicial machinery. It is to these alternatives and issues we now turn.

THE REAL ALTERNATIVES AND THE REAL ISSUES

[T]he judiciary is capable of protecting the defendant's right to a fair trial without enjoining the press from publishing information in the public domain.

Justice Stevens in the *Nebraska Press Association* case[33]

The majority opinion in the *Nebraska* case does not imply that trial publicity can never be prejudicial to a fair trial,[34] but it does call for a consideration of the real issues involved and the more nuanced alternatives needed than the simplistic solution of blanket suppression – one that, in the words of the House of Lords, would indeed be "clearer and easier to apply"[35] – and also for pondering the role of a free press in the legal domain.

It is significant that trial publicity does not apparently constitute any real problem in the case of civil trials in the United States, which indicates that trial publicity restrictions concerning criminal trials are still subconsciously seen as flowing from the "blaze of glory" that has traditionally been thrown around criminal courts. That there may be quantitatively less of a problem in this regard is perhaps true, but it cannot be said that the consequences of a less-than-fair trial in civil matters may not be as important to the litigant as it would be in a criminal trial. The absence of a real concern in the matter of civil trial publicity underlines, in effect, the possibility of solving the problem with reference to logical and democratically acceptable principles. In what follows, an attempt will be made to examine some of the major elements of trial publicity.

The Basic Problem: The Human (and Judicial) Mind

[T]he forces of which judges avowedly avail to shape the form and content of their judgments . . . are seldom fully in consciousness.

Benjamin Cardozo[36]

The crux of the supposed antithesis of free speech-fair trial lies in human psychology (more particularly judicial psychology) and in the ability, or inability, to arrive at certain decisions one is obliged to make without being unduly or improperly influenced by factors one is not entitled to consider. Looked at from another angle, the question is ultimately that of knowing the extent to which it is possible for a member of the judiciary to exercise rational control over his or her thinking processes, particularly in so far as the overcoming of prejudices, preconceptions, and popular pressures are concerned.[37]

In their origin, formal trial publicity restrictions in the Anglo-Saxon world flowed from within the penumbra of awe built up around the judicial office. Until quite recently, the notion of the *pervasiveness* of publicity played no role concerning statements that could not conceivably influence any judicial officer who is endowed with but the vaguest social understanding of his or her position.[38] From this attitude derives the attraction of a "clearer and easier" rule of no comment whatever concerning pending or proceeding litigation. That this clear and easy test somehow contradicts the qualities subsumed in the judicial office is probably at the root of the standard contention, repeated de rigueur and ad nauseam in almost every case, that the protection is of course not at all needed by the judges concerned in view of their training and other qualities. The emphasis is then invariably shifted to the public's distrust in the ability of judicial officers to remain unaffected by trial publicity.[39]

Trial publicity only presents a problem because of a judge's (or juror's) inability – or *suspected* inability – to do what his or her judicial capacity obliges. The underlying assumption of trial publicity restrictions – whether formal or voluntary – is that the judicial mind cannot by itself be relied on to do what it is legally obliged to do, or at least to get the public to believe that it can. The absence until very recently of any attempt in the English-speaking world outside the United States to use a more subtle criterion than outright banning is a clear indication that the democratic premises of legal free speech played essentially no role whatever in the question.

Of course, the truth is that for all the salutary iconoclasm of the modern realists we still know very little of how a member of the judiciary reaches conclusions. The result is that such restrictions, whether formal or voluntary, that have traditionally been imposed on trial publicity have been imposed somewhat blindly and without any real attempt to probe into the fundamental issues involved and with practically no consideration for the democratic values affected.

Ignoring for the time being such cases where the publicity reaches such an intensity that it constitutes a kind of mental intimidation or creates a carnival atmosphere in court, it must at least be doubted whether direct and open and even blatant publicity is necessarily more corrosive to the independent thinking of an honest and critical person than less overt, more subtle, and less obvious forms of publicity or extraneous influences emanating from sources that are leaglly acceptable. Examples include the adducing of irrelevant and even inadmissible but highly impressionable evidence in court, evidence that must then (at least theoretically) be disregarded and psychologically expunged from the particular judicial mind; subtle reliance by lawyers on facts that have a certain importance for the particular mental makeup of the judicial officers concerned; writing or speaking in a legally acceptable way ("the *alleged* perpetrator") but that is a transparent camouflage for saying something that cannot be said but is nevertheless clearly understood; etc. In brief, an impressionable mind may be as deeply and prejudicially corroded by such indirect or less-overt kinds of extraneous persuasion as would be the case with more blatant attempts of overt influencing. Indeed, it may well be that, in the case of highly publicized trials, certain blatant forms of trial publicity or prejudgment may well carry in their very blatantness, exaggeration, or impropriety the major cause for their ineffectiveness by triggering a kind of internal early warning system in honest, critical, and competent judges.[40]

One strange phenomenon regarding free speech in the West is that the strong belief in the actinic, self-correcting, and socially cleansing powers of free speech finds very little application in the legal domain as a consequence of the general application of formal or informal speech restrictions on the basis of highly unproven assumptions. Essentially on the basis that one can never exclude the *possibility* of trial publicity affecting the judicial mind – and henceforth we will be concerned mainly with *judges* and not with juries – Western societies have been willing to exclude from the actinic operation of free speech significant areas of justice administration. The social cost of these restrictions is naturally increased where there is no likelihood of any detrimental influence emanating from publicity, even in terms of the views of the courts.

The dubious nature of the reputed beneficial effects of publicity restrictions becomes apparent when crimes of overwhelming notoriety are committed in societies such as Britain or South Africa, countries that practically have a total ban on all forms of trial publicity. There is nevertheless no serious move to challenge the competence or the fairness of the ultimate court despite the fact that from the moment the courts become involved newspapers start the ritual of referring, for instance, to the "alleged" perpetrator instead of "the gunman X" or "the hijacker Y."[41] In a country such as Germany, where, as we will see below, trial publicity regarding sensational trials is often speculative and can attain great intensity, there is little concern about the fairness of the ultimate trial. And does anyone seriously question, at least on the basis of trial publicity, the fairness of the trials of the accused Watergate conspirators in the United States, where prejudicial publicity probably reached an unparalleled intensity?

It is really when societies with strict sub judice restrictions, whether formal or informal, are compared with societies such as Germany and the United States, where the restrictions or inhibitions are minimal, that the untenable basis of the underlying principle becomes very clear. Unless one seriously supports the notion that in these systems justice is manifestly unattainable because of trial publicity, the case for such restrictions *as a prerequisite for justice* becomes slender. There is also the practice in countries like Britain, which tends to exclude the operation of the sub judice principle regarding appeal courts.[42] And, very strangely, Lord Denning in a recent work underlined a view he had expressed in a judgment by excluding from the operation of the sub judice rule those courts manned by *nonlawyers* who would, as would be the case with jurors, by definition almost be least able to resist the corruptive pressure of trial publicity.[43]

There is another admittedly more subtle reason why trial publicity restrictions ought to be viewed at least with some suspicion. Democratic governments function on the fundamental premise and assumption that *more* rather than less information is helpful to rational thought and decision making. Artificial speech restrictions in the legal domain – which in any event seek and are able to control only overt and extraneous influences on a judiciary while leaving informal influences unchecked – would on this assumption be corrosive rather than promotive to the dictates of justice. In crisp terms, the choice is not between free speech on the one hand and a fair trial on the other, but between a judicial system that is able to live with the full panoply of free speech and one that cannot. In terms of this analysis, there is no problem relating to publicity or information that cannot be mastered by truly independent judicial minds. Where such independence and intelligence are lacking or deficient, the likelihood of *any* speech restrictions serving its purpose in terms of the traditional sub judice assumptions is in any event very slim and problematic in view of the very real danger of other possibly more corrosive influences affecting the independent and rational judgment of such a judiciary.

Naturally, this discussion of the real alternatives is heavily premised on the availability of judicial officers of the said qualities of independence and intelligence, although, to quote Lord Denning again, there is the oft-repeated assumption in even the strictest sub judice jurisdictions that "[n]o professionally trained judge would be influenced by anything he read in the newspapers or saw on television."[44] Some jurisdictions, as we have seen, seem to cope quite acceptably with the problem and others, as we have likewise seen, seem to be able to ignore it quite blithely under circumstances relating to crimes of overwhelming notoriety. It is a basic part of the makeup of any competent judge in any court anywhere in the world to be able to ignore certain facts or impressions in arriving at certain conclusions. A not insignificant part of the law of evidence, particularly in the very Anglo-Saxon countries where sub judice restrictions apply most stringently, concerns the various kinds of evidence that cannot be led, and if led, must be ignored. That the effect of certain impressions improperly imparted, can *never* be effaced is, of course, trite. But the essential submission here is that the control of overt information or publicity is but a small part of this reality of human justice, especially if regard is had to the vast unexplored realm of the unconscious part of the judge's mind.

That certain kinds of trial publicity may detrimentally affect the course of justice, for instance, by making it difficult or dangerous for witnesses to give evidence, or may affect other valuable rights in a democratic society, especially that of the privacy of the individual, may well call for certain controls, as will be argued later. But simply to ban such publicity to protect competent and independent judges from receiving and abusing extraneous stimuli is patently unflattering to their judicial ability. Although clearly only applicable to some top judges, the following statement of Lord Reid in the *Sunday Times* thalidomide case should be true of all truly competent and independent judges: "But I must add ... that comment where a case is under appeal is a very different matter. For one thing it is scarcely possible to imagine a case where comment could influence judges in the Court of Appeal, of noble and learned Lords in this House.[45]

Of course, there may finally be the argument that trial publicity going beyond mere reporting of what actually happened in court is a luxury that in the interests of a pure stream of justice can be dispensed with, especially since it would involve merely a *deferment* of criticism or analysis. That such a "mere" deferment could mean a question of many months and even years is at least clear from the *Sunday Times* thalidomide case and also as regards most cases going on appeal and often in cases involving long delays. That certain kinds of speculative or investigative legal journalism may well be of a socially useless nature must be conceded, but no system of democratic free speech concerning the legal domain can properly and viably function if too many fine distinctions are drawn between potentially useful and useless information and publicity. That the history of the application of sub judice restrictions is studded by the suppression of extremely useful information is at least clear from the general experience in Holland – to be referred to below[46] – where informal restrictions inhibit practically all critical or investigative trial publicity; from the *Sunday Times* thalidomide case where the very belated publicity prevented a continuation of an endless trail of injustice, from the second *Van Niekerk* case in South Africa where a total ban was imposed on public discussion in *general terms* on possible psychological (and a fortiori physical) torture of detainees; and even from the *Tonks* case in New Zealand where a particular view, whether valuable or otherwise, was suppressed as regards a particular crime that had attracted great public interest. A recent case against a British television company where a public discussion on medical matters was penalized with a massive fine under circumstances where there could not conceivably have been a prejudice to a fair trial illustrates the possible impact of these restrictions on education and public discussion on television.[47] The Canadian case of *Radio OB* also underlines this relatively new angle of television publicity as regards pending trials and the potentially stifling effect on public discussion of matters of vital public concern – in this case the inadequate facilities for housing retarded children – with no meaningful advancement of the cause of justice.[48]

Jury Trials and Publicity

It is not asking too much to suggest that those who exercise First Amendment rights in newspapers or broadcasting enterprises direct some effort to protect the rights of an accused to a fair trial by unbiased jurors.

Chief Justice Burger in the *Nebraska Press Association* case[49]

The presence of juries or lay judges in the decision-making processes within the administration of justice is undoubtedly a factor meriting serious consideration and care against the backdrop of trial publicity, constituting as it does a potential danger to the achievement of justice. In the United States, this aspect is generally regarded as the crux of the free speech-fair trial debate, but it is often alluded to also in other Anglo-Saxon jurisdictions with sub judice restrictions with the paradoxical consequence that although the danger of jurors being influenced by trial publicity is taken to be one of the real bases for the preservation of sub judice restrictions there has not been a total scrapping of restrictions for publicity in nonjury trials. In Britain, however, there has been of late a willingness to limit the rigidity of the restrictions in nonjury trials.[50]

The question of how juries arrive at their verdicts and of the factors influencing their minds is enveloped in much uncertainty and cannot even approximately be broached in this study. Writing in the Kansas City *Star*, Dr. Gerald A. Ehrenreich, a clinical professor of psychiatry, pointedly sums up the free press-fair trial debate in relation to juries[51]:

We all agree that a democracy requires a fully-informed citizenry to function most effectively and that freedom of the press and the more recent companion right of the public to know are central to our democratic way of life. Why is it assumed that those same well-informed citizens, once they become jurors, are not capable of judging their fellow men fairly on the basis of all the available evidence?

Is there convincing evidence that jurors are usually, or frequently, unable to weight the evidence and bring about justice? If such evidence exists, it does not necessarily mean that pretrial information is the sole or even the main cause.... We are sadly lacking, I understand, in information about the way in which jurors come to their decisions.

What evidence is there, for instance, of the relative effect of pre-trial information upon the juror as compared to the effect of the emotion-provoking, fact-befuddling antics of some lawyers as they carry out their version of our adversary system of justice?

If the jurors, with the help of the judge, are assumed to be capable of reasoned weighing of evidence in an adversary trial, why cannot the prejudicial effects of pre-trial information be counteracted in the courtroom?

Whatever importance the absence of reliable empirical information on problems relating to jury selection and jury qualifications may have on the present debate, it seems natural to assume on the basis of simple human experience that lay judges or jurors will not always, if indeed ever, possess the qualities of rigorous spiritual independence normally attributed to competent incumbents of judicial office. The ability to be self-critical concerning preconceptions and prejudices and of being able to expunge or countervail such preconceptions, prejudices, and prior knowledge from one's own decision-making processes can not be assumed to be inherent in most persons to the degree required for judicial decision making, especially in cases involving certain categories of "unpopular" or "contemptible" persons in criminal trials. It is, of course, possible that careful jury selection may obviate the worst kinds of bias or other improper qualities and the very elaborate voir dire proceedings in the United States in the case of a cause célèbre are manifestations of concern in this regard. However, it undoubtedly remains a fact of life that in cases of great notoriety that have been subjected to pervasive publicity, the decision-making qualities of juries may often not measure up to what is ideally required and reasonably expected of human justice. This is a multifaceted problem and one that has perhaps still to be assessed in terms of certain social demands in societies where juries or lay judges operate.[52]

Essentially, the question here is less that of the counterposing of free speech and fair trial but of the viability of the jury system in a modern state with free and active media. In those societies where the right of a jury trial is regarded as a basic civil right, it is of course almost impossible to find an audience for the proposition that the time may perhaps have come to question the existence of that system in contemporary circumstances, partly as a consequence of the possibly unreasonable demands made on it by modern media. Excluding once more the question of saturation publicity, the question must surely be faced whether very pivotal rights of society as regards free speech and access to information should be prejudiced and diluted by an institution that, for all the merits it may have had in the past, has a ready substitute available: trial by able and independent judges. At least in those instances where a realistic peril exists regarding the ability of a jury to cope with problems of publicity, it is submitted that in lieu of resorting to restrictions crippling to the interests of free speech, a litigant must avail himself of the ready alternative of trial by judges – an alternative that in any event is the rule in higher tiers of judicial decision making. This kind of situation will of course arise most definitively in those relatively few criminal cases involving notoriously unpopular people or people whose guilt is widely assumed. In the vast bulk of cases, the sentiments of Dr. Ehrenreich quoted above will probably constitute a nearer approximation of the truth. Jurors, like judges, are made of brittle human stuff, and as in the case of judges we must assume that if all reasonable precautions are taken with the selection and guidance of these jurors, they will do what is humanly possible to measure up to the expectations that their society has of them, despite possibly improper attempts to influence them, whether in the media or elsewhere.

A pivotal point generally overlooked is that where a society deliberately chooses the jury or lay judge system as its basic method of fact-finding to the exclusion of using trained judges, it is done with the main objective of achieving an input into the legal processes of the common sense of values of the proverbial common person. However, one of the most important formative factors of this common-sense or common-person values in contemporary society is the influence of the media. In short, the role of the media in a democracy in the exercise of free speech is one of the potent factors that for better or for worse would necessarily influence the juror – and legitimately so in terms of the underlying principles of the jury system. It is submitted that where the operation of the jury system in terms of its own inherent premises is incompatible with the achievement of a fair trial due to trial publicity, the restriction of legal free speech would be too high a social price to pay where an alternative palliative – trial by judges – is readily available.

In the last decade and more, the tendency in U.S. case law has been to stress the alternative remedies that must be adopted before a significant inroad into the rights of free speech would be tolerated, a threshold that has now become almost impossible to cross. In the now seminal judgment of *Nebraska Press Association*, Chief Justice Burger (on behalf of the full Supreme Court) addresses himself to this problem of alternatives. Speaking about the carnival atmosphere in the notorious Lindbergh kidnapping trial he states:

> Responsible leaders of press and the legal profession – including other judges – pointed out that much of this sorry performance [at the trial] could have been controlled by a vigilant trial judge and by other public officers subject to the control of the court.[53]

And later the chief justice restates the position in more general terms in a formulation that is pivotal to the underlying philosophy of the judgment: "In the overwhelming majority of criminal trials, pretrial publicity presents few unmanageable threats to this important right [to a jury trial]."[54] The chief justice then proceeds to spell out more specifically the possibilities of the trial judge other than publicity restrictions to prevent a miscarriage of justice in cases even of massive trial publicity.[55]

An interesting and paradoxical gloss to the situation of juries within the free speech-fair trial debate was written in 1977 and 1978 in the form of applications to various courts on behalf inter alia of the civil liberty-oriented New York State Trial Lawyers Association to ban advertisements doing no more than informing society – and obviously potential jurors drawn from society – that excessive awards in personal injury litigation are paid for by insurance premiums. The protection was sought under various fair advertisement statutes on the basis inter alia that they were directed at potential jurors who constitute "an especially vulnerable audience," that they were incomplete, that they offended public policy because of their unfair and unscrupulous "tendency" to influence jurors by substituting a concern about their own insurance premiums for their duty to award just compensation to injured plaintiffs," that they "pose a serious threat to the integrity of the judicial process" and that they undermine "due process of law, equal protection of the law and access to an impartial and unprejudiced jury."

At the beginning of 1981, the outcome of a motion by the defendants to dismiss on First Amendment grounds was still awaited, but the advertisements had been withdrawn some two years before. Not only is this novel threat to free speech from some unexpected sources interesting, what is also noteworthy is the unspoken assumption of the plaintiffs concerning the greater vulnerability of jurors to corruption by advertisements than by press reports and editorial comments and their mistrust of the viability of the jury system in the face of a threat that seems infinitely less imminent than mildly pervasive press coverage.[56]

Important as the American experience and pronouncements on trial publicity concerning jury trials are in their own right, emphasizing as they now mostly do the fact that remedies and palliatives must be sought that do not involve the suppression of basic rights of free speech, they become even more relevant when they are used as a backdrop to the suppression of free speech as regards *trials by judges*, where in most contempt jurisdictions, from New Zealand and India in the East to Canada in the West, the selfsame problems concerning trial publicity are identified in relation to trials by judges. Considering once again that certain countries like Germany can apparently quite tolerably get by without any controls whatever, and considering also that in the United States (and peripherally also in Britain) the problem of trial publicity is largely seen in the context of the jury system, it is not difficult to conclude that in these contempt jurisdictions just alluded to the real justification for sub judice restrictions must ultimately be sought more in the sociopolitical sphere as an effort to keep the judiciary and their operations removed from the scrutiny of ordinary humanity than in an attempt to achieve a fair trial.

Ultimately, the question of the exposure of juries to the real or imaginary perils of trial publicity is, as is the case also with judges, a question steeped in the realities of justice meted out by human beings. We can expect no more of human beings than human justice, impregnated with the frailties and imperfections of humanity itself. One such frailty is being subjected to the potentially warping influence of trial publicity. A pervasive ban on trial publicity, however, would be a very high social price to pay where alternative remedies are available with which to curb undue corruption of jurors' minds and where in any event so little is known about the relative influence of such publicity on jurors when compared to other influences,[57] and where, finally, media publicity is actually one of the influences on which a juror's common-sense approach is predicated. Infallibility and perfection are simply not requirements for human justice.[58]

Saturation Trial Publicity

> *The trial of Bruno Hauptmann . . . for the abduction and murder of the Charles Lindberghs' infant child . . . produced widespread public reaction. Criticism was directed at the "carnival" atmosphere that pervaded the community and the courtroom itself.*
> Chief Justice Burger in the *Nebraska Press Association* case[59]

It is especially in the case of saturation publicity where very legitimate doubt exists as to the possibility of a just coexistence of fair trial procedures on the one hand and free speech on the other. It is a problem that is closely intertwined with the use of lay jurors and lay judges.

One aspect of trial publicity that should in theory at least present no insuperable problems – paradoxically perhaps in view of the amount of attention and emotion expended on it in the United States – is where the quest of the media for litigation news results in a "carnival atmosphere" in court (to use the words of the Supreme Court in the *Sheppard* case[60]) or even in an atmosphere where a considered and independent judgment becomes imperiled. One of the inherent powers of any court of law is to maintain the order and decorum of its proceedings, and any prejudice in this regard would merit appropriate suppression in terms of readily identifiable social interests, the chief of which being in fact the simple smooth functioning of a fair system of procedure,[61] and also the protection of the personality rights of the various dramatis personae, especially the accused. The crude unfairness and confusion manifested in a case such as *Sheppard* – a case that merits its place in the very long line of "can you believe it" American cases – has substantially nothing to do with freedom of any kind and least of all with a democratically based freedom of speech in the legal domain. A judge who allows such a carnival to take place must be seen for what he or she really is: a judicial clown and improper incumbent for judicial office. In the opinion of the Supreme Court in the *Sheppard* case, Justice Clark itemizes the dreary catalogue of acts of confusion, impropriety, and unfairness and conjures up a mental picture of a trial of a kind that could only be adequately described by Franz Kafka.[62]

It is not necessary to analyze each and every bit of confusion and hysteria to arrive at the conclusion that the *Sheppard* trial was indeed a circus. Individual items quoted here of media behavior may perhaps in isolation not amount to fatal defects, but the global picture that emerges is one of a concert of confusion, orchestrated by the media as well as by a judge and court officers lacking in elementary understanding of the mechanics of decent courtroom and procedural behavior. The blatant examples of the atmosphere of hysteria preceding and surrounding the trial and the conscious way in which the officers of the court contributed to its fomenting in lieu of endeavoring to control it puts the *Sheppard* case outside the ambit of any serious discussion of free speech, despite the fact that it remains to this day an oft-quoted example of so-called trial by the media.

The facts of the *Sheppard* case are deeply embedded in the realities of the world of modern communications with which the question of trial publicity restrictions has become interwoven, despite the fact that these restrictions originated under very different circumstances and also despite their continued enforcement under circumstances not remotely reminiscent of the kind of abuse committed in *Sheppard*. The same kind of problem arose as regards the use of television cameras in court – a situation only indirectly connected to trial-reporting restrictions and their possible corruptive influence on jurors – in the case of *Estes* v. *Texas*.[63] This other seminal American case also grappled with the supposed dichotomy of free speech and fair trial but the facts giving rise to a narrow 5-4 majority in favor of a retrial once again do not point to an insuperable impasse between the legitimate demands respectively of free speech and fair trial. The basis of the problem in *Estes* was really not so much the question of free speech but the free use of television in the courtroom – a question that is related but not crucial to the problem under discussion. Although there was once again some indication of confusion and disturbance as a consequence of the activities of the media in court, this factor seems to be merely of peripheral importance. The major disturbance seems to have occurred at the time of a pretrial hearing on the permissibility of live television and radio coverage. In his opinion concurring with the opinion of Justice Clark, Chief Justice Warren appended seven photographs to convey an impression of the impact of the television and media activities in and around the courtroom. From Justice Clark's opinion, it transpires that both televising as such as well as the particular methods used in the trial were regarded as constitutionally suspect on the ground of the possibility and perhaps the likelihood of inherent unfairness through the introduction of a factor irrelevant to the search for truth.[64]

The problem of *Estes* is really that of the direct access to court proceedings by the electronic media and not that of their right of legal free speech, although the problem was once more projected against the background of the possible frailty of the jury to arrive at a true verdict.[65] In recent times, as we will later see, the question of the televising of trials has been raised again in the United States with several courts allowing such televising under controlled conditions.[66]

This concern for access of the electronic media to the heart of the courtroom is not readily shared or felt in most other Western societies and flows not unexpectedly from some of the consequences of keeping intact what is now called a First Amendment society. A decade and a half after the *Estes* case, it would, therefore, seem that the fair trial objections to the televising of trials has been substantially diluted, although some reservations remain.

That the media should for reasons other than the achievement of a fair trial be prevented from invading every aspect of courtroom procedures will be argued later.[67] An aspect of this restraint that is called for and will not affect the core area of legal free speech is highlighted in the decision of *Rideau* v. *Louisiana*,[68] where the U.S. Supreme Court ordered a new trial after a trial court had refused an accused's application for a change in venue after a televised confession.[69] However, based implicitly on the premise that even a jury system can coexist with the ravishes of full glare media publicity of trials, the minority held strongly to the belief that in the absence of proven prejudice a new trial was not called for.[70] The crux of the majority decision and of their unwillingness as much as to look at the voir dire examination on the selection of a jury was the strange fact that the police interrogation in which the confession was made (and that ultimately resulted in a death sentence) was screened three tmes on a local television station. For the majority of viewers, that screening was in fact the trial and there was undoubtedly a punitive element in the majority decision directed at the prosecution authorities.

The American examples of saturation publicity described here all point in the direction of a failure of the prosecuting and judicial authorities to institute an intelligent but not crippling control over the exercise of their rights by the media. Partly, they also point to a failure of those authorities to control their own zeal to catapult themselves into the limelight of the media.

Much as one may value the full thrust of free speech, there are nevertheless certain things that the media need not do or need not be allowed to do. Where a society in its wisdom or otherwise chooses the jury or lay judge system as its fact-finding process, it does so with the knowledge that some of the problems flowing from an expanding use of free speech would make such lay people less than ideal instruments of factual decision making, but it does so because of its allegiance to the jury or lay judge system as a higher value than having the best possible system of fact adjudication. And if the American experience with saturation publicity has a lesson, it is that there are methods available that fall short of gagging writs or contempt citations with which to control the excesses of trial publicity without affecting the essence of a vital system of legal free speech. We turn now to some of these alternatives.

ALTERNATIVES TO TRIAL PUBLICITY RESTRICTIONS

In the overwhelming majority of criminal trials, pretrial publicity presents few unmanageable threats to this important right [to a fair trial].

Chief Justice Burger in the *Nebraska Press Association* case[71]

Between, say, the South African and Canadian situation on the one hand, where the full repressive sweep of the sub judice rule applies in its pristine purity, and, say, the German situation, where no formal trial publicity restrictions apply at all, one finds a host of intermediate possibilities of restraining or inhibiting trial publicity. In most developed countries, there seems to have been a recognition that trial-publicity restrictions ought to be limited to the minimum and the judgment of the European Court of Human Rights on the *Sunday Times* thalidomide case,[72] together with less formal moves restricting the invocation of the full sub judice rule, even put British law in this respect on a modest road to reform. Since the *Nebraska Press Association* case, the barriers against trial publicity restrictions on the media have become almost insuperable, with the result that along a different and more painful avenue just about the same situation of freedom has been attained as the one prevailing in Germany. There has also been a gradual, albeit somewhat ungenerous, recognition that the freedom of the media, especially of the press, to pursue their métier also as regards trials flows essentially from a recognition of the public interest in legal free speech.[73]

If the public interest, carefully stated and carefully analyzed, were to be taken as the basic yardstick for an assessment of the need for and application of trial publicity restrictions and inhibitions, few problems would be insuperable and very little compromise would be necessary either as regards the public's demand for fair trial procedures or for legal free speech. However, one important caveat is necessary: the recognition that legal free speech inherently deserves the widest possible application in terms of the democratic ethos and that the essential solution to the so-called free press-fair trial problem must be sought in ways other than blanket or draconian restrictions or inhibitions that limit the core area of legal free speech. In all conscience, however, the democratic ethos cannot allow the media to have an unlimited liberty in this sphere.

The French Experiment

What are you telling me; I never realized we had such a [sub judice-type] provision in our law!

French journalist to the author

Article 227 of the French Penal Code[74] created a kind of sub judice rule that, at least in its overt operation hitherto, has been of a less-intimidating nature than the contempt counterpart that inspired it. Indeed, most journalists seem to be ignorant of its existence. It reads:

> The same penalties as those of article 226 shall be imposed on whomever has published, before a definitive court decision, commentaries which tend to exert pressure on the statements of witnesses or on the decisions of the judge of instruction ["of the instruction jurisdiction"] or on the judgment. The provisions of the three last paragraphs of article 226 are also applicable.[75]

Looking at the application of the French sub judice rule in practice, one is first struck by the dearth of precedent and, second, by the integrated fashion in which articles 226 and 227 are applied. As is the case with article 226 on scandalization, there are very few documented instances of prosecutions, successful or otherwise, under article 227.[76] In a number of instances, for example, the *Schroedt* case and the *Papeete* case discussed above,[77] the prosecution was brought under both articles simultaneously with little distinction between the reasoning given under one or the other heading. It is also clear from the court reporting of major newspapers like *Le Monde*,[78] *France Soir*, and *Le Figaro*, especially when sensational trials are involved, that the French sub judice rule is not, like its English counterpart, overly feared.[79] No national newspaper had in fact been prosecuted under article 227 until late in 1980 with the prosecution of *Le Monde*.[80]

The requirement of pressure (*pressions*) makes article 227 something especially different from the contempt sub judice rule. In his commentary on the article, Professor Vitu states that the word "pressure" must be given the same meaning as "pressure group" in political science, but to fall under the purview of the article the pressure must be "reprehensible," a term that he conveniently leaves unanalyzed.[81] If, however, the concept is defined within the context of an awareness of basic civil liberties, it is not an entirely unmeaningful conceptual tool with which to devise limitations to trial publicity that are both socially defensible and promotive of libertarian values. Taken literally and also in the sense in which it is generally understood, the term denotes no more than the protection of the legal value of the *uncorrupted* functioning of the judicial process. In this respect, the special mention of witnesses, often the most vulnerable of all dramatis personae in emotional trials, is significant. It is submitted that no doctrine of democratic free speech can accommodate the corruption or the pressurization of witnesses, the key elements in the onerous judicial search for truth. The emphasis of this aspect in the French provision puts it apart from its contempt counterparts.

Properly construed with reference to civil libertarian values, only such pressures that amount to threats or intimidation would fall within the reach of the provision. For obvious reasons, a clear and crisp distinction can be made between judges and other professional officers of the administration of justice on the one hand and witnesses and jurors on the other. Only such pressures that would entail a palpable and realistic risk of prejudice to the inherent fairness of the proceedings of a case would then fall under this provision. One can easily conceive of many moral pressures that may conceivably affect the outcome of a case that should very properly be permissible in terms of this approach. The strongly held views of a section of the community on a certain kind of crime would be an obvious and common example. Undoubtedly, there naturally would be borderline situations that constitute the stuff of which future precedents will be made and determine whether the spirit that transpires from the provision will be one of liberty or repression. Conceptually, the provision is a much more nuanced and subtle tool of speech control in the legal domain than sub judice contempt, to which it constitutes a meaningful alternative. However, it was announced in November 1977 that new legislation would be enacted to underpin "the presumption of innocence" of the accused, making it possible to prosecute newspapers that report in a manner that presupposes the guilt of an accused.[82] What is particularly envisaged by the legislation is reporting that does not amount to pressure in terms of article 227 but casts doubt on the innocence of an accused. It is clear that a number of sensational murder cases, in particular that of Patrick Henry, moved the government to take this step, which has been unabashedly compared with the English sub judice contempt law.

Restrictions on Particular Persons Disseminating Trial Information

> *Effective control of [the lawyers on both sides of the case] – concededly within the court's power – might well have prevented the divulgence of inaccurate information, rumors, and accusations that made up much of the inflammatory publicity, at least after Sheppard's indictment. More specifically, the trial court might well have proscribed extrajudicial statements by any lawyer, party, witness, or court official which divulged prejudicial matters.*
>
> From *Sheppard* v. *Maxwell*[83]

Following the virtual demise of gagging writs in the *Nebraska Press Association* case,[84] a new form of sub judice press curb was devised in the United States involving the imposition of certain speech restrictions not on the public or the press but on persons who are directly subject to the control of the court.

In the robust atmosphere pertaining to legal free speech in the United States, statements are sometimes made by certain dramatis personae in a criminal trial that may not only be in bad taste but may also be indicative of inherent unfairness to the defendant. This would in the first place apply to statements of the presiding judicial officers.[85] It would almost seem to speak for itself that statements by judicial officers (including jurors and lay judges) that display a manifest absence of concern for impartiality or for the objectivity and decorum associated with the quest for justice can hardly qualify for protection, although circumstances may well arise in cases of great notoriety where, for instance, certain statements implying technical guilt would be more honest than a sepulchral silence and protestations of lack of bias that manifest dishonesty rather than objectivity. Given the ideal leadership role of judges in Western society, it must always be remembered that judicial officers also have rights of free speech, which rights will (as will be shown in the next chapter) often be grievously inhibited by informal societal taboos and susceptibilities and official difficulties.[86]

The kind of statement by officers of the court or by dramatis personae in the trial that may well be dispensed with are utterances (or behavior) that tend to give the proceedings into a carnival atmosphere, depriving them of the decorum commonly regarded as necessary for the taxing search for justice. It can in fact be said that the carnival cases referred to above[87] really fell short on this ground and not so much on account of being subjected to the penetrating publicity of the media. By contrast, a detailed case study that will be undertaken below[88] of a German cause célèbre that was engulfed in cheap publicity-mongering of the worst kinds will show that, in the absence of carnival behavior in the court or on the part of officers of the court, massive publicity by itself does not necessarily corrode fair trial procedures. Nevertheless, one would expect that for reasons of decorum rather than for fair trial considerations certain forms of verbal discretion would prevail as regards the utterances of judicial officers concerning trial matters, if only to avoid a further burdening of the defendant. Such discretion or detachment does not have to reach the pitch of uninvolved silence, but in the quicksand of the inevitable borderline area the test for judicial officers – as opposed to other dramatis personae – concerning utterances regarding a trial ought to be strict rather than liberal.

It is especially regarding restrictions on the utterances of defense lawyers that genuine free speech considerations arise. Both in the United States and in Germany[89] defense lawyers have traditionally been particularly rich sources of trial publicity in causes célèbres. In the *Sheppard* case, the court proposed "remedial measures that will prevent prejudice [by way of trial publicity] at its inception,"[90] particularly by subjecting counsel, "concededly within the court's power," to what it termed "effective control."[91] It continued: "Collaboration between counsel and the press as to information affecting the fairness of a criminal trial is not only subject to regulation, but is highly censurable and worthy of disciplinary measures."[92]

Partly as a consequence of the censure and recommendations in the *Sheppard* case, the American Bar Association adopted certain "recommendations relating to the conduct of attorneys in criminal cases" within its wider report on *Standards Relating to Fair Trial and Free Press*.[93] The long and somewhat tortuous set of rules[94] incorporating restrictions on the liberty of a lawyer to make certain statements is seemingly at the basis of a number of decisions imposing a mandatory gagging order on lawyers in particular cases. These decisions brought about, in fact if not in theory, the introduction of a diluted but still relatively potent sub judice contempt rule applicable to lawyers.[95] Since the *Nebraska Press Association* case, recourse to this novel and indirect speech control has become quite popular, and in February 1978 it was reported in the New York *Times* that the U.S. Supreme Court had refused to grant certiorari and thus to rule on two such cases of gagging orders that had been imposed on the attorneys of accused in criminal cases.[96]

Apart from circumstances where a lawyer's statements involve a direct interference with the course of justice – an intimidation of potential witnesses would be an obvious and crass example – it must at least be doubted whether these gagging orders on lawyers can stand the test of logic and necessity in a viable system of legal free speech. One is ultimately dealing not so much with the free speech of the lawyer but of the media and hence of the public, and assuming a sound case can be made out for an absence of trial publicity restrictions on the press, the same case can logically be made for a similar absence of restrictions on the statements that attorneys can make for the benefit of the press. What is solely at issue here is the question of the perils to fair trial procedures, not questions of the professional good taste of the lawyer concerned, a matter that may be dealt with in a different forum and largely on other principles. If, in other words, a legal system can without mortal peril to its substance live with trial publicity in the press, it should be able to live with one of the obvious sources of such publicity. The reality must also be faced that in a real life situation it will, in any event, be highly unlikely that such a gag will be effective if the lawyer concerned is determined to pass on information to the press, either directly or through third parties.

Because of the reality repeatedly alluded to in this book that lawyers – together with journalists – constitute one of only two groups in society with a professional interest in the critical scrutiny of the justice administration, the gagging provisions would in most countries constitute serious attentuation of legal free speech. That this is so is clear, especially from the effect that formal speech restrictions on lawyers has had on legal free speech in Germany and from the pervasive nature that informal taboos may have in many societies. In the United States, it is true, legal free speech readily finds outspoken champions in the media, a situation without real counterpart anywhere in the world. Elsewhere, cutting off the free speech of lawyers may well constitute – if effective – a backdoor device for restricting the press generally on legal matters. In any event, it seems incongruous that an accused (or his or her appointed agent or attorney) can by judicial fiat be prevented from expressing him- or herself on *his* or *her* case relating to *his* or *her* liberty in a way that, although barred to the accused is permissible as far as the press is concerned. Unless the principle, not entirely unknown to be sure but certainly not unchallenged, is pushed to unendurable lengths that the press has rights in excess of those of the citizenry,[97] there seems no merit in curbing a person (but not the press) from speaking out when his or her own liberty is in question before the courts. Poison – if it be such – can surely not be rendered socially safe merely because it is filtered through a journalist's copy. Indeed, it seems probable that publicity emanating from the accused's lawyer would almost inevitably be more germane to the issues in the trial and hence socially more relevant than media publicity in general emanating from other sources. Only under exceptional circumstances would the dice not be loaded in favor of the prosecution, and media publicity emanating from the defense may at least slightly correct this imbalance.

There is, however, a largely unspoken and indefinable premise on which the arguments advanced here, and indeed all arguments in favor of a relaxed attitude toward trial publicity presented in this work, are based: the need either for an unpoisoned social atmosphere in which a trial itself takes place, or alternatively, the undoubted ability of the judicial and other authorities within the administration of justice to cope with a critical or even poisoned social atmosphere, whether occasioned by publicity or otherwise. It is no doubt possible that extracurial publicity campaigns, fanned or inspired by defense lawyers, may contribute to or even cause substantial miscarriages of justice in their actual effect on the court proceedings, as many kangaroo court judgments not so long ago in the American South involving racial matters prove. Under those circumstances, one may be able to justify even the most vigorous and draconian sub judice restrictions in the rather forlorn hope that they would contribute to a defusing of the poisoned atmosphere in court. In such a case, there is really little hope of achieving justice in any ordinary sense of the word, and a legal system where such measures are imposed may just as well underline its inability in that respect by enacting and enforcing oppressive speech restrictions in the field of trial publicity.

Nevertheless, there is a narrow category of circumstances applicable to lawyers and others that in any country would justify serious speech restrictions and sanctions. These circumstances would involve what may be broadly termed obstructions to the course of justice. What is envisaged here is not the amorphous and amoebic institution of that name in English law,[98] but that which may cause serious miscarriages of justice by the illegal disclosure of certain facts or the making of certain statements that cause an *irremediable* or *substantial* impairment of the possibility of either a fair trial or the achievement of justice. Statements that may fall in this category would be those amounting to a threat or an improper inducement to witnesses or officials to act contrary to their legal duties; those that would lead to the perpetration or the concealment of crimes; and those that would disclose information legitimately protected by the law, such as the content of police records and investigation reports. The limited case law on the subject of attorneys' gagging orders in the United States does not suggest that these narrow and vital considerations played a role. It is clear that the major consideration was simply the circumvention of the virtual ban on newspaper gagging orders. As suggested by a New York *Times* report on the subject, the consideration of the U.S. Supreme Court has been to achieve "a kind of trade-off": "[P]rint what you have, the Court is saying [to newspapers], but we will try to keep secret what you don't."[99]

Unlike celestial justice, courtroom justice remains justice by and for people, and in the final analysis nothing more than human justice with its built-in imperfections can ever be expected. At the basis of all sub judice regulations (of which attorney gagging orders are but a novel variant), there is, however, a notion that some isolation from stimuli from outside the courtroom is a prerequisite for an approximation of the ideal of perfect justice. So, for instance, did the Warren Commission on the assassination of President Kennedy also opine that a fair trial for Oswald would have been unlikely as a consequence of the massive publicity surrounding his arrest.[100] It is submitted that a fundamental error of thinking is at fault for that view, widely supported as it may be in the most respectable of circles. Fairness here is confused with pristine ignorance of the facts and absence of prejudged views – in most instances a situation that will have nothing to do with the humanly taxing task of the pursuit of justice. Moreover, in certain European jurisdictions – Germany being one – judicial officers in fact start that onerous pursuit with precisely the same situation of exposure to the risk of prejudgment because the full record of the investigations and previous convictions of the accused is available to them. In these societies, the hopes and aspirations of society are put where they rightly belong: on the fearless and robust independence of the judicial officers concerned. Therefore, it is not farfetched to submit, especially as far as the United States is concerned, that the continuous tinkering with trial publicity restrictions, including the new form of selective gagging orders, has detracted attention from the area where the major danger to justice will always lie with or without these restrictions: the quality of the judicial process, including the jury.

Concerning restrictions on other persons within the administration of justice, the same considerations as those just described do not necessarily apply. Police officials and prosecutors are particularly important in this regard. Apart from jury trials where the danger exists – at least in terms of popular beliefs and judicial pronouncements – that an extracurial poisoning of the jurors' minds cannot ever be undone, there is the seemingly unanswerable consideration that, if a legal system can live with carte blanche as far as trial publicity in the media is concerned, it should also be able to live with statements originating from these other sources. However, certain considerations unrelated to an ultimate fair trial may militate strongly in favor not only of inhibitions but even of outright bans on dissemination of information (and particularly sensational and speculative information) by these persons and agencies.

Despite their undoubtedly partisan role of "getting their man," police officers and prosecutors also have a wider role within which to consider their duties: that of guarantors of justice both toward suspects, accused, and convicts as well as toward the reputation of uninvolved persons and the administration of justice. Despite the obvious need to keep the public informed about crime detection, there seems under normal circumstances to be no reason that demands that these officers should also constitute press informers or press agents. In most instances, simple considerations of professional decorum should inhibit and prohibit them from assuming such a role. Concerning those cases that displayed a kind of official exhibitionism – the Oswald arrest and surrounding events after the murder of President Kennedy is a telling and monstrous example – considerations of simple justice demand that these officers respect certain basic rights, including personality rights, of the suspect or the accused. Society at large can demand of such officers as it can of judges and jurors that they would not fail to contribute to the attainment of a calm atmosphere surrounding one of humanity's most difficult tasks: the search for justice in a court of law. Part of that search involves the duty of those engaging in it to behave responsibly, decorously and fairly. In essence, one is dealing here more with a problem of intelligent public relations than with a problem related to the free press-fair trial debate.

Voluntary Media Codes

All the news that's fit to print.

Daily caption of the New York *Times*

Not all the news and all the stories that may be legal or interesting to print or broadcast ought to be printed or broadcasted if regard is given to standards of decency, discretion, decorum, fairness, and justice that one would associate with civilized forms of government and behavior. This is true also of news involving the administration of justice. In what follows, attention will primarily be focused on the role of the press, although most considerations would apply with equal, if not greater, force to other media, especially television.

One of the consequences raised by the realization that certain matters are not in the public domain is the institution of press codes enforced by press councils who would "keep their own house in order." These codes relate to trial reporting.

The essential backdrop to the institution of press councils as a partial solution to the problem under discussion is the realization, on the one hand, that what Justice Learned Hand called the "black art of publicity"[101] has assumed an increasingly pervasive nature, reaching out with a potency into the lives and minds of entire populations and their decision-making processes, although it is controlled by relatively small groups of individuals who are not necessarily disinterested philanthropists or practicing democrats. On the other hand, there is also the fact that the livelihood and basic personality rights of individuals also occupy an important place in the hierarchy of social values in a democratic society. Coupled to this fact, there is the bitter experience that under the banner of free speech these personality rights can easily become victims to a quest for sensation for its own sake without any meaningful promotion of indentifiable or overriding social considerations.

As far as trial reporting generally is concerned, the rationale of a voluntary press code enforced by a press council can be summarized by an invasion of the famous daily caption of the New York *Times*: *not* all the news concerning legal matters is fit and worthy to be printed, and a press council must, in the interest of both the reputation of the press and of other essential democratic values, guard against an overreach into spheres in which the public either has no real interest or where such interest is outweighed by society's interest in allowing the individual a domain in which sovereignty and privacy can be retained. Underlying this rationale, there also are the two interrelated notions that the journalistic profession is a better and more socially alert arbiter of its own activities and ideals than legal processes and prohibitions and that problems of social balancing are often better solved before they reach the stage of legal adjudication.[102]

The major and almost exclusive function of a press code and press council within the legal domain would be to lay down guidelines and interpret such guidelines with the backing of some professional sanctions of a meaningful magnitude as regards the publication or otherwise, or the publication in a particular mode, of information relating to individuals enmeshed in litigation. The basic problem confronting press councils in the legal domain is to balance the social interest of having an unrestricted "free trade in ideas"[103] on the one hand and certain primary expectations relating to a fair trial and privacy on the part of the individual on the other. It is especially the fair trial expectation that in recent times has received attention concerning trial publicity in the United States, whereas it would seem that the more important danger of irremediable damage to the interests of the individual is to be found under the second category of expectations. By contrast, the free speech-fair trial debate in Germany has to a significant extent been focused on the privacy aspect.[104]

What has been said above about the narrow category of cases relating to obstructions to the course of justice that may merit the existence and enforcement of legal speech restrictions[105] would apply with even greater force to the self-controlling duties of the press. However, beyond this narrow category of circumstances so imperatively demanding a certain form of inhibitive restrictions and sanctions, there may well be other categories of circumstances into which a press that regards itself as being committed to certain forms of fairness and decency would only venture in instances of extreme social necessity. Many of these circumstances may be covered peripherally by certain aspects of the English sub judice rule, although that rule in the excessive form of its general application would bear little resemblance to the application of a responsible press code of the kind tentatively advocated here. Of basic importance would be the recognition by the press that its reporting in the legal domain can involve fundamental rights and expectations of individuals and that the invasion thereof can only be entertained under exceptional, if any, circumstances. Without any attempt being made here to be exhaustive, one can easily think of a number of restrictions that the press can impose and enforce on itself without in any way unduly endangering free speech and free access to information in the legal domain. Four categories of restrictions readily spring to mind.

Decorum of Proceedings

> *This is a court, not a circus.*
>
> Common courtroom saw

Difficult as it would be to define the borderlines, one would expect that a responsible press would attempt to protect the decorum of the proceedings and refrain from indulging in reporting and activities that would tend, without real and urgent social justification, either to render the search for justice more onerous or to brutalize the persons involved in that search. One would expect that, unless serious social cause exists for more sensational forms of reporting, the press would avoid building up a climate that would manifestly impede the search for justice around trials and their preparations. In short, one would expect a responsible press to behave in a way that an individual journalist would expect others and the media to behave if such a journalist were to be on trial for his or her own liberty.

The Dignity of the Accused and of Other Persons
and Their Claim to Human Compassion

> *The dignity of man is inviolable. To respect and protect it is the duty of all state power.*
>
> Article 1 of the German Constitution

The question of trial publicity has traditionally been almost exclusively seen in the context of the endangerment of an accused person's right to a fair trial, with little or no concern being expended on the fact that certain forms of publicity really constitute the modern version of the pillory, with the consequence of profound dangers to the basic personality rights of the individual. In a society where the freedom to speak and publish is matched by the responsibility to maintain basic standards of fairness and compassionate decency, one would expect that the media, with due regard being given to society's information rights in matters of substantial public importance, would endeavor to avoid impinging more than what is absolutely necessary on an individual's essentially private domain or sense of decency. This would probably be so as regards matters pertaining to the individual's sexual sphere where society has no real interest in such information, even where such information has some relevance to a trial. In a detailed case study of the *Ingrid van Bergen* murder trial in Germany and the attendant trial publicity, we will see below that a considerable amount of the publicity generated around that case served no societal right to information and could well have been dispensed with, not in the interest of a fair trial but in the interest of simple decency to the personality rights of the persons involved, including the accused.

In perhaps the only instance where the South African legislature has generated a press restriction with social merit, a ban was put on the publication of the names and the evidence in divorce proceedings – matters that had previously been a particularly rich and ready source for massive and socially irrelevant press coverage of the most salacious nature.[106] It is submitted that this ban could have been avoided if press reporting had voluntarily refrained from identifying parties in divorce proceedings where lurid personal and especially sexual details were brought into the open. A similar ban – generally applicable only to the identity of minors and certain victims in most countries – would on social balance also seem to be appropriate in such criminal cases where intimate sexual details concerning victims, witnesses, and the accused are involved, unless overwhelming social reasons compellingly dictate otherwise – for example, through the use of violence or as a consequence of the particular position of the accused. The almost total carte blanche given the media in the United States as regards public persons would, however, on this basis not always and necessarily be acceptable. In this regard, it is instructive to recall how in the *Lebach* judgment of the German *Bundesverfassungsgericht*[107] that court went so far as to protect the privacy of a convicted criminal who was about to be released after serving his sentence, on the basis inter alia of his legitimate expectations of being reintegrated into society.[108]

Whatever hesitation there may well be concerning the preservation of the anonymity of an accused, one would expect that irrelevant and undue invasions of privacy of uninvolved relatives and acquaintances of the accused or convicted persons would only be justified under the most exceptional circumstances. One would likewise expect that a special effort would be made to respect the privacy and the dignity of witnesses, often the persons with the most thankless and even dangerous task in the judicial process. The undue exposure of certain witnesses' private or even business life to the glare of pervasive publicity may also result in a reluctance by such witnesses to come forward with their evidence or to be less than cooperative. In even greater need of genuine protection against invasions of privacy are the victims of crimes and their families, whose need and right to society's understanding ought to find a ready echo in a responsible press.

One would further expect that a certain measure of discretion would prevail concerning the naming of suspects and witnesses under certain circumstances. In most legal systems, there are obligatory rules concerning the naming of juveniles, rules that may well under certain circumstances be applied in other cases, especially in relation to highly private matters and to the victims of certain embarrassing crimes.

Obligation to Exercise Discretion and Caution When the Protection of Vital Private and Societal Interests Are at Stake

> *The forces allied against the individual have never been greater.*
> Supreme Court Justice William O. Douglas

Rare as it may be, it is not difficult to conceive of circumstances where even a total news blackout on legal matters can be justified, as happened in recent times in Germany during the Mogadishu raid to free hijacked passengers and the kidnapping of the industrial leader Hans Schleyer in 1977. In October 1977, the mother of a kidnapped child successfully petitioned a Hamburg court for an injunction requiring all local newspapers to refrain from publishing any story on the kidnapping for five days.[109] Voluntary cooperation with police authorities in delaying publication of a story to assist crime detection is a feature not uncommon in the responsible press of most countries. One would think that apart from legal aspects – and this case clearly belongs to that narrow category of cases where trial publicity can be legitimately curbed to ward off irremediable harm to vital interests of society – this kind of ban must also automatically flow from any code of conduct of a press that is responsive to the needs of a free society. Strangely enough, a number of Hamburg papers opposed the granting of the injunction. One would expect that in most countries the ethical dictates of the journalistic ethos would demand that under these circumstances free speech considerations should temporarily make way for considerations of fundamental justice. In most instances, the only social price that would be payable would be a delay in the publication of a story.

Obligation to Avoid Brutalization of Society

Is that really necessary?

Moving now into an area of considerable dissension, there may well be a case for not countenancing the publication of everything to do with the legal domain, although no particularly identifiable social interest would be involved. For instance, pictorial depictions of gory details of crimes of violence, victims of violence, and exceptional brutality may well qualify for a self-imposed ban, backed possibly by professional sanctions for no particular reason beyond their social obscenity and their possibly brutalizing effect on individuals.

Voluntary Press Control: The German Model

The law can guarantee a free press, but it is incapable of guaranteeing a fair press.

John A. Ritter and Mathew Leibowitz[110]

Although unable to back its discipline with meaningful sanctions since it can merely issue a *Rüge* or censure, the Press Code (*Pressekodex*) of the German Press Council[111] contains a number of interesting provisions pertaining to trial publicity. These provisions are of particular interest because there are really no effective legal restrictions whatever on trial publicity in Germany. The three provisions in the code of fifteen principles concerning trial publicity relate to the protection of the privacy and intimate sphere of individuals and especially of uninvolved persons[112]; the depiction of unduly brutalizing scenes of violence and the protection of juveniles[113]; and the public prejudgment of defendants with special reference to the protection of juveniles.[114]

In terms of these broad publicity principles (*publizistische Grundsätze*) the German Press Council issues guidelines (*Richtlinien*) from time to time of which one, that of April 29, 1958, has elaborated on principle 12 as regards trial publicity. This guideline sets out what may be seen as the ideal in media coverage of trials, but as even a cursory reading of some German newspapers would show it is observed largely in the breach. It reads:

> The object of court reporting is to enable the public to obtain unbiased information by means of careful and nonpartisan reports. The press must therefore in its reports and headlines avoid taking a one-sided, tendentious or prejudicial position whether it be before or during court proceedings and it must refrain from publishing anything which may be calculated to impair either the impartiality of persons involved in the proceedings or the independent judgment of the court. Criticism and commentaries after judgment should be visibly separate from the actual report of the proceedings and a crisp distinction should be drawn between mere suspicion and proven guilt.[115]

Having no power to enforce its decisions and largely lacking the prestige that would be necessary to constitute an effective check on abuse to press freedom in the legal domain, the German Press Council cannot be considered as an adequate instrumentality of control. Since its inception, the German Press Council has endeavored to stress the protection of the rights of personality of the dramatis personae that flow from the power of the press and have been less concerned with threats to the independence of the judicial processes.[116] It is especially in this sphere in which the individual may at times be particularly defenseless against the power of the media to create impressions or impart hints that can never again be eradicated that the essential role of the press council must be sought in a viable democracy. There is no indication that it fulfills this task in Germany, especially in relation to what is called the boulevard press, with its heavy concentration on scandal.[117] In this respect, the reporting techniques of *Der Spiegel* – to be discussed in some detail below – constitutes something of a paragon in the Western world in its compassionate understanding of an unpopular and exposed defendant's interest in the protection of his personality rights.

In contrast to the German Press Council's concern with the protection of individual rights, the press council in South Africa has been used – and wittingly or unwittingly has allowed itself to be so used – to protect governmental authorities from embarrassment in relation to certain justice administration matters, especially in relation to abuse of security legislation. The lamentable record of the South African Press Council in understanding press freedom in the legal domain within its Western context[118] has no further importance here beyond underlining the need for a press council to be manned by people who are endowed not only with formal independence – in South Africa, the chairman for a considerable period of time has been an ex-judge of the Supreme Court of Jewish extraction with no overt links with the ruling white establishment – but also with a robust spiritual independence in the widest sense. It follows that the best, albeit necessarily imperfect, guarantee for such independence would be a body consisting of representatives of the media and a number of knowledgeable outsiders (not necessarily lawyers), not of persons appointed by governmental fiat. Such a body would in all likelihood be alive on the one hand to the demands of free speech in relation to the use of power in the legal domain and, on the other hand, to the responsibilities with which the power of the media ought to be wielded in relation to the highly penetrable domain of the vulnerable individual.

The British Press Council, established in 1953, interestingly and by contrast to the German model issues guidelines on specific complaints only and on the basis of undefined principles of equity. These guidelines may vary with the changing mood and the evolving needs of society. Apart from representative members of the press, it consists also of some twenty lay members and an independent chairman.[119]

Ultimately, even press councils working under broad and democratically inspired criteria would not necessarily be the panacea to so-called First Amendment problems relating to the ability and wisdom to balance the personality rights of litigants with societal demands of free speech and information.[120] If too powerful and too establishment minded, as is undoubtedly the case in South Africa, a press council can very easily become a vehicle for transferring the unreasonable and socially damaging inhibitions and restrictions from the legal level to the professional level, leading almost invariably to a debilitating degree of self-censorship on the part of the press. Where a press council is devoid of any real power (as in Germany), it will inevitably run the risk of becoming a piece of decorative trimming on the journalistic landscape.

TOTAL ABSENCE OF TRIAL PUBLICITY RESTRICTIONS IN LAW

[A] defendant is entitled to a fair trial but not a perfect one.
Justice Minton in the *Lutwak* case[121]

On a purely analytical basis, the total or semitotal absence of trial publicity prohibitions is the most dramatic alternative to sub judice restrictions. There is such a situation only in a few countries, if one includes indirect or informal restrictions. The one salient example is the United States, where the residual presence of inhibiting devices and their possible efficacy in limited areas do not affect the overall situation, so that it has become practically meaningless to talk of trial publicity restrictions. This is particularly true where trials of public or political significance are concerned. The trials, for instance, of the Son of Sam murderer in New York, the Watergate personalities, and Patty Hearst are symptomatically telling in this regard.

The Watergate trials constitute a watershed of sorts in the American experience relating to trial publicity, since they effectively swept away any lingering publicity restraints without causing, it would seem, any serious doubt regarding their inherent fairness and, hence, their constitutionality. This acceptance of the fairness of these and similar trials flows not from an indifference to the rights of public figures to a fair trial – an argument put forward in certain quarters[122] – but from an apparent realization that the fairness of a trial must be based on more durable foundations than formal speech restrictions. That certain forms of trial publicity can influence judicial decision making is probably not in dispute, but apart from that narrow category of cases previously alluded to where a real obstruction of the course of justice is involved, the general realization seems to be that in a society based on the free trade of ideas such influencing is part of the democratic scenery and that there is no inherent linkage between fairness and pervasive trial publicity. An indication of the arrival of the United States at this juncture is the judgment of the Fifth Circuit in the appeal against the reversal of the conviction of Lieutenant Calley, who commanded the American troops during the infamous My Lai massacre during the Vietnam War. Said the Fifth Circuit: "[T]he military court did the best it could to control publicity."[123] No more can be expected of any court.

The idea that all possible precautions against unfairness and bias must be taken on a level other than the legal imposition of trial publicity restrictions is nowhere better translated into reality than in Germany, and it is to the situation in that country concerning the various aspects of trial publicity that we now turn our attention.

Trial Publicity in Germany: A Case Study

The problem of achieving a satisfactory system of reporting of crime and criminal proceedings resides especially therein that on the one hand any kind of censorship must be avoided so that the gravamen of the control of such reporting would lie in the voluntary self-control of the information media (press, radio and television). On the other hand there exists in most countries a certain kind of press which is financially very strong and which to some extent exists from sensational crime reporting and from unfactual reporting of criminal trials with the result that one cannot at all expect any comprehension for any voluntary self-control which is directed at the achievement of objectivity.

Professor Hans-Heinrich Jescheck[124]

Of all the countries in Europe, Germany affords the observer with the most interesting case study of a situation where a well-nigh total speech freedom reigns as regards trial publicity. Germany also constitutes the one country in the world – apart from the United States – where there is an unquestioned willingness on the part of the working press to refer to any matter that forms the subject of litigation and where no real attempt is made, either formal or informal, to curb such freedom of speech. Therefore, if there is any substance to the charge that so-called trial by newspaper constitutes a fatal impediment to justice, the perils of such unbridled freedom should be very apparent in Germany.

The situation relating to pretrial and trial publicity in Germany is broadly similar to that of the United States after the virtual demise of gagging orders, but there are a number of differences. Some of the differences and similarities will be alluded to here as backdrop to a study of the German situation.

The contemporary situation in Germany and in America regarding trial publicity, at least in the postwar period, developed from essentially different legal and social backgrounds. In the United States, the melody of the ancient contempt institution was still lingering on, and as late as 1941 in the case of *Bridges* v. *California*[125] there were still three justices[126] on the Supreme Court who sided with Justice Felix Frankfurter in his strong dissent over the constitutionality of contempt.[127] The melody, as we have seen in a previous chapter, continued to linger on for a long time in such practices as gagging orders on newspapers and still does peripherally in the present practice of subjecting defendants and/or their lawyers to such orders to cut off potential sources of trial publicity.

In Germany, on the other hand, the free speech provision in the 1949 constitution was immediately interpreted *in practice* as an insuperable barrier to any possible attempt to introduce *any* form of restriction on trial publicity. In one instance, short shrift was made of an attempt to obtain the recusal of jurors in a murder trial because they had read newspaper articles that clearly presupposed the guilt of the accused, the rejection of the recusal application being upheld by the *Bundesgerichtshof*.[128] Said the latter court: "One must assume that the lay judge will know and uphold his duty to prevent such publicity from influencing him and to arrive at his opinion only on the basis of the proceedings in court."[129]

However, the situation of absolute freedom of speech in relation to trial publicity has not been unquestioned. One of the country's most respected legal academics, Eberhard Schmidt, raised a number of fundamental objections as far back as 1947,[130] and in one of the seminal documents on the topic, *Justiz und Publizistik*, he returned to the topic two decades later with a spirited and outspoken dissent concerning unfettered trial publicity.[131]

The presence of a single legal system in Germany – as opposed to the constitutional proliferation in the United States – greatly facilitates an overview of the German situation both in a legal and a societal context. In addition, there is the significant fact that the most important journals and newspapers all enjoy a wide national or at least supraregional coverage. Therefore, contrary to the situation in the United States, where a gagging writ may still be imposed in clear violation of the spirit of the constitutional guidelines,[132] or where the news media of a particular region may in their coverage of trials differ totally from the news media in other regions and jurisdictions, the situation in Germany is infinitely simpler, less contradictory, and more amenable to analysis. A news magazine like *Der Spiegel*, for instance,[133] is read by almost *every* legislator and important opinion maker in the country and in all likelihood also by the vast majority of judges.[134] Therefore, when a publication like *Der Spiegel* – and to a lesser extent one of the three or four major dailies or a weekly such as *Die Zeit*[135] – adopts a certain approach toward comments on the administration of justice, its impact is instantaneously felt in every single legal and judicial nerve center of the country. Likewise, if the most widely read national exponent of the so-called "boulevard press," *Das Bild*, or a national family magazine such as *Der Stern*, indulges either in the most lurid and descriptive sensationalism concerning a court case or in the most caustic but reasoned comments about the conduct or finding of a judge of a trial in progress, the report is read and talked about in literally every part of the nation. In addition, the country's national television service covers the whole country with the same information – including occasional information and commentaries on pending and proceeding trials. All these factors combine to give the German media an infinitely greater influence over the country *as a whole*, including obviously the judiciary and lay judges or jurors, compared with the media in the United States.

Another significant difference between the American and German situation as far as trial publicity is concerned is that in the United States the consensus of criticism toward trial publicity is directed at the undermining of the *fairness* of the trial procedures, whereas in Germany a substantial part of the critique is directed at the undermining of the *personality rights* of the persons involved in criminal trials, especially of defendants. It will be recalled that in the *Lebach* judgment of the Federal Constitutional Court[136] the personality rights of a prisoner who was about to be released were given precedence over the rights of the public to information and free speech about the crime concerned. The jurisprudential basis of the *Lebach* judgment – a judgment that as such is not pertinent to the question of trial publicity restrictions – is also basic to the spirited lament of Professor Eberhard Schmidt on the absence of sub judice restrictions in Germany. In his critique,[137] Schmidt lambastes the practice of permitting the photographing of the accused in court as a basic infringement of the accused German person's personality – especially his or her dignity – as guaranteed in the German constitution.[138] Regarding excessive trial publicity – especially of the kind that is concerned with a newspaper's own investigation and assessment of facts – Professor Schmidt bases his criticism partly on undermining of the accused's *Menschenwürde* or human dignity, especially in relation to the protection of the individual's reputation.[139]

As for the salient features of the German situation concerning the limits of trial publicity, one can sum up the position with reference to a number of distinctions: first, the distinction between the legal position and the actual position; second, the distinction in practice between the mainstream quality press and the mass circulation boulevard press; third, within the quality press, the distinction between a small group of periodicals that take a burning interest in legal matters, including trials, and the others – the vast majority – that generally show a remarkable lack of incisive concern for such matters, a predisposition reflected in low-key trial publicity; and finally, the distinction between a pious expression of theoretical concern and disquiet by many commentators about certain journalistic phenomena in a particular type of publication on the one hand and the acceptance by the very same people – and by society in general – of the status quo toward other comparable phenomena in respectable publications.

The legal position of criminal sanctions relating to trial publicity in Germany can be simply stated: there is in reality no direct restriction prohibiting commentary of any kind regarding pending or proceeding litigation. Such restrictions that do exist relating to certain kinds of comments about certain aspects of litigation are based either on societal or professional considerations or, at most, on vague and (as far as the press is concerned) essentially meaningless legal considerations based on the protection of certain personality rights of the litigants. However, this well-nigh limitless freedom to publish almost anything concerning pending or progressing trials is only one side of the coin, and although that freedom is manifested in the willingness of a number of news media to go almost any length in their covering or uncovering of the news behind a trial, it is contradicted again by the practice of the majority of quality news media. These quality or mainstream news media will generally speaking refrain from the kind of intensive publicity in which the more venal boulevard press would at times indulge in relation to certain types of criminal trials. Indeed, there is ample ground for criticism that these quality papers are indeed far too reticent in their reporting of contentious or sensational trials. These newspapers in fact display a similarly cautious attitude toward general reporting on controversial legal issues.[140]

However, there is, as will be noted below, a small number of quality publications – notably *Der Spiegel*, *Die Zeit*, and, on a different level, *Der Stern* – that not only indulge in vigorously iconoclastic reporting on legal matters and personalities[141] but also from time to time ignore many customary restraints and subject certain trials, while pending or still in progress, to a kind of publicity that would be unheard of not only in the contempt jurisdictions but even in other contempt-free European jurisdictions, such as France, the Netherlands, Scandinavia, Italy, or Spain.

The principle that the German news media should refrain from any commentary or analysis that may influence the outcome of a trial is not only contained in a relatively oft-expressed academic wish but, as we have seen, is actually enshrined in a guideline of the German press code, enacted by the

German Press Council. However, as indicated above, this sanguine expression of principle and theory is starkly contradicted in some form or at some time or another by the practice of all major newspapers and the electronic news media. Indeed, on the basis of the regular contradiction of this guideline in the practice of the German news media, it came as no surprise to me to find that most lawyers, both academic and practicing, whom I addressed on the topic were substantially oblivious of the very existence of these guidelines and even of the German Press Council and that without exception they expressed the view that the guideline is a mere *brutum fulmen*.[142] The undeniable correctness of this reaction will presently be examined. It must be stressed again that the German Press Council has no more than moral authority, and not a very strong one at that, consisting of the possibility of issuing a so-called *Rüge* or admonishment. This authority is of such little practical consequence that a *Rüge* issued by the council would not even be reported in the daily press – not even by the offending newspaper![143]

There is widespread theoretical, and mostly academic, concern in Germany about the absence of limitations on trial publicity. As is also the case in the United States, the problem is considered only within the context of criminal matters, because only criminal matters really catch the fascination of the public.[144] That any dangers that may obtrude vis-à-vis criminal trials will also do so in the civil sphere is obvious, although it would seem that there has been no recognition whatever of this reality in Germany. Of even greater relevance in the German situation, but equally undiscussed and unpondered, is the vast jurisdiction of the administrative courts and of the Federal Constitutional Court. The subjects decided in these jurisdictions are not only of immense import to all citizens but they are often also of a highly controversial nature, touching on many raw nerves of sociopolitical and economic realities. This has particularly become the case as far as the *Bundesverfassungsgericht* with its ever-expanding social engineering role is concerned.[145] There has been no visible concern in Germany over the possibility that on the basis of the reasoning inherent in the debate on trial publicity concerning criminal cases in Anglo-Saxon countries, there may well be an even greater danger of a corrupting pressure being brought to bear on these courts. It is perhaps possible to explain the absence of any apparent concern concerning the ability to influence those courts either on the basis of the undoubted prestige that the judges enjoy on the one hand – a prestige that is no longer unquestioned[146] – and, more cynically, on the widely accepted notion that as a consequence of the "political" nature of the jurisdiction of administrative courts and the constitutional court judicial lawmaking is entirely shot through with extraneous influences![147]

Specifically, when a matter is referred to the Federal Constitutional Court for adjudication, it has almost invariably already been the subject of widespread public debate and heated political controversy. While the court is seized of the matter, the controversy continues unabatedly. In at least one recent instance, the mere decision of the Organization of German Employers to take the highly controversial matter of state-ordained *Mitbestimmung* (that is, the participation of employees in decision making in private enterprises) to the constitutional court for adjudication led to industrial unrest and even threats of strikes. It is difficult to believe that such threats, quite apart from the publicity surrounding them, would not potentially weigh heavily on an individual judge at least as much as would a campaign of massive publicity surrounding a criminal trial, with the one essential difference being that the effect of such publicity in the former case would not only influence one individual but may influence the basic distribution of power in the state as a whole. In this particular matter,[148] as well as in matters such as the abolition of compulsory military conscription,[149] the use of government money for propaganda purposes during election time,[150] the inquiring into the constitutional legitimacy of the treaties with East Germany on the status and definition of German nationals,[151] and the extension of decision-making powers within universities to nonacademics and nonprofessional members of staff,[152] the atmosphere in which the court had to adjudicate was charged with emotions, dissension, and bitter controversy. Nonetheless, no serious academic or practical argument was advanced impugning the integrity of the decisions on the basis of the massive amount of emotionally charged publicity preceding these and many other landmark decisions. It seems that as far as this court is concerned a mature attitude prevails that is worthy of a mature society: that, when one is dealing with judges of integrity and spiritual independence, more rather than less information would better serve the cause of the liberty of society. It must nevertheless be conceded that my search in the extensive newspaper archives of the *Bundesverfassungsgericht* in Karlsruhe produced no example of any *direct* appeal to the court in any quality newspaper to decide a matter in a particular way. Undoubtedly such appeals have been made.

The philosophy behind the reticence prescribed by the guidelines of the German Press Council was actually incorporated in an official draft for a new German criminal code in 1962.[153] That particular provision was never translated into law, but the mere fact that a kind of contempt of law rule was officially advocated and even elaborated by the German Penal Reform Commission did much to warm the hearts of many critics of the situation in Germany regarding trial and pretrial publicity.[154] The provision, which need not be discussed here,[155] would have been very far-reaching and would, at least in its outward form, in most respects have been similar to the institution of sub judice contempt in England. Interestingly, one writer suggested that the contempt instrumentality would somehow not have suited the German judicial mentality, inexperienced as it is by comparison to its English counterpart with its long and continuing tradition in that field[156] – a statement probably more relevant as an unintentionally accurate description of the proclivities of the English judiciary than as an assessment of German potential in that area!

The German Press Council sub judice guideline, as stated, is not fully observed by any major news medium, not even by the so-called quality newspapers. However, the problem of potentially prejudicial trial reporting is customarily focused only on the mass circulation boulevard press, on the tacit but erroneous assumption that the responsible press in Germany would refrain from indulging in practices of such kind. When writing about excessive trial publicity – in this case particularly as regards the use of pictures of the accused in criminal trials – Professor Eberhard Schmidt issued a generous certificate of good conduct to certain members of the mainstream German press.[157] However, as any reader of the mainstream German newspapers during the long and agonizing period in which the cases of the so-called Baader-Meinhof gang made their cumbersome way through the courts would know, there was often no such reticence in relation to these cases. There also is no inherent reticence on the part, for instance, of *Der Spiegel* when it comes to reporting on trial or pretrial issues. Although it would be impossible to assess or quantify the effect of a scathing report of *Der Spiegel* – a journal that has succeeded in bringing down a number of ministers in its day by its vigorous reporting and disclosures – on a judge, jury, or witness, it is certainly fair to assume that its potential effect is infinitely greater than that of even the most lurid exponent of the boulevard press, which would undoubtedly be taken much less seriously by people in authority (if they are read at all) and possibly even by people in the street. Probably because of the high quality of its reporting, *Der Spiegel* seems to have totally escaped any serious criticism on the basis of constituting a possible source of extraneous influences that would be corrosive to the intrinsic requirements of justice.[158] In what follows, a tentative survey will be attempted of trial reporting in sections of the quality press, followed by a case study of reporting in the boulevard press.

In surveying the trial reporting of *Der Spiegel* over a period of two years, I had no difficulty in finding numerous examples of articles and reports that patently contradict the guidelines of the German Press Council and would constitute clear cases of contempt in England. These articles to a lesser or greater extent all display a willingness to scrutinize or comment on material that are or will be subject matter in trials. A few examples will illustrate the point.

When writing about a murder trial that had just started, *Der Spiegel* reported Gerhard Mauz[159] excoriated the presiding judge for "destroying the atmosphere" and being unreasonable and obstinate.[160] Mauz goes on to demand the dismissal of the judge for bias but concludes: "But these applications, we are sure, will be rejected." The reporter then proceeds to attack the evidence of the police and states categorically that one of the accused refrained from using his weapon at the time of the crime when he clearly could have done so. Somewhat curiously he then states: "However let us not anticipate the finding of the court much as we are disturbed by the irregularities and the contradictions!"

From this report, chosen from a host of possible examples, one can identify a number of rather typical characteristics of legal reporting in *Der Spiegel*. First, there is theoretical concern in the journal about media prejudgment of trial issues that constitute subjects on which a court has to adjudicate,[161] but a concern predicated on the willingness at times to throw inhibitions in this regard to the wind and to say what it believes has to be said in the interest of justice. Second,

Der Spiegel can always be counted on, despite public hysteria, to speak the unspeakable and to mention the unmentionable. In this case the trial concerned persons connected with the urban terrorist scene in Germany and specifically involved the death of a policeman – "a trial which is concerned with the violent death of a policeman is not just any old case." This trial took place in the midst of general press speculation as regards the guilt of the accused. In this atmosphere, *Der Spiegel* dared to question the popular assumptions concerning the accused and to give its own interpretation of the facts. Third, as it often does when the occasion presents itself, *Der Spiegel* does not hesitate to go for the judicial jugular vein of an apparently insensitive judge, criticizing not only his law but also his humanity. Concern for the weak is a particular characteristic of the magazine's legal reporting. Fourth, *Der Spiegel* can always be counted on to publish well-researched articles, descending at times into the depths of both legal and philosophical discussion and imbued by the transparent desire to educate society in the finer points of justice and the law. Finally, apart from its obvious interest in the personalities of the court, *Der Spiegel* would at times take to task all the other personalities involved in a case: the witnesses (as in this case), the prosecution, and also the defense.[162]

Apart from circumstances relating to a cause célèbre or to a trial engulfed in public emotions, it is also usual to find *Der Spiegel* reporting week after week on interesting trials that will usually escape the interest of the national dailies. Although it is not difficult to detect in such reporting a concern *not* to prejudge either legal or factual issues, many exceptions prove this rule. In many of these exceptions, comments and criticism are directed at *judgments* at the termination of court proceedings that in any event would not be covered by the German Press Council's guideline, since the cutoff point of the latter's reach is judgment of the first instance. However, whenever circumstances militate in favor of aggressive scrutiny of the proceedings of a trial that is still in progress, there is no hesitation to publish even the most outspoken criticism or value judgments. So, for example, we find in one instance a detailed legal analysis and criticism of an interim judgment on the rights of a prosecutor concerning the choice of the appropriate legal provision under which an accused is charged on the one hand and on the necessity of detaining him on the other, with arguments relating also to probable motive, all questions that would be relevant to the ultimate question of the guilt or innocence of the accused and of the appropriate sentence.[163]

Sharp irony, biting sarcasm, or simply a pointed dig are often reserved for the decisions of judges or prosecutors in a trial that is still proceeding. "Despite investigations stretching over years and despite extensive wire-tapping operations the prosecution has a problem in obtaining evidence," says the lead-in subtitle of a report on a trial that was about to open against attorney Groenewold for his alleged "assistance to a criminal association" as a consequence of his role as attorney.[164] In the report following this lead-in, there is a well-documented analysis not only of the problems that will be encountered in the trial both for the prosecution and the accused but also of the essential defense of the accused that his activities were all legal. The report leaves no doubt about the fact that the charges are of a kind that stretches the wording of the particular article in the criminal code beyond its legitimate meaning. Or, in a report on a murder trial that had just started, Mr. Mauz criticizes what he regards as the obvious manipulation by prosecutor and judge of the psychiatric evidence relating to the accused's fitness to stand trial. Quoting at length from a speech of the German State-President on the abuse of legal procedures and the unconscionable search for loopholes in the law by certain German lawyers in political cases, he accuses the particular judge and prosecutor of similarly abusing their position by their attempts to have the accused stand trial at all cost.[165]

From these examples and from literally scores of others that can be adduced with the greatest of ease from the files of *Der Spiegel* over any given period of time, it is clear that with sufficient concern on the part of the journal there would in fact be *no* decision and no aspect relating to *any* trial that would not be scrutinized, analyzed, and criticized by the journal. The trial reporting of the journal constitutes a unique blend of in-depth reporting (often on trials completely ignored by the national news media), comment, education, and critique of a kind that to my knowledge is not found in any other journal in the world. The trial reporting of *Der Spiegel* must be seen within the context of its general concern with legal matters that received attention above and is in fact inseparably connected therewith.

There would naturally be no feasible way of establishing any direct correlation between trial publicity on the one hand and the outcome of a trial. In this respect, the situation in Germany is not different from that in any other country. An interesting example of a *possible* influence on a court case – in actual fact on a civil trial – occurred in 1977 on the question of the responsibility in tort of doctors for negligence at the operation table. On April 18, 1977, *Der Spiegel* carried as its main cover story a long article under the title: "Medical Mistakes: 'Conspiracy of Silence.'" In the article, which constituted a discussion of a dire catalogue of cases where doctors had committed errors in their treatment of or operations on patients, a withering and well-documented criticism is made of the difficulties of such patients to pierce through the conspiratorial veil of secrecy and silence of the medical profession to obtain the necessary evidence needed to succeed in civil actions and of the highly inadequate (especially by American standards) damages awarded by the courts in Germany. In a development that may of course be entirely fortuitous but on the other hand may likewise not be entirely unrelated to the possible shock effect that this article in *Der Spiegel* caused in the minds of its readers – in reality almost every person in Germany above a certain professional level – an award of DM 1 million, the highest award for such damages ever pronounced in Germany, was awarded a patient in the following week.[166] The award was given by a court in Berlin three days before a well-publicized seminar for criminal lawyers was to take place in the same city on the topic of "The Doctor and Criminal Law."

Another German journal that regularly contradicts the notion that it is only the boulevard press that indulges in aggressive and uninhibited trial reporting is *Der Stern*. Unlike *Der Spiegel*, which is directed at the higher intellectual strata of society or, at least, at the more discerning tastes of the general public, and unlike the boulevard press, which caters either to the lower intellectual groups or to the less-sophisticated tastes of the general public, *Der Stern* is a high-quality family journal catering to the entertainment tastes and proclivities of the more critical members of society. It is a quality popular magazine comparable to *Paris Match* or the now-defunct *Life*. Although mainly geared to entertainment, *Der Stern* nevertheless also sees part of its role as a vehicle for the education and enlightenment of society and for investigative journalism, sometimes on legal matters.[167] And in relation to reporting and critique of trials, *Der Stern* plays a role – regular, critical, and educational – unlike any similar type of magazine in the English-speaking world. As is the case with *Der Spiegel*, the sub judice guideline is a dead letter for *Der Stern* in its very regular columns on the administration of justice. As examples the following must suffice.

In writing about the same trial in Cologne as did *Der Spiegel*, *Der Stern* accused the presiding judge of prejudice, obstinacy, unreasonableness, and a lust for power.[168] One critical commentator, Wolfgang Reiss,[169] cites as his prime example of *Stimmungsmache* (or the "creation of an adverse atmosphere") a rather mild report in *Der Stern* on the trial of a policeman on the killing of a student demonstrator:

> As far as students are concerned who demonstrate against the Shah [of Iran], this guardian of democracy [i.e. the accused] has already had his own opinion for a long time: They are not really students in any case. The fifth column are nowadays no longer the proletariat. With this attitude in mind the police officer arose at 5.30 hours on 2 June and proceeded well rested to his work.

In almost every third or fourth edition of *Der Stern* a more blatant example of such *Stimmungsmache* can be found!

Despite the patent way in which the German Press Council guidelines are ignored or traduced in reality, also by the quality newspapers, the boulevard press[170] remains – quite unfairly on the basis of the facts adduced above – in the center of discussion concerning the question of trial publicity. Almost invariably after every sensational criminal trial, the alarm is sounded either in the quality press, the academic journals, or the official organ of the German judiciary, the *Deutsche Richterzeitung*. In fact, it would seem that it was the sensational press coverage of the *Brühne* murder trial in 1962 that was the direct cause of the attempt by the German Penal Reform Commission to have a contempt provision written into German law.[171] However, it is not without relevance to note that in the outcry that followed the *Brühne* case in the *Richterzeitung* the boulevard press was actually ignored, with long extracts quoted from commentaries and letters in the most prestigious newspaper in Germany, the *Frankfurter Allgemeine Zeitung*, as well as in other mainstream newspapers.[172]

If sub judice restrictions or inhibitions have any merit as one of many factors steering a case toward establishing the truth and achieving a just solution, there will, so one must axiomatically assume, be no attainment of justice and no discovery of truth in almost any sensational case in Germany if regard is had to the pretrial and trial reporting of the German boulevard press. If sufficiently motivated, there is in reality not a single self-imposed restriction or inhibition on trial reporting as to what and how that section of the press would publish their story.[173] After closely following the murder trial in 1977 of former film idol, *Ingrid van Bergen*, including the publicity attendant on the murder and the subsequent revelations about and by the killer and her flamboyant lawyer[174] in the boulevard press, it is difficult to conceive of *any* limit as understood in a contempt jurisdiction that was not grossly exceeded. In what immediately follows, a few specimen examples of the highlights of pretrial and trial reporting of this cause célèbre will be noted, especially from the columns of *Das Bild*, as a graphic case study of sensational and saturation pretrial and trial reporting at its best.

The Ingrid van Bergen Case

On February 4, 1977, all German boulevard newspapers carried the story of the death of Miss van Bergen's lover, millionaire businessman Klaus Knaths, as their main story. "Ingrid van Bergen shoots her lover! Bullet in heart: Witnesses on telephone," proclaimed *Der Abendpost*, Germany's biggest evening newspaper. In the detailed report, the fact is mentioned that the deceased's parent had heard the shooting through a live telephone connection and that Miss van Bergen had explained that her objective had been to frighten the deceased. On February 6, *Bild am Sonntag*, (one of only two Sunday newspapers in Germany) uses a quote from a friend of the accused in its headline: "'He charmed her to the marrow.'" The report mentions inter alia that her lawyer had stopped his client from speaking to the press: "After weapon experts had found that it is almost impossible to fire shots 'by mistake' [as the accused had reportedly alleged] from the weapon used in the killing ... the defense is now embarking very clearly on a new line: That the deceased was at least partly responsible [for his own death]. In contrast to this version the family of the deceased ... speak unreservedly of a premeditated act." On February 7, *Bild* publishes under a one-inch banner headline – "Ingrid van Bergen: I'm dreaming of him in a coffin. The widow: I reveal everything" – a report ostensibly describing the sight of "the woman who killed for love" in jail and revealing her thoughts. In an inside page follows a detailed interview with the widow of the deceased, concentrating on her experience with and impressions of Miss van Bergen.[175] On February 8, *Bild* opens its main headline story on the case with the subtitle: "Is [the accused's] menopause responsible for the killer shots?" The report proceeds to answer the query as follows: "Ingrid van Bergen (45) is in the menopause period of her life. Her lawyer does not exclude that this critical period of bodily and mental strain, in conjunction with alcohol and jealousy, could have caused the deadly shots. . . . [Attorney] Bossi's suspicion is not unrealistic. There have been cases in the German criminal annals of women who had their menopause recognized as a mitigating circumstance." Then follow two examples of such cases and a quote from a book on forensic medicine in support of the proposition. On February 9, the main story is once more directed at the accused, quoting the deceased's widow on two previous occasions where the accused had threatened the deceased with a pistol. On February 11, *Bild* reports a new development under the headline: "Ingrid van Bergen: she shot with two pro-mille [alcohol in her blood]." The report then quotes the speculation of a professor of forensic medicine on the alcohol content of her blood at the time of shooting. In the meantime, *Bild* had also started a series of articles by the widow of the deceased. On February 13, *Bild am Sonntag* announces over banner headlines, taking up a third of the front page of its tabloid format: "Sensation in the case of Ingrid van Bergen: Wild struggle with lover before the killer shots." In the inside pages of the paper starts the first of a series of revelations – "Now I will talk" – by the accused, starting with a description of the death scene. On February 14, *Bild* follows with an article on the love affairs of the accused, an exercise that it continues for the next few days. On March 12, *Bild*'s main story headline asks: "Will Ingrid van Bergen be acquitted?" The report then speculates that the various circumstances that had come to light made it possible that the accused could either be acquitted or given a suspended sentence. On May 17, *Bild*'s main story echoed the same question: "Ingrid van Bergen: Not guilty?" The report starts: "Ingrid van Bergen will under all circumstances not have to go behind bars for the rest of her life." Then follows a speculation by a lawyer on the probable outcome of the imminent trial.

On July 20, 1977, the trial of Ingrid van Bergen started in Munich to the accompaniment of main-story banner headlines in the entire boulevard press. *Bild* exclaimed: "Ingrid van Bergen: 'The day of destiny is here!'" From page one the reader is invited to turn to page five for "the big trailer on the court case" (*Prozessvorschau*). The van Bergen story on the day consists of a last rehash of the fateful day under the title: "The day [of the killing] began with a passionate kiss [between the accused and the deceased]," followed by another installment in the series by the wife of the deceased, which had begun at the time of the killing but was interrupted in the interim, under the title: "'I am afraid to look at that woman. . . .'" Said the widow: "Yes, I am afraid. How stupid. I've done nothing. It is she who is on trial for killing my husband." Under the title "These four men will decide the fate of Ingrid van Bergen," there follows a brief pen sketch (accompanied by photographs) of the presiding judge, the prosecutor, the defense counsel, and the expert psychiatric witness: "Does he [the presiding judge] know Ingrid van Bergen personally?" . . . [Replies the judge] "Only from her film '*Roses for the Prosecutor*.'" A small inset photograph of the Munich palace of justice carries the caption "Vera Brühne was also put on trial here."[176] A short pen sketch of the career of the accused is accompanied by a photo of the film star at the height of her career with the subtitle: "Parties and sex played a crucial part in her life." The "trailer" ends with a slightly caustic description of her life style as member of the Munich theatrical and nouveau riche society. The story ends on a note of pathos: "Ingrid van Bergen was a good mother. This must also be said."

The reports – all first-story front-page reports with the usual (for *Bild*) $1^{3}/4$-inch headlines – of the following week concentrated mainly on the revelations in the case, particularly on the married and sexual life of the accused flowing from her own evidence and that of her lovers, associates, and acquaintances. Built into these factual reports and accompanied by the requisite headlines, there is the continuation of the stream of personal details and pictures that characterized *Bild*'s reporting from the day of the fatal shooting: the mother's embrace of her children; a kiss of an ex-husband in court, impressions of the trial and the continuation of her story by the widow of the deceased; the interlinear descriptions of the personalities appearing in the case – "a bull of a man" for instance in relation to a lover of the accused giving evidence – and the plaintive cry of a child of the accused (enshrined in a headline) when interviewed by the judge – "Please judge, I want my mommy back!" – and an interview with the accused: "I hope to get a just, a humane verdict. . . . In recent times I have been reading a lot from the Bible. It has helped me a lot." A psychic is quoted: "It will be a mild sentence." A handwriting expert states: "Her handwriting discloses that Ingrid van Bergen hides her sensitivity and her vulnerability behind a hard exterior." A former colleague in filmmaking is quoted: "I met her during the shooting of a film. . . . She was in the nude and her body fascinated me. She was the greatest optical delight of my life." And then the end, encapsulated in the *Bild*'s headline of July 28, 1977, covering a third of the page: "Seven long years." The main story of the day is concerned with the views of persons, prominent and unknown, on the sentence.

The backlash to the sensationalism of the van Bergen case was bound to come and inevitably in the center of the reaction was the dichotomy of free speech (and a free press) versus fair trial. Said *Der Spiegel* in a passage already quoted: "That this criminal trial did not become a catastrophe under the howling of the press must be attributed to the prosecution, the court and especially the chairman, Judge Wilhelm Paul.[177] In what must surely rank as a praiseworthy example of open judicial government, Judge Paul made a statement on German television in the course of a program significantly titled "The Lust for Sensation: The Ingrid van Bergen Trial and the Independence of a Court."[178] Also appearing on the program with the presiding judge was the defense lawyer, Mr. Rolf Bossi. The program summarized in a nutshell the dichotomy of views on the subject.

For an opening gambit, perhaps somewhat paradoxically, the program organizer quoted Mr. Gerhard Mauz of *Der Spiegel*: "What the public did and what the press did was a disgrace. It was a circus. It was an act of inhumanity towards the accused and towards the victim." Interestingly, Mr. Mauz stressed not the fairness of the trial but other civilized values. Explaining the sensationalism and her own contribution in activating it, Miss van Bergen commented briefly that her only consideration was to correct false impressions. Attorney Bossi likewise justified his activities.[179] More impressive and important was the comment by the presiding judge about the way in which the publicity affected – or failed to affect – judicial deliberations and from his statement it is clear that such danger as there might have been was to interests other than the achievement of a fair trial.[180] According to a public opinion poll in *Der Spiegel*, some 57 percent of Germans questioned believed that "too much had been written" on the case with 38 percent considering the coverage adequate.

Although the concept of an independent court was used in relation to the van Bergen case, it is clear that such objections as are raised in Germany are really based on other considerations – the undermining of the formal presumption of innocence, the degrading of the judicial process, the degrading of the accused and of the memory of the deceased, and the like. It is mostly with considerations such as these in mind that an accusing finger is pointed at the sensational boulevard press. If, however, saturation publicity of the present kind constitutes a danger to the independence of a court, such danger would clearly have been very present here. In any event, there was no serious allegation that there was at any stage such danger in the case of this court, a court that consisted also of two lay judges.

Amid the rather general and strident complaints against the boulevard press, the fact is mostly ignored that a potentially far greater source of pollution of the clean stream of justice in the sense of an undermining of the independence of the courts will emanate, albeit perhaps in other kinds of trials, from the quality press. A relatively detailed analysis has already been made of prejudgment trial reporting of what must be regarded as the most influential and also the most intellectual news medium in Germany, *Der Spiegel*. It is submitted that no amount of reporting in the boulevard press of the kind documented here in the *van Bergen* case would either consciously or unconsciously be potentially as relevant to the outcome of a case as would be a well-argued report and critique in a journal such as *Der Spiegel*. While this is merely a speculation, it will be clear to anybody familiar with the situation that an average German judge would be more amenable to be influenced by the peculiar kind of trial and legal reporting of *Der Spiegel* than by the extravagant sensationalism of the *Bild* variety as documented above.[181] Interestingly, unlike the situation after the *Brühne* case, when the *Richterzeitung* was flooded by complaints about the publicity, there was no such reaction in that journal after the *van Bergen* case.

Controlling the German Press

That there is a subliminal hankering in certain recesses of the German legal psyche after some form of sub judice control is clear not only from the cry of a few academic voices in the wilderness that culminated in the 1962 contempt draft, or even from the somewhat paradoxical criticism of Gerard Mauz, but also from a wholly unexpected quarter: an application in 1978 by Mr. Kurt Groenewold in the prosecution against him for "supporting a criminal association" by his use of certain aggressive defense tactics. Mr. Groenewold (as we have seen) had become known inter alia for a host of publications that all heavily infringe the sub judice ethos.[182]

In one of a number of preliminary applications to the trial court, the *Oberlandesgericht* of Hamburg, Mr. Groenewold petitioned the court in effect to introduce a sub judice principle through the back door and to "stop proceedings since it is impossible to achieve a fair trial in conformity with the rule of law."[183] The applicant lists a considerable number of instances where government and prosecuting spokesmen had made statements critical to his defense methods that contributed to subject the "proceedings to very serious public and political pressures" of a kind amounting to a *Vorverurteilung* or prejudgment. In the details of his application, the applicant also lists a number of press reports that contributed in his opinion to the *Stimmungsmache* or adverse atmosphere that had been built up around his trial.[184] As legal pegs for his attempt to introduce what he termed the Anglo-Saxon concept of *fair trial* into the German situation, he used article 6 of the European Convention of Human Rights (which is binding law in Germany)[185] and article 2(1) of the German Grundgesetz.[186]

Naturally, this quixotic attempt to translate a sub judice rule into the fabric of German law was doomed to failure, although the application underlines the fact that the boulevard press finds itself, as far as the infringement of the sub judice ethos is concerned, in the rather illustrious company of ministerial authorities and state prosecutors!

In any event, the interim judgment (*Beschluss*) of the Third Chamber of the *Hanseatisches Oberlandesgericht* constitutes an interesting contribution to the debate in Germany on the desirability or otherwise of introducing some form of control over the free flow of information regarding facts and views concerning litigation matters. While not denying the generally negative feature of exposing the judicial process to extraneous pressures and influences, the court put the emphasis on the only place where it can in fact theoretically be put in a democratic society: the independence and quality of the judiciary.

The court held that the European Convention on Human Rights was binding, but it found that the relevant part of article 6 of the convention did not preclude the trial from proceeding. The court nevertheless expressed considerable sympathy for the applicant's anxiety, although it could not accept his thesis that it was unable to discharge its duties effectively.[187] More interesting are the court's views on an even more problematic influence of trial publicity: the subconscious penetration of the judicial mind by external stimuli. Once more the Hamburg *Oberlandesgericht* did not deny the possible relevance of this subliminal source of psychological influence, but dealt with it in what is really the only possible way that would accord with the requirements of a *Rechtsstaat*:

to stress the need of a court to counteract consciously the possibly pernicious influence of this potential source of psychological pollution on the proverbial clean stream of justice:

> Now the defence quite correctly pointed out that there is always the danger also of an unconscious influencing of judges by some form or another of prejudgment. The court considers this problem of so-called subliminal influencing in a very serious light and it seriously considered this problem in the present case — a problem which as a psychological as opposed to a medical phenomenon applies to all persons, whether [for instance] as consumers or as voters. It is not necessary to assess the importance of the problem by means of expert psychological evidence. The members of the court are, after renewed critical self-examination, of the opinion that they are devoid of any subliminal bias against the accused.[188]

The court finally draws attention to a fact that is also of great significance for contempt jurisdictions: that exaggerated or unfair trial publicity carries within itself its own antidote when one is dealing with a competent judiciary.

> Finally, the concern of the accused and of the defense [concerning unconscious influences] fails to take account of an important aspect of judicial psychology: biased statements or even value judgments concerning court trials which are in progress and which are made by outsiders, provoke almost as of necessity a critical [psychological] defence mechanism on the part of any judge who consciously sees his functions within the concept of the rule of law [*Rechtsstaatlichkeit*].[189]

Conclusions

It is worth emphasizing that the German case study of trial publicity underlines the concern in some circles about the undermining of certain personality values as opposed to the concern with the achievement of a fair trial in the jurisdictions where sub judice restrictions apply. In this context, it is instructive to refer to the *Lebach* judgment of the *Bundesverfassungsgericht*,[190] which constitutes an important jurisprudential landmark in the limitation of the right of free speech in the interests of personality rights of the individual. It will be recalled that the judgment, although as such not concerned with trial publicity, created a potentially far reaching limitation on the freedom of the media – a television chain in this instance – to subject an individual who was about to be released from prison to the embarrassment of having his crime reconstructed on television. The underlying jurisprudential principle on which this decision is essentially based is one that is also inherent in the general complaint often directed at excessive pretrial and trial publicity in Germany: the need for society to balance the protection of its right to information with the protection of certain fundamental personality rights of the accused (or the suspects) and indeed also of other parties in criminal trials.

In German law there is, subject only to considerations of public interest, an absolute prohibition on the publication of personal details and pictures during criminal investigations before an arrest or before a charge has ben laid. Academic attempts to extend this protection of the personality of an individual – flowing partly from the presumption of innocence – to cover in addition the form, tone, and content of pretrial and trial publicity have not been successful and it would seem that the *Lebach* judgment will continue to remain a lone warning buoy on the turbulent sea of German legal journalism.

An interesting case to extend the protective reach of the *Lebach* philosophy to a suspect of a crime occurred when an unsuccessful attempt was made to interdict the Second German Television Chain – the ZDF – from screening one of the most popular German television programs: "Aktenzeichen XY – ungelöst."[191] The ZDF, hooked up to the television chains of Switzerland and Austria, regularly broadcasts reconstructions of unsolved crimes with the object of inviting clues from the public toward the solution of the crimes. The facts were that a suspect in the commission of rape and robbery obtained a temporary injunction restraining the ZDF from broadcasting his identity in an effort to fill in certain lacunae in the police dossier of the crime. Although restrained from publishing the *name* of the suspect, the ZDF nevertheless, in conformity with the injunction, proceeded to screen a *picture* of the suspect. In the ultimate proceedings, the injunction was not only revoked but the ZDF succeeded with its contention that even after the release of the suspect from custody, it would still be entitled to broadcast both his name and picture in an effort to promote certain important public interests.[192]

In its judgment, the court attempted to balance the undoubted interests of the individual against "the interest of the community in solving a crime and . . . in crime prevention."[193] Only subliminally present were free speech considerations based on education, entertainment, and the like. As an obvious prerequisite for this massive technological invasion of privacy of an individual and for the corrosion of the presumption of innocence, the court required that the crime must be one of considerable magnitude. It goes without saying – the court was silent on this, however – that a person who has been put in this technological pillory will retain all the rights that he or she may have in civil law to compensate for the indignity inflicted on him or her if it turns out that the exposure to the media was in fact unjustified.[194]

For practical purposes, however, it can finally be said that for all the concern that is sometimes expressed in Germany in certain academic and journalistic circles, as well as in certain courts and in judicial circles, about trial or pretrial publicity,[195] the situation remains that such concern has little real effect on the media if the latter are seriously concerned about pursuing a certain issue. The legal restraints for their part bear no resemblance whatever to the sub judice contempt rule. Often voices of concern may be heard, but they remain comparatively muted and devoid of much conviction. Essentially these expressions of dissent are nothing more than the symptoms of a necessary and even healthy uneasiness over the relationship between the media on the one hand and the administration of justice on the other.

4

Informal Restrictions and Indirect Sanctions on Free Speech in the Legal Domain

The freedom of speech — which includes the freedom to print — is a facet of civilization which always presents two well-known inherent traits. The one consists of the constant desire by some to abuse it. The other is the inclination of those who want to protect it to repress more than is necessary. The latter is also fraught with danger. It is based on intolerance and is a symptom of the primitive urge in mankind to prohibit that with which one does not agree. When a court of law is called upon to decide whether liberty should be repressed . . . it should be anxious to steer a course as close to the preservation of liberty as possible. It should do so because freedom of speech is a hard-won and precious asset, yet easily lost.

Appeal Judge Rumpff dissenting in the
censorship case *Heinemann* in South Africa[1]

INTRODUCTION

If freedom of speech generally has been a "hard-won and precious asset," it has even been more so in relation to freedom of speech in the legal domain, where in most societies that freedom is still far from completely won. It is so little understood in such wide and respectable circles that knowledge about its virtual nonexistence or attenuation is very often totally lacking, and it is in this lack of knowledge about the understanding of legal free speech that we find one of the most basic reasons why this freedom is so easily lost, often before it has ever flowered at all. The struggle in this field to overcome "the primitive urge of mankind to prohibit that with which [he] does not agree" has as often as not been directed as much at the informal restrictions and at social inertia than at overt official attempts to stifle verbal dissent in the legal domain. Not surprisingly, the memorials of this struggle are not as visible and as easily documentable as is the case with legal restrictions, and it is therefore also much less susceptible to analysis than is the case with the struggle against formal rules, studded as the latter usually are with judgments, convictions, rhetoric, and even high drama.

At various junctures, reference was made to the concept and effects of informal restrictions on legal free speech, and in what follows an attempt will be made to analyze this concept more clearly on the basis of examples (or suspicions) that are documentable from such sources in a number of mostly European countries as were available. Because of my personal familiarity with the situation in South Africa, special reference will be made to the situation in that country.

The problem of sources in relation to informal censorship is a serious one, since it will naturally always be difficult to document a phenomenon that has as its very basis a nonexistent entity. The intrinsically different nature of the phenomenon of informal censorship to formal speech restrictions calls for an analytical approach different from the one used when documenting formal restrictions. The inquiry into the field of informal restrictions will have to be directed at ill-defined symptoms and at phenomena lurking behind the scenes and behind glib theories. At times one must also make use of deductive guesswork.

Both as point of departure and as an overall summary concerning informal legal taboos, it can be said as far as the inhibitive and destructive *effect* is concerned that such informal taboos or restrictions are in most Western countries probably more important than formal restrictions and direct legal sanctions. This would be so particularly in those countries where there are practically no legal sanctions involving speech in the legal domain or where there is a reluctance to enforce sanctions. The mere fact, as repeatedly noted, that sanctions are infrequently invoked in a particular society does not necessarily signify the presence of a robust degree of free speech. Especially in those countries with a tendency toward authoritarianism, experience shows that there would mostly be only a peripheral need to invoke legal sanctions since the informal sanctions and influences would already have exacted their toll as far as coercion is concerned. It is instructive to recall here not only the dearth of recent English cases of the scandalizing type of contempt – as did the Phillimore Report[2] – but also the virtually total absence in reported case law of defamation of officials vis-à-vis judicial officers in Poland and Hungary.[3] The same holds true, although for different reasons, for countries like Germany and the Netherlands, where the self-discipline of the legal profession is so effective as regards critical or robust utterances that such formal restrictions that afford protection to officialdom and state institutions do not generally enter into the picture at all.

Regarding this phenomenon of a kind of *professional precensorship*, it is appropriate to point again to the effective concatenation, cross-pollination and mutual reinforcement of formal and informal sanctions and prohibitions. Although this phenomenon has been referred to at various points in this work, it is a fact that is crucially relevant to a proper understanding of the entire complex of issues pertinent to the reality of informal restrictions of legal free speech.

Free speech generally, including the actual and effective use made of it and the restrictions and inhibitions imposed on it, is intrinsically interwoven with the general atmosphere or intellectual climate of a particular society. It flows largely from and is substantially predicated on something that can, albeit vaguely, be termed the spirit of liberty in a given society. So much is trite and needs no emphasis here. For its part, however, free speech in the legal domain – in its full legal and societal, formal and informal sense – depends on and is shaped by something additional. Although itself obviously emanating from and a product of the spirit of liberty prevalent in a particular society, freedom of speech in the legal domain is also intimately bound up with factors and forces even more subtle and evasive than the amorphous spirit of liberty of such a society.

One such factor would be an understanding in informed circles of the subtleties, vulnerability, bases, and implications of a dynamic system of legal free speech. This understanding, albeit intuitive, is very rarely present in the majority of democratic countries. Among other things, it involves the awareness that the administration of justice and its officers have traditionally escaped the close scrutiny reserved for political questions and politicians; it also involves an awareness of the need to educate the public at large in all the aspects and implications of that freedom; it further involves knowledge of the need for a consistent alertness about and an unimpeded access to the maze of decision-making powers in the vast network of the administration of justice; it must involve the presence on the part of interested parties of a committed doggedness that can penetrate behind the generally placid façade and the gentle myths of the judicial administration, and it must also involve the willingness on the part of at least some individuals to drop some of the fragile porcelain in that domain. Indeed, much more is still involved, especially as far as an enlightened and motivated press and a concerned public opinion are concerned, but even as depicted here the requirements for an understanding of the full concept of legal free speech constitute a tall order.

Important as the spirit of liberty may be in understanding legal free speech in a particular society, it must also be realized that the spirit of liberty will often have very little to say about the more specialized concept of legal free speech, a concept that seldom, if ever, enters into the private world of even the most informed citizen. The parameters of the spirit of liberty in most democratic societies may encompass questions such as free speech in the political field, the treatment of offenders, access to government, and the like, and it will be mostly on the basis of these parameters alone that the *Weltanschauung* of the commentator, judge, or critic will be shaped. The effective ignorance or nonconcern about the more nuanced nature of the concept of free speech in the legal domain, or the unwillingness to see it in a different light from free speech in the general sense, will largely explain how even in deeply democratic societies decisions have been taken concerning vital aspects of legal free speech that are fundamentally corrosive to liberty and the essential interests of society. Put differently and more pointedly, the spirit of liberty or the spirit of the constitution, which is at times such a potent and conscious creative force in judicial lawmaking, will often be substantially silent on a question involving speech in the legal domain.

Now it is precisely because the spirit of liberty (or the constitution) will mostly constitute such a weak and ineffective constraining influence on suppressive forces on free speech on legal matters that the potential influence of critical legal commentators and individuals is so relevant, first, as far as creating the intellectual climate in which courts of law would mold their decisions relating to speech, and second, as far as determining the degree of legal free speech that is effectively prevalent in society. Newspapers that regularly indulge in robust scrutiny of the legal administration, practicing lawyers who speak their mind freely about the inadequacies of or irregularities within the administration of justice, and legal academics who do not fear to tread on the sensitive corns of venerable legal personalities and institutions or to destroy the respectable myths in the administration of judges will be the forces that would effectively shape (or fail to shape) the atmosphere in which formal speech restrictions will be interpreted. In those countries where formal restrictions are seldom enforced or are practically nonexistent, these forces, and practically they alone, will decide the extent to which the administration of justice will receive the scrutiny needed in terms of the premises of a vital and democratic system of legal free speech. Against the backdrop of these considerations we will look briefly again at the situation in a number of countries.

Starting at the one extreme with a country that has substantially abolished and overcome both formal and informal restrictions on speech in the legal domain, the United States, it is not difficult to detect a close relationship between liberalizing court decisions on legal free speech on the one hand and the intellectual atmosphere created by the press, the legal profession, and academics on the other. These decisions have practically eliminated the most pernicious forms of speech restrictions in the legal domain and were molded and shaped by the atmosphere in which those groups mentioned above – but particularly the press – successfully and sometimes painfully asserted their right and duty to scrutinize and analyze as energetically as possible the decision-making processes in the legal field as they did in the political field. As far as those trial publicity cases that have deeply eroded the residual speech restrictions in that field are concerned, it is almost self-evident that they were largely predicated on the inescapable reality that the role that the press had carved out for itself in that field is one that it will not willingly yield again. The vigorously and persistently critical and even defiant attitude of the press must, as a simple reality of human psychology, contribute significantly to shape the atmosphere in which those decisions were handed down and to the tenor and content of those decisions.[4]

In contrast, it is not very difficult to see how the traditional (but certainly changing) aloof and overly respectful attitude of the British press toward the judiciary facilitated the molding of some of the strange decisions of that country's contempt law. In the remarkable *Sunday Times* thalidomide case,[5] Lord Reid was clearly right when he stated: "There has long been and there still is in this country a strong and generally held feeling that trial by newspaper is wrong and should be prevented."[6]

Of course, not many people in the West would see the offending articles as constituting anything remotely resembling a trial by newspaper, and in the very use of that emotional term there is an indication of the strange isolation of the British judiciary from the ordinary operation of and exposure to democratic principles of free speech. A more accurate statement would have been that the media in England have traditionally not claimed for themselves the right to exercise an independent judgment on matters, including those of vital national importance, which formed the subject of litigation or related to sensitive issues concerning the judiciary.

It is also not difficult to speculate about the possible causal connection between some of the scandalization contempt decisions and the still-prevailing (but not unchallenged) attitude of genteel aloofness of British journalism and academic scholarship toward the judiciary. That this aloofness, although no longer as strong and undifferentiated as Brian Abel-Smith and Robert Stevens pointed out a decade ago,[7] is still of a very real nature is evident from the unchallenged way in which the essentially elitist and socially detrimental suggestion of the Phillimore Report was apparently received in both journalistic and academic circles. The suggestion[8] concerns the proposed new contempt legislation in which truth alone will not be a defense unless public policy so dictates. Suffice it to say that in terms of the premises of this work, truth about legal matters will *always* be in the public interest unless countervailed by a much higher social interest of immediate and compelling importance.

In other European countries, but certainly in the case of Germany and the Netherlands, the indirect *legal* restrictions applicable to speech in the legal domain do not appear by themselves to exercise any overly significant inhibiting effect on practicing and academic lawyers and on journalists, the groups most likely to keep a watching brief on the law. In these countries, informal restrictions and taboos really constitute the most important restrictions and inhibitions and as such are of great importance. These restrictions, whether of an informal or of a professional nature, are at times so effective and inhibitive in the ambit of their operation that they really approximate the status of formal restrictions. Under these circumstances, the distinction between the two broad categories of restrictions loses much of its practical importance. More aloof, subtle, invisible, and unfathomable as these informal restrictions may well be compared with the vast array of formal restrictions referred to, it would be fundamentally erroneous to assume that they are necessarily less effective, and especially, less erosive of the premises of a democratic system of legal free speech.

Various examples of the elevation of informal taboos to a level where their *effect* is as potent as that of formal restrictions or sanctions will be noted in this chapter but none is so obvious as the situation in the Netherlands concerning the sub judice convention there. A recent study, surprisingly enough initiated by the arch conservative Dutch Guild of Advocates, noted the reality that although there is no direct legal rule whatever comparable to the sub judice rule in English law, the informal convention in the Netherlands in that respect is just as strong and that during trials a kind of anxious silence prevails in the press as regards matters dealt with in the trials.[9] Therefore, for all it matters there might as well have been a sub judice rule backed by sanctions.

THE INFORMAL RESTRICTIONS AND TABOOS: AN OVERVIEW

> *'Publish and be damned' may perhaps at times seem to be an article of faith of some of our newspapers but it is most definitely still not the case with most of our law journals as far as judges are concerned.*
>
> An English academic to the author

As repeatedly stated, it is mainly lawyers and journalists who, in answer to their professional ethos or to the public interest concern themselves with the controversial aspects of justice and who therefore mostly land in the cross fire of the law and taboos of their societies. Nonetheless, these two groups need clearly not be the only groups in a democratic society who will make the scrutiny of the law their business. Inasmuch as informal restrictions and taboos do, however, apply to these two groups in exercising an inhibitive influence on them, they will apply in most instances with even greater force and effect to other groups within society.

THE LAWYERS

> *At the opposite end of the spectrum is the attitude of a conscientious and punctilious member of the bar who looks at his job through shrivelled up professional spectacles. One case is like another, in the sense that his job always remains the same: to create maximal conditions for a favorable outcome for his client. Hence his insistence that neither the client himself and still less an outside body would be entitled to interfere with his system of defence; he alone would carry the responsibility, with the defendant contracting, so to speak, to conform to a line determined by him.*
>
> Otto Kirchheimer[10]

Looking at the legal professions of the West as a whole, it would seem that the attitude described by Otto Kirchheimer as regards certain lawyers in political trials also characterizes the activities and statements of the vast majority of lawyers out of court in relation to the scrutiny of the administration of justice. Looking at their job "through shrivelled up professional spectacles" and thus ignoring wider social perspectives is very much a fact of life of the legal profession as a whole. On the whole it seems that the inhibitions and taboos and other informal restrictions that lead to some form or another of self-imposed or socially enforced censorship are extensively stronger as regards lawyers than journalists. This is so partly because of a number of important internal professional reasons applying to journalists, but partly because the legal profession has traditionally lacked a rallying cry such as freedom of the press with which to justify a commitment to strong verbal dissent toward the established order.

As a backdrop to a discussion of the informal speech inhibitions within the legal profession, it is useful to posit the outlines of the theoretical model and ideal of the fully mature and democratically oriented lawyer in the West concerning legal free speech. This model would in the first place possess an imaginative grasp and intuitive understanding of the way in which the ideals of his or her métier are intertwined with full and fearless scrutiny of the administration of justice. Such a lawyer would also be conscious of the fact and of its implications that in the ultimate analysis his or her profession must shoulder the major part of the burden to impart to society knowledge and understanding of the workings and the imperfections of the justice machinery. He or she would be sensitive to the knowledge that without constant and penetrating and at times even ruthless public scrutiny of all aspects of that machinery and its personnel, the achievement of justice in its fullest sense will invariably be thwarted. And he or she will be intuitively alert to subtle pressures emanating from his or her profession to be discreet and gentle about its imperfections and myths. Above all, he or she will make it his or her personal business, openly and unequivocally, to speak the truth as it is seen about all aspects of the justice machinery and to spare no delicacies, taboos, and comforting myths. In short, he or she will provide leadership in matters legal and will flay injustice in all its permutations. The only rare compromise that would be tolerated in this regard would be one dictated by social considerations where, on a careful balancing of conflicting social values, a temporary and clearly imminent and irremediable peril exists to a higher social value. His or her voice will be the voice that when convenience dictates otherwise will say "NO"; silence will never be an option when things are ill done.[11]

Taking this ideal as a yardstick, it is not difficult to conclude that in most Western countries the legal professions as a whole have seldom measured up to this degree of commitment to the dictates of free speech concerning the administration of justice. With many felicitous exceptions, one of the overriding phenomena characterizing legal professions in the West has been that of substantial silence on many burning legal and social issues where the particular verbal and professional skills of lawyers would have been helpfully illuminating. If there is truth in the accusation of silence once made by Supreme Court Justice Douglas concerning the American legal profession as a whole on the question of civil rights of the minorities, the charge must surely hold true for the West generally: "In American history lawyers have often rallied opinion outside of courtrooms in support of the despised minorities.... A few lawyers still speak in that tradition. But most lawyers have remained silent."[12] A similar lament was intoned by the great German legal scholar, Gustav Radbruch at the end of World War I, when he tried to peer through the mists of the future to visualize the new model of the ideal socially responsive lawyer: "The lawyers of the future ... will not in the first place be people who blindly execute the law but they will be creative architects of the law."[13] And in more recent times, the first of the postwar sociologically inspired judicial iconoclasts in Germany, Theo Rasehorn, after analyzing the contributions in the 1962 volume of the *Deutsche Richterzeitung* came to the doleful conclusion that the German judiciary is primarily interested with self-congratulatory laudations and with its own uncritical peace of mind: "In short, what is sought is not a debate with the public but simply self-justification."[14]

It is submitted that a substantial part of the cause for this uncritical attitude of social aloofness and self-deception described by Rasehorn was the general absence of effective and critical scrutiny of the administration of justice. The situation has substantially changed over the last decade concerning scrutiny by the press, although important and even crucial pockets of nonconcern for legal matters remain extant in many quarters of the quality press as will be noted later. However, as regards the critical scrutiny of the administration of justice by the legal profession itself, and particularly by the judiciary, the situation has really not materially changed since Rasehorn published his essay in 1962. Freedom of speech in the wider sense of a willingness to indulge in fundamental criticism of the administration of justice couched in direct and robust terms remains very much an exception as far as mainstream German legal literature is concerned, and a survey of the current issues of the *Richterzeitung* would reveal no significant change from the one undertaken in 1962. Indeed, a similar survey by Rasehorn in 1969 produced substantially the same conclusions as the 1962 survey.[15] In what follows a more detailed analysis of the contemporary German situation will be provided.

Legal Taboos in Germany: A Case Study

It is a matter of common knowledge that in the last few years a new breed of German lawyers has come to the forefront who, in an effort to hit at the legal system as one of the pillars of the German society as presently organized, have availed themselves of a variety of aggressive tactics of litigation to further their ideological aims in the defense of a group of urban guerillas loosely known as the Baader-Meinhof gang, a defense that put considerable strain on the country's overburdened and time-consuming legal machinery. The tactics of some of these lawyers have led to a spate of repressive measures, both professional and criminal, unprecedented in any Western country as far as scale and intensity are concerned. Some of these measures have been noted at various junctures of this work in so far as they relate to speech.[16] Outrageous as *some* of these verbal outbursts of *some* of these lawyers may well seem to have been, they were often matched by totally extravagant professional measures taken against critics of the administration of justice. One of the results of this spate of measures was that the mainstream practicing legal profession in Germany virtually abandoned any scrutinizing role and any role of vigorous but loyal dissent as regards the administration of justice, leaving the field almost totally to criticism of a revolutionary nature and to that of isolated pockets of journalists specializing in legal affairs. In many instances of those criminal and disciplinary cases already referred to in which lawyers were subjected to official harassment on account of their critical verbal statements, there was an underlying reproach that the lawyers concerned (in the words of the charge sheet in one disciplinary case) indulged in "campaign[s] of hatred and vilification of the administration of justice of the democratic rule of law."[17] The result has been that an atmosphere of dissuasion and repression was created that has been equated in certain Western quarters with the spirit of the McCarthy era in the United States.[18] Regardless of the correctness or otherwise of this unflattering assessment, no informed observer of the German legal scene can have any doubt about the considerable degree of inhibition and self-imposed censorship prevalent in the German legal profession as regards critical dissent.

The copious available examples of professional restrictions on the legal free speech of German lawyers relate only to members of the practicing profession. The overall result of these measures has been a blunting of the willingness of practicing lawyers to express themselves outspokenly on controversial aspects of the administration of justice. In a profession that in any event has traditionally been considered to be highly conservative, both in Germany and in the West generally, it is not difficult to visualize the extent to which individual cases of repression would ripple out into the profession generally, inducing lawyers to remain silent rather than speak out and to opt for the safe harbor of agreement or silence rather than the stormy seas of dissent and controversy. The net result of the application of these semiformal speech restrictions has been to remove the German legal profession even further from the ranks of outspoken watchdogs over the finer points of the administration of justice, with the strict attitudes displayed by the disciplinary courts constituting the perfect pretext to justify, and thus reinforce, the general noncritical and nonoutspoken atmosphere in the profession. It is useful to recall here that these professional sanctions are imposed substantially removed from any journalistic or academic scrutiny and outside the purview of the ordinary legal system and its constitutional guarantees.

Concerning *the judiciary*, the situation in Germany relating to informal taboos and restrictions on free speech can be accurately analyzed in view especially of the action taken against Dr. Theo Rasehorn entirely for the expression of critical and mildly iconoclastic views on the administration of justice.[19] It will be recalled that the *Richterverband* of the Province of Hesse had objected to the provincial ministry of justice about the promotion of Dr. Rasehorn to the chairmanship of the *Oberlandesgericht* of Frankfurt on the basis that he had "indefatigably propagated, both in writings and in speeches, extremist views which question the existing legal order and the fundamental constitutional principles [of Germany]."[20] In a vain attempt to obtain an injunction against the *Richterverband*, Dr. Rasehorn succeeded at least in bringing this clear attempt at the stifling of mildly critical speech into the open and in so doing to illuminate a few aspects of the evasive concepts of informal speech restrictions on the German judiciary.

At first blush, the intolerance shown in judicial quarters to Dr. Rasehorn may seem quite paradoxical in view of the fact that, unlike the situation in most Western countries, members of the German judiciary occupy a prominent place in legal scholarship, indulging at times in strong criticism of the judgments of their peers. In this important, albeit strictly limited and technical, sense, the German judiciary indulges in public dissent and even controversy to a degree quite unthinkable in the United Kingdom and in English-oriented legal systems, where a special virtue is made of so-called judicial detachment.[21] However, on closer analysis it becomes clear that this commendable degree of outspoken independence on the part of individual German judges has always been profoundly characterized by a basic orientation toward the social status quo and by a concern to eschew fundamental criticism of the administration of justice as such. When a judge like Rasehorn started to direct regular and incisive criticism at some of the fundamental questions of the legal system in Germany, especially on the status of the judiciary itself, the commendable tolerance normally shown toward critical views of judges in academic writings came to an abrupt end. Normally, of course, the professional blackballing or informal sanctioning of such a dissenting judge would take place behind the scenes and would seldom be documentable, and then merely speculatively. In this instance, the matter was laid bare in public by the considerable degree of publicity surrounding Rasehorn's writings and by the latter's attempt to enjoin the *Richterverband* from disseminating its critique.

What is particularly revealing is the list of complaints that the *Richterverband* detailed against the applicant in its original declaration. These refer to writings and speeches that on the basis of any criteria applicable, for instance, in the United States since the time at least of the rise of the school of modern realism can only be regarded as extremely mild. However, considering the outcry caused by Rasehorn's work in some of the media and considering also the biting criticism directed at it in the representations of the *Richterverband* and the way in which it sought to influence his career, it is not entirely difficult to understand why there is generally such a dearth of *outspoken* and *fundamental* criticism of the administration of justice in judicial and mainstream legal circles in general and of the German judiciary in particular. The spirit of small-minded vindictiveness and uncritical pettiness that emanates from the *Richterverband*'s attitude cannot, if it is in any way indicative of the thinking among a significant section of the ranks of the German judicial officers, be conducive to the fostering of a spirit of critical independence and dissent among judicial officers. Against this background, the preparedness of individual judges like Rashorn and a few others to challenge the status quo becomes almost astonishing.

The degree of intolerance toward the ideas of Dr. Rasehorn becomes pathetically evident when, as a kind of *pièce de résistance*, the *Richterverband* quotes an extract from an essay, "Grandpa's Justice Is Still Alive," to bolster its claim that he had been propagating ideas that undermined the constitutional order. However, what emerges from a reading of the extract is in fact nothing more than a somewhat fanciful futuristic speculation – a far cry from anything one would even begin to call undermining or revolutionary.[22] It is when one ponders the potency of the reaction to a statement of this innocuousness that one obtains some indication of the depth of the spirit of intolerance within the German legal profession generally regarding radical criticism and dissent as it is mirrored in the dire catalogue of disciplinary cases that have occurred in recent years. One cannot as a simple proposition of human psychology expect professional people like judicial officers to be prepared to ride out storms of protest and abuse and risk subtle perils to their careers to promote a somewhat amorphous spirit of inquiry and dissent in the interest of the edification of society as a whole.

What is also clear from this episode is that any overt act of suppression of free speech in a domain such as the administration of justice has inhibitive consequences far in excess of what one may normally expect by simply looking at the sanction itself. The sanction in the Rasehorn episode was outwardly of a trivial nature – a mere representation to the provincial government as regards the unsuitability of a judicial promotion – but it must be assumed that the mere fact that such representation was deemed necessary under the particular circumstances relating to Dr. Rasehorn's writings was in itself a manifestation of the rarity of robust comment in judicial quarters in Germany. This reality is further underlined by the *total* absence in the major German legal journals of critical comment on the attempt of the *Richterverband* to expunge a critical voice from the judicial scene, and the deduction therefore seems a fair one that it fairly represented general judicial opinion. The actual step undertaken by the *Richterverband* merely puts a semiofficial seal of respectability on an existing state or pattern of informal inhibitions, reinforcing them, and adding to the creation of an even greater unwillingness on the part of individuals to risk detrimental consequences in challenging current ideas within the administration of justice. The risks of such consequences would not be made known so unsubtly and so hamhandedly as in the case of the *Richterverband*'s intervention, but it does not follow that such risks would not be well appreciated among those potential critics whose interests are potentially involved. As is the case with all subtle forms of sanctions or discrimination – and one only has to think about parallels concerning discrimination against women or members of certain racial groups – we are here in a twilight zone where views would very seldom be openly expressed and where it will be virtually impossible to track down with any degree of accuracy actual instances of critics being penalized for the expression of dissident views. It is against this background that the Rasehorn episode affords such an illuminating and rare insight of how freedom of speech concerning the administration of justice can be inhibited without too many overt signs of suppression while the democratic institutions of a society remain outwardly unimpaired.

To see the atmosphere in which the Rasehorn episode occurred in its full perspective, it is also necessary to consider the fact that among his otherwise outspoken colleagues (outspoken on technical or penological matters) there was an almost total lack of any support for Dr. Rasehorn.[23] This lack of judicial support, especially in the *Deutsche Richterzeitung*, the official organ of the German judiciary, or simply of an attempt to ponder the deeper implications of the event is tellingly indicative of the extent to which the unwillingness to question certain notions and principles and certain traditional values has insinuated itself into the legal profession, including the academic legal profession. It must also be remembered that the object of the exercise of the influential *Richterverband* was not to raise the general demerits of Dr. Rasehorn's promotion and it was not an attempt to counter by way of an inherently democratic right of reply the heretical views of Dr. Rasehorn, but the entire exercise was essentially geared toward the eradication of those views (and the views of others who may think along similarly critical lines) by way of professional sanctions. In other words, its plea was not for more free speech in relation to judicial appointments, a traditional taboo subject.[24]

From yet another point of view the Rasehorn episode illustrates heuristically the socially destructive tendency to treat legal matters, particularly as far as they relate to personalities, with velvet gloves. This time, the negative tendency is manifested on the part of Dr. Rasehorn himself and his attempt to issue an injunction against the further dissemination of the *Richterverband*'s resolution. This attempt comes perilously close to the *Richterverband*'s own misguided initiatives. The court's refusal to go along with Dr. Rasehorn's contention, although largely justified on other grounds – particularly on the ground that controversial statements will evoke controversial reactions – can clearly also be justified on the ground that matters crucially concerned with the administration of justice such as judicial advancements, cannot yield to sensitive personal susceptibilities. The court also approached the matter partly in that way.[25] This approach of frank and robust openness as regards the judicial process invited strong criticism on the part of another outspoken maverick judge and social critic, Helmut Ostermeyer, who bitterly deplored the lack of protection given to Rasehorn.[26]

Under ideal circumstances, one would at least expect the academic section of the legal profession to retain its critical independence toward justice administration and refuse to inhibit itself from mentioning the unmentionable. As we will see, this is not the case in a number of countries and it certainly is not effectively the case in Germany. As already stated, the Rasehorn episode did not at the time figure as a source of *any* academic concern in relation to academic free speech and as a perusal of the major legal periodicals would indicate there is generally not much concern for the matters that moved Dr. Rasehorn. In any event, there is on a less observable level an amorphous but very widespread belief in certain academic circles in the existence of some unobtrusive form of editorial censorship on academic journals in relation to certain subjects, although as can be expected the charge is extremely difficult to document. The very existence, however, of a firm *belief* in the phenomenon would of course almost invariably be self-fulfilling, since the potential academic critic would consciously endeavor to avoid falling foul of the suspected or known susceptibilities of the editors. Given the relatively small number of legal periodicals in Germany and also the reality of the publish-or-perish principle, and given also the notoriously conservative attitudes prevailing in legal academic circles, it is wholly unrealistic to expect that young academics would simply mount the barricades and start challenging the attitudes and decisions of the editors of the German legal periodicals. Nor can one expect that this phenomenon would be readily recognized or openly debated, least of all in the academic journals themselves!

In a conversation with me, Dr. Theo Rasehorn admitted that there was a time when he had difficulty in publishing some of his critical essays in mainstream academic periodicals and this fact has also been documented elsewhere.[27] Reference has also been made above to Rasehorn's study of the kind of article *not* published in the official organ of the German judges, the *Richterzeitung*. The gravamen of his charge, it will be recalled, was that if regard is given to some of the important social and legal events that occurred during the time under review, one finds that there is little or no echo of them in the contributions of the judges' official organ. A cursory glance at the index of any recent volume of one of the major academic journals in Germany would also show that this tendency of keeping an uncritically low profile in sensitive matters concerning the judiciary, particularly as regards the making of robustly critical comments about the quality and the performance of the judiciary and about judicial incursions into fundamental civil rights, is as much the norm there as it is in Britain. Whereas the inhibitive spirit of the contempt institution may still be held partly responsible for the low-keyed comments in vogue in Britain and other English-speaking countries, this excuse clearly is as irrelevant in Germany as it would be in the United States. Ultimately, we are simply witnessing here the German equivalent of the worldwide phenomenon that lawyers as a group, and academic lawyers particularly, are not known for their propensity to avail themselves of the full measure of speech freedom available to them and that they show little intuitive understanding of the effect of their failure.

That extreme situations often lead to opposite extremes is a common human experience, and the somewhat colorless respectability of the German legal periodicals and their unwillingness to portray fundamentally critical views constituted an important factor in the establishment in 1968 of what really is an alternative law journal, *Kritische Justiz*. As the name of this journal implies, it is primarily dedicated to a systematic subjection of the administration of justice

– the *Justiz* – to *critical* examination and analysis. As far as this objective is concerned, the journal has indeed been an effective voice of very fundamental dissent. However, a very clear Marxist orientation probably underlies the majority of articles and other contributions of this journal. By itself, this orientation does not of course nullify the relevance of the criticism, but it certainly has the effect of being primarily directed at a particular kind of reader, of not fully achieving the palliative or reformative results the contributions may inherently deserve, and of being associated with revolutionary forces aimed at the overthrow of society. It is no exaggeration to say that the influence in Germany of *Kritische Justiz* is at most very marginal.

On another level of analysis, however, it is possible to say on the basis of a careful scrutiny of all the issues of *Kritische Justiz* over the last decade that the long and somewhat painful tradition of esoteric German legal scholarship is still very much alive in the pages of this journal, albeit clothed in a new garb. It actually can be said that only a very small number of the contributions manifest any degree of robust criticism directed at specific individuals or at the real sacred cows of the German administration of justice. Perhaps not quite surprisingly, the one article that clearly falls in this category is by Dr. Theo Rasehorn, in which he critically analyzes the nature of the contributions in the official journal of German judges concerning their social relevance.[28] This article portrays the very limited extent to which the guardians of the legal order in Germany, the judges, are prepared to use (and, especially, to refrain from using) their freedom of speech to broach controversial subjects within the administration of justice and to exert a leadership role.

Critical as is the tone of most articles in *Kritische Justiz*, barely half a dozen articles appearing in *Kritische Justiz* during the first decade of its existence qualify as containing really pointed critique. In this connection, one would consider first and foremost the article, "The Adulteration of the Constitution by Its Foremost Judge: Ernst Benda," on the views of the president of the Federal Constitutional Court of Germany. In this article, Joachim Perels analyzes certain views of Dr. Benda and concluded that the latter, ostensibly eschewing all considerations of class, tries to synchronize the German constitution with existing economic conditions.[29] Constituting as it does a pointed attack on the constitutional integrity of the president of the highest court in Germany, the article is nevertheless couched in very restrained language, with only a very faint hint at judicial impropriety amid the involved ideological arguments. The same trend toward an ideologically oriented critique, largely obscuring the essential points to an average non-Marxist reader characterizes the balance of the handful of contributions that one would define as highly critical according to general Western standards. In short, critical as *Kritische Justiz* certainly is, it somehow falls far short even of approaching the kind of direct and pointed criticism that in Anglo-Saxon countries would qualify for the invocation of the contempt power, and it has contributed less than marginally to the creation of a critical academic atmosphere around the administration of justice.

Judicial Self-Censorship

Silence is not an option when things are ill done.

Lord Denning in the *Quintin Hogg* case

Germany is, of course, by no means the only Western country where judicial officers have in recent times fallen victim of the unexpressed but nevertheless potent taboos as regards matters that ought to be entirely acceptable topics for judicial comment. If anything, given the considerable degree of latitude claimed by certain sections of the German press in their reporting on legal matters, one can only assume that the forces of subtle persuasion on judges in other societies where no such journalistic traditions of critical scrutiny exist would be significantly greater. Two incidents in recent times, one in the United States and the other in Britain, illustrate the strength of certain taboos as far as the judiciary is concerned and, in so doing, reveal the extent to which informal speech restrictions imperceptibly but probably very effectively take their toll in the liberties of the public. These incidents also illustrate the tendency on the part of wide circles in the legal profession not to express themselves candidly and robustly on certain matters in a manner demanded by the public interest. It is not suggested that the views presently to be documented necessarily merit unstinted support, but merely that they are views that potentially have sufficient social merit and even popular support to qualify for open debate, also by judges, in a democratic society. The fact that these views met with the reaction they did shows how even in two of the most liberal Western societies freedom of speech in legal matters is at times severely circumscribed by informal and invisible restrictions that for all their informality and their invisibility are not necessarily less erosive of the public interest. These cases also make one wonder about the submerged part of the iceberg whose presence they clearly indicate.

An incident concerning Judge Archie Simonson, county judge in Madison, Wisconsin, vividly illustrates the subtle (and not so subtle) limitations to which judges at times would be subjected as far as their own right of comment. These restrictions may emanate at times (as happened in this case) from a dedicated interest lobby or even from society as a whole. In setting a fifteen-year-old youth free on a probated sentence for the rape of a sixteen-year-old girl, Judge Simonson commented, somewhat loosely, on the possible link between the victim's provocative clothes and the rape. Although he denied saying or meaning it in that way, his words were taken as implying that "rape was a normal reaction for a young man in Madison's sexually permissive climate and provocative no-bra and mini-skirt female fashions." Together with his subsequent explanations it would seem that he intended to say no more than that "whether women like it or not, they are sex objects" and had to take certain precautions not to be unduly provocative to men.[30] An outraged group of feminists started a campaign against the judge by picketing the courthouse and enforcing a recall provision permissible in terms of Wisconsin law. In the ensuing election, Judge Simonson scored almost 9,000 votes fewer than the winner, a female.

The Simonson recall highlights in almost exaggerated fashion the strong societal pull toward verbal conformism and silence that will often be exerted on judicial officers but will only very seldom surface so dramatically and openly. It illustrates particularly how easily a view that a judge may have, which is by no means logically indefensible or intellectually outrageous and can be entirely germane to a matter of public concern or to a matter in hand, can be self-censored out of existence by fear – legitimate or otherwise – of controversy, unpleasantness, or other detrimental consequences. Although a recall (as happened in the instance of Judge Simonson) or an official blackballing attempt (as happened with Dr. Rasehorn) are rare, it does not follow that such inhibitions are not effective or general since the infrequency of their surfacing may well indicate the pervasiveness and effectiveness of those inhibitions, taboos, and informal restrictions on judicial officers. Although the necessity for judicial aloofness on controversial issues has always had an inherent popularity in certain circles, particularly in English-oriented legal systems, it can hardly be doubted that informal censorship of this or other kinds deprives the societies concerned of valuable leadership in a host of issues closely tied up with the quality of justice. The consequences of such informal sanctions are not entirely incomparable to the consequences of the enforcement of formal speech restrictions. It is also worth noting that I was traveling in the United States at the time of the recall election of Judge Simonson, and numerous legal academics and judges openly opined that the recall request constituted a most serious incursion into the right of free speech. One very eminent senior state judge in Michigan went so far as to say that, based on the reported facts, he believed Judge Simonson was perfectly right to say what he did in the way he did. To my knowledge, however, no judge or academic organization deemed it necessary to express any outrage openly and candidly. Indeed a case of compounding censorship!

Apart from topics relating to obvious and not so obvious ramifications of women's liberation, the issue of race with its many subtle implications will often constitute an equally off-limits issue in a number of impeccably democratic societies with great traditions of free speech. There is little doubt that especially in the United States there will always be an assiduous attempt to avoid any critical comment that could invite the disfavor of any of the black lobbies, as an incident in relation to the Detroit *News* in 1980 would seem to show.[31] The 1978 incident, which involved a British lower echelon judge, Neil McKinnon, illustrates very graphically the depth of the racial taboo in the United Kingdom, a situation that includes the United States.

As backdrop to the McKinnon incident, it is necessary to emphasize again that what is defended here is not only the right of a judicial officer to say the *right* thing (whatever that may mean) or the *popular* thing, but indeed at times to say the *wrong* and particularly the *unpopular* thing, especially when such statements are relevant for a matter which is subject to adjudication. It is an important underlying premise of a vital democratic system of free speech in the legal domain that more, rather than fewer, opinions should be channeled both into society and the judicial decision-making process to assist in facilitating the striking of delicate balances between conflicting societal rights and expectations. Whatever limits there may be for this premise, one would expect that in a matter *relating to free speech itself* this premise would not only find application but also general acceptance on the democratic expectation that so-called unreasonable or wrong opinions would be moderated or corrected within the overall system of the justice machinery. The McKinnon incident shows that even at the present time such a tolerance to judicial free speech in a sensitive matter such as race, even where the original cause itself revolved around matters of free speech, is still very much a distant mirage, even in a country so deeply impregnated with a democratic consciousness as Britain. Of course, it is no doubt possible to argue in relation particularly to the McKinnon case that what is at fault here is much less the democratic consciousness of the people than that of some of the media and pressure groups taking an interest in racial issues.

The facts of the McKinnon incident were unexcitingly trivial but not so trivial as to avoid an outpouring of angry printer's ink and the inevitable dismissal move among a vociferous group of House of Commons members — consequences that may be disastrous enough as far as their immediate inhibiting effect are concerned but must inevitably tend to reinforce even more strongly the very potent taboo that inspired the outcry. In instructing a jury in a racial incitement case, Justice Neil McKinnon stated that the words "niggers, wogs and coons" were not in themselves unlawful. He added: "You have got to look at the circumstances and you have got to allow toleration and freedom of the individual, otherwise we are all caught in the vice of dictatorship, repression and slavery." To underline his point, he referred to the fact that a number of innocuous nursery rhymes contained the expression "nigger" and, referring specifically to the accused whose speech advocating the repatriation of black immigrants had given rise to the prosecution, he stated:

> He is obviously a man who has had the guts to come forward in the past and stand up in public for the things that he believes in. You and I may disagree with him wholly and entirely, and might well vote for almost anybody who stood against him. That is not to say he has committed any criminal offence.[32]

It may well be arguable that these remarks and others that tended to influence the jury in a particular direction contained an element of impropriety as far as their forcefulness was concerned, but there can be little doubt that all the remarks conveyed nothing more than a strong plea for recognizing a degree of tolerance toward language and against the undue criminalization of language, even in controversial racial matters. One might even have thought that the comments of the judge would not only be clearly permissible but would indeed be welcomed in liberal and tolerant circles as a potentially useful contribution (misguided as some may nevertheless consider them to be) toward attaining a fully informed and balanced public opinion and also – as far as the actual trial was concerned – a jury displaying the same qualities. This was not the opinion of sixty Labour Members of Parliament, who supported a motion calling for the judge's dismissal, not to mention the collection of demonstrators, letter writers, and editorialists who spoke and acted along similar intimidatory lines.[33] Whether or not one regards the qualification of "eccentric," which the sober *Times* reserved for the words of Mr. McKinnon,[34] as entirely apt, there can be no doubt that the viciousness of the attacks made on the judge and the sheer unpleasantness of the episode will effectively prevent even the bravest judges from venturing into the thicket of race, even under circumstances where such attempts may make an invaluable contribution to the public's state of information. There may well be other such topics, too. Unlike speech restrictions based on the sanctions of criminal law that are openly imposed and whose deterrent effect thus has a certain degree of predictability, these informal taboos and the formidable professional and social sanctions bolstering them have an inherent unpredictability and amorphousness that make their operation and effect more devastating from the point of view of achieving a full consciousness on the part of the interested public of some of the more controversial aspects of the administration of justice. The price for the virtual extermination of a bit of verbal eccentricity and exuberance will be an attenuation of leadership on the part of persons highly qualified to give it and the undermining of one of the most precious assets of a free society: the *atmosphere* of free speech.

The McKinnon incident illustrates in a somewhat curious way one of the expectations that many Anglo-Saxon societies have of their judiciaries: detachment and self-imposed silence on certain matters, especially of a controversial nature. In 1954, Sir Winston Churchill spoke as follows about the judicial conduct generally expected of judges:

> A form of life and conduct far more severe and restricted than that of ordinary people is required from judges and, though unwritten, has been most strictly observed. They are at once privileged and restricted. They have to present a continuous aspect of dignity and conduct.[35]

Undoubtedly a substantial part of their "restricted" conduct relates to speech, both in court (as exemplified by the McKinnon incident) and out of court. That there is no uniformity of views on what subjects should be off-limits on which occasions must be accepted as inevitable. It seems obvious nevertheless that as a consequence of these judicial taboos there may be a serious attenuation of leadership potential in legal matters at times when such potential may be particularly called for. In societies where for whatever reason the other branches of the legal profession are likewise unable or unwilling to give such leadership, such attenuation of leadership will be especially lamentable in terms of the premises of legal free speech. Needless to say, such inhibitions will strongly promote dishonesty and hypocrisy on the part of judicial officers as regards their statements and silence. This situation is particularly clearly illustrated by the situation in South Africa, of which many elements may be reflected in the legal systems of other countries in the English-speaking world where the spirit of the detachment ethos regarding the judicial ethos prevails. Nowhere in the world, however, have spokespeople for the judiciary been so assiduous in proclaiming this self-emasculation as a positive virtue of their métier as in South Africa.

The problem of the self-negation of a leadership role by the South African judiciary must be seen against the backdrop of two facts: first, the utter state of decay of the South African legal system vis-à-vis the civil liberties of the individual, in which judges have either positively aided and abetted the process or where they have been largely eliminated by the legislature as a meaningful force of control of executive abuse of power; and second, the continued spiritual and theoretical allegiance of most members of the judiciary to the outward forms of the Western democratic legal ethos. Knowing full well that they either positively underwrite the structure of suppression of civil liberties or at least lend considerable respectability and legitimacy to it, judges have found it comfortably expedient to resort to a form of pristine Austinian positivism, as far as their judicial role and status and as far as contentious matters are concerned, and withdraw into their judicial ivory towers. The same phenomenon is observable in almost all African as well as in many South American countries during periods of general political repression.

The utterances on a number of occasions by South African judges on the need for detachment followed appeals – largely from academic quarters – directed at the judiciary to play a more dynamic role of leadership and critical scrutiny toward executive invasions of fundamental human rights. In these reactions, of which three will be briefly documented here, we see what is probably the purest examples possible of yet another form of restraint on judicial officers to speak their minds and to give leadership in sensitive areas – censorship of a self-imposed nature and based on a very narrow interpretation of the role of the judicial office. The narrowness of this role was especially clearly put in 1967 by former Chief Justice Dr. L. C. Steyn when he reacted to academics who had urged the courts to play a more dynamic role in speaking out and mitigating the hardships of certain security legislation:

> It is a very . . . improper [thing] for a judge to rush into a political storm or into the wake of it, in a strongly contested matter in which Parliament has, by way of firm deliberate policy, knowing what it is about and in the valid exercise of its legislative powers, laid down what is to be done. In such a matter, it is not our function to write an indignant codicil to the will of Parliament. If, in the eyes of some, there is any blame in avoiding such a course, I have no doubt that our

judges, one and all of them, will not thereby be pressed into unwise participation, before or after the event, in a political conflict.[36]

The inherent philosophy of the above statement and its relevance within the ambit of legal free speech speak for themselves. Fundamental to this statement is the categorization of crucial matters relating to fundamental principles of justice as *political* matters in order to avoid all argument. By the same token, no doubt, judges in the Third Reich and Uganda would have had no difficulty in hiding behind the same argument. We know what history's verdict on such attempts was.

In 1971, the successor to Chief Justice Steyn, Mr. Newton Ogilvie-Thompson, was even more pertinent in his comments about the need (according to him) for judges to remain verbally discreet in relation to controversial matters no matter what the occasion:

> [I]t behoves a judge not only to conduct himself in a manner compatible with his office but also to endeavour at all times to avoid creating, however, unintentionally, any impression that he holds views which might, albeit perhaps unwarrantedly, be construed as evidence of some sort of prejudice regarding, or prejudging of, some issue which, directly or indirectly, may conceivably subsequently fall for decision in his court. For all these reasons, the expression in public, and in particular in the press or other media, by judges of opinions on controversial issues, whether or not such issues have political overtones, is to be deprecated. Independence, detachment and impartiality are of the essence of judicial office. Justice, it is often rightly said, must not only be done; it must also be seen to be done. It is likewise highly desirable that the independence, detachment and impartiality of judges should be seen to be observed.[37]

That views such as these, emanating as they do from the very top rung of the judicial hierarchy, accurately express the general judicial ethos in South Africa is clear to anyone conversant with realities in that country. Nowhere is this philosophy better demonstrated than in the strongly worded statement of the presiding judge of the Natal Division of the Supreme Court of South Africa in the 1971 *Van Niekerk* contempt case. In making a public speech after the death under mysterious circumstances of yet another detainee who was in solitary confinement on the fiat of the executive, I directed an appeal to lawyers – including judges – to stand up and be counted in protest against a law that made such a situation possible. I was charged with contempt of court, first in relation to scandalizing the courts with the appeal to judges, and second, with infringing the sub judice rule, and found guilty on the second count. The judgment does not have to detain us here again. What is relevant here is only the considered statement of the presiding judge on the appeal to the judiciary to criticize and neutralize the statute under which such injustice was possible. Calling such a view "illogical, perverse or . . . just plain silly," the judge lamented the "misunderstanding of the functions of a judge in a society such as ours."[38] On appeal, Chief Justice Ogilvie-Thompson substantively accepted the philosophy of the statement of the judge.[39]

From these three judicial utterances concerning the proper reaction of a judiciary to an appeal to stand up and be counted in the defense of basic Western legal values, it should be clear at least why the characteristic of silence is so deeply impregnated into the judicial makeup in South Africa. The effect of this philosophy of abdication is not, however, limited to the judiciary, since the kind of excoriation reserved for those academic opponents of that philosophy who favor a more outspoken role for judges would naturally not be willingly courted by academics, who in but a few countries stand in a much weaker position socially than does the senior judiciary. The result of this almost aggressive reaffirmation of the need to maintain judicial silence in controversial matters has been a virtually total lack of outspoken and critical scrutiny of the judicial office, both on the part of the press and lawyers. Naturally enough, the use of the contempt power has underlined this spirit of silence and abdication toward the judicial domain.

Ultimately, it must be accepted as a simple dictate both of experience and survival instinct that judicial officers in most Western countries would maintain considerable discretion as regards their utterances in the legal domain. This attitude would be proper inasmuch as their discretion does not deprive society of a valuable leadership input and merely underlines their formal and spiritual independence from other forces in the state and society. However, silence in the face of injustice or even in the face of situations where their silence will be transparent hypocrisy cannot be accepted as an option open to any lawyer, including judges, in societies where a viable doctrine of legal free speech obtains. Whatever degree of detachment may be required in terms of these beliefs, there remains in all conscience a very considerable area for judicial free speech.

Academic Censorship

The arts and sciences, research and education are free.
Article 5(3) of the German *Grundgesetz*

As a result of the oft-repeated rhetoric relating to academic freedom, one would expect that the one branch of the legal profession that will carve out and retain for itself a very viable degree of legal free speech would be the academics. The overall situation in this regard, as already shown in relation to Germany, is not overly rosy and considerable scope for a greater commitment exists in most Western countries, with only the United States being a substantial exception.

Whereas in a country like the United States, the academic legal profession has attained what may be termed a status of full intellectual sovereignty vis-à-vis other members of the legal profession, particularly the judiciary, this is clearly not the case in all other English-speaking countries in the world and in Europe as well. Passing reference has been made to the British situation as described by Abel-Smith and Stevens (at least as it was a generation or so ago), where legal academics conceived of themselves as a kind of lesser breed in relation to the judges, prompting the former to view the latter from a vantage point of "complete inferiority."[40] Such a spirit of deferential abdication toward the judicial power would obviously provide very infertile soil for the growth of a robust spirit of independence vis-à-vis legal free speech generally, and it comes as no surprise, therefore, to find (with more and more felicitous examples proving the rule) a somewhat censorious attitude toward overly critical material in certain law journals. This attitude is reflected – *visibly* would be a misleading term! – in the apparent nonpublication of material sensitive to judicial susceptibilities. That there has traditionally been a subtle form of self-censorship on British law journals in relation to the kinds of material welcomed and published is not seriously doubted. This is especially true concerning critical comments about individual judges and the quality of the judiciary as a whole. It is clear that the fear of contempt proceedings hardly enters into the picture, since the prospect of such proceedings against publishers, editors, or even contributors of academic journals is inconceivable. The caution simply flows from the general taboo as regards outspoken comments about judges. It is naturally difficult to obtain hard evidence about the practice, and a sufficient number of critical articles do actually appear from time to time to cast some doubt at least on the veracity of such allegations. Shetreet, who has done research into the matter, speaks here of the "inherent reluctance" to criticize English judges.[41] Of course, the contempt power contributed to the general spirit of abdication toward the judicial power, and in other countries this fear may well be stronger than the "inherent reluctance" to criticize judges. The truth of the matter is that the formal and the informal powers of persuasion reinforce each other significantly.

As regards informal censorship in legal journals, it is necessary to stress that the infrequency of its open manifestation is not necessarily indicative of its inefficacy as an inhibiting force. It is simply a fact of life that academics, if it is known that certain expressions or lines of thought are subject to some form of editorial taboo, would prefer to write in a way that would neither risk a rejection slip nor an unedifying correspondence about words and expressions, a tussle from which they can in any event only emerge second best. It is a well-known but as yet substantially undocumented phenomenon in many countries – but certainly according to my observations and inquiries in Germany, France, Holland, Switzerland, Spain, and Belgium, as well as all Commonwealth countries and South Africa – that potential contributors to mainstream legal periodicals are not, as one may ideally hope, in a strong bargaining position of getting articles published in the first place, let alone getting articles published that editors disapprove of on grounds of basic policy or ideology.

Documentable instances of law journal censorship would by definition be almost impossible to come by. Strangely enough, it is from the United States that I have been able to find one of the choice examples of impermissible editorial censorship on legal periodicals aimed almost certainly at the avoidance of embarrassment to specific members of the judiciary. In an article entitled "'Je Recuse!': The Disqualification of a Judge," which appeared in the *Louisiana Law Review*,[42] Professor Ralph Slovenko reviewed the Louisiana statute on recusation. In the course of his article, the author published the results of a poll among attorneys in the New Orleans area on their views regarding the predisposition of specific judges in the city as to whether they were lenient or severe in their punishment policies for certain offenses. The poll, which was entirely germane to one of the themes of the article, attempted to demonstrate that judges are partial on certain issues. In its published form, the poll was neatly excised from the article and not mentioned at all, and but for the fortuitous chance of my hearing of the incident there would have been no record of the event. Informal censorship by its very nature operates unobtrusively and discreetly, with all parties being interested in the preservation of silence.

It is, of course, undeniably true that the womb of the mainstream American legal periodicals, the law schools, have traditionally by their very nature constituted the basic mode for the law teacher. These elitist institutions substantially reflect the status-quo values of the practicing legal profession that remains the career ideal of the vast majority of persons making their way through them. This situation prevails at possibly the vast majority of important law schools in the country. Under these circumstances, it must simply be expected that there will be a natural tendency toward conformism, a tendency that will not fail to rub off onto the legal periodicals that are published there and will almost invariably entail at least a subtle amount of self-censorship on the part of both contributors and editors. This form of informal restriction on free speech, important as it may well be, will not detain us here, pertaining as it does more to the inherent nature of humanity than to a conscious decision to restrict the free flow of speech.[43]

Informal censorship on academic contributions relating to the legal domain will not always be as subtle as the examples or indications that have been referred to. The threats behind the censorship will often be of dire importance to the persons to whom they are directed. This was certainly so in the Rasehorn episode in Germany. It is also well known that in some countries – and South Africa is one example – the authorities possess a powerful instrument of persuasion in the form of printing contracts that they may, if they so wish, quite openly and formally steer away from those publishers who have fallen into disfavor with the authorities on account of the publication of one or more critical works or articles. To the initiated in South Africa, it is for instance an open secret that certain government officials have made a number of very direct threats to the publishers of at least two journals over the publication of articles critical of the administration of justice; in one case known to me, the threat concerned printing contracts and in another the possible cancellation of subscriptions.

An almost bizarre attempt on the part of government authorities to intimidate legal academics from being active in matters relating to contentious issues occurred recently in Arkansas.[44] The facts of the case can be summarized as follows: Professor Gitelman of the University of Arkansas at Fayetteville successfully defended a professor of Marxist economics in a suit aimed at his removal from the staff of a university in the state. Professor Gitelman had already previously incurred the wrath of the state government on account of his involvement as counsel in a number of controversial cases and his latest victory induced the state legislature to pass a law, *applicable only to the law school* on which Professor Gitelman was serving, banning the handling of law suits by law professors. It was generally seen as an attempt to thwart the unpopular activities of a particular legal academic. The first attempt to have the legislation declared invalid failed but not unexpectedly the Supreme Court of Arkansas ruled in December 1977 that the particular statute was unconstitutional. This case constitutes a good, albeit slightly uncommon, example of the lengths to which officialdom will go to suppress unpopular ideas emanating from lawyers, and particularly legal academics.

That an inhibiting censoring effect may at times emanate from establishment sources is observable from a rather remarkable documented incident in Switzerland that illustrates the interwoven nature of government authorities and the ruling establishment of elite. Although Switzerland was a neutral country during World War Two, authorities there nevertheless had seventeen Swiss citizens executed for treason during this period. These events were not candidly reexamined after the war, and when Niklaus Meienberg endeavored to publish the full story of one of these executed persons in 1974 he encountered a total unwillingness on the part of reputable Swiss publishing houses to touch the subject. Meienberg's work, *Die Erschiessung des Landesverräters Ernst S,*[45] was published in Germany. In the preface to the second edition, the author sketches the difficulties he had in attempting to interest Swiss publishers in the work despite its undoubted merits. At work was something in the nature of a conspiracy among people in high places – governmental and private – not to assist in the publication of a work based on the thesis that in the Swiss legal system of the time "the small fry got hanged and the big fish went free."

A comparable combination of official and unofficial instances *attempting* to prevent the publication of a report embarrassing to people in high places, in this case judges, occurred in England regarding the report on contempt of court of JUSTICE, the very reputable British section of the International Commission of Jurists.[46] The report, which advocated certain reforms concerning the English judiciary, constituted the result of the investigations and research of a high-powered unofficial committee. Because of the implied criticism of the existing judicial setup, some members of JUSTICE objected to the publication on account of its possible effect of undermining confidence in the judiciary. It was eventually published after it had been leaked to the press. It is also important to note that the Council of Justice is made up of some of England's most prominent lawyers. Therefore, it is not farfetched to assume that if this kind of self-censoring attitude prevails concerning something as important as the results of such an inquiry, one can expect a far greater amount of self-imposed restraint on more controversial or personal matters relating to the behavior or performance of judges.[47] Partly on the basis of this incident and partly on the basis of the very infrequent use of outspoken speech concerning the performance or qualities of individual English judges both in academic and popular writings, I submit that there is a deep and widespread reluctance in Britain to submit the administration of justice to the kind of scrutiny reserved inter alia for politicians and political matters. This impression also seems to be borne out by the research made by Shetreet in the form of questionnaires directed to academics, practicing lawyers, judges, and journalists.[48] Although one must guard against being too conspiratorial concerning such a speculative matter as this, it would nevertheless seem that in Britain, as well as in other English-speaking countries with the exception of the United States, there exists a curious web of interrelated and mutually supporting taboos and restrictions emanating both from official and unofficial sources that inhibit free, open, and outspoken discussion of controversial issues relating to the administration of justice and especially the judiciary.

A study of attitudes prevailing in the legal profession, including the academic legal profession, in other West European countries would not show considerable variations in comparable attitudes in Germany and England. Inquiries in Sweden, generally considered to rank among the most liberal countries in the world concerning free speech, produced a consensus about the fact that the legal profession does not excel in keeping a critical tab on the administration of justice. If this is so – and language barriers prevented me from inquiring into the substance of that verdict – there is little likelihood of the situation being different elsewhere in the Nordic countries. In Holland, as we have seen, a scrutiny of all the postwar volumes of the *Advocatenblad* in which the merest whiff of fundamental or incisive criticism of the administration of justice invariably finds some echo produced a picture of placid coziness of idyllic dimensions. From various contributions as well as from reported disciplinary decisions against lawyers, it is very clear that there is – as regards criticism of judicial officers – "a boundary which cannot be crossed,"[49] and from some decided disciplinary cases and the general tenor of contributions, it is clear that the threshold is very low indeed. And in Switzerland, quite rightly regarded as possibly the most democratic state in the world if regard is had to institutional factors, probing inquiries on my part and extensive readings of academic journals produced a picture of a legal profession utterly and totally at peace with itself and the situation of the country's legal processes.

With its interesting setup in relation to the peculiar combination of authoritarianism and liberal Western democratic concepts, South Africa offers an interesting case study on self-censorship and editorial censorship on the part of law journal editors. There is overwhelming evidence of such censorship, although it is very seldom, if ever, discussed. Like the situation depicted in Britain by Abel-Smith and Stevens,[50] academics have traditionally accepted the status of a lower breed of legal animal in relation to the judiciary. As a result, academic references to the excellence and near perfection of the judges abound, with editors of legal periodicals often leading the chorus of praise-singing by the use of laudatory articles and the eschewing of truly critical articles. Even otherwise critical academics tend to defer excessively to the judiciary.[51]

Against the background of more than a quarter of a century of institutionalized racial injustice committed under the penumbra of the South African legal system, it still remains a relatively rare phenomenon to find the multitude of symptoms of injustice portrayed or analyzed in academic writings or teachings. Civil rights issues and even the attenuation of the academic's right of free speech are never discussed at academic conferences, and where it is done it is often regarded as unnecessarily polemical and political.[52] Over the last decade, not more than four articles appeared in the two major law periodicals that could be described as controversial or outspoken in relation to the judiciary.[53]

What is particularly chilling for individual critics who do from time to time speak out is the fact that they can rely on so little meaningful support when the panoply of formal and informal powers in the state is rolled out to silence them. In many instances, they can really only rely on time and history for their vindication.[54] Such open academic concern as there marginally was for the issues involved in relation to the attempts to silence this author evaporated after the first case that ended in an acquittal.[55]

An extremely telling indication of the abdication of academic responsibility in relation to the judiciary was the total nonreaction to the attacks on academic scholarship made by two successive chief justices, which were noted above.[56] The one chief justice, Dr. L. C. Steyn, in effect assailed not only the substance of the right of scrutiny in sensitive issues, but he also attacked "the disparaging tone in which this has been done." The handful of attacks he could have referred to are all available in print, and if they have one stylistic character in common, it is their almost excessive deference to the judiciary.[57] No academic journal deemed it necessary to generate a response to what was generally regarded as an unjustified judicial smear on academic scholarship (or rather that minute part of it that had taken a concern in civil rights matters) and even in the journal that published the diatribe one senses something of an attitude of a cap-in-hand peccavi.

Unfortunately, it is the trilogy of cases in which I was involved that highlights more than any other factor the very important role of academic scrutiny as regards the administration of justice, despite the fact that it has in so many ways become an unwieldy bludgeon of injustice in terms of general

Western standards to which the majority of South African academics theoretically at least regard themselves as adhering. These cases have already been detailed,[58] but taken together they created a very extensive no-go area for academic scrutiny around a vast area of the justice domain. Apart from the warning issued by the law teachers' organization at the end of the first case for contempt[59] that the "result [despite the acquittal] is to leave academics and legal authors, editors and researchers with a most disquieting sense of insecurity," the academic profession as a whole either failed to see how their rights would be involved (as they mostly would not be in view of the noncontroversial nature of their ordinary research and statements) or lacked the conviction to register their dissent in more than just a superficial mouth-behind-the-fist sort of way.[60] With this kind of a priori abdication of a role of academic dissidence and unwillingness even to militate for the preservation of the traditional academic domain of fearless scrutiny over all aspects of the justice administration, it is not difficult to see why ungolden silence has become the major trademark of legal academics in the realm of meaningful free speech, with exceptions from a small and predictable handful occasionally underlining the rule.

Academic censorship on the editorial level of the major legal periodical is no secret, and I have partly documented such censorship in one of the main offenders, the *South African Law Journal*, the only South African journal which can be said to have an international standing.[61] The practices of course will be subtle, unobtrusive, and largely done with a skill that at times would even leave the editor unaware that his or her gentle and benevolent hand, which "does so much for academic scholarship," has unbeknown to him or her also wielded a sledgehammer with which to crush the incipient flower of a critical academic literature.

It is common knowledge among the handful of civil-rights-oriented academic lawyers in South Africa that articles containing certain criticisms on certain topics would simply not be tolerated. This is especially so as regards the holiest of sacred cows, the judiciary, and any article criticizing the overall performance of the judiciary or of a particular judge in more than just polite and superficial terms activates an elaborate early warning alarm system in the editorial office so that few such articles will ever emerge in print.

Naturally enough, academics are not always made of the stuff of believers in the making of empty gestures and their contributions will therefore be written with the direct object of invoking the editorial imprimatur. This has the result that certain articles will not be written in the first place and others will be written in such a way that they will successfully mount the informal censorship barricades. This phenomenon, referred to above in relation to Britain and Germany, would in any event not involve more than at most a half-dozen academics who would have an interest in the first place in embarking on research that could fall foul of the editorial censor. They would tend to be more knowledgeable about the subtle rules of the game than anyone else and would simply refrain from writing in the first place or would seek publication abroad.[62]

Undoubtedly, a substantial and growing part of the justification for editorial censorship is simply academic cowardice, often dressed up on spurious grounds with an academic ring – a phenomenon noted likewise as regards the earlier writings of Dr. Theo Rasehorn. My short note on an extraordinary statement by a judge about the unsurpassed merits of the South African judiciary, pronounced in open court as justification for not allowing foreign representatives into in-camera proceedings in a security matter, was sent to the editor of the major Afrikaans academic journal. In returning the article to me, the editor wrote:

> I do not in any way intend to bar all contentious issues from the *Journal*; on the contrary. I find your style of writing bombastic and therefore unacceptable for a journal which strives to attain high scientific standards . . . [and which eschews] a manner of writing more appropriate to a political pamphlet.[63]

In any event, the *South African Law Journal*, known for its almost excessive concern with style, published the note intact.[64] In perusing the articles of the *Tydskrif* since its inception, one is hard put to find one single article that could by any stretch of the imagination be regarded as raising any fundamental issues concerning the judicial office.

I have on numerous occasions been subjected to censorship of a greater or lesser extent in the *South African Law Journal* as regards the use of expressions or arguments concerning the judicial office that would be commonplace in the United States. In two cases, however, entire notes were sent back *not*, as the editor explained, because they were unworthy of publication but simply because they touched issues that were too hot to handle. In the one instance, the chief justice let slip a comment in an otherwise enlightened judgment that clearly indicated to what extent his thinking in sensitive areas was unconsciously colored by racial factors.[65] The editor's comment was that it was really a good judgment and it would be regrettable to pick out this foolish statement. The second instance concerned a much more substantial issue and one that was crying out for analysis: sentencing in cross-racial rape. Whereas statistics show an undeniable and massive obtrusion of the racial factor as a criterion for punishment, Mr. Justice Hiemstra (now chief justice of Bophuthatswana, an independent Bantustan enclave within South Africa) used the opportunity of two cross-racial rape cases for propagating the idea that the differential sentencing patterns in South Africa flowed not from differences of race but of class. My note on this case was returned with the note that although the editor agreed with it and with the need for it to be published, it had better not be published. It has since been published elsewhere where the reader can arrive at his or her own conclusions as to its merits.[66] It will be recalled that my critique at an academic conference about the obtrusion of the racial factor in sentencing evoked a sharp reaction from Mr. Justice (now Chief Justice) Hiemstra.[67]

In a candid exposé at a symposium, the longtime editor of the *South African Law Journal* openly admitted that certain fears can override his own initial inclination to publish certain contentious material: of contempt of court (he was personally nearly charged with me in the first *Van Niekerk* contempt case), of legal consequences for the publishers, and of simple unpleasantness.[68] It is well known, however, that the threat of withdrawing government printing orders from printing firms and cancellation of journal subscriptions for government agencies also take their toll in this twilight world of threats that will never surface in print but will be contained rather in the secret hint and the knowing smile. There is also the phenomenon behind the scenes of judicial arm-twisting (of academics!) to behave in a certain way as regards sensitive topics or personalities.[69]

There is a theory often expressed to me by liberal judges that reference to certain taboos and self-censorship would be self-fulfilling, since they tend to harden and even to glamorize the taboos, thus making it more difficult to weaken the stranglehold of the taboos and particularly of the contempt law. However, experience has taught me within the South African context that genteel silence not only reinforces taboos but that it turns the occasional critical utterance – and they are very occasional indeed – into something of a freakish event for which neither the mediator nor the courts have sympathy. Where on the one hand the air is filled with strident dissent and rambunctious criticism on one of the core topics of the no-go areas, on the other hand there has been a tendency of late to let things be and even to welcome such extravagant criticism because it shows the toleration level of dissent within the legal system. In opening a law teachers' conference in 1980, one Appeal Court judge went so far as to say that academics should not be deterred by the first *Van Niekerk* contempt judgment from saying what has to be said.[70]

Of course, in the final analysis, legal academics see their major role in the field of teaching from where, both in the short and long run, their influence may insinuate into the legal profession as a whole and especially into the attitudes of that profession. Ultimately, one would thus assume his or her influence would be a crucial determinant of the future shape of the law itself. In this context, the picture in South African academe is largely still a depressing one, despite improvements in the teaching of certain subjects in certain faculties and despite the more clinical and critical approach to law in most recent times. In this narrow area, there are many similarities between the situation in South African law faculties and in other Western countries, where a more-or-less narrow and technical approach is in vogue. When completing my own legal education in South Africa in 1962, I cannot recall that at the University of Stellenbosch where I had studied I was ever on a *single* occasion meaningfully confronted in my lectures by any critical *reference* to the inherently unjust aspects of South African public law relating to race, class, or poverty. Anything political was entirely excluded from the ambit of teaching, a situation that remained unchanged for about fifteen years afterward, during which period I often had the opportunity of exchanging ideas with colleagues and students there. Ironically, criticism of judicial findings on politically and socially neutral issues, particularly in the field of private law, was made regularly, robustly, and almost viciously – sometimes also in print, to the obvious chagrin of the judiciary – a situation rarely and probably never found in any other law school at the time.[71] The underlying philosophy of the law school was the protection of class and the breeding of the ideal of the "well-heeled, bowler-hatted individual with striped pants and walking stick umbrella who hangs out at the Inns of London or their equivalents in South Africa."[72] Reared and trained in a spirit of aloofness of this kind and exposed to so few winds of dissent during their education, the South African legal profession as a whole continues and will for a long time hence still continue to reflect an uncritical and status-quo-oriented approach to the law, including a great many controversial aspects of the law relating to basic issues of justice. Exposed to nothing but eulogies in the press about the administration of justice, especially the judiciary, and reared largely on nothing stronger than academic pap and deprived (mostly by voluntary action) of the excitement of indulging in the rewarding exercise of keeping institutions of power democratically in check by a fearless and determined use of free speech, the South African legal academic sees his role as that of an ignominious being commentator on other concentrations of power, especially those of the legislature and the judiciary. Unique as this situation may seem to be, it has its parallel in probably the majority of countries described as Western.

THE JOURNALISTS

Were it left to me to decide whether we should have a government without newspapers, or newspapers without a government, I should not hesitate a moment to prefer the latter.

Thomas Jefferson

Difficult as it was to pinpoint the evidence and elucidate the reasons for the reluctance of lawyers in various times and climes to express themselves outspokenly on certain issues relating to the administration of justice, it is even more difficult regarding the journalistic profession and the news media. Whereas there are a number of general qualities that all lawyers everywhere display at least in some measure – commitment to the peace within the profession being one and a general ideological commitment to the social status quo being another – this would clearly not apply to journalists as a whole in democratic countries. The traditions and structures of the press in the West are such that one would expect a vigorous degree of robust scrutiny of the administration of justice as an important source of power over the state and the citizen. In reality this ideal is seldom achieved.

It is not necessary to expatiate on press freedom as the fundamental theoretical ideal of the press in all democratic countries. Suffice it to say in relation to our study that most journalists operating in countries with a free press would react violently to any suggestion that an important segment of public life either be shut off from them or subjected to strict controls concerning what may or may not properly be published. The reasons that could be proffered for the outrageous nature of such a suggestion are numerous but invariably revolve around the argument concerning the social need to scrutinize and control the exercise of power. And yet, it is one of the minor marvels of the story of freedom in the West that as a whole the press has often been willing to impose such restrictions on itself as regards one of the most vital and uncontrolled centers of state power: the administration of justice. The general result is that the administration of justice, more particularly its controversial aspects, receives far less critical attention than the dictates of freedom and of common sense would demand.

The reasons for the reluctance on the part of large sections of the Western press to subject the administration of justice to adequate critical scrutiny are multifarious and multifaceted and would clearly differ from society to society. A cluster of reasons does seem to exist, however, that seems to apply in most countries. It would be appropriate to outline these reasons before proceeding to document the symptoms and instances of such reluctance. Once again, some of these reasons are of a highly subtle nature, based often on psychological realities.

That journalists would also fear legal repercussions concerning the exercise of their métier seems obvious. Apart from the effect of formal speech restrictions, we also encounter here something in the nature of a radiation or fallout effect of legal sanctions that extends far beyond the point of immediate impact of the sanctions themselves. Because speech offenses or other legal restrictions on free speech in the legal domain are always by their very nature vague and amorphous and often depend for their invocation and interpretation on highly personal critieria, it is simply human to expect that those persons who may be drawn into the firing line of the restrictions would tend to exercise a degree of care and reticence that would avoid, as far as possible, the very risk of legal repercussions arising in the first place. We are confronted here with the proverbial chilling effect of speech restrictions, but where a major part of the chill derives more from personal or psychological factors than from the actual sting of the law. Formal and informal restrictions and taboos unite here into a mutually supporting and circuitous mesh of inhibitions with potentially crippling consequences for a dynamic concept of legal free speech.

The decision to publish or otherwise, or to publish in a particular way, material concerning the administration of justice will often be taken by legal advisers who may have little intuitive understanding of or concern for the wider social implications of their decisions. The consequence may well be a legal opinion based on an interpretation of the law that is much wider than one that an eventual court may opt for. Although one is clearly dealing here with a general consequence of the intimidatory effect of legal sanctions, this fear and reluctance to test the law are in a more immediate sense based on a subtle form of self-censorship, with the law acting as convenient pretext and immediate catalyst for the particular decision.

The phenomenon of self-censorship justified on legal sanctions will obtain in any country where there are serious legal restrictions concerning the administration of justice. It is in this ambit that I submit that the diametrically opposed views of English editors regarding the existence or otherwise of a serious intimidatory effect of the contempt institution must be seen.

In a report of JUSTICE,[73] the editor of the London *Evening Standard*, Charles Wintour, is quoted regarding the effect of the contempt sanction: "I probably spend more time worrying about the possibility of contempt of court than I do about all the other legal restrictions put together."[74] Despite this pessimistic assessment of a senior journalist, the members of the joint working party issuing the report stated that they were "nevertheless of the opinion that the law of contempt was not nearly as threatening as some editors and journalists imagined it to be, and need not be as inhibiting."[75] This statement means effectively that certain English journalists really use the contempt law as a facile pretext for refraining from commenting incisively on the administration of justice. The working party goes on to state even more clearly their opinion as regards the need on the part of newspapers to break loose from the exaggerated fear of the contempt law:

[A] large measure of responsibility rests upon the press to keep a constant watch on the proceedings in the courts at all levels and to make such criticisms as appear necessary in the interests of justice. We therefore support the view of one editor who said that if a criticism needed to be made, the press should have the courage to make it and risk the consequences.[76]

Shetreet[77] also records the fact that although there was a general feeling among judges, barristers, solicitors, academic lawyers, and journalists in England that the "press was afraid to criticise the judges," one journalist "surprisingly" suggested the opposite.[78]

Another factor relating to the realm of self-imposed psychological restraints concerns what may be termed general ignorance of the law on the part of nonlawyers in general, especially in those societies where legal restraints on the press are important. Legal speech restraints concerning the administration of justice are inherently vague and shifting, even for lawyers, and it is only to be expected that journalists would even be more reticent than lawyers to probe the outer limits of such restraints.[79] In any event, it is simply to be expected that the well-known self-restraint of lawyers in controversial legal matters would not fail to be reflected and indeed emulated by journalists. After all, why expect journalists to risk their professional necks if the experts, the lawyers, display such a notorious lack of concern to scrutinize their own métier and field of operation for fear of risking a confrontation with the law?[80]

In many developing countries where the democratic ethos is still in an embryonic stage, one of the major reasons for a hands-off policy on the part of journalists toward the administration of justice flows simply from the general weakness of the press vis-à-vis government. In these countries – and they would include virtually all African countries, the vast majority of Latin American countries, and all the countries in the East with perhaps a half-dozen exceptions – the administration of justice is tacitly understood as an integral part of the government structure and the same reluctance toward trenchant criticism of the government would manifest itself as regards the administration of justice. In many of these developing and/or semidemocratic countries, the judiciary in reality constitutes a group of islands of relative enlightenment in comparison with the government administration and hence their claim to respect from the media would find ready support with a resultant reinforcement of the informal taboos around the administration of justice. It is revealing to note that one of the major psychological barriers that prevents the so-called liberal South African press from subjecting the judiciary to trenchant criticism is undoubtedly the fact that outwardly the judiciary remains the most respectable part of the governmental structure. An additional barrier is the fact that the liberal ethos of those journalists places great stress on judicial as opposed to executive determinations, a situation that has the psychological effect of rendering the liberal journalist inherently reluctant to tear into the one shred of decent government surviving relatively intact amid the ruins of Western standards of government.[81] The situation in South American autocratic societies seems similar.

Despite considerable assistance given me, it was not possible to find any worthwhile examples of the press indulging in free criticism of the administration of justice in countries like Nigeria, Senegal, the Ivory Coast, and Ghana. The examples of robust criticism of the administration of justice in these countries all concerned criticism of sentences in actual criminal cases or of laws and institutions. It was particularly in Nigeria and Senegal – the latter now being a multiparty democratic country in the broad Western sense of the word and the former being a military regime but with the survival of many democratic traditions, including one relating to the existence of a relatively free nongovernmental press – that I could through very well-informed and well-connected persons establish the correctness of the above-mentioned principals. In Senegal I was able to study the situation during numerous visits over the last decade. A very informed observer of the legal scene in Nigeria provided one reason for the absence of any meaningful scrutiny of the administration of justice: "criticism of the judges comes too near to the bone of the regime itself" and would therefore neither be seriously contemplated by journalists nor tolerated by the regime. Even in a democratic country like Costa Rica, a law professor there informed me, newspapers are very reluctant to pierce the veil of awe around the judiciary for fear of some unspecified unpleasant reaction.

One important but subtle factor that in developed democracies tends to inhibit the consistent and outspoken scrutiny of the administration of justice, particularly of the higher echelons of the judiciary, relates to the existence of informal but very real personal connections between the judiciary and the top people in the press world. What this really means is that because the top echelons of the judiciary and of the press would often belong to the same social class and may even be personally known to one another or to friends of one another by subtle lines of communication, there would be a natural tendency on the part of the press not to use the same aggressive methods of scrutiny normally employed for other incumbents of power. These lines of communication would be difficult to establish, but it is not at all difficult to detect the relevance of this factor at least in all English-speaking countries – the United States once again partially excepted – and also in countries like Holland, Switzerland, and the Scandinavian countries where the ruling establishment is relatively small and where the lines of communications between the top journalists and the top judges are more direct and less amorphous than what is seemingly the case in a highly decentralized country like Germany.

In South Africa, where I have been able to observe the operation of these subtle forces from close quarters – and where indeed I have been privy to many surreptitious tip-offs during my own confrontations with speech laws – this phenomenon of what may be termed social in-breeding at the top levels of the judicial and journalistic profession can be seen in its purest form, and although it is clear that the situation there would probably not be fully paralleled in any other country, it undoubtedly has considerable heuristic value. All South African judges and all the editors of the top newspapers would in the first place be drawn from substantially the same middle-class white society and they would, for all the superficial political differences that may at times separate them, reflect very similar views on a number of essential questions, among which would be an exaggerated belief in the need to maintain both the dignity of the judiciary and its independence. Members of the judiciary and the top echelons of the press clearly constitute the most enlightened guardians of Western traditions, particularly in their own eyes, and as a simple proposition of human psychology almost instinctively endeavor to avoid treading on each other's corns. The leaders in both fields would in almost all cases also be directly or indirectly familiar with each other, would possibly belong to the same cultural organizations, would as VIPs in a small, racially compartmentalized society often physically meet each other at functions and share certain perquisites, and would also quite likely have similar social customs, likes, and dislikes. Against this background, it must come as no surprise that there will arise a kind of spiritual communion between judges and top journalists that would tend to reinforce greatly the already potent inhibitions on the press to direct outspoken criticism of the judiciary, more specifically at individual members of the judiciary. And when criticism does in fact emerge from across this subtle threshold, it will be of a kind that is markedly different to that reserved for other mortals who are incumbents of positions of power.

In Britain, the traditional reluctance on the part of the quality newspapers to subject the judiciary to robust criticism may also partially be explicable with reference to considerations such as those just mentioned, with the result that the editors of newspapers would be reluctant at times to vent on the incumbents of the bench the same kind of criticism reserved for other persons at the levers of power. When it is facilely said, as does Shetreet, that there is an "inherent tendency [on the part] of the English to avoid criticism of their judges,"[82] the statement in fact informs us less about an allegedly intrinsic British trait, than it does about the profession that normally does the criticizing, the press. In a recent work on the English judiciary, the following was stated:

> [I]t is demonstrable that on every major social issue which has come before the [British] courts during the last 30 years – concerning industrial relations, political protest, race relations, government secrecy, police powers, moral behaviour – the judges have supported the conventional, established and settled interests.[83]

Assuming at least the partial correctness of the above statement, it will not be at all farfetched to assume that the media, which have similar views or inclinations to judges on those social issues, would at least be hesitant about probing into any controversial aspects of the judiciary. This would be so, not on account of any conscious policy of journalistic dishonesty because the values for which the judiciary seems to stand are values that are largely similar to those that the editors of the British quality papers also aspire to defend. The result would be that, apart from more-or-less peripheral criticism and apart from the inevitable exceptions, fundamental criticism of the judiciary would be muted and infrequent. In the same way as the judiciary would be subtly and informally linked to fundamental ideological values of the state and those persons of all political parties representing such values in public life, they would have links with top journalists. This tacit communion of ideology would by itself obviously not be sufficient to restrain more activist newspaper writers and editors, but it must be seen as merely one factor among many – including the legitimate or exaggerated or feigned fear of legal repercussions – that has led to such a situation in Britain that it can be said that even today there is still "an inherent tendency" to avoid criticism of judges. A glimpse of the subtle operation of such lines of communications between the press and the judiciary may well have been manifested in the aftermath of a bitingly critical article from the outspoken pen of Bernard Levin in the *Times* of London. In a letter to the *Times*,[84] a correspondent significantly wrote: "[W]hat should not be lost sight of is that had Goddard still been among us, Levin's perfectly justified expression of opinion on a matter of public importance would probably not have been printed as it stood." The correspondent then continued by relating how a review by him of a biography of Lord Goddard in which he took a similar although "milder" position on Goddard was "panned" by the editor of "a national journal."[85]

Those appointed as judges in most English-speaking countries are mostly from a small group of top barristers. Even before their elevation to the bench, there would already in all likelihood be a system of direct or indirect personal contacts between them and the top people in the press. After their elevation to the bench, senior judges in all English-speaking countries of the world form part of a very closely knit society that is bound together by a web of ties of professional loyalty and common interests. These common interests would inter alia involve a commitment to the defense of the ethos and the ésprit de corps of the judiciary, particularly in the face of criticism or opposition. It is in this atmosphere that just a few close personal contacts between top journalists and top judges could have a disastrously inhibitive effect, at the very least subconsciously, on the willingness of sections of the press to direct anything akin to strong criticism or investigative journalism at the judiciary. On one occasion, when a comment of mine had angered a particular judge, the senior judge of the particular division of the Supreme Court in South Africa "invited" the editor of one of South Africa's major newspapers, an acquaintance of his, into his chambers and prevailed on him to publish what in effect amounted to an abject retraction of a critical statement that had been fully justified by the facts that had preceded (and gave rise to) the criticism. There is practically no chance of anyone but a senior judge achieving such a result with an editor.

Naturally, the symptoms of this conscious and unconscious self-censorship on the part of the press are not easy to detect. This is so, first, because of the general denial on the part of the press of the very existence of the phenomenon and, second, in view of the well-known difficulty to record facts that have their basis in the nonexistence of something. In what follows, a tentative outline will be furnished of a few of the evasive symptoms of this phenomenon.

As can be expected, the United States offers by far the most liberal picture concerning outspoken and robust journalistic comment on the administration of justice. The situation will obviously greatly vary from state to state, from community to community, and from time to time, but there is generally no reluctance on the part of most newspapers to speak with outspoken vigor and robust blandness on anything and everybody concerning the administration of justice. This situation is at least partly a consequence of the exceptional growth and vitality of the system of legal free speech in the wake of the disappearance of virtually all legal restrictions. It is partly no doubt also an aspect of the wider phenomenon of legal realism that since the early thirties has so deeply influenced American legal thinking. And in part it is simply a reflection of the growth of the concept of what is sometimes termed "a First Amendment Society."[86]

Speaking generally, there is effectively no bar on any inquiry or criticism and almost no bar even on the kind of language that can be used in American newspapers. It is, for instance, difficult to imagine that any newspaper in Britain, a Commonwealth country, or even in the European continent of the importance of the San Francisco *Examiner* would print the following comment of a correspondent as regards a particular judge's action: "It is incredible that someone who appears to be a knife-wielding mental case was released on bail. Judge Louis Garcia either lacks the commonsense of a 5-year-old or is looney himself."[87] The columnist in whose column this signed letter appeared went on to support the sentiments of the letter writer concerned.

The extent to which the American press shows and promotes an interest in the administration of justice was clear from its robust methods of reporting on pending or proceeding court cases documented above in another context.[88] The efforts of the American press to eliminate all sub judice curbs is also indicative of its general concern not to be inhibited in matters relating to the administration of justice, and although one will often find abuse under the banner of free speech, especially as far as the invasion of privacy is concerned, it is possible to say that as far as the quality press is concerned one has reached a situation of maturity that befits a society of free people where the only inhibitions would be those dictated by good taste.

As important as the absence of any meaningful informal inhibitions on journalists in America to comment freely on all aspects of the legal domain is the extent to which a positive effort is made to promote public interest in the law and legal machinery. It is in this wider and perhaps more subtle sense of journalistic commitment to legal free speech by the heightening of general expectations that *some* American newspapers play a vitally important social role. In this context, there is first and foremost the very detailed and at times erudite background articles, topical analyses, and editorials in the New York *Times* on practically all aspects of the administration of justice, including controversial ones relating to personalities and shortcomings in the judiciary. This kind of open, analytical, and robust reporting and analyses on legal matters in the New York *Times*, although not paralleled in its incisiveness by any other American newspaper – indeed by no other newspaper in the world – is also found in the Washington *Post*. In view of the continental dimensions of the United States, it does not of course follow that the extent of information on legal matters available to readers of the New York *Times* and the Washington *Post* is matched in all major concentrations of population. The very opposite really seemed to be the case when I studied American papers on a thirty-state U.S. visit in 1977. However, from the point of view of influencing the major political and judicial decision makers in the country whose decisions and views may in turn filter into the more isolated nerve centers of the land, the very considerable amount of critical reporting on the administration of justice in these two quality newspapers has the indubitable effect of achieving a degree of consciousness about legal matters in the leading sociopolitical echelons of the United States that has its counterpart only in Germany, as will be shown later. It does not mean that this consciousness extends to all walks of life and to all the communities in the United States, but it does mean that there is essentially no major area of the law shrouded in mystery or ignorance and that decision making takes place in an atmosphere where, relatively speaking, it would be knowledge and fact and not ignorance and myth that would hold sway. It is in this atmosphere of a free availability of knowledge and a willingness to carry all legal matters, including embarrassing and sensitive ones, into the open that legal free speech assumes a dynamically creative role befitting a democratic system of government. Only in such a society is it possible for a chief justice to state, as happened in 1978, that more than half the lawyers in the country are unfit for practice! It is also in such an atmosphere that some lawyers would be more easily able and willing and better equipped to assume a role of leadership in the scrutiny of legal matters for which they are arguably the most ideally suited group in society. In the United States, the media and the organized legal profession have in the wake of this openness developed a new discipline: the monitoring of the qualities and the behavior of judges. Tom Goldstein, a regular writer on legal affairs on the New York *Times*, put it this way:

> With judicial behavior being scrutinized as never before, judges are finding it harder to favor friends and relatives with impunity or accept favors themselves. If they act erratically, someone is likely to blow the whistle. In New York State, which had a full-time commission on judicial conduct for the last three years, a new, but not entirely consistent, body of decisional law is developing. . . . [The decisions taken in this regard] illustrate what is becoming increasingly clear: injudicious conduct falling short of criminal activity is less likely than it was a few years ago.[89]

The greater freedom that has now become the vogue about judicial matters in America is not without its own perils to free speech. The more critical and sometimes ill-informed attention expended on the performance of the judiciary may well invoke a proclivity on the part of the latter to popular conformism, inhibiting them from giving the kind of leadership that only they can give and from honestly speaking their minds on their own judging processes. The incidents concerning Judge Archie Simonson in the United States,[90] Judge Neil McKinnon in Britain,[91] – not to mention the Rasehorn episode in Germany[92] – clearly illustrate the perils in this regard. These perils, however, are inherent to the ongoing struggle in which any democracy is engaged of a never-ceasing endeavor to strike sensible and acceptable but intrinsically imperfect and always delicate balances between conflicting social interests. Ultimately, more rather than less information flowing from the availability of more rather than less free speech and from a bigger rather than a smaller diversity of opinion would – in terms of a democratic ethos of free speech in the legal domain – better serve the achievement of those precarious balances.[93]

One potential area of taboo in the United States that remains and may in fact be growing as regards journalistic scrutiny of the administration of justice is that which relates to certain racial connotations of the legal domain in America, particularly those dealing with blacks. The psychological burden of centuries of dsicrimination against American blacks has left a scar on them that has yet to heal and it would seem that one consequence of the healing process is an intolerance toward certain critical views relating to the position of blacks within the justice administration. The McKinnon incident in Britain gives a pointer to the kind of situation that may be involved here. More to the point would simply be the recognition and enunciation that certain crime phenomena may in crude statistical terms be black – or conversely white – phenomena. In simple terms, therefore, there may be matters relating to the legal domain that may need to be said but will not be said or will not be said in the way in which many people candidly conceive of them if there is a risk of offending with sensitive groups within certain minorities, especially blacks.

A significant glimpse of this potentially vast taboo area as regards legal reporting was obtained in 1980, when it was reported that black ministers of religion and other leaders were campaigning for a boycott of the Detroit *News*, America's largest afternoon newspaper, over that paper's exposés about corruption among black lawyers and judges in Detroit. When the furor broke, one crucial fact quickly emerged from the welter of accusations: no one had seriously challenged the basic facts of the articles. That being so, there can be no doubt that the Detroit *News* was being subjected to strong persuasion to remain silent for racial reasons; and there can be little doubt that other sources of critical scrutiny of the justice domain that lack the resources of a major newspaper would find it even harder to publish their views if there is but the least likelihood that a well-organized racial lobby would label such views as being racist. Paradoxically, there is a similar racial taboo in operation on the antiracist opposition press in South Africa as regards certain embarrassing facts about blacks, including facts relating to the quality of black lawyers and the treatment of indigent blacks by black lawyers. The lesson that part of the benefit of freedom is the benefit to be criticized has still to be learned on both sides of the Atlantic, where diametrically opposed racial policies prevail.

A few chilling conclusions seem justified based on a review of many cuttings from the Detroit *News* incident and a long interview with the editor, Mr. William Giles. First, there was more than a prima facie case of improper practices in the Detroit Recorder's Court and about the person of its chief judge, relating inter alia to the expunging of records, favors to friends, and overpayment to certain favored lawyers. Some of these defects were later admitted and rectified. Second, the allegation of racial bias was not made by the *News* but the charges were given that connotation by the chief judge, certain black lobbies, and by a rival newspaper the Detroit *Free Press* essentially because the persons charged happened to be black. Third, using any yardstick that would be generally applicable to other investigative reporting in the United States, the stores seem to have been adequately and responsibly researched and presented, with due cognizance taken of the problems involved and the lack of cooperation of the judicial authorities concerned. Fourth, again using the above yardstick, the Detroit *News* would have been guilty of a cover-up had it failed to report what it knew, although the essential purpose of the pressure brought to bear on the *News* was to achieve such a cover-up. Fifth, the approaches made to and pressures brought on the editor by prominent blacks to refrain from pursuing the story, essentially because of the negative impression people would have of black intellectual leaders, illustrate the pervasiveness of the taboo and the dangers for those who choose to ignore it. Sixth, the total lack of concern in the national media for this obvious peril to free speech and of support for the Detroit *News* demonstrates in an even clearer fashion the profundity of the lack of concern to put certain embarrassing racial aspects of American justice on the free marketplace of ideas.[94]

In Britain, there is no doubt that there generally still is a substantial measure of reluctance on the part of the quality press to be robust and outspoken about some aspects of the administration of justice, particularly the judiciary, and the deterrent presence of the contempt power is only part of the reason for this attitude. Nevertheless, many exceptions proving the rule have been multiplying over the last two decades, with the result that the rule itself has become seriously attenuated. This has come about less as the result of an overall change in outlook and direction of the British press than as the result of the endeavors of individual editors or writers who at considerable inconvenience and even peril to themselves and their newspaper set out to challenge some of the taboos in the legal field. In this context, reference must once more be made to the remarkable *Sunday Times* case on the thalidomide tragedy that was extensively discussed above.

Naturally, it is against the background of the awesome contempt power that the *Sunday Times* thalidomide case must be seen in the first place, and it was therefore in that context that attention was chiefly given to this bizarre manifestation of lack of freedom of speech in the legal domain. However, given the truly strange facts of the case – the manifest injustice to scores of malformed children, the patently unreasonable delays in reaching a humane settlement, the enforced silence of the press on a matter of overwhelming public importance, the need for informed public debate, and so forth – I submit that something more than just the fear of the contempt power was involved here. It is not difficult to see an exemplary manifestation of a combination of genuine fear of or respect for the law and legal processes on the one hand and a deep reluctance on the part of the press as a whole to challenge one of the sacred cows of English justice on the other. It must be remembered again that at stake in this wrangle was *not* the protection of any meaningful social value, and there was no question of a trial by newspaper in any intelligent sense of the word. Seen in this light, it must be concluded that the thalidomide tragedy also constituted a total abdication of journalistic responsibility of the entire British press, until the *Sunday Times* started the publication of its series of exposures. If ever there was an occasion where the vast majority of British subjects would have condoned an open and clear technical breach of the law, this was it. It is inconceivable that these facts were not appreciated by the top leaders in British journalism, and the fact that the abdication of responsibility nevertheless took place over such a long and agonizing period is as telling an instance of self-censorship on burning social issues relating to the administration of justice as can possibly be found anywhere. In short, the *Sunday Times* case in fact occurred many years too late.

Looking at the English situation more positively, one is struck particularly by the fact that one paper took a profound and wide and often critical interest in most aspects of the administration of justice. The *Times* of London, it is trite to say, constitutes a paragon of excellence in a number of fields; it is also so in relation to the scope and depth of its legal reporting. Together with *Le Monde* in Paris, it is the one major daily paper in Western Europe that has a clear policy of devoting regular and detailed attention, both reportorial and analytical, to the administration of justice. Although its reports and comments on legal matters are possibly not as wide in scope and as critical as is the case with the New York *Times*, it must be borne in mind that British society itself presents a more homogeneous and hence a less problematical picture as far as the administration of justice is concerned. It can nevertheless be said that the *Times* of London fulfills a uniquely important role in Britain to keep the top leadership of the country – the majority of whom are probably daily readers – informed about most issues within the administration of justice and in so doing to promote the growth of a critical spirit toward justice machinery in society as a whole. However, in keeping with the general low-keyed approach of the *Times* of London, an approach that at times seems clearly geared toward avoiding any unduly harsh criticism of any important segment of the social and political leadership in the country with which it is not entirely unconnected, the reporting of the *Times* is mostly less robust or vigorous than that of the New York *Times*. In this conscious effort to achieve what the editors and publishers may regard as a "balanced approach," the *Times* of London at times manifestly fails to generate the kind of criticism that a particular legal matter may deserve. However, with possibly only one exception in Europe and two in America, the *Times* provides the widest critical and analytical coverage of legal matters in the Western world, with the result that what it lacks in outspokenness it makes up for in its wide coverage.[95]

It is not possible to speak meaningfully about the demystification of legal matters by the *Times* of London without mentioning the regular column of Bernard Levin in which legal matters are often discussed. It can certainly be said that Mr. Levin's columns make up in outspokenness, robustness, and even abrasiveness what the editorial columns of the *Times* lack. The healthy irreverence of Mr. Levin's wit, especially when directed at certain judges and the legal profession, constitutes a potent counterbalance to what is certainly by U.S. and German standards an excessive reverence in the *Times* and other British newspapers for the dignity and pomp of the law and its officers. Mr. Levin's articles have on various occasions inflicted devastating verbal body blows at the legal profession[96] and the judiciary,[97] and his caustic wit has certainly contributed more than peripherally to promoting a more healthy disrespect for some of the sacred cows of British society. A choice example of Mr. Levin's devastating demystification technique in action is found in his article "The ritual game of licence in court," in which he excoriates the impunity with which lawyers and judges alike have been able in court proceedings to assail the characters of noninvolved outsiders.[98]

In referring to Mr. Levin's role as one of Britain's chief iconoclasts in the legal field, it is almost impossible not to mention what must be the most biting bit of iconoclasm ever published in a mainstream newspaper – this time in the conservative *Spectator* – about none other than Lord Chief Justice Goddard during the latter's lifetime.[99] Published in 1958,[100] at a time when the contempt power still held its awesome sway over comments about the judiciary – a full decade before the *Quintin Hogg* contempt case[101] – the article is unique for its reasoned acerbity in relation to any of the legal systems studied in this work:

> It is true that Lord Goddard's law is generally quite good; though he is far from being one of the great jurists. The trouble with Lord Goddard begins precisely where his law books end; in so many of the things, apart from knowledge of statutes and case-history, which a judge ideally needs, the present Lord Chief Justice is woefully deficient. Most notorious of his blind spots is his astonishing ignorance of mental abnormality. . . . Along with this deficiency goes the girlish emotionalism which seems to be his only reaction to such subjects as capital and corporal punishment.
>
> In detailing to the House of Lords, during one of the debates on hanging, two particularly dreadful cases, he said of one (in which a man had raped and mutilated an old woman whose house he was burgling), "The prisoner, thank God, was not a British subject." . . . What is so alarming about this kind of emotional spasm is not that anybody should be so silly as to imagine that terrible crimes are more terrible when committed by British subjects, not even (though this is bad enough) that these remarks should be made by the premier judge on the English bench. What is so shocking about it is that Lord Goddard's citing of these examples was prefaced by the astounding assertion that they were examples of murders "where there is no question of insanity." That anybody in any judicial position at all should be so blinded by his feelings so seriously as to believe that men capable of such acts are men in whose make-up "there is no question of insanity" would

be deplorable; that a judge of Lord Goddard's rank should cleave to such fantastic beliefs is indeed a wretched blot on the English legal system, far out-weighing such trivia as, for instance, the appallingly indiscreet vulgarity of his speech to the Savage Club (much of which seemed to be taken up by an interminable tale about a man who made lavatories), or his curious liking for what the authors of this study call "masculine" or "belly-laugh" stories, but which most of us know as dirty jokes.

And indeed, on the question of insanity in murder, Lord Goddard walks hand in hand with ignorance on one side of him and barbarism on the other. . . . Still, it would be idle, even if agreeable, to maintain that Lord Goddard is, as far as general opinion goes, anything but typical. Muddled, narrow, overwhelmingly emotional, with a belief, the roots of which he is a thousand light-years from understanding, in retributive punishment and the causing of physical pain to those who have caused it to others – in all this he represents only too well the attitudes of most people in the country whose judiciary he heads. Perhaps every country gets the Lord Chief Justice it deserves.

Finally, concerning the *Times* of London, one may note the salutory custom from time to time of senior British judges being interviewed[102] or of such judges writing relatively critical articles.[103] Any address by a member of the judiciary containing elements of criticism of the legal system will invariably receive generous coverage in the *Times'* news columns[104] and often in the editorial columns as well. On the basis of an analysis of the most important legal reports in the *Times* between 1973 and 1978, having evaluated all the issues of the *Times* over a four-month period in 1976, and having daily studied the legal reporting of the *Times* for a period of fourteen months in 1977 and 1978, I have no doubt in submitting that, as a vehicle for imparting a very substantial amount of information and as a watchdog over any abuse in the administration of justice, the *Times* plays a uniquely important role, and with the possible exception only of *Le Monde* in Paris it has no peer among the dailies in those respects in Europe. It constitutes a veritable paragon in Europe as far as the consistent coverage of legal matters by a daily is concerned and as regards the creation of the kind of critical social atmosphere in which an informed and dynamic system of freedom of speech in legal matters can more easily flourish.

In surveying the quality press in the Netherlands, Germany, Italy, and Switzerland, and the Jerusalem *Post* in Israel, one is struck by the relative lack of interest in legal matters displayed in leading daily newspapers, both in their news coverage and in their editorial commentaries and background articles. The result is undoubtedly that something in the nature of an information vacuum on many aspects of the administration of justice exists in those societies. A study of leading newspapers such as *Corriera della Sera* and *La Stampa* in Italy, the *Neue Zürcher Zeitung* in Switzerland, the *Frankfurter Allgemeine Zeitung* and

Die Welt in Germany, the *Figaro* in France, and the *De Telegraaf* in the Netherlands would immediately reveal that in none of these major European newspapers is there any consistent system of legal reporting and journalistic scrutiny of the administration of justice of the kind found in the *Times* of London, *Le Monde* of Paris, or in the New York *Times*. As can be expected, all these newspapers carry full reports on important cases and judgments and reports of problems in the justice domain, but what is substantially absent is the kind of critical and informative articles and reports that on a regular basis illuminate and sometimes castigate controversial aspects and personalities of the administration of justice. Regular readers of these newspapers would obtain at most a sketchy impression of some of the important aspects of justice, especially concerning topics such as the selection and quality of members of the judiciary, miscarriages of justice, penal institutions and mental asylums, class justice, and the like. Their attitude concerning issues within the administration of justice can best be described as detached, and it will come as no surprise that this outlook will also be translated into the public opinion, leading in turn to a general and imperceptible blunting of the critical faculties of the community at large in the legal domain. In such an atmosphere of relative unconcern for some of the more controversial aspects of the administration of justice, one can expect to find a relatively high degree of unwillingness on the part of interested parties, including the legal profession, to challenge the administration of justice on fundamental legal issues and hence to contribute to the demystification of law and its processes. This atmosphere of unconcern can in turn contribute to the determination of the extent of the exercise and hence ultimately of the legal limits of the right of legal free speech.

It is difficult enough to assess the effect on the general critical consciousness about legal affairs flowing from the kind of reporting of a medium such as the *Times* of London; it is even more so when dealing with a supposed *absence* of such interest in relation to a lack of incisive reporting on such matters. It is on the basis of a close personal observation of the above quality newspapers over relatively long periods, ranging from at least three weeks to periods of several months, that I submit that my conclusions above will stand the test of a more scientific scrutiny. Even with due allowance made for my subjective views, which strongly favor libertarian principles in speech matters, I contend that my basic submission cannot be faulted that all over Western Europe there is a lamentable tendency on the part of the quality press to avoid confronting incisively and regularly many sensitive legal issues. In many of these publications, which are of a uniquely superb quality as far as breadth and depth of general reporting and editorial commentaries are concerned – and here I should mention especially *Die Welt*, the *Frankfurter Allgemeine Zeitung*, and the *Neue Zürcher Zeitung* – this restraint seems particularly lamentable, and it underlines heavily the imperceptible web of social and political restraints as well as simple indifference that work as inhibiting factors on these media, which otherwise constitute veritable citadels of Western libertarian traditions in the press world.

At this juncture, reference must be made again to a journal that in its class can only be described as a unique institution in the realm of legal reporting and legal analysis, *Der Spiegel.*[105] As a periodical of unsurpassed quality as regards in-depth reporting and as a vehicle of investigative and demystifying reporting and analyses, *Der Spiegel* does not have its peer anywhere in the world. Within its very wide range of articles and reports, the justice administration receives regular, ample, detailed, and incisive attention. Many of its in-depth legal articles border on the scholarly and are often written by experts in the fields. Whether the contribution concerned is a background study,[106] or is an account of a trial (a matter studied in detail above), or relates to the documentation of events of a legal nature, it is bound to spare no one and soft-pedal no issue. When seen against the fact that *Der Spiegel* is literally read by almost every decision maker of importance and by the vast majority of legal academics and probably by almost all journalists in Germany, the influence that this journal radiates in legal matters can only be described as phenomenal. Whereas the daily press in Germany, as already noted, often seems to give legal matters a wide berth, *Der Spiegel* has a different policy in that regard, largely compensating for such deficiency on the part of other news media by the regularity, incisiveness, and comprehensiveness of its legal reporting. All *Bundesverfassungsgericht* members who responded to a questionnaire of mine had praise for *Der Spiegel*'s legal reporting.

It is not possible to provide an adequate overview of critical legal reporting in Europe, and especially Germany, without referring tangentially to another fine product of European journalism, the weekly newspaper, *Die Zeit*, which plays the role in Germany that the quality Sunday press plays in Britain and America. Although the legal reporting of *Die Zeit* is less regular and less detailed than *Der Spiegel*'s, no important legal development will be unreported and unanalyzed. Most of the contributions of a legal nature over the last eight years have been submitted by a qualified lawyer, Dr. Hans Schueler. After surveying the major articles from the pen of this legal journalist since 1971,[107] it is clear that the working of the Federal Constitutional Court has attracted his regular, detailed, and often quite critical attention.[108] Considering that *Die Zeit* has an appreciably more conservative image than *Der Spiegel*, its consistent concern for legal matters has the undoubted consequence that together with the more robust and regular legal analyses of *Der Spiegel*, the educated public opinion as a whole in Germany is probably better informed about legal matters than any other in the world, with all that that implies for a sharpening of the critical faculties, at least among the intelligentsia, toward most aspects of the administration of justice.

The extent to which the typically bourgeois attitudes toward sensitive legal issues have in most countries in the world been almost universally accepted becomes strikingly apparent when the legal reporting of the official newspaper of the Italian Communist Party, *Unità*, is analyzed. On a purely theoretical basis, one would have assumed that the combination of the press and speech freedom that Italians enjoy, the rejection of bourgeois values by the Communist Party, and the incredible corruption and disarray of the legal system in Italy would combine to produce highly critical legal reporting in that medium. The very contrary is true. A study of this newspaper over several weeks revealed no significant difference in the amount of meaningful legal analysis or reporting from that of any of the other non-Communist dailies. An analysis of all major legal reports between 1975 and 1978 as furnished by the editor indicates that the most critical reports would only qualify as mildly critical by Dutch or South African standards, and the most outspoken one related to the acquittal of a number of terrorists.[109]

Difficult as it is to quantify this phenomenon of self-imposed reticence on legal issues in the major newspapers of the world, it is clear from an inquiry with senior journalists in Europe that many of them are keenly aware of the situation and they also readily concede the detrimental social consequences of such reticence. Four editors of major newspapers in the Netherlands and one in Britain agreed with my proposition that too little critical attention is devoted to the administration of justice in their countries. None of them thought that legal restrictions were significantly responsible for the situation. In the case of liberal journalists from a country like South Africa – a country that despite the presence of a mine field of press restrictions still retains a relatively outspoken and independent press – the first and invariable reaction is to explain their reticence in controversial legal issues with reference to legal restrictions, and it is only after deeper probing that they concede that even within the legal restrictions they may just perhaps be too restrictive when writing about a host of highly relevant but controversial legal issues on the legal and social scene in South Africa. The same legal pretext is not so readily available to journalists in Western Europe, and one often finds top journalists quite willing to concede that the press has largely failed to expend on legal matters the same degree of critical scrutiny that they reserve for other areas of social activity. In a very candid letter to me, one of the editors of a major Dutch newspaper stated that most papers in his country – a country that after all is regarded by many as being one of the most socially tolerant and democratically enlightened in the world – "do not even try to scrutinise or cover adequately questions relating to the quality of the administration of justice." Speaking about "criticism of judicial decisions," the same editor states that such "criticism ... is a more delicate affair than criticism in the realm of political affairs" in view of the essentially different character of the two areas and, he concludes, "I would not treat them as equal or directly comparable objects" as far as criticism is concerned.[110] In an interview, a prominent Swedish journalist simply described the attitude of the Swedish press toward the sacred cows in the justice domain as "disgusting."

Two further sources of legal and especially judicial scrutiny, one in Germany and the other in the Netherlands, merit special reference. In Germany,

Der Stern, a type of glossy family type magazine, regularly addresses itself very outspokenly to legal problems, contentious judgments, and miscarriages of justice. In this context, the wave of judicial protest that was directed at *Der Stern* after the publication of its article on the German judiciary will be recalled.[111] In the Netherlands, there are regular legal articles in *Het Parool*, formerly by Jac van Veen[112] and more recently by a lawyer, Mrs. de Konig. In these articles, a somewhat pedagogical motive is pursued whereby the layperson can be introduced to legal problems relating mostly to specific cases.[113]

As far as endeavoring to play a positively educational role in legal matters is concerned, another unique journalistic beacon in the West, *Le Monde*, must be singled out. It can certainly be said of *Le Monde* – in the same way as it can be said of *Der Spiegel*, the *Times* of London, and of the New York *Times* – that it has created its own almost unbeatable standards of excellence in legal reporting and commentaries. *Le Monde* in this respect is simply in a unique league of its own concerning the quality, scope, regularity, and incisiveness of its contributions on the law. *Le Monde* is read by a very large proportion of the most important decision makers in France, and as such its influence on legal matters will filter through to the major social and political nerve centers of the country. Considering the breadth of legal reporting in *Le Monde*, it can therefore be said that at least among the readers of that newspaper there is no lacuna as regards critical information about the justice machinery, leading undoubtedly to a more critical attitude toward the administration of justice in those nerve centers. On the basis of discussions, it would seem that a more critical and skeptical attitude toward the justice machinery exists in those groups in France than in similar groups in England, the Netherlands, and Germany.

From a survey of practically all the legal articles and commentaries of *Le Monde* over a period of two years, it is possible to make a number of deductions relating to the creation of an informed and critical public opinion about the administration of justice. First, the sheer *regularity* of the legal contributions is impressive. With a few exceptions, there is practically a legal column every day. Although many of these columns will be chiefly concerned with reports of cases, a substantial number of them – about one-half – will contain editorial or specialist comment. Second, the regularity of informed and critical background articles and comments about the law is likewise impressive, and this characteristic particularly puts *Le Monde* in a special category as far as West European dailies are concerned. Many articles are written by practicing lawyers and judges and a fair percentage of them can be described as critical or mildly antiestablishment and thus destructive to the creation or survival of myths in the legal domain. Third, although most of these articles can best be described as having an explanatory or educative nature, some of them are mordantly critical.[114] Finally, it is necessary to note that the articles and commentaries are always concerned with an extensive range of subjects related to the administration of justice, from a series on the "snakepit justice" of the summary courts dealing with *flagrants délits*,[115] the "conveyor belt justice" of a particular court,[116] police violence,[117] the pompous style of legal speech,[118] to the perennial charge of courts being too soft on criminals,[119] to mention just a few topics from my collection of clippings. Written in a semiacademic style interspersed with commentaries that characterizes most of the reporting in *Le Monde*, these articles constitute a veritable mirror of practically all aspects of the legal scene of France and a potent instrumentality of keeping the administration of justice under active and continuous scrutiny.[120]

In a multistratified country such as Israel, a country moreover that in its present configuration has been under continuous threat for a third of a century, the justice administration would naturally tend to reflect the siege mentality of the dominant groups of society. One would also expect a conscious effort on the part of the press not to rock the boat overly, lest criticism undermines (in terms of popular beliefs) the confidence in one of the pillars of the state, the justice administration. Language barriers compelled me to look only at the role of one newspaper, the Jerusalem *Post*, which, together with a Hebrew contemporary *Ha'aretz*, apparently constitutes the major source of critical legal comment.[121] The above expectation of reticence is essentially fulfilled when one peruses the legal reporting of the *Post*. Such a survey of legal reporting over a period of five years prior to 1978 is nevertheless revealing from a number of angles relevant to the questions being surveyed here.[122] First, there are regularly background articles or analyses of good quality about legal matters that at times have a relatively strong critical flavor, as far as legal provisions and the ministry of justice are concerned. However, such articles are rare and never even approximate the kind of mordant or simply outspoken criticism of *Der Spiegel*, *Le Monde*, and Bernard Levin's columns in the *Times* of London. There is certainly a willingness to report in detail on any legal scandal or inadequacies such as questionable police methods and long delays in the courts, but the comments fall short of questioning basic policies and personalities of the judiciary. Second, the Jerusalem *Post* makes a conscious effort by way of specialist articles and interviews to play an educational role in legal matters and is particularly wont to give members of the judiciary a forum for their ideas. As a general proposition, it is true that a newspaper with as small a circulation as the Jerusalem *Post*, appearing to boot in one of the most provincial capitals of the West, nevertheless concerns itself more regularly and intensively (albeit not too critically) with the administration of justice than any daily in Germany, Switzerland, Holland, Italy, or Spain. Nonetheless, there are clear limits beyond which the Jerusalem *Post* clearly does not venture, a consequence possibly of the inherent and understandable ideological inhibition referred to above. This inhibition, at least concerning the judiciary, was referred to somewhat unwittingly in an article entitled "Destroying the Rule of Law," in which the proposition was propounded that judges must not be unduly criticized since it would undermine the "rule of law."[123] A member of the Knesset, not surprisingly perhaps, soon afterward spoke about "the growing danger to democracy in Israel as a result of the increasing number of attacks on our courts and judges"[124] when he referred to the same instances referred to by the Jerusalem *Post* – that is, industrial disputes and reactions to commissions of inquiry – where members of the judiciary came in for strong criticism.[125]

Underlying what has been hitherto said about the degree of intensity of legal reporting and scrutiny of the justice administration is the assumption that there will ultimately be something in the nature of a causal connection between such reporting and scrutiny (or absence thereof) and the quality of justice in terms of the premises of legal free speech. This connection is more easily stated and assumed in theory than substantiated in practice, and in the final analysis one returns to one's democratic article of faith with the feeling that such connection does in fact exist despite difficulties in proving or disproving it. In a candid and wide-ranging interview with the Jerusalem *Post* – the interview itself was a rare and felicitous example of a high judicial officer outspokenly speaking his mind on controversial issues – Justice Yoel Sussman of the Israeli Supreme Court directed a shaft of excoriating criticism against several ills of the legal scene and the standards of the people involved therewithin. However, even more significant was his belief in the need for judicial officers and the media to scrutinize intelligently the workings of the courts in the interest of justice.[126]

A Case Study: South Africa – The Myth of a Free Press

One of the most skilfully nurtured South African myths is that there is a genuinely free press. This myth is perpetuated by the apparent freedom with which the English-language press criticizes governmental policies and practices in certain legally and conventionally defined areas; by the praise of foreign critics who are continually surprised to find any criticism tolerated and, particularly, by the shower of abuse poured upon the English-language press by government spokesmen who regularly accuse it of disloyalty and subversion and threaten to deprive it of its "freedom."

Professor John Dugard in *Human Rights and the South African Legal Order*[127]

The situation in South Africa regarding the scrutiny of sensitive legal topics by the press naturally would not have its exact parallel elsewhere in the world, but it is also clear that many aspects of that situation have heuristic value in other societies in the Western world, especially (but by no means entirely) in those states where government rules with a heavy hand. In many respects, the situation in certain so-called Western countries – the whole of South and Central America would largely fall in this category – is appreciably worse than in South Africa.

As a general background to what follows, it is important to consider that the *belief* in and commitment to press freedom is very much alive in South Africa, particularly in large sections of the press itself. Language and other connections with the freest press in the English-speaking world – notably Britain and the United States – have the effect of sharpening and deepening this belief. Although grievously hampered by a plethora of unnerving laws couched in ambiguous and expansive language and often unimaginatively applied by courts that have little understanding of the underlying issues, this belief and commitment have at times flowered into action and revelations not incomparable to the best the free world has to offer by way of illustrations, including the uncovering in recent times of a governmental scandal of a scale greater than Watergate, which lead to the resignation and disgrace of the president.[128] However, instances of a vigorous demonstration of independence vis-à-vis the administration of justice, especially the judiciary, are few and far between, and the South African press offers an almost perfect laboratory example of the observance of certain important taboos in relation to the administration of justice. More significantly, it constitutes a rare case study that can be documented with tolerable accuracy of the social and legal consequences of the observance of these taboos in the legal domain.

Two important phenomena characterize the South African press as a whole concerning its role as a vehicle of free speech in the legal domain: first, its purely voluntary abdication (as opposed to a legally or governmentally induced abdication) from playing a meaningful and dynamic role as regards many – but not all – aspects of the administration of justice; and, second, the unawareness and even denial among many journalists that such abdication is taking place. Both these phenomena assume overriding significance when viewed against the backdrop of the state of the administration of justice, a state of affairs with which more than half of the leaders of the South African press would strongly disagree privately and publicly. It is perhaps only this last point that makes the situation in South Africa as regards the role of the press in the legal domain markedly different from the situation in most countries in Western Europe, where the administration of justice is likewise not given sufficient outspoken attention. The analogy in this respect with most Latin American countries and perhaps Italy would be more accurate. Whereas leaders in journalism in most West European countries may at times be critical of aspects of the administration of justice and yet refrain from speaking out at all or speaking out as they would in relation to other ills in their society, they do not overtly or covertly reject as vehemently and as avowedly the basic tenets and configuration of their respective administrations of justice as is the theoretical case with a large percentage of their South African counterparts.

In terms of the consensus of international opinion in the journalistic and academic worlds, the South African legal machinery falls very far short of acceptable standards, particularly in the field of the protection of basic human rights and more especially when those rights are interwoven with problems concerning race and political dissent.[129] I submit that the majority of editors and senior journalists of the English-speaking press in South Africa[130] would largely support the international consensus, a submission I base on personal knowledge and on direct information from those quarters. Yet we witness, now and in the past, the incongruous situation that, in a press known at times for its strident opposition to the ruling political order, there is virtually no whisper of dissent or even a trace of outrage when things are ill done by the South African judiciary.[131]

Equally important and concomitant to the abdication of responsibility regarding the legal domain is the fact that the policymakers of the press are either unaware of such abdication or, if they are aware (as I submit they are largely on the basis of my close contact and many discussions with them over a number of years), they take great pains at concealing or denying it in their copy. This unawareness or concealment of self-censorship is from the point of view of the defense of the fragile concept of free speech in the legal domain of possibly greater importance than an involuntary or reluctant abdication of responsibility, since it reveals, in effect, either a basic agreement with the status quo or at least a conscious subordination of the value of free speech to other values. Personal inquiries in a number of South American countries reveal a different approach on the part of responsible journalists, inasmuch as there is generally a candor about their unwillingness or inability to penetrate the taboos around the justice machinery. The analogy with France and Germany is much more apposite, where in certain influential journalistic circles a similar abdication or simply disinterest concerning the legal domain would likewise either be denied or ignored.

Generally, the unawareness of the situation of self-censorship in the legal domain or its denial take place against the backdrop of considerable reporting – including critical reporting – on legal matters in the South African press. These legal matters, however, mostly concern either executive actions (of the justice ministry, for instance) or the state of the law or actual judgments. In this respect, the South African situation is very comparable to the situation in Holland or Britain, as described by Abel-Smith and Stevens,[132] before recent improvements. In short, the charge of abdication in sensitive legal matters is countered by pointing to consistent scrutiny in less sensitive (but perhaps still controversial) legal affairs.[133] Also significant – in regard to an analogous situation in most Western countries where informal legal taboos are observed – is the reluctance by academic scholars or journalists to concern themselves with the phenomenon.[134] Editorially, there has been a considerable reluctance even to admit the existence of a problem or to take responsibility for shouldering the burden of a vigorous scrutiny of sensitive aspects of the judicial order.[135]

What is not in doubt today is the overall *theoretical* commitment of the South African press as a whole[136] to press freedom generally as well as to contentious statutes. However, the considered charge that is made here – and that is made with deep respect and considerable reluctance for an institution that has done more than any other to keep the tatters of Western ideas fluttering in an inclement clime – is a rather nuanced one; it is that the press has gone much further than a "strictly enforced law on contempt" (in the words of the *Star*) seems to demand or than is justified in terms of another ubiquitous but seldom expressed catchall alibi: "local circumstances."[137] That the contempt laws and other press restrictions have contributed to the atmosphere of awe and aloofness around the judicial administration is decidedly true, but the crucial point is that the press – and, as we have seen above, the entire legal profession – has been far too willing to hand over to the law much more than its legitimate pound of flesh on the one hand and, on the other, to indulge in far too much unqualified praise-singing in favor of the judiciary. In addition, the truth is that the concept of legal free speech has not been seen by the press as the militant doctrine it certainly is – one that necessitates at times the making of a painful stand or the use of skill and ingenuity. In any event, there is a strong reluctance on the part of authorities to prosecute over issues where the defense of truth and public interest would inevitably be raised. This would particularly be so where the quality of the bench or its individual members is pertinently raised or where the racial element within judicial policymaking is isolated.

It would not be difficult to compile a debilitating list of matters in South Africa that could very justifiably be subjected to vigorous scrutiny by the press, but are mostly not given the critical attention they deserve beyond mere reporting at most. Such matters are, for instance, overall discriminatory sentencing patterns among races; the obtrusion of conscious or unconscious racial premises among members of the all-white Supreme Court judiciary and overwhelmingly white lower court magistracy; blatant discrimination going back for generations in many interracial crimes, particularly where the death sentence may be imposed; possible lack of understanding between judges and the judged due to differences measurable in light-years as far as cultural chasms are concerned[138]; the way in which factors of avoidable and discriminatory class justice permeate the legal system; the quality of individual judicial appointments and incumbents; the traits of particular judges (so-called hanging judges, for instance) as regards sentencing; the ability of certain judges to be independent in certain political matters in view of their identifiable predispositions; the total breakdown of almost all procedural guarantees in cases involving undefended accused – that is, the vast majority of accused in South Africa; the narrow social and political *Weltanschauung* of most judges in view of their narrow training and their commitment to elitist values in a predominantly proletarian society; and so forth. On the basis of these and many other similar matters, it may well be possible that opinions will differ widely, but it is impossible to deny that every single point of possible criticism alluded to here can in fact be substantially supported. Yet one will very seldom hear but the faintest echo of these matters in even the most liberal newspapers. Criticism, particularly narrow technical criticism of individual judgments, is found from time to time, albeit rarely, but there is for all practical purposes a total silence on criticism of a fundamental nature. Narrow technical criticism of judgments can of course be found even in East European socialist states.

The virtual absence of any proclivity or willingness on the part of the South African press to subject the administration of justice, especially the judiciary, to vigorous scrutiny is particularly clear from a statement made as far back as 1955 by the most liberal newspaper – both then and now – the *Rand Daily Mail*, as regards the reason for the lack of scrutiny of judicial appointments at a time when the contempt power was still largely dormant:[139]

> No one who respects the dignity of the judiciary would lightly criticise the system by which judges are appointed. Clearly there is a danger that comment on this subject might give the impression that the judges themselves were being criticised. That would be the first step towards undermining confidence in the bench, a disaster that no sane citizen would court.[140]

It is important to note, first, that what was deprecated was not criticism of actual appointments but criticism of the *system* of judicial appointment – a *system* that in practice is based on the unfettered discretion of the minister of justice and has often been grievously abused and by its very nature is racist in its effect. Second, in this bit of unwitting honesty, which will probably never be repeated, there is a strong adherence to the belief, assailed at numerous junctures of this work, that respect for and confidence in a judiciary are contingent on an absence of criticism. It is particularly relevant in this context to note that, of all South African newspapers, the *Rand Daily Mail* has traditionally displayed more independence and courage toward the ruling order, including the legal order, than any other newspaper.[141]

The taboo around the vitally important matter of the quality of judicial appointees, with which the *Mail* editorial was concerned, has rarely been pierced, and then only very tangentially or obliquely, despite the fact that there seems to be no relevant contempt case law in South Africa or Britain making such an exercise overly perilous. Only the Johannesburg *Sunday Times* has at times gingerly entered this thicket with mild criticism.[142] I am aware of only one instance – and then surprisingly on the part of an Afrikaans newspaper – where the appointment of a certain judge who obviously fell far short of being judicial material was roundly condemned.[143]

Coupled to the lack of scrutiny of judicial appointments and incumbents, there has traditionally been a concomitant indulgence in effusive praise of the judiciary as a whole, with little concern for accuracy and in terms that to my knowledge are not found in any other country.[144] Almost any patently correct or courageous step on the part of a judge can be counted on to draw a volley of unstinted praise *for the judiciary as a whole*. Such praise is understandable in purely psychological terms, since the judiciary unquestionably constitutes the least contaminated part of the body politic and a considerable part of the ethos of the press is also predicated on the use of judicial procedures (as opposed to administrative procedures) in the maintenance of state security, so that it is felt criticism of the judiciary may undermine this ethos.

Apart from the operation of the combined force of the taboo around the judicial office and of psychological deference to the judiciary, a third factor undoubtedly plays a role as it does in most Western countries, but then merely as regards specific media: shoddy reporting of persons not sufficiently knowledgeable about or interested in some of the subtleties of judicial lawmaking. There is a tendency in most societies to afford legal processes more respect and awe than they may inherently deserve, and flowing from this tendency there seems to be a widespread reluctance on the part of nonlawyers to probe into some of the more involved aspects of the legal machinery. Judicial lawmaking would certainly fall in that category. In short, the failure on the part of journalists to afford the judicial process the attention it deserves may at least partly be based on negligence and incompetence.

Such lack of competence is by far not an exclusively South African phenomenon, and in several letters by Dutch and British editors to me it was deprecated in relation to their own countries. Nonetheless, this unwholesome combination of negligence and incompetence is potently present in the workings of the South African press. On many occasions, senior journalists and editors explained to me their failure to analyze or report a legal event by their lack of expertise in the subject. The press reactions to the three free speech cases in which I was involved graphically illustrates the situation. All three cases pertinently concerned the role of the press, and the precedents created there apply today with greater force to journalists than to anyone else.

The first case,[145] ending as it did in an acquittal for scandalization contempt after a short and dramatic trial, was followed in all English dailies by an outpouring of critical comments, some scathing in the extreme, about the prosecuting authorities and the judgment.[146] The second case concerning sub judice contempt was finally disposed of in the Appellate Division of the Supreme Court, at which time the case had lost its topicality. Moreover, the case and the conviction revolved around both controversial and involved aspects of judicial influencability that went beyond the immediately available expertise of the press at the time. Despite the fact that the judgement constitutes one of the most oppressive precedents for the press to live with, not a single critical commentary was forthcoming.[147] The same happened in the *Van Niekerk* defamation case, where a newspaper was codefendant and where it was ultimately held that in effect the *government* can be defamed.[148] What came into play here was obviously a combination of subtle factors in which negligence and lack of expertise would only constitute two, perhaps minor, elements. The taboo factor interconnected with them was obviously based on exaggerated respect for judge-made law or on fear of legal complications. In any event, the result for South Africa has been a debilitating silence on matters vitally important to society.

Not astonishingly, there is a strong taboo about the taboo in the press in view of the unflattering connotations affecting the reputation of an institution that has very successfully cast itself in the role of a vigorous upholder of free speech. Some of the reactions to my accusations have been noted above. Only the *Sunday Times* has ever approached something akin to a willingness to put part of the blame on the press. Its willingness flowed in large part from the presence of a courageous and legally trained person in the editorial chair.[149] Inter alia, the newspaper stated as follows:

> It is possible that judges in South Africa have been edged into aloof isolation. Criticism of their judgments and verdicts has been muted to the point of extinction. The fundamental assumptions that they make are never questioned in public.... [T]he Appeal Court and the Bench in general are regarded with awe by the government and the establishment which surrounds it. This reverence descends through the radio and, to a slightly lesser extent, through the press, to the public in general, who have come to believe that our judiciary is as near perfect as makes no difference. This belief is not discouraged by the bench itself.[150]

This taboo about the taboo concerning the role of the press within the administration of justice naturally has its basis in the psychological reality that no institution gladly parades its inherent defects, least of all if such defect goes against the grain of its raison d'être and declared principles. This taboo also exists in the United States, as proved by the Detroit *News* incident documented above in relation to racial aspects of the American judicial system. No newspaper, it will be recalled, came out in support of the Detroit *News* when it decided to challenge the taboo of the quality of certain black judicial personnel in Detroit.[151]

The extent of the mental subservience of the South African press to the judicial establishment can at times reach grotesque proportions, as is illustrated in the abject and totally undeserved apology of a newspaper for simply publishing a photograph, taken during filming operations in the precincts of a court, of a shapely girl (a former Miss World) seated on the judge's chair playing a game of cards. It was pointed out that such a picture could have "the effect of bringing the Supreme Court into disrepute."[152] One might have assumed that at least one national newspaper would have had the courage to tell the particular judge that it was he who was bringing ridicule, if not contempt, on his bench. There was no such statement.

An aspect curiously interlinking formal and informal speech inhibitions in the legal domain and that is also demonstrative of the imperceptible flow of one set of inhibitions into the other concerns the role of legal advisers to the South African press. The important but invisible role of these advisers has still to be investigated, but they are undoubtedly highly relevant in setting the tone for reporting and commenting on legal matters.[153] Speaking on the basis of personal experience over a period of more than a decade during which a multitude of statements and contributions of mine have landed on the desk of the legal advisers of newspapers and also on the basis of numerous discussions with journalists and editors, I think it is manifestly clear that perhaps the most important éminence grise in the South African newspaper world as far as critical legal reporting is concerned is the legal adviser. In most instances involving the slightest doubt as regards either the legality or even the propriety of statements relating to the administration of justice, he will be referred to. Largely on the basis of his own hunch as regards likely consequences of publication, the adviser then would decide whether or not to publish or decide the form of the publication. The role of legal advisers in South Africa in setting the tone of journalism in the legal domain is apparently embarrassing. I am aware, for instance, that in a book review a reference to the fact that the book concerned ignored the role of the legal advisers in setting the tone for reporting was excised from the review in a newspaper!

The monuments to the role of legal advisers to newspapers consist not so much in what appears in the newspapers but in what *fails* to appear, despite social circumstances that militate strongly in favor of airing the questions concerned. It is not difficult to understand how legal advisers of newspapers, by being members of a profession that in South Africa at least is notorious for its narrow legalistic approach, would mostly advise their clients to exercise caution and prudence rather than forthrightness and courage. With the relevant common law or statutory provisions as elastic and wide as they are and with lines of decisions often based on amorphous principles, the advisers would naturally be perfectly right to argue that a particular formulation *may* be regarded as unlawful by a court. However, by so often taking such a restrictive line under circumstances where prosecutions would be either very unlikely or socially and politically very costly to the authorities, they have perhaps contributed more than any group of persons apart from editors to dilute the essence of free speech in the legal domain and to deprive society of some of its beneficial consequences. That this problem is not typically South African is clear from and implicit in the statement, already quoted, of a joint committee of British lawyers and journalists in 1965: "We support the view of one editor who said that if a criticism needed to be made, the press should have the courage to make it and risk the consequences."[154]

Apart from the very rare reference to a matter that has been censored for legal reasons, one would not readily be able to identify the operation of the legal adviser's role. However, on one occasion a skit on the evidence of a police officer before a judicial commission of inquiry by the now exiled editor of the East London *Daily Dispatch*, Mr. Donald Woods, was withdrawn by the legal advisers of at least three newspapers to which the article had been circulated by telex. By mistake, the telex message containing the legal advice was not received by one newspaper, which published the report on the agreed day. No consequences ensued. Several months later, the other newspapers in the syndicated pool published the article, obviously also without bringing the wrath of officialdom down on them. At the time Mr. Woods had already become the bête noire as far as the government was concerned, and an attempt to prosecute him would not have been surprising. The incident graphically demonstrates the excessive caution of legal advisers to the press and the way in which their excessively cautious approach allows a far greater diminution of press freedom in the legal domain than what may reasonably be expected. Ostensibly, we are confronted here by the debilitating operation of the law, but in actual fact one is witnessing the operation under legal guise of extralegal inhibitions. Needless to say, there was no indication in this instance of the decision of the advisers.

The identifiable social consequences of the operation of extralegal taboos in the South African press concerning the administration of justice are not difficult to identify. Some of them merit brief mention. First, there is the logical fact that silence in these matters breeds ignorance, which in turn generates myths. The allegedly color-blind nature of the law and the reputed excellence of the judiciary are two obvious examples. Second, flowing from this ignorance and the oversensitive approach toward the judiciary, the latter institution invariably starts believing in its own unsurpassed excellence. If the judiciary's normal journalistic fare is unqualified silence on contentious aspects of their métier and/or unqualified praise, it is inevitable that in time certain incumbents would act as if such silence or praise were totally merited, a fact that would also affect their approach to legal matters, as will presently be shown.[155] Third, there is a general blunting in society as a whole and in the press specifically of critical faculties in relation to the administration of justice. One of the most striking features of self-censorship in the South African legal domain is the widespread ignorance about or denial of its existence. Because the press is not really expected by public opinion or critics to do more in that field, it very expectedly does not tend to strain its nerves and resources in an exploit that may turn out to be both perilous and controversial. Fourth, and most important, in time social taboos tend to harden into legal restrictions. This has undoubtedly happened in South Africa.

The elevation of societal taboos into legal taboos is a phenomenon that has already been referred to.[156] In South Africa, the situation is particularly clearly documentable in relation to legal free speech. When in all three cases in which I was involved the highest courts of the land were called on to lay down the outer limits of legal free speech in the three most important areas of the law regarding free speech in the legal domain, they were doing so essentially on a clean slate as far as the three different issues were concerned and without any interference whatever from statutory law. However, the general atmosphere as depicted in the press in relation to legal free speech was not that of a robust spirit of inquiry that had manifested itself over many years. Therefore, on the basis of simple propositions of realist jurisprudence, it is not difficult to understand why they chose highly restrictive rather than liberal interpretations of the law. When some kind of criticism is rare or nonexistent, it is almost axiomatic to expect that judicial authorities would also regard it as unreasonable, and when laying down the *legal* limits of free speech such unreasonableness would consciously or unconsciously color the findings of such authorities, who would quite naturally tend to interpret amorphous speech restrictions in the ambit of societal beliefs and expectations. Where a certain kind of criticism or a certain line of inquiry on the part of the press have been sanctioned by long and consistent usage, a judicial officer would be deeply wary and very hesitant to decide a matter in a way that would go contrary to a strong existing trend and interfere with something akin to vested rights and expectations. However, because the South African press had over a period of decades failed to educate the public about some of the finer aspects of legal free speech, the judiciary could step into a virtual vacuum as regards public expectations and generate new restrictions with impunity. In a sense, the fight for legal free speech was lost before it ever began.

Likewise, regarding the willingness or otherwise of the legislature to enact restrictions on free speech in the legal domain, there is a lesson to be learned from the actual use made by the press of their rights to free speech and especially from their failure to use such rights. The Prisons Act restriction in South Africa on reporting on prison affairs did not result from a long tradition of vigorous reporting on prisons; on the contrary, it was enacted after generations of neglect of prison affairs.[157] The same holds true of similar restrictions imposed on reporting on mental institutions[158] and, very recently, police activities.[159] When a few embarrassing reports started appearing on these matters, the government could with relative ease and minimal outcry push through the legislation concerned.

Concerning restrictions imposed in 1980 on the reporting of police matters, it is quite possible that the fact that the act was roundly condemned by *all* sections of the South African press at the time of its enaction may carry considerable weight when the concept of reasonable steps to verify the accuracy of a report has to be interpreted. This may be the case especially in view of the known and regular abuse by police of their powers as highlighted in many press reports. It is not without interest to note that the South African censorship authorities, largely using standards derived from popular concepts of ordinary citizens, have in recent times also clamped down on writings critical of the police.[160] The price for failing to use free speech undoubtedly leads in more ways than one to its legal erosion and even eradication.

Finally, reference cannot be omitted to the institution of civil defamation, which constitutes a formal, albeit indirect, source of verbal restraint on potential critics of judicial officers (or other officers of the justice administration) with an inhibiting potential of almost infinite dimensions. Whereas the institution of criminal defamation in a continental system such as Germany constitutes a hazard to the prospective critic that would hardly entail a greater risk element than a traffic infraction, the very opposite is true with civil defamation in Anglo-Saxon societies, with their well-nigh limitless and totally open-ended punitive potential. This is particularly so in view of the obligation to pay costs for a kind of case that is notorious for its built-in possibilities of delays and abuse of procedures. Although the suggestion for English law was made in the *McLeod* case,[161] where it was ruled that an impugned judicial officer had to seek his balm for criticism like any other citizen, and although there is something inherently fair *sounding* in this statement of equality, the situation in practice would give the strong a highly unfair advantage and would impose on the weak – mostly the critic – a burden of almost infinite and astronomical dimensions. Whatever the possible or even probable outcome of an eventual case, few critics would be willing to risk their very economic existence in the interest of free speech.

It would seem that in only two cases in the English-speaking world has the civil law of defamation been used to silence criticism of legal policy. In the case of *New York Times* v. *Sullivan*,[162] the Supreme Court made short shrift with the argument that the Alabama police chief could claim (as the Alabama Supreme Court had said he could) massive damages for criticism over the handling of a civil rights demonstration by his police department. In ringing language and with a vision that made some believe this judgment to be among that court's finest,[163] the U.S. Supreme Court ruled that criticism of the government could not be transferred onto the plane of personal damage to an individual official:

> For good reason ... no court of last resort has ever held, or even suggested, that prosecution for libel on government have any place in the American system of government.... The present proposition [that personal libel was possible] would sidestep this obstacle by translating criticism of government, however impersonal it may seem on its face, into personal criticism, and hence potential libel of the officials of whom the government is composed. There is no legal alchemy by which a state may thus create the cause of action.... The proposition strikes at the very centre of the constitutionally protected area of free expression.[164]

In the *Van Niekerk* defamation case against me and a Sunday newspaper, the Natal Court and later the highest court of the land held that as a legal proposition – the matter never came to trial in view of the plaintiff's death – the Minister of Justice, Mr. Pelser, could sue for libel in his personal capacity for criticism directed not only at an *official* act of his, but indeed at an act for which the entire cabinet was co-responsible and despite the fact that he was not directly or indirectly named.[165] The case revolved around my accusation that the government had in the execution of a black and the reprieve of a white for the same crime failed "to avoid the obvious inference of discrimination."[166] Although one of the usual libel defenses might have prevailed if the matter had gone to trial, by its decision on the law – which is devoid of any realistic assessment of the intimidatory potential of the case[167] – the Appellate Division opened up an entirely new gamut of legal restrictions on the scrutiny of policy, particularly – *as happened in the present case* – when the plaintiff's case was totally backed by the resources of the state.[168]

My plea to history on the *Pelser* case has been made elsewhere,[169] and it remains to record merely the ominous reality, so vividly appreciated by the Supreme Court in the *Sullivan* case, that at stake for the critic under the above circumstances is not just a fine or even a few days or weeks in prison but his very economic existence. Devoid as the atmosphere in South Africa has traditionally been of pointed personal criticism of legal officers, this new technique has added an ominous new dimension to the legal restraints against the critic because – as so pointedly stated by Justice Black in the *Sullivan* case – "this technique for harassing and punishing a free press – now that it has been shown to be possible – is by no means limited to cases with racial overtones; it can be used in other fields where public feelings may make ... newspapers easy prey for libel verdict seekers."[170] Only someone who has been subjected to this technique can fully understand the meaning of intimidation. The precedent and the threat may perhaps be directed in the first place at South Africans, but the awesome implications may well be universal.

CONCLUDING REMARKS

A people gets the government it deserves.

Old cliché[171]

If there is some truth in the cliché that a people gets the government it deserves, there is a fortiori even more truth in saying that a people gets the press it deserves, and on the basis of what has been argued in this chapter, a press will ultimately get the speech law it deserves. In a society where a press, reflecting or leading the societal mores in that area, strenuously pursues legal free speech and probes its outer legal limits, there will be little danger to that concept and even legal restrictions will constitute no insuperable barrier. The same may hold true, but to a lesser extent, of a legal profession considering itself the watchdog over the law and legal processes.

It seems that only in very few Western societies – and then seemingly in certain pockets of such societies – is the administration of justice regarded as an arm of government that must be as vigorously spoken and written about as the political executive. The result is inevitably that important powers are exercised without the countervailing benefit of the actinic qualities of free speech on which Western democratic government is predicated. Even more important, failure in the medium and long run to fully exercise rights of legal free speech harden into formalized restrictions with their attendant social cost to society. The existence of a greater or smaller web of informal taboo in the legal domain in *every* society induces one to ponder the elusive truth that ultimately it may perhaps not so much be society that is threatened by the law, but the law that is threatened by society.

5

Conclusion: The Unending Struggle

What then is the spirit of liberty? I cannot define it; I can only tell you my own faith. The spirit of liberty is the spirit which is not too sure that it is right; the spirit of liberty is the spirit which seeks to understand the minds of other men and women; the spirit of liberty is the spirit which weighs their interests alongside its own without bias.
                                                          Justice Learned Hand[1]

The achievement of free speech in general and legal free speech in particular is never complete, nor should it be. The light beckoning at the end of the tunnel is often a mirage or a firefly briefly lighting the path of those relatively few souls who make legal matters the object of their contemplations and, especially, their outspoken criticism. Sometimes, there is indeed light that will only in very few instances mean the emergence, albeit temporarily, from the tunnel. More often than not, the light signifies no more than a turning or a twist or a light vent in a tunnel, which for the vast majority of societies in the West will seemingly never end in the sunlight of a vital, dynamic, and responsible system of free speech in the legal domain, a system that responds to the needs of a democratic society and also responds to the protection of certain other vital interests of the individual in a humane society.

In most respects, one society has to a significant extent emerged in the sunlight of a system of legal free speech that is responsive to the needs of a free society, especially because of the theory of the law as handed down by its highest court. The same holds true concerning unfettered access to information about legal matters. Moreover, this is a system where individuals and the media have the ability (both legal and societal) and the willingness to speak freely and forthrightly on all matters within the vast structure of the country's just machinery and to obtain information thereof. But even in that country, the United States, the struggle to achieve such a dynamic system has not yet been finally won, although it can certainly be said that the legal framework for the attainment of that goal has been firmly laid. However, even on the legal plane a reentry is still made from time to time into the tunnel of formal restrictions that are impermissible and unjustified in terms of fundamental democratic requirements. Notwithstanding the *Nebraska Press Association* decision, courts in the United States continue to impose general gagging orders[2] that, although impermissible in terms of Supreme Court guidelines and ineffective as regards the national media, will not fail to impose a chilling penumbra of silence on a local level where, in any event, interest in most trials will mostly begin and end. Moreover, on the level of informal and invisible inhibitions that are built up around subtle lines of communication or mutually accepted no-go areas between local legal and judicial officers and local media, the picture even in the United States is very far from perfect.[3] And so it can be said that even in the one country where the most dramatic strides have been made to light up the legal processes and subject them to the actinic beam of fearless and open scrutiny, the proverbial light at the end of the tunnel also at times turns out to be a mere fata morgana.

However, true to the belief that in legal matters Pliny's aphorism about *semper aliquid novi ex Africa* is really more appropriately applied to the United States today, a recent example of semiformal and semiinformal restrictions combining in the United States to inhibit legitimate legal free speech illustrates how unending the search for the evasive *graal* remains even in the most liberal First Amendment society[4] in the world. A series of advertisements by an insurance company were informally withdrawn after complaints by the New York State Trial Lawyers Association to the Federal Trade Commission and after a class action suit had been filed by a Connecticut law firm specializing in insurance cases. The advertisements, in one instance headed "Too bad judges can't read this to a jury," simply informed the reader of the obvious truth "that money does not grow on trees" and that massive personal injury and other awards by juries "must be paid through insurance premiums from uninvolved parties, such as yourself." The advertisement, which had been placed in the New York *Times* and *Newsweek*, were clearly geared to the education of potential jurors[5] and, so one might think, would be totally legitimate and even desirable in a First Amendment society in which the so-called free marketplace of ideas operated. Once again, the suppression of what seems perfectly legitimate and even desirable legal free speech was repressed without an iota of attention being given in the national media and elsewhere to the deeper implications involved. The tunnel simply stretches on – and no similar advertisements have to my knowledge been inserted again.

On balance, the gist of this work has not been one of excessive optimism about the state of legal free speech when we take a broad and dispassionate look at the West as a whole or even those few societies that make up its most democratic kernel. Free speech as it is universally understood in the better and more democratic moments of the most democratic countries has in relation to sensitive aspects of the legal domain not generally been given the same meaning and applied in the way it is understood and used in relation to political matters and political personalities. Although isolated and very meaningful steps have been taken at times in various countries toward the goal of seeing the administration of justice as merely another source of power inherently deserving to be subjected to open and uninhibited scrutiny, it cannot truthfully be said that legal free speech is thriving and blooming anywhere in the Western world outside the United States. Too many restrictions, although seemingly of peripheral importance only to the more dramatic interests of society, still cast their inhibiting shadow – silently and mostly unnoticed and almost always unlamented – over those very few people in society who under ideal circumstances would be inclined or able to take a critical interest in the law. And even more sadly, far too many reasons, subtle and otherwise, dictate to and impose on those few people (mostly in the journalistic and legal professions) a regime of discretion, circumspection, inhibition, and silence concerning the more sensitive and often seamier aspects of the administration of justice. And so as we scan the legal and societal horizons of the West, we find with only certain felicitous and limited exceptions proving the rule that there are still vast pockets of relatively uncontrolled power that are seldom if ever subjected to the scrutiny that, by democratic definition, is necessary to control all power in all societies. Two examples, already peripherally referred to, must suffice here to illustrate this point, which in its almost universal application in the West detracts profoundly from the democratic substance of the individual's liberty mostly without his or her even being aware of it.

Example one: The Netherlands, as we have seen, does not have any sub judice restrictions and yet we find, whether it be out of deference to judicial susceptibilities, old traditions, professional inertia, or for whatever reason, a situation of almost total abdication by the press of its responsibilities of keeping a close and uninhibited scrutiny over trial proceedings on a day-to-day basis. This abdication or discretion is of an intensity that effectively makes the existence of a sub judice rule superfluous. That even the arch-conservative Dutch legal profession finds this self-emasculation of the press intolerable transpires from a report of a work group of that profession.[6] The situation in the Netherlands is to a significant extent repeated in all other continental West European countries, with the partial exception of a number of periodicals in Germany, and that despite the fact that only France has a meaningful legal prohibition in this regard.[7] The picture that therefore emerges from the North Cape to Gibraltar and from Reykjavik to Nicosia is hardly one that befits the kind of governmental ethos associated with Europe. Impressive theories about fee speech and a free press lose much of their substance and gloss in the face of the almost unrelieved monotony of this fact of life in the heartland of the Western world. And even more important and more depressing, there is very little overt recognition and concern about this fact.

Example two: Search as much as one may through the columns of what will be regarded by many as the best daily newspaper in Europe – the *Neue Zürcher Zeitung* – one will find no echo of critical and inquiring scrutiny of the personalities, performance, and inadequacies of the Swiss judiciary or even of many other aspects of the Swiss administration of justice, at least not of a kind that one would find all over Europe as regards the performance and quality of politicians and other incumbents of power. Once more, this situation in what can possibly be described as the world's most viable democracy is not very different from that of the media of most other democratic countries in Europe. It is true that there are many more exceptions proving the rule than in the first example and these have been duly noted in this work, but the overall picture in

Europe as regards the consistent, close, and outspoken scrutiny of the personalities of the administration of justice by the media is not very different from that which obtains in the contempt jurisdictions of the English-speaking world. Once more one must conclude – albeit not as gloomily as before – that the global view presenting itself from our survey of the West European media for evidence of the *use actually made* of free speech as guaranteed theoretically in the various legal systems is far from impressive as regards the legal domain and hardly inspiring in terms of the democratic ethos.

And looking beyond the confines of Western Europe and assessing the state of legal free speech, both in a legal and in a societal sense, the picture is bleak indeed. Legal free speech in the wide and dynamic sense that underlies the premises adumbrated at the outset exists only fitfully and in isolated pockets in only a very small number of states. And when considered in the framework of the commitment *especially of lawyers* to speak out loudly for justice and against injustice it is well-nigh nonexistent. The inspiring exceptions from countries such as Argentina, Yugoslavia, India, and others, which have been duly documented when they occur by the newly founded Centre for the Independence of Judges and Lawyers in Geneva, shine forth all the more brilliantly over the dark and lugubrious scene on account of their rarity. As a group, lawyers all over the world have largely shown themselves to be unconcerned about free speech in the legal domain and the free speech barricades they man have proved to be the most vulnerable and most easily surmountable. Therefore, the scene in the realm of legal free speech in the world at large is not inspiring, a situation that makes those exceptions, when and where they do exist and manifest themselves, inspiring indeed.

Several of the reasons, some legal, some societal and others again psychological, that tend to produce the overall situation of uninvolvement and unconcern about matters relating to legal free speech were noted at various junctures in this work. One additional reason to which some attention must still be given is that of access – *or lack of access* – to information about the law as a factor compounding the difficulties of attaining a situation of maturity in legal free speech. Because this important matter pertains to an entirely different complex of issues, the attention given to it here will at most be cursory.[8]

The proposition that all free speech depends substantially and perhaps overwhelmingly on free information to achieve a status of full viability and vitality is too trite a proposition to merit detailed argument here. The right of access to information has in the more enlightened societies come to be regarded as being one of an individual's basic constitutional rights and also as a prerequisite for a meaningful exercise of free speech. That the relationship between free speech and access to information cannot be regarded as an absolute one in the sense that the demand of free speech will justify the access to *all* information stands to reason. One may think here of instances such as access to jury and judicial deliberations. An absolutist interpretation here would make of the right to *speak* something almost tantamount to the right also to *do* certain things, an interpretation that would intrinsically change the foundations on which a democratic system of free speech is ultimately based. Such a system, as was argued early in this work, rests on the fundamental distinction between speech and action, with the limits to speech drawn much more generously – if they have to be drawn at all – than the limits to action. The same principles would also hold true as regards free speech on the one hand and access to information that will enable better-informed speech on the other hand, with the important qualification that in terms of certain matters limitation of access may indeed substantially mean an intrinsic ban on speech.

The proposition that is argued here is not that one of the major reasons for the doleful picture of legal free speech in the West is due to the impediments placed on access to information, but only that such impediments (whether institutional or societal) have an important bearing on the quality of legal free speech in the West and that a vital and democratic system of free speech can ignore the problem of access of information only at the peril of being unrelated to reality. The particularly crass but heuristic example of the South African Prisons Act and the pall of silence that fell over the entire prison system on its invocation in the *Rand Daily Mail* prosecution were noted above.[9] What really in effect happened here was that an institutional or formal barring of access to a particular part of the administration of justice effectively placed a *ban* on speech, and the effect in South Africa has been that prison services – and because of a similar recent enactment also mental institutions and police services[10] – have become enveloped in well-nigh total silence. Free speech as regards these institutions has become practically meaningless. In other situations, difficulties of access will not necessarily lead to such catastrophic results, but they would nevertheless not fail to burden further legal free speech.

The kind of crude provisions of the South African Prisons Act and the blunt way in which it has been interpreted in the *Rand Daily Mail* case will admittedly not easily find their direct counterpart elsewhere in the West in times of peace, and as such it merely represents a high point of censorship flowing from difficulties of access to a vital institution within the justice machinery. However, all over the Western world we find restrictions on access to legal information that *in their effect* may at least be comparably inhibitive to the draconian provisions of the South African Prisons Act in terms of information being withheld from the system of legal free speech.

As recently as July 1980, the U.S. Supreme Court ruled definitively in *Richmond Newspapers* v. *Virginia*[11] that the crudest form of ban on access to information – the holding of proceedings in camera without sufficient cause – violated inter alia the free speech guarantee of the First Amendment. However, the *Richmond Newspapers* case is an important landmark not only within the confines of the narrow question that had to be decided but especially in relation to the underlying philosophy on which the judgment was clearly based: that of an adherence to the fundamental premises of legal free speech. Quoting Bentham that "[w]ithout publicity, all other checks are insufficient" as far as justice administration is concerned, the court underlined the "nexus between openness, fairness and the perception of fairness" and proceeded to frame a proposition totally in line with the demands of a democratic system of legal free speech:

> The early history of open trials in part reflects the widespread acknowledgement, long before there were behavioral scientists, that public trials had significant community therapeutic value. . . . Thereafter the open processes of justice serve an important prophylactic purpose, providing an outlet for community concern, hostility and emotion. The crucial prophylactic aspects of the administration of justice cannot function in the dark. . . . It is not enough to say that results alone will satiate the natural community desire for "satisfaction". A result considered untoward may undermine public confidence, and where the trial has been concealed from public view an unexpected outcome can cause a reaction that the system at best has failed and at worst has been corrupted.

The court went on to acknowledge that access to the administration of justice is mainly provided by the media and that access to that administration is crucial to free speech:

> It is not crucial whether we describe this right to attend criminal trials to hear, see, and communicate observations concerning them as a "right of access" . . . or as a "right to gather information", for we have recognized that "without some protection for seeking out the news, freedom of the press could be eviscerated".

The need under most circumstances of *physical access* to court proceedings[12] would seldom present problems, but the situation becomes dramatically different with some of the wider aspects of the administration of justice. For a variety of formal and informal factors prisons and mental institutions escape the interest of the media and hence fail to become an object of forceful scrutiny. The formal restrictions will mostly relate to physical access to the institutions, especially by the media, and restrictions on the possibilities of interviewing inmates. In the recent case of *Sheriff of the County of Alameda* v. *KQED et al.*,[13] the U.S. Supreme Court refused to extend to the media an absolute right of access to prisons in excess of that of other citizens. In the course of the majority judgment, Chief Justice Burger stressed how "important" the "role of the media" was as "a powerful and constructive force, contributing to remedial action in the conduct of public business."[14] The dissenting opinion of Justice Stevens, who would have granted the access sought, stated that the "preservation of a full and free flow of information to the general public has long been recognized as a core objective of the First Amendment."[15]

That unreasonably strict or cumbersome access formalities or restrictions to vital areas of the administration of justice will substantially deprive freedom of speech vis-à-vis such areas of its life-giving sustenance stands to reason, and it is clear that as far as prisons and mental institutions are concerned, most Western countries do not nearly approximate the ideal or even an acceptable situation in this regard. From a study of difficulties concerning access to prisons in Switzerland documented in an alternative journal, *Schwarzpeter*,[16] it is very clear that the silence on these issues in the quality Swiss press can come as no surprise. These difficulties of access relate not only to bureaucratic red tape but also and perhaps primarily to the difficulties that inmates themselves experience when they become involved with the media in an attempt to attract critical attention to prison conditions.[17]

One must not lose sight of the fact that the conditions in institutions such as prisons and mental asylums, constituting as they do the end station of the judicial process within the administration of justice, are concerned ultimately with the rights of mostly unsavory, unpopular, uninfluential, or uninteresting people – and a limitation of the speech rights of these very people will be pivotal to an undermining of the rights of free speech vis-à-vis those institutions. For obvious reasons these people will have few if any champions for their cause. It is only in recent times and mostly only hypothetically that the direct concatenation between the free speech of these outcasts of society and the free speech of the community at large has been recognized in a few communities. On the supposition that society has the legitimate democratic right and expectation to expect its media to say or disseminate everything worth saying and hearing, it follows logically that constitutionally unconscionable restrictions on potentially the most knowledgeable sources of information – that is, the inmates of institutions – will inherently affect the quality and quantity of what is or can ultimately be said by the media. This problem has still only been very inchoately recognized as a vital factor affecting the quality of free speech.[18] At the time of writing, a number of cases emanating from Britain are winding their time-consuming way through the Council of Europe's human rights structure at Strasbourg, in which the censorship of prisoners' correspondence is being tested inter alia against the guarantees relating to freedom of expression in the European Convention of Human Rights.[19] It is possible that if and when the Court of Human Rights eventually pronounces on these complaints, it would also consider the problem in its wider connotation relating to the concatenation of the rights of these prisoners and the free speech of society. Ironically, the appalling prison conditions in Britain – previously the major reason for encloistering them from the public gaze – has in recent times caused the authorities to relax media access regulations in the hope of achieving amelioration.[20]

Important as bureaucratic or statutory restrictions on news gathering may be as regards access to sources of vital information concerning the administration of justice – a problem still in its infant stages of recognition – more important for the ultimate substance of legal free speech in society is the *disinterest on the part of the media to seek out* the news in the less-glamorous institutions of the administration of justice, such as prisons and mental asylums. Compared with the sensitive aspects relating to the operation of the courts and the quality of the judiciary – subjects about which I have documented an ignominious degree of self-censorship or simply disinterest on the part of the media in the course of this work – the press in the West as a whole displays an even greater degree of disinterest vis-à-vis prisons and mental institutions. In fact, so great is the disinterest at times that it assumes *in its effect* the nature of an almost insuperable obstacle to the dissemination of information. Even if one takes the paragons of the exercise of legal free speech in Western Europe – *Der Spiegel*, the *Times* of London, and *Le Monde* – the degree of journalistic concern expended on these vast pockets of semiuncontrolled power is minimal. We hark back here simply to another aspect of one of the major points of this work: the vast array of subtle and indirect influences and reasons – not all related to controls or inhibitions – that bring about a situation of substantial silence on certain topics, a silence that in its effect will not be different from that caused by strict legal provisions restricting access. Much as secrecy in certain legal institutions is dictated by direct or indirect formal and bureaucratic considerations, the problem must also be faced that the success of the authorities in *maintaining secrecy* is often based more on the inertia of the media than on the strength or force of any bureaucratic measures.[21] At issue here is the difficulty of giving sustenance and content to a vital system of legal free speech, but it is a difficulty largely dictated by the lack of concern both in society at large and in the media for problems that for most ordinary citizens either have unpleasant connotations or possess little intrinsic interest.

The problem of self-imposed limitations on the part of the media to seek out information on the entire structure of the administration of justice can be placed in yet a wider framework: that of the *education of the public* in matters relating to the administration of justice.[22] The quality and vitality of legal free speech will most quintessentially depend on the measure of education, concern, and enlightenment of a given community. The process of cross-pollination between the quality of enlightenment of a society in legal matters and the quality of free speech is not a simplistic one, and seemingly contrary to the democratic ethos, the major influence on legal free speech will not necessarily or even mostly emanate directly from society. Most societies are notoriously unconcerned about legal issues other than sensational ones, and the major input into society of these issues will come from leadership groups with an interest in the legal domain, notably lawyers and journalists. However, it is important to realize that the activities of these leadership groups are not unrelated or uninfluenced by the state of legal knowledge and legal conscience in society as a whole. Free speech in the legal domain must thus be seen both as a method of enlightenment of society and as the product of the enlightenment of society. The underlying premises of a system of legal free speech, based as they largely are on the expectation of the amelioration of society, can therefore not be separated from the long-term goal of educating society about the law and, especially, about its right to exercise a full measure of free speech in the legal domain.[23]

The use of legal free speech for the education of society is a question that in terms of some of its *technological implications* will undoubtedly receive greater attention in the near future. Hitherto, the question related mostly to the possibility and the interest of newspapers to have access to and take an active interest in all legal matters and, in so doing, whet the critical faculties of society at large on those matters. When seen in a wider time frame and in relation to new problems that will flow from the technological changes to which the communications media have been subjected, it is clear that new solutions will have to be sought to new dimensions of the problem of access of the media to the full legal domain.

Television has become the developed world's most important form of communication of news and ideas, and most societies are only very slowly, if at all, coming to grips with some of the implications of its use as a form of communication in relation to the legal domain. The *Lebach* judgment in Germany[24] and the *Estes* judgment in America[25] both illuminated a number of aspects of this medium in relation to free speech, but both judgments have now been overtaken by the realization that the use of television in relation to legal free speech has become a reality that must be seen through a different general philosophy than that on which those judgments were based. Some basic considerations that will be relevant in the future within a dynamic and democratic system of free speech will be adumbrated here.

The use of television in the courts and journalism relating to legal matters is a development that can no longer realistically be shelved in any society that endeavors to be true to the premises of a system of legal free speech. In this sense, the *Estes* judgment – inasmuch as it was predicated on the impermissibility of televising trials – can no longer be seriously defended. A blanket ban is comparable to frowning on the use of unobtrusive tape recorders in certain courts. In the wider sense again, in relation to the use of television as far as legal journalism is concerned, the judgment in the interesting *X Y Ungelöst* case in Germany[26] seems by comparison to be based on a better understanding of the beneficial social use to which the television medium, if subject to certain controls, can be put in relation to reporting on legal matters that infringe on the personality rights of individuals.

The courtroom use of television has suddenly become the vogue in the United States, despite serious reservations in certain quarters[27] and despite the warning light of the *Estes* judgment.[28] In April 1980, it was reported that the U.S. Supreme Court was ready to review the constitutionality of such use.[29] At least one situation need not be in dispute in terms of the premises of this work, although dissension about it is still rife: the permissibility of the use of television in courts of appeal where no testimony of witnesses is given. This would seem to be even more overwhelmingly the case when matters concerning constitutional or basic rights are being decided in such courts. A court of appeal that deliberately excludes the unobtrusive use of television cannot be regarded as an *open* court, in the same way as a court where the press is excluded cannot be so regarded. Any artificial distinction between press and television reporting is an affront not only to the intrinsic idea of an open court interpreted in contemporary terms but also against society's democratic expectations to *see* how government (including judicial government) operates.[30] The majority judgment in the *Estes* case did actually foresee the possibility of a need for a change arising in future, and it seems like a statement of common sense to suggest that the situation as regards the need for the use of television in legal matters has indeed changed.[31]

The pivotal part of the majority judgment in the *Estes* case is the fact that the "use of television . . . cannot be said to contribute materially" to ascertain the truth in what the court described as the "chief function of our judicial machinery."[32] This statement is inexplicable as it stands but is not sufficiently nuanced. I submit that the better point of departure would be that where the use of television does not *obstruct* the search for truth there can be no case in logic or justice why it should not be as acceptable in court as a journalist's notebook. This seems to be the clear direction of things in the United States. On the basis of this reasoning, it follows that the failure of the overwhelming part of the Western world to allow the use of television in courts where no testimony is heard constitutes a gaping lacuna in the need to introduce the citizen to the operation of the processes of justice. Indeed, in no other society has the problem yet presented itself.

Two major clusters of considerations may nevertheless militate against the use of television in courts on the basis of socially defensible principles that would be in line with the basic premises of a democratic doctrine of legal free speech. First, one must accept the fact on which the *Lebach* judgment of the German *Bundesverfassungsgericht* was partly predicated, namely, that television can indeed constitute the modern version of the pillory and that certain unconscionable and socially indefensible invasions of privacy by this medium would in no way contribute to the long-term and relatively amorphous educative advantages accruing to society. One may indeed question whether the social considerations at cross-examination or the testimony of the accused and certain witnesses can ever be sufficiently justified to prevail against the social duty to guard against the unnecessary and avoidable humiliation of a fellow human being before the most pervasive technological medium of our time.[33] Second, where the use of television can lead to *any appreciable risk* of encumbering the search for truth and justice, there can be no justification for the use of television. In such a case, the traditional open-court procedures and access of the press to proceedings seem to be sufficient guarantee that the dictates of justice are met. It is not difficult to visualize how the ability or willingness of witnesses to give truthful or satisfactory evidence may be severely curtailed in televised trials on account of the additional publicity angle of television with no meaningful social benefit accruing to society.[34] In short, the use of television in the courtroom is long overdue in certain cases and would be a potential disaster in others. Under any circumstances where the use of television is permitted, however, there is a strong case for an enforceable code of professional and judicial control over its use.[35]

The question of controls over televised access to courts inevitably raises the much wider and more involved question of controls that may be introduced to curb free speech in the legal domain in general on the basis of defensible social considerations. This question has been touched on tangentially at various junctures of the work, but it merits final adumbration at this point as an important counterbalance to the vigorous defense of the liberty of speech insinuated throughout this work.

The idea that there need be no or only very minimal speech controls over matters and personalities in the legal domain is perhaps too utopian an idea to sell to many societies, although elements of such a situation of total speech freedom do in fact exist in various countries: in Germany, for instance, as regards trial publicity; in the United States as regards scandalization of judicial officers; in Italy as regards the verbal steam that lawyers may wish to blow off in court concerning matters in hand; progressively in the United States also as regards the access that is allowed to journalists in practice (although not demandable as of right) to various traditionally sacrosanct parts of the justice administration such as prisons, mental asylums, scenes of crises,[36] police blotters and reports,[37] and, in several states in the United States, as regards the use of television in court. The attainment of this situation of maturity in a particular area of the law or regarding societal practices can by no means be equated with the attainment of a balanced system of justice or a balanced outlook as regards that particular area of the law. Some thoughts are overdue on the vital but complicated question of balancing total speech freedom in the legal domain with the responsibility required for attainment of other values to which the Western democratic ethos is hitched.

In certain societies, one consideration that may justify various kinds of speech restrictions in the legal domain and one that is consciously (albeit unobtrusively) used at times as the *real* (as opposed to the *stated*) basis for speech restrictions is the inability of a legal system to cope with open scrutiny and criticism and the fear of the public's reaction to this inability. A justification of this kind will obviously not be one that will be openly paraded by courts, constituting as it does the testimony of their inability to remain mentally uncorrupted by the influence of publicity or criticism. The fact must nevertheless be faced that courts in certain countries and at certain times may well be so unable to withstand the cleansing qualities of speech; hence their defense and application of speech restrictions that are manifestly devoid of social merit. It is clear that a substantial number of criminal cases documented in this work will fall in this category, if one could probe behind the façade of the prosecutors' offices and the judicial reasonings. Speaking on the basis of my own experience in South Africa and from my peculiarly interesting position there of being both a dramatis persona and a ringside seat observer as it were of three court dramas relating to the limitation of legal free speech and being moreover by dint of my position and contacts privy also to many bits of confidential information that would normally escape documentation, I have no doubt about the applicability of this rationale in at least two and possibly all three of the cases. Given the overwhelming truth of racial discrimination in the imposition of capital punishment in South Africa, I submit that there was simply no way in which the courts and the government authorities could allow me to parade in public the patent inability of the courts and the executive to distribute nonracist justice. There was, in crude terms, simply not enough confidence in the courts and the executive concerning the role of racism and its influence of the use of capital punishment to allow with impunity any further attenuation thereof.[38]

The reasons that courts all over the West, which ostensibly function on the basis of democratic principles, cannot simply ignore criticism of statements of the kind referred to here and also documented at various junctures of this work ultimately have their basis in judicial psychology. Constituting as they do the more gentle and more genteel part of government, judges cannot, unless they possess total confidence in their own spiritual sovereignty and their own status in society, easily summon the courage to admit that they are often an integral part of a system of repression and injustice and are used in effect for the oiling of its cogs. Inquiry, scrutiny, scathing comments, embarrassing questions, and investigative probing are therefore better stopped at a very early stage because the system of which judges and other legal processes form part simply cannot endure the escalation of scrutiny that would otherwise ensue. This would have been a conscious or subconscious consideration in several of the cases documented in this work. Needless to say, there is no conscionable way in which a democratic system of legal free speech would justify limitations of speech on the embarrassing basis of the fragile nature of popular confidence in the courts and justice machinery.

However, it is possible on a slightly different level of analysis to justify legitimate speech restrictions in the legal domain. This may be the case in a society where popular hysteria and pressure tend to invade the judicial and legal processes and where one may well justify speech restrictions as the lesser of several evils. Such restrictions may also act as a constant reminder of the inability of the legal system to cope with the problems of a particular society. Once again this justification is hardly one that can furnish the philosophical underpinning for any limitations that may be legitimately required in a vital and functioning democracy for a system of legal free speech. However, as a logical deduction from many socially indefensible speech restrictions, this justification can usefully be applied by a critic of speech restrictions!

Ultimately, a vital and democratic system of legal free speech that upholds a crisp distinction between *speech* and *action* can entertain serious restrictions on legal free speech only on the basis of one of three not entirely unrelated constellations of considerations. The mark of the degree of enlightenment achieved by a system of legal free speech will largely depend on the extent to which these considerations can be built into the system with the least possible loss of essence of the fundamental premises of such a system. These considerations in their probable order of importance are the following: first, considerations relating to the protection of the essential personality rights of individuals against socially indefensible or avoidable or unnecessary incursions flowing from the use of legal free speech; second, considerations that will, unless heeded, vitally and manifestly detract from the search for and the achievement of justice; and third, considerations that are based on and are defensible in relation to the maintenance of generally acceptable and basic standards of decorum, delicacy, and good taste.[39] The integration of these considerations into a system of legal free speech will, so one may hope, take place by a process of careful social balancing. This balancing will mostly take place on the basis of evils or negative attributes (rather than positive attributes) being balanced against each other on social scales or analysis criteria that are carefully attuned to the qualities inherent in the premises of legal free speech and democratic government in the widest context of that word.

A system of legal free speech that gives the media the unmitigated possibility to invade in a substantial sense *any* personality right and expectations of privacy at *any* time will undermine basic expectations of the members of a refined democracy.[40] At stake here is not the impairment of the smooth functioning of the justice machinery but the infringement of a basic expectation of democratic government that is every bit as important as the achievement of due legal process – the expectation of society that the individual will be able to retain a substantial degree of spiritual sovereignty, privacy, and individuality. That there may be delicate distinctions to draw is inevitable and flows partly from the ever-growing complications of life in Western society with its potent attachment to the freedom of the media, but I submit that no system of legal free speech should claim for itself a dispensation whereby *all* speech at *all* times relating to the legal domain will be totally free. Even the man who has grievously sinned against society must be allowed, if at all defensible in terms of vital social interests, to reclaim for himself his right to be left alone – a problem with which the *Lebach* judgment in Germany impressively grappled and that in recent times has again given rise to controversy in Britain, where statutory protection has been created for the protection of the honor and privacy of convicted prisoners.[41] The problem of protecting spheres of privacy of the individual can only be solved imperfectly by recourse to the law and my submission thus stands that responsible media would be better and more effectively able to give substance to this cluster of considerations by an adherence to a code inspired by the totality of democratic values and not merely that of free speech.[42]

It is perhaps ironic that in this one respect the South African legislature has in recent times come up with a speech restriction totally within the ambit and

222 / THE CLOISTERED VIRTUE

spirit of a legitimate defense of privacy within the legal domain. The prohibition on the publication of details of matrimonial litigation[43] has drastically changed not only the lurid back pages of the Sunday press but also the delicate balance within the divorce law. The threat that one spouse could use "nice juicy publicity" against the other – a particularly potent weapon in the case of professional and public figures – has been eviscerated with no observable loss to the common good of society but with an appreciable gain for the achievement of justice.

That unrestricted publication of all facts relating to the administration of justice can in a certain kind of case thwart the interests of justice can likewise not be denied, and therefore, there should in any overall system of legal free speech be a place for a narrow category of restrictions, mostly temporary in nature, that would ensure that the question for justice in a particular case is not irretrievably or substantially prejudiced by publicity. The object here would mostly be related to the avoidance of great peril to the life of individuals or the safety of the community, the detection of crime, and the attempt to safeguard the truthfulness of testimony in court.[44] The protection of witnesses and difficulties in procuring witnesses – a problem not yet fully recognized in all its implications – may be of particular relevance.[45] The restriction that may be sought here will relate not to the incorruptibility of the judicial process – a value that in any event can only very superficially and ineffectively be protected by speech restrictions – but to the edification of wider societal interests concerning the efficacy and the smooth functioning of the administration of justice in its widest connotation. It is not impossible, for instance, to visualize the taking of exceptional steps, such as the hearing of the certain witnesses in camera, when wider societal interests are legitimately involved. Legal free speech is one of the most important goods of a free society, but of greater importance still is the functioning of an effective system of justice for the protection of vital social interests. The same consideration would manifestly apply in most instances to the invasion of the privacy of judicial and jury deliberations.

Third, and finally, not all the words that can be pronounced by the human tongue need be printable, transmissible, or usable in a society that desires to maintain civilized standards.[46] I have insinuated into the core of this work a plea for the possibility to use a certain amount of forthright robustness of language and speech vis-à-vis the administration of justice, provided that at no time the Rubicon into action is crossed. This plea stands but is qualified here to the extent that there is no need and no social justification for the subjection of the public to the lack of civilized standards of speech by individuals when they address themselves to the administration of justice. I have in my possession the record of a scatologically obscene diatribe by a lawyer against a Detroit judge where the professional body refused to take steps against the lawyer concerned on the basis that he was protected by his right to free speech. The answer could well have been – as it could be for journalists as well – that at issue in such a case was not the right of the lawyer to say what he did but the basic adherence of the particular individual to civilized standards demanded by his profession. This may have been a legitimate case for professional sanctions, due allowance always made for legitimate or understandable anger and for the basic need to be tolerant toward speech as opposed to action. The law remains a bad vehicle with which to enforce refined standards of behavior, and in most instances the law would best ignore outbreaks of this kind, leaving it to professional bodies under the umbrella of legal guarantees to generate and enforce standards of speech that would be acceptable to a modern public as opposed to cavepeople. Such bodies, however, must be profoundly conscious of the dangers of enforcing standards of moral behavior on individuals and of the way such enforcement can be abused and has been abused in the past in undermining legal free speech.[47]

In his separate opinion of only one paragraph in the seminal *Nebraska Press Association* case, Justice Stevens rhetorically puts a question that also presents itself at the conclusion of this work. Said Justice Stevens:

> Whether the same absolute protection [given to trial publicity] would apply no matter how shabby or illegal the means by which the information is obtained, no matter how serious an intrusion on privacy might be involved, no matter how demonstrably false the information might be, no matter how prejudicial it might be to the interests of innocent persons, and no matter how perverse the motivation for publishing it, is a question I would not answer without further argument.[48]

I submit that no democratic society can burden its citizens with an unqualified affirmative answer to these and similar questions. In the final analysis, the answers will be spawned and determined by the continuous struggle that must inevitably go on in a vital democracy between the warring ideals to which the democratic ethos is hitched. However strong one's adherence to free speech may be, and particularly free speech in the legal domain, there are vital values of another and not necessarily inferior kind with which one's commitment to legal free speech must be tempered and integrated into a relationship that can and must never be entirely comfortable and that will also never be stagnant. If I have tried to do one thing in this work, it was to indicate that in the West as a whole legal free speech has in the past been shortchanged far too often and far too much. Nonetheless, its belated claim for full recognition cannot be interpreted as an absolute and limitless one. Nor can we believe that a strong allegiance to the doctrine of legal free speech can bring us all the answers to the problems with which we are confronted as a consequence of the position of the media in society. But we must persist in our endeavor to catch sight of and work toward reaching the light at the end of the tunnel and in so doing accept that, as with the attainment of other basic rights, we can never expect to arrive at a final destination or find simple answers to all the problems besetting us on our journey over the perilous social terrain of democratic societies. At the very least, we must demand that also regarding the justice administration in our societies, we "shall not yield a foot upon demanding a fair field and an honest race to all ideas."[49]

NOTES

INTRODUCTION

1. See note 55 (Ch. 1) and the text.

2. Thomas I. Emerson, *The System of Freedom of Expression* (1970) 12.

3. Legislatively, no action has in fact been taken, but there have been recommendations by the Committee on Contempt of Court (Phillimore Committee) for changes – see note 66 (Ch. 2) – and as will be documented in various parts of the work, there have been considerable relaxations in the law of contempt in Britain. See Colin Munro, "Contempt Becomes Less Strict," in (1977) 40 *Modern Law Review* 343.

4. Unless otherwise indicated, reference to Germany means the Federal Republic of Germany (West Germany).

5. Gordon J. Borrie in a preface to *Shimon Shetreet Judges on Trial. A Study of the Appointment and Accountability of the English Judiciary* (1976) xvii.

6. See Jac van Veen, *De Rechten van de Mens. De Mensen van het Recht. Opstellen over de Praktijk van de Nederlandse Rechtspraak* (1971). See on this work, Marijke Reinsma, "Heilige Koeie in Toga" in (1972) 13 *Codicillus* 41.

7. This idea has been well developed in an essay by that rugged nonconformist Justice William O. Douglas, "The Bill of Rights is not enough," in *The Great Rights* (ed. Edmond Cahn) 117 ff (1963).

8. Reference may be made here to a protest of Spanish lawyers in 1972 when about 1,500 Madrid lawyers declared a state of permanent protest over certain acts of governmental interference and the entire college of advocates resigned. See *International Herald Tribune* (Paris) December 18 and 19, 1972.

9. See the *Times* of London of June 27, 1977. For more details of this incident see note 59 (Ch. 3).

10. Douglas op. cit., pp. 127-28 is not so sanguine as regards the American lawyers: "In American history lawyers have often rallied opinion outside of courtrooms in support of the despised minorities. . . . A few lawyers still speak in that tradition. But most lawyers have remained silent."

CHAPTER 1

1. From an address to the University of the State of New York in 1952, reprinted in Irving Dilliard (ed.), *The Spirit of Liberty. Papers and Addresses of Learned Hand* (1959) 216.

2. Niklaus Meienberg, *Die Erschiessung des Landesverräters Ernst S* (1977) 7. See the text to note 10.

3. From the introduction to the essays by Theo Rasehorn, Helmut Ostermeyer, Fritz Hasse, and Diether Huhn, *Im Namen des Volkes? Vier Richter über Justiz und Recht* (1968) 9. The name of Theo Rasehorn, chairman of the *Oberlandesgericht* in Frankfurt, and veritable enfant terrible of his profession and precursor of a tradition of more robust free speech in legal matters in Germany, will figure repeatedly in this work.

4. Brian Abel-Smith and Robert Stevens (with the assistance of Rosalind Brooke), *Lawyers and the Courts. A Sociological Study of the English Legal System 1750-1965* (1967) 126-27 and 289, respectively.

5. See the text to note 49.

6. See Norman Fowler, "Prison security and freedom of the press," in the *Times* of London of August 12, 1968, where the restrictions on the press to report freely on prisons is criticized. Martin Wright, "Why all the secrecy about what goes on in prison," in the *Times* of London of June 12, 1974, laments the basic disinterest on the part of the press in the prisons.

7. Admittedly Thomas Emerson, op. cit., pp. 449-65, deals specifically with the "administration of justice" as one of the "other social interests" – in addition to national security and the internal order – that the U.S. constitutional system is desirous of protecting against possible abuse of freedom of expression. However, he does not regard the administration of justice in a different light from other interests that may come into conflict with freedom of expression.

8. Two recent works on contempt of court in England, that of C. J. Miller, *Contempt of Court* (1976), and of Gordon Borrie and Nigel Lowe, *The Law of Contempt* (1973), do not at all contain a value-oriented discussion of the basic legal value or *Rechtsgut*, which is limited by the protean institution of contempt. Neither do we find any substantial discussion of the public interest in a fearless scrutiny of the administration of justice. In comparing the two works concerned with the treatment of the same subject in the first edition of *Oswald on Contempt* of 1892 and with the scattered articles of Sir John Fox in the *Law Quarterly Review* between 1908 and 1924, one is not particularly alerted to the important sociopolitical changes that have taken place in the interim in most Western societies concerning the right and expectation of the individual, in the interest of the public at large, to speak his or her mind freely on matters of importance to the individual and society.

9. Elaine Potter, *The Press as Opposition. The Political Role of South African Newspapers* (1975).

10. A collection of cuttings on legal problems emanating over a two-year period from the *Neue Zürcher Zeitung*, the country's most prestigious and influential newspaper, produced not a single instance of a really strong criticism of the justice administration.

11. Informal and indirect sanctions will be discussed in Chapter 4.

12. Borrie and Lowe, op. cit., 3.

13. Jerome Frank, *Courts on Trial. Myth and Reality in American Justice* (1950) 2.

14. 328 U.S. 331 [1946].

15. Emerson, op. cit., 7-8

16. Idem 10.

17. Douglas, op. cit., 128. See note 10 (Introduction).

18. See the text starting with note 110 (Ch. 2).

19. See the text starting with note 253 (Ch. 2).

20. See the text starting with note 237 (Ch. 2).

21. See the text starting with note 206 (Ch. 2).

22. See, for instance, the cases from Fiji (note 168), the Bahamas (note 170), Trinidad (note 117), or St. Vincent (note 165).

23. Several instances of criminal defamation of critics of the judiciary or the administration of justice will be documented. See the text to note 129 (Ch. 2).

24. See the *Sunday Times* thalidomide case alluded to in note 49.

25. Gustav Radbruch (1878-1949), *Ihr Jungen Juristen* (1919) 12, quoted and discussed by me in "The Warning Voice from Heidelberg – The Life and Thought of Gustav Radbruch" (1973) 90 *South African Law Journal* 234 at 243.

26. Article 2(1) of the *Grundgesetz*.

27. *Die Verteidigung auf der Anklagebank* [The Defence in the Dock] *Informationen über Ehrengerichts- und Strafverfahren gegen Verteidiger in politischen Strafsachen*, published by a group of Hamburg lawyers (1977). A number of the cases instanced in *Verteidigung auf der Anklagebank* have not been disposed of at the time of writing and in a country notorious for the delays in judicial proceedings, final judgments may still be a long time away. However, as far as the inhibiting effect on the vigorous execution of their duties by lawyers is concerned, these ultimate judgments will be of relatively little significance. The mere fact of the charge will in itself constitute a sufficiently potent inhibiting factor militating toward the silence of the legal profession. See the text to note 116 (Ch. 2).

28. Idem 26. The full statement reads:

Statement. Jürgen H. Bäcker, 1 Berlin 31, Alt Moabit 12a, Awaiting trial jail. Today, 4.2.76, 5 years awaiting trial prisoner. The undersigned wish to draw attention to the following: That spending a period of five years as an awaiting trial prisoner is unique in the Federal Republic of Germany. That it was the intention of the Legislature that as a rule no one should be an awaiting trial prisoner for more than half a year. That awaiting trial detention should be of a less onerous nature than ordinary criminal detention. That the awaiting trial prisoner should be regarded as innocent until he has been duly sentenced. In the awaiting trial jail of Moabit pre-trial detention is more onerous than ordinary criminal detention since it always constitutes solitary confinement. This in effect means that Jürgen Bäcker has been alone for five years, 23 hours per day in an area of 8 square meters, a physical torture which contradicts the regulations of pre-trial detention, the Basic Law [of the Constitution] and the [European] Convention on Human Rights. An application by Bäcker to be transferred to the ordinary jail in Tegel has been turned down. We appeal to the public to concern itself with this case.

29. Idem 27.

30. No. 83 of 1967.

31. The case will be referred to again in relation to the sub judice rule of contempt. See note 70 (Ch. 2).

32. A substantial part of the text is reprinted in the Helen Silving *Festschrift*. See note 93.

33. The judgment of the court of first instance, which has not been fully reported, is published as Appendix Two. The appeal court judgment is reported as *S* v. *Van Niekerk* [1972] (3) SA 711 (AD). For an analysis of the second *Van Niekerk* contempt case, see John Dugard, "Judges, Academics and Unjust Laws. The Van Niekerk Contempt Case," in (1972) 89 *South African Law Journal* 271 and John Dugard *Human Rights and the South African Legal Order* (1978) 293 ff.

34. *S* v. *Van Niekerk* 1972 (3) *SA* 711 (AD) at 720. The statement of a former chief justice, Dr. L. C. Steyn, to which the chief justice referred approvingly constituted a strong attack on certain members of the academic profession for their indulgence in critical analysis of certain aspects of the law. In a country where the social (and now the legal) pressures on professional people to remain silent on controversial issues is particularly great, the intimidating effect of the wrath of the chief justice is extremely severe. No comment was forthcoming from any law journal at the time. The statement, in the form of an address, was published in full in 30 (1967) *Tydskrif vir Hedendaagse Romeins-Hollandse Reg* 105. See the text to note 36 (Ch. 4).

35. My first contempt case in 1970 – to be alluded to below in the text to note 88 – also has relevance to the self-fulfillment of the academic lawyer. I was prosecuted for a serious and restrained academic article in a legal periodical on the death penalty. Concerning this case, Frank Bates, "Contempt and the Criminologist," in (1971) 6 *The Criminologist* 75 at 78-79, states:

The second major point which arises from *S* v *Van Niekerk* concerns the general right of the scholar to comment on the administration of penal justice. *Van Niekerk's* case is alone, in all cases relating to contempt in that it arose out of a serious study published in an internationally known legal periodical. . . . *S* v *Van Niekerk* does not, therefore, recognise a right *per se* to comment on apparent instances of judicial bias. It is suggested that such a right should be recognised in principle both in South Africa and England.

In his commentary on the judgment, "S v Van Niekerk," in (1970) 33 *Tydskrif vir Hedendaagse Romeins-Hollandse Reg* 302 at 303-04, Professor J. E. Van der Walt states the following about the academic's claim to legal free speech:

> It is in the interest of every democracy that academics should have the right, if they act without improper motives, to do their scientific research without hindrance and to publish the results thereof without prejudice, notwithstanding the disturbing nature of such results to individuals or the state. In a case such as the one under discussion the public interest must enjoy considerable priority when weighted against other interests such as the dignity of the courts, respect for judicial officers and for the administration of justice. After all, the knowledge, insight and criticism of the scientific researcher are essential prerequisites for the healthy growth of community institutions.

36. See Otto Kirchheimer, *Political Justice. The Use of Legal Procedure for Political Ends* (1961) 252-58.

37. See, for example, Kirchheimer, op. cit., 256.

38. Ultimately reported as *Dennis* v. *U.S.* 341 U.S. 494 (1951).

39. Consisting of Judges Jerome Frank, Augustus N. Hand, and Charles E. Clark.

40. See Emerson, op. cit., 112 ff.

41. Op. cit., 112.

42. As recorded in *U.S.* v. *Sacher* et al. 182 F.2d 416 (2d Cir 1950), 343 U.S. 1 (1952). On this case and particularly on the suitability of the contempt instrument under those circumstances, see Fowler Harper and David Haber "Lawyer Troubles in Political Trials" (1951) 60 *Yale LJ* 1 at 4-5.

43. On the French cases, see Kirchheimer, op. cit., p. 253. The kind of contempt involved in the *Dennis* case – that is, *in facie curiae* – is discussed in the text to note 21 (Ch. 2). It is crucial to note that the contempt sanction was invoked not at the time of the alleged infringements of the order of the court but at the conclusion of the case when the sanctions could no longer be said to serve the maintenance of order.

44. Cf, for instance, the case of Attorney Cassel (*Verteidigung auf der Anklagebank*, op. cit., 12) where the judgment speaks inter alia of "a general insult of senior judges" and of conduct calculated to bring "the pressure of street protests" on court decisions. More examples will be furnished in Chapter 2.

45. See the text to note 171 (Ch 2). Kirchheimer, op. cit., pp. 252-53, briefly describes the difficulties of French defense lawyers in the late fifties and early sixties in the political trials spawned by the bitterness of the decolonization of Algeria.

46. Article 24 of the Italian Constitution. This article and its role as a haven of refuge for Italian lawyers will receive attention in the text to note 245 (Ch. 2). The suggestion has been made in France to give lawyers a kind of

immunity similar to that of parliamentarians. Cf Conzalez de Gaspard "L'imunité de la défense" in *Le Monde* February 28, 1960.

47. (1832-1904), British scholar, poet, and journalist. From *The Tenth Muse*, stanza 18.

48. See the text to note 31 concerning this writer's second contempt case and the comments made there, but see especially the text to note 38 (Ch. 4).

49. *A-G* v. *Times Newspapers Ltd* (1973) 1 QB 710. The judgment of Lord Denning is reprinted as an appendix. For a lively commentary on the legal wrangle surrounding the thalidomide tragedy, see Harvey Teff and Colin Munro, *Thalidomide. The Legal Aftermath* (1976), particularly pp. 65-100 dealing with contempt of court and the freedom of the press. The facts, very briefly stated, are that around 1960 some 451 deformed babies were born to mothers who had taken the drug thalidomide. A long legal tussle ensued regarding compensation claims against the marketing firm. After yet another abortive attempt to win the support of all the parents, the editor of the *Sunday Times* decided to publish the details of the failure of the marketing company to honor (what he considered to be) their moral obligations, despite the fact that a number of court cases on the issue were pending. A first article appeared on September 24, 1972, headed "Our Thalidomide Children: A Cause for National Shame." The company immediately complained to the Attorney-General that the article was in contempt. Before publishing a second and even more detailed article, the *Sunday Times* requested the comments of the Attorney-General and the company. The Attorney-General then proceeded to issue a writ against the *Sunday Times* , claiming an injunction to restrain the newspaper from publishing the draft. The application was granted by the Queen's Bench Division of the High Court with the Lord Chief Justice (Lord Widgery) and Judges Stevenson and Brabin concurring ([1972] 3 All ER 1136 and repeated in [1973] 1 QB 717 ff). On appeal to the Court of Appeal, the writ was set aside by Lord Denning MR, Lord Justice Phillimore, and Lord Justice Scarman. On further appeal by the Attorney-General to the House of Lords, that body delivered judgment on July 18, 1973 and in a return to the pristine purity of the law of contempt as described by Oswald at the close of the nineteenth century, the House of Lords unanimously held that the injunction had been properly issued in the first place – *A-G* v. *Times Newspapers Ltd* ([1974] *AC* 273). With a commendable perseverance coupled to a considerable commitment of economic resources, the *Sunday Times* took its struggle with the authorities (and really with the substance of the English contempt law) to an international arena by invoking the protection of Article 10 of the European Convention on Human Rights, which guarantees freedom of speech. In its report, the European Commission of Human Rights declared the application of the *Sunday Times* admissible (Application no. 6538 of 1974). In August 1977, the commission referred the matter to the European Court of Human Rights. As far as the substance of the original writ is concerned – to prevent a court from being prejudiced by publicity of a pending case – it had long since lost all practical relevance, although the legal ban on one of the articles was only lifted

in August 1977. For a full documentation of the legal implications of the thalidomide tragedy – including the contempt case – see *The Thalidomide Children and the Law. A Report by the Sunday Times* (1973). Concerning the hearing, the following documentation is available: Proceedings of 24 April (morning) 1978 Cour/Misc (78) 37; idem (afternoon) Cour/Misc (78) 38; Proceedings of 25 April Cour/Misc (78) 39; Memorial of the Government of the UK Cour (77) 61; Supplementary Memorial of the UK Government Cour (78) 13; Memorial of the Applicants Cour (78) 5. The latter document of 287 pages constitutes a withering attack on the contempt institution as applied in this case.

50. *A-G* v. *Times Newspapers Ltd* [1973] 1 QB 717 at 735.

51. See the text to note 51 for a discussion in this case in terms of the sub judice rule.

52. See his statement at 737:

On October 12, 1972, the Attorney-General issued a writ against *The Sunday Times* claiming an injunction to restrain them from publishing the draft article. This step was welcomed by *The Sunday Times* as being "both sensible and constructive". So it seemed at the time, because it would enable *The Sunday Times* to see where they stood. But, as things have turned out, I think it was a pity.

53. At 739.

54. At 739-40.

55. At 741-42. My emphasis.

56. See note 49. The Strasbourg decision will effectively do much to relieve the problems of journalists as regards certain kinds of court reporting. In his work, *Pressures on the Press: An Editor Looks at Fleet Street* (1972) 129, Charles Wintour (editor of the *Evening Standard*) once wrote: "I probably spend more time worrying about the possibility of contempt of court than I do about all the other legal restrictions put together."

57. *Ambard* v. *Trinidad and Tobago* [1936] *AC* 322. See note 113.

58. At 335.

59. At 337.

60. *New York Times* v. *Sullivan* 376 U.S. 254 at 277 [1964]. This seminal decision as regards the suppression by means of civil action of freedom of speech in relation to the administration of justice will be considered in the text to note 162 (Ch. 4).

61. See the text to note 44 (Ch. 4).

62. *Entscheidungen des Bundesverfassungsgerichts* [1974] Vol. 35 at 202. (case no. 16 of June 5, 1973).

63. The judgment of the Oberlandesgericht Koblenz is reported in (1973) 26 *Neue Juristische Wochenschrift* 251.

64. At 206-07: "eine rechtswidrige Verletzung seines Persönlichkeitsrechts, seines Namensrechts, und seines Rechts am eigenen Bild." The

applicant's case was based on article 1(1) and article 2(1) of the German Basic Law, which read respectively:

> Article 1(1) The dignity of the human person shall not be infringed. To respect and protect that dignity is the duty of all state authority.
> Article 2(1) Each individual has the right to an unimpeded development of his personality to the extent that he does not infringe the rights of others, transgress against the constitutional order or violate the moral code of society.

65. At 209. A further complicating factor was the intended depiction in the program of the homosexual relationship between the applicant and his coperpetrators.

66. Summary of the respondent's case as contained in the judgment of the court. At 212, it was inter alia contended thus:

> If only *one* single potential perpetrator is prevented from the commission of similar criminal acts, the production [of the documentary] would be justified. The fundamental rights of potential victims and of potential criminals have no lower standing than the rights vested in the personality of the already sentenced applicant.

67. At 230-31.

68. Extracts of the judgment are reprinted as an appendix.

69. At 231, the court states laconically:

> Last but not least, one must also seriously consider the legitimate democratic need for control over the relevant state organs and officers who are responsible for security and order, over the prosecuting authorities and over the criminal courts. It is self-evident that television broadcasts because of their extensive coverage are peculiarly suitable to satisfy these information needs.

70. See article 5(3) of the Basic Law.

71. At 227, it is stated that as regards the television medium there is "as a rule a much greater incursion into a private sphere than would be the case with the transmission of information in word or writing, through the medium of radio and press."

72. Concerning the hundred or so persons who would really have mattered, the printed word, easily conserved and passed on from hand to hand, would have been of more durable effect than a television show. To those who knew him before incarceration, the documentary would have brought nothing new.

73. The question of the virtual futility and counterproductivity of certain protective devices will be discussed in the text starting with note 182.

74. This case is again discussed from the sub judice angle in the text to note 190 (Ch. 3).

75. *R* v. *Metropolitan Police Commissioner: Ex Parte Blackburn* (no. 2) [1968] 2 All ER 319, p. 320. This famous contempt judgment involving Mr. Quintin Hogg, O.C. (as respondent) will be discussed below. This case will henceforth be referred to as the *Quintin Hogg* case.

76. Cf Emerson, op. cit., 6-7:

[F]reedom of expression is an essential process for advancing knowledge and discovering truth. An individual who seeks knowledge and truth must hear all sides of the question, consider all alternatives, test his judgment by exposing it to opposition, and make full use of different minds. Discussion must be kept open no matter how certainly true an accepted opinion may seem to be; many of the most widely acknowledged truths have turned out to be erroneous. Conversely, the same principle applies no matter how false or pernicious the new opinions appear to be; for the unaccepted opinion may be true or partially true and, even if wholly false, its presentation and open discussion compel a rethinking and retesting of the accepted opinion. The reasons which make open discussion essential for an intelligent individual judgment likewise make it imperative for rational social judgment.

77. Jerome Frank, op. cit., 1:

The rulers of America, the numerous John Q. Citizens who have no intention of becoming lawyers, should be taught what their courts do and why.

For alas they know too little of that subject. American journalism, on the whole, does a poor job of accurately reporting court-doings. Our lawyers have made little effort to explain to the laymen, in intelligible terms, the working of our judicial system. The resultant public ignorance is deplorable. Our courts are an immensely important part of our government. In a democracy, no portion of government should be a mystery. But what may be called "court-house government" still is mysterious to most of the laity.

To a considerable extent, that is true because too few lawyers and judges have been willing to speak out plainly, even to other lawyers, about the actualities of court-house behavior. In most law-schools, many aspects of that behavior are disregarded.

78. Idem 2. He continues (at 3):

Some persons suggest that candor about court-house ways is unwise, that it is undesirable to let the public know the imperfections ... in our judicial doings. I confess I have little patience with, or respect for, that suggestion. I am unable to conceive, I repeat, that, in a democracy, it can ever be unwise to acquaint the public with the truth about the workings of any branch of government. It is wholly undemocratic to treat the public as children, who are unable to accept the inescapable short-comings of man-made institutions. The public, I think, can "take it". Our people need not be coddled, and should not be deluded. It is the essence of democracy that the citizens are entitled to know what all their public servants, judges included, are doing and how well they are doing it.

79. See, for instance, a commentary like that of David Riley, "The Mystique of Lawyers," in *Verdict on Lawyers* (ed. Ralph Nader and Mark Green) (1976) 82: "Every self-respecting law school fills a thousand law review pages a year with articles bearing titles like. ... Meanwhile important matters go unexamined. The closer a topic gets to an honest look at the role of lawyers in our society, the less research is done on it."

80. *The Law and the Press* ("The Report of a Joint Working Party or representatives of JUSTICE [British section of the International Commission of Jurists] and of the British Committee of the International Press Institute which in the view of the Council of Justice clearly contains important recommendations and provides a basis for informed discussion") (1965) 2. See also note 46 (Ch. 4).

81. At 11 and 17 of the report.

82. Borrie and Lowe, op. cit., 161 ff; C. J. Miller, op. cit., 186 ff; *Contempt of Court (A Report by JUSTICE)* (1959) 14 ff.

83. At 15:

Our view is that, while the press should not be free to allege partiality or corruption on the part of a judge, it should not be prevented by the law of contempt from criticising his competence. Clearly if someone wishes, in good faith, to make a charge of partiality or corruption against a judge he ought to have the opportunity of making it; but we do not consider the press to be the appropriate organ for this purpose. We consider that he should be able to do so by letter to the Lord Chancellor or to his member of Parliament without fear of punishment, and would deplore the use of the law of contempt to prevent him from doing so. The charges could then be considered either administratively or in the House of Commons or the House of Lords.

84. The facts of the case, *R* v. *Editor of the New Statesman* [1928] 44 *TLR* 301, were that Dr. Marie Stopes, an advocate of birth control, had been involved in a libel action brought against her by the editor of a newspaper. (The

libel, it should be added, was of a surprising nature as will appear from the offending statement itself.) The verdict of the court invited the ire of Mr. Sharp's words in the *New Statesman*. To convey what seems to be the utterly responsible way in which the editor of the *New Statesman* interpreted his duties, the offending words are repeated in full:

> We cannot help regarding the verdict given this week in the libel action brought by the editor of the *Morning Post* against Dr Marie Stopes as a substantial miscarriage of justice. We are not at all in sympathy with Dr Stopes' work or aims, but prejudice against those aims ought not to be allowed to influence a court of justice in the manner in which they appeared to influence Mr Justice Avory in his summing-up. Dr Stopes found one of her advertisements in the *Morning Post* suddenly stopped. Accordingly she wrote to the Duke of Northumberland suggesting that Roman Catholic influence was at work. The Duke passed the letter on to the editor, who chose to regard it as a reflection upon his own honesty – which was patent nonsense – and brought an action. He was awarded £200 damages. The sum is not large, but the principle is important. We do not think the action ought to have been brought. Dr Stopes' letter was foolish, partly because it is always foolish to write to a proprietor behind a trusted editor's back and partly because it is always foolish to talk of "Catholic plots" – or of "Bolshevik plots" for that matter. But Dr Stopes obviously intended no reflection upon the editor personally – did not even know who he was. And from what we ourselves know of newspaper practice there could be no injurious reflection upon him, first because he may never have heard of the censoring of the advertisement, and, second, because the suggestion that a man is influenced by Catholic ideas of right and wrong is surely not an "injurious reflection". That certain advertisers threaten to boycott any paper which accepts Dr Stopes' advertisements is a fact for which we can vouch. Their exclusion may therefore be no more than a matter of commercial policy, implying no reflection at all upon an editor, since he may not even know what has happened. The serious point in this case, however, is that an individual owning to such views as those of Dr Stopes cannot apparently hope for a fair hearing in a court presided over by Mr Justice Avory – and there are so many Avorys.

85. At 303:

> [T]he court had no doubt that the article complained of did constitute a contempt. It imputed unfairness and lack of impartiality to a judge in the discharge of his judicial duties. The gravamen of the offence was that by lowering his authority it interfered with the performance of his judicial duties.

86. The sentence was payment of the cost of the proceedings, which may nevertheless be a rather hefty penalty for a private individual to defray.

87. It is clear from the works cited in note 82 that the *New Statesman* precedent is still substantially intact in England itself. It is interesting to find that in his *The Road to Justice* (1955) at 75, even Lord Denning (as he later became) cites the *New Statesman* judgment with apparent approval. See the text to note 41 (Ch. 2).

88. Miller, op. cit., 191. See note 8.

89. Idem.

90. Questionnaires were sent to advocates (barristers) only and not to attorneys (solicitors), since only advocates have right of appearance before the Supreme Court, the forum in which death sentences are imposed. Most advocates have considerable experience of capital cases under the system of *pro deo* defense in capital trials of indigents who constitute the vast preponderance of candidates for death row.

91. Herewith the full text of the questions, results, and accompanying comment:

In a country where the element of race plays such an important role in so many spheres it would indeed be surprising if that element does not also have some bearing on the pattern of executions. The question "Do you consider, for whatever reason, that a Non-European [Black] tried on a capital charge stands a better chance of being sentenced to death than a European [White]?" elicited the following responses: Abolitionists, Yes 24; No 18; Only for certain crimes 22; Uncertain 6. Retentionists, Yes 10; No 46; Only for certain crimes 10; Uncertain 3. Doubtfuls, Yes 5; No 3; Only for certain crimes 7; Uncertain 3. The following question was related to the previous one: "If your answer (to the previous question) is 'Yes' or 'Only for certain crimes', do you think that the differentiation shown to the different races as regards the death penalty is conscious and deliberate?" The response was: Abolitionists, Yes 18; No 14; Uncertain 14. Retentionists, Yes 6; No 12; Uncertain 2. Doubtfuls, Yes 8; No 2; Uncertain 2.

Whatever conclusion one may draw from the results of these two questions, the fact which emerges undeniably is that a considerable number of replying advocates, almost 50 per cent in fact, believe that justice as regards capital punishment is meted out on a differential basis to the different races, and that 41 per cent who so believe are also of the opinion that such differentiation is "conscious and deliberate".

The article concerned, ". . .Hanged by the Neck until You are Dead," appeared in two subsequent issues of the *South African Law Journa*:(1969) 86 *SALJ* 457-75 and (1970) 87 *SALJ* 60-70.

92. The case, henceforth to be referred to as the first *Van Niekerk*

contempt case (to distinguish it from the second *Van Niekerk* contempt case referred to in the text to note 32), and the *Van Niekerk* defamation case (to be discussed in the text to note 165, Ch. 4) is reported as *S* v. *Van Niekerk* 1970 (3) SA 655 (T). The full transcript of the trial, together with the undelivered address of counsel for the defense and an explanatory introduction by "Rhadamanthus" has been published in (1970) *Acta Juridica*. This transcript affords a mine of information on the discriminatory application of the death penalty in South Africa and the attempt to stop discussion thereof. See also note 35.

93. Barend van Niekerk, "Freedom of Speech Concerning the Administration of Justice – A Personal View from South Africa," (1977) *Revista Juridica de la Universidad de Puerto Rico* 647-720 [Festschrift for Helen Silving] 647.

94. Between 1911 and 1966 (inclusive), the article revealed, 2,107 persons terminated their lives on the South African gallows. In the following decade, about 600 more were executed. In the offending article, it was also recorded that about half of the executions between 1911 and 1966 had taken place after 1953, during a time when almost the entire civilized world had largely turned its back on capital punishment. On the statistics, see also Ellison Kahn, "The Death Penalty in South Africa" (1970) 32 *Tydskrif vir Hedendaagse Romeins-Hollandse Reg* 117 and (1970) *Acta Juridica* (note 89).

95. Regarding the possible unconscious obtrusion of the racial factor, the following statement by Professor John Dugard is revealing:

> South African judges are all drawn from one small section of the population – the white group. Whether they support the government or not, most have one basic premiss in common – loyalty to the *status quo.* . . . Inevitably there will sometimes be a subconscious communion of opinion between members of the judiciary and the executive drawn from the same privileged white élite, in cases involving disputes between individuals bent on radical change and the state. This is what is at the root of the accusation that the South African judiciary has become "establishment-minded".

From "The Judicial Process, Positivism and the Civil Liberty," in (1971) 88 *SALJ* 181 at 190-91. See also the present writer, "Mentioning the Unmentionable. Race as a Factor in Sentencing," in (1979) 3 *SA Journal of Criminal Law and Criminology* 151.

96. In *S* v. *Van Niekerk* 1970 (3) SA at 658-59 it is stated:

> A reasonable person reading the article in question would understand that advocates are persons who have an intimate knowledge of the way justice is meted out and their opinions are entitled to great respect and if the reader accepted the views set out he could possibly hold the judges and the administration of justice in low esteem. . . . Of course then it

would have been no defence to say: "I did not say that; I merely recorded what others thought" ... I say all this as to the possible interpretation of the article to indicate that in the opinion of the Court the representative of the state cannot be blamed for having brought this matter to court.

97. See my article, "Mentioning the Unmentionable," op. cit., for examples of the obtrusion of the racial factor in judicial attitudes. Writing in a more honest albeit more overtly racist age in South Africa's history, Mr. Justice William Pittman, *Criminal Law in South Africa* (1950) at 96, states bluntly as follows about the influence of race in cases of criminal injuria:

A feature of a large number of cases falling under this last-mentioned group [concerning male insults upon females] has been that the accused was a black man and the complainant a white woman. Such difference of race must needs aggravate the seriousness of any *injuria* committed; under certain circumstances there is no doubt that it makes "injurious", what in its absence would not have been so.

More modern textbooks are less explicitly candid about this situation. The most detailed study of "judicial attitudes towards race in South Africa" is that by Albie Sachs, *Justice in South Africa* 123 ff. See also M. A. Milner, "Apartheid and the South African Courts," in (1961) 14 *Current Legal Problems* 280.

98. The situation regarding the defense of truth in the law of contempt in South Africa is perhaps essentially the same as that which obtained in England in the eighteenth century for the related crime of seditious libel. As Leonard W. Levy, *Freedom of Speech and Press in Early American History. Legacy of Suppression* (1963) 13, puts it:

The judges also refused to permit the defendant to plead the truth as a defense. Indeed, they proceeded on the theory that the truth of a libel made it even worse because it was more provocative, thereby increasing the tendency to breach of the peace or exacerbating the scandal against the government.

It is possible that the refusal of the court to hear the counsel for the defense – despite its important findings on the law – must be understood in this context. See note 133.

99. See note 152.

100. See note 138 (Ch. 4).

101. See Barend van Niekerk, "The Uncloistering of the Virtue. Freedom of Speech and the Administration of Justice – A Comparative Overview," in (1978) 95 *SALJ* 362-93 and 534-73, especially 554 ff; also idem "Silencing the Judges: A Comparative Overview of Practices Concerning Restrictions and Inhibitions

on the Free Speech of Judges," in (1979) 4 *Journal of the Legal Profession* (Alabama Law School) 157 at 166 ff, where the Rasehorn episode – presently to be discussed – is detailed.

102. Dr. Rasehorn's assistance is gratefully recorded. An extract of the judgment is reprinted in (1973) 51 *Deutsche Richterzeitung* (June 1973) 203. Strong criticism of the failure of the court to come to Dr. Rasehorn's assistance was published by another maverick on the German judicial scene, Helmut Ostermeyer, "Ein klassischer Fall richterlicher Befangenheit," in (1973) 12 *Vorgänge* 16-18 – a somewhat ironic indication of the widespread intolerance toward the implications of legal free speech in Germany. See the text to note 137 (Ch. 2).

103. In concluding its judgment, the court issued a kind of partial vindication of Dr. Rasehorn's pioneering work:

> In conclusion the following point must once more be made clear: The Senate [of the Court] does not state that the applicant [Dr Rasehorn] entertains opinions which cannot be reconciled with the Basic Law. This is the view only of the respondent, a view which the respondent is however entitled to express on the basis of a balancing of values and of interests, despite the disparaging nature of that view as regards the personality of the applicant.

104. Cf my article "Silencing the Judges," note 101.

105. The examples quoted referred to sociological analyses of the conservative attitudes of the German judiciary.

106. From the extract of *Opas Justiz lebt*, which is quoted in the *Richterverband*'s memorial, the following can be described as the most controversial and outspoken:

> This would not be the place to deliver a graveside eulogy for the administration of justice (*die Justiz*), but it can be pointed out that we are living in times in which the administration of justice must be questioned – in which the question may – nay, must! – be posed whether the profession of the judge remains a fundamental profession [Ürberuf] or whether it has become a dying profession; whether in the place of the judge there will not in the near future be welfare officers, social workers and computerized justice. . . . The chance of renewal by means of reform appears to have been lost. It is possible that a new [kind of] administration of justice and a new type of judge may break into the scene with revolutionary force. It seems unlikely though. The administration of justice would always move to the sidelines and away from the centre of revolutionary change and away from the educational system.

107. For a discussion of the Rasehorn episode in the context of informal taboos, see the text to note 19 (Ch. 4).

108. See note 75, at 310-21. Mr. Quintin Hogg, in *Punch*, made a devastating attack on the Court of Appeal, inter alia for the "blindness which sometimes descends on the best of judges." Unfortunately for Mr. Hogg, the attack, which has become a veritable classic in the contempt literature, was directed at the wrong court! See also the text to note 173.

109. Emerson, op. cit., 7, states concerning this participatory premise of freedom of speech generally:

> [F]reedom of expression is essential to provide for participation in decision making by all members of society. This is particularly significant for political decisions. Once one accepts the premise of the Declaration of Independence – that governments "derive their just powers from the consent of the governed" – it follows that the governed must, in order to exercise their right of consent, have full freedom of expression both in forming individual judgments and in forming the common judgment. The principle also carries beyond the political realm. It embraces the right to participate in the building of the whole culture, and includes freedom of expression in religion, literature, art, science, and all areas of human learning and knowledge.

110. *New York Times* v. *Sullivan* 376 U.S. 254. The reliance on the public interest by the Alabama Supreme Court was indirect but undoubtedly present.

111. See note 49. In *A-G* v. *Times Newspapers Ltd* [1974] AC 273, Lord Reid put it as follows (at 300):

> If this material [which would have been published by the *Sunday Times* but for the injunction] were released now, it appears to me almost inevitable that detailed answers [to the issues such as negligence that the court may have to determine] would be published and there would be expressed various public prejudgments of this issue. That I would regard as very much against the public interest. There has long been and there still is in this country a strong and generally held feeling that trial by newspaper is wrong and should be avoided.

See the text to note 12 (Ch. 3) for a more technical discussion of the *Sunday Times* thalidomide case, which has probably done more than any other case in recent times to enwrap parts of the British justice administration in a cloak of untouchability. The situation may, however, change in view of the judgment of the European Court of Human Rights in 1979 – see the text to note 145.

112. In the second *Van Niekerk* case – see the text to note 31 – Chief Justice Ogilvie-Thompson echoed the inevitable public interest refrain thus:

[I]t is important to bear in mind that the true basis of punishment for contempt of court lies in the interests of the public, as distinct from the protection of any particular injured Judge or Judges. . . . [U]nless those last-mentioned interests clearly so require, genuine criticism, even though it be somewhat emphatically or unhappily expressed, should, in my opinion . . . preferably be regarded as an exercise of the right of free speech. *S* v. *Van Niekerk* 1972 (3) SA 711 AD at 720-21.

113. *In Re C Abayomi Cassell*, Vol. 14 Liberian Law Reports 391. See note 125.

114. The article in *Der Stern* that gave rise to the furor will be referred to in the text to note 168 (Ch. 3). The *Richterbund* is the authoritative professional organization of German judges.

115. On informal restrictions, see Ch. 4.

116. On the effect of noncomment or nonscrutiny on judicial lawmaking concerning free speech see the text to note 40 (Ch. 4).

117. *Ambard* v. *Attorney-General for Trinidad and Tobago* [1936] AC 322 (PC). The case concerned a newspaper article in which the topic of discrimination in sentences was discussed. The article itself was mild and reasoned, and the list of qualifications in the judgment of Lord Atkin to the right of criticism of judicial actions detracts considerably from the force of a doctrine of free speech in legal matters. Amid the euphoric praise normally surrounding reference to the *Ambard* case, these qualifications are always overlooked.

118. See the passage quoted on the title page of this work.

119. At 335.

120. In government systems based on the so-called rule of law principle much thought is expended on the judicial control of the legislature, especially of the executive, but practically none on the control of the judicial arm of government.

121. On the subtle influence on the judiciary of public opinion, see Roscoe Pound's classic comment in *The Nature of the Judicial Process* (1921) 168:

[I]f there is anything of reality in my analysis of the judicial process, [it is that judges] do not stand aloof on these chill and distant heights; and we shall not help the cause of truth by acting and speaking as if they do. The great tides and currents which engulf the rest of men, do not turn aside in their course and pass the judges by.

122. See the text to note 115. It can be argued that *Ambard*'s qualifications make the decision as useful to the repression of legal free speech as it is for its edification.

123. James Madison stated in *The Federalist* (No. 48):

It will not be denied that power is of an encroaching nature, and that it ought to be effectually restrained from passing the limits assigned to it.... [T]he ... most difficult task is to provide some practical security for each [class of power], against the invasion of the others. Everyman's Library edition (1942) 252.

124. See the text to note 216 (Ch. 2).

125. The gist of the article was that instead of elaborating on the seriousness of the crime (injuries, drunkenness, etc.), the prosecutor made a great play of the high position of the accused and his morality when he asked for the imposition of a mild sentence. See (1961) *Juris-Classeur Périodique: La Semaine Juridique Doctrine-Jurisprudence-Textes* no. 12233.

126. As will be seen later, these provisions are very seldom invoked. I have been able to find at least two other cases where repressive precedent-creating convictions were obtained. See text to note 215 (Ch. 2).

127. *A-G v. O'Ryan and Boyd* 1946 IR 70.

128. A few extracts from this letter are indeed worthy of record (at 72-73):

As a humble member of the Catholic community of the diocese of Waterford and Lismore, I take exception to your taunt and sneer at the Most Venerable Dean Byrne, PP of Sts Peter's and Paul's Church, Clonmel, from your exalted? perch on the Bench of the Court in Waterford last Monday, 5th inst – that he thought and expected that crime perpetrated outside his church should be exonerated. I fling that taunt back into the face of the worthy representative of the seed and breed of Cromwell. You, Sir, were foisted on the judicial Bench at a time when legal ability was not the qualification best fitting to lead to it. To the foreign, hostile administration of that time there were better qualifications evidently well known to your Lordship. I well remember, in the Spring of 1917, when acting as advocate for Lord Ashtown in a claim for compensation for the burning of his wood, you stated that perhaps it was done to celebrate the anniversary of Easter Week, 1916, although all in the district knew that the burning was accidental. ... At any rate you were elevated to the Bench by the Lord French-*cum*-Hamar-Greenwood regime to administer "true British Amelioration" in Ireland. You remember how the IRA chased you off the Bench at Clonmel. Notwithstanding all that you were tolerated and retained by an Executive Irish Government predominantly national and Catholic. And your return for all that was to taunt the second highest dignitary in the Diocese of Waterford and Lismore that he would condone crime which was committed outside his church. You are as poor at marshalling your facts as you were mediocre at law. ... Your ilk and breed in this country are the inheritors of lands, castles and wealth secured by the brute laws of robbery, spoliation and confiscation of the property of Catholic Ireland!

129. See note 113. The judgment in the *Cassell* case has been discussed by the present writer in "Contempt of Court: A Little-Known Liberian Case," in (1974) 62 *SALJ* 248. It formed the subject of a special pamphlet of the International Commission of Jurists, *The Cassell Case. Contempt in Liberia* (1961). Excerpts from the judgment are reprinted as an appendix. The facts of the case briefly are that Mr. Cassell, a former Attorney-General of Liberia, made a speech at an international conference in which he spoke about various aspects of law reform. In those parts where he referred to the judiciary he stated inter alia that he considered the judiciary to be the weakest link in the chain for the achievement of justice and although there were no great injustices the sum total of many little things might nevertheless be considered a menace to the rights of the individual. It could not be honestly stated that the judiciary and the bar were doing their utmost to change these conditions and he regretted that nothing had been done to secure the tenure of judges and to ensure their fitness for office by an investigation into the character or ability of nominees. Because judges were removable only by a joint resolution of both houses of the legislature, Mr. Cassell considered that the bar association had not done its duty by ensuring that only properly qualified persons be appointed to the judiciary.

130. The following is a selection from some of Justice Pierre's pungent formulations in the *Cassell* case (note 129). At 404-05:

> Counsellor Cassell spoke about reforms, perhaps implying that these might be needed to strengthen the judiciary. The Constitution has provided ample means, and has laid down the methods by which reforms should be brought about.

At 405:

> There is no law which authorizes a citizen who wants reforms in the institutions of the government of Liberia to resort to foreign countries or international forums to effect them. Since when have Liberians become incapable of instituting reforms if and when they are needed?

At 409:

> In the enjoyment of basic rights ... the individual in Liberian society has as much freedom under our Constitution as any citizen in any country in the world, without excepting the most avowed and professed democratic nations.

At 410:

> One would have been prepared to shout hallelujah from the housetop in support of Counsellor Cassell, had he advocated that we begin to find ways and means of showing the world the wisdom of some of our native laws and customs.

At 415:

> [R]aising the question of the qualifications of Liberian judges at an international conference seems irrelevant, unpatriotic and strange under the circumstances.

At 419:

> As Attorney-General, Counsellor Cassell should have known whether or not particular statutes infringed the rights of citizens; and ... should have advocated the necessary steps to correct the alleged evils in the law. This was his duty morally, professionally, and officially. But to have known the laws to be evil, as he has now claimed, and yet to have prosecuted citizens under them ... is to call into question the said judgments and that is to belittle them.

131. Op. cit., 7.

132. *Areopagitica.* From the edition by Northrop Frye (ed.), *Paradise Lost and Selected Poetry and Prose by John Milton* (1951) 501.

133. In looking at all restrictions on speech in the legal domain as a whole, it is not difficult to conclude that in the majority of instances where free speech has been restrained it has been done to prevent the truth – or at least a reasonable version of the truth – from reaching public knowledge. This tendency to subvert the truth has very respectable historical roots, as we have seen in the quotation from Levy about seditious libel quoted in note 98.

134. See the Chicago *Tribune* of September 9, 1977, and the New York *Times* of the same date; *Time* September 19, 1977.

135. I have documented this case in "Silencing the Judges," op. cit. (see note 101) 162.

136. See the text to note 102.

137. Ulrich Sonneman (ed.), *Wie Frei ist unsere Justiz?* (1969) 263.

138. His first work, *Im Paragraphenturm* (literally, In the Tower of Paragraphs), was published under the pseudonym Zaver Berra and was scathingly received in judicial and academic quarters. For instance, a reviewer in the influential *Juristenzeitung* (1967, p. 22) stated:

It must be conceded that Berra is literally bubbling over with ideas and suggestions but at times one cannot escape the impression that these [ideas etc] have in fact taken control of him. . . . Is it surprising, therefore, if much is one-sided, exaggerated, overdrawn, generalized, over-simplified, warped or just plain untruthful?

When it became known that he was the author of the work, preliminary steps were taken to have him disciplined. These were later abandoned.

139. Under the impact of neo-Marxist criticism of the law, the name and role of Rasehorn has, however, almost been forgotten in Germany.

140. It would seem that most, and perhaps all, of the great legal innovations by the U.S. Supreme Court in recent years – for example, on race and criminal defendant rights – had some of their origins in realist-oriented writings.

141. See note 77.

142. Naturally, there are still voices proclaiming that parts of American justice are mystified or left unresearched – cf Nader and Green, op. cit. 82, quoted in note 78.

143. See note 49.

144. See the text starting with note 88. The case concerned, it will be recalled, was the publication of a law journal article on the death penalty in which questions were asked concerning the influence of racism in that area.

145. See *The Sunday Times Case* (judgment) of April 26, 1979. References are to the official transcript of that date.

146. *Report of the Committee on Contempt of Court* (1976) Cmnd. 5794. Cf paragraph 60 of the report, where it is stated: "We have no doubt, however, that the change in the course of the thalidomide proceedings which occurred in the months following September 1972 was the result of the campaign of moral pressure against Distillers triggered off by the first two articles in the *Sunday Times*."

147. Article 10(2) of the European Convention on Human Rights provides for the restriction of the freedom of expression:

The exercise of these freedoms, since it carries with it duties and responsibilities may be subject to such formalities, conditions, restrictions and penalties as are prescribed by law and are necessary in a democratic society, in the interests of national security, territorial integrity or public safety, for the prevention of disorder or crime, for the protection of health or morals, for preventing the disclosure of information received in confidence, or for maintaining the authority and impartiality of the judiciary.

At the time of the drafting the last proviso concerning the judiciary was specifically inserted to retain the British contempt institution.

148. The court held by eleven to nine votes that there had been a breach of Article 10 of the Convention.

149. At 31.

150. The minority did not as such support the contention that the sub judice rule was legitimately enforced under the circumstances but merely that the matter was of a kind that was best left to the national courts to interpret.

151. See the text to note 88. See on these effects Van Niekerk "Freedom of Speech Concerning the Administration of Justice," op. cit., 677 ff. Professor John Dugard, "The Judicial Process, Positivism and Civil Liberty," in (1971) 88 *SALJ* 181 at 190, stated that "State v Van Niekerk has generally been interpreted as a warning against academic enquiry into the judicial process in sensitive areas."

152. Cf D. J. Pavlich in (1972) *Annual Survey of South African Law* 458:

In the House of Assembly the Minister of Justice revealed that during the calendar year 1971, 76 persons were hanged. . . . It is interesting to note the decline in the number of executions since the publication of the article "Hanged by the Neck until You are Dead" by B v D van Niekerk (1969) 86 *SALJ* 457.

The changed statistics of capital punishment in South Africa were these: At the time of the publication of the article the average number of executions for the decade 1957-1966 was 89.3. During the calendar year of 1968, 119 persons were executed, and from 1971 to the statistical year 1973-1974 the hangman's toll decreased from 76 to 43. The number of executions, undoubtedly as a consequence of the lull in abolitionist activities, has since increased again to 59 for the statistical year 1974-75 and in 1978 the hangman's toll reached an all-time high of 130. There had over the previous five years been no significant agitation about capital punishment.

153. *U.S.* v. *Schwimmer* 279 U.S. 644 at 654 [1929].

154. Sensational trials obviously fall in a category of their own in terms of attracting attention not normally enjoyed by the administration of justice generally. On sensationalism in trial reporting see the text to note 175 (Ch. 3).

155. See text to note 63 (Ch. 3).

156. The robust use of speech by defense counsel in political trials to give the accused some sense of equality is a well-known phenomenon. See Kirchheimer, op. cit., 252 ff.

157. See, for instance, the *Dennis* case in the text to note 38.

158. For instance in a judgment of the *Bundesgerichtshof* for criminal cases of March 30, 1955, a judgment of a lower court was upheld in which the accused had been found guilty of the crime of defamation (*Beleidigung*) because of his use of the term terror judgment to describe the finding of a judge. And in an unreported judgment of November 19, 1976, a judgment that is probably not

entirely unsymptomatic of the attitudes of lower echelon German courts at the present time, the *Amtsgericht* of Freiburg sentenced an accused to a fine of 10 daily units (at DM 55 per unit) and costs for the *Beleidigung* of the *Oberlandesgericht* of Karlsruhe, which had accorded custody over his son to his estranged wife. The insult was contained in a letter addressed to the court concerned:

> Further to your catastrophic misjudgment of 23 October. ... although your judgment is constitutionally correct it is my opinion that from the human point of view the action taken was barbaric and irresponsible. ... by robbing the child of his ward and his contact person and by having him deported. ... Such act of deportation constitutes in my opinion an act of inhumanity which is in line with the spirit of terror. ... I would like to make it clear also that it is a lie that my mother is 70 years of age when in fact she is 66 years old. ...

159. The Irish case of *O'Ryan and Boyd* – see note 127 – is a minor classic. A near textbook example is the South African criminal defamation case of *S* v. *Revill* 1970 (3) SA 611 (C), where the accused had indulged in a prolonged and vicious letter-writing campaign against the finding of a particular judge in which he, the accused, had been involved.

160. Cf Walther Isele, *Bundesrechtsanwaltsordnung: Kommentar* (1976) 692.

161. Some of the spate of professional misconduct cases in Germany clearly fall in this category and would therefore on the premises of this argument fail to qualify for free *speech* protection.

162. See note 75 (at 320 of the judgment).

163. In the judgment of the Irish High Court in the *O'Ryan* case, Gavan Duffy, J., starts his separate opinion with the following remark: "The reputation of His Honour Judge Sealy for integrity stands after his twenty years in the Bench since his appointment in the year 1924, as high as that of any judge in this country and needs no vindication of this court." (at 83)

164. See the text starting with note 109.

165. *McLeod* v. *St Aubyn* [1899] AC 549.

166. The Privy Council, rather prematurely, stated as follows: "Committals for contempt of court by scandalising the court itself have become obsolete in this country. Courts are satisfied to leave to public opinion attacks or comments derogatory or scandalous to them." In the colonies the situation may, however, be different (at 561):

> But it must be considered that in small colonies, consisting principally of coloured populations, the enforcement in proper cases of committal for contempt of court for attacks on the court may be absolutely

necessary to preserve in such a community the dignity of and respect for the court.

In the *Ambard* case – see note 117 – Lord Atkin without as much as a murmur referred (at 335) approvingly to this authority.

167. In the *McLeod* case, the acting chief justice of St. Vincent had the appellant arraigned before court for inadvertently passing on to a friend a newspaper published in the neighboring island of Grenada. The newspaper contained a scathing but apparently factual attack on the acting chief justice of St. Vincent in the form of a headline and a letter. Prevented from laying his hands on the editor of the newspaper, the chief justice sought balm for his hurt pride in action against a completely innocent purveyor of the newspaper. The juiciest parts of this tropical island verbal cocktail merits documentation:

> Kindly grant me space in your unfettered and fearless journal to expose the scandalous state of things that has existed here since Mr Geoffrey Peter St Aubyn's appointment as Acting Chief Justice in November last.
>
> The public career of this gentleman is interesting. A briefless barrister, unendowed with much grain who religiously attended with his empty bag at the several courts of London in the forlorn hope of picking up a case he, after long weary years of waiting exchanged the law for the stage (being a good amateur actor) and tried to earn an honest penny by turning his undoubted histrionic talent into account. . . . [I]n an evil moment for St Vincent, he was appointed police magistrate of the Kingstown District in May, 1891, at a salary of £450 a year. His demeanour in the Magistrate's Court has been anything but dignified, and he has indulged in offensive expression to the litigants before him which were discreditable to one in his position. A man of the Torquemada [a Spanish inquisitor] type, narrow, bigoted, vain, vindictive, and unscrupulous he takes advantage of his position to vent his spleen upon those whom he hates.

The editorial in the *Federalist* referred to the correspondent's letter and stated inter alia as follows about the acting chief justice:

> He has apparently been too wrapped up and intermingled with personal disputes and squabbles of a questionable character to allow him to deal honestly and impartially with questions which come before him to be judicially settled. To nod and wink to counsel engaged in cases is not at all dignified in a judge; it becomes double criminal when he who performs these grievances and gymnastics is solemnly adjudicating questions of the utmost importance, involving the liberty, almost the life, of British subjects.

168. Reported as *In the Matter of One Vijaya Parmandam* (Case no. 90 of 1972). A photocopy of the judgment has been made available to me by the court.

169. The accused stated inter alia as follows:

This particular gentleman, Sir John Nimmo, an Australian, who was appointed Chief Justice of Fiji, you will recall his salary or part of his salary is paid by the Australian Government. Have we sold our independence for a few measly thousand dollars to Australia?

He concluded his speech by stating: "There . . . are different aspects of the judiciary which need clearing up. And if you vote NFP into power, the judiciary will be cleaned up once and for all." In a pamphlet distributed later, the speech was reproduced and the following statement was recorded: "It was under the Alliance Government that two Suva lawyers were condemned in absentia in a court of law. Vote Federation for the protection of your fundamental human rights."

170. *In the Matter of a Special Reference from the Bahama Islands* [1893] AC 138. This decision was handed down before the *McLeod* case, which, it will be recalled, revived contempt for the colonies. See note 166.

171. The Privy Council held that although the offending letter "might have been made the proceedings for libel" it was not, in the circumstances, "calculated to obstruct or interfere with the course of justice or the due administration of the law, and therefore did not constitute a contempt of Court."

172. The offending letter in the Nassau *Guardian* followed two earlier letters from the chief justices relating to questions of health. Herewith some extracts from this gem of contempt satire:

Sir,

The combined wisdom and vigilance of "Governor Shea, Providence, and the Board of Health" being insufficient to preserve the health of this community, Mr Yelverton has come to the rescue, and it is but fair to him that his protest should be echoed by every citizen of this city.

What is the good of increasing the salary of the Chief Justice if his mind is to be disquieted and alarmed through fear of fever? For our additional £300 a year we have all that our souls yearned for, viz, an English barrister, and we should do all that lies in our power to preserve the health and life of this luminary of the English bar. . . .

Search the annals of the bench of every country, of every age, and I defy creation to produce a more noble, more self-denying, and more virtuous exhibition of a tender conscience than was afforded by our Chief Justice in refusing to accept a gift of pine-apples! Some cynic has said, "Every man has his price". It is assuring to this community to know that the "fount of justice" in this colony is above the price of even one dozen pine-apples. Mr Yelverton's noble words of scornful renunciation should be graven in letters of gold upon the walls of every magisterial office in this colony; then, and not till then, will sweet potatoes, pigeon peas, etc., cease to exert their baneful influence on the administration of justice in this colony. . . .

But I must not confine myself to words of heartfelt commendation. Duty and esteem call upon me to speak words of warning; and it is well that Mr Yelverton should know that a great many people of this city are mean enough to say that "He should risk his valuable life and attend to the duties of his office in summer as well as winter." They contend that the day of non-resident officialdom is over, and that a man should reside in the colony that pays him his salary. . . .

Not being an Englishman, I am not afraid of noxious gases or destructive microbes. We colonists have had many camels of incompetence forced down our throats. We cease to strain over a microbe more or less. For myself, and on behalf of others who consider health of paramount importance, I thank Mr Yelverton for his unselfish protest; and more, that as he has sided with Providence, Governor Shea, and the Board of Health, we are certain to enjoy immunity from fevers this summer.

(Sd) Colonist.

173. See note 75 for the reference. The full offending passage reads thus:

The recent judgment of the Court of Appeal is a strange example of the blindness which sometimes descends on the best of judges. The legislation of 1960 and thereafter has been rendered virtually unworkable by the unrealistic, contradictory and, in the leading case, erroneous, decisions of the courts, including the Court of Appeal. So what do they do? Apologise for the expense and trouble they have put the police to? Not a bit of it. Lambaste the police for not enforcing the law which they themselves had rendered unworkable and which is now the subject of a Bill, the manifest purpose of which is to alter it. Pronounce an impending dies irae on a series of parties not before them, whose crime it has been to take advantage of the weaknesses in the decisions of their own court. Criticise the lawyers, who have advised their clients. Blame Parliament for passing Acts which they have interpreted so strangely. Everyone, it seems is out of step, except the courts. . . . The House of Lords overruled the Court of Appeal . . . it is to be hoped that the courts will remember the golden rule for judges in the matter of obiter dicta. Silence is always an option.

174. At 320.

175. Prominent German criminal defense lawyer.

176. *Pardon* Nov. 1968.

177. It was entitled: "Who laughed over there? Concerning the punishability of mirth."

178. Extracts from the article quoted in the indictment read thus:

Rod wielding family homes, certain schools and business concerns, the army and the police are not the only authoritarian institutions to which citizens, in terms of the Constitution of our democratic state are subjected. Any person also who enters a courtroom in which law is handed down in the name of the people, must leave the democratic part of his personality outside – that part of him which is willing and entitled to indulge in open dissent – if he wishes to leave again as a free man. He must know that authoritarian rule is humourless. He who laughs at the demand of the rulers to be taken seriously must be taught a lesson. He must be taught that the crime of overthrowing ancient authoritarian conditions starts with the attempt to ridicule those conditions. . . .

Mirth in the courtroom cannot be. The judge records the mirth like an old fashioned schoolmaster recording the pranks of his boisterous pupils in his class register. It is impossible for the judge to comprehend that young people who have been trying for a number of years to kill this old fashioned school through the use of ridicule have to laugh over his meticulous fashion of recording the proceedings. He dictates: "While the judge is dictating this passage, the public laughs anew". "Look Chief, look", says one of the accused, "record also that the accused cannot suppress a smile". . . .

The subject of the charge presupposes a judge who is very moral, somewhat uninitiated into the realities of real life, responsive to authority and humourless, and who is endowed with some pedagogical ambitions. The Bremen juvenile judge Dr A combined these characteristics in an almost ideal degree . . .

. . . it is all quiet now, the judge can now at last address himself to the matter at hand. But no, he relishes in his victory and indulges in pedagogical monologues which are addressed to the public, the accused and the defence lawyer . . . and then follow endless monologues with samples of thought inspired by authoritarian principles which of course cannot be inculcated early enough into the youth of today.

179. On the German *Ehrengericht* jurisdiction in matters concerning contempt of court, see the text to note 110 (Ch. 2).

180. The *Cassell* case from Liberia, the *Parmandam* case from Fiji, both *Van Niekerk* cases from South Africa, and the *Hannover* case from Germany. This attitude was also implicit in the treatment of Dr. Rasehorn and of the

attorneys by Judge Medina in the *Dennis* case. In the second *Van Niekerk* contempt case, the position was put as follows:

> Whether one regards this point of view as illogical, perverse or just plain silly, the words do not, in my opinion, constitute a contempt of or insult to the court. They do, however, express a point of view with which I, as judge and as one of those to whom the words were addressed, profoundly disagree and which, in my humble opinion, exhibit a misunderstanding of the functions of a judge in a society such as ours which, especially in the case of a man in the accused's position, is both surprising and, indeed, disturbing.

See the text starting with note 31.

181. Individual lawyers who display the quality of outspokenness are really the exception and the ideal rather than the rule and the reality in Western countries. Cf Wolfgang Friedmann Law in (1972) 2 ed *Changing Society* 519: "Predominantly ... the lawyer in the western world has been a defender of the established order and of vested interests."

182. See note 146.

183. Cf the text to note 15 for a quote in this regard by Emerson, op. cit.

184. On this selectivity of victims, see the text to note 6 (Ch. 2).

185. See the text to note 289 (Ch. 2).

186. See the text to note 171 (Ch. 2).

187. *Attorney-General* v. *Tonks* 1939 NZLR 533 at 538. See also the text to note 7 (Ch. 3).

188. Myers C. J. said this about such stimuli: "Nor, indeed, is a common-law Judge in the least likely to be affected consciously by any such publication. But can it be said with certainty ... that any man, even a Judge, may not possibly be in some way unconsciously affected?" A generation later, in 1971, in South Africa the following interesting views were expressed by Fannin J. (*S* v. *Van Niekerk* 1972 (1) PH H19 (D)): "Who can say, with any confidence, that consciously or unconsciously, the court, even as so constituted [the judge president sitting with two assessors], would not be affected by the suggestions which the accused made?"

189. With the exception of the United States, where a series of cases culminating in the Supreme Court decision of *Nebraska Press Association* v. *Stuart* 423 U.S. 1327 (1975) has effectively although not entirely put an end to restrictions on pretrial and trial publicity, some form or another of sub judice restrictions exists in all English-speaking countries in the world, as well as in Israel.

190. Articles 226 and 227, especially the latter, of the French Penal Code, adopted in 1958, created a kind of crime of contempt of court in both major senses of the concept. Toward the end of 1977, the French government introduced legislation to bolster what was called the *presumption d'innocence*

against pretrial publicity (cf *Le Monde* November 8, 1977). See note 206 (Ch. 2).

191. In both Germany and Holland, for instance, there have been moves to introduce sub judice restrictions, and in both countries there is from time to time an outcry over pretrial publicity. In Holland, the press largely succeeds in disciplining itself in this regard; in Germany, the relevant press code provisions have become dead letters. In Germany, an official draft amendment to the criminal code in 1962 proposed the introduction of sub judice restrictions. On these and related matters, see, generally, Wolfram Reiss *Störung der Strafrechtspflege durch Berichterstattung in den Massenmedien* (Doctor of Laws thesis, Bonn 1975) and *Pers en Rechtspraak* (*Rapport van een werkgroep gevormd op initiatief van de Nederlandse Orde van Advocaten*) (1977).

192. As in the Liberian case of *Cassell* – see notes 113 and 129.

193. Such as the interesting Canadian cases of Nichol (re Nichol et al. [1954] 3 DLR 690) and *Hébert* (A-G of Quebec v. *Hébert* [1967] 2 CCC 111), both involving pointed and emotional criticism in writing of specific cases where the death penalty was imposed and executed.

194. As in the *Quintin Hogg* case, where the criticism was directed at the wrong court. See the text to note 173.

195. As in the Irish case of *O'Ryan*. See note 127.

196. As in the *Hannover* disciplinary case in Germany. See note 179. More recently, it was reported again (*Der Spiegel* July 17, 1978) that Mr. Hannover had been sentenced to a fine of DM 3,000 by the *Ehrengerichtshof* of Hamburg on three charges of importance to free speech in the legal domain. One concerned his statement in a trial that class justice [meaning injustice as between classes] is not tripped up by the fine mesh of legal guarantees of the Criminal Procedure Code.

197. *Mishra* v. *Registrar of Orissa High Court* (1974) 1 SCC 374 at 409.

198. See note 150.

199. See note 151.

200. See the text to note 102.

201. See the text starting with note 39 (Conclusion).

202. The case is documented in (1953) 6 *Neue Juristische Wochenscrift* 1722. In an article in his newspaper, the accused, an editor, had printed a report in which it was alleged that a meeting had taken place between the president of the Federal Constitutional Court and an official in the office of the German Chancellor to discuss the text of an advisory opinion that the Court was due to present to the government; the object of the consultation, so it was stated, was to facilitate the passage of a bill through the German Parliament. With the permission of the president of the *Bundesverfassungsgericht*, the editor was successfully prosecuted in the *Landsgericht* of Hannover for criminal defamation in terms of article 186 of the penal code. The technical appeals of both the accused and the prosecution need not detain us here, except insofar as the appeal court now found that article 187a of the penal code would have

been applicable to the circumstances of the case. Article 187a(1) of the Criminal Code reads:

> If a defamatory falsehood (*üble Nachrede*) (in terms of article 186) is disseminated either publicly, or in a meeting or by the dissemination of writing against a person in the political life of the people, for motives which relate to the position of the insulted person, and if the act is calculated to embarrass his public activities, the penalty will be imprisonment between three months and five years.

203. The fact of the matter is that governments are known to consult judges privately, and a prosecution of the present kind would do nothing about the unobservable and potentially more detrimental silent communion that sometimes exists between executives and judiciaries.

204. See the text starting with note 109 (Ch. 2).

205. See the comment by Professor Dugard in note 151.

206. In terms of Section 44 of the South African Prisons Act of 1959, a person commits a crime if he

> publishes or causes to be published in any manner whatsoever any false information concerning the behavior or experience in prison of any prisoner or ex-prisoner or concerning the administration of any prison, knowing the same to be false or without taking reasonable steps to verify such information (the onus of proving that reasonable steps were taken to verify such information being upon the accused).

In *S* v. *SAAN* 1970 (1) SA 469 (W) the editor, a reporter, and the publishing company of the *Rand Daily Mail* newspaper was successfully prosecuted under this provision for a report on prison conditions that contained some inaccuracies, although elaborate efforts had been made to verify all allegations about misconduct of officials or about prison conditions. Although the fine was nominal, the trial lasted about six months and cost the company a record sum in costs. This judgment, probably wrongly decided even in terms of South African law, was not taken on further appeal and it has since *totally* inhibited the press in South Africa from concerning themselves with the prisons where, as is common in all societies, injustices and abuse are rife. On this case and its chilling effect see A. S. Mathews, *Law, Order and Liberty in South Africa* (1971) 216, and Dugard, *Human Rights* op. cit., 182. Ironically again, the bad publicity flowing from the revelations in court resulted in modest but meaningful improvements in South African prison conditions.

CHAPTER 2

1. See note 52.

2. See, for instance, the view of Abel-Smith and Stevens and Professor Goodhart referred to in notes 62 and 63, respectively, and in the text to note 77.

3. Cf the Prisons Act No. 8 of 1959. See note 2026 (Ch. 1).

4. This inhibition flows specifically from the interpretation put on the particular provision in *S* v. *South African Associated Newspapers* 1970 (1) SA 469 (W). See note 206 (Ch. 1). More than a decade after this case, I was informed by the editor of the newspaper concerned *that on advice of their legal advisers* the paper could not provide me with photocopies of the original articles, since such dissemination may be covered by the Act – a proposition that seems patently absurd. See note 23 (Conclusion).

5. *John Fairfax and Sons* v. *McRae* (1954) 93 CLR 351 at 370-71. See the text to note 180.

6. A clear case of a blatantly differential approach has been documented by John Dugard in (89) *SALJ* 364. His reference is to the second *Van Niekerk* contempt case (see note 3, Ch. 1) where a prosecution for sub judice contempt was instituted where there was no direct reference to a trial in progress and where a contemporaneous critical statement of the minister of police in relation to the same trial was not prosecuted. See also on this discrimination A. S. Mathews and Barend van Niekerk, "Eulogizing the Attorney-General. A Qualified Dissent," in (1972) 89 *SALJ* 292.

7. Cf note 49 (Ch. 1). In paragraph 40 of the judgment, it is documented that "in their submissions on the merits, the applicants [the *Sunday Times* et al.]" made the following allegations: "that there had been discrimination . . . by reason of the fact that similar press publications had not been restrained. . . ." In any event this point was not pursued.

8. Sebastian Soler, *Derecho Penal Argentino* (1973) V 120.

9. See the text to note 116.

10. Walter Schwarz, "Le Monde could be another Dreyfus," in *The Guardian* of November 30, 1980. Cf also *Time* of December 22, 1980, and *Le Monde*, November 1980. One of the offending articles was published on September 18, 1980, and attacked the detention without trial of one Roger Delpey who had information embarrassing to the government. See the text to note 229.

11. Brian McKenna, "The Judge and the Common Man" (1969) 32 *Modern Law Review* 601 at 602.

12. See note 16.

13. Ronald L. Goldfarb, *The Contempt Power* (1963) 11-12:

With the rise of the feudal system in England, accompanying the preeminence of royal power after the Norman Conquest, there developed manifestations of the idea of the complete ownership, authority, and power of the king. This was but another, though not different, step from the sanctity of the medicine man, the priestly character of primitive royalty, and the Christian concepts of obedience. . . . The contempt power is understandable when seen through the perspectives of its age of inception, an age of alleged divinely ordained monarchies, ruled by a king totally invested with all sovereign legal powers and accountable only to God.

14. At 11.

15. James Francis Oswald, *Contempt of Court, Committal and Attachment and Arrest upon Civil Process in the Supreme Court of Judicature* (1892) 1. At 3-4, Oswald defines contempt thus:

Speaking generally, contempt of court may be said to be constituted by any conduct that tends to bring the authority and administration of the law into disrespect or disregard, or to interfere with, or prejudice parties litigant, or their witnesses during the litigation.

16. *R* v. *Almon* [1765] Wilm 243 at 270. Quoted by Oswald, op. cit., 9. On the *Almon* case, see also Goldfarb, op. cit., 16 ff, and Oswald, op. cit., 2. The notes of the undelivered judgment by Wilmot J. were posthumously published in 1802, but through judicial repetition it assumed the nature of binding authority despite the fact (in the words of Oswald, op. cit., 3) that the "judgment . . . will be found on examination to depend rather on a somewhat turbid rhetoric than on ratiocination or the examination of authorities."

17. Civil contempt relates essentially to disobedience to court orders or undertakings given to court. Cf Borrie and Lowe, op. cit., 314 ff, and Miller, op. cit., 232.

18. Concerning these technical rules, see, for instance, Oswald, op. cit.; George Stuart Robertson Oswald's *Contempt of Court; Committal, Attachment and Arrest upon Civil Process* (1910); Miller, op. cit.; Borrie and Lowe, op. cit.

19. *Pennekamp* v. *Florida* 328 U.S. 331 [1946]. For a synoptic view of the American practice before *Pennekamp*, see Goldfarb, op. cit., 89 ff. The case concerned the publication of two editorials and a cartoon in a newspaper criticizing certain actions of a Florida court. The Supreme Court unanimously struck down the contempt conviction, which had been upheld by the Florida Supreme Court and applied the clear and present danger test as regards the kind of risk to a fair and orderly administration of justice that may justify intervention. In effect, both sub judice and scandalization contempt were involved.

20. Goldfarb, op. cit., 10-11:

Though centuries later men were to accept the self-righting process, recommended by the writings of men like Locke and Milton, as the more democratic way to resolve individual-governmental conflict, the contempt power was more suited to the early English rulers and their style of government. And the law of contempt is not the law of men, it is the law of kings. It is not law which representative legislators responsibly reflecting the *vox populi* originally wrote, but is rather evolved from the divine law of kings, and its aspects of obedience, cooperation, and respect toward government bodies. Though this is not the only source of the power, it is the seed from which the power grew, if later adopted and cultivated by men not adverse to its exercise. Later institutions agreeably accepted it, less as adjuncts to the king than to protect their own dignity and supremacy.

21. On this species of contempt, see Robertson-Oswald, op. cit., 39 ff; Miller, op. cit., 48 ff; Borrie and Lowe, op. cit., 5 ff. Perhaps the most vicious verbal assault of this kind in the annals of contempt was made during the so-called Chicago Conspiracy trial in 1969, during which 175 contempt citations were issued. See Judy Clavir and John Spitzer, *The Conspiracy Trial* (1971).

22. See Robertson-Oswald, op. cit., 41-42, for a description of some of the classical cases of overt acts of unkindness of litigants to judges. In 1877, a man who had just been convicted was jailed for five months for throwing an egg at a judge leaving court. Robertson continues: "The Vice-Chancellor [the target of the egg] had sufficient presence of mind and sense of humour, it is said, to remark that the present must have been intended for his brother Bacon, VC, who was sitting in an adjoining court."

23. See the text to note 38 (Ch. 1).

24. *R* v. *Davies* [1906] 1 KB 32 at 40. Reference to this quote, which comes from a much older source, has practically become part of the obligatory routine of all judgments for scandalization contempt.

25. On such criminal defamation cases involving judges, see note 156 and also the text starting with note 125.

26. See the text to note 301.

27. An instance in England where the judicial officers concerned showed a commendable degree of philosophical fortitude to a calculated insult (albeit of a nonverbal kind) is documented by Miller, op. cit., 49-50, based on the *Times* of February 12, 1970. It concerned the reaction of a litigant who had conducted her own case on hearing of the dismissal of her appeal. She thereupon threw her law books at the judges: "Lord Denning MR and his colleagues did not make an issue of the matter, but left the court with carefully measured tread."

28. *Parashuram Detaram Shamdasani* v. *King-Emperor* [1957] AC 264 (PC). The appellant, a layman to the law, had appeared in person before the High Court of Bombay to object to a taxation order for court costs. When opposing counsel alleged that the appellant was misleading the court, the appellant replied: "I do not keep anything back at all. My fault is that I disclose everything, unlike members of the bar, who are in the habit of not doing so and misleading the court." When faced by the protest of opposing counsel, the appellant

immediately apologized. However, at the end of the proceedings, counsel again raised the matter and despite a renewed apology, the appellant was sentenced to a fine of one thousand rupees and three months imprisonment; subsequently after another apology the imprisonment was reduced to eight days. At 268, the Privy Council states: "[T]heir Lordships would, indeed, go further, and say that it would have been more consonant with the dignity of the bar to have ignored a foolish remark which has been made over and over again, not only by the ignorant, but by people who ought to know better."

29. See the text to note 42 (Ch. 1).

30. On this form of contempt, see generally Miller, op. cit., 182 ff; Borrie and Lowe, op. cit., 152 ff.

31. *In the Matter of a Special Reference from the Bahama Islands* [1893] AC 138 at 149. See the text to note 170 (Ch. 1).

32. On Mr. Levin's unique role, see the text to note 95 (Ch. 4). The present incident is documented by Miller, op. cit., 53, who quotes Levin:

> Mr Bangs has recently had his rates increased, and is, understandably enough, displeased in consequence. When, therefore, a large and official-looking car passed him, in which he saw a gentleman in colourful, not to say ridiculous, clothes, he suited his action to his feelings and extended the first and second fingers of his right hand, knuckles outwards, in its direction, believing that the gorgeously-caparisoned traveller was the Mayor. In this, it speedily appeared, he was mistaken, for the man at whom he had made his rude gesture was not only blameless in the matter of the rates; he was Mr Justice Lawson, on his way to clock in for the morning shift at Teesside Crown Court.

Miller continues:

> Mr Bangs was, it appears, taken along to the Crown Court and brought before Lawson, J, some two hours later to be informed that it was a serious matter and that there was jurisdiction to send him to prison. He was thereafter released. The incident has, perhaps, a more serious side for even assuming that Mr Bangs had intended to direct his time-honoured gesture at a person whom he knew to be a judge – and this seems likely for a similar occurrence had apparently taken place the previous day – it would seem quite wrong to treat such conduct as a contempt.

The incident occurred in 1973.

33. See the reference in note 24.

34. *McLeod* v. *St Aubyn* [1899] AC 549. See the text to note 165 (Ch. 1).

35. See note 166 (Ch. 1) and the text there concerning this "racial"

justification for invoking contempt powers.

36. At 561. In one of the classic articles on contempt, Arthur E. Hughes, "Contempt of Court and the Press," in (1900) 16 *Law Quarterly Review* 292 at 300, echoes these sentiments and states: "[T]he authorities ... show that the privilege of a judge for the protection of his personal and judicial reputation is no greater and no less than that of every subject of the Queen."

37. *R* v. *Gray* [1900-03] All ER 59.

38. At 62. The full article, "A Defender of Decency," reads thus:

> Mr Justice Darling, having so few prisoners to try in Birmingham, and feeling the inspiration strong upon him to be a terror to evildoers, filled in a pleasant five minutes yesterday by "giving fits" to the reporters. If anyone can imagine Little Tich upholding his dignity upon a point of honour in a public house, he has a very fair conception of what Mr Justice Darling looked like in his warning to the press against the printing of indecent evidence. His diminutive Lordship positively glowed with judicial self-consciousness. He was determined there should be no reporting of improper details in the case before him. He felt himself bearing on his shoulders the whole fabric of public decency. Under the evident impression that newspapers were always on the prowl for unseemliness, he warned their representatives against giving a full report of what was about to transpire in their hearing. He hoped his words would be sufficient, but, if not, he warned them of the penalties which he should make it his business to enforce in the event of disobedience. The terrors of Mr Justice Darling will not trouble the Birmingham reporters very much. No newspaper can exist except upon its merits, a condition from which the bench, happily for Mr Justice Darling, is exempt. There is not a journalist in Birmingham who has anything to learn from the impudent little man in horse-hair, a microcosm of deceit and empty-headedness, who admonished the press yesterday. It is not the credit of journalism, but of the English Bench, that is imperilled in a speech like Mr Justice Darling's. One is almost sorry that the Lord Chancellor had not another relative to provide for on the day that he selected a new judge from among the larrikins of the law. One of Mr Justice Darling's biographers states that "an eccentric relative left him much money". That misguided testator spoiled a successful bus conductor. Mr Justice Darling would do well to master the duties of his own profession before undertaking the regulation of another. There is a batch of quarter sessions prisoners awaiting trial, who should have been dealt with at this assize. A judge who applies himself to the work lying to his hand has no time to search the newspapers for indecencies.

39. See the text to note 84.

40. See the text to note 169.

41. Lord Denning, *The Road to Justice* (1955) 73. On this case see also Lord Denning, *The Due Process of Law* (1980) 32. See note 88.

42. *R* v. *Wilkinson* reported in the *Times* of July 16, 1930, alluded to by Miller, op. cit., 186. In this case, a sentence of nine months' imprisonment was imposed on persons responsible for the publication in the *Daily Worker* of a report containing the following passage:

> Rigby Swift, the judge who sentenced Comrade Thomas, was the bewigged puppet and former Tory MP chosen to put Communist leaders away in 1926. The defending counsel, able as he was, could not do much in the face of the strong class bias on the judge and jury.

43. *R* v. *Colsley* reported in the *Times* of May 9, 1931, alluded to by Borrie and Lowe, op. cit., 162. In this case, the editor of a periodical, the *Truth*, was fined for publishing an article containing the following passage: "Lord Justice Slesser who can hardly be altogether unbiased about legislation of this type maintained that really it was a very nice provisional order or as good as one can be expected in this vale of tears." The significance of the latter remark as regards the bias that lay therein was that Slesser, as solicitor-general, had previously steered the relevant legislation under which the order was made through Parliament. According to Miller, op. cit., 188, quoting a bibliographical work, Justice Slesser was against the prosecution.

44. For instance, in his judgment in the celebrated *Quintin Hogg* case, Lord Denning also makes the point:

> All we would ask is that those who criticise us will remember that, from the nature of our office, we cannot reply to their criticisms. We cannot enter into public controversy. Still less into political controversy. We must rely on our conduct itself to be its own vindication.

The Phillimore Report on contempt (see note 1426, Ch. 1) states: "[J]udges commonly feel constrained by their position not to take action in reply to criticism, and they have no proper forum in which to do so as other public figures may have." (at 69)

45. *A-G of Quebec* v. *Hébert* [1967] 2 CCC 111 at 138. The facts of this case were that the accused had published a polemical book on the trial, more than five years before, and subsequent execution of a person convicted of murder. It was more the general disparaging tenor of the book, *J'accuse – les assassins de Coffin*, and not specific sections that seemed to have swayed the trial court. The gravamen of the accused's criticism was that the court had leaned too heavily toward the prosecution.

46. At 137-38. Commenting on the *Gray* case (see note 37), Hughes, op.

cit., 300, makes essentially the same point: "The gross vulgarity of the article ... appears to have led both Court and Counsel away from the legal aspect of the matter."

47. See, for instance, the *Ambard* case (note 117, Ch. 1), the first *Van Niekerk* case (note 92), the *Daily Worker* case (note 42), and the *Truth* case (note 43). See also *A-G for New South Wales* v. *Mundey* [1972] 2 NSWLR 887, concerning an allegation of racism that was prosecuted.

48. In the first *Van Niekerk* case (note 92, Ch. 1), the judge ended his judgment (in which he found that contempt had been committed by the making of a poll on the possible race prejudices of South African judges) by stating in effect that there was often discrimination in favor of blacks!

49. Cf Jacob S. Ziegel, "Some Aspects of the Law of Contempt of Court in Canada, England and the United States," in (1960) 6 *McGill Law Journal* 229 at 245-46:

> The cherished right to speak one's mind freely on all topics of public interest is founded in the belief that men are fallible beings, and judges no less so, and that only a vigorous stream of criticism "expressed with candour however blunt" can ensure that those who are entrusted with immense power and great responsibilities do not abuse their privileged position. History and the occasions on which libels on the courts have been punished give substance and justification for this belief.

50. At 69 of the report. Concerning the Phillimore Report, that is, the *Report of the [British] Committee on Contempt of Court*, see note 146 (Ch. 1).

51. A recommendation by JUSTICE in its report, *Contempt of Court* (1959) 10, makes a similar recommendation as regards reporting to the Lord Chancellor but also adds the complainant's member of Parliament as a possible recipient of such complaints. On this report, see notes 80 and 81 (Ch. 1).

52. *Pennekamp* v. *Florida* 328 U.S. 331 [1946]. For a synopsis of the American position before *Pennekamp*, see Goldfarb, op. cit., 89 ff. The facts of the *Pennekamp* case were that the appellants had been found guilty of contempt in a judgment that was confirmed by the Supreme Court of Florida for the publication of two editorials and a cartoon in their newspaper that criticized and ridiculed certain actions of a Florida court. Two of the three cases criticized had been finally dismissed, and in the third a new trial was pending. This distinction was, however, of no great concern in terms of the court's ultimate finding. The gravamen of the criticism was that the court concerned dismissed criminal cases too easily on technical grounds and a number of specific cases were cited as evidence. The language used cannot be said to have been particularly strong. The cartoon in question "caricatured a court by a robed compliant figure as a judge on the bench tossing aside formal charges to hand a document marked 'Defendant dismissed', to a ... criminal type. At the right of the bench, a futile individual labeled 'Public Interest' vainly protests" (at 338-39).

53. *Bridges* v. *California* 314 U.S. 252 [1941]. On this case, see Emerson, op. cit., 451.

54. At 347.

55. At 346. The judgment of the Court was delivered by Justice Reid.

56. At 320 of the judgment. See note 75 (Ch. 1) for the reference and the text to note 73 (Ch. 1) concerning this case.

57. At 349, the Court states:

It is suggested, however, that even though his intellectual processes cannot be affected by reflections on his purposes, a judge may be influenced by a desire to placate the accusing newspaper to retain public esteem and secure reelection presumably at the cost of unfair rulings against an accused. In this case too many fine-drawn assumptions against the independence of judicial action must be made to call such a possibility a clear and present danger to justice. For this to follow, there must be a judge of less than ordinary fortitude without friends or support or a powerful and vindictive newspaper bent upon a rule or ruin policy, and a public unconcerned with or uninterested in the truth or the protection of their judicial institutions. If, as the Florida courts have held and as we have assumed, the petitioners deliberately distorted the facts to abase and destroy the efficiency of the court, those misrepresentations with the indicated motives manifested themselves in the language employed by petitioners in their editorials. The Florida courts see in this objectionable language an open effort to use purposely the power of the press to destroy without reason the reputation of judges and the competence of courts. This is the clear and present danger they fear to justice. Although we realize that we do not have the same close relations with the people of Florida that are enjoyed by the Florida courts, we have no doubt that Floridians in general would react to these editorials in substantially the same way as citizens of other parts of our common country.

58. Charles Wintour (editor of the *Evening Standard*), op. cit., 130, writes that more recently "the courts have been much more tolerant regarding very outspoken comments about the bench." See note 56 (Ch. 1).

59. Op. cit., 68.

60. See the text to note 41 for a reference to Lord Denning's support for the institution. Cf also Borrie and Lowe, op. cit., 161 ff, and Miller, op. cit., 186. Lord Denning, *The Due Process of the Law* op. cit., 31 ff, also reports these cases without critical comment.

61. Cf the text to note 2 (Ch. 4).

62. Op. cit., 389:

As the judges removed themselves from sensitive areas . . . criticism
of the judiciary, which earlier in the century had been open, began to
disappear. The absence of criticism was partly the result of the
development of what many felt to be an excessive power to commit for
contempt of court those who criticised judges.

See the text to notes 4 and 5 (Ch. 1) for a fuller quotation on this topic.

63. See Arthur L. Goodhart, "Newspapers and Contempt of Court in
English Law," in (1935) 48 *Harvard Law Review* 885 at 1033:

And nothing, clearly, is so likely to interfere with . . . [the] production
[of criticism] as an attitude to criticism which fails to provide occasion
for its proper explanation and defence. That attitude is necessarily
present whenever the judges themselves decide upon the fitness of
criticism passed upon them. . . . An authority so wide and so
uncontrolled must necessarily act as a limitation upon the willingness
of men to criticise at all. The knowledge that the person challenged is
to act as the judge of whether the challenge be reasonable, or, at the
best, that his colleagues are so to act, is a dangerous hindrance for
effective public criticism.

64. Working paper no. 20 *Contempt of Court. Offences against the
Administration of Justice* (1977) at 31:

Curiously enough, contempt for scandalising the court is rarely invoked
in England, but it is still quite frequently used in Canada. Some might
attribute this to a greater sensitivity on the part of Canadian courts or to
greater feelings of insecurity in the face of criticism. It may be, as well,
that the very existence of the offence has had a preventative effect in
England. . . . Although one cannot hope to assess the exact impact of
its preventive effect, it cannot be ignored.

65. *Ex parte A-G of New Brunswick* [1969] 4 CCC 147. The offending
statement reads:

The courts in New Brunswick are simply the instruments of the
corporate élite. Their duty is not so much to make just decisions as to
make right decisions (i.e., decisions which will further perpetuate the
élite which controls and rewards them). Court appointments are
political appointments. Only the naive would reject the notion that an
individual becomes a justice or judge after he proves his worth to the
establishment.

66. At 31:

[It would, all things considered, probably be best] to retain this type of contempt but clarify its limits so as to ensure that it does not overlap or duplicate other forms of contempt. If this were done, it would be necessary to make sure that both the limits of the right to criticise and the procedure to be followed in the event of a violation are defined as clearly as possible.

67. At 31.
68. See note 45.
69. On this aspect, see note 27 (Ch. 1).
70. See the text to notes 33 (Ch. 1) and 88.
71. For a more detailed examination of the social results of the invocation of the contempt law in my cases, see my articles in Helen Silving's *Festschrift* (note 93, Ch. 1) and in the 1968 *SALJ* (note 98), as well as "The Taboos in Legal Research – A Personal Case History," in (1976) 2 *Social Dynamics* (University of Cape Town) 44.
72. Cf the references to Abel-Smith and Stevens in notes 4 and 5 (Ch. 1) and Professor Goodhart in the text to note 63.
73. Concerning this interrelationship between informal taboos and the interpretation of the law, see the text to note 1 (Ch. 1). See also van Niekerk, "The Uncloistering of the Virtue," op. cit. (note 101, Ch. 1) 567 ff and the conclusion of Ch. 4.
74. Reprinted in (1970) 87 *SALJ* 467. Part of the statement reads thus:

The Council notes the conclusion arrived at by the learned Judge – and that without hearing argument by the defence ... on a most significant potential finding on the question of law. . . . The result is to leave academics and legal authors, editors and researchers with a most disquieting sense of insecurity. There is every prospect that in future no one will be prepared to discuss even tangentially or indirectly, and without personal agreement, the possibility that the actions of the judiciary might imply bias, albeit unconsciously, against certain races, classes or groups, for fear of a prosecution for contempt of court. This sort of discussion, it is well known, takes place in overseas countries without prosecutions following.

75. See the text to note 33 (Ch. 1). However, the charge sheet also alleged that the *same words* constituted a scandalization of the bench. On this allegation an acquittal was achieved on the basis of considerations of free speech!
76. Professor John Dugard, "The Judicial Process," op. cit., 190 (see note 92). In *S* v. *Gibson* 1979 (4) SA 115 (D), an attempt was made to extend contempt protection to the Bar as part of the justice administration. Although

the acquittal was a relatively strong one – "it is relevant to bear in mind that the Bar is not a profession of shrinking violets" that would be deterred from assuming its *pro deo* duties (at 130), and although this writer's ideas on legal free speech are described as "thought-provoking" (at 136) – the judgment nevertheless produced an apology to the prosecution with the regrettable result that a similar kind of prosecution in the future would not be rendered more difficult: "There is no reason to believe that the proceedings in this case were commenced with any other object than that of ensuring impartial administration of justice" (at 140).

77. In at least three recent instances South African judges conferred on themselves and their peers verbal certificates of merit proclaiming that they are among the best – and perhaps even *the* best – in the world. See C. J. Claassen, "Retain the Bar and the Side-Bar," in (1970) 87 *SALJ* 25; (1971) 88 *SALJ* 520 (reviews of Justice Eksteen); especially J. Curlewis in *S* v. *Mothopeng* 1979 (4) SA 368 (T) at 369:

> The Courts of this country have for over a century acted fairly and competently and honestly and independently of improper influence. They do so today; they will do so in future. This is not a matter for debate; it is a fact. In this regard the Courts of no other country surpass our Courts and very, very few equal them. If the two gentlemen in question do not know that, that has nothing to do with me. I do not need, the Courts of this country do not need, any latterday Mrs Jellaby poking and prying about.

On this statement see my article referred to in note 155 (Ch. 4).

78. On the unmentionability of one such aspect — race — see my article, "Mentioning the Unmentionable," op. cit. (above note 92). See also the text starting with note 124 (Ch. 4).

79. See note 52 and the text to that note.

80. See the text to notes 165 (Ch. 1) and 34.

81. At 69 of the *McLeod* case.

82. See again here the revealing statement of Tremblay J. in the Canadian case of *Hébert* in the text to note 45.

83. Cf the text to note 13 (Ch. 1).

84. Cf the text following note 13 (Ch. 1) on the definition of the concept of legal free speech.

85. See the text to note 125.

86. See the text to note 64.

87. See note 197 (Ch. 1) and the longer quotation there from this leading Indian case. For a striking statement by Emerson on the actinic power of free speech, see note 76 (Ch. 1).

88. Cf Goldfarb, op. cit., 1-2:

[T]o the lawyer from a non-common-law country the contempt power is a legal technique which is not only unnecessary to a working legal system, but also violative of basic philosophical approaches to the relations between government bodies and people. Neither Latin American nor European Civil law legal systems use any device of the nature of proportions of our contempt power.

89. Foremost German criminal reporter. From a preface to a book cited in note 123. Concerning Mauz, see the text to note 164.

90. Herta Lienert, *Der Contempt of Court im Anglo-Amerikansichem Recht* (unpublished Ph.D. thesis of the University of Freiburg) (1956) 1-2. At two important gatherings of lawyers shortly after World War Two, the introduction of contempt provisions was propounded in the hope, according to Lienert, "that existing conditions of tension between the administration of justice and the press would be relaxed and the way opened for fruitful co-operation" (at 2).

91. Cf the critical note of the president of one of the chambers of the *Oberlandesgericht* of Frankfurt, Joachim Greiff, on the need to interpret criminal defamation provisions in Germany in the contempt fashion, discussed the text corresponding to note 144.

92. Cf M. Grünhut, "Contempt of Court," in (1948) 2 *Monatsschrift für Deutsches Recht* 442, and Eberhard Schmidt, *"Richtertum und Staatsdienst"* (1952) 30 *Deutsche Richterzeitung* 37 at 38:

It would be in the interest of the administration of justice to wish that further institutional consequences were drawn [from the need to achieve the independence of the judiciary] by the creation of an effective protection of the judicial office against unfactual and malevolent reporting and criticism in the press.

93. One of Germany's most respected judges, writing in (1969) 24 *Juristenzeitung* 150. See note 105 for the full quotation.

94. See "So lebte Richter P.75 Tage in Beton," in *Die Welt am Sonntag* of May 1, 1977. For other choice examples from previous trials of the gang, see Schwind (note 101) 133. The hardening of attitudes toward judges as manifested in the use of scandalous language is described by Hanno Kühnert, "Richter über neuartige Angeklagte," in the *Süddeutsche Zeitung* of January 10, 1973.

95. Cf Goldfarb, op. cit., 297: "Courts and any other governmental agency should have plenary summary physical control of their proceedings. The control is necessary as a matter of self-defence and common sense."

96. Articles 176, 177, and 178 of the *Gerichtsverfassungsgesetz* (*GVG*; law on the constitution of courts) read together with article 231b of the Criminal Procedure Code (on the exclusion of prisoners) contain the major provisions concerning the maintenance of order in courts.

97. Article 231b of the Criminal Procedure Code.

98. Because most *Ungebühr* cases will be dealt with in the lower courts and will not proceed on appeal, there is a dearth of reported cases.

99. Here the accused refused to stand when the court entered or when questioned; instead of addressing the judge with his full title, he addressed him simply as "Judge" and, when reprimanded for irrelevant utterances, he remarked to the judge: "If you wish to be so stuffy." On appeal, the penalties were confirmed. The decision is reported in (1969) 24 *Juristenzeitung* 150. In his defense, the accused maintained that compulsory standing would be an infringement of his constitutional rights (dignity of the person and free development of his personality) and that it represents a "remnant of authoritarian thinking from the 19th century which is out of touch with the improved position of the accused." In a commentary to this decision, a very senior and respected German judge, Dr. Werner Sarstedt, criticizes all the grounds on which the sentence was confirmed. See the quotation in the text to note 93.

100. Reported in (1966) 44 *Deutsche Richterzeitung* 356. The facts here are interesting. Appearing before a judge in an open-neck shirt and overcoat, the accused was warned by the judge that he was guilty of an *Ungebühr*. Thereupon, an adjournment was obtained to allow the accused to appear properly dressed. The accused lodged a constitutional complaint against the warning and adjournment with the Federal Supreme Court, which ultimately refused to receive the complaint and also imposed a fee for the abuse of procedure. In a case reported in (1969) 22 *Neue Juristische Wochenschrift* [*NJW*] 627, a higher court, although upholding a conviction for *Ungebühr*, wondered aloud whether the concept should at all be tied to the "infringement of the dignity of the court" as is common in the decided cases and in the commentaries.

101. Article 183 of the *GVG*.

102. Cf Theodor Kleinknecht, *Strafprozessordnung* 33 ed (1977) 1119, who documents the criminalization of the remark that with his questions, a judge, wished "to catch" the accused and of an exclamation "then you will have to face a disciplinary hearing."

103. See, however, the remarks in the text to note 35 (Ch. 1).

104. Some commentators come near to adopting the contempt idiom. For instance, Hans-Dieter Schwind, "'Ungebührliches' Verhalten vor Gericht und Ordnungsstrafe," in (1973) *Juristische Rundschau* 133 at 134, states:

> The protected legal value of art 178 is [according to contemporary opinion] not only the maintenance of peace in the court, but also the protection of the judicial reputation which is interpreted as judicial "dignity".

There is almost a ring of the *Almon* case (see the text to note 16 [Ch. 1]) in the comment of Fritz Baur, "Die Würde des Gerichts," in (1970) 23 *Juristenzeitung* 247:

What is meant with "Ungebühr" .... is the conscious deprecation of the functions of the administration of justice entrusted to the court, especially the manifestation of an absence of seriousness.... A person who has undertaken the onerous duty of judge and who fulfills these duties conscientiously and according to the law, deserves our respect and support.

105. Op. cit., 153:

In the reasons of the present judgment the "dignity of the court" plays an important, indeed too important a role.... "The Court" is no magical bearer of dignity; the court is no more than the judge who fortuitously happens to be presiding. The matters above which they as judges ought to be elevated, are matters above which "The Court" can also be elevated. Dignity, according to Schiller [the German poet], is the manifestation of a lofty mind. Its expression is all the easier the loftier the mind is. If this is not the case, dignity becomes a hollow dignity; and that is particularly bad for the reputation of the court. The dignity of the court lies not in the hand of any boorish individual who behaves improperly before the court; and the judge must guard against entrusting it to him.

106. Adolf Arndt, "Die Freiheit des Verteidigers," in (1964) 27 *NJW* 2146. The late Adolf Arndt is regarded as one of Germany's most respected lawyers in the post-War period.

107. Concerning contempt by counsel, see Miller, op. cit., 53, and Borrie and Lowe, op. cit., 20. As regards contempt committed *ex facie curiae* by lawyers, it may be recalled that in the cases of *Cassell* in Liberia, *Parmandam* in Fiji, and *Van Niekerk* in South Africa the fact that the accused were lawyers constituted a kind of aggravating circumstance. See note 180 (Ch. 1).

108. The United States constitutes an exception.

109. It has been suggested that as a type of self-defense measure a court has inherent powers to eject counsel. Cf Manfred Rehbinder, "Das Ordnungs- verfahrensrecht wegen Ungebühr vor Gericht," in (1963) 17 *Monatsschrift für Deutsches Recht* 640 at 642.

110. On this allowance in Germany, see the text to note 160 (Ch. 1).

111. Articles 43 and 113(2) of the *Bundesrechtsanwaltsordnung, (BRAO)* respectively read:

The attorney has to exercise his profession conscientiously. In his conduct both in the exercise of his profession and outside his professional duties he must show himself worthy of respect and of trust as demanded by his position as attorney.

Behaviour of an attorney outside the scope of his duties is a breach of
duty to be punished by a disciplinary court if it is peculiarly calculated,
according to the circumstances of the particular case, to reduce the
respect and the trust necessary for the exercise of his duties as attorney
or the reputation of the attorneys' profession.

The standard commentary is that by Walther Isele, *Bundesrechtsanwaltsordnung*
(1976), which constitutes a mine of information on most aspects of the official
code of lawyers. It does not deal with any of the problems of speech control that
we will discuss and it does not deal with the problem within a sociological
framework.

112. In 1923 (cf *Entscheidungen des Ehrengerichtshofs für deutsche
Rechtsanwälte* [1923] 122) the following statements were punished:

Class Justice is practised by judges today exactly as in the past, indeed
more so.

Where in the last few days papers stated ... that 1500 workers
in the Ruhr area were given amnesty, I can only say to the contrary: it
is a disgrace that 1500 workers had been charged at all.

113. See the text to note 179 (Ch. 1).

114. Cf *Entscheidungen des Ehrengerichtshofs der Reichs-Rechtsanwalts-
Kammer* [1936] 40. Here a disbarment of an attorney was upheld for three jocular
remarks concerning the established order. The appeal tribunal held at 45:

The attorney's profession, as necessary and full organ of the German
administration of justice, cannot tolerate in its midst members who
give expression to their hostile attitude towards the state by way of
their biting and humiliating criticism.

115. See the facts in the text to note 27 (Ch. 1).

116. See the text to note 68. Cf also note 26 (Ch. 1). The threat of civil
action, irrespective of outcome, would be considerably more ominous in certain
countries – cf the text to note 161 (Ch. 4).

117. See the text preceding note 25 (Ch. 1).

118. For a critical and balanced description of the backdrop of these
political or, perhaps more accurately, *politicized* cases, see the contribution of
Josef Augstein, "Anwälte und Terroristen. Zur Behinderung der Verteidigung
durch 'Anti-Terrorgesetze'," in the collection of essays *Terrorismus contra
Rechtsstaat* (1976) 188 (ed. Rudolf Wassermann). For a description of the
political and legal atmosphere, see in the same collection (245 ff) the essay by
Theo Rasehorn, "*Jenseits des Rechtsstaats?*" For the views of a number of the
lawyers involved in these politicized cases, see Wolfgang Dressen (ed.),
Politische Prozesse ohne Verteidigung (1976), especially the contribution by

attorney Christian Ströbele, "Verteidiger im Verfahren gegen die RAF. Zu den Vorwürfen, zur Praxis und zum Selbstverständnis" 41 ff. More particularly on the professional cases, see *Die Verteidigung auf der Anklagebank* – discussed in note 26 (Ch. 1) – and a similar collection published by the same group of lawyers, *Die Einschränkung der Verteidigung* (1976).

119. Cf. *Verteidigung*, op. cit., 41. Mr. Groenewold's statements here can be compared with the offending statements in the second *Van Niekerk* contempt case in South Africa – see note 32 (Ch. 1).

120. In terms of article 129 (1) and (2) of the penal code. The trial lasted many months and ended in July 1978 with a conviction. The *Oberlandesgericht* of Hamburg conceded that in many ways Mr. Groenewold's defense methods involved negotiating uncharted territory that would have taxed anyone and that he even "enriched" the legal system by his original methodology. In the course of the trial, former U.S. Attorney-General Ramsey Clark testified that he would have used comparable defense tactics in the United States. On the trial and judgment, see William H. Schaap, "Auf Wiedersehen to Civil Liberties," in Oct./Nov. (1978), *Juris Doctor* 36. On the aspect of pretrial publicity that was prominently raised by Mr. Groenewold in his defense, see the text to note 183 (Ch. 3). Mr. Groenewold intends to appeal his case, if necessary to the Council of Europe. I gratefully wish to record my indebtedness to Mr. Groenewold for considerable assistance in the research of these disciplinary cases.

121. *Verteidigung*, op. cit., 150.

122. Idem 162. In writing in a circular to imprisoned clients, he described the role of attorneys committed to the popular front as having to render judges and prosecutors "as naked as possible as to that what they really and always are under their trappings: politicians, and as politicians also dark reactionaries, capitalist knaves, imperialist pigs, communist devourers, desk activists, murderers."

123. Idem 164. As regards nightly controls in a prison Dr. Croissant stated: "What is practised here under the stamp of legality by the prison authorities . . . is in fact nothing other than Gestapo methods. This is no longer creeping fascism but real fascism."

124. Messrs. Langmann, Niepel, and Wächtler. Documented briefly in *Verteidigung*, op. cit., 90. The writer had at his disposal a copy of the 30-page indictment.

125. *Einschränkung der Verteidigung*, op. cit., 111. The offending statement in the letter reads:

> Your reference to the possibility of lodging a complaint with the same body as the one which I accuse of having acted arbitrarily in my case, must surely be a joke. . . . The reason why I preferred to report the incident to the state authorities was that I had the impression that the committee of the chamber of attorneys at Bamberg was simply trying to anger me and to subject me to a demonstration of its power.

In its judgment, the court opines as follows about the speech of attorneys:

> One must be able to presuppose and to expect on the part of an attorney that he would consider whom he is addressing himself to and that he would thus differentiate between the various methods with which he defends his rights. By reference to his conscience and by exercising a duty of care, he would have had no difficulty in establishing that he was using expressions of an insulting nature without regard to the personality of the recipient, something which, even according to the feelings of a man from the ranks of the common people, . . . would be prohibited.

126. See the text to note 179 (Ch. 1).

127. Cf the text to note 39 (Ch. 1). Mr. Otto Schily, the only lawyer defending the Baader-Meinhof group who (at least at the point of this research) had not been subjected to disciplinary changes, wrote about a "psychological war" being waged against the lawyers who defended adherents of this group. Cf Otto Schily, "Antrag zur einstellung des Verfahrens in Stammheim," in Claus Croissant, Kurt Groenewold, Ulrich K. Preuss, Otto Schily, and Christian Ströbele, *Politische Prozesse ohne Verteidigung* (1976) 57 at 77 (with a preface by the legal reporter of *Der Spiegel*, Gerhard Mauz).

128. Concerning selectivity of contempt victims, see note 6 and the text there.

129. Eberhard Schmidt, "Richtertum und Staatsdienst," in (1952) 30 *Deutsche Richterzeitung* 37. In this article the writer, a prominent German lawyer, advocated the introduction of the crime of contempt. Cf the text to note 131 (Ch. 3).

130. Cf note 125.

131. In terms of articles 253 and 847 of the German Civil Code.

132. In some of the older English authorities, there was a distinct call for a deemphasis of the elitism of the contempt law. In the *Bahama* case (see note 179, Ch. 1) and in the *McLeod* case (see note 165, Ch. 1), the Privy Council intimated that the scandalized judges had to look essentially to civil law for their vindication, an attitude warmly supported at the time by Hughes (see note 36).

133. Because prosecutions for defamation would all be dealt with by courts of first instance and would not be reported unless they go on appeal to higher courts, one finds few reported instances of defamation for *Richterkritik*.

134. Cf the text to note 68.

135. Cf the text to note 116.

136. See note 158 (Ch. 1).

137. Cf the text to note 103 (Ch. 1). In that note, reference is made to the scathing criticism from a fellow judicial critic for the court's *failure* to issue an injunction against the organization of judges.

138. Attorney Croissant, see *Verteidigung*, op. cit., 16.

139. Idem. The statement reads: "The behaviour of the police officers and of the doctor must, when compared with the methods of the former GESTAPO and the avowedly fascist regime, offend any critical observer of the incident."

140. Attorney Ehrig, *Verteidigung*, op. cit., 24. The conviction was for a qualified form of defamation *üble Nachrede*, in terms of article 186 of the criminal code. See note 202 (Ch. 1) concerning *üble Nachrede*.

141. Attorney Goy, *Verteidigung*, op. cit., 37: "I am always grateful when the prosecutor, Mr Przytarski, opens his mouth because one is then able to notice that he is totally devoid of any knowledge about the law."

142. AttorneyStröbele, *Verteidigung*, op. cit., 86.

143. See the text to note 202 (Ch. 1).

144. Attorney Croissant, *Verteidigung*, op. cit., 19-20. The charge was brought under article 90a of the Criminal Code. The offending statement reads:

> The Federal Republic stands alone for having introduced torture by means of the justice machinery and to declare legal that which every security policeman tells a tortured prisoner. . . . With this decision of the highest court the Federal Republic must be the first state which practices torture in the administration of justice and which has glorified torture in a court judgment.

145. Cases of defamation of prosecutors have been noted above. The unsuccessful prosecution for defamation against Attorney Schily for laying a charge (at the behest of his client) against prison doctors for refusing to give timely treatment to a cancer patient adds a novel dimension to the contempt aspect of defamation. The case is documented in Frank Rühmann, *Anwaltsverfolgung in der Bundesrepublik 1971-1976* (1977) 81-82. This work gives an interesting factual overview of the spate of lawyers' cases and of the atmosphere (particularly the atmosphere created by the public media) surrounding these cases. On Schily, see note 127.

146. On the *Lebach* judgment, see the text to note 62 (Ch. 1).

147. See the text to note 202 (Ch. 1).

148. Reported in (1962) 15 *NJW* 64. The strongest part of the statement reads:

> If, however, juridical brains in the Federal Republic consider the "elimination of unnecessary mouths to feed" – the object of the murder of mental patients – as being dictated neither by "base motives" nor as being gruesome, then one has to ask oneself whether such brains really ever comprehended and whether they are at all able to comprehend the struggle to renew the moral foundations of the state and to re-introduce human rights. The killing upon state order of defenceless and helpless people was an infamous and perfidious betrayal of the humane tradition which has characterised the West over two millenia. Anyone who

assails this elementary truth with crafty sophistry alerts the attention all those people who are still concerned about preventing the return of the rule of injustice and of criminals.

149. Idem. The commentator was Joachim Greef, president of one of the chambers of the *Oberlandesgericht* in Frankfurt:

> If the citizen of a democracy wishes to honour a state based on the rule of law, it is necessary also to protect the judge in office against disparagement. . . . The journalist who wishes to defend a public interest by his warning against considering euthanasia in too mild a light is at the same time infringing another public interest: the necessary general respect for judicial office. . . . Such questionable "defence" of public interests . . . must be resisted by the use of the method permitted and indeed required by German criminal law, by countering such acts which in Anglo-Saxon criminal law constitutes a separate offence: contempt of court.

150. See the text to note 65. In South Africa, student publications have been especially singled out for intimidatory action under various political censorship laws.

151. Criticism in these alternative newspapers can at times be downright scatological. A relatively mild example thrust into the writer's hands at the University of Freiburg and emanating from the official student newspaper, *Asta Info* no. 112 of May 5, 1977, reads:

> Once again the court demonstrated where it belongs. The Administrative Court of Mannheim confirmed . . . that Kurt Faller "correctly" had had his services as teacher terminated on 30.6.76. It is clear that this court which is known for its professional banning orders based its decision not on the Constitution but on the interests of a reactionary provincial government and on the views of those people who have a material interest in preventing the spread of any thoughts which question our capitalistic order. In the almost incomprehensible lingo of juridical German, progressive citizens are being robbed here of their rights and of their existence.

152. A glossy but relatively serious family magazine of the type and appeal of the now defunct *Life*, with perhaps a slightly more generous sprinkling of pictorial but tasty depictions of the female anatomy than was the case with its more staid erstwhile American counterpart.

153. A news magazine of the *Times* and *Newsweek* genre, but with an appreciably deeper and more scholarly coverage especially of national subjects, which really constitutes the only example of this kind of magazine in the world.

154. Cf the text to note 111 (Ch. 4) and the text to note 167 (Ch. 3).

155. Heinrich Bremer, "Deutschland Deine Richter" [Germany thy Judges], in *Der Stern* no. 13 of March 19, 1972.

156. Published in (1972) 50 *Deutsche Richterzeitung* 181. Inter alia the letter stated:

> We believe, however, that the justice ministers and justice senators must undertake the necessary steps in accordance with their duties of guarding over the interests of the judiciary, for the maintenance of respect for the judiciary . . . since lack of confidence on the part of the population towards the Third Estate also means lack of confidence towards the legal order of the Federal Republic.

157. In (1972) 50 *Deutsche Richterzeitung* 162.

158. See especially the case of Croissant in the text to note 140. The relevance of the article will be referred to in the text to note 114 (Ch. 4).

159. "Die Hässlichen Deutschen," in *Der Stern* of June 10, 1976.

160. In terms of article 336, a judge who consciously thwarts the operation of the law commits *Rechtsbeugung* and is guilty of a serious crime.

161. For instance, "Griff der Doktor noch zur Waffe," in the issue of January 27, 1977. The following is said about the presiding judge in a specific case:

> The Cologne judge Dr Armin Draber is not to be envied. He has to judge a man who has already been judged by popular prejudice as a "police murderer". . . . Not for a moment can the judge allow the impression to arise that he is prejudiced against the accused. In this judge Draber is only partially successful. Whatever the defence requests in order to alleviate the situation of the ill accused, the judge rejects. . . . Equally obstinate is the behaviour of the judge as far as co-operation with the defence is concerned. He denies them the use of a tape recorder. . . . And he further rejects the application of the defence to have the decision which he had taken in a display of lust for power reviewed by the full court although the procedural code demands this as a compulsory requirement.

162. For instance, in "Rettet den Rechsstaat," in the issue of January 27, 1977, it excoriates the presiding judge of the main Baader-Meinhof trial: "During the twenty months that Judge Prinzing was enthroned on the seat of glory in the Baader-Meinhof trial the law experienced a decline which concerns us all."

163. Cf. Schily's comment in note 127.

164. See note 156. The letter mentioned a statement by Mauz in *Der Spiegel* in which he had contended that certain questions of the judge in a particular case could only be described as "obscene," a comment that would "lower the judge in the esteem of the public."

165. See the text to notes 133 and 158 (Ch. 3) and note 105 (Ch. 4).
166. Cf *Der Spiegel* no. 4 of January 17, 1977:

It would have been bad for the West German administration of justice, if Prinzing [the presiding judge] would have had to go [after a recusal application]. However, the oft discussed principle of the rule of law in the Stammheim trial suffered, so it seems, even greater damage by the fact that he is allowed to stay. Because there can no longer be any doubt that the Chairman has quite a few prejudices.

167. *Der Spiegel* no. 10 of February 28, 1977.
168. See the text to note 106 (Ch. 4). All eight judges of the Federal Constitutional Court who replied to my questionnaire were readers of *Der Spiegel*. Cf the text to note 134 (Ch. 3).
169. A weekly newspaper catering especially to intellectuals. Legal reporting can be extensive and is of a less polemical nature than with *Der Spiegel*. See the text to note 107 (Ch. 4).
170. See the text to note 296 concerning the remarkably tolerant attitude toward verbal indiscretion of Polish lawyers.
171. Editorial "Careful," in *Advocatenblad* March 1977. See note 189.
172. Article 266 of the criminal code. The article refers to various kinds of infringement of a person's honor.
173. Cf W. H. Schreuder, A. L. H. van den Berg, and J. A. Dunnewijk, *Het Wetboek van Strafrecht* (1951) I 434.
174. Bribery of judges is an aggravated form of bribery – article 178.
175. Reported in detail as Case 258 in (1953) *Nederlandse Jrisprudentie* 389 under the name *Schurer*. The presiding judge had refused to call an interpreter since no foreign language was involved. Other parts of the offending report read:

The answer to the question, why Mr W was so immeasurably irritated when hearing the language of the people whose legal problems he has been adjudicating for so long, lies more in the domain of a psychiatrist than ours. But the fact that he is so incapable of hiding his irritation whilst publicly executing his duties is something which concerns us all. We may also suddenly find ourselves before his bench. . . . We wonder whether it is the intention of the minister of justice that the canton judgeship be used by a judge for repeatedly displaying his personal inferiority complexes against free Dutch citizens who insist on their popular rights of centuries.

176. See the text to note 84 (Ch. 1).
177. Concerning the causal connection between informal taboos and formal speech restrictions, see the text to note 2 (Ch. 4).
178. The provision, article 137(a), reads:

Whosoever expresses himself intentionally and publicly – whether orally in writing or in image – in an insulting manner as regards public authority [openbaar gezag] or a public body or institution, shall be punished with imprisonment not exceeding two years or a fine.

179. The offending publication contained the following sentence: "The Bench of Amsterdam [de "Recht" – bank te Amsterdam] expressed itself very openly and very clearly as to the fact that it sees itself as being a servant of our class enemy, in other words in favour of class justice." Pivotal to the conviction was the pun on the word Rechtbank, that is, bench. From the fact of putting Recht into inverted commas, presumably indicating that the justice emanating from the Rechtbank was not recht, that is, just, the court inferred the presence of criminal intention.

180. Reported as Case 482 in (1958) Nederlandse Jurisprudentie 1144.

181. The crux of the article, "Not even a court case," reads as follows:

Although major K has been sentenced to imprisonment . . . I refuse to view the sinister farce produced by the military tribunal in the Hague as either a court case or even a military case. Right from the time of his arbitrary arrest . . . I have had the impression that the officials of our war ministry have been using Gestapo or MVD methods. . . . And then finally the proceedings started . . . during which the military judges stubbornly clung to the evidence of two highly unsavoury characters. . . . Documents which tend to exonerate major K were either ignored or were missing. . . . Journalists at the hearing were placed with their backs to "the judges", in a minute little hall where the representatives of the public could only breathe with difficulty and where, with the speed of an express train, a dash was made for the goal, i.e. putting the troublesome major behind bars. . . . The proceedings before the military tribunal which one can hardly call a court case proved only one thing to me, namely that guided from high places a bureaucratic-judicial murder was being committed upon a person who . . . had realised that something was wrong and who had tried to oppose it.

182.

The press . . . must enjoy a considerable measure of freedom and it must be entitled even to publish facts which could constitute an assault on the honour and reputation of the public authorities but precondition for this impunity is that the publication, regardless of the factual basis, must not be cast in a disparaging form.

183. The later case is reported as Case 41 in (1960) *Nederlandse Jurisprudentie* 69. The Hoge Raad upheld the conviction of an individual under article 137(a) for an article entitled, "A Dutch Dreyfus Affair," in which he had accused the authorities, quoting defense argument, of having used "Gestapo methods" in a court martial. About the presiding judge he asked: "Why did B [the presiding military judge] commit such improprieties?" The article, which was disseminated inter alia as an advertisement in *De Telegraaf*, concluded thus: "It is really a scandal that one tries with such methods to get a decent man into jail."

184. Following an industrial tribunal decision requiring a cooling-off period for would-be strikers, Mr. Cees Scheling called the judge "hypocritical" and he went on to doubt aloud whether workers could ever receive a fair hearing for their cause in a tribunal over which he presided. On this incident, see (1977) 57 *Advocatenblad* 113 and (1977) *Nederlands Juristenblad* 285. The Dutch press reacted scathingly to the said comments. See *Utrechts Nieuwsblad* of March 4, 1977, *Elseviers Magazine* of February 12, 1977, *Nieuwe Rotterdamse Courant* of February 5, 1977 and *De Telegraaf* of February 9, 1977.

185. The article "Gelet op de persoon van de verdachte . . . ," (1976) 18 *Nederlandse Tijdschrift voor Criminologie* , caused a number of strong reactions that were printed in various issues of the journal in 1977, indicating that speaking the unspeakable – and even the obvious! – is not always well received in Holland in relation to the administration of justice. These reactions raise the question of informal taboos that reinforce or obviate legal speech restrictions. On the situation in Holland in this regard see the text to note 49 (Ch. 4).

186. See Jac van Veen, *De Rechten van de mens: De Mensen van het Recht. Opstellen over de praktijk van de Nederlandse rechtspraak* (1971) 8:

Criticism of the performance of the judicial power, except in the strict juridical sense, is of very recent vintage; only very few years ago it was still unthinkable that officials of the administration of justice and judges would be subjected to a scrutiny in the press on their attitude and behaviour, let alone to be subjected to an "unfavourable review". Also for the journalist the judge in particular was someone who dwelt in a holy shrine [and being] an elevated magistrate about whom it seemed wrong to say anything which may meet with his [the judge's] disapproval.

187. Van Veen laments the lack of courage of lawyers to stand up to judges who abuse their positions in court. He continues (at 15):

Apart from the accused, only the lawyer can emit a word of protest. In practice, however, this will seldom, if ever, happen since the Dutch advocate is bound by a rather strong ethical code and he does not like to create even the impression that he lacks respect for the judicial power.

188. Speaking about the lack of "image" among the public of the Dutch advocate, van Veen states:

> To what extent is the Dutch advocate himself responsible for his frayed image in criminal cases? Undoubtedly this phenomenon can be largely explained with reference to the typical Dutch bourgeois morality [burgermansfatsoen]. . . . We have little comprehension for people who stand accused on offences which we ourselves would never commit. . . . We do not at all tolerate mitigating circumstances for individuals who go off the rails or who rebel against a society which has always suited us just fine.

189. *Advocatenblad* March 1977. The editorial concerned the attack on the alleged partiality of a judge by a trade union leader – see note 180. The editorial stated that such critical commentaries on judges constituted a "danger to the freedom of the judge."

190. J. J. van Wessem, "Balie en rechterlijke mag," in (1974) 54 *Advocatenblad* 288.

191. O. A. C. Verpaalen, "Eerbied voor de rechterlijke autoriteiten," in (1961) 41 *Advocatenblad* 231.

192. At 235-36: "The advocate must then uphold the interests of his client and not allow the judge to get away with his behaviour although it can be very difficult to know where to draw the line and the choice of the right words may demand a lot of tact."

193. "Gevoel voor verhoudingen bij de beginnende advocaat," in (1963) 43 *Advocatenblad* 66.

194. At 67-68.

195. M. I. Roessel, "De verhouding van de advocaat tot de rechterlijke macht," in (1963) 43 *Advocatenblad* 146.

196. This phenomenon of using safe foreign topics as subjects for critical investigation was also demonstrated by the fact that the editor of a national Dutch daily forwarded me as the example of his most robust comment on the judiciary an editorial on the inquest on the death of Mr. Steve Biko in 1977 in South Africa! The same phenomenon has been documented as far as Pakistan is concerned by Professor R. Braibanti, *Research on the Bureaucracy of Pakistan* 261, referred to by H. R. Hahlo, "Scandalising Justice: The Van Niekerk Story," in (1971) 21 *University of Toronto Law Journal* 378 at 387, to the effect that he, Braibanti, had been told by many "able lawyers . . . that they are reluctant to comment analytically on [local] judicial decisions for fear of being found in contempt of court. They assert that this is the reason for research being focused on foreign law, which is 'safer'."

197. Cf B. W. Kranenburg, "Lof der Zotheid in de advocatuur," in (1962) 42 *Advocatenblad* 345 at 345-46. See also (1958) 38 *Advocatenblad* at 371 and an editorial at 473. Kranenburg states inter alia:

Time and again one can only emit a sign when considering the question why it really is necessary at all to wash all this dirty linen in public. . . . The answer is then that the honour of the advocates' profession can best be protected against contamination by the misdeeds of colleagues by punishing these misdeeds under the eyes of the public. . . . Illusions, illusions. From the fact of publication it would seem as if we have regard for the judgment of the public and that the public would admire our courage of [openly] cleansing ourselves. Nothing can be further from the truth. The public finds in the publication of these misdeeds a confirmation of a nagging suspicion. . . . In short, in the eyes of the public our honour is of a highly dubious nature.

198. "Beslissingen van het Hof van Discipline," No. 61, reported in (1958) 38 *Advocatenblad* 191. The lawyer concerned is designated only as "Mr [*Meester*] X." *Meester* is an academic designation.

199. Cf the Liberian case of *Cassell* in the text to note 113 (Ch. 1) concerning contempt committed abroad.

200. As reported in the original English. In answer to a question on the method of election of Dutch judges, Mr. X replied:

Well, they are selected from a rather close-knit group, and they are very inadequately paid. . . . So most of them have some money of their own, and ordinarily an appointment would be made by the Queen only from that select group.

Pressed for more detail, Mr. X continued:

Well, I would like to say that not all the aspects of Dutch life are represented in that group. There is some change now but especially in preceding years these judges have been selected from a very close-knit group. . . . [These are] [p]eople who have some money of their own, belong to a somewhat higher circle in Dutch society and are willing to take the job because it gives them prestige.

201. See the text to note 194.

202. See the text to note 301.

203. Cf A. J. Hoekema, *Vertrouwen in de Justitie* (1971), stating that 50 percent of the Dutch believed that judges applied double standards.

204. *Juridisch Studentenblad Ars Aequi.* A scrutiny of all volumes since 1972 reveals similar attitudes to those in the *Advocatenblad*.

205. Quoted by Maurice Hamburger, "Il faut sauver la critique judiciaire," in (1959) *La Vie Judiciaire* April 6-11, 1959 1.

206. The latter innovation is discussed in the text to note 74 (Ch. 3).

207. Cf. M. Garcon, "De l'infaillibilité de la justice," in *Le Monde* of

December 25, 1959.

208. Cf A. Vitu, "Atteintes à l'autorité de la justice," in *Juris-Classeur Penal* (no. 8 of 1963) (concerning articles 226-27) 2. In one of the first major reported cases under article 226, the prosecutor was reported as follows: "The new art 226 has aroused some emotions amongst journalists, quite unjustifiably since there was never any question of assailing the freedom of the press and to punish anyone who would dare suggest that the courts are not infallible." The *Schroedt* case, reported in (1963) *Gazette* du *Palais* Vol. 2 350. For another apologia see Jean Boucheron, "Prosper Mérimée et l'article 226 du code pénal," (1959) 17 *Recueil de droit pénal* 173 at 176 with an overview of antecedents of article 226.

209. Article 226 reads in full:

Whosoever shall, publicly by acts, words or writings seek to bring discredit upon an act or a decision of the courts [*un acte ou une decision juridictionnelle*] in a manner which impairs the authority or the independence of the administration of justice will be punished with imprisonment of between one month and six months and a fine...

The court may in addition order that its decision shall be announced and published in a manner determined by the court and at the expense of the convicted person provided that the expenses shall not exceed the maximum amount envisaged in the fine.

The foregoing provisions may under no circumstances be applied to purely technical commentaries or to acts, words or writings aimed at the modification of a conviction.

If the offence is committed by the press the provision of article 285 [concerning the liability of directors, editors, printers, etc.] of the present code shall apply.

210. Cf Vitu, op. cit., 3:

Since the press was incapable by itself to observe a measure of professional discipline, it was necessary to impose on it certain express boundaries which it may not cross. Acting as it did the legislature only pursued the objective ... of protecting what one may call the "judicial order" against the attacks directed at it, directly or indirectly, by the bias of the press.

211. See the text preceding note 29 (Ch. 1).

212. The first *Van Niekerk* case in South Africa would have been such a case. See concerning the academic issues involved in that case the comments of Bates, note 35 (Ch. 1); Van der Walt, note 35 (Ch. 1); and of the Council of the South African Society for Teachers of Law, note 74. See also the Canadian case of *Hébert* concerning a prosecution over a critical book in the text to note 45.

There is little doubt that the unique constitutional provision in Germany contained in article 5(3) of the Basic Law could have relevance in this context in Germany: "The arts and science, research and education are free. The freedom of education does not absolve one from loyalty to the Constitution."

213. That ordinary newspaper reports would not qualify for protection under this defense of "technical commentaries" is clear from the *Coulouma* case referred to in note 227.

214. Cf the comments to note 146.

215. See note 204 for the reference and the text to note 216 for the facts. The prosecutor stated as follows:

> Article 226 [in its present form was inserted] ... in 1958 after several press campaigns which endangered the judicial power. Great Britain has known the offence called "contempt of court", the denigration of the administration of justice, for a long time.

216. From the commentary by Pierre Mimin accompanying the judgment, reported as Case no. 12233 in (1961) *Juris-Classeur Périodique. La Semaine Juridique* (not paginated).

217. The *Ambard* case at 336. See the text to note 117 (Ch. 1).

218. Part of the criticism reads as follows:

> Instead of defending the interests of society and of stressing the excessive speed ... the seriousness of the injuries ... and the position of the accused in the local community which excludes mitigating circumstances ... [the prosecutor] argued about the representative functions of the person as a well-known political figure, about his morality, about his [good] criminal record, his position at the head of a semi-administrative body. ... If punishment was determined by the social function of the accused, we shall soon have the financier being acquitted for murder and the dock worker decapitated for treading on the tail of a cat.

219. Because the statement did not interfere with a case proceeding in terms of article 227, the accused was acquitted under that article.

220. Handed down by the Tribunal Correctionel of Montbellard in 1963. See note 204.

221. See the text to note 6 concerning the discriminatory invocation of the contempt power.

222. Part of the criticism reads as follows:

> Following the events of 9.11.1961 [concerning strikes and violence at the Peugeot plant] the [Tribunal] the Conseil de Prud'hommes ... has just delivered its judgment. Management is allowed to dismiss four

delegates. This is a parody of justice, a "Peugeot judgment." . . . To reproach comrade Bourquin that he has not given any indication of "balance" . . . is a mockery of the working class. Like the times of despots and kings those who have the courage to oppose the bosses and the regime are judges and punished.

223. The judgment stated inter alia:

In view of the fact that such judgments and imputations display a manifestly malevolent and injurious nature which reveals the unequivocal wish of Schroedt to discredit the judgment . . . in the eyes of the workers and to incite them to render it ineffective by their action, and in view further of the fact that with this intention in mind he presents the judgment to his readers as supremely unjust and dictated entirely by a desire on the part of the court of defending [the interests of] management, the circumstances are such that the authority and the independence of the justice administration are assailed.

224. On the "rudimentary appeal device," see the text to note 156 (Ch. 1).
225. Per Professor Louis Hugueney in (1960) and (1961), *Revue de Science Criminelle et de Droit Pénal Comparé*, respectively at 76 and 804, expressed before and after the *Papeete* case.
226. See the text to note 178.
227. Reported as Case no. 13155 in (1963) *Juris-Classeur Périodique. La Semaine Juridique*. The crucial parts of the statement read:

Amongst the judgments (very numerous) delivered under the new exceptional procedure of expropriation there is one which merits our special attention. This is so because this judgment appears to us quite frankly as a masterpiece of incoherence and of an extravagant abuse of law the like of which has rarely been witnessed in the annals of French legal history. . . . What remains for Miss Delmas [the aggrieved party]: a handkerchief in which to cry or a revolver with which to defend herself. . . . People expropriated under the 5th Republic can be sure, whether or not their property has buildings, that the judgments of the courts will not compensate them. O! Eternal France, is that thy justice?

228. The judgment states inter alia:

[Although] . . . it is certainly permitted to comment upon and even to criticise any judicial decision both on the law and on the facts . . . but in a case where such criticism is outrageous, abusive and excessive – both in its form and in the terms used – and when it manifests clear intellectual dishonesty on the part of its author, it brings evident discredit upon the law and assails the authority of the administration of justice considered as a fundamental institution of the state.

229. See the text to note 114 (Ch. 4).

230. The basic concept of "outrage" has approximately the equivalent meaning in English. In substance, these provisions of article 222 of the penal code punish an outrage, whether in speech, writing, or drawing, "not rendered in public," in other words privately, against "officials [*magistrates*] of the administrative or judicial order" that "tend to impair their honour or their feelings [*délicatesse*]"; or such act committed "during a session of a court or tribunal"; or an outrage committed with the same effect but directed at an "official" [*magistrat*] or a juror, "by gestures or threats or by the transmitting of any object whatever" while these persons are engaged in the exercise of their functions (article 223). These provisions are substantially similar to the *desacato* provisions in Spanish-speaking countries and *oltraggio* in Italy, which are dealt with later.

231. Alain Peyrefitte, "Pour une justice moderne. Un monde clos?" in *Le Monde* January 12, 1979.

232. See the text to note 10.

233. A study of the newspapers *Corriera della Sera* and *La Stampa* over a period of 6 months in 1977 produced not a single article containing any kind of fundamental or outspoken criticism.

234. A letter to the editor of the Communist Party daily, *L'Unità*, requesting copies of that newspaper's most critical articles and reports produced a number of reports, none of which even approximated outspoken or robust criticism of the kind found in *Der Spiegel* in Germany. See the text to note 109 (Ch. 4).

225. Certain lawyers have been outspoken about what they regard as class justice, especially during and around cases involving the urban terrorists. On the conduct of so-called democratic judges in Italy, see Giuseppe Federico Mancini, "Politics and the Judges – The European Perspective," in (1980) 43 *MLR* 1 at 8 ff.

236. Article 24(2) of the Italian Constitution, which states that "the defence in an inviolable right at every stage of the proceedings" has undoubtedly contributed to an upgrading of robustness of defense strategies of counsel.

237. Translatable as "outrage."

238. Translatable as "vilification."

239. In article 341 of the penal code, *oltraggio* (outrage) of the public administration is defined:

Any person who affronts the honour or reputation [*prestigio*] of a public official, in the latter's presence or as a consequence of the latter's exercise of his functions, is punished by imprisonment between six months and two years.

The same punishment is imposed upon a person who commits the act by means of any telegraphic or telephonic communication, or by means of writing or a picture which is directed officially at the public and in the course of the person's [official's] duties.

If the affront consists in the attributing of a specific fact the punishment will be imprisonment between one and three years.

The penalties are increased if the act is committed with violence or with threats or when the affront is committed in the presence of one or more persons.

240. Article 357 defines "public official" very widely as persons occupying "a public function of a legislative, administrative or judicial nature." Article 343 refers specifically to the commission of "*oltraggio* towards a magistrate in session," which will be discussed later. Article 344 concerns *oltraggio* toward a "public employee." Article 342 concerns *oltraggio* committed against "a political, adminisitrative or judicial body, or of a representative of such body or of a public authority organised in a council." Punishment here is imprisonment between six months and three years. For a synoptic overview of the case law, see Guiseppe Lattanzi, *I Codici Penali con la Costituzione e leggi varie* (1974) 456. Not surprisingly in view of the broad ranks of protected persons, many cases concern attacks on military and police officers.

241. Reported in (1939) 19 *La Scuola Positiva* Vol. 2 177.

242. The note is by Professor Arturo Santaro. Cf 177-78:

The Supreme Court has lost a unique occasion to maintain and proclaim that the incumbents of public office, and primarily the judges, are duty bound to respect in their actions the norms of legality and the principles of basic justice on which such legality is based and also that the reputation of public officials derive not only from their office but more directly from their upholding of correct procedures towards citizens and of the latters' interests and rights.

243. Article 343 reads: "Anyone offending the honour or reputation of a judge [*magistrato*] in session is punished by imprisonment between one and four years." On this form of *oltraggio*, see Gennaro Guadagno, *Manuale di Diritto Penale* (1967) 581:

The act of offending a judge while in session, in other words in the critical moment in which the administration of justice manifests itself in its solemn form, certainly assumes the nature of a grave offence against the very prestige of the state in one of its important functions.

244. From a 1953 case reported by Lattanzi, op. cit., 467.

245. The *oltraggio* institution has been challenged on various other grounds, for instance, in relation to the democratic nature of Italy (article 1 of the Constitution), equality before the law (article 3), the personal basis of criminal responsibility (article 27), direct legal responsibility of officials (article 28), the duties of officials to fulfill their functions "with discipline and honour" (article 54), the impartiality of the public administration (article 97), and the duty of public employees to be "in the exclusive service of the Nation" (article 98). In an *ordinanza* or order of February 20, 1975 (no. 39), the Italian Constitutional Court was again seized of the matter but declined to pronounce on it.

246. Cf the *sentenza* of the Constitutional Court of November 21, 1972 – confirmed by reference in the above-mentioned 1975 *ordinanza* refusing to reconsider the matter – where the Italian Constitutional Court dealt with four different cases in which the *oltraggio* provisions were challenged and concluded that the inequality inherent in the existence of special protection for the honor of certain officials and offices did not infringe constitutional standards. The court restated a 1968 case in which it had held inter alia:

> It is clear that . . . the penal protection of the honour of the physical person holding such a public office, is absorbed into the reputation of the public administration which represents him and that this reputation of the public administration is assailed the moment his authority is affected, which thus brings about a new and different legal situation.

247. In the ten *oltraggio* cases reported in the 1976 edition of the *Revista Penale*, it would seem that in only one instance the judgment concerned itself with the right of free speech, more particularly with the "right of criticism." In none of these cases was the administration of justice directly involved.

248. Article 290 reads:

> Any person who publicly vilifies the Republic, the Legislative Assemblies (or one of these), the Government, the Constitutional Court or the judicial order is punished by imprisonment between six months and three years. The same penalty applies to a person who publicly vilifies the armed forces of the state or those of the liberation.

On the crimes of *vilipendio*, see Nicola Campisi, *I Reati di Vilipendio* (1968).

249. Judgment of the Bologna court of April 22, 1972, reported in (1972) *Critica Penale* 107. Inter alia the court stated:

> Subjecting the institution [of the court] as such to severe and devastating criticism does not constitute the crime of *vilipendio* if such criticism emanates from logical and historically justified premises and is devoid of gratuitous expressions of contempt of mockery.

250. Judgment of December 11, 1972, reported in (1974) *Cassazione Penale Massimario* 126. The court defined *vilipendio* as:

[A] fact which is grossly offensive and which expresses in a particularly effective form contempt for the person or the institution at which it is directed and which manifests more than is the case with *oltraggio*, injuria or defamation, a total denigration of the public function of the aforementioned person or institution.

251. In addition to the constitutional aspect referred to previously, article 598 of the penal code would be relevant here:

Any insults contained in documents or addresses furnished or delivered by parties or by their legal representatives during legal proceedings, before judicial bodies or before administrative authorities, will not be punishable provided the insults relate to the object of the matter or to the object of the administrative appeal.

252. Several of the Spanish and Argentinian works and cases quoted refer to the Italian penal provisions and interpretations thereof when dealing with *desacato* provisions. Somalia has taken over the Italian provisions almost verbatim.

253. Sebastian Soler, *Derecho Penal Argentino* (1973) Vol. 5 120.

254. Cf Jose Maria Rodriguez, *Devesa Derecho Penal Espanol. Parte especial* 6 ed (1975) 7538, who speaks thus about the *bien juridico* or *Rechtsgut* that is protected:

The legal value which is protected is thus the same as with crimes of violence [literally "attack" – *atentato*], namely the principle of authority and of the dignity of [official] function whose relationship with the public order is such that it is unthinkable to have social and political discipline if the organs through which the state fulfills its functions are not respected.

255. Literally translated, article 240 of the Spanish Penal Code reads:

Those who vilify, injure, insult or threaten, (whether by acts or words, and in his presence or in a writing directed at him), at the time of such exercise, commit *desacato*. If the vilification, injury, insult or threat is not serious a sentence of minor imprisonment shall be imposed and a fine of . . . ; if such is not the case the penalty shall be that of major arrest and a fine between. . . . If the convicted person is a public official, subordinate to the offended person in the service hierarchy, penalties higher than those mentioned in the previous paragraph shall be imposed and if there is no subordination the maximum penalties mentioned in the previous paragraph shall be imposed.

The meaning of the terms relating to imprisonment is found in article 30 of the code: "minor imprisonment" being between one month and six months; "major arrest" being between six months and six years.

256. A compendious overview of the case law on the subject of *desacato* is to be found in Aranzadi *Diccionario de Jurisprudencia Penal* (1972) Vol. 2 71-192, each case being illustrative of the kind of words (or acts) that has been considered to be injurious in terms of article 240.

257. In the decided cases, judges occupy a very respectable percentage of the victims of *desacato* but they share this protection with policemen, postal officials, university professors, notaries, municipal guards, and the like.

258. But on new moves against the Spanish press see "Embattled Madrid Editor Snipes at Entrenched Foes" in the *New York Times* of May 30, 1980.

259. Article 244 of the Argentinian Penal Code states:

A person who provokes to a duel or who threatens, injures or in whatever way offends the dignity or decorum of a public official in the course of his duties or at the time of the exercise of these [the official's] duties, shall be punished with imprisonment from fifteen days to six months.

Imprisonment shall be of a duration between one month and one year if the offended person is the president of the Nation, a member of Congress, a provincial governor, a national or provincial minister, a member of the provincial legislatures or a judge.

260. See the statement of Soler referred to in the text to note 253.

261. Reported under the title "Libertad de Prensa," in (1967) 128 *Revista Juridica Argentina* 808. The offending words were: "What we are witnessing here is simply another assault against a work of cinematographic art on which some retarded minds customarily saturate themselves."

262. The judgement's ratio is expressed thus (at 810):

[The criticism] is premised not on an expression of loyal criticism, however strong and wounding, of the activities of the officials, but constitutes an injurious attribution to them of malevolent qualities; it is also (as the judgement which is being appealed indicates) an intrusion into the private sphere of the judges by the gratuitous suggestion that they [the officials] gratify themselves secretly with pornographic films.

263. Article 263 of the Chilean Penal Code reads:

Whosoever, by act or word, gravely insults ['*injuriare*', injures] the President of the Republic, or any of the legislative bodies or their commissions (whether in their public acts in which they are involved or in the execution of their particular duties), or [who gravely insults] the superior courts of law, will be punished with minor imprisonment between the medium and upper limits and with a fine. ... If the insults [*injurias*] are minor the penalty will be minor imprisonment in its minimum degree and a fine ... or only a fine.

Articles 264 to 268 penalize "grave" disturbances of the order of certain bodies, including courts, and the use of threats, violence, or fraud as regards the operation of these bodies.

264. Cf Alfredo Etcheberry, *El Derecho Penal en la Jurisprudencia* (no date – 1971?) Vol. 6 at 271.

265. Idem 272.

266. Article 328 of the Peruvian Penal Code. Different sentences are prescribed than those in Argentina.

267. For an overview of the case law on article 328, see Julio D. Espino Perez, *Codigo Penal* 5 ed (1975) 398 ff.

268. Perez, op. cit., 400.

269. Article 232 of the Ecuadorian Penal Code reads:

Whosoever fails to respect any court, authority ['*corporación*'] or public official when such [body or person] is engaged in its functions, whether by words, gestures or acts of disrespect, or whosoever disturbs or interrupts the act in which such [body or person] is engaged, is punished by imprisonment of between eight days and one month.

270. In a more positive vein, the code proceeds in the following article to punish positive acts of insults, not only of officials, but before "any person being present" in "the courts or the public authorities."

271. Article 162 of the Bolivian Penal Code reads: "Whosoever, by whatever means, insults, injures or defames a public official in the exercise of his functions or as a consequence of those functions, shall be punished by imprisonment of between one month and two years." Where contemptuous acts are directed against the president, the vice preisdent, minister of state, or members of the Supreme Court, or a member of congress, the penalty is increased by one-half.

272. Article 148 of the Venezuelan Penal Code reads:

Whosoever shows disrespect to the President of the Republic, whether in word or in writing or in any other way whatever, or to a person charged with his functions, shall be punished by imprisonment of between six and thirty months in a case where the offence was a serious one and with imprisonment of one half that period if the offence was slight. The penalty shall be increased by one third if the offence was committed publicly. If the offence was directed against the President of one of the Legislative Chambers or against the President of the Supreme Court, the penalty shall be [imprisonment] between four months and two years if the offence was serious and half that period where it was slight.

In terms of article 149 one-half of the penalties of article 148 are prescribed for *desacato* as defined there for acts of disrespect to a number of other dignitaries, including "the incumbents of the Supreme Court . . . and judges of superior courts." A lesser scale of punishment, one-third, is prescribed for a number of other lesser officials.

273. Article 173 of the Uruguayan Penal Code in rather peculiar phraseology prescribes as follows:

Desacato which diminishes the authority of officials can be committed in any of the following ways:
1.   By means of insults which could be either direct ['*reales*'] in writing or verbal and which are committed at the place where the official exercises his functions, or away from such place and not in the presence of such official but committed because of the [official's] function or with the function as object.
2.   By means of open disobedience to the instruction of the official.

Insults which are considered direct ['*reales*'] are the entering while bearing arms into the place of assembly and the use of arms; offensive shouts and gestures, even though these are not directed at the officials concerned.

The crime is punished by imprisonment of between three and eighteen months.

274. Article 150 of the Venezuelan Penal Code.
275. Article 175 of the Uruguayan Penal Code states:

For the purposes of this Code all persons are considered to be officials ['*funcionarios*'] who fulfil a task or exercise a function whether for remuneration or gratuitously, permanently or temporarily, of a legislative, administrative or judicial nature, in the state, in local authorities or in any public body whatever.

276. Article 185 of the Colombian Penal Code reads:

The same sanction [of between six months and four years' imprisonment as in article 184 dealing with *violence* committed against public officials in order to influence the latter's decisions] will be incurred by any person who, by means of violence or threats attempts to prevent or disturb the assembly or the exercise of the functions of legislative, judicial or administrative bodies, or of any other public authority, or who seeks to influence their decisions.

In the event of the person responsible being a public official or employee the sentence shall be imprisonment between one and six years.

277. Article 186 states:

In all instances not specifically regulated otherwise, a person committing a crime against a public official, by reason of or as a consequence of the exercise of the official's functions, shall be subjected to the sentence corresponding to the sentence which can be imposed for the crime committed, increased by between one sixth and one half.

Antonio Vicente Arenas, *Comentarios al Codigo Penal Colombiano* (1969) Vol. 1 211 ff, furnishes a detailed overview of the background of the *desacato* provisions.

278. Op. cit., 208.

279. Jorge Ortega Torres, *Codigo Penal y Codigo de Procedimiento penal* (1975) 192 ff.

280. Cf the decision of October 5, 1959 – Torres, op. cit., 194 – of the Colombian Supreme Court, which put the point thus: "What is protected here is nothing other than the autonomy of the servants of the various branches of public power as far as the execution of those acts are concerned which relate to their authority."

281. Further to the Swiss press, see the text to note 10 (Ch. 1) and the text to note 104 (Ch. 4).

282. See the text to note 16 (Conclusion). The last issue appeared in February 1979.

283. Cf Walter Huber, "Der strafrechtlich geschützte Ehrbegriff in der schweizerischen Rechtsprechung," in (1965) 61 *Schweizerische Juristen-Zeitung* 349 at 350, where the writer states that the ordinary defamation proceedings of articles 173 (infringement of honor) and 174 (slander) are available not to protect a person's "business, political and other interests, but only personal interests. Only at the point where the assailed person is exposed to contempt in his quality as human being does the infringement of honour start."

284. See the text to note 202 (Ch. 1) and note 143.

285. *Rechtsprechung in Strafsachen* (1971), Case 152 83.

286. A perusal of decided cases between 1949 and 1975 clearly indicates a profound lack of interest on the part of Swiss judges to avail themselves effectively of this opportunity, despite the relatively "sensitive" and strict

attitude Swiss courts take vis-à-vis the infringement of honor. See the *Rechtsprechung in Strafsachen [RS] – Bulletin de Jurisprudence Pénale* between these years. For actual cases see, for instance, *RS* (1953) Case 35 14; *RS* (1955) Case 157 62; *RS* (1969) Case 58 38; *RS* (1971) Case 92 52; *RS* (1955) Case 157 62.

287. Article 492 of the Austrian Penal Code reads:

> The preceding punishable acts mentioned in articles 487 to 491 [on impairment of honour, defamation or disclosure of secrets] are also committed by a person who perpetrates the same acts against families, public authorities or individual organs of the government in relation to their official activities, as well as against legally recognised corporate bodies or against the reputation of a deceased person.

Theodor Rittler, *Lehrbuch des Österreichischen Strafrechts* 2 ed (1962) Vol. 2 99, is quite sure of the potential applicability of this provision to judicial authorities. See also Otto Leukauf and Herbert Steininger, *Kommentar zum Strafgesetzbuch* (1974) 576.

288. Cf *Entscheidungen des Österreichischen Obersten Gerichtshofes in Strafsache und Disziplinarangelegenheiten*, in yearly volumes from 1919 onward.

289. Dennis Campbell, "Free Press in Sweden and America: Who's the Fairest of Them All?" in (1976) 8 *Southwestern University Law Review* 61.

290. I derived considerable assistance, however, in relation to the scene in Sweden from a number of well-informed Swedish journalists during a visit to that country.

291. A senior Swedish journalist wrote to me as follows:

> The whole Swedish court system is very much a "holy cow", especially when it comes to the individual judges and their capacity to fulfil their tasks properly. Criticism will be directed quite easily at lawyers who are allegedly incompetent or at the prosecution but never at the judges in a way which can be described as critical.

292. Chapter 17, article 5 of the Swedish Penal Code reads:

> If someone insults a person, who enjoys protection in accordance with section 1, during the exercise of his function or because of such function, such person shall be sentenced for *insulting a public servant* to a fine or to imprisonment not exceeding six months.

Article 1 refers to violence (or threats thereof) inflicted on "an incumbent of a function or of a responsibility connected to an official function."

293. Chapter 17, article 6 reads:

If someone spreads amongst the public any false rumours or any other false allegations of such a nature as to undermine respect towards public authorities or towards any other organ competent to take decisions in public matters, such person shall be sentenced for contempt of the standing of public authority to a fine or to imprisonment not exceeding two years.

294. Cf *Das Schwedische Kriminalgesetzbuch* of Gerhard Simson (*Sammlung ausserdeutscher Strafgesetzbücher in deutscher Übersetzung*) no. 96 (1976) 147. The Swedish Penal Code is available in an official French translation of the Swedish Ministry of Justice as well as in Vol. 17 of the *American Series of Foreign Penal Codes, Sweden* (1972).

295. Article 121 of the Danish Penal Code states:

Whosoever attacks one of the persons mentioned in article 119 during the exercise of his office or his commission, or in relation to such office or commission, by contempt, abusive language or other insulting behaviour, shall be punished by a fine or detention or with imprisonment not exceeding six months.

The persons mentioned in article 119 are all persons "entitled to act in terms of a public office or commission" and "persons to whom official judicial power or the authority to make decisions in connection with legal problems or the penal system are entrusted." See the German translation of Franz Marcus, *Das Dänische Strafgesetzbuch (Sammlung ausserdeutscher Strafgesetzbücher in deutscher Übersetzung*) no. 84 (1964).

296. Article 130 of the Norwegian Penal Code reads cumbersomely as follows:

Anybody who against his own better conscience publicly attributes to the authorities of the state or other public authority acts which they have not committed, or who gives misleading information about the circumstances under which such authorities have acted, or about the methods they have used, or is accessory thereto, shall be punished by fines or by jailing or imprisonment up to one year.

The same penalty is applicable also when the incorrect assertion is made with gross negligence, if the intent was to harm the general reputation of the authorities involved.

If the felony is committed against Parliament, one of its divisions, committees or employees, prosecution is initiated only at request of Parliament. Otherwise prosecution is initiated at the request of the proper ministry or by decision of the King.

The translation is that of Vol. 3 of the *American Series of Foreign Penal Codes,*

Norway (1961).

297. Chapter 16, article 24 of the Finnish Penal Code reads thus:

Whosoever makes unfounded allegations which are calculated to lower the authority of the Government, of the popular representation or of a council of such representation, or of a public official or of the decisions [of these persons and authorities] or [which have the effect] to discredit the established social order or which [have the effect] to endanger the public order, and who makes these allegations publicly to a congregation of people, or in writing, or in any other manner, shall be sentenced to a fine. The same [penalty] applies if someone produces or disseminates information or allegations in the said way which are calculated to bring about the above-mentioned effect by the non-disclosure of certain material facts or by reference to matters out of proper context or by the use of an insulting mode of expression or representation.

The translation is made from Bryholf Honkasalo, *Das Finnische Strafgesetzbuch* (*Sammlung ausserdeutscher Strafgesetzbücher in deutscher Übersetzung*) no. 66 (1954).

298. I wish to state on record the very considerable assistance given me by East European scholars at the Max Planck Institute at Freiburg.

299. A perusal of *Das Neue Deutschland*, the major newspaper in East Germany, over a six-month period produced not a single critical line on the justice adminisitration.

300. Article 220 of the East German Penal Code reads:

(1)   Whosoever publicly insults or renders contemptible

1. the national [state] order or state organs, institutions or social institutions or the activities or decisions of these bodies;

2. a citizen in connection with his national or social activities as a consequence of his adherence to a national or social organ or a social organisation,

shall be punished with imprisonment not exceeding two years, or with a suspended sentence, a fine or with public rebuke

(2)   The same penalty applies to anyone who publicly makes fascist or militaristic statements.

301. The relevant provisions from the Polish Penal Code read:

Article 236. Whoever insults a public functionary or a person called upon to assist him, in the course of and in connection with the performance of official duties, shall be subject to the penalty of

deprivation of liberty for up to two years, limitations of liberty or a
fine.

Article 237. Whoever insults a state organ or a political organisation, a
trade union, an association of higher public utility or other social
organisation of nationwide importance, at a place of its activity or in
public, shall be subject to the penalty of deprivation of liberty for up to
two years, limitations of liberty or a fine.

Translation as in Vol. 19 of the *American Series of Foreign Penal Codes,
Poland* (1973).

302. Judgment of October 8, 1966, reported in (1967) *Palestra* no. 4 123-
24.

303. Roman Lyczywek in (1967) 1 *OSPIKA* (*Journal of the Institute of
Legal Science of the Polish Academy of Science*) 513 ff. In a passage that has a
ring of Lord Denning he states as follows:

> Any other view [of this role] is merely a relic of the past when the
> judge was regarded not as the "representative of society" but as an
> instrumentality which was independent from the society ("the hand of
> the King").... The judge does not fulfill his obligations ... if he
> consciously infringes the respect to which other participants in a trial
> are lawfully entitled. Mere passive resignation to and a general
> prohibition of any reaction to a dishonourable and hence also unlawful
> act of the judge cannot be required by the precept of respecting the
> "reputation and honour" of the court. The general application of the
> principle *noli me tangere* is simply wrong [under these circumstances].
> Reputation and honour of the court do not constitute overriding
> principles in themselves. They serve other more important
> values.... If a chairman of a court behaves untactfully or even
> insultingly towards an attorney it is he and not the attorney who really
> infringes the "reputation and honour" of the court. Any participant to
> court proceedings is entitled and ought to be so entitled to draw the
> attention also of the chairman to infringements of the law.

304. Judgment of November 22, 1969 in (1970) *Palestra* no. 5 85.

305. Judgment of October 26, 1963 in (1964) *Palestra* no. 4 82.

306. Judgment of February 2, 1974 in (1975) *Palestra* no. 1 134. The
attorney stated inter alia as follows:

> Must the accused be made responsible for the *mens rea* of another
> person.... In other words, as happened in the Middle Ages when the
> pigs and not their owners were punished for the damage they did.....
> The judgment [of the court below] infringed not only the rules but in
> fact also all the basic principles of the Polish legal system. It is the

first time that I have encountered such judicial methods. . . . The court simply had no inkling about the case and had not at all looked at the documents. . . . If such a judgment remains in force it merits to be published for educational purposes.

307. The existence of a very influential Catholic Church and a relatively independent Catholic Press in Poland is a factor of immense importance in the creation of the kind of atmosphere in which critical speech can survive. This situation is not paralleled elsewhere in Eastern Europe.

308. *ICJ Review* no. 16 (June 1977) 17.

309. See in this regard the text starting with note 25 (Ch. 1).

310. The court refused to hear witnesses to substantiate the truth of the "hostile propaganda." The most critical statement of Attorney Popovic was his assertion that "one only had to make the journey from Belgrade to Valjevo [where the trial was being held] to see peasants using the same methods as were used 1,000 years ago."

311. Article 174 of the Yugoslav Criminal Code, in the translated version of the Union of Jurists Associations of Yugoslavia (1960) reads thus:

Whoever brings the Federal People's Republic of Yugoslavia, a people's republic, their flag or coat of arms, their highest organs of state authority or the representatives of the highest organs of state authority or the representatives of the highest organs of state authority, the armed forces or the supreme commander into derision, shall be punished with imprisonment of not less than three months.

312. Article 158 of the Hungarian Penal Code reads (in part) as follows:

Whosoever uses an expression which is calculated to point directly to a fact, which [fact] is calculated to undermine confidence in an official body or an official in relation to the activities of such body or official, or which is calculated to diminish the dignity of an official, shall be punished by imprisonment not exceeding one year.

This translation is based on that of Ladislaus Mezöfy, *Der Strafkodex der Ungarischen Volksrepublic (Sammlung ausserdeutscher Strafgesetzbüher in deutscher Übersetzung)* no. 83 (1964).

313. Judgment of 1965 of the Budapest Court sitting in appeal, reported in *Rünteto elvi határozatok* (1973) 574.

314. *Shri Baradakanta Mishra v. Registrar of Orissa High Court* (1974) *Supreme Court Cases* 374 at 413. See the text to note 197 (Ch. 1).

315. Reported as Case no. 873, in (1976) 27 *Pinika Chronika* 313. The case was brought in terms of article 181 of the Greek Penal Code, which in part reads: "Anyone who publicly insults a public, municipal, or communal

authority or a national party leader . . . shall be punished."

316. A representative extract of the long article reads thus:

You, [the judges of the Supreme Court] acquitted the traitors [in a specific case on which the article was based] since you yourselves were guilty and you simply wished to protect yourselves. . . . You who only yesterday judged and punished the militants for democracy by applying then the laws and the orders of the traitors, in effect [by exonerating the traitors] declared them again guilty today. Where do you, who only yesterday were still the court jesters of the tyrants, get the nerve and the gumption to arrogate unto yourselves the status to sit in judgment on these traitors. In order to enjoy status today you would have needed status yesterday. But you have neither status, nor pride nor honesty. Doormats yesterday for the barbarian boots of the tyrants; today you are shy little men in the anaemic arm of democracy.

317.

The constitution by which we live . . . is called democracy because power does not rest with the few, but with the many, and in law, as it touches individuals, all are equal, while in regard to the public estimation in which each man is held in any field, his advancement depends not on mere rotation, but rather on his true worth.

318. Cf the remark on free speech generally by Frede Castberg, *Freedom of Speech in the West* (1960) 423:

A democracy is [at times] capable of showing marked intolerance with regard to political opinions that run counter to the standpoint at the moment enthroned . . . [although] [t]he persons mainly responsible for muzzling freedom of speech are undoubtedly convinced supporters of the principle of the rule by the majority; it is precisely their ardent assertions of the system of the extant democracy which has provoked their often ruthless intolerance to those daring to criticise the system, or rather to those whose opinions and militant political activity is considered to constitute a threat to the actual system.

CHAPTER 3

1. *A-G* v. *Times Newspapers* [1947] AC 273 at 300. See note 49 (Ch. 1).

2. In the now-leading U.S. case of *Nebraska Press Association* v. *Stuart*, presently to be discussed (see note 25), Chief Justice Burger, writing the opinion

for the Supreme Court stated as follows (427 U.S. 548) as regards this modern perspective of trial publicity problems: "The speed of communication and the pervasiveness of the modern news media have exacerbated these problems . . . as numerous appeals demonstrate."

3. The two most recent British books on contempt do not discuss this psychological problem in any depth; cf Borrie and Lowe, op. cit., and Miller, op. cit.

4. The now trite and universally used sociological methodology of social balancing was crisply put as follows in a seminal article by Roscoe Pound, "A Survey of Social Interests," in (1943) 57 *Harvard Law Review* 1 at 39:

> Such in outline are the social interests which are recognized or are coming to be recognized in modern law. Looked at functionally, the law is an attempt to satisfy, to reconcile, to harmonize, to adjust these overlapping and often conflicting claims and demands, either through securing them directly and immediately, or through securing certain individual interests, or through delimitation or compromises of individual interests, so as to give effect to the greatest total of interests or to the interests that weigh most in our civilization, with the least sacrifice of the scheme of interests as a whole.

  5. *Sheppard* v. *Maxwell* 384 U.S. 333 [1966]. See note 30.
  6. See the text to note 49 (Ch. 1) and the text to note 12.
  7. *A-G* v. *Tonks* [1939] NZLR 533 (Supreme Court).
  8. See the text to note 32 (Ch. 1).
  9. At 537.
  10. At 538. Meyers C. J. states as follows:

> [A] common-law judge [is not] in the least likely to be affected consciously by any such publication [in the press]. But can it be said with certainty – especially in a matter of the sentence of a person convicted of a shocking crime in respect of which public opinion has been aroused – that any man, even a judge, may not possibly be in some way unconsciously affected? I can think of few things more calculated to injure the due administration and course of justice in criminal cases in public opinion than that any newspaper or newspapers should be permitted to appear to dictate to the courts what its sentence should be in a particular case.

  11. It will be recalled that in the second *Van Niekerk* contempt case in South Africa – see the text to note 32 (Ch. 1) – the same extended reach into the subconscious sphere was given to the sub judice contempt rule. In that case the test for contempt was stated thus:

Who can say, with any confidence, that consciously or unconsciously, the court, even as so constituted [with very senior and experienced officers in charge] would not be affected by the suggestions which the accused made?

12. See note 49 (Ch. 1).
13. *A-G* v. *Times Newspapers* [1974] AC 273.
14. *A-G* v. *Times Newspapers* [1973] 1 QB 710.
15. Cf the crux of the judgment of Lord Reid at 300:

If this material [on the details of the alleged delaying tactics of the defendant company which would have been published by the *Sunday Times* but for the injunction] were released now, it appears to me almost inevitable that detailed answers [to the issues such as negligence which the court may have to determine] would be published and there would be expressed various public prejudgments of this issue. That I would regard as very much against the public interest. There has long been and there still is in this country a strong and generally held feeling that trial by newspaper is wrong and should be avoided. . . . I think that anything in the nature of prejudgment of a case or of specific issues in it is objectionable, not only because of its effect on that particular case but also because of its side effects which may be far reaching. Responsible "mass media" will do their best to be fair, but there will also be ill-informed, slapdash or prejudiced attempts to influence the public.

16. Idem.
17. Idem.
18. The Phillimore Committee – see note 146 (Ch. 1) and the text there – stated thus about the aggressive role of the press in this case:

We have no doubt, however, that the change in the course of the thalidomide proceedings which occurred in the months following September 1972 was the result of the campaign of moral pressure on [the defendant litigant] Distillers, triggered off by the first two articles in the *Sunday Times* [published in defiance of the contempt law].

19. See note 11. On the inhibiting effect of sub judice contempt in South Africa, see this writer, "The Uncloistering of the Virtue," op. cit., 549 ff, and the text to note 131 (Ch. 4) ff.
20. During the so-called information scandal in South Africa in 1979 – a scandal involving massive misappropriation of government funds – a newspaper that took on the investigative role in the matter à la Washington *Post*, the *Rand Daily Mail*, saw itself and its editor successfully prosecuted for contempt of commission over a report that tended to anticipate the findings of a judicial

commission of inquiry at a time when every newspaper was expending columns to similar reports. See note 144 (Ch. 4).

21. See Borrie and Lowe, op. cit., 296 ff.

22. *Sheppard* v. *Maxwell* 384 U.S. 333 at 342 [1966]:

> Given the persuasiveness of modern communications and the difficulty of effacing prejudicial publicity from the minds of the jurors, the trial judge must take strong measures to ensure that the balance is never weighed against the accused.

On this seminal American case, which introduced so-called gagging writs, see the text to notes 30 and 62.

23. See note 16 (Ch. 2).

24. Robertson-Oswald, op. cit., 5.

25. *Nebraska Press Association* v. *Stuart* 427 U.S. 539 [1976]. On this decision see inter alia James T. Ranney, "Remedies for Prejudicial Publicity: A Brief Review," in (1976) 21 *Villanova Law Review* 819; Edward D. Robertson, Jr., "The Fair Trial – Free Press Debate Continues," in (1976) 45 *UMKC Law Review* 311; Diane E. Burkley, "Ungagging the Press: Expedited Relief from Prior Restraints on News Coverage of Criminal Proceedings," in (1976) 65 *Georgetown Law Journal* 81; Stephen A. Bennett, "Fair Trial v. Free Press," in (Sept. 1976) *Trial* 24; Jack Landau, "Free Press Boon: A Stop to Direct Gag Orders?" in (Sept. 1976) *Trial* 27; Susan M. Peterson, "Collision Course – The First and Sixth Amendment: Freedom of the Press versus the Right to Trial by an Impartial Jury," in (1976) 22 *Loyola Law Review* 1095.

26. Of the decision, Landau, op. cit., 28, states:

> [The decision constitutes] a resounding policy statement in support of broad rights of the public to know information about the criminal justice system [and] a sweeping opposition to prior restraint on press information about the courts.

27. At 561. The facts briefly were that the murder of a family of six had taken place in a small Nebraska town leading to a significant degree of media reporting. With a suspect already arrested, the prosecutor applied for and obtained a "restrictive order" restraining the dissemination of certain facts. An order was granted and it was against this order that the petitioners went to court and ultimately to the Supreme Court.

28. At 547.

29. Justice Brennan with Justices Stewart and Marshall concurring.

30. *Sheppard* v. *Maxwell* 384 U.S. 333 at 358 [1966]. See the text to note 60. On this case and its relevance to free speech, of Alan Grant, "Pre-Trial Publicity and Fair Trial – A Tale of Three Doctors," in (1976) 14 *Osgoode Hall Law Journal* 275.

31. At 559:

The thread running through all these [older] cases is that prior restraints on speech and publication are the most serious and the least tolerable infringement on First Amendment rights. A criminal penalty or a judgment in a defamation case is subject to the whole panoply of protections afforded by deferring the impact of the judgment until all its avenues of appellate review have been exhausted. . . . A prior restraint, by contrast and by definition, has an immediate and irreversible sanction. If it can be said that a threat of criminal or civil sanctions after publication "chills" speech, prior restraint "freezes" it at least for the time.

32. On jury trial problems, see the text starting with note 49.

33. At 617.

34. Justice Stevens at 617 puts the Court's disinclination to devise a blanket rule as follows:

Whether the same absolute protection would apply no matter how shabby or illegal the means by which the information is obtained, no matter how serious an intrusion on privacy might be involved, no matter how demonstrably false the information might be, no matter how prejudicial it might be to the interests of innocent persons, and no matter how perverse the motivation for publishing it, is a question I would not answer without further argument.

35. See the text to note 17.

36. Benjamin Cardozo, *The Nature of the Judicial Process* (1921) 167-68.

37. For the time being the discussion includes juries, to which separate attention will be given later.

38. See Oswald, (3 ed) op. cit., 91, for references to such old cases relating to "offences . . . which . . . prejudice mankind against persons before the cause is heard," all predating the advent of mass media.

39. Cf Justice Frankfurter's celebrated statement in the *Pennekamp* case (see note 52 (Ch. 2):

If men, including judges and journalists, were angels there would be no problems of contempt of court. Angelic judges would be undisturbed by extraneous influences and angelic journalists would not seek to influence them. Naturally, no legal system can work on the above assumptions; nor can it work, however, on the assumption that judges do not have or cannot acquire the mental discipline to exclude or minimize the effect of a possibly pernicious extraneous influence filtering through into or unduly affecting their judging processes.

40. For a statement by a German judge on the operation of such an early warning system concerning trial publicity, see the text following note 186.

41. In South Africa, where, it must be remembered, the potential reach of the contempt power extends even to the unconscious sphere – see note 11 – there have been a number of occurrences, for instance the assassination of Prime Minister Verwoerd or the capture of the Israeli Consulate in Johannesburg by a berserk gunman or the activities of the main dramatis persona in that country's "Watergate" around the Information Department, where media coverage of the occurrences reached saturation point. No allegation was made, however, that the courts subsequently did not reach proper verdicts, something that would be manifestly impossible in terms of the underlying premises of the sub judice rule in that country.

42. The Phillimore Report, op. cit., paragraph 132, proposed that the sub judice rule "should cease to apply at the conclusion of the trial or hearing at first instance, both in criminal and civil proceedings." See also Miller, op. cit., 107:

> At this stage [after the trial at first instance] ... however, the position differs radically from the position which obtains in the period before and during the trial. An appeal will be heard without a jury. Hence one can discount the possibility of prejudice through this medium.

Cf also the statement of Lord Parker C. J. in the *Duffy* case (*R* v. *Duffy, Ex Parte Nash* [1960] 2 QB 188 at 198):

> Even if a judge who eventually sat on the appeal had seen the article in question and had remembered its contents, it is inconceivable that he would be influenced consciously or unconsciously by it. A judge is in a very different position to a juryman. Though in no sense superhuman, he has by his training no difficulty in putting out of his mind matters which are not evidence in the case. This indeed happens daily to judges on assize.

43. Lord Denning, *The Due Process of Law* (1980) 53, refers to his judgment in *A-G* v. *BBC* [1979] 3 WLR 312, where he expressed the view that a local valuation court was not "protected" by contempt:

> It has no one on it or connected with it who is legally qualified or experienced. ... The reason is that a lawyer is, or should be, by his training and experience better able than others to keep to the relevant and exclude the irrelevant ... and not to be influenced by outside information.

44. Idem loc. cit.
45. At 301. Cf note 13.

46. See the text to note 6 (Conclusion).

47. See the *Times* of January 14, 1978. The television company was fined £50,000 (with a number of other fines imposed on the individual producers) for showing a film featuring a photograph of and making reference to a nursing sister due to stand trial in Scotland the next day for obstructing the air supply to a patient in a hospital. The program concerned a debate on whether or not life supports should be withdrawn from patients with certain forms of severe brain damage. It was mentioned in passing that "a jury at Edinburgh Sheriff Court ... will be told that Nurse Atkins twice tried to block the air supply of a 13-year-old girl in her care." The fact that this averment was accompanied by a statement concerning the nurse's intention to plead not guilty did not in the opinion of the court remove the sting. It seems clear from the reported version of the judgment that a slightly more extensive use of camouflage tactics could have made all the difference to the court without changing the substance of the report. Lord Justice-General Emslie stated that the "references to Mrs Atkins ... were in the highest degree likely to prejudice her prospects of a fair and impartial trial."

48. Re *A-G for Manitoba and Radio OB Ltd* [1977] 133 *CCC* (2d) 1. A radio reporter and a radio company were fined for contempt for an interview with the mother of an accused juvenile about to stand trial for murder. The interview took place within a wider discussion of inadequate facilities for housing mentally disturbed children. The woman was interviewed anonymously but sufficient details were given about the crime to identify the juvenile. In the low-keyed and unsensational interview the mother provided some background information about the juvenile and mentioned that he had confessed to the crime. Said Solomon J. in finding the respondents guilty (at 13-14):

> In this day when rapid communication reaches all members of our society, the news media, which enjoys great power in our society, has to exercise a high standard of care in publishing material in respect of pending court proceedings which could prejudice the fair trial of an individual, particularly when the liberty of that person is involved. It gives to the individual, whose cause is before the court, very little comfort to learn that the publication was not intended to prejudice his trial when, in fact, he discovers he might lose his liberty because of such publication. In cases where there is no actual intention to commit contempt of court by the published material, but contempt of court is committed by lack of adequate care, as in the case at bar, a penalty should be imposed in order to prevent recurrence of such publication and serve as a deterrent to others.

49. Op. cit., at 560.

50. Cf here the revealing statement of *Vine Products* v. *Green* [1965] 3 A11 ER 58 at 62:

This is not an action which will be tried by a jury. Although I suppose that there might be a case in which the publication was of a kind which might even be thought capable of influencing the mind of a professional judge, it has generally been accepted that professional judges are sufficiently well equipped by their professional training to be on their guard against allowing any such matter as this to influence them in deciding the case.

The case concerned a future civil case about the right or otherwise to designate certain non-Spanish wines as sherries. Before trial, an editorial in the *Daily Telegraph* ridiculed the naming of non-Spanish products sherry. The court refused to commit the editor for contempt.

51. Gerald A. Ehrenreich, "Is Pre-Trial Publicity Really Bad?" reprinted as a *Report* (no. 24, June 1968) of the Freedom of Information Center, Columbia, Missouri.

52. Cf Anon., "Prejudicial Publicity in Trials of Public Officials," in (1975) 85 *Yale Law Journal* 123 at 128: "The problem of media-induced bias which cannot be purged [by elaborate precautions and procedures] from jurors' minds has yet to be addressed squarely by the courts."

53. 427 U.S. at 549.

54. At 551.

55. Cf, for instance, his statements at 554-55:

Taken together, these cases [of massive trial publicity] demonstrate that pretrial publicity – even pervasive, adverse publicity – does not inevitably lead to an unfair trial. The capacity of the jury eventually impaneled to decide the case fairly is influenced by the tone and extent of the publicity, which is in part, and often in large part, shaped by what attorneys, police, and other officials do to precipitate news coverage. The trial judge has a major responsibility. What the judge says about a case, in or out of the courtroom, is likely to appear in newspapers and broadcasts. More important, the measures a judge takes or fails to take to mitigate the effects of pretrial publicity ... may well determine whether the defendant receives a trial consistent with the requirements of due process. That this responsibility has not always been properly discharged is apparent from the decisions just reviewed.

56. See also the text to note 4 (Conclusion). Because of the novelty of this attack on free speech, the matter has remained largely unpublicized but it seems inconceivable that information filtering through to jurors via modest, relatively rare, and rather haphazard advertisements would be unconscionable in terms of constitutional free speech criteria or in terms of the premises of legal free speech. The quoted sections in the text come from the plaintiff's "Memorandum in support of plaintiffs' Motion for preliminary injunction" of

March 15, 1978 before the U.S. District Court of the District of Connecticut in the case of *Linda Young* v. *Crum and Forster* and *Kevin Naylor* v. *Case and McGrath.*

57. In Britain, the question of the influencability of juries or lay judges by pretrial or trial publicity would normally not arise in view of the strict sub judice rule. In the committal proceedings of the former Liberal Party leader, Mr. Jeremy Thorpe, for conspiracy to kill, held in November and December 1978, the question arose whether, after all the attending publicity of the committal proceedings (which would normally not be reported unless, as happened in this case, one of the accused so wished), Mr. Thorpe could expect a fair trial before an unbiased jury. In the event Mr. Thorpe was nevertheless sent to trial. The *Sunday Times* of November 26, 1978 editorialized under the title "Can Thorpe get a fair trial?":

> Against [this common opinion that juries should come fresh to the facts], however, and against the whole principle of the 1967 [Criminal Justice] Act [demanding non-reporting of committal proceedings] there are important arguments of principle and practice. Justice should not only be done but seen to be done. . . . The case for [secrecy], moreover, probably misrepresents the psychology of jurors, admittedly an under-researched subject, in two important respects. First, it assumes that but for the committal reports [in newspapers] jurors would have untainted minds; whereas the truth is that, well before committal, the media may have been full of rumour and innuendo which the proceedings may play a part in disentangling form real evidence. . . . Secondly, the magisterial dignity of the juror's task should not be overlooked. To assume that when a jury is sworn in it cannot make an honest effort to address itself to what is said in court calls into question the whole jury system; and also contradicts such anecdotal evidence as exists about how jurors behave. . . . Meanwhile, although "fairness" in court proceedings must always be somewhat impalpable, we do not think Mr Thorpe will get less justice because of the publicity than he would have done without it.

58. Cf the *Richmond Newspapers* case (note 11 [Conclusion]), where it is succinctly stated in the majority opinion: "People in an open society do not demand infallibility from their institutions, but it is difficult for them to accept what they are prohibited from observing."

59. Op. cit., 548-49.

60. See note 5.

61. Concerning the perhaps overly elaborate regulation of the problem of courtroom decorum in Germany, see the text starting with note 89 (Ch. 2).

62. Cf the following sampling – at 342 ff of the case – from the judgment of Justice Clark:

With this background [of long, sustained and sometimes vituperative publicity of the most lurid kind] the case came on for trial two weeks before the November general election at which the chief prosecutor was a candidate for common pleas judge and the trial judge, Judge Blythin, was a candidate to succeed himself. Twenty-five days before the case was set, 75 veniremen were called as prospective jurors. All three Cleveland newspapers published the names and addresses of the veniremen. As a consequence, anonymous letters and telephone calls . . . were received by all of the prospective jurors. . . .

The courtroom in which the trial was held measured 26 by 48 feet. A long temporary table was set up inside the bar, in back of the single counsel table. It ran the width of the courtroom, parallel to the bar railing, with one end less than three feet from the jury box. Approximately 20 representatives of newspapers and wire services were assigned seats at this table by the court. Behind the bar railing there were four rows of benches. These seats were likewise assigned by the court for the entire trial. The first row was occupied by representatives of television and radio stations, and the second and third rows by reporters from out-of-town newspapers and magazines. One side of the last row, which accommodated 14 people, was assigned to Sheppard's family and the other to Marilyn's. The public was permitted to fill vacancies in this row on special passes only. Representatives of the news media also used all the rooms on the courtroom floor. . . . Station WSRS was permitted to set up broadcasting facilities on the third floor of the courthouse next door to the jury room, where the jury rested during recesses in the trial and deliberated. Newscasts were made from this room throughout the trial, and while the jury reached its verdict.

On the sidewalk and steps in front of the courthouse, television and newsreel cameras were occasionally used to take motion pictures of the participants in the trial, including the jury and the judge. Indeed, one television broadcast carried a staged interview of the judge as he entered the courthouse. . . . After the trial opened, the witnesses, counsel and jurors were photographed and televised whenever they entered or left the courtroom. Sheppard was brought to the courtroom about 10 minutes before each session began; he was surrounded by reporters and extensively photographed for the newspapers and television. . . .

All of these arrangements with the news media and their massive coverage of the trial continued during the entire nine weeks of the trial. The courtroom remained crowded to capacity with representatives of news media. Their movement in and out of the courtroom often caused so much confusion that, despite the loudspeaker system installed in this courtroom, it was difficult for the witnesses and counsel to be heard. Furthermore, the reporters clustered within the bar of the small courtroom made confidential talk among Sheppard and his counsel almost impossible during the proceedings. They frequently had to leave the courtroom to obtain privacy. And many times when counsel wished to raise a point with the judge out of the hearing of the jury it was necessary to move to the judge's chambers. Even then, news media representatives so packed the judge's anteroom that counsel could hardly return from the chambers to the courtroom. The reporters vied with each other to find out what counsel and the judge had discussed, and often these matters later appeared in newspapers accessible to the jury. . . .

The jurors themselves were constantly exposed to the news media. Every juror, except one, testified at *voir dire* to reading about the case in the Cleveland papers or to having heard broadcasts about it. Seven of the 12 jurors who rendered the verdict had one or more Cleveland papers delivered in their home; the remaining jurors were not interrogated on the point. Nor were there questions as to radios or television sets in the jurors' homes, but we must assume that most of them owned such conveniences. As the selection of the jury progressed, individual pictures of prospective members appeared daily. During the trial, pictures of the jury appeared over 40 times in the Cleveland papers alone. The court permitted photographers to take pictures of the jury in the box, and individual pictures of the members in the jury room. One newspaper ran pictures of the jurors at the Sheppard home. . . . Another paper featured the home life of an alternative juror. . . .

63. *Estes* v. *State of Texas* 381 U.S. 532 [1965].

64. The major premise of this thinking seems to reside in the followin argument as formulated by Justice Clark (at 544-45):

As has been said, the chief function of our judicial machinery is to ascertain the truth. The use of television, however, cannot be said to contribute materially to this objective. Rather its use amounts to the injection of an irrelevant factor into court proceedings. In addition experience teaches that there are numerous situations in which it might cause actual unfairness – some so subtle as to defy detection by the accused or control by the judge.

65. Says Justice Clark in the majority opinion (at 545-46):

The potential impact of television on the jurors is perhaps of the greatest significance. They are the nerve center of the fact-finding process. . . . The conscious or unconscious effect [that the televising of a trial] . . . may have on the juror's judgment cannot be evaluated but experience indicates that it is not only possible but highly probable that it will have a direct bearing on his vote as to guilt or innocence. . . . Moreover, while it is practically impossible to assess the effect of television on jury attentiveness, those of us who know juries realize the problem of jury "distraction".

66. See the text to note 24 (Conclusion).
67. See the text to note 39 (Conclusion) ff.
68. *Rideau* v. *Louisiana* 373 U.S. 723 [1963].
69. Said the majority at 727:

[We] do not hesitate to hold, without pausing to examine a particularlized transcript of the *voir dire* examination of the members of the jury, that due process of law in this case required a trial before a jury drawn from a community of people who had not seen and heard Rideau's televised "interview".

70. Per Justice Clarke at 729:

Unless the adverse publicity is shown by the record to have fatally infected the trial, there is simply no basis for the court's inference that the publicity, epitomized by the televised interview, called up some informal and illicit analogy to *res judicata*, making petitioner's trial a meaningless formality.

71. Op. cit., at 551.
72. See the text to note 56 (Ch. 1) and note 49 (Ch. 1).
73. The Phillimore Report, op. cit., in Britain, following somewhat gingerly the philosophy of the English Court of Appeal in the *Sunday Times* case, formulated a new test for sub judice contempt at 49: "The test of contempt is whether the publication complained of creates a risk that the course of justice will be seriously impeded or prejudiced." See also Colin Munro, "Contempt becomes less strict," in (1977) 40 *MLR* 343, on certain relaxations concerning reporting in wardship cases. But for a less sanguine view, see Anthony Whittaker, "Contempt – The Need for Reform," in (1978) 128 *New Law Journal* 1040. The Law Reform Commission in Canada in its working paper no. 20 *Contempt of Court* (1977) 41 ff makes certain recommendations for future reform. Significantly it states (at 43) that it did "not think it useful to distinguish . . . between jury trials and trials before a judge alone." It also states (at 41) that in "reforming the law the principle of freedom of information must . . . be given first priority."
74. Enacted in 1958 together with article 226, which introduced a kind of scandalization contempt – see the text to note 206 (Ch. 2).
75. The reference to the "three last paragraphs of article 226" is important. They refer to the power of the court to impose special conditions concerning the publication of its judgment, the application of certain articles concerning the

press relating to the liability of directors, editors, and printers and, especially, the indemnity given to "purely technical commentaries or acts, words or writings aimed at the modification of a conviction." This latter qualification has been discussed previously and would naturally be of exceptional importance in the present context. See the text to note 209 (Ch. 2) ff.

76. Cf *Juris Classeur Penal*, articles 226 and 227, especially the updating insertion of 1976.

77. See on these cases the text to notes 220 and 216 (Ch. 2), respectively.

78. On the role of *Le Monde* within the field of legal reporting and analysis, see the text to note 112 (Ch. 4).

79. A sensational kidnapping and murder case in 1976, involving one Patrick Henry, unleashed a spate of articles both before and after his arraignment, many speculating on the need for the imposition of the death penalty. In *Le Monde*, of February 20-21, 1976, extracts are furnished from editorial comments of various newspapers a few days after the discovery of the corpse of the victim and the arrest of the accused. On February 24, 1976, *Le Monde* headlined its report on the case: "The death penalty is already in the centre of debate." The following day a report on the case was headlined: "According to the detectives the confessions of Patrick Henry display certain improbabilities." Detailed analyses followed.

80. See the text to notes 10 (Ch. 2) and 229 (Ch. 2).

81. Vitu, op. cit., 1. See note 208 (Ch. 2).

82. See *Le Monde* of November 8, 1977.

83. 384 U.S. 333. See notes 5 and 62.

84. See the text to note 25.

85. In the notorious Son of Sam case in 1977, Brooklyn Supreme Court Justice John Starkey gave a wide-ranging interview on the accused's guilt months before the trial started. Not surprisingly, the judge in question was forced to withdraw from the case for having in effect displayed a gross absence of judicial detachment. See New York *Post* of November 1 and 4, 1977, and New York *Times* of November 2, 1977. Stated the report in the New York *Times*:

> Lawyers were surprised last week when, in a wide-ranging interview with the *New York Post*, Justice Starkey declared that he would not accept a guilty plea from young Berkowitz if the defendant insisted he had been motivated by demons to kill. "I could not accept the plea", the 71-year-old justice said, "because he would, in effect, be raising an insanity defense whether he knew it or not".
>
> Justice Starkey also said that the former post office employee was almost certain to spend most or all of his life in a maximum security mental institution if he were found innocent by reason of insanity.

86. See the text to notes 30, 32, and 94 (Ch. 4) for recorded instances in England and the United States of massive informal pressure being brought to

bear on judges. Another documented instance that seems to fall in the category of socially defensible utterances by judges and on balance should not be inhibited is the case of a German judge, Mr. Bernd Poelchau. A prosecutor in Berlin had applied for his recusal in a particular case because he, the judge, had written a letter to *Der Spiegel* in which he had countered the argument (likewise published in *Der Spiegel*) of the General Federal Prosecutor to the effect that criminals (in political trials) who confess to their crimes could almost invariably expect leniency. On the basis of this letter, a recusal application was brought in view of the fact that in a particular political case one of the "crown" witnesses was to give evidence. In the *Der Spiegel* report (August 28, 1977) on this incident, it is hinted that the judge's letter to *Der Spiegel* was merely a pretext with which to obtain the removal of someone whose strict views on correct procedures could have been embarrassing in the case. The incident is particularly remarkable in view of the fact that in Germany a great amount of tolerance is shown toward judges writing, even on controversial topics, in academic and other journals.

87. See the text to notes 60, 63, and 68.
88. The Ingrid van Bergman murder trial. See the text to note 174.
89. Idem.
90. The *Sheppard* case at 363 (see note 5).
91. At 361.
92. At 363.
93. American Bar Association Project on Standards for Criminal Justice *Standards Relating to Fair Trial and Free Press* (1968) 1.
94. The recommendations of about 1,000 words stipulate inter alia that a lawyer before a trial shall not disseminate or authorize the dissemination of any information to the media concerning a trial "if there is a reasonable likelihood that such dissemination will interfere with a fair trial or otherwise prejudice the due administration of justice," and that he shall not issue information on certain matters such as the criminal record or character of the accused, confessions, the performance of tests, the identity and credibility of prospective witnesses, opinions as to the guilt or innocence of the accused, and the likelihood of certain pleas being entered. During a trial, a lawyer shall not issue or authorize "any extrajudicial statement or interview, relating to the trial or the parties or issues" and he shall not issue a statement before sentencing if it "will affect the imposition of sentence."
95. As regards some of these cases, see Kathry Houck Sturm, "Judicial Control of Pretrial and Trial Publicity: A Reexamination of the Applicable Constitutional Standards," in (1975) 6 *Golden Gate University Law Review* 101 (especially concerning California); Jeffrey Cole and Michael I. Spak, "Defense Counsel and the First Amendment: 'A Time to Keep Silence, and a Time to Speak'," in (1974) 6 *Saint Mary's Law Journal* 347; David W. Hipp, "Constitutional Law – Free Speech – Attorney Comment on Pending Trial," in (1976) 22 *Wayne Law Review* 1233; and the anonymous note in (1975) 10 *Georgia Law Review* 289 on the case of *Chicago Council of Lawyers* v. *Baur*

552 F2d 242 (7th Cir 1975).

96. The cases were those of *Sigma Delta Chi* v. *Martin* and *Leach* v. *Sawicki*. In the first case, according to the report, a restriction on the making of any statements "which might divulge prejudicial matter not of public record" was made on the lawyers, defendants, witnesses, jurors, and court officials. The second case involved a restriction on the accused and his lawyers, a restriction that was then challenged by the restrictees. See the New York *Times* of February 9, 1978.

97. Concerning, for instance, the right of access to prisons, the U.S. Supreme Court held in recent times that the press has no preferred position. See, for instance, the decision of *Houchins* v. *KQED* [Broadcasting Company] of June 26, 1978, reported in 46 *US Law Week* 4830, in which the Supreme Court held that "the media has no special right of access to the Alamedia County Jail different from or greater than that accorded the public generally" (at 4833).

98. Cf, for instance, Borrie and Lowe, op. cit., 205 ff.

99. Quoting Attorney Floyd Abrams, who is regarded as one of the United State's foremost First Amendment lawyers. See the New York *Times* of February 9, 1978.

100. *Report of the President's Commisison on the Assassinaton of President John F. Kennedy* (1964) 231-42, especially at 239:

> The American Bar Association declared in December 1963 that "widespread publicizing of Oswald's alleged guilt, involving statements by officials and public disclosures of the details of 'evidence', would have made it extremely difficult to impanel an unprejudiced jury and afford the accused a fair trial". Local bar associations expressed similar feelings. The Commission agrees that Lee Harvey Oswald's opportunity for a trial by 12 jurors free of preconception as to his guilt or innocence would have been seriously jeopardized by the premature disclosure and weighing of evidence against him.

101. Learned Hand, in "Mr Justice Brandeis" (address in 1942), in Irving Dillard (ed.), *The Spirit of Liberty* (1959) 127 at 132:

> [T]he day has clearly gone forever of societies small enough for their members to have personal acquaintance with each other, and to find their station through the appraisal of those who have any first-hand knowledge of them. Publicity is an evil substitute, and the art of publicity is a black art; but it has come to stay; every year adds to its potency and to the finality of its judgments. The hand that rules the press, the radio, the screen and the far-spread magazine, rules the country.

102. Cf the statement of Justice Brennan (Justices Stewart and Marshall

joining) in the *Nebraska Press Association* case (op. cit., at 613):

> Voluntary codes such as the Nebraska Bar-Press Guidelines are a commendable acknowledgement by the media that constitutional prerogatives bring enormous responsibilities, and I would encourage continuation of such voluntary efforts between the bar and the media. However the press may be arrogant, tyrannical, abusive and sensationalist, just as it may be incisive, probing, and informative. But at least in the context of prior restraints on publication, the decision of what, when and how to publish is for editors, not judges.

103. Per Oliver Wendell Holmes in his dissent in *Abrams* v. *US* 250 U.S. 616 at 630 [1919]: "[T]he ultimate good desired is better reached by free trade in ideas – that the best truth is the power of thought to get accepted in the competition of the market.

104. See the text to note 129.

105. See the text to note 95.

106. Section 12 of the South African Divorce Act of 1979 provides as follows under threat of punishment. Cf the text to note 39 (Conclusion):

> (1)   Except for making known or publishing the names of the parties to a divorce action, or that a divorce action between the parties is pending in a court of law, or the judgment or order of the court, no person shall make known in public or publish for the information of the public or any section of the public any particulars of a divorce action or any information which comes to light in the course of such an action.
>
> (2)   The provisions of subsection (1) shall not apply with reference to the publication of particulars or information –
>
>   (a) for the purposes of the administration of justice;
>
>   (b) in a bona fide law report which does not form part of any other publication than a series of reports of the proceedings in courts of law; or
>
>   (c) for the advancement of or use in a particular profession or science.

107. See the text to note 71 (Ch. 2) and the text to note 190 concerning the *Lebach* case.

108. In Britain, the Rehabilitation of Offenders Act (1974) penalizes the "unauthorized disclosure of spent convictions" of persons after the lapse of a variable number of years "in the course of . . . official duties" or the obtaining of "specified information" by fraud, dishonesty, or bribe. The repeal of this provision was mooted in relation to persons seeking election to public office when past offenses of neo-Nazis could not be mentioned. See the *Times* of December 12, 1977.

109. Cf *Der Spiegel* of October 31, 1977. See also the text to note 40 (Conclusion).

110. See note 120.

111. On the German Press Council, see the text to note 142.

112. Article 7 reads:

The press respects the privacy ["private life"] and the intimate sphere of the individual. If however the private conduct of an individual impinges upon public interests, it can be discussed in the press. In such a case there must be an examination whether or not the personality rights of uninvolved persons would be infringed.

113. Article 10 reads: "Unreasonably sensational depictions of violence and brutality should be avoided. The protection of juveniles must be considered in reporting."

114. Article 12 reads:

Reporting on proceedings, preliminary investigations and trials must be free of prejudice. The press therefore avoids both before the commencement of and during the period of such proceedings both in reports and in captions any one-sided and prejudicial statement. A suspect may not be depicted before a court judgment as being guilty. In the case of criminal acts of juveniles the press must as far as possible, with deference to the future of such juveniles, avoid the naming of the juveniles and the publication of pictures identifying them in instances where the crimes are not serious. Without serious grounds of justification there shall be no reports on the judgments of courts before their official announcement.

115. Cf Martin Löffler, *Presserecht* (1968) Vol. 2 102. In 1976, a new guideline was issued in which the last two sentences of the 1958 guideline were replaced by an "appeal" to the press "to refrain from publishing statements made by involved parties before the commencement of a court hearing in the proper court" and to refrain from the publication of a judgment before its official announcement.

116. As appears in the guidelines which the German Press Council publish from time to time. See *Deutscher Presserat: Publizistische Grundsätze & Richtlinien für die redaktionelle Arbeit nach den Empfehlungen des Deutschen Presserates* (1976).

117. A report, for instance, in *Der Spiegel* of August 18, 1980 documents a number of instances where sensational reports about criminal investigations into alleged spying activities of certain named individuals caused immense hardship despite subsequent exoneration of such persons on the part of the authorities.

118. The editor of the liberal *Rand Daily Mail* (Johannesburg) sums up the situation by stating that "to the best of my knowledge, no case that has gone to a hearing has gone against either a cabinet minister or a senior official of the government and in favour of a newspaper. No single case." Cf *The South African Press Council – A Critical Review* (1979) 21.

119. Cf, for instance, *Press Conduct and the Thorpe Affair* (1980).

120. Cf John A. Ritter and Matthew Leibowitz, "Press Councils: The Answer to Our First Amendment Dilemma," in (1974) *Duke Law Journal* 845 at 870:

> The law can guarantee a free press, but it is incapable of guaranteeing a fair press. The journalism profession must recognize that while its enterprise is and should remain a private business, free from government regulation, its efforts to define and realize standards of performance are also a community concern. A mechanism is needed through which individuals who understand the complexities of modern journalism and members of the community can meet and discuss press performance and press responsibility. Their discussions should not be restrained by strict interpretations of the first amendment; elementary fairness and high journalistic standards should serve as their guides. A press council satisfies this need.

121. *Lutwak* v. *US* 344 U.S. 604 at 619 [1953]. Cf note 58.

122. Cf Anon., "Prejudicial Publicity in Trials of Public Officials," in (1975) 85 *Yale Law Journal* 123 at 130:

> The essential circumstances governing the question of fairness in trials of public officials is that in our society such defendants are people who have chosen to put themselves and their conduct before the public. Exposure to extensive publicity has for years been an acknowledged fact of public life. It is a prerequisite of campaigning for office and a concomitant of holding it. . . . Unlike most other citizens, public officials can legitimately be said to have assumed the risk of publicity surrounding allegations of misconduct. In the circumstances, it can hardly be considered unfair to make them accountable for their actions in criminal trials (assuming appropriate procedural safeguards), even if the effects of publicity cannot be purged from the jurors' minds.

123. *Calley* v. *Galloway* 17 *Criminal Law Reports* 2500 (5th Circuit September 9, 1975) at 2501, as quoted in (1975) 85 *Yale Law Journal* 123 at 128. The district court, which reversed the military court conviction of the accused stated as follows in justification of its reversal (idem *Yale LJ* 127): "Never in the history of the military justice system, and perhaps in the history of American courts, has any accused ever encountered such intense and

continuous prejudicial publicity as did the petitioner herein."

124. One of Germany's foremost criminal lawyers writing on the resolutions of the Eighth Criminal Law Conference in Lisbon in 1961, in (1962) 74 *Zeitschrift für Gesamte Strafrechtswissenschaft* 186.

125. See note 53 (Ch. 2).

126. Chief Justice Stone and Justices Roberts and Byrnes.

127. *Bridges* v. *California* 314 U.S. 279-80 [1941]:

> Our whole history repels the view that it is an exercise of one of the civil liberties secured by the Bill of Rights for a leader of a large following or for a powerful metropolitan newspaper to attempt to overawe a judge in a matter immediately pending before him. The view of the majority [of the Supreme Court which held that conviction for contempt was unconstitutional] deprives California of means for securing to its citizens justice according to law. . . . This sudden break with the uninterrupted course of constitutional history has no constitutional warrant . . . [and] misconceive[s] the idea of freedom of thought and speech as guaranteed by the Constitution. . . . To be sure, the majority do not in so many words hold that trial by newspapers has constitutional sanctity. But the atmosphere of their opinion and several of its phrases mean that or they mean nothing.

128. *BGHSt* 22 [1968] 289.

129. At 294. Practical considerations played an important role in this decision since the mere fact that a lay judge or juror had read a newspaper article would, if a contrary view were adopted, lead to an almost automatic ground for his recusal. Said the court (at 295): "We would [if this were permitted] give the press an impermissible influence over the way in which courts are constituted and jeopardise the role of laymen in the administration of justice." This generous approach is not without irony in view of the excessively strict precautions taken to avoid other kinds of information, for instance, facts about preliminary investigations, from reaching the knowledge of the jurors.

130. Eberhard Schmidt, "Unabhägigkeit der Rechtspflege," printed in the proceedings of the *Tagung deutscher Juristen* (1947).

131. Eberhard Schmidt, *Justiz und Publizistik* (1968). On some of Professor Schmidt's points, see the text to notes 137 and 157.

132. According to a report of the Freedom of Information Center, some gagging writs have been imposed since the decision in the *Nebraska Press Association* case. This latter case did not stop the actual imposition of gagging writs, most of which would remain unchallenged and substantially unreported in the national media. On the *Nebraska Press Association* case, see the text to note 25. An editorial in *Editor & Publisher* (New York) of December 24, 1977, sums up the situation following the latter case as follows: "News media have lived in a fool's paradise since July 1976 believing they had seen an end to gag orders."

Of the judgment in the *Nebraska* case it says: "The Court's language provided a loophole big enough to drive a truck through. And, the courts either are doing that, or are being requested to do so."

133. See, for example, the text to note 164 (Ch. 2).

134. All eight judges of the Federal Constitutional Court replying to a letter of mine were regular readers of *Der Spiegel*.

135. Concerning *Die Zeit*, see the text to note 107 (Ch. 4).

136. See the text to notes 68 (Ch. 1) and note 190 and note 24 (Conclusion).

137. See the text to note 130.

138. Op. cit., 33 ff.

139. Op. cit., 55 ff.

140. The tendency is particularly evident in the two major national newspapers, the *Frankfurter Allgemeine* and *Die Welt*. See also the comments preceding note 104 (Ch. 4).

141. See, for instance, the text to note 154 (Ch. 2) concerning *Der Stern*.

142. The German Press Council was founded in 1956 and was inspired by the English Press Council. See Martin Löffler, *Presserecht* (1968) Vol. 2, and the note by the same author, "Gemeinsame Tagung der Internationalen Studiengesellschaft für Publizistik ... in Paris," in (1966) 19 *NJW* 2258 on the question of "self-control of the press." See also the text starting with note 111.

143. See Horst Bührke, in (1964) 42 *Deutsche Richterzeitung* 75 at 77. In the *Badische Zeitung* (Freiburg) of December 10, 1976, a news report mentioned that a *Rüge* of the German Press Council had been directed at *Das Bild* for referring to a person as "the woman murderer Honka."

144. It will, however, be recalled that the *Sunday Times* thalidomide contempt case in England concerned a comment relevant to a civil trial. This is an almost unique example of a civil case giving rise to a concern for the maintenance of fair-trial procedures.

145. See, for instance, Barend van Niekerk, "Social Engineering in the German Constitutional Court," in (1975) 92 *SALJ* 298. My own incomplete collection of critical and value-oriented articles on the *Bundesverfassungsgericht*, which, for instance, appeared over the last five years in *Die Zeit* (mostly under the by-line of Hans Schueler) and in *Der Spiegel*, fills several scrapbooks.

146. A series of long and analytical articles in 1978 in *Der Spiegel* – see note 105 (Ch. 4) – constitute a veritable litany of devastating accusations against the assumption by the Constitutional Court of legislative functions.

147. An analysis of this phenomenon, briefly touched upon by me in the article alluded to in note 145, would exceed the confines of this work. In a far-reaching and incisive interview with *Der Spiegel* (June 25, 1973), the then president of the *Bundesverfassungsgericht*, Dr. Ernst Benda, was grilled on – as the subtitle of the report called it – "the boundaries between law and politics." To the question whether "the [political] independence of the Constitutional Court

is more a wish than a reality" in relation to a particularly hotly disputed judgment, Dr. Benda replied: "The notion that in this particular question [relating to the constitutionality of the treaty with East Germany] there could be judges who have not formed some opinion, for or against, is in my view utopian." A similar grilling took place of Judge Martin Hirsch in the issue of *Der Spiegel* of November 27, 1978.

148. At the time of research, the court had not yet pronounced on the matter. See *Der Spiegel* of November 27, 1978, for a graphic description of the economic and political pressures being brought to bear on the court.

149. See the decision of the *Bundesverfassungsgericht* of December 7, 1977.

150. Idem of March 2, 1977.

151. Idem of July 31, 1973. See also note 147 for a reference to the political nature of this question.

152. Idem of May 22, 1973.

153. See Löffler, *Presserecht*, op. cit., 116-17, and, especially, Wolfram Reiss, *Störung der Strafrechtspflege durch Berichterstattung in den Massenmedien* (Ph.D. thesis) (1975) 33 ff.

154. See, for instance, Eberhard Schmidt, *Justiz und Publizistik* (1968) 61 ff; Reiss, op. cit., 72 ff; and Joachim G. Bornkamm, *Contempt of Court and the Freedom of the Press* (unpublished diploma in law thesis, Cambridge) (1975) 82 ff. A different view is taken by Ulrich Rubens-Laarman, *Die Gerichtsberichterstattung im englischen Recht unter vergleichender Betrachtung des deutschen Rechts* (Ph.D. thesis) (1969) 62 ff.

155. The provision in the draft code reads thus:

Whosoever, publicly and during the proceedings of a criminal trial before judgment in the first instance, whether in printed matter or at a meeting or in sound or television broadcasts or in a film

1. discusses the future result of the proceedings or the value of evidence in a manner which anticipates ["vorgreift"] the official result of the proceedings, or

2. makes a statement on the result of unofficial enquiries relating to the matter which is calculated to impair the unbiasedness of the members of the court or the witnesses or the expert witnesses or in any other way impair the process of establishing the truth or arriving at a just decision,

will be punished with imprisonment. . . . This provision does not apply to a discussion which concerns questions relating to the law which has to be applied.

Quoted by Eberhard Schmidt, *Justiz und Publizistik*, op. cit., 62-63. See the text to note 164.

156. Rubens-Laarmann, op. cit., 63-64:

Even though the endangering by certain kinds of trial reporting of an unbiased process of judicial decision making still remains, the idea must be rejected of putting into the hands of the German judge an instrumentality similar to the contempt institution. Although he is no worse a judge than his English counterpart, he lacks the support of a long and continuing legal tradition. And should he make law, he would be subjected in Germany to the serious charge, based undoubtedly on political reasons, that he is judge in his own cause and his decisions would for the same reasons undoubtedly contribute to a further heightening of the tension between the administration of justice and the press.

157. Schmidt, op. cit., 23 (see note 131):

It should be specifically pointed out that one can by no means accuse the German press as a whole [of using excessive reporting techniques]. . . . For 19 years now I have been reading the . . . *Rhein-Neckar-Zeitung,* as well as the *Frankfurter Allgemeine Zeitung,* the *Heidelberger Tageblatt* and the *Neue Zürcher Zeitung.* I can merely say that I have never yet encountered these excesses in these newspapers.

158. In his interview with *Der Spiegel, Bundesverfassungsgericht* Judge Hirsch commends the journal for its incisive series on the Constitutional Court (referred to in note 147), calling it "useful."

159. See the text to note 164 (Ch. 2) for a comment about the role of this foremost court reporter in Germany today.

160. *Der Spiegel* of January 31, 1977, 63. Herewith an extract:

Judicial independence apparently prevents a judge from learning from the mistakes of other judges. . . .

Rule one of the art of destroying the atmosphere of the main trial: As presiding judge one resists an understandable and reasonable request of the defence [concerning the use of a tape recorder]. . . .

Rule two. . . . One can as presiding judge decide matters quite differently from other judges. . . .

Rule three. . . . Scrutinise the brief of the client's lawyer of choice so minutely that he [the lawyer] can have no doubt as regards his own undesirability and as regards the mischief which one expects of him.

Rather paradoxically, in a follow-up article on the same case (*Der Spiegel* May 23, 1977), Mr. Mauz criticizes the conduct of a newspaper prejudging the same case:

What can this report mean but that [the accused] ... are proved to be terrorists, long before judgment and that they play an evil role in the hierarchy of the terrorists [of the Baader-Meinhof gang]. . . ?

In this report of *Bild am Sonntag* it is also mentioned "that [the two accused and their dead companion] ... fell into a police trap and immediately opened fire". . . . However it is undisputed that the two accused did *not* fire any shots.

What will happen with this trial in Cologne which was preceded by massive prejudgments ... and which has now been terribly subjected to outside intervention by way of associations arousing all kinds of emotions?

161. Regarding this concern, one can also refer to the scathing criticism of Gerhard Mauz of the reporting of the boulevard press before and during one of the most sensational murder trials in Germany in recent times, that of the film star Ingrid van Bergen in 1977 *Der Spiegel* of July 25, 1977 (to be discussed more fully):

Like share certificates criminal cases are traded on the publicity market. Whoever fails to get the accused in distress because of losing out to his competitor, simply has to make do with the purchase of the widow of the victim and her sorrow.

In the report following upon the judgment Mr. Mauz wrote in *Der Spiegel* of August 1, 1977: "That this criminal trial did not become a catastrophe amidst the howling of the press must be attributed to the prosecution, the court and especially the chairman, Judge Wilhelm Paul."

162. In the issue in which the judgment of the *Van Bergen* trial was reported, the cover story constituted a violent criticism of the defense lawyer and his tactics in and out of court (*Der Spiegel*, August 1, 1977, 24).

163. *Der Spiegel* of December 19, 1977. The case in question concerned a journalist, Mr. Faust, who had been charged with various crimes relating to state secrets following the leaking to *Der Spiegel* of facts about the illegal wiretapping and electronic eavesdropping of an atomic scientist, Klaus Traube. This event, the Traube affair, caused a heated political crisis early in 1977. See also note 174 for another aspect of the publicity relating to Mr. Faust's difficulties. In December 1978, it was reported that the Faust prosecution had been dropped. In the report in question, *Der Spiegel* speculated inter alia as follows:

Proof of this kind [that the accused prejudiced public interests] would be hard to adduce in the trial stage where matters are not decided so cursorily as in the decision regarding his detention. In fact, the informer [and accused] Mr Faust did not prejudice "public interests" – he did the very contrary since the discussion of the Traube affair in fact served public interests.

But this means in effect that Faust did not act "improperly" ["unbefugt"] but indeed very properly.

164. *Der Spiegel* of January 16, 1978. On Attorney Groenewold and his troubles, see the text to note 119 (Ch. 2). See also the text to note 182 concerning Attorney Groenewold's own paradoxical invocation of the sub judice principle in the trial in question.

165. Mauz ends by drawing the following moral from the particular episode (*Der Spiegel* of October 10, 1977):

Not only are courts at times "tricked" but it also happens that counsel and their clients are trapped.... That there are certain things which one simply does not do even though such things may be permitted by the law or by lacunae in the law is something of which judges and prosecutors must be reminded.

166. See *Die Welt* of April 23, 1977. The operation concerned the erroneous removal of a woman's sole kidney. In the *Der Spiegel* article, the facts of the case – or of a similar case – were tangentially alluded to. No names were mentioned in the report of *Die Welt*, whereas, true to its usual policy, full personal details are given about the patients and the doctors concerned in *Der Spiegel*.

167. See the text to note 154 (Ch. 2) on the pioneering role of *Der Stern* as a scrutinizing agency of the judiciary and the administration of justice in Germany.

168. Herewith an extract (*Der Stern* of January 27, 1977):

The Cologne judge Dr Armin Draber is not to be envied. He has to judge a man who has already been judged by popular prejudice as a "police murderer".... Not for a moment can he allow the impression to arise that he is prejudiced against the accused. In this matter judge Draber is only partially successful. Whatever the defence requests in order to alleviate the situation of the ill accused, the judge rejects.... Equally obstinate is the behaviour of the judge as far as co-operation with the defence is concerned. He denies them the use of a tape recorder.... And he further rejects the application of the defence to have the decision which he had taken in a display of lust for power reviewed by the full court although the procedural code demands this as a compulsory requirement.

169. Wolfgang Reiss, "Störung der Rechtspflege durch Berichterstattung in den Massenmedien" (1975) 54. The report was in *Der Stern* no. 47 of 1967.

170. No attempt at a precise definition will be attempted of the concept of the boulevard press, as the mass circulation yellow press is generally referred to in Germany. Wahrig's *Deutsches Wörterbuch* defines it succinctly but not too helpfully as "sensation [oriented] newspapers and magazines mostly sold on the street."

171. Concerning this draft, see the text to note 155. The case was that of Vera Brühne, who was convicted of murder on circumstantial evidence. The draft soon became popularly known as the *lex Brühne*. See the editorial overview entitled "Der Prozess Brühne-Ferbach," in (1962) 40 *Deutsche Richterzeitung* 252, and Max Kohlhaas, "Reformbedürftigkeit der Gerichtsberichterstattung," in (1963) 16 *Neue Juristische Wochenschrift* 477 at 478.

172. Paradoxically, the general editorial criticism of the *Richterzeitung* again only refers to the boulevard press. Inter alia it stated:

> We merely once more regrettably record that the daily press has once again ignored its duty. Even before the judgment the press portrayed the proceedings in a sensational way and exerted an influence detrimental to the interest of the establishment of truth upon the jurymen and others involved in the case through the reporting of its views and those of the so-called public opinion. Certain journalists even felt themselves emboldened to engage in their own investigations.

173. The most extreme example of this genre is undoubtedly *Das Bild*, whose circulation of several million makes it the newspaper with the largest circulation in Germany.

174. Mr. Rolf Bossi.

175. An extract from the widow's interview: "When I hear talk of the great love I want to scream. Ingrid van Bergen was not searching for love but for money. She wanted to be looked after."

176. On this case see note 171.

177. *Der Spiegel* of August 1, 1977. See note 161.

178. Produced by *Südwestfunk* and broadcast nationally on August 1, 1977. The text of the program was made available to me by the SWF.

179. An extract:

> Immediately upon taking over the defence we were overwhelmed by the press and it was impossible not to avoid reacting to this situation. However, when the trial started to take on [a definite] form and when the trial date was approaching I imposed a total embargo on information in order in principle to avoid anything which could contribute, from the point of view of the defence, to a burdening of the pre-trial atmosphere.

180. The following is the full reply of the presiding judge:

It is undoubtedly so that with this kind of snowballing of opinions the judicial office as well as the independence and the freedom of judicial decisions become involved. To the question, raised at the trial, whether we were not perhaps restricted in our decisions I replied negatively; and even today, with a greater measure of detachment to these hectic days, I can repeat that answer. It was definitely not the case. The deliberations which took many hours proceeded like all others and were devoid of any outside considerations. Nonetheless it is probably correct to say that with surrounding circumstances such as these certain influences – not speaking now about the Van Bergen case specifically but generally – cannot be denied. I considered it particularly bad that value judgments relating to the facts which formed part of the jurisdiction of the court were anticipated in the press, questions such as the trustworthiness of witnesses or, a particularly pivotal question of the trial, the matter of the trustworthiness of the memory gaps of the accused. Also regrettable was the fact that the man in the street was asked: How would you judge? Because this is a question which one can manipulate, because one may omit to mention positive responses or bring a sampling representative of views which would falsify the picture. There should in fact be no sampling of opinion before the judgment of the court.

181. An instance, previously documented in note 156 *possibly* illustrates the point. In *Der Spiegel* of July 31, 1978, an article was published on the case of a journalist Hans Georg Faust concerning various charges about his leaking facts about the illegal wiretapping and bugging of the house of an atomic scientist, Klaus Traube. The article was a scathing condemnation of the prosecuting authorities, accusing them and lower judicial authorities inter alia of manipulating facts, character assassination, misusing the criminal law, etc. Many matters that would have been crucial to an eventual case were discussed in detail, including the motives of the accused. Given the devastating nature of the facts and circumstances alleged in this article of over 2,000 words, read potentially by every politician and every senior judge in the country – and the name of the celebrity author Klaus Traube would almost naturally have ensured such readership – there can be little doubt that a court in Germany would have been hard put either to record a conviction or, at least, to impose any substantial punishment. No boulevard newspaper would conceivably have such influence, either consciously or unconsciously, directly or indirectly. In any event, the prosecution was dropped, *possibly on account of the article.*

182. On some of the activities of this outspoken lawyer, see the text to note 119 (Ch. 2). The very considerable assistance given me by Mr. Groenewold concerning the procuring of documentation on this trial as well as on matters previously discussed is gratefully acknowledged.

183. ". . . da ein rechtsstaatliches Verfahren unter Beachtung des fair trial nicht möglich ist."

184. From the 28-page particulars, the following extracts are illustrative (at 2):

When the necessity of finding a person guilty is made the object of the highest government organs a fair trial is no longer possible.

It is not so much the bias of the individual [judge] that matters but rather the political climate which puts on these proceedings its special stamp, which influences every aspect thereof and which already at this stage regards the prosecution as being right and the defence as being wrong on all points. An equality of arms between prosecution and defence can no longer be achieved. The defamations perpetrated over a period of years have had the effect that nobody can free himself entirely therefrom and a verdict of not guilty of this lawyer who has been prejudged in the public opinion as an accomplice of terrorists now seems to constitute a political impossibility.

185. The relevant part of article 6 of the Convention of 1950 reads:

In the determination of his civil rights and obligations or of any criminal charge against him, everyone is entitled to a fair and public hearing within a reasonable time by an independent and impartial tribunal established by law.

186. Article 2(1) of the *Grundgesetz* of Germany reads: "Every person has the right to a free development of his personality, in so far as he does not impair the rights of others or infringe the constitutional order or the moral code."
187.

The court has a measure of understanding for the concern of the accused and his defence emanating from the events and statements of the past that fair proceedings may be endangered. This concern, however, is without substance. . . . The defence argued and showed . . . that a campaign was unleashed against the accused. This may well be so . . . and the court does not consider that everything which happened in this respect was conducive to the interests of an ordered administration of justice and to a generation of respect therefor. Nonetheless this court, consisting as it does of judges who are level-headed persons who think and judge both soberly and critically, is uninfluenced. This court is aware of the obvious fact that the media and high official quarters are not immune to making erroneous statements or indulging in wrong actions.

188. The extracts of the judgment are from an official typed transcript.

189. Cf the text to note 40 concerning this warning system.
190. See the text to note 62 (Ch. 1) and note 107.
191. Literally "Reference Number XY – Unsolved." During and after the program, members of the public can telephone in to various studios with possible leads in the crimes portrayed. From personal observations, I can record that dramatic breakthroughs are in fact regularly achieved – often before the end of the program. The police cooperate in the program.
192. The judgment is reported in (1971) 26 *Juristenzeitung* 331. See also in the same volume the article by Horst Neumann-Duesberg, "Fernsehsendung 'Aktenzeichen XY-ungelöst' und Persönlichkeitsrecht" (1971) 26 *JZ* 305.
193. The essence of this balancing operation is clear from the following extract:

When in relation to publications and broadcasts prejudicial information of a third party is disseminated, such invasion may be justified when a balancing of the competing public and individual interests shows a preponderance of weight on the side of the interests of the public. . . . The present case is different from the other cases [in which this balancing had to be undertaken] . . . in the sense that on the side of the public interest very different interests are involved. Involved here is not the quest for education, enlightenment or entertainment which has to be balanced against the interests of personality [of the individual], but the interest of the community in solving a crime and the corollary public interest of crime prevention in the future. This interest of the community at large weighs more heavily than its interest in the representation of historical truth or in the entertainment of the television viewers. Where the case law has already tended to expand the limits of the invasion which a person who enters into the limelight of contemporary history [Zeitgeschichte] has to suffer when such interests as the enlightenment and education of the public are involved, this must *a fortiori* happen when an interest so eminently worthy of protection such as the solving and the prevention of crime is at stake.

194. Cf the decision of the *Bundesgerichtshof* in (1963) 16 *NJW* 904, where a person was wrongly described as the key figure in a band of thieves while he had at the time merely been charged with receiving, and the decision of the *Oberlandesgericht* of Braunschweig of October 24, 1974, as reported in (1975) 28 *NJW* 651, where reliance on a police report by a newspaper constituted a sufficient bar to a claim for damages for an erroneous report about a suspect.
195. An interesting and rare example of a court in Germany taking critical note of statements made about its operations was reported in the *Frankfurter Allgemeine Zeitung* of August 2, 1977. Commenting on criticism directed at the *Verwaltungsgerichtshof* (civil service court), among other things about the

latter's alleged failure to allow certain evidence to be adduced, the court issued a statement to the effect "that it objects strenuously to the fact that the DGB [the German Trade Union Council] as an outsider to the court proceedings makes certain demands upon the court with which it apparently endeavours to influence the proceedings and the verdict." The spokesman for the court qualified the statement of the DGB as a "most serious intervention in pending proceedings."

CHAPTER 4

1. *Publications Control Board* v. *William Heinemann Ltd* 1965 (4) SA 137 (AD) at 160. Mr. Rumpff is presently chief justice of South Africa. Justice Rumpff's spirited dissenting judgment in this particular case is one of the very few positive features over the last three decades in the inexorable decline of free speech in South Africa, constituting a lonely but ringing declaration of faith in free speech in the full sense of the term.
2. See the text to note 146 (Ch. 1).
3. See the text to notes 301 and 312 (Ch. 2).
4. As was pointed out previously – see the text to note 95 (Ch. 3) – the recent U.S. decisions concerning gagging orders on attorneys have in reality given the press a preferred position, allowing them in effect to publish what others may not. This preferred position is not unquestioned (see, for instance, the same note concerning access to prisons). See also Anthony Lewis, "Cantankerous, Obstinate, Ubiquitous. The Press," in (1975) 75 *Utah Law Review* 75 at 83:

Some members of my profession [the journalists] believe strongly that freedom of the press should be an absolute value in our constitutional order. I have heard them say that the first amendment's protection of the press always outweighs such other interests as the right to privacy, the individual's opportunity to make whole an unfairly damaged reputation, the right to a fair trial.

5. Anthony Lewis, op. cit., 87, speaks with reference to this case of "outlandish British examples of suppression [of trial comment] by court order."
6. *A-G* v. *Times Newspapers* [1974] AC 273 at 300.
7. Abel-Smith and Stevens, op. cit., 183:

As was the case in some other professions, [law] teachers had a much lower status than practitioners. When judges came in contact with law teachers the former had, according to Laski, "a most amusing sense of infinite superiority, and the teachers as interesting a sense of complete inferiority."

And later (at 289-90):

> As the judges removed themselves from sensitive areas where their discretion or law-making activities had previously been obvious, criticism of the judiciary, which earlier in the century had been open, began to disappear.... The fact that the judges gradually came to be regarded as above any type of criticism, may well have led them to believe in their own infallibility. In 1943, a political scientist listed among the abuses accepted by Englishmen "the immunity from criticism of judges, the most pampered of English officials". In the years after the Second World War ... various factors ... strengthened the feeling of complacent superiority within the judiciary.... Thus, in these years, it became customary to refer to the judges in hushed tones of awe.... In Parliament, too, the mere mention of the English judges led to a whole symphony of cloying praise.

8. See the text to note 51 (Ch. 2).

9. See *Pers en Rechtspraak. Rapport van een werkgroep gevormd op initiatief van de Nederlandse Orde van Advocaten* (1977) 19-21.

10. Op. cit., 246.

11. On this ideal see the present writer, "The Warning Voice from Heidelberg ... ," op. cit., especially at 242 ff: "Radbruch and the Lawyers."

12. William O. Douglas, "The Bill of Rights is not enough," op. cit., 127-28.

13. Gustav Radbruch, *Ihr Jungen Juristen* (1919) 4, reprinted from van Niekerk, "The Warning Voice ... ," op. cit., 242:

> Also on his own terrain, that of the administration of justice, will the duties and the position of the jurist undergo fundamental change. The type of lawyer of the future will not be moulded after the image of the judge, the public prosecutor or the practising lawyer of the past. The judge and the public prosecutor as blind executors of the will of the state, and of course as protectors of the corporate will of the state [*gesetzlicher Staatswille*] against illegal caprice emanating from the machine of state [itself], were in all their duties as servants of the state completely immersed in the spirit of the authoritarian state. The practising lawyer, representative of the rights of the individual and therefore, by dint of his *métier*, the people's spokesman *vis-à-vis* the state authority, was admittedly the personification of the democratic state [*Volksstaat*] in its struggle against the authoritarian state; [unfortunately] however, he was not the personification of the victorious and dominating democratic state. The interests of both groups of lawyers were limited to the legal form.... To probe behind

the state order was, however, not the business of the lawyer; the lawyer of the past intentionally closed his eyes to the purposes which should be served by order and liberty and to the idea of state welfare whence the law of the state emanates. The lawyers of the future, however, will not in the first place be people who blindly execute the law but they will be creative architects of the law.

14. Theo Rasehorn in "Eine – noch – heile Welt? Untersuchung des Jahrgangs 1962 der Deutschen Richterzeitung," in Rasehorn, Ostermeyer, Huhn, and Hasse, *Im Namen des Volkes*, op. cit., 45-46:

Characteristic also is the fact that the section "Overview" is not essentially geared to inform the judiciary dispassionately about discussions in the public concerning the judiciary and to interpret criticism [against the judiciary] in a knowledgeable fashion in order to induce the average judge to indulge in self-criticism or to contemplate his position. Not so, when discussing the public debate [concerning various *causes célèbres*]; the attacks from the public are immediately subjected to counter attack, and self-criticism therefore not considered. Instead the cry goes out that once again the press had failed in its duties. . . . The overall impression cannot be avoided that the "Overview" sees as its main objective not to point to the criticism of the judiciary but to the latter's apologists. . . . In short, what is sought is not a debate with the public but simply self-justification.

Concerning Rasehorn, see the text to note 102 (Ch. 1).

15. See Theo Rasehorn, "Über informierte und formierte Justiz" (1970) 3 *Kritische Justiz* 80. See the text to note 26.

16. See, for instance, the text following notes 27 (Ch. 1) and 118 (Ch. 2).

17. See *Die Verteidigung auf der Anklagebank* op. cit., 80 concerning disciplinary proceedings against Attorney Spangenberg.

18. See, for instance, Peter Weiss, "Joe McCarthy Is Alive and Well and Living in West Germany. Terror and Counter-Terror in the Federal Republic," in (1976) 9 *New York University Journal of International Law and Politics* 61 and William H. Schaap, "Auf Wiedersehen to Civil Liberties," in (October/November 1978) *Juris Doctor* 36.

19. The action taken against Dr. Rasehorn was described in the text to notes 102 and 136 (Ch. 1).

20. From (1973) 53 *Deutsche Richterzeitung* 203.

21. But see note 85 (Ch. 3).

22. From the extract of "Opas Justiz lebt," which is quoted in the *Richterverband*'s memorial, the following can be described as the most controversial and outspoken:

This would not be the place to deliver a graveside eulogy for the administration of justice, but it can be pointed out that we are living in times in which the administration of justice must be questioned – in which the question may – nay, must! – be posed whether the profession of the judge remains a fundamental profession [Urberuf] or whether it has become a dying profession; whether in the place of the judge there will not in the near future be welfare officers, social workers and computerised justice. . . . The chance of renewal by means of reform appears to have been lost. It is possible that a new type of administration of justice and a new type of judge may break into the scene with revolutionary force. It seems unlikely though. The administration of justice would always move to the sidelines and away from the centre of revolutionary change and away from the educational system.

23. Reference will presently be made to the support of a fellow maverick judge, Helmut Ostermeyer. See note 26.

24. The appointment of members of the Federal Constitutional Court has often been a topic of relatively outspoken critical comment in the quality German press, especially in *Der Spiegel* and *Die Zeit*. See, for instance, notes 106 and 108.

25. At 9 of the transcript:

The objective of the respondent [*Richterverband*] was, by means of the statement, to make a contribution to the formation of public opinion and to exert influence on the Ministry of Justice of Hesse and the relevant bodies concerning the filling of the vacant judicial position.

26. Helmut Ostermeyer, "Ein klassischer Fall richterlicher Befangenheit," in (1973) 12 *Vorgänge* 16:

It is therefore – and this makes criticism thereof so invidious – a judgment in favour of freedom of expression, albeit once again the freedom of expression of those on the right. . . . When for instance an industrialist is imputed to be using a stimulant for sexual potency or that a professor believes in the ginseng root they receive damages. When however it is imputed to a judge that he tirelessly expresses views which question fundamental constitutional principles, he is apparently not even being regarded as being sufficiently affected that he can demand the cessation of such utterances, or at least not when they originate from the *Richterverband*.

27. In Rasehorn, Ostermeyer, Huhn, and Hasse, op. cit., 236.
28. See the text to notes 13 and 14.

29. Joachim Perels, "Die Verfälschung der Verfassung durch ihren obersten Richter: Ernst Benda," in (1972) 5 *KJ* at 177.

30. According to a report in the Chicago *Tribune* of September 9, 1977. See also *Time* magazine of September 19, 1977, and the New York *Times* of September 9, 1977. See the text to note 134 (Ch. 1).

31. See the text to note 94.

32. The extract is from the *Times* of January 7, 1978. In the *Sunday Times* of January 8, 1978, the incident is fully documented. The dangers of an oversensitive approach were alluded to in an editorial of the *Sunday Telegraph* of January 8, 1978. See the *Daily Telegraph* of January 10, 1978, concerning the move among parliamentarians to dismiss the judge.

33. For instance, a group of black barristers announced that they would boycott McKinnon's court – see the *Times* of January 11, 1978.

34. Although it made a few polite assertions in favor of free speech, the *Times* for its part spoke editorially of an "eccentric summing-up" and a deplorable insensitivity to the feelings of members of the colored communities in Britain (January 9, 1978).

35. On such judicial detachment in Britain, see generally Shetreet, op. cit., 314 ff and 323 ff. See also Barend van Niekerk, "Silencing the Judges: A Comparative Overview of Practices Concerning Restrictions and Inhibitions on the Free Speech of Judges," in 1979 (4) *Journal of the Legal Profession* 157. See the text to note 85 (Ch. 3) concerning justifiable aloofness of judges.

36. Reprinted in (1967) 30 *Journal for Contemporary Roman-Dutch Law* 101 at 106-07. The passage preceding the quote reads as follows:

My present concern is the reproach levelled at our courts [that ther has been a dereliction of duty due to an inadequate concern for basic rights of the individual], and the disparaging tone in which this has been done. . . . As to our failure strongly to censure interrogation under solitary confinement, I would remind our critics that this provision was politically one of the most controversial on our statute book. . . . In effect we have now been blamed, on the ground *inter alia* of the alleged effects of such interrogation . . . for not entering the political arena and taking a strong stand on a particular side, after the law had been duly passed; for not judging also of the law while, as the oath of a judge requires, we were judging, as we thought, in accordance with the law. Such criticism is perhaps best ignored. . . . It would be an evil day for the administration of justice if our courts should deviate from the well recognised tradition of giving politics as wide a berth as their work permits. It is one thing, and a very proper one, for a judge to point out defects in a statute or to draw attention to results, in all probability not anticipated or appreciated, which work hardship or injustice, i.e. to matters which Parliament might presumably want to rectify.

37. Reported in (1972) 89 *SALJ* 23 at 32.

38. On the facts of this judgment and its relevance to free speech generally, see the text to note 33 (Ch. 1). The full passage of Justice Fannin reads as follows:

> Whether one regards this point of view as illogical, perverse or just plain silly, the words do not, in my opinion, constitute a contempt of or an insult to the court. They do, however, express a point of view with which I, as a judge and as one of those to whom the words were addressed, profoundly disagree and which, in my humble opinion, exhibit a misunderstanding of the functions of a judge in a society such as ours, which, especially in the case of a man in the accused's position, is both surprising and, indeed, disturbing. . . . I feel I should be doing less than justice to my brother judges and myself if I were not to say why I regard the accused's remarks in this part of his speech as singularly misguided.

39.

> For some years past an increasing tendency has manifested itself on the part of certain academic lawyers to criticise the Judiciary from time to time for failing to comment adversely upon certain statutory provisions. That question was, *inter alia*, with special mention of interrogation under solitary confinement, pointedly referred to by Steyn CJ in 1967 . . . and again . . . by myself in 1971. . . . It suffices to say that . . . I disagree with the appellant's concept of the duty of a Judge.

40. See note 7.
41. Op. cit., 195:

> Even more surprising are complaints about "censorship" by the English law reviews. Some young academic lawyers have complained that strong terms and sharp observations on judges have been deleted from case comments and notes which they offered for publication. This practice is not commonplace nor a uniform practice followed by all English law reviews. However, the fact that it takes place, even on rare occasions, illustrates the reluctance to criticise judges which is inherent in the English approach.

42. (1959) 19 *Louisiana Law Review* 644.
43. See, for instance, the radical approach of David N. Rockwell, "The Education of the Capitalist Lawyer. The Law School," in Robert Lefcourt (ed.) *Law against the People* (1971) 90 ff:

At least two factors arising from the nature and limitations of the legal system also have a profound effect on legal education. First, only certain types of disputes, involving, for the most part, a particular class of disputants, receive a fair hearing and are resolved within the legal process. . . . The priorities of legal education are determined more by this distribution than by the pressing need for representation of classes which now receive little or no legal help. Second, as the implicit purpose of the legal system is to maintain the social order, no change which overturns existing power relationships is possible through use of the legal system. Whatever the legal method, it will always reflect a greater concern for the safety of institutions and power structures upon which the stability of the present society depends, than for the creation or restructuring of new or radically different institutions. There is an inherent resistance to sweeping – and often necessary – change and innovation implicit in legal education. . . .

The career pattern ending in a professorship reveals the kind of beliefs held by the law faculty member. Success in both educational and business careers is an indicator of an instructor's ideology. This success is marked by a reluctance to challenge the assumptions of the present role of lawyers in society.

44. See *Brief Amicus Curiae of the Association of American Law Schools* by C. Dallas Sands of the University of Alabama, Tuscaloosa, in the case of *Atkinson* v. *Board of Trustees of the University of Arkansas*. I record here my appreciation to Professor Sands for making the relevant documents available to me.

45. 1974, with an extended second edition in 1977. See the text to note 10 (Ch. 1).

46. *The Judiciary. The Report of a JUSTICE Sub-Committee* (1972).

47. On the controversy, see the editorial, "Justice and the Unpublished Report," in (1971) 121 *New Law Journal* 943. See also the "Council's Foreword" in the report. In the editorial, reference is inter alia made to one of Lord Shawcross's reasons for not publishing the report since it might "shake public confidence in the judiciary." The editorial then continues:

But the question surely is whether the criticisms are valid or not, for if they are valid, they must relate to defects that are no basis for confidence anyway, and whose existence is not in any event likely to remain concealed for long. . . . The reputation which JUSTICE has acquired over the years derives chiefly from its independence; it is highly damaging to it that the impression should be given that it will speak only after it has parleyed with the captains and the kings.

48. See, for instance, Shetreet, op. cit., 193-94.

49. OACV [OAC Verpaalen] "Eerbied voor de rechterlijke autoriteiten," in (1961) 31 *Advocatenblad* 231 at 235. See the case study on legal and informal speech restrictions in the Netherlands and especially the text starting with note 171 (Ch. 2).

50. See note 7.

51. From the pen of one of the few legal academics who has often delivered himself of strong criticism of repressive policies:

> I should like to conclude this lecture by paying tribute to South African judges, who more often than not have employed all the means at their disposal to interpret unjust laws so as to favour the victims of inequality as far as possible. . . . I wish to express my personal confidence that our jduges are worthy of the trust placed in them as the major patron of justice.

J. D. van den Vyver, *Seven Lectures on Human Rights* (1976) 12 and 16. By perhaps not such a strange quirk, Professor van den Vyver became the victim of the ultimate form of informal persuasion to remain silent by being summoned to explain a critical comment in a newspaper article. It was reported that he was subsequently forced to resign from the relatively enlightened University of Potchefstroom.

52. At an international conference, an address by this writer on the obtrusion of racial factors in sentencing was bitterly attacked by a prominent ex-judge from South Africa and chief justice of the host country, Bophuthatswana, not on the basis of any errors but simply on the basis of having alluded to the problems concerned. See *Rand Daily Mail* August 14, 1980, and (January 1981) *Reality*. Cf note 138.

53. Cf Barend van Niekerk, "Speaking Your Mind about the Judges and the Law," in (November 1978) *Reality* 5 at 9.

54. See in this regard Barend van Niekerk, "Freedom of Speech Concerning the Administration of Justice. A Personal View from South Africa," op. cit., 719-20, on the "personal trauma" of the writer concerning official attempts to silence him.

55. See the text to notes 33, 88, and 89 (Ch. 1) concerning the three cases. After the first case, the Law Teachers' Society issued a spirited statement on the academic issues and against the judgment – see note 72 (Ch. 2). Some ten editorials, all critical of the prosecution, appeared in various newspapers after the acquittal. For reference to these comments, see (1970) *Acta Juridica* 79. No such support was forthcoming after the second and third cases, where the writer's guilt/liability was established. On these cases, see Dugard, op. cit., 179-302 ("The Judiciary and Criticism of the Courts"). After the third case, in which vital interests of the press and academe were involved, some four years elapsed before the appearance of the first academic criticism of the judgment. Only one academic criticism appeared after the second case.

56. See the text to notes 34 and 35.

57. Given the strong hand of law journal editors, there is simply no way in which a vicious or disrespectful criticism of judges can find its way into academic periodicals. The same is true of the press. It is also well known that the major *causa causans* of the outburst of Dr. Steyn was the article by Professors A. S. Mathews and R. C. Albino, "The Permanence of the Temporary. An Examination of the 90- and 180-Day Detention Laws," in (1966) 83 *SALJ* 16. The article constitutes a reasoned and restrained but nonetheless withering criticism of the judicial attitudes of the Appellate Division on the country's detention laws. It is almost a masterpiece of respectful writing.

58. See note 53.

59. Idem.

60. The sole exception in an academic journal was an article by Professor Dugard in (1972) 89 *SALJ* 271. It has often been suggested that the judgment and conviction were in effect welcomed by the editors of certain legal periodicals in view of the repeated embarrassment the writer had caused them by referring to the inactivity on the part of legal scholarship in the realm of civil rights. See note 53.

61. "The Uncloistering of the Virtue," op. cit., 559-60. See also my article, "Mentioning the Unmentionable. Race as a Factor in Sentencing," in (1979) 3 *SA Journal of Criminal Law and Criminology* 151.

62. The pioneering sociologically oriented study on the South African administration of justice by Albie Sach, *Justice in South Africa* op. cit., is banned in South Africa and may not be quoted from. In this respect it is also important to note the very extensive banning procedures of books or authors regarded by the authorities as being undesirable.

63. The journal concerned was the *Journal for Contemporary Roman-Dutch Law*. In all fairness, after informing him of my intention of using his letter as an example of unjustified editorial censorship he conceded that his judgment may have been wrong and colored by prejudice. The journal is generally referred to as the *Tydskrif vir Hedendaagse Romeins-Hollandse Reg*.

64. Cf "To Pretoria, Washington and Stockholm ... With Love." See note 155.

65. The statement concerned emanated from Ogilvie-Thompson C. J. in the judgment where the liberal Anglican dean of Johannesburg had often expressed himself critically about the government and political setup. In his judgment, the chief justice avers that "the majority of South Africans" would have seriously disagreed with the statements of the dean for which he was charged. See *S* v. *Ffrench-Beytagh* 1972 (3) SA 430 (AD) at 439.

66. Fully documented in "Mentioning the Unmentionable," op. cit. See Barend van Niekerk, "Class, Punishment and Rape in South Africa," in (1976) 1 *Natal University Law Review* 299.

67. See the text to note 50.

68. At the Witwatersrand University, Johannesburg, on May 7, 1978. See

the Johannesburg *Star* of May 8, 1978, and that newspaper's editorial on May 9, 1978. The contributions of the panel, including the comments of the editor of the *South African Law Journal*, are published by the Law Students Council of the Witwatersrand University. See (1978) *Mutatis Mutandis*.

69. I am aware of an attempt by a now-deceased chief justice to exercise influence over a journal to refrain from using a certain political term that at the time was controversial in South Africa.

70. Mr. Justice Trengove in February 1980 at a conference of law teachers.

71. The role of Professor J. C. de Wet is particularly relevant here. On his contribution as a pioneer of legal free speech, see my note, "JC NOSTER: A Review and a Tribute to Professor JC de Wet," in (1980) 97 *SALJ* 183.

72. See Barend van Niekerk, "The Role and Function of the Radical Lawyer in South Africa," in (1975) 1 *Natal University LR* 147.

73. The report was jointly published in 1965 by JUSTICE (the British section of the International Commission of Jurists) and the British Committee of the International Press Institute and is entitled *The Law and the Press*. In the report, the views of certain editors and journalists are reported concerning the inhibiting effect of contempt. See the text to note 80 (Ch. 1).

74. Charles Wintour, *Pressures on the Press. An Editor Looks at Fleet Street* (1972). See note 56 (Ch. 1).

75. At 11.

76. At 15.

77. Op. cit., 193-94.

78. For a tentative opinion poll on the views of a South African sampling concerning the scrutiny of judges by the press, see my note, "Empirical evidence in court: a Durban case study," in (1980) 4 *SA Journal of Criminal Law and Criminology* 150 at 152, where I record a poll to the effect that 60 percent of the interviewees desired more criticism of judges in the press.

79. Concerning the vague nature of contempt, see, for instance, the text to note 2 (Ch. 2).

80. One of the recurring and understandable answers of the South African press to my criticism that they should be more outspoken in legal matters is that lawyers themselves set a bad example. See note 130.

81. As will be seen, there was outspoken support for this writer after his first case ended in an acquittal; there was no press commentary after the second and third cases, despite their greater relevance to the press. See the text to note 145.

82. Shetreet, op. cit., 193.

83. J. A. G. Griffith, *The Politics of the Judiciary* (1977) 213.

84. Letter by Mr. Peter Black in th *Times* of June 12, 1971.

85. "The Editor confided to me that what I had said was well said; he was equally confident that to publish it was out of the question." Although the correspondent obliquely indicates that the editor may have been afraid of legal

proceedings, it would seem more realistically that the censorship he referred to must be sought elsewhere. On the work of Mr. Levin, see the text to note 96. In actual fact, as we will presently see, the correspondent was wrong, since Bernard Levin had written what must be one of the most damning criticisms of Lord Goddard while the latter was still at the height of his glory. See also on this incident Shetreet, op. cit., 194.

86. Cf Rose Elizabeth Bird (Chief Justice of California), "The Role of the Press in a First Amendment Society," in 1980 (20) *Santa Clara Law Review* 1.

87. San Francisco *Examiner* of October 10, 1977.

88. See Chapter 3, which deals with the American situation at various junctures.

89. See Tom Goldstein, "A New Body of Law: Judging of the Judges," in the New York *Times* of October 16, 1977.

90. See the text to note 28.

91. See the text to note 29.

92. See the text to note 18 and the references in that note.

93. An interesting example of the dangers and challenges of a vital doctrine of free speech in the legal domain is recorded in the St. Louis *Post-Dispatch* of January 26, 1978. Reacting to an article in the *St. Louis University Law Journal*, which alleged and set out to prove "that federal district judges here rule overwhelmingly against civil rights of plaintiffs," the St. Louis Bar Association called the study "highly unfair" to the judges concerned. Reacting to this statement of the Association, Professor Charles B. Blackmar of the St. Louis University Law School said

> that the bar's criticism was unsupported by solid data and "jeopardizes the credibility" of the entire association. Blackmar said that the statement may also "chill" further discussion of issues raised in the article. The ... Bar Association ... asserted that its study of the article found insufficient data to support its conclusions. But the committee's statement did not detail its reasoning, nor would the members do so when interviewed later.

The original article, "Civil Rights Enforcement and the Selection of Federal District Court Judges," appeared in (1977) 21 *Saint Louis University Law Journal* 385.

94. I gratefully record the assistance of the editor. See the incident in the New York *Times* April 13, 1980, *Newsweek* May 19, 1980, and inter alia the following issues of the Detroit *News* April 13 and 27; June 15; September 7, 19, 20, 21 and 22; October 15, 19 and 31, 1980.

95. An interesting example of the "balanced" editorial approach of the *Times*, which may at times amount to unnecessarily gentle treatment of a socially disastrous court decision, is the editorial – entitled "The Silence of the Law" – on the *Sunday Times* decision of the House of Lords. There is little

doubt where the sympathies of the newspaper lay in this particular matter, and from the text of the editorial itself it is clear that the editor regretted the decision of the House of Lords. Nevertheless, in the editorial of some 1,300 words, more explanatory and repetitive of the facts than condemnatory, no attempt at all is made to castigate a decision in terms commensurate to its uniqueness and repressiveness. See the *Times* of July 19, 1973. The three most condemnatory phrases were the following:

> The layman does sometimes find it difficult to penetrate the legal mind. . . .
> It is difficult to find impartial terms to describe the two attitudes [respectively of the House of Lords and of the Court of Appeal]. We would see a contrast between the dry legalism of the House of Lords and the concern for the real world of the Court of Appeal. Others would see respect for law in the House of Lords and the making law bend to cases in the Court of Appeal. . . .
> Might not journalists or politicians in such a case [involving important issues which form the subject of a pending court case] have a duty to test again so great a restriction on freedom of speech?

96. See, for instance, the *Times* of January 6, 1976, "The most generous of men, Bar none" – a scathing and almost vitriolic attack on the reply of the English bar to a study of it. The writer wishes to record here the kind assistance of Mr. Levin.

97. See, for instance, the *Times* of June 8, 1971, "Judgment on Lord Goddard," referred to in the text to note 85.

98. Published in the *Times* of March 20, 1975. The opening paragraphs are indeed worthy of preservation:

> It is, you will agree, rare to find the toast buttered on both sides (and with the best butter, at that) but a row between lawyers on the one hand and Mr Justice Melford Stevenson on the other falls upon my imagination with something of the same feeling that would be engendered in my breast at an announcement that war had broken out between Bulgaria and East Germany: to wit, absolutely pure pleasure, unalloyed by the slightest preference between the contestants, and an earnest prayer that the struggle should be prolonged, ferocious and accompanied by casualty-lists of unprecedented length.
> The judge is the very last living specimen of the long line that stretches, in a kind of unholy apostolic succession, from Lord Ellenborough to Lord Goddard, and which, when the good Melford joins his ancestors, will be extinct. Notable milestones in his career (apart from his appearance as prosecution second-in-command in the Bodkin Adams case) have included his publicly-expressed indignation at the

existence of Acts of Parliament that prevent people like him from handing down punishments even more severe than they already do, his suggestion that the Cambridge students he jailed for their part in the Garden House riot had committed their offences under the "evil influence" (unspecified, of course, but not believed to include opium-smoking) of dons, his recommendation (happily ignored by the authorities) that a South African convicted of an offence in connexion with left-wing political activities should be sent back whence he came, and his description of a rape as "a rather anaemic affair as rape goes". Do I really have to add that lawyers, asked for their opinion of him, have said that he is an "extraordinarily nice man with a good sense of humour" and "one of the warmest of men"?

99. It will be recalled that reference was made above to a correspondent in the *Times* suggesting that the publication of Levin's article, "Judgment on Lord Goddard," would not have been possible during Goddard's lifetime. See the text to notes 84 and 85. In the latter article, Mr. Levin records the fact that there was serious talk of a prosecution after the *Spectator* article and that certain official steps in that direction were in fact taken. That the article was published not in the *Times* but in the *Spectator* must, however, be considered.

100. Printed in the *Spectator* of May 16, 1958, entitled "Brother Savage," it is actually a book review.

101. The *Blackburn* case. See note 72 (Ch. 1).

102. For instance, an interview with Chief Justice Lord Widgery on August 7, 1972, in which the latter spoke freely of his concern to keep track of things for which judges are criticized. On July 3, 1974, another interview with Lord Widgery is published in which he refers to the failure of certain judges to keep abreast of new developments.

103. For instance, an article on "The Age of Reform" by Lord Justice Scarman on January 5, 1977.

104. For instance, on June 26, 1975, where a detailed account of Lord Devlin's Chorley lecture is furnished in which he stated inter alia that judges, by dint of their limited background and experience, are ill equipped for taking a lead in law reform. See also the *Times* of December 14, 1974, where Lord Justice Scarman's Hamlyn lecture is reported in detail on the need to adapt the law to the needs of a changed society.

105. See, for instance, the text to notes 165 (Ch. 2) and 158 (Ch. 3).

106. It is invidious to single out a list of representative background articles on the basis either of quality or incisiveness. A series of articles in 1978 on the *Bundesverfassungsgericht* (October 30 and November 6, 13, and 20) entitled "The Struggle about the Federal Constitutional Court" constitute a veritable mine of information about and critical insights into the controversial political role of that court. Four articles on the undermining of the *Rechsstaat* in the edition of December 5, 1977, constitute a detailed catalogue of reasoned but bitter

criticisms of legal policies in Germany with the length of a short novel. Any number of detailed long articles on the legal problems relating to terrorism or the environment or the challenge to legality by citizens' movements have appeared over the last five years.

107. The assistance of Dr. Schueler is gratefully recorded here.

108. Examples are manifold. The most impressively incisive articles by Schueler on the *Bundesverfassungsgericht* are "Im Namen der Verfassung: Ein Profil des Bundesverfassungsgerichts. Zwanzig Jahre Wirken für die Demokratie" of December 17, 1971; "Das Orakel des Zweiten Senats. Die Verfassungsrichter versagten vor einem Politikum" of June 8, 1973; "Karlsruhe verbietet vorschnelle Ausweisung von Ausländern" of December 21, 1973; "Gewissensgrenze. Karlsruhe prüft das Fristenmodell" (on abortion) of June 28, 1974; "Karlsruher-Urteile. Für alle Ewigkeit?" of April 18, 1975; "Zwei nicht ganz hilfreiche Urteile des Bundesverfassungsgerichts" of May 2, 1975; "Radikale im öffentlichen Dienst. . . . Das Bundesverfassungsgericht versteht sich selbst nicht mehr" of August 1, 1975; "Ostverträge. Karlsruhe übt Selbstbeschränkung" of October 31, 1975; "Zivildienst als Schikane. Das Urteil aus Karlsruhe gibt Rätsel auf" of April 21, 1978; "Die Konterkapitäne von Karlsruhe. Wird Bonn von den Verfassungsrichtern regiert?" of February 24, 1978.

109. Herewith the most outspoken part of the criticism:

> The judgment of the Trento Court provokes indignation not only as a consequence of the scandalous acquittal of the five accused but also because it erects a well-nigh insurmountable barrier against ever ascertaining the truth concerning one of the gravest acts of subversion relating to the [terrorist] strategy of tension.

See the text to note 233 (Ch. 2).

110. In one of the very few instances known to me where a major European newspaper directly broached the question of critical reporting of the administration of justice, the Dutch paper *Het Parool* stated as follows on May 13, 1972:

> The principle of judicial independence does not mean that the administration of justice should be the sacred cow of the community. Apart from being independent the administration of justice is also public. . . . But the principle of the public nature of the administration of justice entails certain consequences, although these have only been recognised in recent years. In principle every person may sit in as a critical spectator in the public gallery. In practice it so happens that the public is more or less represented by the press. And that does not mean that the press does not only have a descriptive and reporting task but it must also critically observe what happens in court.

111. "Deutschland Deine Richter." See note 155 (Ch. 2).

112. A collection of these contributions by Jac van Veen has been published in a work already alluded to, *De Rechten van de Mens – De Mensen van het Recht* (1971). See the text to note 186 (Ch. 2).

113. Parenthetic and commendatory reference must be made here also of the work of Mr. F. Kuitenbrouwer of the *NRC Handelsblad* in the Netherlands, who gives regular and semiacademic attention to legal matters in editorials or signed articles. His point of departure, as he pointed out to me in a letter, is human rights but attention is focused (as is also the case in most countries where either legal or societal restrictions prevail) at the police, prisons, and the Ministry of Justice. A recent study by the Dutch Ministry of Justice – A. W. M. Coenen and J. J. M. van Dijk, *Misdaadverslaggeving in Nederland* (1974) – found that the *NRC Handelsblad* devoted only 1.40 percent of editorial space to crime reports.

114. It is difficult, for instance, to imagine the following concluding sentence in a report of the *Times*, especially in relation to a case still proceeding, relating to allegations of police brutality toward suspects (*Le Monde* of February 10, 1976):

It is not unlikely, so people think at Aix, that [if there had not been a determined effort by the *juge d'instruction* to get to the bottom of the matter] the affair would simply have been recorded as not having produced any results or it would have been handed to a "reliable" magistrate. Once again the Marseilles police would then have been able to commit grave acts of violence with impunity against suspects. Is it mere chance that the prosecutor's office asked for Mr Millet [the *juge d'instruction*] to be replaced by Mr Gironsse, senior *juge d'instruction* who, despite belonging to the trade union of magistrates, is known to be a ferocious defender of the established order?

115. Inter alia on November 15, 1976, and December 11, 1976.

116. On May 10, 1976.

117. On March 8, 1975.

118. On April 4, 1976.

119. On February 7, 1975.

120. Very surprisingly, the French government started an unprecedented contempt case against *Le Monde* at the end of 1980. See note 10 (Ch. 2).

121. See the remarks by Justice Sussman in note 126.

122. I gratefully acknowledge the assistance by the Jerusalem Archives and Mrs. Doris Lankin of the Jerusalem *Post*.

123. Jerusalem *Post* of October 9, 1975, written by David Landau:

Judges *can* err, of course, but it is not for dockers, or trade union officials, or (even) the press to criticise them. There are appeal courts, and the Supreme Court, from which to seek redress. Beyond these there is sometimes the President's exercise of mercy. Other times there is nothing. That is what the Rule of Law is about.

124. Jerusalem *Post* of November 6, 1975.

125. At about the same time, Supreme Court Justice Haim Cohn also had some views on the press. The report in the Jerusalem *Post* of October 20, 1975, stated as follows: "Justice Cohn complained that journalists and newspapers permitted themselves absolute freedom to comment on issues which were *sub judice*, and considered themselves fit to guide and to decide on every matter." It is not quite clear how Justice Cohn arrived at his opinion, since he also noted in the same interview that he *never* read newspapers!

126. Jerusalem *Post* of April 15, 1972. Part of the interview reads as follows:

What are Justice Sussman and his peers doing to alleviate the many ills which he so keenly feels?

"What can I do?" he replies. "When I'm invited, I lecture – in public – or to the Bar Association, or at the universities. They're mostly my pupils, you know, the deans, the professors, the Bar Association officers . . ." – (Justice Sussman is, on the side, a law professor at the Hebrew University, and author of three major works, including the authoritative treatise on civil procedure) – . . . .

The Supreme Court itself, in its judgment, can and sometimes does inveigh against instances of maladministration in government or malpractices elsewhere. But Sussman indicates that the Justices have become disheartened by the negligible effect their fulminations seem to produce – and that this in turn often deters them from comment on broad public, social or ethical issues beyond the narrow confines of the legal issue in point.

In part he blames the press. There is no serious and intelligent coverage of Supreme Court decisions in any newspaper, he says. The *Jerusalem Post* and *Ha'aretz*, granted, print extracts from some judgments, and other papers, too, keep a weather eye open for scandal or sensation. But competent reporting by newsmen with a thorough legal grounding – as is practised in other countries – could encourage the Supreme Court to express its views more frequently on a broader range of social issues – and could enhance its standing and influence in public life.

127. Op. cit., 181.

128. On this so-called information scandal, see note 144.

129. Admittedly, there have in the past been a few international voices of praise of the South African judicial order – see John Dugard, op. cit., 279 ff for examples – but they have become exceedingly rare. For a depiction of the

background situation to the South African judicial system, see Albie Sachs, *Justice in South Africa* (1973), Dugard, op. cit., and the present writer in "The Mirage of Liberty" (1973) 3 *Human Rights* 283.

130. The South African press can be divided into three broad sections with reference to the language and/or race and/or political ideology of their readership: the English press, the Afrikaans press, and the black press. The Afrikaans press is openly wedded to the existing order and the government's racial policies, a situation that affords it a greater measure of protection and confidence should it wish to flout some of the journalistic taboos. Cf *Index on Censorship* Autumn (1976).

131. Reference here to the *judiciary* means primarily the Supreme Court of South Africa (including its Appellate Division, which is the highest court of the land) as opposed to lower echelon civil service judges or magistrates. Judges of the Supreme Court are not civil servants and can only be dismissed by Parliament and are in the constitutional sense independent of the executive. See Dugard, op. cit., 280, for a useful overview of the situation.

132. Op. cit., 289. See note 7 for a quotation.

133. In reply to my charge that the South African press had abdicated its responsibilities to play a critical and creative role vis-à-vis the administration of justice and especially the judiciary, the Natal *Mercury* (August 11, 1978) stated thus:

> The professor, who is nothing if not outspoken, is on his own admission ploughing an exceptionally arid and lonely furrow. Some may regard him as a courageous crusader, while others may feel that the lack of general support for his views provides its own commentary in a society where freedom of speech and the right to criticise are still in a fairly healthy state . . . .
>
> The *Natal Mercury* is content to leave it to its readers to judge the forthrightness and vigour of its comments over the years on legislation in the making and on the Statute Book, as well as on the administration of justice.

134. It would seem that the problem of the informal taboos concerning the administration of justice has so far been raised publicly only by this writer.

135. The country's largest newspaper, *The Star* (May 9, 1978), replied editorially as follows to my public criticism and examples of journalistic abdication vis-à-vis the judiciary:

> It is the press (or at least a section of it) which normally acts as front runner in querying specific decisions, particularly when it comes to seemingly unjust sentences. No doubt it would be a healthy thing if its role could be wider. However, a strictly enforced law on contempt of court gives the bench a high (some would say excessive) degree of

protection. The hard fact remains that judges cannot be treated "no differently from politicians" as the professor suggests.

Where it comes to judicial appointments, or arguable decisions on points of law, we submit that the legal profession and legal academics are the people best qualified to pass informed criticism (although the press, again, would play an indispensable role by acting as vehicle for such comments). Admittedly Professor van Niekerk, who has himself set a spirited example of criticism in the past, did apportion some blame to the academics as well. But his strictures should be addressed to his legal colleagues, more than to the press.

136. Over the last five years or more the government-supporting Afrikaans press has become decidedly more critical of aspects of the reigning sociopolitical order, also on free speech matters.

137. Said the Natal *Witness* of August 11, 1978 concerning the same address that provoked the Natal *Mercury* (see note 130) report: "In criticizing the press for failing – by accepted Western standards – to scrutinise the performance of our judges more energetically, Professor Barend van Niekerk makes little allowance for local circumstances." And said the Durban *Daily News* of August 10, 1978:

[H]is argument was based on the assumption that freedom of speech is a fundamental human right. In some parts of the world this may be so. But there are scores of laws to vitiate that principle in South Africa, as any editor who daily negotiates a web of restrictive legislation knows.

The Natal *Witness* of the same date published the address in full; it has since been reprinted as "Judges and the Law" in *Reality* of November 1978.

138. On some of these aspects concerning race, see Barend van Niekerk, "Sentencing in a Multiracial and Multi-ethnic Society," in *Southern Africa in Need of Law Reform*. These papers were delivered at the Southern African Law Reform Conference Bophuthathswana (1980). See (January 1981) *Reality*.

139. In other words, before the "discovery" of the contempt power in the first *Van Niekerk* case – see note 92 (Ch. 1).

140. *Rand Daily Mail* January 5, 1955. As far back as 1951, the same newspaper displayed the same sensitivity toward the judicial office when it objected to a few remarks on the part of a minister concerning an *obiter* statement of a judge in a politically neutral case. The offending statement, according to the editorial of April 25, 1951 "went so far as to say that the judge's remarks were 'uninformed', 'unjustified', 'uncalled for' and 'most unfortunate' . . . and that it was beyond [the judge's] . . . province to make the statement he had made." Objecting to these statements, although avowing the fact that it is "open to cabinet ministers, as it is open to any member of the public, to criticise a judgment by the courts," the newspaper laid down what it

regarded as the guiding principle for a critic of the judiciary: "[B]ut it is clearly desirable that such criticism should be couched in the most moderate terms and should confine itself to the soundness in law of the decision, or its wisdom from the point of view of the public good."

141. In this context, see note 206 (Ch. 1) concerning the role of the *Rand Daily Mail* as regards the scrutiny of prisons.

142. On a number of occasions, the Johannesburg *Sunday Times* highlighted or criticized the nonappointment of certain judges. A very rare and ingenuous example of criticism of a particular appointment took place in the issue of December 11, 1960. The terse comment, placed below a picture of the appointee, simply reads:

> Mr JS Henning QC, who will become a judge of the Natal Supreme Court next month. Mr Henning, 39, took silk [i.e. became a senior advocate from whose ranks judges are appointed] in February last year. Seven of the other nine Natal QC's are senior to him. They are. . . .

The names of the seven then follow.

143. The appointee was a politician with almost no legal experience.

144. The Natal *Mercury* editorialized on January 18, 1980: "Our present [judicial] system is tried, trusted and widely acclaimed. That is the way it must remain." The virtual deification of the South African judiciary *even in its present shape* reached unprecedented dimensions in 1978 when a particularly courageous judge, sitting as a one-man commission of enquiry, threw the entire government structure into commotion by announcing corruption and malpractices in high government places. But for the high-minded vigilance of one man, Mr. Justice Anton Mostert, this so-called Information Department scandal would undoubtedly not have been brought into the open. The liberal press was especially effusive in its praise, not only of Justice Mostert, but of the *judiciary as a whole*. It was interesting to see that there was no statement of solidarity on the part of his judicial brethren when a few days after his revelations at a press conference he was summarily dismissed by the government as a commissioner. Said the *Rand Daily Mail* of November 3, 1978:

> [I]n the midst of all this sordid mess, at least the status of both the independent press and the independent judiciary has been enhanced. And thanks to these two vital institutions in our society, South Africa may now be saved from the skids of corruption which would have carried it to its destruction like some latter-day Roman Empire.

145. See note 92 (Ch. 1).

146. These press reactions are referred to in (1970) *Acta Juridica* 79.

147. See note 32 (Ch. 1).

148. See the text to note 165.

149. The editor, Mr. Joel Mervis, was undoubtedly the enfant terrible of the journalistic world at the time and was certainly also responsible for the limited scrutiny given to judicial appointments referred to above. During his distinguished editorship of the largest newspaper in South Africa, a considerable amount of attention was given to legal matters generally. Since his retirement, Mr. Mervis has become something of the elder statesman of the journalistic world and has played a most significant part in the defense of free speech. According to well-informed sources, Mr. Mervis often took legal decisions himself without reference to the legal advisers.

150. *Sunday Times* March 28, 1971. The editorial concerned an address by Professor John Dugard in which he had dealt with the judiciary's isolation from criticism. See note 95 (Ch. 1). On the same theme, see John Dugard, *Human Rights and the South African Legal Order*, op. cit., 279.

151. See the text to note 94.

152. Only from the *description* and not from the picture could it be inferred that the beauty queen and her friend were seated "comfortably on a judge's chair in the Supreme Court in Bloemfontein." A telephone call from the acting judge president – the highest judicial officer in the province – produced the following apology (*The Friend* March 1, 1978):

It has been drawn to the attention of the *Friend* that the front-page picture which appeared yesterday, depicting a scene during filming on the set at the Supreme Court, Bloemfontein, could have had the effect of bringing the Supreme Court into disrespect. The *Friend* acknowledges that the use of the picture was regrettable and apologises for any inconvenience or for any unintentional damage caused to the image of the administration of justice.

153. It would seem that my article, "The Uncloistering of the Virtue ...," op. cit., 569 ff, was the first discussion of the topic in South Africa.

154. *The Law and the Press*, op. cit., 15. See note 73.

155. A recent and almost unsurpassable example of a judicial officer's unqualified belief in his profession's own excellence is documented by me in "To Pretoria, Washington and Stock/holm ... With Love. Some Thoughts on a Recent Judicial Pronouncement on the Standing of Our Courts and on Access to Proceedings," in (1980) 97 *SALJ* 389. Incidentally, this article, which can be read and analyzed on its own merits, was rejected for publication by the other major legal periodical in South Africa, the *Tydskrif vir Hedendaagse Romeins-Hollandse Reg.* Cf note 77 (Ch. 2) and the text to note 63.

156. See the text to note 77 (Ch. 2).

157. See note 202 (Ch. 1) concerning this statute. The act penalizes the publication of "any false information" about prisons and prisoners "knowing the same to be false or without taking reasonable steps to verify such information

(the onus of proving that reasonable steps were taken to verify such information being upon the accused)."

158. Section 66A of the Mental Health Act no. 18 of 1973.

159. In 1979, the Police Act was amended to penalize (potentially with a fine of R10,000 and/or five years' imprisonment) "any person who publishes any untrue matter in relation to any action by the Force . . . without reasonable grounds (the onus of proof of which shall rest on such person) for believing that statement is true" (see 27B of Police Act no. 7 of 1958).

160. See Louise Silver, "Criticism of the Police: Standards Enunciated by the Publications Control Board," in (1978) 95 *SALJ* 580.

161. See the text to note 34.

162. For the reference see note 60 (Ch. 1) and note 110 (Ch. 1).

163. Professor Harry Kalven, in "The New York Times Case: A Note on 'The Central Meaning of the First Amendment'," in (1964) 191 *The Supreme Court Review* at 193-94, was of the opinion that the Supreme Court in the *Sullivan* case, "compelled by the political realities of the case to decide it in favor of the *Times*, yet equally compelled to seek high ground in justifying its result, wrote an opinion that may prove to be the best and most important it has ever produced in the realm of freedom of speech."

164. At 291-92.

165. The judgment of the Appellate Division is fully reported as *Pelser* v. *South African Associated Newspapers and Another* 1975 (1) SA 34 (AD). On the judgment in the court, see William L. Church, "Free Speech, Defamation and South Africa: An American Legal View," (Fall 1974) 4 *A Quarterly Journal of Africanist Opinion* 51. See also Dugard, *Human Rights*, op. cit., 179.

166. The offending statement published in the *Sunday Times* of April 15, 1975 reads:

> Two persons of different races commit the same crime and are sentenced to the same punishment by a court of law; yet they are treated differently by the executive on the plea of mercy. One would have expected the Government to save the life of Makinitha to avoid the obvious inference of discrimination; that they did not do so speaks volumes for their lack of concern for justice and the reputation of our law.

167. Although the jurisprudence of the *Sullivan* case was prominently argued, it was not at all alluded to in the Appellate Division judgment. The closest approximation to a jurisprudential statement of the Appellate Division was the following (at 807):

> In my opinion, however, the fact that the Government cannot be defamed, does not assist the defendants in this case. The plaintiff's case . . . is that the article in question is defamatory of him personally, and

not that it is defamatory of the Government and that he, therefore, as a member thereof, has an action for damages.

168. Conservative estimates put the cost of the proceedings had it gone to trial and subsequent appeal at about $150,000.

169. See Helen Silving's *Festscrift* – note 90 (Ch. 1).

170. At 294-95.

171. Cf Bernard Levin's remark (in the text to note 100) concerning Lord Goddard: "Perhaps every country gets the Lord Chief Justice it deserves."

CONCLUSION

1. Learned Hand, "The Spirit of Liberty" (address in 1944) in Dillard, op. cit., 143 at 144.

2. See note 132 (Ch. 3).

3. The Detroit *Free Press* incident (see the text to note 94 [Ch. 4]), with the concomitant lack of understanding in the national media for the important issues involved, is graphically illustrative here, as is the recall of Judge Simonson in Wisconsin – see the text to note 28 (Ch. 4).

4. Cf note 86 (Ch. 4).

5. On the incident, see the New York *Times* of February 6, 1978, "Insurers Sued on Ads about Juries" and of December 11, 1977, "Lawyers Group Contends Insurers Ads Are False." Other advertisements in my possession were headed "What's a Broken Nose Worth Today?"; "Liability Jackpot: And Now, the Big Winners in Today's Lawsuits"; "Everyone is Talking about Insurance Rates and Why They are Skyrocketing. Here are Some Practical Solutions to the Problem." All advertisements, spread out over two pages in *Newsweek* were in impeccably good taste and contained no implicit threat.

6. *Pers en Rechtspraak*, op. cit., 19 ff. See note 191 (Ch. 1) and the text to note 9 (Ch. 4).

7. See the text to note 75 (Ch. 3).

8. See also the comments to note 19 (Ch. 3) concerning access.

9. See the text to notes 206 (Ch. 1) and 157 (Ch. 4).

10. See notes 155 and 156 (Ch. 4).

11. Provisionally reported in 48 *US Law Week* 5008 [1980].

12. Even the problem of the *physical facilities* for the achievement of a meaningful open court may create problems. In the *Newsbriefs* of the State Bar of Michigan of May 1979, the following report appears:

"HALLS OF JUSTICE" NO EMPTY PHRASE – Increase in Federal judges authorized by Omnibus Judgeship Act plus moratorium on building or leasing more federal office space forcing U.S. judges to double up in courtrooms, use makeshift offices.

Two new judges in Baltimore will be housed in library; Miami Federal judges may end up standing in halls, reports Louis J. Komondy, official in charge of Federal court facilities.

Space squeeze also affecting state courts. In Alabama, one district judge has been forced to hold criminal trials outdoors – with crowds of 1,000 watching proceedings – according to *Washington Star.*

13. Provisionally reported in 46 *US Law Week* 4830 [1978]. Now reported as *Houchins* v. *KQED* 438 U.S. 1 [1978].

14. Stated the majority opinion (at 8):

Penal facilities are public institutions which require large amounts of public funds, and their mission is crucial in our criminal justice system. Each person placed in prison becomes, in effect, a ward of the state for whom society assumes broad responsibility. It is equally true that with greater information, the public can more intelligently form opinions about prison conditions. Beyond question, the role of the media is important; acting as the "eyes and ears" of the public, they can be a powerful and constructive force, contributing to remedial action in the conduct of public business.

15. Herewith an extract from the opinion of Justice Stevens (with Justices Brennen and Powell joining) (at 30 and 32):

The preservation of a full and free flow of information to the general public has long been recognized as a core objective of the First Amendment to the Constitution. . . . It is not sufficient, therefore, that the channels of communication be free of governmental restraints. Without some protection for the acquisition of information about the operation of public institutions such as prisons by the public at large, the process of self-governance contemplated by the Framers would be stripped of its substance. . . . While prison officials have an interest in the time and manner of public acquisition of information about the institutions they administer, there is no legitimate, penological justification for concealing from citizens the conditions in which their fellow citizens are being confined.

16. Published by *Aktion Strafvollzug* in Zürich. Difficulties of access to prisoners and especially difficulties of the latter to make their complaints with impunity and efficacy are constant themes of most contributions. Concerning this journal, see the text to note 281 (Ch. 2).

17. See, for instance, the article, "Die Freiheit, die sie meinen. Repression nach der Thorberg-Fernsehsendung," in *Schwarzpeter* June 1976.

18. Speaking about the situation as regards the speech rights of the

inmates of mental institutions in the United States, Lawrence O. Gostin concludes his article, "Freedom of Expression and the Mentally Disordered. Philosophical and Constitutional Perspectives," in (1975) 50 *Notre Dame Lawyer* 419 at 446-47:

> In examining the right of the incarcerated mentally ill to communicate judicial attention has thus far focused on the statutory aspects of the right. The basis for many of these enactments is that communication is necessary to expose cases of wrongful hospitalization. The statutory guarantee of correspondence and visitation is thus often limited to named public officials or attorneys. Simultaneously, where courts have vindicated the right to communicate, they have limited their inquiry to the federal or state constitutional right of *habeas corpus*. This statutory and constitutional treatment of the resident's right to communicate is unnecessarily limited in scope. It protects the resident's right to communicate with his attorney or with officers of the state but does not protect against more pervasive restrictions such as limitations of expression and association with friends and relatives, as well as between residents of the opposite sex. A less restricted reading of the first amendment would insure meaningful communication on a broader front; it has been interpreted in other areas with an adaptability and a sensitivity which should be extended to the problems encountered in mental institutions.

19. The letters were addressed inter alia to lawyers, members of Parliament, officials, public figures, relatives, and friends and related to different subjects, including prison conditions, civil and criminal proceedings, requests for information or help, business transactions, and family problems. See *Communiqué of the Secretary of the European Commission of Human Rights* of February 9, 1978. On the question of the rights of free speech of prisoners, see Gary S. Mobley, "Bans on Interviews with Prisoners. Prisoner and Press Rights after *Pell* and *Saxbe*," in (1975) 9 *University of San Francisco Law Review* 718.

20. See Peter Jenkins, "Punishment too cruel to be condoned," in *The Guardian* (International Weekly edition) June 1, 1980:

> The Home Office and the Prison Service are throwing open their gates to reporters and television cameras in the hope of alerting the public to the true and abominable condition of the prisons and in the more slender hope of making the public care.

On the traditional closed-door policy see note 6 (Ch. 1).

21. I have documented this reality in relation to the situation in South Africa in "Free Speech and Prisons," in (1980) 3 *South African Journal of Criminal Law and Criminology* 209. The crux of my argument here is that the

South African press laid the groundwork and the climate in which the restrictive provisions of the Prisons Act could flourish.

22. Cf note 20 on a dramatic attempt to educate the British public about prisons.

23. Norman Fowler, "Prison Security and Freedom of the British Press," in the *Times* of August 12, 1968, records that a "very senior civil servant" told him that there were "apparently so few journalists who were interested in [prison] policy." Even in South Africa, the widely interpreted secrecy provision of the Prisons Act could have been intelligently circumvented and hollowed out if the media were so inclined by challenging it in a socially and legally defensible case in a division outside the Transvaal, where the precedent of the inhibitive *Rand Daily Mail* judgment does not apply. In any event, after a decade it is well possible that both the prosecuting authorities and a court and ultimately particularly the Appellate Division may show a more enlightened approach than did the particular court in the Transvaal in 1970. On the *Rand Daily Mail* case, see the text to note 157 (Ch. 4).

24. See the text to note 68 (Ch. 1) and the text to note 190 (Ch. 3) concerning the *Lebach* case.

25. See the text to note 63 (Ch. 3). Cf also notes 47 and 48 (Ch. 3) on sub judice cases involving television journalism.

26. See the text to note 183 (Ch. 3). It will be recalled that the case concerned the attempt by a criminal suspect to have a televised reproduction of the crime enjoined in a popular program geared to the solution of unsolved crimes. For a different kind of television case, see the text to note 71 (Ch. 1).

27. In the New York *Times* of February 13, 1979, it was reported that in a "surprise" decision the American Bar Association's House of delegates voted overwhelmingly *not* to support the introduction of television and radio in courts. According to the *Wall Street Journal* of January 7, 1981, twelve states in the United States allow television in the courts.

28. See, for instance, Fred Graham, "Cameras in the Courtroom," in (1978) 64 *American Bar Association Journal* 545; Lawrence W. Burt, "The Case against Courtroom TV," in (July 1976) 12 *Trial* 62; Michael L. Roberts and William R. Goodmann, "The Televised Trial. A Perspective," in (1976) 7 *Cumberland Law Review* 323; Joseph A. Boyd, "Cameras in Court. *Estes* v *Texas* and Florida's One Year Pilot Program," in (1978) 32 *University of Miami Law Review* 815; and Ronald F. Loewen, "Cameras in the Courtroom. A Reconsideration," in (1978) 17 *Washburn Law Journal* 504.

29. Cf. the New York *Times* of April 23, 1980.

30. The president of CBS News, Richard Salant, wrote as follows in the New York *Times* of November 16, 1977:

Dred Scott, Marbury v *Madison, Brown* v *Board of Education of Topeka,* and quite possibly *Bakke* v *University of California* – would public understanding of the great issues involved in those landmark

United States Supreme Court decisions, and of the court itself, have been greater if all Americans had been able to hear and watch the arguments before the court in those cases?

Of course, all Americans who were, are, and will be deeply affected by those decisions would have been better informed. . . .

On the same day that newspapers printed, and television broadcast, pictures of the lines of baseball fans waiting to get Yankee Stadium tickets, they also carried pictures of others waiting in lines outside the Supreme Court to hear the argument in Allan Bakke's case. Those who were able to buy tickets for the World Series could see the whole game, and those who did not get tickets could hear the game, play-by-play, on radio or watch it on television. Those who stood in line at the court were allotted five minutes inside the chambers to hear the arguments, but there was nowhere they could go to hear and see the entire proceedings for themselves. . . .

Powerful and important to our whole democratic system as it is, sometimes shaping the very nature of our society, the United States Supreme Court is an enigma to many Americans – and often an ominous enigma at that. It is time to bring it into the eighth decade of the 20th century. It is time that the American people, who are so deeply affected by these landmark cases, understand just what the grave issues are about.

31. Said Justice Clark for the majority (at 551-52):

It is said that the ever-advancing techniques of public communication and the adjustment of the public to its presence may bring about a change in the effect of telecasting upon the fairness of criminal trials. But we are not dealing here with future developments in the field of electronics. Our judgment cannot be rested on the hypothesis of tomorrow but must take the facts as they are presented today.

32. At 544.

33. One of the first full trials to be televised under the Florida one-year experiment was that of Ronny Zamora on a charge of murder. The major defense of the thirteen-year-old killer was that he was a television addict! See Loewen, op. cit., 506.

34. In the Florida experiment, two exceptions are made as regards the televising of testimony: one involving undercover police informers and the other relocated government witnesses. See Graham, op. cit., 548. An interesting consequence of opening the American courts to television and cameras has been the virtual disappearance of the demand for courtroom artists. See "Growing Camera Access to Courtrooms Provides Competition for Artists Who Sketch for the Media," in the *Wall Street Journal* of January 7, 1981.

35. See Boyd, op. cit., 834 ff, on "The responsibility of the media." There seems to be no possible objection against the televising of *judgments* in important cases.

36. See *Access to Scenes of Crises*. Freedom of Information Center Report no. 28 of April 1969.

37. See *Access to Police Blotters and Reports*. Freedom of Information Center Report no. 27 of January 1969.

38. It will be recalled that the first criminal case concerned an alleged implication by me of racial bias in the imposition of capital punishment, whereas the third case concerned a similar allegation as regards the use of the power of commuting death sentences by the executive. See notes 92 (Ch. 1) and 165 (Ch. 4), respectively.

39. Cf the text to note 105 (Ch. 3), concerning obstructions of justice justifying restrictions.

40. In a passage already quoted in part, the well-known columnist of the New York *Times*, Anthony Lewis, op. cit., 83-84, records that among certain journalists a claim is indeed made to have the right to print everything:

Some members of my profession believe strongly that freedom of the press should be an absolute value in our constitutional order. I have heard them say that the first amendment's protection of the press always outweighs such other interests as the right to privacy, the individual's opportunity to make whole an unfairly damaged reputation, the right to a fair trial. But these interests go to the integrity of the human personality. Any civilized society owes them respect. In an age when perverted technology has found ways to penetrate the secrets of the bedroom ... does one really have to argue that there is value – constitutional value – in the right to be left alone?

41. In terms of the Rehabilitation of Offenders Act in Britain, the offenses of persons cannot be revealed after certain periods of time. Controversy erupted when in December 1977 the *News of the World* published the criminal records of a number of National Front leaders in direct contravention of the Act. It was reported subsequently that there was a move afoot among parliamentarians to withdraw the ban in the case of convicted persons seeking public office. See the *Guardian* of December 12, 1977. See note 108 (Ch. 3).

42. Cf John Hohenberg, *The News Media. A Journalist Looks at His Profession* (1968) 166: "Self-discipline, now and in the future, will be one of the journalist's most necessary qualities if he is to maintain his freedom of action."

43. See note 106 (Ch. 3) and the text there concerning the South African ban on divorce-proceeding details.

44. For a textbook example of such a situation, see the text to note 109 (Ch. 3) where the life of a kidnapped person was impaired by publicity.

45. On the problems of simply getting witnesses to testify, see Les

Ledbetter, "Lack of Witness Protection Poses Problems for Criminal Prosecution," in the *New York Times* of November 14, 1977. In the New York *Times* of September 9, 1977, Howard Blum, "Witness Paying a Price for Federal Protection," paints a frightening picture of the dangers to a particular witness, necessitating around-the-clock protection and the adoption of a new identity. See also the text following note 108 (Ch. 3).

46. By the same token, it may be argued that not every kind of picture ought to be transmissible by the media despite its actual or theoretical relevance to the wider education of the public in legal matters. It may be in this context that one must view the case of *Garrett* v. *Estelle* (U.S. Court of Appeals Fifth Circuit no. 77-1351), where a court turned down a television reporter's application for the filming of an execution for later showing on television. The printing or televising of scenes of particular gruesomeness would fall in this ambit.

47. An interesting variant of this kind of case arose recently as regards a Tennessee judge whose removal was sought by the legislature of the state for using "gutter-type" language in a letter written on official stationery with judicial letterhead to *Hustler* magazine in which he gave "a graphic description of oral sex." See Detroit *Free Press* of April 12, 1978.

48. See the text to note 25 (Ch. 3). At 617 of the judgment.

49. See the text to note 1 (Ch. 1).

Afterword: Freedom of Speech and the Administration of Justice – Recent Developments

INTRODUCTION

If he were alive today, Barend van Niekerk would probably have felt slightly encouraged by recent trends in the area of free speech and the administration of justice. The judiciary and the administration of justice generally are receiving greater attention in legal journals and the lay press. Regrettably, however, many of the old restraints and taboos still loom large. With a few notable exceptions, comment critical of the administration of justice, although appearing with an encouraging frequency, remains polite, restrained, and largely ineffective. Nevertheless, the pioneering work done by Barend van Niekerk has lent encouragement to others to tentatively follow in his footsteps.

In this afterword I intend to discuss recent developments in the area of freedom of speech and the administration of justice in South Africa, Britain, and the United States. Only selected areas of the topic will be dealt with. The emphasis will be on developments in South Africa.

SOUTH AFRICA

Case Law and Legislation

Since the death of Barend van Niekerk, there have been few reported cases that have a bearing on freedom of speech and the administration of justice. The dearth of cases on the subject is indicative of the stifling effect of the judgment in the second Van Niekerk case [S v. *Van Niekerk* 1972(3) SA 711(A)]. The extremely restrictive test for contempt laid down by the Appellate Division in that case has probably caused many commentators to think twice before making pronouncements on matters affecting the administration of justice.

The enforcement of respect for the judicial office reached unprecedented heights in the recent trial of Albertina Sisulu and Thami Mali, both charged with furthering the aims of the outlawed African National Congress. The magistrate presiding at the trial, Mr. J. le Grange, warned spectators to stand up more quickly when he entered or left the courtroom as a delay showed "a certain measure of disrespect" (the *Star* January 21, 1984). In another recent case, the persistent requests of a person charged with a criminal offense to be defended by an attorney were punished as a contempt of court by the Magistrate hearing the case. The conviction was overruled by the Supreme Court as the accused had "replied calmly and courteously, and his only fault lay in his persisting with [his] desire for an attorney after it had been explained to him that no further delay would be countenanced" [per Mullins, J., in *S* v. *Montyi* 1983(2) PH H149(E)].

Although not a decision of a South African court, *S* v. *Hartmann and another* 1984 (1) SA 305 (ZSC) warrants special attention. In this case, the Zimbabwe Supreme Court jettisoned the restrictive and outmoded test for contempt of court laid down in *S* v. *Van Niekerk* (supra). What is of particular interest about the case is that like the *Van Niekerk* case the circumstances giving rise to the charge concerned comments made that had a bearing on legal proceedings.

The appellants, Michael Hartmann and Rhett Gardener, were attorneys retained to represent Air Vice-Marshall Hugh Slatter and Wing Commander Peter Briscoe, both senior officers in the Zimbabwe Air Force. Slatter and Briscoe had been detained on suspicion of being implicated in a serious act of sabotage that had virtually crippled the Zimbabwe Air Force. The appellants had applied to court and obtained an order of access to their clients. Shortly before access was granted, however, Slatter and Briscoe made statements to the police that were confirmed before a magistrate in court. After seeing their clients, the appellants held a press conference attended by journalists mostly representing overseas media. The conference began with the reading of a statement by the appellants detailing the history of their clients' arrests and the application for access. It was alleged that Briscoe and Slatter had been interrogated under conditions of extreme duress, including the use of torture. It was further alleged that the torture allegations were corroborated by medical evidence.

A question-and-answer session followed the reading of the statement. The appellants refused to give details of the torture, stating only that it was psychological as well as physical. At one stage, Hartmann said:

> We are in a society where law and order, and by that I mean the rule of law, is honoured and adhered to and we feel as officers of the Court that, if it comes to our notice that certain personnel have used torture to elicit untruthful, or what our clients say are untruthful, confessions, then we are honour bound to bring that to your notice.

On the basis of the statements made at the press conference, the appellants were charged with contempt of court. It was alleged that these statements were intended to "impair the dignity, repute and authority of a judicial body or to interfere with the administration of justice in the matters of S v Peter Richard Briscoe and Hugh Slatter, matters pending before it." At the trial, Gardener stated that his intention in calling the conference was to prevent a further recurrence of the kind of behavior that had been perpetrated on his clients and to avoid the possibility of the same behavior being meted out to other suspects who were then under arrest or were likely to be arrested.

It is particularly noteworthy that the appellants in the *Hartmann* case as well as Barend van Niekerk were moved to make public pronouncements because of what they perceived to be their duties as lawyers opposed to injustice.

It will be recalled that Van Niekerk's conviction for contempt of court arose out of a speech he made in which he condemned the Terrorism Act as "a negation of what any true lawyer with a basic awareness of decent standards would regard as justice in the accepted sense of the word." At his trial, Van Niekerk's counsel made a statement indicating the basis of his defense, in which he said that

> detention without trial and interrogation of persons detained in solitary confinement are matters of grave public importance on which the fullest opportunities should be available to all persons to express their views, and this applies particularly to lawyers whose views on certain aspects of these matters will in general be more informed than those of others.

Hartmann, Gardener and Van Niekerk belong to that rare breed of lawyers who are not prepared to acquiesce in injustice. For their courage they were charged with contempt of court.

The trial magistrate in the *Hartmann* case, relying on *S* v. *Van Niekerk* (supra), found that the statements made by the accused tended to interfere with or prejudice the administration of justice. He convicted the accused and imposed a fine of $100. When the matter went on appeal, however, both the state and the defense agreed that the test in *S* v. *Van Niekerk* (supra) was wrong and should not be used.

Section 20 of the Declaration of Rights that forms part of the Constitution of Zimbabwe specifically protects the freedom of expression, but nevertheless recognizes that this freedom can be curtailed for the purpose of maintaining the authority and independence of the courts. Georges C. J. expressed the view that the test for contempt laid down in the *Van Niekerk* case (supra) "would make too great an inroad into the right of freedom of expression set out in the Declaration of Rights" (at 311).

After examining recent trends in British law, including the Contempt of Court Act of 1981, the chief justice concluded that the proper test of contempt was "whether there can be said to be a real risk that . . . [the publication] was, likely to prejudice the fair trial of the action discussed" (at 312).

Although the appeal was allowed, the chief justice sounded a note of caution. In 313 E-F, he stated:

> Nothing in this judgement should be taken as casting any doubt on the wisdom of the well-established and long-established custom of lawyers not to discuss in public outside of the courts matters concerning cases in which they are involved. This restraint serves as a useful model to others less knowledgeable or less concerned with the limits of the legally permissible and is in keeping with the spirit which has imbued the practice of the profession and has earned for the administration of justice such respect as it enjoys.

The decision is welcome in restoring a practical and realistic approach to the question of contempt of court. It is hoped, however, that the cautionary note will not inhibit lawyers from speaking out against injustice as and when the occasion arises. Indeed, the administration of justice is done a disservice when lawyers remain silent in the face of iniquity.

The case of *S* v. *Gibson NO* 1979 (4) SA 115(D), although decided when Barend van Niekerk was still alive, is also worthy of special comment. The failure to deal with this case in the main text is probably attributable to the fact that it was reported late in 1979 at a time when the manuscript was at an advanced stage of preparation.

The facts of the case arose out of the publication of an article in the *Sunday Express* in which it was alleged, among other things, that political detainees were being brought to trial without the knowledge of their families or legal representatives. Many detainees who had been tried in these circumstances had received very lengthy sentences of imprisonment. The article further alleged that many detainees, unaware that lawyers had been instructed on their behalf, accepted *pro deo* counsel, that is, lawyers appointed by the court. It was claimed that these lawyers were inadequate for political trials by virtue of their lack of qualifications. The accused were charged with contempt of court on the ground that the allegations contained in the article were "unlawfully calculated to cast suspicion upon the administration of justice in and by the Supreme Court of South Africa and to bring the administration of justice into dispute" (at 119).

In a penetrating and thoughtful judgment, Milne J. pointed out that the article contained no reference to any judge of the Supreme Court and there was no suggestion that any judicial officer had performed his functions inadequately (at 121). He said that the target of the article was the security police. He agreed that "there is a mass of authority that criticism of the police, however vigorous or even unfair, cannot constitute contempt of court, even if it is suggested, in making such criticism, that the consequence of police action has been a failure of justice" (at 122).

The court dismissed the state's contention that there was an indirect attack on the courts in that the article was calculated to inhibit counsel from undertaking *pro deo* defenses. Milne J. thought it

> relevant to bear in mind that the Bar is not a profession of shrinking violets; it is part of the cut and thrust of general practice to encounter sarcastic, sneering and sometimes even insulting or humiliating language from one's opponent or from litigants (at 130 B-C).

The court was confident that, were the article to be read out in a bar common room, "it would not evoke ... a pusillanimous or petulant decision not to appear in *pro deo* cases or to do less than one's duty in such cases" (at 130).

Although the court rejected the submission by the defense that the prosecution was making an undue attempt to interfere with the freedom of the press to comment on the administration of justice, Milne J. warned attorneys-general to be "wary of instituting prosecution for contempt of court lest they have the effect of stifling healthy and legitimate criticism" (at 160). The court was clearly not enamored with the institution of the prosecution, and this was reflected in its approach to balancing the competing claims of freedom of speech and the protection of the administration of justice. It is also significant that on two occasions Mr. Justice Milne referred to Barend van Niekerk's article "The Uncloistering of Virtue," (1978) 95 *SALJ* 362 and 534, which he described as "thought provoking" (at 136).

The application of the common law protection of the esteem and dignity of the courts and judicial officers by means of the contempt weapon has undoubtedly inhibited many commentators from expressing their views on important matters affecting the administration of justice. One could be forgiven for thinking that the courts of law needed no further protection than that afforded by the Appellate Division in the *Van Niekerk* case (supra). Yet, 1982 saw the enactment of one of the most bizarre pieces of legislation designed to give further protection to the courts. Section 2(1) of the Demonstrations in or near Court Buildings Prohibition Act 71 of 1982 prohibits "all demonstrations and gatherings in any building in which a court-room is situated or at any place in the open air within a radius of five hundred meters from such building." Section 1(i) defines "demonstration" as "any demonstration by one or more persons for or against any person, cause, action or failure to take action, and which is connected with or coincides with any court proceedings or the proceedings at any inquest under the Inquests Act."

Among other things, the Act penalizes any person who convenes, organizes, advertises, attends, or takes part in a demonstration. A person so convicted may be liable to a fine not exceeding R1,000 or to imprisonment for a period not exceeding one year or to both such fine and imprisonment.

Where contempt is committed in the face of a court, the matter may be dealt with summarily by the judicial officer to whom the contempt relates. This is a drastic power and has been recognized as such by the courts. Why then was it thought necessary to bolster an existing and drastic common law power with a new statutory offense? The most probable explanation is that the government was dissatisfied with the manner in which judicial officers were exercising their summary jurisdiction to try cases of contempt. It has been stated that political trials tend to evoke a special type of concern (Raymond Suttner, *The Role of the Judiciary in the South African Social Order*, unpublished manuscript [1983] 42):

> People demonstrate (at political trials) because many of those accused of political offences are not regarded merely as individuals but as representatives of organizations or political traditions which often enjoy widespread popular support. It is often argued that these offenders are punished because they have used the only effective, admittedly illegal, means of securing their legitimate rights.

The purpose of the new legislation seems to be aimed primarily at the stifling of any gestures of support for those on trial rather than the protection of the judicial office or the orderly administration of justice. The new statutory powers can operate harshly if the first reported case on the Act, *S* v. *Sithole* 1984 (1) SA 226 (N), is anything to go by. The two appellants were charged under the act with demonstrating within five hundred meters of the Supreme Court building in Pietermaritzburg. They were both convicted by the magistrate who tried the case. The first appellant was sentenced to a fine of R500 or nine months imprisonment, while the second appellant was sentenced to a whipping of five strokes with a light case. An appeal was lodged against both convictions and sentences.

The demonstration giving rise to the charge took place at a time when certain blacks were being tried on charges of high treason and offenses under the Terrorism Act. During lunch time on a particular day of the trial, the appellants and others were alleged to have gathered outside the Supreme Court building. The first appellant was alleged to have said that those on trial were his brothers and that they had recruited people to be sent out of the country for military training to overthrow the government. Following this comment, the second appellant is alleged to have said, "We will shoot them as one." The first appellant then apparently said that the present system was finished, that nothing would stop the blacks as they were already triumphing and that the whole cause of the problem was black education. The first appellant's comments were applauded by the others.

The court of appeal accepted that what had taken place outside the court was a demonstration and that all the elements of the offense had been present. The contention advanced by the defense that the act was aimed at organized rather than spontaneous demonstrations was rejected. The court found that the definition of "demonstration" was not susceptible of distinction between spontaneous and organized demonstrations (at 229). In any event, it was found that appellants' conduct had not been spontaneous (at 229). The convictions were accordingly confirmed but the sentence of a whipping on the second appellant was altered to one of a fine of R100 or 100 days' imprisonment.

The Demonstrations in or near Court Buildings Prohibition Act has further undermined one of the basic premises suggested by Barend van Niekerk underlying the system of freedom of expression in a democratic society, namely, that freedom of speech is a prerequisite for justice and the liberty of the individual. Commenting on this premise, Van Niekerk observed in "The Uncloistering of Virtue," op. cit., 389:

> Allowing an individual – or his supporters – a measure of robust comment in and out of court will, far from undermining the administration of justice redound to its advantage by constituting a kind of crude but psychologically highly effective "appeal" procedure – an appeal, in other words, to the public at large or even to history.

The greatest danger of muzzling the public expression of opinion is that it virtually eliminates peaceful methods for the articulation of dissent. The short-term disadvantages of public embarrassment by displays of solidarity with those involved with political trials are surely outweighed by the advantages derived from a system that permits robust and even outspoken comment on matters affecting the administration of justice.

The Judiciary

In a society where scant respect is accorded to human rights, judges inevitably occupy a controversial position. Although the judiciary cannot be blamed for the enactment of repressive legislative measures by Parliament, judges nevertheless do not simply occupy a position of neutrality. In interpreting statutes, for example, judges undoubtedly have the power to mitigate the harshness of statutory provisions that infringe individual liberties. In the area of subordinate legislation, the Supreme Court enjoys the power to strike down unreasonable and discriminatory enactments, unless the unreasonableness is expressly or implicitly sanctioned by Parliament. From a civil libertarian pe==spective, the performance of the judiciary in the advancement of the cause of human rights in South Africa has, except for a few notable exceptions, proved to be disappointing. Certain judges of the provincial divisions of the Supreme Court, particularly the Natal Provincial Division, have shown themselves both capable and willing to protect the individual from abuses of executive power. The Appellate Division, however, has, for the past twenty-five years, largely shown itself to be executive minded and reluctant to advance the cause of human rights.

The proliferation of harsh legislative enactments has highlighted the role of the judge in an unjust society. It is no longer simply accepted that judges can distance themselves from the laws they are called on to enforce. Questions are increasingly being raised as to the proper course to be followed by a judge with a moral conscience. Notwithstanding the pivotal role that judges play in South African society, they have largely remained immune from criticism. I intend to critically examine the reasons for this immunity and to examine recent trends in comment critical of the judicial function.

Comment critical of the judicial function in the South African context is largely confined to criticism of judicial decisions. Judges, as individuals, tend to enjoy a virtually anonymous existence during their tenure of office. Occasionally after death or retirement, a judge's personal life will be the subject of scrutiny. [See, for example, Edwin Cameron, "Legal Chauvinism, Executive-Mindedness and Justice: L. C. Steyn's Impact on South African Law" (1982) 99 *SALJ* 38; and Ellison Kahn, "Oliver Deneys Schreiner: A South African," in Ellison Kahn (ed.) *Fiat Iustitia: Essays in Memory of Oliver Deneys Schreiner* (1983) 1 ff.] While there exists criticism of judicial decisions in legal journals, this criticism is usually confined to the correctness or otherwise of the decision in question. It is usually couched in sober and temperate terms. Where, however, a judicial decision is criticized as being incorrect, it is, to that limited extent, an implied criticism of the judicial officer himself. Apart from criticism of this nature, the judiciary enjoys a cloistered existence in South Africa. Certain critics have offered strident criticism of judicial decisions. [See, for example, A. S. Mathews, "A Meer Debacle – The Law and Social Gathering" (1982) 99 *SALJ* 1.] Criticism of this nature tends to be the exception to the norm.

Those who have ventured beyond mere criticism of judicial decisions, such as Barend van Niekerk, run the risk of being charged with contempt of court. It has been suggested by Professor Dugard that the first prosecution of Van Niekerk for contempt of court [*S* v. *Van Niekerk* (1970) (3) SA 655(T)], and the resultant rebuke from Claassen J. who tried the case, were "clearly designed to discourage further research into the judicial process, particularly in respect of the influence of race on sentencing policy and practice" [John Dugard, *Human Rights and the South African Legal Order* (1978) 293]. This prosecution arose out of the publication of research conducted by Van Niekerk, which indicated that there was a judicial bias against blacks in the imposition of the death penalty [see (1969) 86 *SALJ* 457; (1970) 87 *SALJ* 60]. On this occasion, Van Niekerk was acquitted for lack of mens rea.

A moment's reflection on the protective barrier that surrounds South African judges will reveal it as being largely unjustified. Judges wield enormous power in South Africa, including the power to impose the death penalty. And let it not be forgotten that South Africa has one of the highest rates of judicial executions in the world. Judges have security of tenure until the age of seventy and may only be removed from office by Parliament on grounds of misbehavior or incapacity. To date, no judge has been removed from office. It has been said that "the procedure for removing a judge from office is so difficult to bring into operation that critics consider that it gives too great security of tenure, making it virtually impossible to terminate the office of one who ought to go" [H. R. Hahlo and E. Kahn, *The South African Legal System and its Background* (1968) 44].

This difficulty has not in any way been alleviated by an unnecessarily restrictive ruling made by the speaker of Parliament. In 1935, a motion of censure on the chief justice, Sir Johannes Wessels, was introduced by Dr. N. J. van der Merwe. It arose out of a comment made by the chief justice while hearing a case in which the Nationalist Party of the Orange Free State had claimed certain funds. The chief justice is reputed to have stated that the court had been established under a monarchical system and added, "you are asking the court to recognise a body, the political purpose of which is to destroy the system." Dr. van der Merwe complained that the impression had been created that the Supreme Court was established to protect a certain political system, namely, the monarchical system and anybody representing a different system would be prejudiced in the eyes of the court. He stated that the chief justice's statement had "occasioned considerable disquiet amongst numbers of people, because the impartiality of our Supreme Court is doubted" (*House of Assembly Debates*, March 11, 1935, cols. 2799-2801).

A ruling by the speaker, Dr. E. G. Jansen, was given two days later. Since the statement complained of was made in the course of the hearing of a case, it was sub judice and could not be discussed. He went on to say that (*House of Assembly Debates*, March 13, 1935, cols. 2943-2945):

> It cannot be doubted that Parliament is entitled to enquire into the manner in which judges fulfil their duties. Such enquiry should, however, not be lightly embarked upon and should in any case be founded upon a clear and definite basis. . . . If . . . the conduct of the judge which is objected to is not of such a nature that he can be dismissed on the ground of misconduct, then I do not think that it would be in the interest of the administration of justice for the House to entertain it. In such a case it should be left to public opinion and to the tact and common sense of the judge in question.

The result of this ruling is that only judicial conduct of sufficient magnitude as to warrant dismissal can be debated in Parliament. The speaker can be forgiven for not anticipating that the law would develop in such a way as to reduce public opinion to an impotent arbiter of judicial propriety.

In exchange for security of tenure, a South African judge is obliged, in terms of the oath of office, to "administer justice to all persons alike without fear, favour or prejudice, and as the circumstances of any particular case may require, in accordance with the law and customs of the Republic of South Africa or the territory of South West Africa" [Section 10(2)(b) of the Supreme Court Act 59 of 1959].

It must surely be self-evident that judges, like other human beings, do in fact have their own fears, favorites, and prejudices. These traits do not simply disappear with the donning of the judicial cloak. It is also surely equally self-evident that judges vary in their ability – there are good judges and thoroughly bad judges. This is a fact of legal life and is not by any means peculiar to the South African legal system. It may be added, however, that the South African system of appointing judges is open to abuse when political factors are allowed to determine judicial positions. It is also striking that in a multiracial country such as South Africa, in which the vast majority of the population is black, the bench is manned exclusively by whites. The term manned is also not inappropriate, for there is only one woman on the bench.

The judicial personality is always a factor to be reckoned with in litigation. Competent practitioners will have regard to all available information concerning the judge before whom they have to appear. They will glean this information from all available sources. Occasionally, they may obtain insight from court decisions, but more often they will consult colleagues who have appeared before the judge in question. Even the reported cases, however, abound with dicta that reveal aspects of the judicial personality. Few practitioners would deny the relevance and importance of the judicial personality. The extent to which personal characteristics influence a judicial decision will vary from judge to judge. The better the judge, the less likely this is to occur. Nevertheless, personal bias does play a part in legal decisions. A striking, and perhaps extreme example is the case of *S* v. *Xhego* 1964 (1) PH H 76(E). The issue to be decided in this case was the admissibility of certain confessions alleged to have been induced by torture. During the course of judgment, Van der Riet A. J. P. said the following:

> The persistency of the evidence of this form of torture was undoubtedly impressive and I hope the Commissioner of Police has satisfied himself that it did not exist. Had the evidence been given by Europeans it might well have prevailed against the single evidence of warrant officer De Beer, for there were many other policemen, one of even higher rank, who were allegedly involved in evidence of assault and of this torture, who gave no evidence in contradiction. But the native, in giving evidence, is so prone to exaggeration that it is often impossible to distinguish the truth from fiction. On the one hand the evidence of this form of torture, persistent as it was, could indicate the genuineness of the complaint, on the other it could show merely a conspiracy. To indicate the guilelessness of the witnesses, for example, they were adamant, when asked, that no-one had ever compared his experience with another while awaiting trial. This is a very common characteristic of the native and only demonstrates the difficulty in arriving at the truth. There are . . . other factors which militate strongly against the acceptance of the allegations of the accused, again resulting largely from the inherent foolishness of the Bantu character.

These dicta reveal an important aspect of the particular judge's racial attitudes. This is not merely a matter of fleeting academic importance. At the time of the decision it ought to have been a matter of outrage. Yet such is the protected position of judiciary that it attracted not so much as a murmur of dissent from academics or practitioners. Fear of a charge of contempt of court may conceivably have been at the root of the ominous silence. Regrettably, instances of apparent racial bias on the part of judges still occur. Even the former chief justice can be accused of racial insensitivity. In *S* v. *Augustine* 1980 (1) SA 503 (A), the accused was a 17-year-old colored youth charged with the murder of a black man, whom he admitted to stabbing in the back. A plea of self-defense was rejected but the trial court found that there could have been a measure of provocation. Rumpff C. J. quoted the trial court's reasoning as follows:

We have come to the conclusion, and I may say the decision of the Court is unanimous on this point, that the version given by the accused might reasonably be true and that there was some element of provocation which provoked him into the action which led to the death of the deceased. Otherwise, as was correctly stressed by Mr Irwin, this would have been the action of a madman because he was sober, there was no evidence of misuse of drink or dagga [marijuana], and in effect if the Court were to accept Rohan's evidence it means that without provocation he simply stabbed this man for an unknown reason.

This eminently sensible approach was met with an extraordinary retort by the chief justice. He stated that it was clear that "the advocate for the defence and the trial court had not yet encountered the experience that Coloureds and Blacks sometimes stab people for no apparent reason other than a type of stabbing lust" (free translation by the present writer). It is extremely alarming that attitudes of this sort should be expressed by the country's highest judicial officer. The administration of justice is done a disservice and is brought into disrepute when judges are allowed to get away with such behavior. If confidence in the courts is to be retained, racial prejudice coming from the mouths of judges should be condemned without reservation.

In the trial court in the second *Van Niekerk* case, [*S* v. *Van Niekerk*, 1972 (1) PH H19], the role of the judge was explained by Fannin J. in the following terms:

The functions of a judge include the duty to do justice between man and man "without prejudice", and it is vitally important that all men should know that they can expect that they will be judged without prejudice on the part of judicial officers. . . . Judges have to do justice between all sorts and conditions of men, of all political, religious and other points of view.

As a statement of the theoretical foundations of the requirement that judges are required to do justice, few people would quibble with this view. But what if practice belies the theory, as it so shockingly did in the *Xhego* case? Is the public and the profession to remain silent in the face of such appalling racial bigotry? The respect we accord to judges is not simply deference to their status. It is respect that is accorded in exchange for the guarantee that they will "administer justice to all persons alike without fear, favour or prejudice." If they do not do so, they do not fulfill the requirements of their office and they accordingly forfeit the respect due to them. Compliance with the judicial oath is the very least that we demand of judges. In addition, we demand the highest standards of competence and basic courtesy. Every practitioner knows that certain judges are more blessed with these qualities than others. Yet critical assessment of judicial behavior in court beyond criticism of decided cases is virtually unheard of in South Africa.

But should this be so? In principle, no one who exercises power of whatever nature should ever be immune from public criticism. This is recognized to some extent by South African courts in respect of that species of contempt of court known as scandalizing the court.

The administration of justice is not per se threatened by comment critical of judges. Kotzé J. in *In re Phelan*, (1877) Kotzé 5 at 9, stated the following:

> Although no scandalous or improper reflection of the administration of justice can be allowed, everyone is undoubtedly at liberty to criticize the conduct of judges on the bench in a fair and legitimate manner. It is only when the bounds of moderation and of fair and legitimate criticism have been exceeded that the court has power to interfere.

In the second *Van Niekerk* case [*S v. Van Niekerk* 1972 (3) SA 711(A)], Ogilvie-Thompson C. J. made two important observations:

> First, it is important to bear in mind that the "true basis" of punishment for contempt of court lies in the interests of the public, as distinct from the protection of any particular judge or judges.... Secondly, unless those last mentioned interests clearly so require, genuine criticism, even though it be somewhat emphatically or unhappily expressed, should, in my opinion ... preferably be regarded as an exercise of the right of free speech rather than as scandalous comment falling within the ambit of the crime of contempt of court.

These views require closer scrutiny. If Ogilvie-Thompson C. J. is correct in stating that the "true basis" of punishment for scandalizing the court lies in the interests of the public, then it is fundamental to establish precisely what the public interest requires. In *R v. Torch Printing and Publishing Co (Pty) Ltd* 1956 (1) SA 815 (C), Ogilvie-Thompson J. dealt at greater length with this notion of the public interest. He suggested that punishment for contempt is imposed in the interests of the public and not for the benefit of the injured judge (at 820).

In similar vein, Claassen J. in the first *Van Niekerk* case (supra) cited with approval the following dictum from *R v. Davies* (1906) 1 KB 32 at 40:

> The real offence is the wrong done to the public by weakening the authority and influence of a tribunal which exists for their good alone.... Attacks upon judges ... excite in the minds of people a general dissatisfaction with all judicial determinations ... and whenever men's allegiance to the laws is so fundamentally shaken, it is the most fatal and dangerous obstruction to justice, and in my opinion

calls out for a more rapid and immediate redress than any other obstruction whatsoever: not for the sake of the judges as private individuals but because they are channels by which the King's justice is conveyed to the people. To be impartial and to be universally thought so are both absolutely necessary for giving justice that free open and unimpaired current which it has for many ages found all over this kingdom.

Claassen J. after considering Van Niekerk's research, expressed the view that, if the reader accepted the views set out in the article, "he could possibly hold the judges and administration of justice in low esteem." As the article apparently included all judges, it was possible that "judges could no longer be treated with due respect for they could no longer be universally thought of as impartial." In the circumstances, the article could be construed as an "attack, not on a single judge or court, but on judges and the superior courts generally with the consequence that it might have been a contempt of court" (at 659).

It seems, then, that the public interest protected by punishment for contempt of court is the need to ensure public confidence in the courts and the dispensation of justice in an impartial manner. No doubt it is desirable for the public to display confidence in the courts, but this is a confidence that must be deserved. If judges behave in a manner that inspires little or no confidence in the administration of justice, public respect is forfeited. This is why research into the performance of judges is of such cardinal importance to the administration of justice. It ensures that judicial behavior is continually under the spotlight and that abuses are exposed. Judges who are aware that their performances are being monitored by professionals are less likely to abuse their power. Notwithstanding the ruling made by the speaker in 1935, Parliament could, if it so desired, exercise an important role in monitoring judicial behavior. It has been suggested of the English practice that [Shimon Shetreet, *Judges on Trial* (1976) 165-66]:

[t]here is overwhelming evidence that in practice Parliament exercizes control over judges short of an address for removal, by criticism, censure and condemnation. Censure is passed in the course of debates upon motions for resolutions criticising the conduct of a particular judge or the judicial decision in a particular case. Parliamentary questions on the conduct of judges, in general and on particular cases, have also been a very effective device. Criticism of individual judges and the judiciary as a whole has likewise been voiced in the course of the debates on Bills and Orders relating to judges.

These devices have not yet been utilized by the South African Parliament. On the contrary, Parliament has frequently been used as the forum for lavish praise of the judiciary.

Cases in which judges display a deliberate partiality are happily rare, although it is reasonable to assume that they do occur. But deliberate partiality is not the only problem. Subconscious partiality is probably more dangerous. Therein lies the importance of Van Niekerk's research on judicial bias in relation to the imposition of the death penalty. The results of his empirical study were horrifying to those who believe in judicial impartiality. The solution, however, did not lie in a prosecution for contempt of court. As Lord Denning M. R. has put it, "silence is not an option when things are ill done" [*R* v. *Commissioner of Police of the Metropolis, ex parte Blackburn* (1968) 2 QB 150 at 155]. Research on judicial bias is of inestimable value, if for no other reason than it serves as a reminder to judges not to be influenced by improper considerations. It has been stated that [Jerome Frank, *Law and the Modern Mind* 2 ed (1949) 138]: "[t]he honest, well-trained judge with the completest possible knowledge of the character of his powers and of his own prejudices and weaknesses is the best guarantee of justice."

South African judges are quick to point out that it is not their intention to stifle all criticism of the judiciary. Claassen J. in the first *Van Niekerk* case [*S* v. *Van Niekerk* (supra) at 657] cited the famous dictum of Lord Atkin in *Ambard* v. *The Attorney General of Trinidad and Tobago,* (1936) AC 322 (PC) at 335: "Justice is not a cloistered virtue: she must be allowed to suffer scrutiny and respectful, even though outspoken comments of ordinary men." Claassen J. went on to say that "such criticism is necessary and in the public interest" (at 657). Notwithstanding the professed commitment to freedom of speech, it is clear that not all criticism of the judiciary will be permitted. Much depends on the manner in which the criticism is presented. "Genuine criticism" is permissible, even though it be "emphatically or unhappily expressed" [per Ogilvie-Thompson C. J. in *S* v. *Van Niekerk* 1972 (3) SA 711(A) at 72]. In similar vein, Claassen J. accepted that "reasonable criticism" would be permissible (at 567).

J. R. L. Milton has drawn a distinction between criticism relating to judicial competence and criticism relating to judicial impartiality. He notes that in the latter case there is a "noticeable reluctance, if not absolute refusal," to recognize a right to criticize. He goes on to call for a reassessment of this attitude since, "in principle, there must be right in the public to comment publicly on instances of judicial bias, apparent or real, and whether relating to personal, political, racial or social factors, and that such comment should not be regarded as *per se* wrongful or in contempt" [J. R. L. Milton, "A Cloistered Virtue?" (1970) 87 *SALJ* 426]. The author, however, in making these welcome comments, goes on to add that

> there will, of course, be obvious and necessary limits on the extent of such a right to comment. Basically these must be that the comment must be bona fide and reasonable, and made in temperate and proper terms, and expressed for the advancement or interest of the better administration of justice.

More recently, Chief Justice Rabie has expressed himself in similar terms. After expressing concern that certain critics have gone so far as to question the impartiality and honesty of judges, he went on to suggest that these critics would have a greater impact if they expressed themselves courteously (P. J. Rabie, "Regbank en Akademie" 1983 *De Jure* 21).

The notion that criticism is permissible only when it is expressed in fair and temperate terms requires closer analysis. Why there should be this special restriction when it comes to criticism of judges is not immediately clear. After all, if criticism degenerates into an attack on personality, a judge, like anybody else, has his remedy, for instance, in the law of defamation. Should judges, therefore, enjoy further protection over and above others in positions of power? It surely cannot be seriously contended that confidence in courts will be promoted if special rules apply to limit criticism of judges. On the contrary, it is likely that confidence in the courts will be undermined if the usual rules are not allowed to apply. Dr. Paul O'Higgins has noted in this regard that [P. O'Higgins, *Censorship in Britain* (1972) 161]:

> it is the very essence of responsibility, which is so often invoked to stifle effective criticism. Judges welcome responsible criticism, and responsible criticism is not contempt. The sober and responsible discussion of the foundations of Christian belief does not constitute blasphemy. But this approach stifles those who are beginning to think critically. Institutionalized, it becomes the old-boy network, which plays such a vital and sometimes unconscious role in ensuring that criticism of the established order should be simultaneously responsible, muted and ineffective.

It might be added that in the area of freedom of expression judicial officers already enjoy special protection. In the first place, judicial officers have a particularly wide latitude of freedom of expression within the course and scope of their official functions. In *May* v. *Udwin* 1981(1) SA 1(A) at 19, Joubert J. A. stated that "public interest in the due administration of justice requires that a judicial officer, in the exercise of his judicial functions, should be able to speak his mind freely without fear of incurring liability for damages for defamation." Although comments by judicial officers in the course of legal proceedings are not protected by an absolute privilege, a litigant or witness who is defamed by a judge may institute action only with leave of the Supreme Court [Section 25(1) of the Supreme Court Act 59 of 1959].

It has been held to be "contrary to public policy to allow a judge to be examined and cross-examined with reference not to facts but to his performance of his judicial duties" (per Mason J. in *Ex parte Wolpert* 1917 WLD 98).

Even if an application for leave to sue a judge for defamation is granted, a plaintiff will face the further obstacle of rebutting the presumption that a judicial officer who defames another in the exercise of his judicial authority does so lawfully within the limits of his authority.

It is not suggested that either the rebuttable presumption of the lawfulness of defamatory remarks made by judicial officers in the exercise of their powers or the requirement that judges may be sued only with leave are necessarily objectionable. They are, however, illustrative of the special protections that surround judicial officers over and above the weapon of contempt. It is sometimes suggested that judges are precluded from replying to adverse criticism by virtue of the nature of their office. To this there are at least two replies. Lord Denning M. R., after noting this convention of judicial silence, said that judges must "rely on (their) conduct itself to be its own vindication" [the *Blackburn* case (supra) at 155]. Second, David Pannick has suggested that there is nothing, apart from tradition, to prevent a judge from replying to criticism that he believes to be unfair or ill informed [David Pannick, in a review of *And Nothing But the Truth* (1983) by Alan King–Hamilton Q. C. in *The Listener* 17 March 1983 p. 21 (Vol. 109 no. 2803)]. It is particularly ironic that, notwithstanding the tradition of silence in the face of adversity, certain judges have seen fit to indulge in extravagant praise of the judiciary with apparent insensitivity to the self-congratulatory nature of such praise [see the remarks of Claassen J. in (1970) 87 *SALJ* 25; Curlewis J. in *S v. Mothopeng* 1979 (4) SA 367(T); and Klopper J. in (1983) *De Rebus* 4].

As the bearers of enormous power, judges do not warrant special protection from criticism, whether concerning their competence or their partiality. Notions such as the "public interest" or "fair and legitimate criticism" should not be employed as subterfuges to protect the judiciary. On the contrary, judges should be continually exposed to the public glare and the judgment of professionals. Research such as that conducted by Barend van Niekerk should therefore not only be welcomed but actively encouraged as one possible method of checking the potential abuse of power.

Judges and Unjust Laws

Any judge who accepts an appointment to the Supreme Court is confronted with the dilemma of the extent to which he will be associated with the laws he is called upon to enforce. For the judge with a moral conscience this is a factor which he must weigh before accepting his appointment. The decision to accept a judicial appointment, while fundamentally a personal decision, cannot simply be viewed in isolation. The extent to which a judge is perceived by the general public to be associated with the injustice of the system he represents is also a factor to be weighed in the general equation. In South Africa, it would not be unfair to observe that there exists a tradition of silence in the face of legislative oppression. A handful of judges have shown themselves willing in the course of their judgments to condemn legislative enactments that infringe on individual liberties. The majority, however, remain silent. When it comes to extracurial comment, very few judges are willing to make public pronouncements on matters affecting human rights. In 1971, Chief Justice Ogilvie-Thompson, stated that "the expression in public, and in particular in the press or other media, by judges of opinions on controversial issues, whether or not such issues have political overtones, is to be deprecated" [(1972) 89 *SALJ* at 32]. As far as the judiciary is concerned, this is the common wisdom. Thankfully, there are some exceptions to this belief.

Mr. Justice Didcott of the Natal Provincial Division is one of those judges who never loses an opportunity, whether in or out of court, to express his views on the racially oppressive nature of many of South Africa's laws. His comments in a recent decision confirming the interpretation of Section 29 of the Blacks (Urban Areas) Consolidation Act 25 of 1945 are typical. The section in question is one of the most notorious of the laws of apartheid. It authorizes the arrest of any black person thought to be "idle or undesirable." The Act defines an "idle person" as, inter alia, a black person who though capable of being employed is not lawfully employed and for a period or for periods in the aggregate of not less than 122 days during the preceding twelve months, has not been lawfully employed and is not bona fide engaged in any business, trade, profession, or other remunerative activity for which he is in terms of any law licensed or registered. A person so arrested is obliged, in terms of the Act, to be brought before a commissioner and to "give a good and satisfactory account of himself." Commenting on this provision, Mr. Justice Didcott said the following [*In re Duma* 1983 (4) SA 469 (N) at 475-76]:

> A number of judgements delivered by the Supreme Court over the years have called Section 29 drastic in its general effect. That seems the least which can be said of it. One has only to read it to feel this. Its harshness is foreign to the idea, cherished by lawyers everywhere, that the law's business is first and foremost to protect the liberties of the individual, that the safety of the public rests largely on the law's success in doing so. No counterpart, nothing at all similar, can be found in any system of jurisprudence with which we would like ours to be compared. The Section has been amended from time to time, on some occasions in apparent reaction to judicial interpretations of it curbing undue exuberance in its enforcement. The amendments have not relaxed its provisions. Instead these have got progressively tighter. The current version is the toughest yet. There is little our courts can do about legislation of this kind. They can make their distaste for such known, for what that may be worth. It is not a great deal. Parliament seldom takes notice once some policy it considers important is involved.

The attitude displayed by Mr. Justice Didcott is unquestionably the exception to the rule. South African judges have by and large lost many an opportunity to express their distaste for legislative enactments that encroach on individual liberty. Nowhere is this more evident than in the field of security legislation. In a seminal article, Professor Matthews and R. C. Albino expressed the view that "in recent years courts have interpreted laws which have cried out for one of those resounding defences of individual liberty and the dignified and majestic language in which judges sometimes speak, but opportunity has been passed by" [A. S. Matthews and R. C. Albino, "The Permanence of the Temporary" (1966) 83 *SALJ* 16].

A handful of judges have seemingly come to realize the importance of public comment on the nature of law in an unjust society. A noteworthy example was the address by Mr. Justice M. M. Corbett to the First International Conference on Human Rights in South Africa. As a judge of appeal, his contribution was the more significant. In the course of a thoughtful address he made some important observations about the curtailment of civil liberties in South Africa [M. M. Corbett, "Human Rights: The Road Ahead" (1979) 96 *SALJ* 192 at 195]:

> Turning to the contemporary scene in South Africa, one cannot avoid the conclusion that in many areas the freedom of the individual and his basic human rights have been severely curtailed. This is particularly evident in regard to such matters as the freedom of movement, equality of treatment, equality of opportunity, freedom of association, freedom from detention and arrest except by due process of law (and here I have in mind the various laws aimed at maintaining the safety and security of the State) and to some extent freedom of speech and assembly. . . . Among the questions we, as South Africans, will have to ask ourselves are whether such curtailment actually promotes the common weal, to what extent dangers, internal and external, justify extraordinary measures and arbitrary powers intruding upon the liberty of the subject; to what extent these dangers are not the product of our own socio-political system; to what extent the risk of injustice or of abuse can be and is being obviated, by checks and controls; whether society can accept measures, normally regarded as temporary expedients in a time of crisis, as a more or less permanent feature of its pattern of life; and to what extent we do not tend in much of our thinking on the subject to identify the interests of South Africa with the interests of the white group in South Africa.

Although resignation is always open to a judge who cannot in good conscience comply with the terms of his oath of office, no South African judge has openly opted for resignation on this account. As already pointed out, however, some judges have taken the opportunity of voicing their distaste to laws that infringe individual liberty. Traditionally, the call has been for judges to make their protest known but not to resign. Professor Dugard, for example, one of the foremost proponents of the liberal legal tradition, has advocated the view that judges should express their views on legislation that runs counter to accepted legal principles. This option is to be preferred to resignation and is one "that accords more with the responsible position he occupies in society" (John Dugard, *Human Rights and the South African Legal Order* 384). A different view was expressed by the Civil Rights League, which suggested that "resignations on grounds of conscience may, looked at retrospectively ... be seen as the sparks which kept alight a fundamental belief in the best traditions of our Western legal heritage" ("Responsibility of Judges in Applying Unjust Laws in South Africa," *South African Outlook*, January 1981, 8).

Recently, the question of the position of a judge in an unjust legal system has received considerable impetus by the debate that arose from the publication of the inaugural lecture of Professor Raymond Wacks, who has been appointed to the Chair previously held by Barend van Niekerk. The significance of Professor Wacks's contribution was his strident call for judges of conscience to resign [Raymond Wacks, *Judges and Injustice* (1983) University of Natal Press, 16]:

> If a judge is to square his conscience with his calling, there would appear to be no choice open to him but to resign. How have I arrived at this conclusion? First, by rejecting the positivist assumption that judges have discretion in the strong sense. Secondly, by recognizing that South Africa conforms in many ways to the model of a repressive legal system. Thirdly, by accepting that a judge in such a system who is unable to reconcile his moral standpoint with the law has three choices: to protest, to lie or to resign. And fourthly (by expressing doubts as to whether protests would bear fruit, and by pointing to the limitations of the judicial lie – caused principally by the severe restraints of the courts' jurisdiction) concluding that there is no compelling alternative to resignation.

Later in his address, Wacks argued that resignation could have a considerable impact [Raymond Wacks, op. cit., 18]:

> A resignation would be a clarion call: a statement of judicial despair and outrage. It would be an assertion of the judge's absolute fidelity to justice, of protest against the abuse of law. In a repressive legal order it would constitute an act of faith in the face of unconscionable legislation.

It is not intended here to canvass all the arguments and counterarguments that were generated by Wacks's thesis. However, Wacks's central proposition, namely that judges lend legitimacy to an unjust system, was strongly refuted, by, among others, Mr. Justice Didcott. He argued that [Mr. Justice J. M. Didcott, Address to the Graduation Ceremony of the University of Natal, April 22, 1983, *Lawyers for Human Rights* Bulletin no. 3, January 1984, 23]:

> there must be something wrong with a proposition which postulates an unjust society, then denies those with the will and ability to improve it such obvious opportunities for doing so. . . . What would be the consequences of resigning from one's post or declining to take it up? Such, it has been suggested, might be a fine protest. I beg to doubt that it would have much effect. The effect, were there any, would moreover be temporary. It would soon dissipate. More certain, and certainly more lasting, would be a different consequence. I mean one's replacement by somebody with no qualms about the injustice which had troubled one.

The Commission of Inquiry into the Structure and Functioning of the Courts

In recent years, the position of the judiciary in the South African legal order has come increasingly under the spotlight. Of particular importance is the publication of the final report of the Commission of Inquiry into the Structure and Functioning of the Courts (hereafter referred to as the Hoexter Commission RP 78/1983).

The idea of an independent judiciary has been sedulously fostered by successive governments. It is argued that regardless of the many shortcomings of government, the judiciary has remained untainted by the racially oppressive policy of the National Party government. This has, of course, been wishful thinking. Regrettably, the once-shining reputation of South African courts of law has been tainted by political appointments to the bench. Already in 1968, the International Commission of Jurists made the following observation concerning the South African judiciary [*Erosion of the Rule of Law in South Africa*, International Commission of Jurists (1968)]:

> In spite of a number of courageous decisions at first instance, the overall impression is of a judiciary as "establishment-minded" as the executive, prepared to adopt an interpretation that will facilitate the executive's task rather than defend the liberty of the subject and uphold the Rule of Law.

To say that an independent judiciary is the cornerstone of a sound legal system is to state the obvious. It is equally trite to contend that to achieve the goal of an independent judiciary only the most able and dedicated people should be elevated to the bench. For the past thirty years or more, there has been an alarming tendency on the part of the executive to appoint judicial officers for political reasons. Occasionally, appointments of this nature have provoked adverse critical comment but by and large the organized legal profession has remained ominously silent. In an important public address, a senior member of the Johannesburg bar recently spoke out forcefully on the topic of political appointments to the bench. In an address to the University of the Witwatersrand, Advocate Sydney Kentridge S. C. made the following observations [Sydney Kentridge, "Telling the Truth about Law" (1982) 99 *SALJ* 648 at 652]:

> [It] must be said that over the past thirty years political factors have been placed before merit not only in appointments to the bench but in promotions to the Appeal Court. This has undoubtably lead in many cases to better qualified men being passed over in favour of others less worthy of appointment or promotion. And it must also be said over the past thirty years a number of appointments to the Supreme Court and enough number of judicial promotions have been made which are explicable solely on the ground of the political views and connections of the appointees and on no other conceivable ground. Fortunately, such blatant political appointments have constituted a small minority of the bench. But there have been enough of them to cause disquiet, especially as this tendency has clearly not yet ceased. Most lawyers know this but do not often publicly discuss it. Some would say that it is best not to talk about these things, because to do so impairs the dignity and reputation of the Supreme Court. I would say just the opposite. It is these appointments which in fact endanger the standing of the Supreme Court. If we truly value that institution for what it is (and not merely because it has a certain image which it is convenient to maintain), these appointments should not be allowed to go unnoticed. . . . I believe that it would be a proper function not only of Bar Councils but of law journals published by university faculties of law to scrutinize the pattern of judicial appointments and, when necessary in the public interests, to comment on them. The knowledge that unworthy appointments will not pass without adverse comment is the best, perhaps the only, protection against them.

Advocate Kentridge was articulating the views and fears held by many. The public expression of such views was, however, of considerable importance particularly when expressed by a senior and respected member of the profession. At around the same time that Advocate Kentridge delivered his speech, John Dugard also made known in public some alarming research findings. In an address to the University of Natal, Professor Dugard revealed the findings of his research into the selection of judges who try cases under the security laws. In a study of security trials held in the Transvaal between 1978 and 1982, there were some twenty-five trials of persons charged with treason, terrorism, sabotage, or serious offenses under the Internal Security Act. His research revealed that about 17 percent of the Transvaal judiciary heard 84 percent of the cases in question. Commenting on these findings, he observed [John Dugard, "The Judiciary and National Security" (1982) 99 *SALJ* 655 at 658]:

> both the public and members of legal profession are deeply troubled by the allocation of certain judges to such trials. . . more important, there is no evidence to suggest that the judges who have heard political trials enjoy any greater expertise on the subject then those who have been overlooked. On the contrary, several of the judges so overlooked did have some experience in this field of law, both as counsel for the state and for the accused – before their appointment to the bench.

Professor Dugard's research as well as the views expressed by Advocate Kentridge were presented to the Hoexter Commission. The commission accepted that "in the assessment of possible candidates for elevation to the Supreme Court bench, individual merit has not always been the decisive factor. Judicial appointments sometimes betray an element of arbritrariness" (p. 59, paragraph 1.3.2). Commenting specifically on Advocate Kentridge's allegations of political appointments to the bench, the commission stated that "it is prejudicial alike to the efficient administration of justice, the image of the bench and public confidence if the manner in which the judges are appointed leaves any room for gossip about the independence of those who are elevated to the bench" (p. 60, paragraph 1.3.5). The commission obviously took Advocate Kentridge's comments to heart because it recommended that judicial appointments should no longer simply be left to the state president acting on the advice of the minister of justice (p. 36, paragraph 4.2.1).

With regard to Professor Dugard's submissions on the selection of judges for political trials, one would have thought that his findings cried out for an explanation. In fact, the commission submitted full details of Professor Dugard's research to the judge president of the Transvaal and requested him to furnish the commission with comments on the matter. No comments were forthcoming (p. 64, paragraph 1.3.8.2). The failure of the judge president to comment on Professor Dugard's submissions can only undermine public confidence in the method of selection of judges for particular cases. In the absence of an explanation, the commission was not able to make any final findings on Professor Dugard's research. Nevertheless, the commission was constrained to observe that [pp. 64-65, paragraph 1.3.8.4]:

> It is vitally important that the general public should have confidence that our courts will maintain absolute impartiality at all times and especially in cases involving subject and State. Judges should guard against a belief that those exalted notions regarding the administration of justice which they themselves may cherish are shared by the general

public. The latter, as the evidence before this Commission repeatedly showed, often regard the administration of justice with a jaundiced and even cynical eye. Confidence in the law is a fragile plant. Any noticeable tendency for only certain judges to be assigned to preside at criminal trials involving the security of the State would run counter to the proud tradition of our administration of justice; it would debase the judicial office and inevitably breed suspicion and disquiet.

The commission accordingly recommended that [p. 65, paragraph 1.3.8.5]:

in the assignment of judges to preside at sensitive criminal trials, it is in the interests of the proper administration of justice that, so far as may be practicable, an attempt should be made to achieve an even distribution of such work among all available judges.

It is commonly assumed that one of the reasons for the refusal of appointments to the Supreme Court bench is the comparatively poor remuneration of judges. The Johannesburg Bar Council submitted a memorandum to the Hoexter Commission in which it pointed out that the unavailability of the senior counsel for appointments to the bench is not only because of the inadequate salary. In its memorandum, the bar council mentioned other reasons that make practitioners reluctant to accept judicial appointment. These included the "necessity to impose death penalties," the existence of provisions regarding criminal procedure that effectively preclude proper investigation by the court, and a feeling that judicial appointments were not made on merit (p. 69, paragraph 1.3.11.5).

For reasons that were not stated, the Hoexter Commission decided not to examine the validity and cogency of the various grounds for refusing judicial appointments indicated in the memorandum (p. 70, paragraph 1.3.11.5). Nevertheless, the commission made the following observation [p. 71, paragraph 1.3.11.8]:

It calls for no great prophetic gift . . . to see that the Bar will remain the primary source of judicial appointments in the future only for so long as the eminent silks are prepared – as in the past their conscientious predecessors at the Bar were prepared – to make the sacrifices which appointment to the Bench demands. If ever the judiciary in South Africa should lose its independence, the country will have lost, never to regain, an asset beyond price. In the light of this inescapable reality it would be short-sighted for the Bar to parade too piously too many reasons for declining judicial appointment.

For the commission to reject as pious the reasons for declining judicial appointment advanced by the Johannesburg Bar Council was unfortunate. In a far-ranging inquiry, one would have thought it incumbent on the commission to take seriously what senior advocates perceived to be problems in participating in a repressive legal system. It is regrettable that an important opportunity was lost to investigate fully the important factors outlined in the memorandum of the Johannesburg Bar Council.

The Press

It is a misnomer to talk of a free press in South Africa. It is true that one encounters vigorous and often vituperative criticism of the government in the opposition press. That, however, is a dangerous and misleading index of press freedom. A more appropriate index is to pay attention to what does not appear in the press, because of the many statutory provisions restricting press freedom. Some of the most important institutions of society, the police, the prisons, and the defense force, enjoy a virtually anonymous existence because of statutes curbing disclosure of their activities. But what of comment relevant to the administration of justice? Save for those exceptional cases where trials are heard in camera, the press is free to report on the proceedings in courts of law. The press must of course keep an ever-vigilant eye on the law of contempt.

By and large, it would not be unfair to say that the South African press has sought out the most sensational trials and given them widespread coverage. Often, important trials that have a bearing on the liberty of the individual have been all but ignored at the expense of the more sensational and gory high society murders. That is not to say that the press has ignored human rights issues but that the record of the opposition press in this regard has been somewhat patchy. In this section, certain general observations will be made concerning the conduct of the press in relation to coverage of matters affecting the administration of justice.

When carrying reports of persons arrested on suspicion of committing offenses, the press is generally astute to ensure that no comments are made that are suggestive of the arrested person's guilt. This is as it should be. However, a different set of standards seems to apply in relation to the arrest of persons suspected of engaging in the activities of the African National Congress. It is by no means uncommon for the press to publish the verbatim statement of a spokesman for the South African Police in which the guilt of the arrested person is a foregone conclusion. Statements emanating from the police often refer to "the arrest of a prominent ANC member" (see, for example, the *Rand Daily Mail* December 12, 1983 and *The Star* December 16, 1983). The mere fact that these newspapers are carrying the verbatim reports of senior police officers does not make this practice any less offensive. Those detained under the security laws are at a tremendous disadvantage, being denied access to their legal advisers, family, and friends. These people are invariably detained in solitary confinement for lengthy periods. Security detainees, even if not mentioned by name, are done an immense disservice if they are convicted by the police and the press before they reach a court of law.

Obviously, not every story can be given front page prominence by the press. Newspaper editors have to make important decisions as to which stories are relegated to the middle pages. In this regard, sensationalism often tends to be the overriding criterion. For example, most of the English newspapers regarded the death of an escaped fugitive from justice, Andre Stander, as being of greater importance than the trial of Sergeant Van As, who was charged with the murder of a security detainee, Paris Malatji. The trial and subsequent conviction of Van As for culpable homicide was a landmark legal case. It was the first time that a security policeman had been found responsible for a death in detention. The trial was given some prominence but not the sort of prominence one might have expected for a case of such importance.

An alarming and potentially dangerous feature of the South African press is the emergence of special editions of newspapers aimed at black readers. This phenomenon has given rise to a situation where the black editions carry items of news that do not appear in the white editions and vice versa. A form of press apartheid has thus come into being in South Africa. What is particularly distressing is that the opposition press is the worst offender. Both the *Rand Daily Mail* and the *Star*, purportedly liberal newspapers, have special editions for black readers. The black edition of the *Rand Daily Mail* appears as the *Rand Daily Mail Extra* and the black edition of the *Star* appears as *The Star Africa*.

A comparison of the black and white editions of these newspapers on any given day yields startling results. Certain items of news that appear in one edition make no appearance whatsoever in the other. In other instances, the degree of prominence given to stories varies markedly according to the edition in which it appears. The selection of news according to editorial perceptions of racial preferences is the inevitable by-product of this new and insidious form of apartheid. For example, the *Rand Daily Mail*, pandering to the white obsession with sport, gave excessive coverage to the rebel tour of the West Indian cricket team. The *Rand Daily Mail Extra* largely underplayed the tour (Anton Harber, "Here is the news, well, some of it," *The Journalist* February 1984, 4). The most pressing political issues that affect the majority of the population, such as forced removals, resettlement, and black education, are highlighted for the benefit of black readers. These issues, although not ignored by the white editions, are certainly underplayed. The result is that white readers are ill informed and in some cases deliberately kept ignorant of the needs, demands, and ongoing resistance of the black community. In this way, an already complacent white community is lulled into a false sense of security.

Press apartheid has a direct bearing on the reportage of matters affecting the administration of justice. At the simplest level, reports on court cases often receive a remarkably different degree of prominence. The most glaring and obvious example is the manner in which the press covers the trials of political offenders. Casual readers of the white press could be forgiven for thinking that the only people charged with high treason are whites. The press coverage given to the trials of Barbara Hogan, Carl Niehaus, and Jansie Lourens, all charged with high treason, received widespread and justified press coverage. The spectacle of whites on trial for high treason is undoubtedly the stuff of which news is made. However, the mistaken impression was created that trials involving white political offenders are the only political trials with which the courts have to deal. In fact, political trials involving blacks are an everyday occurrence in the South African courts. Even trials of high treason are by no means uncommon. In 1982 and 1983, for example, at least 23 people stood trial for treason, and by April 1984 at least 16 people have been so charged. An analysis of the coverage afforded these trials indicates that they are all but ignored (Anton Harber, "Political Trials: Shade of Difference," *The Journalist* December 1983, 4). The difference in emphasis accorded by the white press to trials of political offenders is further emphasized by comparing the coverage given to such trials in black newspapers such as the *Sowetan*. Political trials involving blacks undoubtedly have their fair share of drama. For newspapers with a flair for the sensational, many of these cases contain all the necessary ingredients. Why then are they ignored by the white press? Perhaps it is because white newspaper editors think that white readers should not be jolted from their comfortable reverie by reading about armed insurgents on trial for acts of sabotage.

BRITAIN

Since the completion of *The Cloistered Virtue*, the most significant development in the English law of contempt was the promulgation of the Contempt of Court Act 1981. This statute was the culmination of a drawn-out debate beginning with the appointment in 1971 of a committee under the chairmanship of Lord Justice Phillimore to consider whether any changes were required in the law relating to contempt. The Report of the Committee on Contempt of Court (the Phillimore Committee, cmnd. 5794), which was tabled in December 1974, made certain far-reaching recommendations. It recognized that the existing law of contempt contained uncertainties that impeded and restricted reasonable freedom of speech. It recommended that the law be amended and clarified by statute so as to allow as much freedom of speech as is consistent with the maintenance of the rights of the citizen to a fair and unimpeded system of justice and the protection of the orderly administration of the law.

Before the Phillimore Committee had tabled its report, the House of Lords delivered their speeches in *Attorney-General* v. *Times Newspapers* (1974) AC 273. The House of Lords held that a contempt was committed when any publication prejudged the issues in a pending case. It mattered not that it was a technical offense involving no more than a small likelihood of prejudice. The prejudgment test was criticized by the Phillimore Committee, which recommended that the test for contempt should be whether the publication creates a serious risk of prejudice to the course of justice (paragraph 113). The matter did not rest with the report of the Phillimore Committee. In 1978, a Green Paper on Contempt of Court (cmnd. 7145) expressed certain reservations about the recommendations of the Phillimore Committee. It was suggested that the central recommendations of the Phillimore Committee "raise difficult and important issues of public policy about the proper balance between the freedom of the press and the right of a citizen to a fair trial." It was therefore decided that "satisfactory conclusions cannot be reached on these issues without informed Parliamentary and public discussion" (paragraph 4). The green paper was intended to provide a basis for such discussion. In the meantime, however, the *Times Newspaper* case (supra) had been taken on appeal to the European Court of Human Rights. The European Court held that the test for contempt enunciated by the House of Lords contravened Article 10 of the European Convention on Human Rights, which enshrines the principle of freedom of expression (see Eur. Court HR, Series A, Vol. 30, Judgement of April 26, 1979). As a signatory to the European Convention on Human Rights, the British government was under an international obligation to give effect to its provisions. However, a decision emanating from the European Court of Human Rights is not binding on English courts. Hence, a conflict arose between the English domestic law on contempt (as reflected by the House of Lords) and the ruling by the European Court. It was against this background that the Contempt of Court Bill was introduced by Lord Hailsham, a past victim of the law of contempt [*R* v. *Metropolitan Police Commissioner, ex parte Blackburn (no. 2)* (1968) 2 QB 150].

Contempt of Court Act (1981)

The Contempt of Court Act (the Act) became law in August 1981. It is not intended to give a detailed commentary on all aspects of the Act but only to highlight certain aspects of relevance to the present work. [For a detailed commentary, see Anthony Arlidge and David Eady, *The Law of Contempt* (1982) and S. H. Bailey, "The Contempt of Court Act 1981," 1981 *Modern Law Review* 301.]

The Strict Liability Rule

In terms of Section 1 of the Act, the strict liability rule is defined as "the rule of law whereby conduct may be treated as a contempt of court as tending to interfere with the course of justice in particular legal proceedings regardless of intent to do so." The strict liability rule applies only in relation to "publications" defined in Section 2(1) to include "any speech, writing, broadcast or other communication in whatever form, which is addressed to the public at large or any section of the public." Section 2(2) provides that "the strict liability rule applies only to a publication which creates a substantial risk that the course of justice in the proceedings in question will be seriously impeded or prejudiced." The strict liability rule applies only if the proceedings in question are "active." Schedule 1 to the act lays down the times when proceedings are "active" for the purposes of the application of the strict liability rule.

The Act creates various defenses to a charge of contempt. For example, innocent publication constitutes a defense provided that at the time of publication and after taking all reasonable care the accused does not know and has no reason to suspect that the relevant proceedings are active [Section 3(1)]. The burden of proving this defense lies with the accused [Section 3(3)]. It is specifically provided in Section 4(1) that a "fair and accurate report of legal proceedings held in public, published contemporaneously and in good faith" does not constitute contempt. A court may, however, order that the publication of the report of proceedings be postponed "where it appears necessary for avoiding a substantial risk of prejudice to the administration of justice" [Section 4(2)].

Section 5 of the act provides:

> A publication made as or as part of a discussion in good faith of public affairs or other matters of general public interest is not to be treated as a contempt of court under the strict liability rule if the risk of impediment or prejudice to particular legal proceedings is merely incidental to the discussion.

The defense created by Section 5 of the Act is in accordance with the recommendations of the Phillimore Committee (paragraph 142). In *Attorney-General* v. *Times Newspapers Ltd* (supra) Lord Reid anticipated the existence of a defense of this nature when he stated at 296:

> Suppose that there is in the press and elsewhere discussion of some question of wide public interest, such as the propriety of local authorities or other landlords ejecting squatters from empty premises due for demolition. Then legal proceedings are begun against some squatters, it may be by some authority which had already been criticised in the press. The controversy could hardly be continued without likelihood that it might influence the authority in its conduct of the action. Must there then be silence until that case is decided? And there may be a series of actions by the same or different landlords. Surely public policy does not require that a system of stop and go shall apply to public discussion.

Section 7 of the Act contains the purported safeguard of requiring the consent of the attorney-general before proceedings are instituted under the strict liability rule. The original bill contained no such provision and the requirement of the attorney general's consent was introduced by way of amendment. The utility of a safeguard of this nature is certainly open to question. In this regard, the comments of Lord Edmund-Davies in *Attorney-General* v. *British Broadcasting Corporation* (1980) 3 WLR 109 are particularly apposite. Responding to the assertion that the attorney-general, as the guardian of the public interest, is able to ensure that contempt proceedings are not oppressively or otherwise abused, Lord Edmund-Davies commented at 123:

> My Lords, in so far as the Attorney-General invites the courts to rely on his ipse dixit in the confidence that all holders of that office will always be both wise and just about instituting proceedings for contempt, acceptance of his invitation would involve a denial of justice to those who on occasion are bold enough to challenge that a particular holder has been either wise or just. And it would doom this appeal to failure from the start.

In terms of Section 8 of the Act, it is a contempt of court "to obtain, disclose or solicit any particulars of statements made, opinions expressed, arguments advanced or votes cast by members of a jury in the course of their deliberations in any legal proceedings." The inclusion of this section is a direct response to the decision in *Attorney-General* v. *New Statesman and Nation Publishing Ltd* (1980) 2 WLR 246. That case was a shining example of how the disclosure of jury deliberations could operate in the public interest. It will be recalled that the case concerned the publication of comment on the conduct of a juror, Peter Bessell, in the trial of Jeremy Thorpe. With regard to the offense created by Section 8 of the Act which prohibits any disclosure of a jury's deliberations, it has been stated [Geoffrey Robertson, "The Contempt Bill and Press Freedom," in *The Listener* February 5, 1981, p. 162 (Vol. 105 no. 2698)]:

> It may be desirable to spare defendants acquitted in notorious trials the double jeopardy of jurors prepared to announce that their doubts, though reasonable, were not many. But there are cases – the Thorpe trial was one – where the public interest can be well served by an identifiable revelation. There, it will be remembered, Peter Bessell was "bought" by the *Sunday Telegraph* with an escalation clause in his contract which doubled his money on conviction. Demands to outlaw this practice were met with arguments that jurors would not be influenced by it – until the *New Statesman* interview with a juror demonstrated that the deal had, in fact, effectively discredited Bessell's testimony. That revelation served the public interest because the trial was identified. The moral of the story is, surely, to extend the law of contempt to punish newspapers which make pre-trial financial deals with witnesses, rather than those which expose the evils of such deals in the most effective way. This new crime, requires at very least a "public interest" defence.

It should be added that at the time of Robertson's comments, the bill allowed publication of jury deliberations if neither juror nor case were identified. The bill was amended to prohibit entirely disclosure of jury deliberations.

Section 9 of the Act provides that it is a contempt of court "to use in court, or bring into court for use, any tape recorder or other instrument for recording sound, except with the leave of the court." Section 9(2) prohibits absolutely the publication of recordings of court proceedings.

Section 10 of the Act provides:

> No court may require a person to disclose nor is any person guilty of contempt for refusing to disclose, the source of information contained in a publication for which he is responsible, unless it be established to the satisfaction of the court that disclosure is necessary in the interests of justice or national security or for the prevention of disorder or crime.

This section is merely a codification of existing law and does not afford journalists any greater protection than previously existed [see *British Steel Corporation* v. *Granada Television Ltd* (1891) 1 All ER 417].

An important innovation appears in Section 13 of the Act that empowers the court to grant legal aid in respect of proceedings for contempt in the face of the court. This follows the recommendations of the Phillimore Committee (paragraphs 32-33).

The passing of the Contempt of Court Act necessarily raises the question whether it brings British law into line with its obligations under the European Convention on Human Rights. In this regard, it is significant that the Act has omitted to deal with certain important areas of the law of contempt.

The Act contains no general defense of publication for the public benefit. This defense was considered and rejected by the Phillimore Committee [paragraph 145]:

> To decide whether, in respect of a particular matter a defence of public benefit could be successfully advanced would . . . be extremely difficult. Public benefit is notoriously difficult to define; the creation of a defence on that basis would introduce a fresh area of uncertainty into the law. Moreover, the ventilation of a misconceived defence on these lines could well exacerbate the risks of prejudice.

In the *Times Newspapers* case (supra), the European Court was required to consider whether the interference with freedom of expression was necessary in a democratic society for maintaining the authority of the judiciary. The court made the following finding:

> Having regard to all the circumstances of the case . . . the Court concludes that the interference complained of did not correspond to a

social need sufficiently pressing to outweigh the public interest in freedom of expression within the meaning of the convention. The Court therefore finds the reasons for the restraint imposed on the applicants not to be sufficient under Article 10(2). The restraint proves not to be proportionate to the legitimate aim pursued; it was not necessary in a democratic society for maintaining the authority of the judiciary.

The approach of the European Court necessarily involved the balancing of competing interests. In so doing, it was effectively determining whether the publication in question was for the public benefit. It has accordingly been suggested that the omission from the Act of a defense of publication for the public benefit has created the risk of further decisions in breach of Article 10 of the European Convention on Human Rights (see Arlidge and Eady, op. cit., 147).

The Act also does not specifically deal with the question of whether it is lawful to bring pressure to bear upon litigants. This question lay at the very heart of the *Times Newspapers* case (supra). The Phillimore Committee stated that "criticism of a litigant, whether public or private, is not something from which the law of contempt should protect him" (paragraph 61). It was accordingly recommended that bringing pressure to bear upon a litigant should not constitute contempt of court unless such pressure amounted to intimidation or unlawful threats to his or her person, property, or reputation (paragraph 62). The failure to incorporate this recommendation into the Act has left open the question of the legitimacy of attempting to pursuade a litigant to change his or her mind. It has also given rise to an interesting debate as to whether the result in the *Times Newspapers* case would have been different had it been heard in accordance with the provisions of the Contempt of Court Act. On this there is a divergence of opinion [see, for example, Arlidge and Eady, op. cit., 144-46, and Patricia Hewitt, *The Abuse of Power* (1982) 91].

Another omission from the Act is the failure to deal with the question of scandalizing the court. Again, an important recommendation of the Phillimore Committee was ignored. The Phillimore Committee had recommended that scandalizing the court should cease to be part of the law of contempt. Instead, it should be made an offense to defame a judge in such a way as to bring the administration of justice into disrepute. Proof that the allegations were true and that publication was for the public benefit should be a defense (paragraphs 159-67).

Although the Act is clearly open to criticism, it is generally regarded as a liberalizing measure. It is unfortunate, however, that important opportunities for further improvement were lost. One of the first cases to be tried under the Act was *Attorney-General* v. *English and another* (1982) 3 WLR 278. The case arose out of the publication in the *Daily Mail* of an article written by Malcolm Muggeridge entitled "The vision of life that wins my vote." The article was written in support of a parliamentary candidate who was seeking election as a pro-life candidate. The article was concerned with the necessity for preserving the sanctity of human life. It asserted that handicapped babies were unlikely to be allowed to survive and had either been or were likely to be allowed to die of starvation or by other means. The article appeared on the third day of the trial of Dr. Arthur, charged with the murder of a handicapped baby by starvation. Charges for contempt of court were instituted against the editors of the newspaper under the Contempt of Court Act.

The case raised for the first time the scope of the strict liability rule and the ambit of the defense afforded by Section 5. The Divisional Court found that the publication of the article constituted a contempt of court, but the decision was reversed by a unanimous House of Lords. Lord Diplock, speaking on behalf of the court, held that it was clear that the article was capable of prejudicing the jury against Dr. Arthur. The question that then fell to be decided was whether the article was published as part of a discussion in good faith of public affairs as envisaged by Section 5 of the Act. Lord Diplock has no doubt that Section 5 afforded a good defense:

> Such gagging of bona fide public discussion in the press of controversial matters of general public interest, merely because there are in existence contemporaneous legal proceedings in which some particular instance of those controversial matters may be in issue, is what s5 of the Contempt of Court Act 1981 was in my view intended to prevent.

This decision illustrates the importance of the defense created by Section 5 of the Act. In the absence of such a defense, the appeal would clearly have failed. It is also significant that the House of Lords held that the attorney-general bore the burden of proving that the risk of prejudice to the fair trial of Dr. Arthur by the publication of the article was not merely incidental to the discussion of the matter with which the article dealt. This is a significant departure from the decision of the Divisional Court, which had held that the burden of proof fell on the accused.

The decision in *Home Office* v. *Harman* (1982) 2 WLR 338, although not concerned with the Contempt of Court Act, warrants special attention. Miss Harman, a solicitor, had been retained by one Williams, a prisoner serving a lengthy prison sentence. She had been instructed by Williams to seek a declaration that his detention in a special isolation cell was unlawful. After an interlocutory application for discovery, the Home Office disclosed some 2,800 documents of which 800 were read out in open court at the ensuing trial. Some of these documents contained the minutes of Home Office meetings and objection was taken to their admissibility. A decision on the question of their admissibility was reserved. In the interim, Miss Harman showed the 800 documents to David Leigh of the *Guardian*, who was doing research on the prison service. The documents that were the subject of the dispute on admissibility were among those shown to Leigh. Leigh then published an article based on the documents he had been shown. Thereafter, the objection to the admissibility of the documents was upheld.

Miss Harman was successfully charged with contempt of court. The House of Lords, by a majority of 3 to 2, confirmed the conviction. It was contended on behalf of Miss Harman that the discovered documents, although initially confidential, entered the public domain once they had been read out in open court. Furthermore, a journalist who attended the hearings or who purchased a transcript of the record could quite legitimately make use of the information for the purposes of writing an article. Lord Diplock would have none of this. At 341, he stated:

> It may assist in clearing up misconceptions if I start by saying what the case is not about. It is not about freedom of speech, freedom of the press, openness of justice or documents coming into the "public domain".... What this case is about is an aspect of the law of discovery of documents in civil actions in the High Court.

The dissenters (Lord Scarman and Lord Simon) took a very different approach. In his speech, Lord Scarman emphasized that what was at stake was the principle of freedom of communication [at 553]:

> Can it be good law that the litigant and his solicitor are alone excluded from the right to make that use of the documents which everyone else may now make, namely, to treat them as matters of public knowledge? In our view, this is not the law. We do not think that a system of law which recognises the right of freedom of communication in respect of matters of public knowledge can decently or rationally permit any such exception.

Lord Scarman also gave consideration to the question of obligations imposed by Article 10 by the European Convention on Human Rights. He concluded that there was no pressing social need to exclude the litigant and his solicitor from the right available to everyone else to treat as public knowledge documents that have been produced and made part and parcel of legal proceedings (at 558).

Prior to the decision by the House of Lords an unsuccessful attempt was made to reverse the effects of the decision by an appropriate clause in the Contempt of Court Bill. It still remains possible that the decision will be taken on appeal to the European Court of Human Rights.

UNITED STATES

It is difficult to speak of recent developments in the area of freedom of speech and the administration of justice in the United States. The tradition of free speech and open government on which the modern United States is based has facilitated vigorous public debate on all matters of national importance. The courts and the administration of justice generally have not escaped the glare of public scrutiny. The principle that justice is not a cloistered virtue has long been recognized by the U.S. Supreme Court. When speaking of recent developments, therefore, it is really only a matter of examining current refinements to a long-established principle.

For South African and British lawyers, reared in the conservative tradition, the extent to which the legal profession is subjected to public scrutiny in the United States is a source of constant amazement. This is particularly true of comment critical of judicial officers. Critical assessment of judicial competence and behavior beyond criticism of decided cases is virtually unheard of in South Africa and is unusual in Britain. If a journal entitled *The American Lawyer* is anything to go by, such criticism seems to be the order of the day in the United States.

The July/August 1983 edition of the journal includes a 54-page supplement described as "The Complete Guide to Federal District Judges." The supplement, which can conveniently be removed from the main body of the journal, includes a brief profile of each of the 560 active federal district judges, as well as notes on the "background, major rulings, philosophy and court room style" of the judges in question. The editor informs readers that a "litigator in Cleveland who suddenly finds himself with a case in Atlanta can now turn to our Directory to get a sense of the judge's background (is he a former insurance defense lawyer or a former NAACP lawyer?); his prior experience (is he famous for a pro-plaintiff ruling in an anti-trust case?); the president who appointed him; and his age, law school, and general political philosophy."

In an article entitled "The Best and Worst," the performances of all the federal district judges are critically assessed. The best and worst judges of each of the twelve judicial circuits are discussed in some detail. This is the second time in its five-year history that a survey of this nature has been conducted by the journal. Four basic criteria were utilized for the purposes of the assessment: legal ability, temperament, willingness to work hard, and integrity. The authors apparently spoke to "hundreds of lawyers," read "dozens of decisions" rendered by the judges who were tentatively considered, and "sifted through hundreds of pages of trial records." In addition, they consulted "law professors, local courthouse reporters, prosecutors, even judges." If a judge seemed to be falling into the "worst" category, they "aggressively sought out those who might provide a different view." Despite the difficulties in making the assessments, the authors found "a broad consensus as to the two or three best or worst judges in each region."

The results are illuminating, particularly for South African lawyers. Andrew Caffrey, voted the worst judge of the First Circuit, was found to have "a volatile temper and severe prosecutorial bias." A partner in a major firm said that "there are times you have the feeling you're appearing before the god of vengeance and tasting his wrath." A litigator who frequently appears before Caffrey described him as "petty, venal, arbitrary, capricious and totally unsuited to being a federal judge. He thinks he was anointed not appointed." A criminal defense lawyer stated that "everyone walks in with the presumption of guilt." A former prosecutor said that Caffrey "decides that the defendant is guilty and then he decides all discretionary rulings against him."

Joe Fisher was voted the worst judge of the Fifth Circuit. His biggest problem according to those who have appeared before him is his "pro-plaintiff bias." A defense lawyer, who is able to cite three recent examples, said that Fisher will "rule for the plaintiff no matter what, and if the jury brings in a defense verdict, he'll grant a new trial." Another defense attorney noted that "the only difference between winning and losing in Fisher's court is if you win, you settle cheaper." Lawyers were agreed, however, that when it came to civil rights, Fisher was not proplaintiff. One lawyer explained that "he takes you into chambers, and tells you he is going to rule against you, and berates you for wasting the court's time." The authors also note that "it sometimes takes multiple reversals to convince Fisher to revise his opinions." On the other hand, in his favor is his success in reducing the delay in the hearing of cases.

Commenting upon J. Robert Elliot, voted the worst judge of the Eleventh Circuit, the authors stated the following:

> Judges like J. Robert Elliot of Georgia's Middle District are, fortunately, a vanishing breed. An old-line segregationist who flaunts his deep rooted prejudices against blacks, unions and criminal defendants, Elliot is less a judge than a despot.

He too was not without redeeming features, however. Thus "in civil cases where [his] considerable biases are not stirred, lawyers say he is not a bad judge – smart enough, and even tempered."

The biographical sketches of the best judges reveal qualities possessed by the finest judges in the world. Typical remarks are "a model jurist – intelligent, impartial, hardworking, and independent" (Joseph Tauro); "Lasker gives the appearance as well as the substance of fairness . . . a warm and well rounded individual" (Morris Lasker); "He does a tremendous job. He can take a complicated case and go right to the heart of it . . . brilliant . . . witty, patient" (John Fullam); "sharp witted efficiency . . . brilliant and practical and always fully prepared" (Alexander Harvey II); "sheer legal ability . . . widely acclaimed as a jurist" (Jerry Buchmeyer); "His industry is legendary . . . an absolutely ideal judge in terms of temperament and scholarship" (William

Thomas); "lauded ... for his extreme sense of fairness, his diligence and scholarship, and his innate decency" (Prentice Marshall); "universal praise for his fairness, consistency and scholarship" (Harry MacLaughlin); "a businesslike intentness in being impartial, consistent and courteous" (David Winder); "thoughtful, incisive, evenhanded, and unfailingly gracious to the lawyers who come before him" (William Hoeveler).

Judges are not the only targets of *The American Lawyer*. The legal profession as a whole is regarded as fair game. The performance of lawyers in court is subjected to critical scrutiny, and boardroom intrigue of the major firms of attorneys receives widespread coverage. The journal is not without its critics, however. Tom Goldstein, the well-known legal writer has commented that *The American Lawyer* "has transformed legal journalism" and "in the process ... has pushed to the very edge questions of journalistic taste and ethics" [(1983) 83 *Columbia LR* 1351]. The propriety of the journal aside, *The American Lawyer* is illustrative of the extent to which the administration of justice may be commented on in a society that respects the freedom of expression.

One of the issues that has attracted judicial attention and generated new doctrines is the extent to which there exists a constitutionally protected right of access to judicial proceedings. Two recent decisions of the Supreme Court warrant special comment. It had previously been decided in *Gannet Co.* v. *De Pasquale*, 443 U.S. 368 (1979) that the Sixth Amendment, which guarantees the accused the right to a public trial, does not confer on the press or the public at large any right of access to pretrial hearings. Whether or not any other provisions of the Constitution guaranteed a right of access was specifically left open by the Court. The significance of the Court's decision was clouded by the fact that members of the Court were divided in their reasoning (there were separate concurring opinions by Justices Powell and Rehnquist) and by inconsistent public statements by Chief Justice Burger and Justice Blackmun as to what they thought the decision meant [see Archibald Cox, *Freedom of Expression* 30 (1981)].

In *Richmond Newspapers Inc.* v. *Virginia*, 448 U.S. 555 (1980) the Court was called on to decide for the first time whether [per Chief Justice Burger at 564]:

> a criminal trial itself may be closed to the public upon the unopposed request of a defendant, without any demonstration that closure is required to protect the defendant's superior right to a fair trial, or that some other overriding consideration requires closure.

The case arose out of the fourth trial of one Stevenson, indicted for the murder of a hotel manager who had been found stabbed to death. At Stevenson's first trial, a bloodstained shirt purportedly belonging to him was held to have been improperly admitted into evidence. The two subsequent trials ended in mistrials due to jury irregularities. At the fourth trial, the court granted defense counsel's motion that the trial be closed to the public without any objections having been made by the prosecutor or two reporters from Richmond Newspapers, who were present in court. Defendant's counsel had moved that the court be closed to the public because he did not want "any information being shuffled back and forth when we have a recess as to . . . who testified to what." Later that day the appellant newspaper's motion to vacate the closure order was denied by the trial judge, who ordered the trial to continue with the press and public excluded. A petition for appeal to the Virginia Supreme Court was denied.

After a lengthy historical excursus, Chief Justice Burger concluded that "the historical evidence demonstrates conclusively that at the time when our organic laws were adopted, criminal trials both here and in England had long been presumptively open" (at 569). While conceding that historical practice is insufficient to establish a constitutional right and that the Constitution nowhere explicitly guarantees the right of the public to attend trials, the chief justice concluded that a right of access is implicit and "indispensable to" the expressly guaranteed rights of freedom of speech and freedom of assembly (at 580). These freedoms, he stated, "share a common core purpose of assuring freedom of communication on matters relating to the functioning of government," including the criminal justice system (at 575) [see generally Mary Cheh, "Judicial Supervision of Executive Secrecy: Rethinking Freedom of Expression for Government Employees and the Right of Access to Government Information" (1984) 69 *Cornell LR* 201].

The chief justice also made some interesting criminological observations [at 571]:

> When a shocking crime occurs, a community reaction of outrage and public protest often follows. . . . Thereafter the open processes of justice serve an important prophylactic purpose, providing an outlet for community concern, hostility, and emotion. . . . Civilized societies withdraw both from the victim and the vigilante the enforcement of criminal laws, but they cannot erase from people's consciousness the fundamental, natural yearning to see justice done – or even the urge for retribution.

Although the First Amendment was found implicitly to guarantee the right of access to trials, this did not mean that the right was absolute in all cases. The justices' difficulty in formulating the standard of the newly announced right of access was illustrated by the fact that of the seven justices who agreed with the result, six wrote separate opinions. Justice Brennan, for example, suggested that national security concerns about confidentiality may sometimes warrant closures during sensitive portions of trial proceedings, such as testimony about state secrets. Justice Stewart, foreshadowing problems that were later to arise, suggested that the sensibilities of a youthful prosecution witness in a criminal trial for rape might also justify closure.

These exceptional cases notwithstanding, there were certain features of the criminal justice system that, in the opinions of the various justices, explained why a right of access is protected by the First Amendment. Justice Brennan, for example, observed that [at 595]:

> Open trials assure the public that procedural rights are respected, and that justice is afforded equally. Closed trials breed suspicion and arbitrariness, which in turn spawns disrespect for law. Public access is essential, therefore, if trial adjudication is to achieve the objective of maintaining public confidence in the administration of justice.

The issue of access to trials involving minor victims of sexual offenses came to the fore in *Globe Newspaper Company* v. *Superior Court for the County of Norfolk* 102 SC 2613 (1982). The case arose out of an attempt by the Globe Newspaper Company to gain access to a rape trial in which the defendant had been charged with the forcible rape and forced unnatural rape of three girls who were minors at the time of trial. Relying on Section 16A of the Massachusetts General Laws, which requires the exclusion of the press and the general public from the courtroom during the testimony of victims of specified sexual offenses under the age of 18 years, the trial judge ordered the courtroom closed. The Supreme Court of Massachusetts dismissed Globes's appeal.

The state interests advanced in support of Section 16A were twofold: the protection of minor victims of sex crimes from further trauma and embarrassment; and the encouragement of such victims to come forward and testify in a truthful and credible manner. Both these interests were considered by the Supreme Court. In delivering the opinion of the court, Justice Brennan (joined by Justices White, Marshall, Blackmun, and Powell) conceded that the interest in safeguarding the physical and psychological well-being of a minor was a compelling one. He added, however, that "as compelling as that interest is, it does not justify a *mandatory* closure rule. . . . A trial court can determine on a case-by-case basis whether closure is necessary to protect the welfare of a minor victim." With regard to the assertion that Section 16A is designed to encourage minor victims of sexual offenses to come forward and provide accurate testimony, Justice Brennan rejected this claim as "speculative in empirical terms" and "open to serious question as a matter of logic and common sense."

In his dissenting opinion, Chief Justice Burger berated the courts' "cavalier disregard of the reality of human experience." He added that Section 16A was intended

> to prevent the risk of severe psychological damage caused by having to relate the details of the crime in front of a crowd which inevitably will

include voyeuristic strangers. In most states, that crowd may be expected to include a live television audience, with reruns on the evening news. That ordeal could be difficult for an adult; to a child, the experience can be devastating and leave permanent scars. . . . If, as psychologists report, the courtroom experience in such cases is almost as traumatic as the crime itself, a state certainly should be able to take whatever reasonable steps it believes are necessary to reduce that trauma.

The chief justice also pointed out that Section 16A did not deny the press and the public access to information as to what takes place at trials. The verbatim transcript of the rape victim's evidence is made available to the public and the media and may be used without limit.

The importance of *Globe* lies in the fact that for the first time a majority of the Court was able to agree on a standard to govern trial-access issues. Speaking for the Court, Justice Brennan announced that under the First Amendment criminal trials are presumptively open and that closure is permissible only on a state showing a compelling need to inhibit the disclosure of sensitive information. Regrettably, in applying this standard to the case before it, the majority in *Globe* failed to take sufficient account of the problems experienced by the victims of sexual violence. The secondary victimization of rape victims has been well documented. Many such studies were in fact referred to by Chief Justice Burger. To dismiss these claims as "speculative" borders on willful blindness. It was particularly disappointing that Justice O'Connor, the only woman on the Supreme Court bench, did not even address herself to these issues. Perhaps naively, one would have thought that a woman would have been sensitive to the ordeal of rape victims. The majority opinion notwithstanding, "logic and common sense" do indeed dictate that the chances of reporting sexual assaults are considerably reduced if the victim knows that she may be exposed to the humiliation and degradation of reliving the ordeal before a group of curious onlookers. It would seem that only an automatic closure rule can assure rape victims in advance that they will not suffer the psychological trauma of trial publicity.

The intrusion of the media on a victim of sexual violence is graphically illustrated by the recent case of a 22-year-old woman, Cheryl Arauso, who was stripped and gang raped on a pool table by six men in Big Dan's Tavern, Fall River, Massachusetts. The trial of the six men was broadcast live on national television. It was the first time a rape trial had been given national television coverage. The ordeal of Cheryl Arauso, whose face was never shown, was "enjoyed" by millions of avid viewers, many of whom probably only had a prurient interest in sex and violence.

It is doubtful that the interest of the media in instant access to criminal trials outweighs the need to protect the victims of sexual violence from public humiliation, trauma, and degradation. Thus, while one may applaud the exacting open-trial rule enunciated in *Globe* as consistent with First Amendment protection accorded to vigorous public debate on all matters concerning the administration of justice, it remains unfortunate that the rule was misapplied in that case.

Gilbert Marcus
Advocate of the Supreme Court
Senior Research Officer
Center for Applied Legal Studies
University of the Witwatersrand
Johannesburg, South Africa

INDEX

background of, 98–100; conflict in, fundamental, 100–5; and dissemination of trial information, 119–24; in France, 117–19; in Great Britain, 107–8; and human mind, 106–10; issues in, 105–6; and jury trials, 110–14; and media codes, voluntary, 124–28; and press control, voluntary, 128–30; and saturation, 114–16; in South Africa, 107–8; term of, 98
trials by judges, 113
truth, 24–28
Truth case, 54

U
Ungebühr, 64–65, 66
Ungelöst case, 217
United States: academic censorship in, 172; contempt of court in, 49, 56–57; freedom of speech in, 209–10; journalists in, 184–88; judges in, 386–88; and judicial proceedings, access to, 388–92; McCarthy era in, 157; scandalization of judges in, 56–57; and self-fulfillment of lawyer, 16; trial publicity in, 131
unjust laws, in South Africa, 368–72
unused freedom, 5

Uruguay, 89. *See also* Hispanic countries

V
Van Niekerk case: and case law, 353–55; and criticisms of judiciary, 59–60; and formal restrictions of freedom of speech, 42–44; and freedom of speech, 35–36; and journalists, 207; and judges in South Africa, 360, 363–64, 366; and self-censorship of judicial officers, 168; and trial publicity restrictions, 101, 103, 109; and truth, 26
Van Veen reports, 77–78
Venezuela, 89. *See also* Hispanic countries
vilipendio, 81, 85–86

W
Warren Commission, 123
Watergate trials, 131

X
Xhego case, 362

Y
Yugoslavia, 94. *See also* Eastern Europe